ENVIRONMENTAL LAW & NATURE, LAW, AND SOCIETY

SUPPLEMENT

ZYGMUNT J.B. PLATER
ROBERT H. ABRAMS
WILLIAM GOLDFARB

AMERICAN CASEBOOK SERIES
West Publishing Company

1994

The enclosed materials provide timely new text, questions, and information for courses in environmental law using the coursebook Environmental Law and Policy: Nature, Law, and Society (West Publishing Company, 1992). The materials of this Supplement are keyed to the coursebook text: Each entry is prefaced, within the table of contents and within the text, with a coursebook cross-reference, by page, and a notation on subject matter.

Publication of this Supplement would not have been possible without the perceptive minds, research and drafting abilities, and unflagging energies of Louis DiPietro and Renita Ford, both of the Boston College Law School's Class of 1996, with able and much-appreciated occasional research help from William Mendelsohn of the same class.

 TEXT IS PRINTED ON 10% POST CONSUMER RECYCLED PAPER    PRINTED WITH SOY INK   ∞

© 1994

by

West Publishing Company

ISBN 0-314-04693-3

Table of Contents

TABLE OF CASES.. vii

COURSEBOOK PAGE REFERENCE		SUPPLEMENT PAGE
xxxvi	INTRODUCTION..	1
CHAPTER 1	THE ENVIRONMENTAL PERSPECTIVE	
20	Critical response from the highway salting industry...........	3
23	Environmental justice as a new theme in environmental law...	4
23	Contending forces: the appearance of the anti-environmental "Wise Use" movement and "the Unholy Trinity"...	5
CHAPTER 2	LAW AND ECONOMICS, UNCERTAINTY AND RISK	
54	Wise Use anti-regulation initiatives.................................	17
89	Risk assessment in setting administrative policy..............	18
89-100	Cancer risk and causation, *Corrosion Proof Fittings*......	26
CHAPTER 3	ENVIRONMENTAL TORTS AND REMEDIES	
121	SLAPPs and SLAPP-Backs..	37
148, 168-169	Remedies: Restoration damages, *Escamilla v. ASARCO* ..	40
150	Assessing permanent damages.......................................	51
159	Punitive damages, *TXO* and *Honda v. Oberg*..................	53
CHAPTER 4	TOXIC TORTS	
182-93	Proving causation: *Landrigan v. Celotex*.........................	55
196	Expert Testimony: *Daubert v. Merrill-Dow*.....................	62
221	Statutes of limitation...	70
223	Compensation for toxic exposure and fear, *Potter v. Firestone*...	72
223	Community reaction and injury to land values.................	87
223	Settlements: the role of judges.....................................	89
CHAPTER 5	ENVIRONMENTAL REMEDIES DRAWN FROM OTHER FIELDS OF LAW	
228	Maxxam and redwood clearcutting..................................	96
229	"Socially-responsible corporations" and CERES.............	96
239	Property cases and environmental law............................	99
CHAPTER 6	THE INTERPLAY OF COMMON LAW AND STATUTES	
260	Statutory interpretation..	101
277	CERCLA liability of "arrangers" and "operators".........	101

279	CERCLA amendments	102
277	"Disposal" under CERCLA , *Aceto*	104
280	CERCLA liability of lenders.	109
283	Corporate succession – choice of law	110
284	Landowner liability	111
292	CERCLA joint and several liability	112
295	Contribution actions	114
295	Attorneys fees	115
295	CERCLA: insolvent PRPs and insurance	115
299	CERCLA and bankruptcy	117
304	Statutory pre-emption defenses	118

CHAPTER 7 ENVIRONMENTAL CRIMINAL LAW

335	Federal sentencing guidelines, *U.S. v. Rutana*	120
347	Liability of corporate officials	124

CHAPTER 8 FUNDAMENTAL ENVIRONMENTAL RIGHTS: CONSTITUTIONS, AND THE PUBLIC TRUST

405	A new form of public trust mechanism	125

CHAPTER 9 PUBLIC POWERS AND PRIVATE PROPERTY RIGHTS: CONSTITUTIONAL AUTHORITY AND LIMITATIONS

442	EMF radiation as inverse condemnation?	127
449	The geography of Maine v. Johnson	127
473	Amortization, and time baselines	129
468	The Supreme Court, *Lucas*, and regulatory takings	129
474	Regulatory exactions, *Dolan* v. *City of Tigard*	161
475	Property rights political initiatives	173

CHAPTER 10 ENVIRONMENTAL AUTHORITY, FEDERAL AND STATE GOVERNMENTS

503	State Sovereignty as a limit on federal power, *N.Y v. U.S.*	175
503	Dormant commerce clause, *Chem. Waste Mgmt.*	179
520-523	Protectionist challenges, *Swin Resources*, and *Carbone v. Clarkstown*	188

CHAPTER 11 ENVIRONMENTAL ADMINISTRATIVE LAW

569	Citizens oversight councils	199
570	Citizen enforcement attorneys fees and the Supreme Court: *City of Burlington v. Dague*	206
574	Restrictions on standing, *Lujan v. Defenders of Wildlife*	209
593	Re-adjusting regulatory mechanisms, *AFL-CIO V. OSHA*	224
593	Regulatory reform and the unholy trinity	226

CHAPTER 12 THE NATIONAL ENVIRONMENTAL POLICY ACT

596	NEPA overview	230
644	The *NAFTA* case	231

TABLE OF CONTENTS

CHAPTER 13   ROADBLOCK STATUTES, ENDANGERED SPECIES

673   The ESA's prohibition on "taking" species by harming them: the *Sweet Home* case 236

680   The old-growth forest/ Spotted Owl controversy 239

683   Under-enforcement of the ESA? 241

685   A statutory roadblock comparison: the Delaney Clause and *Les v. Reilly* 244

CHAPTER 14   PUBLIC RESOURCE MANAGEMENT STATUTES

688   Public resource management theories 252

700   The national forests planning case, *CEQ v. USFS* 253

CHAPTER 15   PERMIT PROCESSES, AND MODERN STANDARD-SETTING APPROACHES

737   Pollution-prevention, and "cause-based" regulation 261

CHAPTER 16   REGULATORY CONTROL OF MARKET ACCESS: PESTICIDES AND TOXICS

748   FIFRA's administrative process 265

CHAPTER 17   DIRECT LEGISLATION OF SPECIFIC POLLUTION STANDARDS, AND TECHNOLOGY-FORCING : AUTOMOBILE AIR POLLUTION

772   Overview of technology-forcing 268

CHAPTER 18   ADMINISTRATIVE STANDARD-SETTING STATUTES: THE CLEAN AIR ACT'S HARM-BASED AMBIENT STANDARDS

773   Complexitiesof the Federal Clean Air Act 273

801   U.S. primary air standards 280

CHAPTER 19   ADMINISTRATIVE STANDARDS BASED ON AVAILABLE TECHNOLOGY: THE FEDERAL CLEAN WATER ACT

825   The return of WQSs 282

835   EPA multimedia regulation 284

845   CSOs and industrial overflows 285

852   Nonpoint sources and CZMA 286

852   Water quality standard-setting 287

856   Upstream/Downstream, *Arkansas v. Oklahoma* 288

858   Citizen enforcement issues 288

   Exercise: the Average River, a complex hypothetical 291

CHAPTER 20   ECONOMIC INCENTIVE AND ARTIFICIAL POLLUTION MARKET STATUTES

870   Market incentives as an alternative to regulation 293

CHAPTER 21   A STATUTORY SYSTEM FOR MANAGING AND FUNDING ENVIRONMENTAL REMEDIATION: CERCLA

897   The cost of cleanups 294

898	CERCLA'S continuing evolution	295
919	De micromis settlements	304
923	CERCLA contribution litigation	304
CHAPTER 22	A COMPOSITE APPROACH : RCRA	
940	Hazardous waste statutory systems	307
946	Harm-based variances	315
CHAPTER 23	LAND-USE-BASED ENVIRONMENTAL CONTROL STATUTES	
953	"Consistency" analysis	316
967	Wetlands regulation and the scope of the commerce clause	318
971	Attempts at comprehensive watershed management	319
CHAPTER 24A [INSERT AT 978]	ENVIRONMENTAL JUSTICE — RACE, POVERTY, AND THE ENVIRONMENT	
	East Bibb Twiggs Neighborhood Assoc.	320
	Simulation Exercise	335
CHAPTER 24B	ALTERNATIVE DISPUTE RESOLUTION	
985	Map of the Hudson River settlement negotiatons	338
CHAPTER 25	INTERNATIONAL ENVIRONMENTAL LAW	
1023	"Extraterritoriality": the *Antarctica* case, and *Lujan v. Defenders* excerpt	339
1024	Environmentalism and free trade	347
1030-31	UNCED, the United Nations Conference on Environment and Development – the Rio Earth Summit	347
	The Rio Declaration	350
	Agenda 21	353
APPENDIX 1	FEDERAL ENVIRONMENTAL STATUTES OVER 100+ YEARS	Reference page 2
APPENDIX 2	(A) ENVIRONMENTAL ON-LINE ELECTRONIC RESOURCES, AND (B) PERIODICAL-LOOSELEAF SERVICES	18
APPENDIX 3	FEDERAL ENVIRONMENTAL JUSTICE MATERIALS	33
APPENDIX 4	AN ENVIRONMENTAL JUSTICE BIBLIOGRAPY	40
APPENDIX 5	EPA CHART OF SALT DISTRIBUTION	33

Table of Cases

Aceto Agric. Chem. Corp., U.S. v., (CERCLA)........................104
AFL-CIO v. OSHA, (OSHA, consolidated rulemaking)..........................224
Arkansas v. Oklahoma, (CWA)........................288
C & A Carbone, Inc. v. Town of Clarkstown, (solid waste, dormant
    commerce clause)........................191
Chemical Waste Management v. Hunt, (RCRA, dormant commerce
    clause)........................181
Chicago v. Environmental Defense Fund, (RCRA, toxic ash from
    household waste)........................313
Citizens for Environmental Quality v. United States, (NFMA)...............253
City of Burlington v. Dague, (CWA, SDWA, attorneys fees)..................206
Corrosion-Proof Fittings Co., v. EPA (asbestos risk)...................28
Dague, City of Burlington v., (CWA, SDWA, attorneys fees)................206
Daubert v. Merrill-Dow Pharmaceuticals, (causation, Bendectin)...........63
Department of Energy v. Ohio, (RCRA, CWA, sovereign immunity)......283
Dolan v. City of Tigard, (regulatory exactions)........................162
East Bibb Twiggs Neighborhood Council v. Macon-Bibb County,
    (waste siting, environmental justice)........................322
Environmental Defense Fund v. Massey, (Antarctica, NEPA)...............339
Escamilla et al. v. ASARCO, (restoration damages)........................40
Fort Gratiot Sanitary Landfill v. Michigan Department of Natural
    Resources, (solid waste, dormant commerce clause)........................185
Hoffman Homes v. U.S.EPA, (CWA, §404)........................318
Honda Motors v. Oberg, (punitive damages, due process)........................54
Jefferson County and City of Tacoma v. Washington Department of
    Ecology, (CWA and FERC, state-federal roles)........................290
Landrigan v. Celotex Corp., (asbestos causation)........................55
Les v. Reilly, (FDCA, zero risk, and the Delaney Clause)........................244
Loveladies Harbor v. U.S., (CWA §404, regulatory takings)...................150
Lucas v. South Carolina Coastal Commission, (regulatory takings).......130
Lujan v. Defenders of Wildlife, (standing, ESA)........................210, 344
New York v. U.S., (radioactive waste, Tenth Amendment)........................176
Nollan v. Calif. Coastal Comm., (regulatory exactions)........................162
Oberg, Honda Motors v., (punitive damages, due process)........................54
Oregon Waste Systems v. Dept. of Environmental Quality, (solid waste,
    dormant commerce clause)........................186
Potter v. Firestone Tire and Rubber Co., (cancerphobia)........................72
Public Citizen v. U.S. Trade Representative, (NAFTA, NEPA)................231
Public Util. Dist. No. 1 of Jefferson County and Tacoma v. Washington
    Dept. of Ecology, (CWA and FERC, state-federal roles)................290
Rutana, U.S. v., (sentencing guidelines)........................120
Shults v. Champion International, (class settlements)........................90
Seattle Audubon v. Robertson, (spotted owl, NEPA)........................240
Sweet Home Chap. Comm. for a Great Oregon, v. Babbitt, (ESA §9)....236
Swin Resource Systems Inc. v. Lycoming County, (solid waste, dormant
    commerce clause)........................188
TXO v. Alliance Systems, (punitive damages, due process)........................53
U.S. v. Aceto Agric. Chem. Corp., (CERCLA)........................104
U.S. v. Rutana, (sentencing guidelines)........................120

Introduction

PAGE xxxvi   **A compilation of federal statutes**

Over the years a remarkable number of statutes relevant to environmental law practice has been put on the federal statute books. For students who want to get an overview of this wide array of statutes, and a sense of the legal history of federal environmental legislation, a chronological compilation of some representative federal acts over the past century, most of which are still with us in original or amended form, is included at the back of this Supplement as **Appendix 1, Federal Environmental Statutes....**

PAGE xxxvi   **Information resources for studying environmental law:**

Loose-leaf services
The Internet and the environment
Treatises
Computer-based clipping services

LOOSE-LEAF SERVICES

In the casebook's introduction, at page xxxvii, several loose-leaf services are noted for students who want to follow up specialized questions in the field. The range of environmental loose-leaf services now available is quite astonishing. A fuller compilation of current loose leafs appears as **Appendix 2B** of this Update Supplement.

THE INTERNET AND THE ENVIRONMENT

Electronic databases have become basic tools in modern legal research. Many environmental attorneys and law students, however, are also becoming increasingly at ease with electronic research networks beyond WESTLAW and LEXIS. There are active environmental law e-mail networks, and a seemingly endless number of specialized Gopher sites on the Internet that make a personal computer into a global research tool.

For readers interested in exploring these networks, **Appendix 2A** of this Supplement contains an essay on E-Law, and a guide to environmental research on the Internet.

•TREATISE

An interesting new treatise has been published by the Environmental Law Institute and West Publishing Company — C. Campbell-Mohn, B. Breen, and J.W. Futrell, Environmental Law: From Resources to Recovery (1993). The book applies a new approach to presenting domestic U.S. doctrine, organizing it by problem areas, and considers resource and pollution prevention issues beyond traditional pollution regulation. The hornbook should help students integrate the diversity of statutes and regulatory approaches that characterizes our existing rather ad hoc environmental law system.

COMPUTER-BASED CLIPPING SERVICES

To follow the ongoing course of environmental law, it is now possible to use on-line electronic clipping services to produce customized scheduled printouts of information on a chosen particular topic or pending judicial decision, or a summary of a daily news service — for example, a daily printout of all items on the BNA Environment Reporter National Environmental Daily service, with each item in 50-word or 75-word format, a similar clipping printout from BNA's International Environment Reporter Daily, or a clipping service search awaiting a particular imminent appellate decision.

Both WESTLAW and LEXIS/NEXIS offer this clipping service function. On WESTLAW the service is called "PDQ." On LEXIS, the service is called "ECLIPSE." For instructions on how to place a standing order for daily, weekly, or other scheduled printouts on desired topics, contact your WESTLAW or Mead Data Central representative.

[The standard ECLIPSE printing format unfortunately generates a great deal of waste paper — sometimes five sheets of nonfunctional output for a single sheet of information. Until Mead chooses to correct this problem, users can minimize the excess page output by using a Laser Printer format and requesting a simplified download without front and end sheets.]

Chapter 1,   The Environmental Perspective

PAGE 20   **Update: critical response to Chapter 1 analysis from the highway salting industry**

Shortly after publication of the coursebook, with its overview analysis of highway salting as a case study in environmental externalities, at pages 15-27, a highly critical letter was received from Mr. Richard L. Hanneman, president of the Salt Institute, the highway salt industry lobby. The letter announced a study released in January, 1992, by the Transportation Research Board, (an arm of the National Research Council, which is a large private nonprofit research organization affiliated with the National Academy of Sciences). The study concluded that the benign salt substitute CMA has not — or at least not yet — been proved to be a sufficiently economical substance for highway de-icing to justify a switch away from rock salt. According to Mr. Hanneman, the report indicated that

> there is a strong relationship between the application of de-icing salt and the prevention of about 80% of the fatalities and serious injuries that would otherwise occur on untreated highways.... Using highway de-icing salt may prevent huge numbers of tort recoveries, but it still might be of interest to aspiring attorneys.

Readers may wish to review this report. Given the coursebook's analysis, it is not at all clear however that untreated highways are the appropriate comparison, rather than highways treated with CMA or cinders and sand.

The study also seems to contain some potentially serious gaps:

The special committee that issued the report , in using an overview accounting and monetary estimation approach to compare salt and CMA, excluded several public costs that may indeed be significant. Excluded from their calculus were all human health problems, particularly those from salt infiltration into drinking water supplies, and "environmental damages" — both of potentially large magnitude and both excluded on grounds of "insufficient information."

The citation for the report is: Transportation Research Board, Highway De-Icing: Comparing Salt and Calcium Magnesium Acetate (Special Report 235, 1991) (TRB, 2101 Constitution Ave. NW, Washington DC 20418).

Distibution of highway salt in the environment

A U.S. EPA schematic diagram showing the distribution of highway salt in the environment — U.S. EPA, D. Murray and U. Ernst, An Economic Analysis of the Environmental Impact of Highway Deicing, EPA-600/2-76-105 (1976) is printed at the back of the Appendices to this Supplement.

PAGE 23   **Environmental Justice as a new theme in**
                   environmental law study and research

The sprawling bulk of modern environmental law doctrine, as the coursebook often reflects, has in most if not in all cases been developed and incorporated within the legal system in response to citizen efforts, not by the initiative of legislatures and the administrative branch. In many areas of environmental law, the citizen actions that impelled the development of doctrine began in neighborhoods of low-income citizens and people of color. The Love Canal chemical poisoning case arising in a working class neighborhood of industrial Buffalo, is only one case in point.

Until recently, however, focused attention has not been paid to the fact that such communities not only do not seem to get their share of environmental enforcement efforts by government, but also that they seem to attract a disproportionate amount of environmental problems, often including toxic threats to health and safety.

Over the last several years, many people have begun to see a pattern in the distribution of toxic harms and the characteristics of the people who were most often exposed to them. The correlation was highlighted in Charles Lee's 1987 study, "Toxic Wastes and Race in the United States," sponsored by the United Church of Christ Commission for Racial Justice. The exposure of racial minorities and low-income groups to environmental hazards appeared to be both quantitatively and qualitatively greater than that of the general public. The U.S. GAO reached tentative conclusions along the same line in its 1983 study "Siting of Hazardous Waste Landfills and Their Correlation with Racial and Economic Status of Surrounding Communities." The chart reprinted after the following case surveys some of the data that has emerged. The National Law Journal published a comprehensive study showing disparate federal enforcement of environmental law especially as it affected low income communities of color. Coyle and Lavelle, "Unequal Protection: the Racial Divide in Environmental Law," National Law Journal, Sept. 21, 1992 at S4.

Whatever the cause of the disproportionate burdens felt by communities of low income and color — from the inevitabilities of the political and economic marketplace to occurrences of environmental racism — issues of environmental justice have renewed environmental law's focus upon community effects and conditions.

A variety of attempts have been made to bring the problem of disparate environmental protection directly into the legal process. In Chapter 24A of this Supplement textual materials are collected examining the law of the environmental justice issue, including recent executive orders and attempted litigation. This is one area, however, in which existing rules of statutory, nonstatutory, and constitutional law do not yet readily appear to be effective in addressing perceived problems.

If desired, the themes of environmental justice analysis — and a focus on the community impacts of the various environmental law doctrines explored in the coursebook's chapters — can provide a coherent theme to be carried throughout the study of environmental law.

To facilitate that perspective, one may choose to review the materials of Chapter 24A at this point, rather than later on in the course.

PAGE 23   **Contending forces: an environmental perspective on the dramatic appearance of the anti-environmental "Wise Use" movement, and "the Unholy Trinity"**

> "Environmentalism is the new paganism, trees are worshipped and humans sacrificed at its altar.... It is evil...and we intend to destroy it." *Ron Arnold, chairman of the Center for the Defense of Free Enterprise,* Boston Globe, *January 13, 1992.*

> "The preservationists are like a new pagan religion, worshipping trees and animals and sacrificing people.... It's a holy war between fundamentally different religions." *Charles Cushman, founder of the National Inholders Association/Multiple Use Land Alliance, U.S. News & World Report, October 21, 1991.*

> "Property is that which is peculiarly yours, whether it's your money, your wife, your children, your house, your car or your real estate." *Don Gerdts, founder of The Property Rights Council of America, Albany Times Union, April 11, 1992.*[1]

An overview of current environmental affairs would be delinquent if it did not include recognition of the rambunctious emergence of the so-called "Wise Use" movement, a loose but high-profile anti-environmental coalition of mostly Western populist groups funded by industry to advance an antiregulatory agenda.[2]

Before the advent of the Wise Users, it could be said that there was no organized national opposition to public interest environmentalism operating at a populist level.

Appropriating their name from the words of Gifford Pinchot, a grand old conservationist who worked with Teddy Roosevelt in founding American environmental ethics with a call for "wise use of the nation's resources," the Wise Use movement groups over the past several years have had a remarkable impact in the media and on the national political scene, operating, like the environmental movement, without any central organization.

---

1. From THE WISE USE MOVEMENT: Strategic Analysis and Fifty State Review.
2 The financing of the wise use groups is not readily disclosed. One such group, "People for the American West!" is reported to receive most of its financing from the mining and minerals industry, with a contributors list of more than 60 companies – Homestake Mining, Kennecott Copper, Crown Resources, Cyprus Minerals, NERCO Minerals, Hecla Mining, Pegasus Mining, Chevron, and others – some of which have given more than $100,000 to this grassroots populist group.

Beyond fundraising, the Wise Use movement incorporates three major sectors of action: a media initiative, a political initiative, and a legal implementation initiative.

MEDIA

In the media the Wise Guys, as they are ruefully called by many pro-environment citizen groups, have been able to put forward a parade of vivid images of down-home Americans suffering private property losses owing to governmental high-handedness — leading to the conclusion that national regulatory efforts across a wide range of issues must be rolled back. Most Americans have a gut sympathy for the little guy, and unlike most Europeans do not instinctively incorporate a fundamental recognition of the necessity of government. With well-chosen images, the Wise Users have enlisted the media in their David and Goliath caricature. When a rugged ranch wife tells how public land grazing restrictions are closing down the family ranch (see Chapter 9B of this Supplement), or protected endangered species are killing her cows (coursebook at 442), or David Lucas walks his barrier beach house lot for which he paid $1 million and then was forbidden to build on (see Chapter 9C of this Supplement), the media story has typically been "little guy gets hit hard by governmental zeal," notably ignoring the public subsidies being soaked up by Wise Use individuals and industries, and the public harms caused by their unregulated actions.

As a self-described "movement" rather than a coordinated organization, the Wise Users media presence incorporates voices ranging from Rush Limbaugh to the Rev. Moon's Washington Times.

POLITICAL ACTION

Beyond media, which in America today is emphatically part of the political process, Wise Users operate at the local as well as state and national levels. In the Pacific Northwest they have successfully elected their members to local office and organized county secession movements, with the aim of circumventing resource management ordinances. They have organized more than a hundred lobbying groups at all three levels of government. This, of course, is the stuff of American politics. They have fit effectively into the existing anti-environmental interests entrenched in the political establishments. What is not so straightforward has been the groups' evasiveness about political linkages to various resource exploitation industries and about where the money comes from.

The Wise Use movement will continue to be a fascinating case study of how national environmental policy gets made, and remade.

LEGAL IMPLEMENTATION

The Wise Users' political agenda has been represented in the legal process in legislatures and the executive branch as well as in court litigation.

The central issue in the Wise Use legal agenda has been strenuous assertion of private property rights against government regulatory restrictions — the fight against "regulatory takings" — an area in which regulated industry's arguments can often strike a chord in grass roots citizens as well.

In litigation, Wise Users have supported litigation like the *Lucas* case, resistance to endangered species protection in national forests, and various mining and grazing law challenges.

The Wise Users' legislative and administrative themes have focused on attempts to legislate requirements that any regulatory burdens on private property must be compensated. This initiative is noted further in Chapter 9 of this Supplement.

"THE UNHOLY TRINITY"

Concurrently with the rise of the Wise Use movement and the congressional travails of the Clinton Administration, there has emerged a triple-headed set of anti-regulatory political initiatives that has been described as "the Unholy Trinity," attempting to force government to back off in three general sectors:

> • Private property rights, with calls for administrative compensation to regulated parties, noted later in Chapter 9.
>
> • "Unfunded mandates," echoing state and local governments' frustration with federal programs that particularly after 1980 required them to pay for implementation of federal laws. This initiative is noted further in Chapter 11 of this Supplement.
>
> • Cost-benefit analysis/risk assessment, an initiative for requiring all public interest regulation to be preceded by a thorough-going analysis of overall economic rationality. This initiative is noted further in Chapter 2 of this Supplement.

In themselves, of course, these three themes are appropriate and logical public policy inquiries. Cost-benefit analysis, for instance, including risk assessment, is a recurring theme in the coursebook's policy analysis. The environmentalists' jaundiced reaction to the Unholy Trinity comes from their highly selective application — to resource regulations, not to the massive subsidy programs that provide their political backdrop — and their tactical implementation in bills requiring so much administrative procedure and reporting that it appears really to be seeking not answers and assurances, but "paralysis by analysis."

The following articles provide further skeptical views of the Wise Users.

Margaret Knox,[3] **Meet the Anti-Greens:**
The Wise-Use Movement Fronts for Industry

The Progressive, October 1991, 21

When David Heatwole of Arco, Alaska, suggested at the 1988 American Mining Congress that industry "organize a grass-roots movement" to counter environmentalism and oppose new wilderness, it sounded laughable. But since then, a lot of money, time, and energy have gone into doing just that. A determined band of organizations is working — with help from the Unification Church, oil, mineral, and timber companies, and political allies in the Senate — to defeat environmentalists who wish to

---

3. Margaret Knox is a free-lance writer in Missoula, Montana.

restrict corporate encroachment and motorized recreation on public lands.

The coalition hopes to unite industry with farmers, ranchers, snowmobilers, motorcyclists and hunters. By some estimates, that's a potential anti wilderness constituency of more than fifty million Americans.

To the extent such a movement exists, it does so under the banner of "wise use" or "multiple use" of public lands, a name chosen to imply that we can simultaneously clear-cut forests and preserve them, motor through wilderness and keep it wild, and extract a profit from the land without damaging it. Wise-use activists employ a number of familiar right-wing tricks to stampede people into action. They equate environmental protection with lost jobs, question the Christian morality of their opponents, raise gas-guzzling to the level of a constitutional right, and elevate anti-intellectualism to a virtue.

The wise-use movement was launched in 1988 at a huge conference in Reno, Nevada, sponsored by the Center for the Defense of Free Enterprise (DEFE) of Bellevue, Washington. Before that, CDFE's forty-five year-old president. Alan Gottlieb was national director of Youth Against McGovern, a board member of Young Americans for Freedom, founder of the Second Amendment Foundation, and chairman of the Citizens Committee for the Right to Keep and Bear Arms. Gottlieb, who is on the board of the American Conservative Union, considers himself an anti-tax hero, having been convicted in 1984 of filing a bogus tax return. "A badge of honor," he calls the conviction.

Gottlieb and his vice president, Ron Arnold, coined the term "wise use." In 1989 they published a slim volume called *The Wise Use Agenda* that lists twenty-five goals, including open all public lands — including wilderness areas and national parks — to mineral and energy production; rewrite the Endangered Species Act to remove such "non-adaptive species as the California condor"; make almost anyone protesting corporate activities liable for civil damages; make it a felony for any national forester to let a natural forest fire burn usable timber, prescribe immediate logging of all old-growth forests, and build national-park concessions under the direction of "private firms with expertise in people moving such as Walt Disney."

Who sign on to such an agenda? George Bush, for one. The Agenda's cover features a photo of Gottlieb and Bush in a warm embrace, and the book contains a congratulatory telegram from the White House. Also listed inside are sympathetic organizations such as the DuPont Co., the National Rifle Association, James Watt's Mountain States Legal Foundation, Exxon Corporation's exploration and drilling subsidiary Exxon Co. USA, and Louisiana Pacific Corporation.

But some 200 tiny clubs signed on, too, mainly recreationists with such titles as the Treasure Valley Trail Machine Association, the Issoula Snowgoers, and the Yakima Valley Dust Dodgers — the "grassroots" David Heatwole was talking about.

Anyone who has driven through the Northwest lately knows this boom-and-bust territory harbors a good deal of fear and animosity toward the environmental movement. Yellow ribbons on car aerials and chartreuse signs in store windows — to say nothing of EAT A SPOTTED OWL bumper stickers — pledge allegiance to the timber industry and all its works.

It is the goal of the wise-use organizers to channel that anger into action. "They're not that effective in the legislature yet, but they're stirring up rallies in limber communities and getting their views heard with the long-term goal of effecting legislation," said Sheryl Hutchison, deputy press secretary to Democratic Governor Booth Gardner of Washington.

Last year, Gardner vetoed a wise-use-sponsored bill that would have restricted the state from regulating business, such as clear-cutting on private land.

Ron Arnold defines the fight as class warfare. The environmental movement, he says, is made up of "rich, educated people so high up the needs hierarchy that they actively seek to mock and disdain the lower needs, such as food and shelter." Now, he says, "loggers who have an average education of the ninth grade are trying to figure out why these educated people want to put them out of work."

The theme of educated against uneducated, rich against poor, comes up again and again. Mike Nickols is a slash contractor to the timber industry in Darby, Montana. Ask him why he started "Grassroots for Multiple Use" — a 1,400-member wise-use organization of loggers, ranchers, and snowmobilers — and he inevitably gets around to railing against the "Ph.D's" who [are drawn] to sexy green causes because they don't have anything real to worry about. Working people are being left behind, Nickols complains. "We're living in a full-stomach America, and they're after cake and ice cream while we're scrambling for meat and potatoes," he says.

In this view, environmentalists are not only Ph.D's; they're pagans, Earth-worshipers, and druids "willing to sacrifice people to save trees," says Ron Arnold. According to Ed Wright, editor of the newsletter of the Blue Ribbon Coalition, "Where the Sierra Club tells the truth and deals in practical issues, more power to them," But, says Wright, "When they start mixing in their weird science and Earth religions, that's where I say enough is enough."

"It's very serious, very ugly," says John Gatchell, program director for the Montana Wilderness Association. Wise-use "is deliberately and purposefully trying to drive a wedge between people who should be natural allies. Tree huggers and tree cutters both have an interest in sustained yield. The wise-use folks are trying to make out as though it's un-Christian to have a reverence for nature."

Arnold says corporate sponsorship of wise-use activities has been thin. "They're scared of us," he claims. "We've gotten no more than $500 in contributions from any one company." But Exxon, Chevron, and the timber giant Georgia Pacific helped sponsor the third-annual Wise Use Conference in Salt Lake City in April, 1990. And representatives from Kawasaki, Yamaha, and Honda are on the Blue Ribbon Coalition's advisory board, says Wright, and have given substantial support.

Wise-use activists vehemently deny any support from the Unification Church of the Reverent Sun Myung Moon and carefully guard their financial secrets. But one of the biggest promoters of the wise-use philosophy is the arch-conservative American Freedom Coalition (AFC), with 300,000 members and offices in all fifty states. According to AFC president Robert Grant, almost one-third of all the money the AFC has collected since it was founded three years ago has come from Unification Church "business interests." (In a letter published in The Washington Post last year, Grant in one breath denied being "controlled" by Moon and in the next admitted that of almost $17 million AFC has raised, more than $5 million is Moon money.) AFC has its own environmental task force which promotes wise-use in the AFC newspaper and which, in 1989, hosted wise use rallies and conferences in four states. Gottlieb and Arnold both say they have served on AFC advisory boards.

The wise-use philosophy also has powerful friends in the U.S. Senate. In April 1989, six Republican Senators sent a letter to 120 "opinion leaders" — including Interior Secretary Manuel Lujan, requesting funds for the Our Land Society, a wise-use group based in Idaho. Written on Senate stationery, the letter warned that "advocates of environmental paranoia, locked-up resources, and costly regulation have never lacked a forum for their views," and urged that "this imbalance must be corrected."

The letter, which included Our Land Society materials, was signed by Republican Senators Steve Symms and James McClure of Idaho, Conrad Burns of Montana, Strom Thurmond of South Carolina, Jesse Helms of North Carolina, and Ted Stevens of Alaska. Wise-use activists take credit for a bill Symms introduced that would channel a portion of gasoline-tax receipts to build trails for off-road motorized vehicles (item twenty-four of The Wise Use Agenda), and another introduced in July of 1990 by Representative Bob Smith, Republican of Oregon, that would require Federal agencies to consider the economic stability of communities when they adopt plans for forest and resource management.

The wise-use movement was well enough organized in September 1989 to pressure all the sponsors of Turner Broadcasting System's logging documentary Rage Over Trees to withdraw their support, Arnold claims credit, and Joel Westbrook, Turner's vice president for nonfiction development, describes a "creepy" campaign of calls from people all over the country objecting to the film before it aired. "Often they were identical letters or fax trees. They already had the system together to get at this show. They couldn't have organized it that fast."

Ford Motor Company, one of the key sponsors, pulled its ads after receiving "urgent requests from our dealer associates in the Pacific Northwest," says Ford spokesman Michael Parriss. "They said it would really hurt their business." Turner aired the film anyway and lost $100,000, Westbrook says. Arnold, who says he was a "peripheral" organizer, celebrated a wise use victory. In June, Ford yanked $60,000 worth of ads from The New Range Wars, a documentary Turner aired about cattle grazing on public lands. Ford said it did so because it anticipated controversy. The National Inholders Association, a wise-use lobby for holders of grazing permits on public lands, is planning a boycott of the General Electric Company, which underwrote the production. Both Rage Over Trees and The New Range Wars were produced by the National Audubon Society.

Arnold also claims credit for a lawsuit filed last November by the Washington State Apple Growers Association against the Natural Resources Defense Council and CBS News. He says the "Alar Scare" —

in the revelation that people were getting sick from eating apples sprayed with chemicals — damaged hundreds of mom-and-pop growers. Arnold raised money for the lawsuit, which he hopes will set a precedent of holding environmentalists responsible for the "disparagement" of industry.

The wise-use movement is no more monolithic than the environmental or peace movements. It doesn't have a central headquarters. But it does try to identify people and organizations sympathetic to the cause and then move them to unified action. Myron Ebell, who runs the one-man Washington office of the National Inholders Association, says he figures wise-use is about fifteen years behind its nemesis, the environmental movement.

But he's patient, "The radical environmentalists didn't win many at first, either," he says.

THE WISE USE MOVEMENT: Strategic Analysis and Fifty State Review[4]

...At the most elementary level of analysis, the national Wise Use Movement uses three distinct messages to communicate.

> **Conspiracy Message:** Environmentalists, a group comprised mostly of elite intellectuals, are in league with big government bureaucrats to put the needs of nature before man. Their cabal believes economic activity is less important than preserving a pristine natural environment, and they are ready to sacrifice the basic needs of you and your family on the altar of environmental purity.

> **Mainstream Message:** Man and nature can live together in productive harmony.

> **Vanguard Message:** It is man's inherent right to exploit nature, no matter what the environmental cost.

The *vanguard message* is the central precept of the movement's national organizers. In the early stages of the development of the Wise Use Movement, it occupied center stage and was used to organize an elite group of "true believers" under the Wise Use tent. The *vanguard message* is still used to keep the core right wingers within the movement, and it reflects the...philosophy of the movement's national leaders.

The *conspiracy message* is used as a tool to organize at the local level or to convince people, already involved in local Wise Use groups, of the need for a national movement. While this message is directed at a larger audience than the *vanguard message*, it is not for common consumption. It is political rhetoric devised to play on peoples' emotions and fears, polarize people into an us versus them mentality and incite those who feel at risk.

The *mainstream message* is Wise Use dogma packed for popular consumption. It is Wise Use with a moderate face, carefully calculated to appeal to the broadest possible audience. As Wise Use has received

---

4. A Special Report of The Wilderness Society, reprinted by permission.

more national media attention, its leaders have increasingly used a *mainstream message* to communicate. A prime example of this is Ron Arnold's recent definition of the Wise Use Movement's core principles.

> We in the Wise Use Movement have a few core beliefs...that we all believe. Man and nature can live together in productive harmony. Human values, culture and tradition are more important than other living creatures. Economic activity should not be damaged to protect nature. Nature can be properly protected by wise management of economic activity. Beyond that, every segment of the Wise Use Movement has its own specialized belief that are not shared by other segments. Speech, Maine Conservation Rights Institute, April 20, 1992.

Comments made by Wise Use leaders incorporate elements from each of these three basic messages. But the mix of messages has changed dramatically over time with the sugar-coated mainstream message ascendant.

Environmentalists, who focus on Wise Use's conspiracy and vanguard messages and say the movement is too extreme to become a major force in America, overlook the power of the mainstream message. They also fall to see that the underside of the mainstream message paints a convincing portrait of environmentalists as the extremists in the debate over striking a balance between man and nature.

There is nothing new about extremism in American politics, [or] anti-environmental organizations advocating the exploitation of public lands.... What is new is the success that the anti-environmental movement has had in popularizing their message.

One ploy the national Wise Use Movement has used effectively to popularize their appeal is to put a human face on their message by parading local victims of overzealous environmental regulators and law before the media. This technique enables wise Use to put a David and Goliath spin on their message — a sure winner with the press...

Some typical examples of "environmental victims" whose stories have been transformed by the Wise Use Movement into modern n day parables of the results of environmental extremism include:

> •Steve Nelson of Burnt Ranch, California. Nelson is a rancher who owns property adjacent to a National Forest. Nelson learned that the Forest Service was resurveying his area because topographical maps of the area were incorrect. When the survey was completed, the Forest Service claimed Nelson's property and that of two of his neighbors, were in the National Forest. The government promptly served Nelson with an eviction notice and put a sign on his front lawn reading "Property of the National Forest Service."

> •Albert Cusick of Pembroke, Maine. Cusick is worried the U.S. Fish and Wildlife Service will take his 100 acres along Maine's coast and make it part of the Moosehorn national Wildlife Refuge. Cusick told the New York Times, " The Constitution of the United States said we can own this property, and my family has for 206 years, then the government turns around and said they can manage it better. I'm no college

boy, but that doesn't make sense to me. What's happening to us just isn't right...."[5]

•Sue Sutton of California. Sue Sutton is a farmer in California. When water was taken from the Sacramento River to save salmon, it endangered her farm. She said on ABC News: "Are we going to sacrifice human beings for a fish or a bird or a snack or a rat? We need to ask ourselves that question,"[6]

•Robert Brace of Erie County, Pennsylvania. Brace, a farmer, was accused by EPA in 1987 of filling 35 acres of his land and draining another 75 acres to build a golf course. Brace states that he planned to grow cabbages. Outraged, Brace's family and friends formed the Pennsylvania Landowners Association. The group now claims over 135,000 members. Brace's daughter, Rhonda McAtee, is the director of the organization.

What do these typical stories have in common? The victims live in rural areas and work in resource dependent jobs....

The ambitions of national Wise Use leaders, however, stretch well beyond the horizons of rural America. And while exaggerating their actual reach at this time, they have been involved in and are responsible to varying degrees for:

•killing the Synar grazing bill, which would have raised grazing fees from $1.92 to $5.39 per animal unit,

•adding $30 million to the highway bill for the construction of off-road vehicle (ORV) trails on public lands,

•defeating the Montana Wilderness bill in the Senate,

•passing through the Senate the Symms private property bill and

•effecting environmental regulatory proceedings through former President Bush's Council on Competitiveness (a staff aide for former Vice President Quayle's Council on Competitiveness attended the 1992 Wise Use Conference in Reno).

THE STRUCTURE OF THE WISE USE MOVEMENT

The Wise Use Movement was officially founded in August of 1988 at the Multiple Use Strategy Conference in Reno, Nev. The conference was sponsored by the Center for the Defense of Free Enterprise (CDFE) — Alan Gottlieb and Ron Arnold's group.

The *mainstream message* of the Wise Use Movement is often the most prominent communication in a given community of a can-do, entrepreneurial philosophy that promotes stewardship and husbandry and reaffirms the morality of rural life. The core arguments of the positive message are:

---

5. *New York Times*, August 2, 1992.
6. ABC American Agenda, Spring 1992.

1. Balance: Man and nature can exist in productive harmony. Nature can be properly protected by the wise management of economic activity.

2. People Come First: Man is the preeminent species. Nature exists for man. Man's needs come first.

3. Can-Do Attitude: Science, technology and our own ingenuity can solve our environmental problems.

4. Freedom of Choice Is Our Individual Right: The best government is the government that governs the least. Individual freedom, individual choice must be predominant.

There is obviously a contrasting or underside to each one of Wise Use's core arguments. According to Wise Use, environmentalists are extremists who believe:

1. No Balance: Economic activity is less important than preserving pristine nature.

2. People Do Not Come First: All life is sacred. Man is no more important than a grasshopper or an amoeba.

3. Can't Do Attitude: American science and technology along cannot solve environmental problems (nattering nabobs of negativism!). In fact, environmentalists use bad science like Chicken Little to say, the 'sky is falling.'

4. Public Needs Supersede Individual Rights: The rights of the many are more important than the rights of the individual. And government regulation enforces this hierarchy.

The contrast drawn by these positive and negative messages is quite effective.

Tactics

Below is a list of tactics...National Wise Use leaders...commonly employ:

Telling the Big Lie: Wise Users are not averse to stretching the truth, telling outright lies and using fear tactics to make their case more persuasive and compelling.

Using Deceptive Language and Names: Wise Use leaders borrow much of their language from environmentalists. They also give their organizations benign names like Maine Conservation Research Institute, Davis Mountain Trans-Pecos Heritage Association, National Wetlands Coalition, and the Wilderness Impact Research Foundation.... In some cases, Wise Use groups have even been known to steal an environmental group's name.... The Friends of the Bow (FOB), a local environmental group in Wyoming, has been active for several years on issues relating to the Medicine Bow National Forest. Last year, a multiple use group discovered that FOB had never registered their name with the Wyoming Secretary of State,.[so they] paid the trademark and nonprofit corporation fees, and legally became the Friends of the Bow.[7]

---

7. The anti-environmental FOB is run by Larry Bourret, executive vice president of the Wyoming Farm Bureau, Carolyn Paseneaux, Wyoming Woolgrowers

Describing All Opponents as Part of the Status Quo or Extremists: ...code words for out of touch with the realities of every day life and average people and part of the problem with government....

Describing Wise Use As the Defender of the Constitution: Wise Use bolsters it arguments by employing powerful symbols like the Constitution....

Questioning Opponents' Patriotism: Wise Users present themselves as true Americans while questioning, both directly and indirectly, environmentalists patriotism....

One California farmer remarked, "I was born and raised in America, and I can't believe this [environmental regulation] is coming from the government that I went to war to defend.... The most common gambit is to call environmentalists communists. Cliff Gardner vice president of Nevada Farm Bureau said, "The enemy is the hard-core groups that are using the environmental movement to their advantage... I'm talking about those people who would destroy the free enterprise system of the United States and set up a tyrannical socialist or collectivist type government...."

Wolves in Sheep's' Clothing: Wise Use advocates are rarely seen in suits.... Many of the most ardent Wise Use advocates...drop their professional titles and are...referred to as ranchers, rather than as attorneys. In addition, they are almost always interviewed by the news media in natural surroundings — out on the farm, out on the range. By contrast environmentalists in the news reports...reviewed for this study, wore suits or jackets and ties and were filmed or interviewed in offices crammed with books and computers.

Using Influential Politicians and Those with Credibility to Buttress Their Positions:

Wise Users solicit op-eds and letters of support from influential politicians, Farm Bureau executives and labor leaders to lend credibility to their cause.

Packing Hearings: In some situations Wise Users pay attendees [or give] workers paid days off... and provide buses to ensure large turnouts at particular hearings....

Pre-Hearing Pep Rallies: ...to stir up their troops to a fever pitch. People for the West! has used this technique effectively in several states.

Using Video Cameras At Hearings: ... filming every meeting, every hearing and every rally...to intimidate environmentalists and those convening the meeting....

Using Fear To Dissuade Environmentalists From Action: ...There have been several incidents nationwide where people were physically and verbally threatened for their pro-environmental views.... In the weeks after an appearance by Cushman, vandals slashed tires and sprayed swastikas on Park Service vehicles.... Robert Barbee, Yellowstone National Park Superintendent, said, "I went to a meeting in Bozeman, Montana, and...I was a communist, everything else you could think of. One lady got up,

---

Association, Sharon Nicholas, Wyoming Trucking Association and Jack Ratchye, formerly of the Wyoming Mining Association.

used her time to say the pledge of allegiance, then looked at me and called me a Nazi."

Maintaining A Grassroots Image: Arnold has long warned resource industry executives to provide money for political fights and then "get the hell out of the way" to allow the money to be used for grassroots organizing and communication....

While Arnold is actively working to diminish the [visibility of the] role corporations play in Wise Use, he is forcing corporate sponsors of environmental groups into the spotlight. In 1991, NIA/MULA called for a boycott of General Electric as a result of their sponsorship of Audubon documentaries.   The boycott was so successful in its letter-writing campaign and grassroots appeal that GE withdrew its annual $1 million contribution to Audubon.

Chapter 2, Law and Economics, Uncertainty and Risk, in Environmental Decision-Making

---

Page 40   More on the tragedy of the commons

3A. An array of strategies for protecting the commons. Professor Carol Rose has suggested that many environmental problems are properly conceived of as involving overuse ("congestion") of common resources. In a recent article, Rethinking Environmental Controls: Management Strategies for Common Resources, 1991 Duke L.J. 1, she attempts first to create a catalogue of ways in which common resources can be regulated and thereafter attempts to construct a calculus that will discern which of the management approaches is most appropriate. Her four basic strategies are encapsulated by the terms **do nothing**, **keep out** (prohibit additional use after an acceptable limit is reached), **right way** (control the methods of resource exploitation), and **property**. She posits that the objective should be to select the approach that results in the lowest total social costs, which she defines as the total of administrative costs, user costs (of complying with the regulatory scheme) and overuse or failure costs (arising to whatever extent the system fails to achieve the desired limitations on use). Finally, she describes the general prospects for each regulatory strategy and finds that the key variable in selecting the least cost system will be "how far we have traveled along the...line of resource pressure [over-use]." *Id.* at 24.

PAGE 54   Wise Use anti-regulation

3. Contending forces and opposition to governmental regulation. As noted in Chapter 1, most environmental controversies pit contending forces against one another, whether it is salt manufacturers and their allies against the car and water using public, or the Kepone profiteers against the users of James Bay. A broader effort to resist pro-environmental government regulation of pollution and other incursions on the commons appears to be underway, flying under the expropriated banner called "Wise Use."[8] Capitalizing on instances of heavy-handed government regulation, the Wise Use Movement has created a facade of national unity among numerous groups who have opposed environmental regulation in their own localities. At the national level, particularly for media consumption, the leaders of the Wise Use Movement espouse the message that man and nature can live together in productive harmony. The groups leaders, in other settings also urge that it is man's inherent right to exploit nature without regard to environmental cost, and add a conspiratorial tone to their message by blaming environmental elitists and

---

8. The term "wise use" is originally associated with Gifford Pinchot, father of the Forest Service, who was a great conservationist.

big government for sacrificing the economic interests of the ordinary people on the altar of environmental purity.

Plainly, not all governmental regulation in the name of the environment is good, but equally plainly, the organization's name is surely a misnomer when it seeks to characterize as an conspiracy so much of the requisite "mutual coercion" that prevents the tragedy of the commons from becoming even more commonplace. What often escapes notice in the rhetoric of the particular conflict are the external costs imposed by those who desire to continue their "wise use." Even less well known is the extent of public subsidy that is often being collected by wise use proponents. As an example, three major off-road vehicle (ORV) manufacturers are major contributors to the Wise Use Movement, whose leaders lobbied hard for legislation that funded $30 million in trails for ORVs.

A political analysis sponsored by the Wilderness Society canvasses the structure and philosophy of the Wise Use Movement, its strengths, and the extent of its activities. See MacWilliams Cosgrove Snider, The Wise Use Movement: Strategic Analysis & Fifty State Review (revised edition, March, 1993).

PAGE 89   Risk assessment in setting policy

2c. Risk Ranking in Policy Making

The breadth and scope of environmental concerns have burgeoned in recent years with the result that they cannot all be addressed simultaneously. Even if there were agreement that all environmental problems are worthy of action, to take on all of the perceived problems at once would demand more resources, human and fiscal, than society is willing to commit to the task. Inevitably, priorities must be set that select some problems for more immediate attention while leaving others for more remote action. Setting those priorities is, rather plainly, a vital form of policy making. Setting priorities in addressing environmental problems may not be as simple as it appears:

- What problem is in greater need of remediation, indoor air pollution or outdoor ozone?

- How would $1,000,000 be better spent, cleaning up contaminated groundwater in Wichita, Kansas, or removing lead-based paint from aging single family homes in Detroit, Michigan?

- Which is a more urgent problem, species eradication resulting from urban sprawl in Southern California, or marginal reduction of air toxics emissions from smelters?

There does not seem to be a ready common denominator for making such policy decisions, but to some extent relative risk reduction fills that void. At least when the risks involved relate to human health, it seems that setting priorities that maximize risk reduction offers a form of cross-medium comparison. The greatest amount of risk reduction means, in effect, that the aggregate environmental hazard has been reduced by the greatest amount.   EPA, in response to demands for consistency and rationality in priority setting, began to embrace risk reduction as a priority setting mechanism in the late 1980s.   In 1987 it published a document titled "Unfinished Business: A Comparative Assessment of Environmental Problems" that began an attempt to make relative risk reduction a part of EPA's policy making process.   William Reilly, EPA Administrator wrote, "To the extent permitted by our statutory mandates, sound science can help us set priorities based on risk.   Indeed, the rigorous analysis of risk is fundamental to all of EPA's regulatory programs. Without some way of determining relative levels of risk, we would quickly become mired in a regulatory swamp, wherein all problems were equally important; all risks would have to be addressed with equal urgency; and accordingly, nothing would get done."[9]   A more substantial EPA document soon followed, a portion of which is excerpted below.

Reducing Risk: Setting Priorities and Strategies for Environmental Protection
Environmental Protection Agency, Report of the Science Advisory Board: Relative Risk Reduction Strategies Committee (RRRSC) to William K. Reilly, Administrator
Science Advisory Board A101, SAB-EC 90-021, September, 1990

...Risks to Human Health

The Human Health Subcommittee limited its assessment to those problems addressed by Unfinished Business. On reviewing the rankings in Unfinished Business, the Subcommittee identified those problems that represented major types of human exposure known to be associated with significant impacts on human health. In four such instances, relatively high-risk rankings were supported more firmly by the available data than they were for other health problems. The Subcommittee also noted that the development of better methodologies and more complete data could lead to a different approach to the assessment of human health risks, and that such an approach would involve the selection of specific environmental toxicants that warranted detailed assessment and major risk reduction efforts.

•   Ambient Air Pollutants

Stationary and more mobile sources emit a range of different air pollutants to which large populations are exposed.   Some have toxic and/or carcinogenic effects following direct inhalation exposure (e.g., carbon monoxide and benzene).   Others, such as lead and arsenic, reach humans by a variety of pathways including direct inhalation, inhalation of re-suspended dust, and ingestion of dust deposited on food products. Still others are important precursors that can lead to compounds such as ozone, acid aerosols, and carcinogenic hydrocarbons that form in the atmosphere over large areas of North America.

•   Worker Exposure to Chemicals in Industry and Agriculture

---

9. William Reilly, Taking Aim Toward 2000: Rethinking the Nation's Environmental Agenda, 21 Envtl. Law 1359, 1363 (1991).

Industrial and agricultural workers are exposed to many toxic substances in the workplace. Such exposures can cause cancer and a wide range of non-cancer health effects. Due to the large population of workers directly exposed to a range of highly toxic chemicals, this problem poses relatively high human health risks.

• Pollution Indoors

Building occupants may be exposed to radon and its decay products as well as to many airborne combustion products, including nitrogen dioxide and environmental tobacco smoke. Indoor exposures to toxic agents in consumer products (e.g., solvents, pesticides, formaldehyde) also can cause cancer and a range of non-cancer health effects. due to the large population directly exposed to a number of agents, some of which are highly toxic, this problem poses relatively high human health risks.

• Pollutants in Drinking Water

Drinking water, as delivered at the tap, may contain agents such as lead, chloroform, and disease-causing microorganisms. Exposures to such pollutants in drinking water can cause cancer and a range of non-cancer health effects. This problem poses relatively high human health risks, because large populations are exposed directly to various agents, some of which are highly toxic.

Other problem areas also involve potentially significant exposure of large populations to toxic chemicals, e.g., pesticide residues on food and toxic chemicals in consumer products. However, the data bases to support those concerns are not as robust as they are for the four areas listed above.

Relatively High-Risk Environmental Problems

The RRRSC not only reviewed the risk rankings contained in Unfinished Business, but it also identified several environmental problems as relatively high-risk, based on available scientific data and technical understanding. This effort was challenging for a number of reasons. Ecological, health, and welfare risks can be manifested in a number of different end points; it is difficult to compare risks with widely different time scales and spatial dimensions; because of data gaps and methodological inadequacies, it is rarely feasible to quantify total risk. In other words, the RRRSC faced many of the same hurdles that faced the authors of Unfinished Business when they developed their risk rankings.

Consequently, the RRRSC did not rank risks in the same manner as Unfinished Business did. The Ecology and Welfare Subcommittee grouped environmental problems into high-, medium-, and low-risk areas; the Human Health Subcommittee identified environmental problem areas where existing data indicated that risks could be relatively high. Additional data might identify additional high-risk problems. Both Subcommittees developed their assessments in light of the latest scientific and technical knowledge and using their best professional judgment, and both caution that their assessments are based on incomplete and often inadequate knowledge about 1) the extent of human and ecological exposures to pollutants and 2) exposure-response relationships.

The Ecology and Welfare Subcommittee identified areas of relatively high, medium and low risk, despite gaps in the relevant data. The four environmental problems that it considered high-risk even after data and analytical methodologies are improved because the geographic scale of all four is very large (regional to global), and because the time that could be required to mitigate all four is very long, and some effects are irreversible.

The Ecology and Welfare Subcommittee did not limit their assessment to the environmental problems listed in Unfinished Business. The order of problems listed within each of the three different risk groups shown below is not meant to imply a ranking.

- Relatively High-Risk Problems

    — Habitat Alteration and Destruction

    — Humans are altering and destroying natural habitats in many   places worldwide, e.g., by the draining and degradation of wetlands, soil erosion, and the deforestation of tropical and temperate rain forests.

- Species Extinction and Overall Loss of Biological Diversity

    — Many human activities are causing species extinction and depletion and the overall loss of biological diversity, including the genetic diversity of surviving species.

- Stratospheric Ozone Depletion

    — Because releases of chlorofluorocarbons and other ozone-depleting gases are thinning the earth's stratospheric ozone layer, more ultraviolet radiation is reaching the earth's surface, thus stressing many kinds of organisms.

- Global Climate Change

    — Emissions of carbon dioxide, methane, and other greenhouse gases are altering the chemistry of the atmosphere, threatening to change the global climate.

- Relatively Medium-Risk Problems

    — Herbicides/Pesticides
    — Toxics, Nutrients, Biochemical Oxygen Demand, and Turbidity in Surface Waters
    — Acid Deposition
    — Airborne Toxics

- Relatively Low-Risk Problems
    — Oil Spills
    — Groundwater Pollution
    — Radionuclides
    — Acid Runoff to Surface Waters
    — Thermal Pollution

The Ten Recommendations:

1. EPA should target its environmental protection efforts on the basis of opportunities for the greatest risk reduction. Since this country already has taken the most obvious actions to address the most obvious

environmental problems, EPA needs to set priorities for future actions so the Agency takes advantage of the best opportunities for reducing the most serious remaining risks.

2. EPA should attach as much importance to reducing ecological risk as it does to reducing human health risk. Because productive natural ecosystems are essential to human health and to sustainable, long-term economic growth, and because they are intrinsically valuable in their own right, EPA should be as concerned about protecting ecosystems as it is about protecting human health.

3. EPA should improve the data and analytical methodologies that support the assessment, comparison, and reduction of different environmental risks. Although setting priorities for national environmental protection efforts always will involve subjective judgments and uncertainty, EPA should work continually to improve the scientific data and analytical methodologies that underpin those judgments and help reduce their uncertainty.

4. EPA should reflect risk-based priorities in its strategic planning processes. The Agency's long-range plans should be driven not so much by past risk reduction efforts or by existing programmatic structures, but by ongoing assessments of remaining environmental risks, the explicit comparison of those risks, and the analysis of opportunities available for reducing risk.

5. EPA should reflect risk-based priorities in its budget process. Although EPA's budget priorities are determined to a large extent by the different environmental laws that the Agency implements, it should use whatever discretion it has to focus budget resources at those environmental problems that pose the most serious risks.

6. EPA — and the nation as a whole — should make greater use of all the tools available to reduce risk. Although the nation has had substantial success in reducing environmental risks through the use of government-mandated end-of-pipe controls, the extent and complexity of future risks will necessitate the use of a much broader array of tools, including market incentives and information.

7. EPA should emphasize pollution prevention as the preferred option for reducing risk. By encouraging actions that prevent pollution from being generated in the first place, EPA will help reduce the costs, intermedia transfers of pollution, and residual risks so often associated with end-of-pipe controls.

8. EPA should increase its efforts to integrate environmental considerations into broader aspects of public policy in as fundamental a manner as are economic concerns. Other Federal agencies often affect the quality of the environment, e.g., through the implementation of tax, energy, agricultural, and international policy, and EPA should work to ensure that environmental considerations are integrated, where appropriate, into the policy deliberations of such agencies.

9. EPA should work to improve public understanding of environmental risks and train a professional workforce to help reduce them. The improved environmental literacy of the general public, together with an expanded and better-trained technical workforce, will be essential to the nation's success at reducing environmental risks in the future.

10.　EPA should develop improved analytical methods to value natural resources and to account for long-term environmental effects in its economic analyses. Because traditional methods of economic analysis tend to undervalue ecological resources and fail to treat adequately questions of intergenerational equity, EPA should develop and implement innovative approaches to economic analysis that will address these shortcomings.

COMMENTARY & QUESTIONS

1.　EPA's steps toward risk analysis.　EPA's general approach to quantitative risk assessment got a blue-ribbon stamp of approval in early 1994 when the National Academy of Sciences, Committee on Risk Assessment of Hazardous Air Pollutants released a 600-page report that found EPA's approach to be sound.　Despite this endorsement, the report went on to offer 70 recommendations for changes in EPA's risk assessment practices.　The report, "Science and Judgment in Risk Assessment," was mandated by § 112(o) of the 1990 Clean Air Act Amendments.　Overall, the report advocates use of a range of approaches for evaluating risks of hazardous air pollutants, as is mandated under the Clean Air Act.　The most elaborate evaluative methods would be used for chemicals shown by relatively inexpensive techniques to possess the most significant health risks.　Additional stress was urged for chemical risks that arise through multiple exposure pathways or exposures to multiple chemicals.

2.　EPA's two-track use of relative risk as a policy making tool.　How far in the direction of using relative risk as a unified policy making tool does EPA seem willing to go?　When activities create commensurate risks, such as human health dangers, recommendation 1, 4, and 5 indicate that EPA wants to increase the role of relative risk in setting its priorities.　Likewise, several of the recommendations apply to ecological risk issues somewhat apart from health risk.　In contrast, however, EPA seems unwilling to try to mesh "ecological risk" with "human health risk" in a single all-encompassing calculus.　Instead, EPA seems to make a qualitative decision that ecological risks are also quite important, and then seeks to improve ecological risk assessment tools so that relative risk analysis can be used to set priorities among those risks.　In this fashion, EPA seems to have avoided the problem of trying to compare ecosystem harms with human health harms.

3. Competing proposals for setting environmental priorities.　In November 1992, Resources for the Future sponsored a national conference on potential uses of risk-based analysis in setting the federal regulatory agenda.　Several competing paradigms emerged from that conference.[10] Barry Commoner, director of the Center for the Biology of Natural Systems at Queens College, offered a pollution prevention-based approach to setting priorities. He proposed that the general public should set U.S. environmental priorities, based on what it decides are the most important opportunities to transform industries from polluting to non-polluting.　John Graham, professor of health policy at Harvard

---

10. The conference proceedings were published in July, 1994.　A 16-page synopsis of the conference is available from Resources for the Future, 1616 P St. N.W., Washington, D.C. 20036, by facsimile machine at (202) 939-3460.

University, argued that pollution prevention and comparative risk assessment-based approaches are complementary. Robert Bullard, professor of sociology from the University of California-Riverside argued that justice dictates that environmental protection is not a privilege to be doled out but is a right for all individuals. He argued that a strictly risk-based priority system may perpetuate the failure to identify and remediate so-called hot spots of environmental risk that exist in communities with a significant minority population. Instead, EPA's priority should be to clean up hazardous waste sites in communities where minorities and the poor face multiple risks from multiple sites and to limit imposition of new risks in these areas. A third alternative, directed innovation, which focuses on evaluating the cause of environmental problems was urged by Nicholas Ashford, a professor of technology policy from the Massachusetts Institute of Technology. He argued that strict regulation, properly designed, can trigger technological innovation, allowing for more risk reduction at equal or lower costs. This view was contested by James Wilson of Monsanto, who argued that individual companies do not always know when a particular innovation will succeed, and, therefore, it is folly to believe that the federal government can reliably choose targets for directed innovation.

4. Is a risk-based grand strategy a good plan? On the surface, the concept of risk management by risk ranking is so simple as to seem self-evidently correct. Somewhat like benefit-cost analysis, the end product of comparative risk analysis is information that says, "The most pressing environmental problem (i.e., the one involving the greatest risks) is problem X. The next most pressing problem is problem Y." And so on. The comparative risk methodology creates a common denominator for assessing the importance of environmental problems. Comparative risk analysis appears to have a triad of virtues, it partakes of the rationality of scientific measurement of the risks involved, it maximizes utility, and it allows for the integration of environmental management strategies.

On more careful scrutiny, there is reason for extreme caution in embracing comparative risk analysis. In a beautifully-researched article Professor Hornstein, after canvassing the virtues of comparative risk analysis, provides an array of arguments against uncritical reliance on comparative risk analysis as anything more than a useful datum in setting environmental protection priorities and policies. See Donald Hornstein, "Reclaiming Environmental Law: A Normative Critique of Comparative Risk Analysis," 92 *Colum. L. Rev.* 562 (1992). The article is a difficult one because it tends to be very exacting in marshaling arguments developed in social sciences literature to illustrate its points. Its thesis, however, is important in showing that (like "efficiency"), the comparative risk analysis process is sufficiently problematic that it should not be adopted uncritically as a normative touchstone. Among the most salient areas for caution in relying on comparative risk analysis are (1) the welter of uncertainty and unsupported simplifying assumptions that undergird the risk calculus itself, (2) the failure of the comparative risk methodology with its emphasis on expected values (measured in terms of losses) to account for the divergence between those values and the expected utility (perceived and real benefits) of various outcomes, (3) the indifference of comparative risk to the equity effects of alternative environmental protection choices, (4) the lack of a role for significant public participation in the decisional process, and (5) the failure of comparative risk analysis to frame environmental alternatives adequately.

See also Shifrin, Not by Risk Alone: Reforming EPA Research Priorities, 102 Yale L. J. 547 (1992), L. Winner, The Risk of Talking about Risk, in Winner, The Whale and the Reactor (1986)

Many economists, including participants at the November '92 conference noted above, apparently believe deeply in the fundamental topic of risk assessment — and are developing even more sophisticated tools to measure potential harms and uncertainties — yet do not advocate risk assessment as a strict technical process for setting public policy. "Risk assessment does not provide answers," said one conference participant. "It only helps define considerations that should be part of the public political debate." Cf. Stephen Breyer, Breaking the Vicious Circle (1994) (asserting that risk assessment can be objectively applied to guide national administrative agendas, through decisional structure similar to an agency of experts on a military command process).

5.   Risk assessment/ cost-benefit analysis, and the anti-regulation movement. It should be noted, finally, that there are two quite different concurrent tracks upon which discussions of risk assessment and cost-benefit analysis generally proceed. One one hand are economists and policy analysts concerned with the extremely difficult and important planning and policy questions posed for longterm rationality and effectiveness of national regulatory programs. These experts, as noted above, often believe deeply in the process of analyzing risk as a component of rational publc debate, but not as a mechanistic substitute for value-based policy debates.

On the other hand, those who most vociferously espouse risk assessment and cost-benefit analysis in the political arena are often broad-brush anti-regulationists who take the opportunity to push intra-agency regulatory risk reviews as a way to block administrative action. This was often the charge levelled against the Reagan cost-benefit Executive Order 12291, that it sought to emphasize corporate expenses involved in pollution control, not to achieve an analysis of public subsidies in the private sector or of the diffuse public harms motivating regulation.

When Rep. Billy Tauzin of Louisiana sponsors a succession of risk/ cost-benefit amendments providing that–

> In promulgating any final regulation relating to public health and safety or the environment...the administrator of the Environmental Protection Agency shall publish...in the Federal Register:(1) An estimate, performed with as much specificity as practicable, of the risk of the health and safety of individual members of the public addressed by the regulation and its effect on human health or the environment and the costs associated with implementation of, and compliance with, the regulation, (2) A comparative analysis of the risk addressed by the regulation relative to other risks to which the public is exposed, and (3) The administrator's certification [of all relevant data on the above],

and this provision is fully litigable by regulated industries, it is easy to see why many observers suspect that at least one of the goals of the required process is not better information but bottlenecked regulatory action, paralysis by analysis. See Chapter 11 of this Supplement.

PAGE 89-100   **Text Replacement for pages 89-100, on legal consideration of cancer risk and causation.**

Section 3. THE SPECIAL CASE OF CANCER RISK AND CAUSATION

It should come as little surprise that regulation of cancer risks is an area of special concern in modern environmental law. There is a growing body of scientific evidence that correlates exposure to a wide variety of hazardous materials with cancer in humans and other species. Moreover, as many of the preceding materials have pointed out, the public is significantly risk averse to the sorts of cancer risks that are generated by exposure to hazardous materials that have been released into the environment as pollution or discarded waste. Cancer seems to serve as an "indicator disease" identifying and arousing particular public concern about unhealthy conditions that may create public risks of other diseases as well.

Using the legal system to regulate cancer-causing materials and to provide remedies to those who have been injured by its release requires an unusual effort to marry scientific evidence and legal doctrine. The crux of the problem lies in trying to satisfy legal norms of proof of causation with evidence of the sort that scientists have adduced that link exposure to a hazardous material with the subsequent onset of cancer.[11] Moreover, the nature of the available knowledge still leaves significant gaps in understanding the linkage between toxic exposures and cancers. The precise etiology of diseases is often unknown and will vary depending on the carcinogen and the type of cancer involved. Presumably, sufficient exposure to a carcinogen precipitates a change in genetic or cellular structure. Over time, perhaps a very long time, the change is replicated and eventually alters the functional qualities of cells involved, causing them to multiply or attack other cells. The law has always functioned best with better-understood paths of causation, as when the smoke and particulate pollution from a neighboring factory cause immediate, observable physical and health damage to nearby neighbors.

Scientific inquiry into the linkage between exposure to suspected carcinogens and the subsequent onset of disease employs several quantitative techniques that estimate the magnitude of carcinogenic risks. In Leape, Quantitative Risk Assessment in the Regulation of Environmental Carcinogens, 4 Harv. Envtl. L. Rev. 86 (1980), the rudiments of how science approaches these problems is laid out in a straightforward fashion. Data on the carcinogenicity of a particular substance is usually developed in one of three ways — epidemiological studies, animal bioassay studies, or single cell tests. Data on exposure is even more difficult to develop because it involves generating a catalogue of sources of a particular carcinogen and a modeling of pathways by which that substance reaches humans. Only then can a guess about actual doses be made.

---

11. This problem is addressed in greater detail in Chapter 4.

The uncertainty involved in estimating the potency of carcinogens and the degree of exposure to them is not the only lack of precision in assessing the risks of exposure to potential carcinogens. To translate those figures into a population-wide risk assessment is even more daunting. This latter step generally involves two sorts of extrapolation. First, the risk assessor must extrapolate from observed effects on subgroups of the population to the population as a whole. If a subgroup is, for some undisclosed reason, particularly susceptible or particularly resistant to contracting cancer, the extrapolation magnifies the degree of inaccuracy of the underlying data. Second, because most data is derived from high exposure settings, the risk assessor must attempt to predict the degree to which lower doses result in lowered cancer rates. Here the question of "threshold" doses becomes acute; that is, the risk assessor must decide if there is some level of exposure for which it will be assumed that there is literally a zero risk of contracting cancer. Given the relatively large numbers of persons who may be exposed to low-level doses, the threshold safe level question holds the potential to influence profoundly the risk assessment.

COMMENTARY AND QUESTIONS

1. The anthropocentric nature of risk assessment. Cancer risk assessment usually includes only human health effects. Should risk assessment also consider ecosystem effects? Are ecosystem effects more, less, or as important as human health effects? Assuming that an accounting for ecosystem effects is appropriate, do some environmental losses count more than others? Are, for example, unusual or endangered ecosystems more important than relatively common ones?

2. Outrage and cancer risk. Why does quantitative cancer risk assessment, as described in the text above, systematically ignore "outrage" factors? Presumably, their absence is not indicative of their insubstantiality; rather, it should be taken as a sign that outrage is more in the nature of a qualitative factor. How are quantitative and qualitative factors to be compared? Even if outrage factors are not a part of risk assessment, at a minimum, they can be used to frame policy decisions regarding risk management strategies.

3. The fallacy of numeration. Is quantitative risk assessment viable, in light of the profound scientific uncertainties inherent in predicting carcinogenicity? Leape asserts that in many cases the uncertainties so confound the quantification process that it is even impossible to measure the extent of potential error (much less the risk itself) reliably. Does expressing such crude estimates in numerical form create a "fallacy of numeration" by which risk assessments are given undue credibility because they seem to be so precise?

4. Turning quantitative measures of risk into legal causation. As has long been understood, moving from quantitative risk assessment data to a claim of causation that will satisfy judicial decision-makers, requires a step beyond that act of quantification. In discussing the linkage of cigarette smoking to cancer, for example, a 1964 report of the Surgeon General's Advisory Committee stated:

> Statistical methods cannot establish proof of a causal
> relationship in an association. The causal significance of an
> association is a matter of judgment which goes beyond any

statement of statistical probability. To judge or evaluate the causal significance of the association between the attribute or agent and the disease, or effect upon health, a number of criteria must be utilized, no one of which is an all-sufficient basis for judgment. These criteria include: (a) the consistency of the association; (b) the strength of the association; (c) the specificity of the association; (d) the temporal relationship of the association; and (e) the coherence of the association.[12]

5. How safe is safe enough in dealing with cancer risks? Once risk is quantified insofar as is possible, the regulatory concern switches to the judgmental process of deciding what level of risk is little enough so that the risk should be encountered.

•

How does this work in specific cases? What is the regulator to do in trying to protect the public from harm? What is the relevance in regulation of the cost of avoiding risks? One of the principal efforts to control toxic exposure created health risks is embodied in the Toxic Substances Control Act of 1976 (ToSCA), 15 U.S.C.A. §§ 2601-2692, as amended. As its name implies, ToSCA attempts to regulate the risks posed by toxic substances. The case that follows considers regulation of cancer risks posed by asbestos under that law, a carcinogen for which an unusually large body of data about its effects is available. The operation of ToSCA is explored more fully in Chapter 16, but for present purposes very little about ToSCA or administrative law[13] need be known to focus on the problem of cancer risk management by an administrative agency (the United States Environmental Protection Agency (EPA)) as it is presented by the following case:

Corrosion Proof Fittings v. Environmental Protection Agency
United States Court of Appeals for the Fifth Circuit, 1991
947 F.2d 1201

SMITH, J. The Environmental Protection Agency (EPA) issued a final rule under section 6 of the Toxic Substances Control Act (ToSCA) to prohibit the future manufacture, importation, processing, and distribution of asbestos in almost all products. Petitioners claim that EPA's rulemaking procedure was flawed and that the rule was not promulgated on the basis of substantial evidence....

Asbestos is a naturally occurring fibrous material that resists fire and most solvents. Its major uses include heat-resistant insulators, cements, building materials, fireproof gloves and clothing, and motor vehicle brake linings. Asbestos is a toxic material, and occupational exposure to asbestos dust can result in mesothelioma, asbestosis, and lung cancer.

[EPA, after an elaborate seven-year review of the scientific evidence of asbestos carcinogenicity, concluded in 1986 that asbestos exposure

---

12. See U.S. Surgeon General's Advisory Committee on Smoking and Health, Smoking and Health 20 (1964).
13. A primer on administrative law appears in Chapter 11, at pages 539-544. Those wholly unfamiliar with how agencies function may wish to preview that material before reading the *Corrosion Proof Fittings* case.

"poses an unreasonable risk to human health." It proposed a series of regulatory options for asbestos usage and, for two more years collected more data and received comments on its regulatory proposals. In 1989, EPA announced its final rule, imposing a staged ban on most commercial uses of asbestos. A number of affected firms challenged the rule as violative of TOSCA ' 6.]

[Section 6] of ToSCA provides, in pertinent part, as follows:

> (a) Scope of regulation.—If the Administrator finds that there is a reasonable basis to conclude that the manufacture, processing, distribution in commerce, use, or disposal of a chemical substance or mixture, or that any combination of such activities, presents or will present an unreasonable risk of injury to health or the environment, the Administrator shall by rule apply one or more of the following requirements to such substance or mixture to the extent necessary to protect adequately against such risk using the least burdensome requirements.

...Congress did not enact ToSCA as a zero-risk statute.[14] The EPA, rather, was required to consider both alternatives to a ban and the costs of any proposed actions and "to carry out this chapter in a reasonable and prudent manner [after considering] the environmental, economic, and social impact of any action."

We conclude that EPA has presented insufficient evidence to justify its asbestos ban. We base this conclusion upon two grounds: the failure of the EPA to consider all necessary evidence and its failure to give adequate weight to statutory language requiring it to promulgate the least burdensome, reasonable regulation required to protect the environment adequately. Because the EPA failed to address these concerns, and because the EPA is required to articulate a "reasoned basis" for its rules, we are compelled to return the regulation to the agency for reconsideration.

LEAST BURDENSOME AND REASONABLE

ToSCA requires that EPA use the least burdensome regulation to achieve its goals of minimum reasonable risk. This statutory requirement can create problems in evaluating just what is a "reasonable risk." Congress' rejection of a no-risk policy, however, also means that in certain cases, the least burdensome yet still adequate solution may entail somewhat more risk than other, known regulations that are far more burdensome on the industry and the economy.. The very language of ToSCA requires that the EPA, once it has determined what an acceptable level of non-zero risk is, choose the least burdensome method of reaching that level.

In this case, the EPA banned, for all practical purposes, all present and future uses of asbestos—a position the petitioners characterize as the "death penalty alternative," as this is the most burdensome of all possible

---

14. Cf. Southland Mower Co. v. CPSC, 619 F. 2d 499, 510 (5th Cir. 1980)("It must be remembered that 'the statutory term "unreasonable risk" presupposes that a real, and not a speculative, risk be found to exist and that the Commission bears the burden of demonstrating the existence of such a risk before proceeding to regulate.'

alternatives listed as open to EPA under ToSCA. ToSCA not only provides the EPA with a list of alternative actions, but also provides those alternatives in order of how burdensome they are. The regulations thus provide for EPA regulation ranging from labeling the least toxic chemicals to limiting the total amount of chemicals an industry may use. Total bans head the list as the most burdensome regulatory option.

By choosing the harshest remedy given to it under ToSCA, the EPA assigned to itself the toughest burden in satisfying ToSCA's requirement that its alternative be the least burdensome of those offered to it. Since both by definition and by the terms of ToSCA the complete ban of manufacturing is the most burdensome alternative—for even stringent regulation at least allows a manufacturer the chance to invest and meet the new, higher standard—the EPA regulation cannot stand if there is any other regulation that would achieve an acceptable level of risk as mandated by ToSCA....

The EPA considered, and rejected, such options as labeling asbestos products, thereby warning users and worker involved in the manufacture of asbestos-containing products of the chemical's dangers, and stricter workplace rules. EPA also rejected controlled use of asbestos in the workplace and deferral to other government agencies charged with workplace and consumer exposure to industrial and product hazards such as OSHA, the [Consumer Product Safety Commission], and the Mine Safety and Health Administration. The EPA determined that deferral to these other agencies was inappropriate because no one other authority could address all the risks posed "throughout the life cycle" by asbestos, and any action by one or more of the other agencies still would leave an unacceptable residual risk.[15]

Much of the EPA's analysis is correct, and the EPA's basic decision to use ToSCA as a comprehensive statute designed to fight a multi-industry problem was a proper one that we uphold today on review. What concerns us, however, is the manner in which the EPA conducted some of its analysis. ToSCA requires the EPA to consider, along with the effects of toxic substances on human health and the environment, "the benefits of such substances or mixtures for various uses and the availability of substitutes for such uses," as well as "the reasonably ascertainable economic consequences of the rule, after consideration for the effect on the national economy, small business, technological innovation, the environment, and public health."

[The court then reviewed EPA's methodology and calculation of the benefits and costs of the regulatory options. It found a number of problems. One had to do with discounting to present value the future costs to industry of the regulation but not always discounting the benefits of lives saved at future dates. The court indicated that both costs and benefits must be discounted to preserve an "apples-to- apples" comparison. Even when it did discount the benefits of its proposed regulation, EPA used the time of exposure instead of the time of injury as the point in time from which to discount.[16] Beyond that, EPA declined to

---

15. .These agencies leave unaddressed dangers posed by asbestos exposure through product repair, installation, wear and tear, and the like.
16. Eds.: This substantially increases the benefits having them accrue twenty to forty years earlier than they would if the date of onset of cancer is used

compute benefits and costs beyond the year 2000, but listed lives saved after that point in time as "unquantified benefits."]

Of more concern to us is the failure of the EPA to compute the costs and benefits of its proposed rule past the year 2,000...   In performing its calculus, the EPA only included the number of lives saved over the next thirteen years, and counted any additional lives saved as simply "unquantified benefits."   The EPA and interveners now seek to use these unquantified lives saved to justify calculations as to which the benefits seem far outweighed by the astronomical costs.   For example, the EPA plans to save about three lives with its ban of asbestos pipe, at a cost of $128-227 million (i.e., approximately $43-76 million per life saved). Although the EPA admits that the price tag is high, it claims that the lives saved past the year 2000 justify the price.

Such calculations not only lessen the value of the EPA's cost analysis, but also make any meaningful judicial review impossible.   While ToSCA contemplates a useful place for unquantified benefits beyond the EPA's calculation, unquantified benefits never were intended as a trump card allowing the EPA to justify any cost calculus, no matter how high.

The concept of unquantified benefits, rather, is intended to allow the EPA to provide a rightful place for any remaining benefits that are impossible to quantify after the EPA's best attempt, but which still are of some concern.   But the allowance for unquantified costs is not intended to allow the EPA to perform its calculations over an arbitrarily short period so as to preserve a large unquantified portion.

Unquantified benefits can, at times, permissibly tip the balance in close cases.   They cannot, however, be used to effect a wholesale shift on the balance beam.   Such a use makes a mockery of the requirement of ToSCA that the EPA weight the costs of its actions before it chooses the least burdensome alternative....

REASONABLE BASIS

...Most problematical to us is the EPA's ban of products for which no substitutes presently are available.   In these cases, the EPA bears a tough burden indeed to show that under ToSCA a ban is the least burdensome alternative, as ToSCA explicitly instructs the EPA to consider "the benefits of such substance or mixture for various uses and the availability of substitutes for such uses."   These words are particularly appropriate where the EPA actually has decided to ban a product, rather than simply restrict its use, for it is in these cases that the lack of an adequate substitute is most troubling under ToSCA.

As the EPA itself states, "when no information is available for a product indicating that cost-effective substitutes exist, the estimated cost of a product ban is very high."   Because of this, the EPA did not ban certain uses of asbestos, such as its use in rocket engines and battery separators. The EPA, however, in several other instances, ignores its own arguments and attempts to justify its ban by stating that the ban itself will cause the development of low-cost, adequate substitute products.

As a general matter, we agree with the EPA that a product ban can lead to great innovation, and it is true that an agency under ToSCA, as under other regulatory statutes, "is empowered to issue safety standards which require improvements in existing technology or which require the development of new technology." Chrysler Corp. v. Department of Transportation, 472 F.2d 659, 673 (6th Cir. 1972). As even the EPA acknowledges, however, when no adequate substitutes currently exist, the EPA cannot fail to consider this lack when formulating its own guidelines. Under ToSCA, therefore, the EPA must present a stronger case to justify the ban, as opposed to regulation, of products with no substitutes.

[The court then concluded that EPA's ban waiver provision for industries where the hoped-for substitutes failed to materialize in time did not relieve the agency of its heavy burden of justifying a total ban, in the face of inadequate substitutes, by shifting the burden to the waiver proponent.]

We are also concerned with the EPA's evaluation of substitutes even in those instances in which the record shows that they are available. The EPA explicitly rejects considering the harm that may flow from the increased use of products designed to substitute for asbestos, even where the probable substitutes themselves [such as PVC pipe] are known carcinogens. The EPA justifies this by stating that it has "more concern about the continued use and exposure to asbestos than it has for the future replacement of asbestos in the products subject to this rule with other fibrous substitutes." The agency thus concludes that any "regulatory decisions about asbestos which poses well-recognized, serious risks should not be delayed until the risk of all replacement materials are fully quantified."

This presents two problems. First, ToSCA instructs the EPA to consider the relative merits of its ban, as compared to the economic effects of its actions. The EPA cannot make this calculation if it fails to consider the effects that alternate substitutes will pose after a ban.

Second, the EPA cannot say with any assurance that its regulation will increase workplace safety when it refuses to evaluate the harm that will result from the increased use of substitute products. While the EPA may be correct in its conclusion that the alternate materials pose less risk than asbestos, we cannot say with any more assurance than that flowing from an educated guess that this conclusion is true....

In short, a death is a death, whether occasioned by asbestos or a toxic substitute product, and the EPA's decision not to evaluate the toxicity of known carcinogenic substitutes is not a reasonable action under ToSCA. Once an interested party brings forth credible evidence suggesting the toxicity of the probable or only alternatives to a substance, the EPA must consider the comparative toxic costs of each. Its failure to do so in this case thus deprived its regulation of a reasonable basis, at least in regard to those products as to which petitioners introduced credible evidence of the dangers of the likely substitutes.[17]

UNREASONABLE RISK OF INJURY

---

17 . We note that at least part of the EPA's arguments rest on the assumption that regulation will not work because the federal government will not adequately enforce any workplace standards that the EPA might promulgate. This is an improper assumption. The EPA should assume reasonable efforts by the government to implement its own regulations. A governmental agency cannot point to how poorly the government will implement regulations as a reason to reject regulation. Rather, the solution to poor enforcement is better enforcement, not more burdensome alternative solutions under TOSCA.

...Even taking all of the EPA's figures as true, and evaluating them in the light most favorable to the agency's decision (non-discounted benefits, discounted costs...), the agency's analysis results in figures as high as $74 million per life saved. For example, the EPA states that its ban of asbestos pipe will save three lives over the next thirteen years, at a cost of $128-227 million ($43-76 million per life saved), depending on the price of substitutes; that its ban of asbestos shingles will cost $23-34 million to save 0.32 statistical lives ($72-106 million per life saved); that its ban of asbestos coatings will cost $46-181 million to save 3.33 lives ($14-54 million per life saved); and that its ban of asbestos paper products will save 0.60 lives at a cost of $4-5 million ($7-8 million per life saved)...

While we do not sit as a regulatory agency that must make the difficult decision as to what an appropriate expenditure is to prevent someone from incurring the risk of an asbestos-related death, we do note that the EPA, in its zeal to ban any and all asbestos products, basically ignored the cost side of the ToSCA equation. The EPA would have this court believe that Congress, when it enacted its requirement that the EPA consider the economic impacts of its regulations, thought that spending $200-300 million to save approximately seven lives (approximately $30-40 million per life) over thirteen years is reasonable....

The EPA's willingness to argue that spending $23.7 million to save less than one-third of a life reveals that its economic view of its regulations, as required by ToSCA, was meaningless. As the petitioner's brief and our review of EPA case law reveals, such high costs are rarely, if ever, used to support a safety regulation. If we were to allow such cavalier treatment of the EPA's duty to consider the economic effects of its decisions, we would have to excise entire sections and phrases from the language of ToSCA. Because were are judges, not surgeons, we decline to do so....[18]

COMMENTARY AND QUESTIONS

1. Who is in charge? Who is the appropriate decision maker in this case? The four candidates are, the entities who use asbestos, Congress, the EPA, and the reviewing court. The political theory answer is that Congress has made the policy choice to protect against unreasonable health risks and authorized EPA to act in that regard by circumscribing the untrammeled freedom of action of the asbestos using community, subject to judicial review (at the behest of aggrieved parties such as the asbestos users) to ensure that EPA's action conforms to congressional policy as set forth in ToSCA. How well did the actors play their roles?

2. Risk assessment and regulation (risk management). One way to think about the *Corrosion Proof Fittings* case is in terms of how §6 of ToSCA sets out a methodology and process of risk assessment and risk management. In the end, both are assigned to EPA, but there is a substantial question of what latitude EPA has in acting to fulfill those

---

18. ...As the petitioners point out, the EPA regularly rejects as unjustified, regulations that would save more lives at less cost. For example, over the next 13 years we can expect more than a dozen deaths from ingested toothpicks–a death toll more than twice what the EPA predicts will flow from the quarter-billion dollar bans of asbestos pipe, shingles, and roof coatings.

mandates, particularly the management function. Consider these two competing interpretations of how the law is supposed to work:

> In a very open-ended way (when there is a "reasonable basis" for believing that there is "an unreasonable risk of injury to health or the environment," EPA shall act "to protect adequately against such risk"), Congress has assigned to EPA both risk assessment and risk management functions.

> Only after performing a risk assessment that reasonably finds "an unreasonable risk of injury to health or the environment"[19] is EPA empowered to engage in risk management and then only "to the extent necessary," "using the least burdensome requirements."

Who is to determine which view of ToSCA is correct? Notice that the basic political theory structure discussed above does not really address this latter question. It tells us that the right thing to do is what Congress intended, but here, it is not easy to be sure which type of system Congress was trying to erect EPA, acting pursuant to what it thought was its statutory mandate, took the position that the statute accorded it more discretion to act as it saw best. In its decision of the resulting challenge to EPA's action in regard to asbestos risk, the court of appeals viewed ToSCA as more nearly in the latter camp. The court's opinion does not make a significant effort to discern congressional intent, citing the statute's legislative history only once. Is it clear that, as between EPA (the administering agency) and the court (the process of judicial review), that the court's interpretation of an ambiguous statute is more likely to be correct than that of the agency that has the expertise in the area that is being regulated? Isn't that Huber's point? Even though Huber might prefer the real world result in this case (because it appears to be risk reducing on balance) he would not approve of the degree of second-guessing of the (expert) agency engaged in by the court.

3. EPA's burden of proof. Do you agree with the court that EPA's burden of proof should increase proportionately to the harshness of the remedy? Does this test violate ToSCA's "substantial evidence" rule of judicial review? The court's interpretation requires EPA to produce more evidence in cases where the agency considers the risk to be particularly severe, whereas most risk management systems work in just the opposite way. Recall, for example, the position taken by Talbot Page, calling for minimization of false negatives when dealing with toxic risks. (Main volume at pp.88-89.) Using the court's test, will EPA ever be able to impose a complete prohibition under §6 if doing so dictates gathering the information necessary to perform cost-benefit analyses on all less burdensome alternatives?

4. The failure to consider technology-based regulation. Among its points of criticism, the court chastens EPA for not considering how much risk could be reduced by requiring the use of the best asbestos handling

---

19. Note here that the assessment function is the "objective" number crunching type inquiry that does not consider outrage factors. Moreover, the phrase "reasonable basis" can be used to mount attacks on each of the elements of the risk assessment, including the estimates of exposure, the dosimetry extrapolations, and so on.

technologies in the various manufacturing and workplace settings. What sort of a risk management strategy is implicit in requiring the best technology to be used? Here, recall that the court is less persuaded than is EPA about the hazard posed by low-level exposures. Again using Page's terminology, employing the best technology to limit the number and extent of asbestos exposures is a significant step toward minimizing false negatives, i.e., avoiding toxic exposures where the outcomes (hazards) are uncertain.

5. **The value of a life**. Do you agree with the court that the avoidance of cancers should be treated like any other economic benefit, i.e., the benefits accrue at various points in time and should be quantified in dollar terms and discounted to present value? Once quantified, the value of lives saved can be plugged into a benefit-cost analysis and compared to the costs that must be expended to attain the reduction in mortality. Can a benefit-cost analysis in a situation like this ever be an "apples-to-apples" comparison, or does this approach so debase the dignity of human life as to be offensive? The benefits calculus is notably incomplete, it omits placing a monetary value on the avoided pain and suffering and health care costs of those who never become victims and it also takes no account of costs associated with those who are made ill but who do not die. The court is both critical and skeptical of EPA's reliance on "unquantified benefits" that will accrue in the more distant future. The court refers to a proper role for unquantified benefits, can you describe what that would be?

6. **How safe is safe enough in dealing with cancer risks? Part II.** The regulatory zeal of EPA in *Corrosion Proof Fittings* appears to be unusually stringent, at least in regard to the thirteen year period for which EPA quantifies both benefits and costs. Investigators have found that federal agencies are relatively consistent in defining "acceptable risk." More often than not, if a substance is expected to increase the number of cancer cases by more than four in 1000 over a lifetime of exposure, federal agencies decide to regulate that substance to reduce the risk below that level. If a substance is expected to increase the number of cases by less than one in a million, the chemical is rarely regulated. Between these extremes, federal decision-makers conduct cost-effectiveness analyses, which weight the cost of the regulation against the number of lives that regulation is likely to save. If the cost falls below $2 million per life saved, the substance is regulated. Travis, Richter, Crouch, Wilson & Klema, Cancer Risk Management, 21 Envtl. Sci. Tech. 15 (1987). The mere fact that the norm of agency behavior has been more lenient is not in itself proof that the more lenient approach is appropriate, but it is irrefutable evidence of how risk managers have responded to "life and death" choices in the past.

What justifies the choice of any particular level for regulatory action and forbearance? Should zero risk levels be set for carcinogens with no known safe levels of threshold exposure? Given the uncertainties involved in quantifying acceptable risk, should an "ample margin of safety" be factored in to compensate for uncertainty? Should the relevant population consist of the general public? The most sensitive persons? The most exposed persons? See, Marchant and Danzeisen, Acceptable Risk For Hazardous Air Pollutants, 13 Harv. Envtl. L. Rev. 535 (1989). In the view of Professor Harold Green, Congress is "the primary authority guiding the risk-management decisions of the courts and regulatory agencies," and

Congress defines acceptable risk in "more a political than a scientific, or even a rational" way. "Although scientific analysis and quantification may have some input into legislative considerations of risk reduction strategies, the final statute will usually be influenced more heavily by subjective and political factors than by objective, scientific ones." The Role of Congress in Risk Management, 16 ELR 10220 (1983). Should Congress be more scientific, or is this inconsistent with the nature of the political process? Should Congress establish broad public policy and allow expert administrative agencies to set the actual numbers, or would this approach result in Congress abdicating its legislative responsibilities in favor of agencies?

7. Technology-forcing effect of a ban. EPA attempted to justify a complete ban on asbestos for uses where no substitutes existed in terms of promoting technological innovation through technology-forcing. Given the rarity of technology-forcing devices in environmental law (see Chapter 17), EPA was on shaky ground in utilizing a technology-forcing strategy without express congressional authority.

8. Nonenforcement as a factor. Was EPA's reliance on government's chronic nonenforcement of OSHA regulations as one factor justifying an absolute prohibition on asbestos as silly as the court makes it sound? In fact, absolute prohibitions, although they are crude devices, do avoid many of the implementation difficulties inherent in more sophisticated remedies. See the discussion of roadblock statutes in Chapter 13.

9. Risk : the no balancing approach. Later in this text situations are considered where no cost-benefit risk balancing occurs — stark prohibitions govern. Closest to the *Corrosion Proof Fittings* case is Les v. Reilly, in chapter 13 *infra*, applying the "Delaney Clause" of the federal Food, Drug and Cosmetic Act, which flatly prohibits the presence of **any** known carcinogen in foods. Such stark prohibitions have undeniable value in getting serious industry and administrative attention paid to a congressional concern, but often are accused of mindless, expensive overkill. Compare the flat congressional requirement of 90% auto emission rollbacks in chapter 17.

Chapter 3, Environmental Torts and Remedies: Fitting Environmental Cases into Common Law Theories

PAGE 121 SLAPPs and SLAPP-Backs

SLAPPing in the courts. Judicial willingness to use procedural rules censuring or constraining attorneys and plaintiffs who file SLAPP suits appears to be increasing. In a recent case, the judge awarded the maximum sanction allowable under New York law, $10,000, against a developer and his attorneys for a SLAPP suit brought against the Nature Conservancy. Gordon v. Marrone, 590 N.Y.S. 2d 649 (1992). The SLAPP suit was based upon the developer's challenge of the Nature Conservancy's tax exemption for its offices located near the Mianus River Gorge, a wildlife refuge and botanical preserve managed by the non-profit organization. The court declared the developer's challenge "frivolous on the basis that it was brought primarily to harass or maliciously injure the Conservancy for opposing [the developer's] efforts to develop the area near Mianus River Gorge by forcing it to incur the expense of defending the [rationally-based tax] exemption." *Id.* at 650. In the proceedings reviewing the award, the court rejected the developer's First Amendment and Due Process arguments.

For more on SLAPP-backs, see the California anti-SLAPP statute, 1991 Cal. S.B. 341 § 425/66(a), Leonardini v. Shell Oil, 216 Cal. App. 3d 547 (1989), Wegis v. J.G. Boswell Co., 1991 Lexis 4641 (1991), and the article by the father of SLAPP jurisprudence, Professor George "Rock" Pring, in 7 Pace Envtl. L. Rev. 3 (1989), in a symposium on SLAPPs.

Does judicial concern with the chilling effect of SLAPP suits upon the speech of public-interest groups argue for granting these groups a special immunity from lawsuits? A recent Florida appellate decision said no, reversing a trial court's dismissal of a SLAPP suit filed by an agricultural group. Florida Fern Growers Assoc., Inc. et al. v. Concerned Citizens of Putnam County, 616 So. 2d 562 (Fla. App. 1993). The complaint charged the Concerned Citizens with, among others, intentional and malicious interference with advantageous business relationships for its role in challenging the issuance of consumptive water permits to members of the fern growing industry. In the face of the environmental argument that this was a SLAPP suit chilling their 1st Amendment right to petition government, the court held that this did not justify granting immunity from such suits or requiring heightened pleadings by the Fern Growers Association. Such rulings, the court said, would grant the citizens' group "broader protection than the Constitution itself guarantees," and sent the case back for trial. Given the limited monetary sanctions that can be awarded under many states' procedural rules for instigating frivolous litigation, it seems important to public interest groups to have SLAPP suits dismissed as early as possible. Note, however, that federal Rule 11 does not impose limits on the amount the judge may award. For further reading on SLAPP suits, see Note, "Silencing SLAPPS: An Examination of Proposed Legislative Remedies and a Solution for Florida," 20 Fla. St. U. L. Rev. 487

(1992); Note, "SLAPP Suits: Weakness in First Amendment Law and In the Courts' Response to Frivolous Litigation," 39 U.C.L.A L. Rev. 979 (1992); Tobias, "Environmental Litigation and Rule 11," 33 Wm. & Mary L. Rev. 429 (1992).

PAGE 129   **Added chart — Spur v. Webb case**

The photograph and map below, illustrating the *Spur* case, were
inadvertently separated at the press during the coursebook's printing.
Here they are, for coursebook page 129.

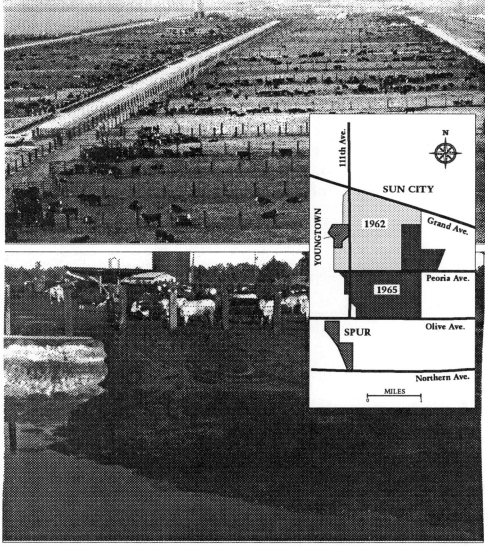

USDA PHOTOS

*Inset map from Spur decision, 494 P.2d 702, and two views of feedlot operations like those
involved in Spur. Rather than grazing, the cattle have feed and water brought to them.
Densities sometimes reach 400+ per acre, with predictable liquid and solid waste and
animal health consequences. Note the manure runoff in lower photograph; in some feedlots
the wastes do not drain off but accumulate where the cattle stand.*

Section 1A. RESTORATION COSTS AS A MEASURE OF REAL PROPERTY DAMAGES

In some cases, as noted in the text at 148 and 168-169, remedies based on the amount of market value lost because of defendant's actions do not accurately reflect the plaintiffs' perceived injury, or the defendant's blameworthiness. Fascinating possibilities arise when courts consider remedies based on restoration of land to the condition it held prior to the wrongdoing.

The following case was successfully litigated, against the odds, on behalf of residents of Globeville, a low-income working class ethnic minority community in northern Denver. It considers the major escalation of tort recoveries when damage awards are based on the actual cost of restoring, or "remediating," injured land:

The Restatement of Torts 2d §929 reads:

> §929, Harm to land from past invasions
>
> (1) If one is entitled to a judgment for harm to land resulting from a past invasion and not amounting to a total destruction of value, the damages include compensation for (a) the difference between the value of the land before the harm and the value after the harm, *or at his election in an appropriate case, the cost of restoration that has been or may be reasonably incurred....*[emphasis added].

Restoration awards are an evolving, useful, and problematic form of damages. Under Restatement 2d of Torts §929, damage awards based on the cost of returning the land to its prior status quo can redress the balance — or skew it.

Robert and Margaret Escamilla, et al. v. Asarco, Inc.
District Court for the City and County of Denver, Colorado
No. 91 CV 5716, 23 April 1993
ORDER

Hoffman, D.J. This case is before me on the parties' post-verdict briefs concerning the appropriate measure of the damages to Plaintiff class members' properties caused by Defendant's negligence.[20]

---

20. Plaintiffs' negligence claims were the only claims presented to the jury. Plaintiffs' Fourth Claim for Relief (Medical Monitoring) and Fifth Claim for Relief (Strict Liability) were dismissed on summary judgment by my Order dated December 4, 1992. Plaintiffs subsequently withdrew their First Claim for Relief (Trespass), Second Claim for Relief (Private Nuisance), and Sixth Claim for Relief (Injunction), leaving only their Third Claim for Relief (Negligence) [and the jury found liability in negligence].

I.   INTRODUCTION

On March 12, 1993, following a six week trial, the jury returned verdicts in this class action [arsenic and cadmium] pollution case in favor of the Plaintiff class and against Defendant based on two alternative damage theories. For the reasons I more fully articulated when the record was made on jury instructions, the evidence of property damage in this case was so disparate that in order to avoid invading the jury's fact finding province, I felt compelled to submit the case to them on the two alternative theories advanced by the parties, and then to select between those theories post-verdict.

Plaintiffs argue that the appropriate measure of damages to their real property is the cost to remediate that damage.[21] The evidence on this remediation cost ranged from as high as $38 million according to Plaintiffs' witnesses, down to $0 according to Defendant's witnesses.[22]

On the other hand, Defendant argues that the proper measure of damages to Plaintiffs' properties is the difference between the market value of those properties before and after the contamination. The evidence on this market value diminution came essentially unrebutted from Plaintiffs' real estate expert, Mr. Wayne Hunsperger, who testified to a pre-contamination value of approximately $17.5 million, and a post-contamination value of from $12.25 million to $14 million, for a diminution in market value ranging from 3.5 million to 5.25 million.[23]

The jury returned its verdict as to the Plaintiff class in the following alternative amounts:

	Market Value Alternative	Remediation Alternative
Property Damage	$ 4,159,000	$20,125,000
Annoyance and Discomfort	8,000,000	8,000,000
Total	$12,159,000	$28,125,000

II   MARKET VALUE VERSUS REMEDIATION A. THE MARKET VALUE RULE AND ITS EXCEPTIONS

It is well-settled in Colorado and many other states that the basic measure of damages for injuries to real property is ordinarily the so-called "market value measure"—the difference between the market value of the property immediately before and immediately after the injury...

---

21. I use the term "remediation" in this case because that was the term used by the witnesses, by counsel, and by me in the instructions and verdict forms. This term is meant to be synonymous with the term "restoration," which is the term used by the Restatement and by our Supreme Court.

22. Defendant's principal theory in this case was that any contamination of Plaintiffs' properties will be fully and adequately remediated in any event by the Colorado Department of Health pursuant to a Record of Decision they issued in conjunction with a related federal case. See Part III. F below.

23. As discussed in Part III.D below, Hunsperger estimated that the contamination of Plaintiffs' properties resulted in a 20 percent loss in value (yielding the $14 million post-contamination number), but also indicated that loss could go as high as 30 percent (yielding the $12.5 million post-contamination number).

However, beginning almost as soon as the general rule was first recognized, and more recently with its decision in *Zwick v. Simpson*, 572 P. 2d 133 (1977), our Supreme Court has acknowledged that this general measure is not written in stone, and that under certain circumstances the broader tort policy of making sure victims of torts are adequately compensated may require the market value measure to yield to the so-called "remediation measure," under which a plaintiff is entitled to recover the costs of restoring his property to its pre-tort condition.

The *Zwick* Court recognized several particular situations in which remediation might be more appropriate than market value, but until its opinion in *Board of County Comm'rs v. Slovek*, 723 P. 2d 1309 (Colo. 1986), these collections of narrowly defined exceptions never coalesced into any broad remediation principles.

B.   The *Slovek* case

In *Slovek*, which involved a private landowner's claims that an adjoining County landowner negligently caused the plaintiff's lands to become flooded, the trial court, despite unrebutted evidence of remediation damages, and in the face of quite incomplete evidence of market value, nevertheless held that it was required to assess damages by the market value method. The Court of Appeals reversed, holding that under the circumstances of the case, where the plaintiff was a private landowner residing on the premises, the plaintiff was entitled as a matter of law to remediation damages. 697 P. 2d 781 (Colo. App. 1984).

The Supreme Court reversed and remanded the question back to the trial court for consideration in light of several principles articulated in the opinion.

First, the Supreme Court rejected outright the County's suggestion that the *Zwick* list of exceptions was dictum, and reiterated the general notion recognized in *Zwick* that the market value measure is not necessarily the only appropriate measure of damages to real property.

The Court went on to discuss Restatement (2nd) of Torts §929, which also recognizes, at least in a trespass context, that redemption may in appropriate circumstances be the measure of damages to real property, and which at comment b states as follows:

> [I]f a ditch is wrongfully dug upon the land of another, the other
> normally is entitled to damages measured by the expense of
> filling the ditch, if he wishes it filled. If, however, the cost of
> replacing the land in its original condition is disproportionate
> to the diminution in the value of the land caused by the
> trespass, unless there is a reason personal to the owner for
> restoring the original condition, damages are measured only
> by the difference between the value of the land before and after
> the harm.

Under this Restatement protocol, the first inquiry is whether the use of the property was "personal." If not, then remediation costs may exceed the amount of market value diminution only if that excess is not "disproportionate." Presumably, if the use of the property *is* "personal," then the plaintiff is entitled to remediation under §929 regardless of whether the costs of remediation are "disproportionate" to the diminution in value.

Although the *Slovek* Court expressly recognized the importance of these comment b factors, it expressly rejected the particular analysis contained in comment b:

> We agree that the factors enumerated in Restatement (Second) of Torts §929 comment b are important in determining whether a case is appropriate for application of "cost of restoration" rather than "diminution of market value" as the measure of damages for tortious injury to land. We conclude, however, that the considerations governing what is an "appropriate case" for departure from the market value standard are not susceptible to reduction to a set list and that no formula can be devised that can produce litmus test certainty and yet retain the flexibility to produce fair results in all cases. 723 P. 2d at 1315-16.

Instead of any particular mechanical approach, the Court outlined several broad principles to be considered.

First, the Court rejected the notion that remediation damages ipso facto may not exceed market value damages, noting that it is precisely because the market value measure may not adequately compensate land owners that the remediation measure may come into play. 723 P. 2d at 1316.

The Court then rejected the notion that remediation damages can never exceed the pre-tort market value of the property to be remediated:

> If the damage is reparable, and the costs, although greater than original value, are not wholly unreasonable in relation to that value, and if the evidence demonstrates that payment of market value likely will not adequately compensate the property owner for some personal or other special reason, we concluded that the selection of the cost of restoration as the proper measure of damages would be within the limits of a trial court's discretion. 723 P.2d at 1317.

Finally, the Court articulated two cardinal principles that must be kept in mind in making the market value/remediation decision: On the one hand, the award must make the plaintiff whole; on the other hand, it cannot so exceed the goal of full compensation that it constitutes in effect a punishment of the defendant, or encourages wasteful remedial expenditures by the plaintiff *Id*....

III.   APPLICATION OF *SLOVEK* Let me now apply the general principles outlined in *Slovek* to the particular facts of this case.

A. Nature of Plaintiffs' Property By definition of the Residential Property Owners Class, Plaintiff class members all own residences in the Globeville neighborhood. In particular, each class member owns a private residence, duplex, or trailer in the class Geographic Area. Both *Slovek* and §929 of the Restatement recognize that the personal nature of a plaintiff's property is an important factor which militates toward remediation.

Defendant's suggestion in its briefs that Plaintiffs have failed to prove the personal nature of their property misapprehends the clear import of §929. Comment b specifically recognizes that a personal residence is precisely the kind of "personal use" of property that tends to make the market value measure inadequate. In fact, I find it noteworthy, given the evidence in this case of Plaintiffs' inability to grow vegetables safely in their gardens, that one of the examples of personal use contained in comment b is the following:

> So, when a garden has been maintained in a city in connection with a dwelling house, the owner is entitled to recover the expense of putting the garden in its original condition even though the market value of the premises has not been decreased by the defendant's invasion. Restatement (2nd) of Torts §929, comment b, p. 546 (1977).

I cannot imagine a more inherently "personal" piece of property than the home in which an owner raises his family, nor a more classic example of the type of property for which remediation may be the more appropriate measure of damages.

B. Nature of the Injuries There are two important aspects about the nature of the injuries in this case which must be considered in any decision about damages—the type of injuries and the time span over which the injuries were suffered.

Plaintiffs proved that microscopic particles of airborne arsenic and cadmium drifted off Defendant's plant site and landed on Plaintiffs' properties. As a result, Plaintiffs' soils suffer from levels of these two harmful metals many, many times higher than background levels.

This is not a case like *Slovek*, which involved rather discrete and knowable damages consisting of broken dikes, fences and trees, and the depositing of silt and debris. Because of the very nature of the microscopic contamination in this case, and what remains to a great extent unknown about the future health effects of that contamination, I have serious concerns about whether the market value approach could ever adequately compensate Plaintiffs. Phrased another way, and as suggested by the testimony of both Plaintiffs' and Defendant's real estate experts, the market may be particularly inefficient in digesting and reacting to a disclosure that property has been contaminated with heavy metals. At bottom, the problem with the market value approach in a contamination case like this one may be the fact that the impact of the contamination is so inherently uncertain that any market valuation based on that impact is likewise inherently uncertain.

On the other hand, the contamination is clearly not "permanent." It was undisputed that full use of the property can be restored simply by removing and replacing the contaminated topsoil. In this regard, I find the following language from Professor Dobbs instructive:

> If salt water is discharged onto land or into water supplies, the land or water may be ruined, but the land's function can probably be restored in *some* manner by bringing in new topsoil or piping in new water...

> [W]here the topsoil can be reasonably restored, and the owner wishes it, the cost of restoration is allowed on the ground that the injury is not permanent. Dobbs *on Remedies* 314 (1973) (emphasis in original, citations omitted).

As for the timing of the contamination, the damages in this case were suffered over a 70 year period, not during a single episode of flooding as in *Slovek*. Therefore, the market value approach, which requires a consideration of the value of the property immediately before and immediately after the loss, is not technically capable of being undertaken, since there is no discrete point in time when the loss was suffered. Instead, the market value testimony in this case compared the current value of the contaminated properties (the "post-loss" value) with the value of hypothetical uncontaminated properties (the "pre-loss" value). Market value testimony like this is by necessity significantly more speculative than market value testimony in a case like *Slovek*, where the fact finder simply compares the pre-loss value with the post-loss value.

I recognize that the remediation measure of damages also required the jury to consider evidence regarding hypothetical uncontaminated properties. It was necessary for the jury to determine what levels of these two metals would have been present in these properties in the absence of the contamination by Defendant (the so-called "background levels"), and to consider the appropriate clean-up levels. However, there was an enormous amount of technical evidence regarding background levels and appropriate cleanup levels, including the so-called Skyline Study (as reflected in the testimony of Plaintiffs' soils expert, Richard Trenholme) done by an independent sampler years before this dispute arose between Plaintiffs and Defendant, from which the jury could make its determination of background and cleanup levels. The jury had substantial data as well as expert testimony on these issues.

C. Remediability The evidence in this case was uncontroverted that remediation, though expensive, is certainly feasible, and indeed quite simple. Experts for both sides testified that remediation could be accomplished simply by removing and replacing topsoil in the contaminated areas. Indeed, when one adjusts for the disputed costs of dumping the contaminated soils off site, and relocating Plaintiffs during remediation, Plaintiffs' and Defendant's experts were in remarkably close agreement about the base cost of such remediation.

D. A Comparison of the Remediation Costs to the Market Values The jury found that it would cost $20,125,000 to remediate Plaintiffs' properties. The jury found that Plaintiffs' properties suffered a diminution in market value of $4,159,000, from which I infer that the jury found the uncontaminated market value of Plaintiffs' properties to be approximately $17.5 million (Hunsperger's unrebutted testimony), and the contaminated value to be approximately $13.4 million.

Thus, the remediation costs exceed not only the diminution in market value, but also both the pre-and post-tort market values themselves. Under *Slovek*, this excess does not necessarily preclude remediation, but does require me to consider carefully whether the remediation costs are "wholly unreasonable" in relation to the properties' market values. 723 P. 2d at 1317.

Although the remediation costs do exceed the uncontaminated market value, they do so only by approximately 13 percent.[24] This compares with an excess in *Slovek* of up to 19 percent.[25]

My survey of the case law under §929 of the Restatement reveals no particular ceiling beyond which courts seem to refuse to go in ordering remediation costs which exceed a property's market value, nor indeed any particular floor below which courts require remediation. At the extremes, remediation costs have been awarded which exceed the property's value by 1250 percent, *G&A Contractors, Inc. v. Alaska Greenhouses, Inc.*, 517 P. 2d 1379 (AK. 1974), yet remediation damages continue to be denied in a handful of jurisdictions if those damages exceed even by one dollar the value of the property, or, even more extreme, the diminution in market value. See *Newsome v. Billips*, 671 S.W. 2d 252 (Ky. App. 1984).[26]

Here, although I am certainly concerned about the $2,625,000 absolute number by which the remediation costs exceed uncontaminated market value, I must view this excess not only in absolute terms but also relative to the total uncontaminated market value. When viewed in this way, and as discussed above, the excess represents only 13 percent of the total market value. Even in absolute terms, the excess represents roughly only $4,600 per class family. For all of these reasons, and under all of the circumstances of this case, I cannot say that the remediation costs are "wholly unreasonable" in relation to the market value.

E. Class Issues   I agree with Defendant that among the factors I must consider in this case in choosing an appropriate measure of damages is the fact that Plaintiffs' property damage claims were brought, tried, and reduced to verdicts as class claims. Although neither Plaintiffs nor Defendant cite any case law discussing the impact this factor should have on the market value/remediation inquiry, Defendant does argue that an award of remediation damages would present unique allocation problems between class members, and therefore would create unacceptable risks of excess recovery. Although I acknowledge these risks, I do not view them, under all of the circumstances in this case, as unacceptable.

In the first place, I am not entirely convinced that Defendant is in any position to raise any argument about allocation. Defendant will be paying X amount to the Plaintiff class, and how these Plaintiff class members divide that amount seems to me to be a concern for Plaintiffs and not for Defendant.

Moreover...the risks of misallocation are inherent in the class nature of these claims, and are certainly not creatures of remediation...

---

24. 20,125,000 - 17,500,000) + 20,125,000 = 0.1304. The calculations Defendant uses in its post-trial brief are palpably incorrect. At pages 10-11 of that brief, Defendant compares the $28 million total in damages under the remediation measure (which included $8 million for annoyance and discomfort) to the $17.5 million in uncontaminated market value(which of course did not include the $8 million for annoyance and discomfort).

25 This percentage reflects the high end of the *Slovek* remediation range of $36,100 to $86,500, as follows:
(86,500 - 70,000) + 86,500 = 0.1907.

26. Both of these hard and fast limits, of course, were expressly rejected in *Slovek*.

F. The Record of Decision Defendant argues that Plaintiffs will be grossly overcompensated if they are awarded remediation damages, because Plaintiffs' properties will in any event be remediated under [a pending CERCLA cleanup]...Record of Decision ("ROD") (Exhibit A-54) currently pending approval in the federal case which the State of Colorado brought against Defendant. *Colorado v. Asarco, Inc.*, Case No. 83-C-2393 (D. Colo., filed December 9, 1983) ("the Federal Action"). The fallacy with this argument is that it ignores the fundamental fact the jury in this case has already considered that ROD in reaching its verdict on remediation.

Indeed, Defendant's central defense in this case was that Plaintiffs will suffer no damages because under the ROD their properties will be remediated. However, the ROD calls for the properties to be remediated down to 73 ppm for cadmium and 28 ppm for arsenic,[27] despite evidence that the background levels for these two metals may be an order of magnitude lower. (For example, Trenholme testified that background for cadmium was as low as 1.7 ppm.) By awarding any damages at all in this case, and particularly at the levels that were in fact awarded, the jury resoundingly rejected the notion that the ROD will fully mitigate Plaintiffs' damages. The jury's verdict represents their conclusion, fully and fairly supported by the evidence, that the settlement between the [government agencies] and Defendant was woefully inadequate, at least with regard to Plaintiffs' state common law rights to be compensated for Defendant's negligence.[28]

Defendant also invokes the CERCLA policy of avoiding double recovery. This is not a CERCLA case, and in any event the policy against excess recovery is already well-embedded in this state's tort law, as recited by the entire *Slovek* discussion contained in this Order. 42 U.S.C. §9614. There simply is no significant risk of excess recovery in this case because the jury here has already determined that even considering what the state proposes to do under the ROD, it will nevertheless take $20 million to remediate Plaintiff's properties. What Defendant and the State of Colorado wish to do under the ROD with regard to any Plaintiff class member who may receive remediation damages as a result of this judgment, is a matter to be resolved under the ROD and in the Federal Action, not here.

IV. CONCLUSION

Considering all of the factors discussed above, and with due regard for the overarching principles of full and just compensation on the one hand, but no windfalls on the other, I find and conclude: that the losses which Plaintiff class members have suffered to their residences as a result of Defendant's negligence are remediable; that the cost of that remediation, as found by the jury, is not wholly unreasonable in relation to the

---

27. The base ROD action level for arsenic is actually 70 ppm, with the landowners having the option to go down to 28ppm.

28. I do not mean in any way to suggest that the ROD is or is not protective of the general public health, or does or does not comply with the requirements of CERCLA. That, of course, is a question before the federal district court, and one over which I clearly have no jurisdiction. But I do have jurisdiction to decide how best to compensate Plaintiffs for the damages which this jury has determined they have suffered at the hands of Defendant, and the jury has already concluded that the ROD is inadequate to insulate Plaintiffs from these losses.

uncontaminated or "pre-tort" market value of the Plaintiff class members' residences; that the market value measure will not adequately compensate Plaintiff class members for the damage to their residences; that there is no significant risk that the Plaintiff class will be overcompensated by a remediation award, that Defendant will be punished by such an award, or that such an award will encourage wasteful expenditures by Plaintiff class members; and therefore that the jury's remediation award is the more appropriate measure of damages to compensate Plaintiff class members for their property losses....

[After this decision Asarco decided to drop plans for an appeal and began negotiating a settlement for plaintiffs claims, presumptively hoping to pay somewhat less than the jury award.]

COMMENTARY AND QUESTIONS

1. Balancing restoration as a measure of damages. As noted, the Restatement of Torts 2d §929, Harm to Land from Past Invasions, says:

> (1) If one is entitled to a judgment for harm to land resulting from a past invasion and not amounting to a total destruction of value, the damages include compensation for (a) the difference between the value of the land before the harm and the value after the harm, or at his election in an appropriate case, the cost of restoration that has been or may be reasonably incurred....

In the casebook on page 148, examples are given of proposed restoration remedies that were intuitively quite beneficial and useful on one hand (the example of the defendant who maliciously destroys a private arboretum, thereafter claiming to have actually *increased* the real property value thereby), and on the other extremely drastic, undesirable, and unnecessary.

The *Escamilla case* attempts to balance the beneficial use of Restatement §929 restoration as a measure of damages against the obvious prospect for misuse and miscarriages of justice. Does the *Escamilla* court succeed?

The court holds that "the market value measure is not necessarily the only appropriate measure of damages to real property." In a situation where restoration will produce a dramatically greater damage recovery, however, plaintiffs are altogether likely to "elect" the §929(1)(a) restoration measure, and the only question becomes whether it is an *appropriate* case for the award. The *Escamilla* court does not explain whether restoration should be the exception or can become the rule where plaintiffs make out the requirements it describes.

The court requires a showing by plaintiff:

> (1) That the court must find that the injury to the land is not "permanent," i.e. that it is indeed remediable.

> (2) Whether the use of the property was personal. If it is not personal, the court will not allow restoration damages that are "disproportionate" to the difference in market value. But if it *is* personal, then the requirement of rough parity disappears.

Note however how the court has changed this threshold term: The court does not require proof of a "*reason* personal to the owner [for remediation instead of traditional damages]," but only personal "*use.*" The Restatement Comment's language, however, seems to require a special rationale for restoration; by converting the test merely to personal use, the plaintiff is given a much easier road toward the higher damage recoveries.

(3) The court must find that restoration damages do not "exceed the goal of full compensation to the extent that it constitutes in effect a punishment of the defendant, or encourages wasteful remedial expenditures by the plaintiff." These twin considerations are scarcely discussed by the *Escamilla* court.

(4) If the plaintiff's use was personal, apparently the court must further determine whether remediation costs are "wholly unreasonable" in relation to the property's market value. This phrasing clearly puts the burden on defendants to show that the extra costs are unreasonable. The *Escamilla* court analysis does closely analyze the proportionality of the excess amount of restoration damages over market value diminution, a useful discussion.

If all the above are found, then remediation damages will apparently be granted. This analysis leaves further questions.

2. Why should a court grant restoration damages? The *Escamilla* court does not establish clearly that restoration was necessary or desirable. One reason the court gives for this restoration award is the difficulty of quantifying "before and after" market values where pollution has continued for a long time. But that is not the typical evaluative comparison. In market value diminution cases real estate experts are routinely asked to establish the value of a parcel of land *with and without* the particular contamination, an evaluation technique that is well developed, using "comps" — review of comparative sales of comparably situated parcels.

The court also notes that it is difficult to establish true market value injury where pollutants are microscopic in size and "the impact of the contamination is so inherently uncertain that any market valuation based on that impact is likewise inherently uncertain." Where damages are being assessed for injury to property rather than to personal health, however, market value tends to be a generally accepted measure of injury, and is quite responsive to information about potentially dangerous conditions.

Was it a review of actual dangers that brought the court to order the drastic remedy of remediation restoration? The court never discusses why the diminished contamination left after the federally-ordered statutory cleanup required a further level of cleanup under the common law remedy. The judge deferred to the jury's implicit decision that the contamination would continue to be injurious to health or to the use of property. It would seem important to consider the proportionality between potential effects and the costs of a "Cadillac cleanup" (see coursebook at 896). Ultimately, is this a case where a jury responds to the scary word "toxics" by attempting to legislate a skewed remedy, or do the facts represent a context in which the drastic costs to an embattled neighborhood justify remediation?

Standards for when restoration is to be the measure of the remedy will undoubtedly be developed for this and other environmental settings. Beyond toxic contamination lie examples like the killing of fish in a river, the wrongful cutting of trees noted at page 148, or the wrongful partial demolition of an old, sentimentally-held house or historic building lacking market value, and so on. When and for what kind of plaintiffs are injunctions or damages based on restoration justified and desirable?

3. Must remediation damages actually be spent on remediation? In the *Escamilla* court's test, there is no consideration of whether plaintiffs will actually use the money recovered to restore the condition of the land. If they do not, restoration damages are just a fortuitous way of giving plaintiffs a windfall. They also raise the further question whether subsequent purchasers will thereafter be estopped from suing defendants for the same contamination if their litigious predecessors in title did not actually cleanup the land. (Defendants would be well-advised to record the judgment in the land titles registry.) Some courts discussing remediation have considered the likelihood of plaintiffs actually remediating the land as part of the test, but *Escamilla* does not. There is no reason, is there, why a court could not require actual remediation as a condition of allowing plaintiffs to use remediation as the measure of damages?

4. The *Escamilla* settlement. On remand, ASARCO decided to settle the *Escamilla* case. The jury award had been for $20 million for remediation and $8 million for plaintiffs' discomfort and inconvenience. In the settlement the plaintiffs agreed to allow ASARCO itself to do the supervised remediation — reducing the defendant's cost to as little as $11 million — and the recovery for discomfort was raised to another $11 million.

In a fascinating twist on the problem raised in the prior comment, the settlement included a provision that plaintiffs who did not agree to actual remediation of their land — ASARCO's removal of the top twelve inches of contaminated soil, replacing it with fresh topsoil — would not recover a penny for remediation, and would have their discomfort recovery docked by 40%! The plaintiffs' attorneys clearly did not want the *Escamilla* settlement to serve in subsequent community-based restoration cases as an example of cynical nonremediation, where subsequent defendants could argue against similar restoration-based awards by saying that the *Escamilla* plaintiffs had taken the restoration money and run. This policy, however, raised an ethical issue that had to be fully discussed with the named plaintiffs.

5. Restoration as redressing the balance: punishment? The court quickly rejects the possibility of levying restoration as a punishment, but it should be noted that the Restatement in its §929 comment (b) considers that in some cases defendants' willful and malicious actions deserve special remedial attention. Where defendants are willful trespassers, plaintiffs can recover the value of any ill-gotten profits made thereby (this deserves a term paper). In cases where the defendant has acted maliciously, willfully or with gross negligence, isn't the need and cost for restoration a suitable consideration for the grant of damages in the nature of punitive damages?

6.   Sidenotes on *Escamilla*: Early in the litigation, responding to ASARCO's motion, Judge Hoffman issued a gag order preventing plaintiffs' attorneys from mentioning that Globeville, the contaminated community, was primarily a community of color — 60% Hispanic, 10% African-American, 5% Native American.

Prior to the settlement, the lead attorney bringing this path-breaking case, Macon Cowles of Denver, had had to re-finance his home in order to support the litigation.   Subsequently his practice has developed an environmental specialty caseload.

7.   Municipal restoration-based awards.   In a case involving the contamination of a potable water source in Florida, the Florida Supreme Court found that damages measured by diminution in value were inappropriate to compensate the municipality for the loss of 5 of its 6 water wells.   The court stated that, in this instance, public policy supported restoration costs as the measure of damages because the court was "dealing with the single most necessary substance for the continuation of life.... Any danger to that primary necessity is ecologically and humanly unacceptable."   Indicating that it thought it was diverging from the general rule on damages for wrongful injury, the court stated that extending damages beyond the loss of value of the property was further justified in this case because neither over-compensation nor overlapping of recoveries was likely.   Davey Compressor Co. v. Delray Beach,   7 Toxic Law Reporter 97 (Fla., March 3, 1994).

PAGE 150   **More on assessing permanent damages**

1A. Setting permanent damages in *Boomer*.   As noted in the coursebook, on remand the trial court in *Boomer* set damages according to a subjective guesstimate that was quite difficult to describe.   To illustrate the problem of assessing permanent damages in cases where the plaintiffs are unwilling sellers of a pollution easement to private defendants, here is a brief excerpt from the trial court's opinion:

BOOMER v. ATLANTIC CEMENT COMPANY
72 Misc. 2d 834, 340 N.Y.S.2d 97 (1972)

HERZBERG, J.,   [T]he plaintiffs contend that we should use a "special" market value rule and a so-called "contract price" theory..., the amount that a private corporation would have to pay where it needs such servitude to continue in operation as against a seller who is unwilling to sell his land; plaintiffs ask "heavy damages as will set notice to all the world that an industry cannot move into a town for the first time, an unindustrialized town, with a rural suburban setting, and cast the substances, pollute the air and the lands of its neighbors, and to blast without any thought of compensation".

[Simply stated, this is asking for punitive damages and invoking the aid of equity to formulate policy.   The Court of Appeals, in this case (Boomer v. Atlantic Cement Co.,   26 N Y 2d 219, 223), has rejected the latter, and the present court rejects any notion of punitive damages, since we do not see that the "wrong complained of is morally culpable, or is actuated by evil and reprehensible motives". (Walker v. Sheldon, 10 N Y 2d 401, 404.)]

The defendant, insisting on strict compliance of the market value rule, urges that any other considerations would be speculative and uncertain. We disagree....

As to the so-called "contract price" value, it appears highly speculative. On cross-examination Mr. Boomer testified that he arrived at the price of $350,000 thusly:

"Q. Now, this price that you put on this land of $350,000, how did you arrive at that figure?...

A. I have got two small boys that would like to go in the salvage business. The youngest one is 11 years old. Now, between the time he gets to where he can run this salvage business and the time he retires at 65, there is a lot of space in between. $350,000 falls in there.

BY MR. TRACY (continuing):

Q. That's what you based it on?

A. On my children, yes, sir."

And plaintiffs' expert Mulligan, having put a value of $92,700 on the Boomer property, when asked on cross-examination how he arrived at the so-called "contract price" of $250,000, testified:

"Q. You would put a figure of two to three times the valuation of the $92,700, correct?

A. I stated first that I would not sell for market value, that I would use a factor of two or three times the market value.

Q. And you said something about $250,000?

A. Yes.

Q. Now, you could have said four or five times the valuation, correct?

A. Yes.

Q. You could have said six or seven times the valuation, correct?

A. No, I don't think I could have gone that high."

Again, plaintiff Boomers' expert Meisner valued the property at $10,000 an acre, total $80,000, without the nuisance; and with the nuisance he testified:

"A. There wouldn't be no value".

And Boomers' witness Mulligan testified to a value of $97,700 without the nuisance. With the nuisance he testified:

"A. Under all the conditions that you stated, as a second hand and used parts enterprise, probably $5,000."

It is no easy task, under the conditions of this case, to determine the amount of permanent damages, past, present and future. In a particularly difficult decision involving the valuation of an entire railroad system, including tunnels and subways, where an award of $55,000,000 was made, after exhaustively reviewing different methods of valuation, the court finally wrote: "If analogy is found in Newton's experiment with prisms showing that white light is composed of all the colors of the spectrum, each lending its own characteristics to a degree when passed through a prism, all the approaches to valuation entering into the informed mind and sensitive conscience of the court lend to an appropriate degree in the resulting decision." (Matter of Port Auth. Trans-Hudson Corp., 48 Misc 2d 485, 535).

In determining permanent damages we have noted:

1. The temporary damages already found insofar as they assist us.

2. The damage from September 1, 1962 to date.

3. The fair market value with and without the nuisance.

4. The consideration of plaintiffs' theories.

5. The future damages.

And applying the statement above quoted from the Port Authority case, we find the permanent damage to the [Kinleys, Boomers having settled,] to be:

Kinley: $175,000.

We find the fair market value without and with the nuisance to be:

Without nuisance $265,000

With nuisance   125,000.

In accord with the decision of the Court of Appeals, the plaintiffs Kinley are granted an injunction which shall be vacated upon payment by the defendant of the sum of $175,000....

PAGE 159   Punitive damages and due process: *TXO* and *Honda v. Oberg*

5A. Constitutional checks on punitive damage awards. Are punitive damages subject to substantive due process limits? Two relevant Supreme Court cases have been decided since the coursebook was published. In TXO v. Alliance Resources, 113 Sup. Ct. 2711, the Court scrutinized a punitive damages award in due process term, but rejected any 'mathematical' brightline test to determine the constitutionality of such damages. The case involved a lawsuit by TXO against Alliance Resources to remove an alleged cloud on the oil and gas rights title for 1,000 acres of land in West Virginia; Alliance successfully counterclaimed against TXO for slander of title and was awarded $19,000 in compensation and $10 million in punitive damages. By affirming punitive damages that were 525 times the compensatory damages, the justices made clear that a violation of due process in the punitive damage area is not solely determined by the size or ratio of an award.

In his opinion, Justice Stevens acknowledged that the punitive award was in fact large. He noted, however, that it was not *grossly* excessive "when one takes into account the magnitude of the potential harm that the defendant's conduct would have caused to its intended victim if the wrongful plan had succeeded, as well as the possible harm to other victims that might have resulted if similar future behavior were not deterred." The use of such a reasonableness test in *TXO* makes this ruling consistent with that of *Haslip* (see coursebook page 159).

The first Supreme Court decision actually to *strike down* a punitive damages award as a violation of 14th Amendment due process, it appears, is the recent Honda Motors, Inc. v. Oberg, 1994 WL 276687 (U.S. Sup. Ct., June 24, 1994).[29] Like *TXO*, *Oberg* also echoed the *Haslip* holding. In *Oberg*, an Oregon case, Justice Stevens held that due process imposes a substantive limit on the size of punitive damages awards, that judicial review of the size of punitive damages awards was a necessary safeguard against excessive awards, and that Oregon law provides no procedure for reducing or setting aside a punitive damages award where the only basis for relief is a challenge to the amount awarded. A state's common law or statutory law must provide a set of standards for the size of a punitive award, and providing for possible remission of punitive damages along the lines of the seven tests noted in the coursebook at 159. Although Oregon is the only state that has no such tests in place, the Court's tone bespeaks stricter review of state practices in other punitive damage cases to come.

---

29. *Oberg*, since it involved an injury to the rider of a three-wheeled all-terrain-vehicle, might in a stretch be called a quasi-environmental case.

Chapter 4,   Toxic Torts : Beyond The Traditional Common Law Setting

Pages 182-93   **Update on proving causation**

Landrigan v. Celotex Corp.
127 N.J. 404, 605 A.2d 1079
Supreme Court of New Jersey, 1992

Pollack, J. Plaintiff, Angelina Landrigan, sued defendants Owens-Corning Fiberglass Corporation and Owens Illinois, Inc. for the personal injuries and death of her husband, Thomas Landrigan, claiming that exposure to defendants' asbestos had caused his death from colon cancer....

Decedent worked as a maintenance man and pipe insulator at the Bayonne Terminal Warehouse from 1956 until December 1981, when he was diagnosed as suffering from colon cancer. From 1956 until 1972, he allegedly worked with insulation containing asbestos supplied by defendants. In January 1982, he underwent surgery but the cancer spread, and he died in December 1982. The cause of his death was adenocarcinoma, "a malignant adenoma arising from a glandular organ," the most common type of colon cancer. Generally speaking, colorectal cancer is the second most common cancer in the United States, striking 140,000 persons and causing 60,000 deaths annually. In 1984, plaintiff filed this survivorship and wrongful death action, asserting that exposure to asbestos had caused decedent's death.

At the trial in 1989, plaintiff relied on two experts, Dr. Joseph Sokolowski, Jr., a physician who is board certified in both internal medicine and pulmonary medicine, and Dr. Joseph K. Wagoner, an epidemiologist and biostatistician but not a physician. Dr. Sokolowski never treated or examined decedent He based his conclusions on a review of decedent's history of exposure to asbestos, the absence of other risk factors in decedent's history, and on various epidemiological, animal, and in vitro studies. Stating that physicians regularly rely on epidemiological studies, Dr. Sokolowski testified that asbestos can cause colon cancer in humans. He also described the path asbestos fibers take from inhalation to the gastrointestinal tract. Dr. Sokolowski testified that exposure to asbestos was the cause of decedent's colon cancer...[and] further that decedent would not have contracted colon cancer if he had not been exposed to asbestos.

Plaintiff also offered Dr. Wagoner to testify that asbestos exposure had caused decedent's colon cancer. After conducting a hearing pursuant to Evidence Rule 8, the trial court ruled that as an epidemiologist and not a physician, Dr. Wagoner was not qualified to testify that asbestos had caused decedent's cancer. The court, however, permitted the witness to testify about epidemiological methods and studies linking colon cancer to asbestos exposure. It also allowed Dr. Wagoner to state his opinion that asbestos causes colon cancer in humans....

At the close of plaintiff's case, the trial court granted defendants' motions for a directed verdict. The court ruled that Dr. Sokolowski's testimony was a net opinion because it was supported only by epidemiological studies and the exclusion of other risk factors, explaining: Epidemiological evidence can only be used to show that a defendant's conduct increased a plaintiff's risk of injury to some measurable extent but it cannot be used to answer the critical question did the asbestos cause Mr. Landrigan's colon cancer.

In recent years, we have sought to accommodate the requirements for the admission of expert testimony with the need for that testimony. See Rubanick v. Witco Chem. Corp., 593 A.2d 733 (1991); Ryan v. KDI Sylvan Pools, Inc., 579 A.2d 1241 (1990). Nowhere is that accommodation more compelling than on the issue of causation in toxic-tort litigation concerning diseases of indeterminate origin. Many such injuries remain latent for years, are associated with diverse risk factors, and occur without any apparent cause. Steve Gold, Note, Causation in Toxic Torts: Burdens of Proof, Standards of Persuasion, and Statistical Evidence, 96 Yale L.J. 376, 376 (1986) (hereinafter Gold). In that context, proof that a defendant's conduct caused decedent's injuries is more subtle and sophisticated than proof in cases concerned with more traditional torts....

Traditionally, plaintiffs have established a connection between tortious conduct and personal injuries through the testimony of medical experts who testify that the defendant's specific conduct was the cause of the plaintiff's injuries. Toxic torts, however, do not readily lend themselves to proof that is so particularized. Developments in the Law—Toxic Waste Litigation, 99 Harv.L.Rev. 1458, 1620 (1986). Plaintiffs in such cases may be compelled to resort to more general evidence, such as that provided by epidemiological studies. A basic understanding of some fundamentals of epidemiology is essential for an assessment of the admissibility of such evidence.

Simply defined, epidemiology is "the study of disease occurrence in human populations." Gary D. Friedman, Primer of Epidemiology 1 (3d ed. 1987) (hereinafter Friedman). Epidemiology studies the relationship between a disease and a factor suspected of causing the disease, using statistical methods to determine the likelihood of causation. Bert Black & David E. Lilienfeld, Epidemiologic Proof in Toxic Tort Litigation, 52 Fordham L. Review 732, 750 (1984) (hereinafter Black & Lilienfeld). By comparison to the clinical health sciences, which are directly concerned with diseases in particular patients, epidemiology is concerned with the statistical analysis of disease in groups of patients. The statistical associations may become so compelling, as they did in establishing the correlation between asbestos exposure and mesothelioma, that they raise a legitimate implication of causation. "[S]tatistical associations," however, "do not necessarily imply causation.... It is important, therefore, to have some basis for deciding whether a statistical association derived from an observational study represents a cause-and-effect relationship." Friedman, supra, at 182-83. See Austin B. Hill, The Environment and Disease: Association or Causation?, 58 Proc. Royal Soc. Med. 295 (1965) (criteria to assess likelihood of causal relationship from statistical associations).

At oral argument, defendants, for example, stressed two criteria, among others, that are crucial in determining whether a statistical association will give rise to an inference that a particular substance causes a certain disease in people who are exposed to it. The two criteria are the strength of the association and the consistency of any such association with other knowledge. The argument is sound. As Professor Friedman explains: In general, the stronger the association, the more likely it represents a cause-and-effect relationship. Weak associations often turn out to be spurious and explainable by some known, or as yet unknown, confounding variable.... Strength of an association is usually measured by the relative risk or the ratio of the disease rate in those with the factor to the rate in those without. The relative risk of lung cancer in cigarette smokers as compared to nonsmokers is on the order of 10:1, whereas the relative risk of pancreatic cancer is about 2:1. The difference suggests that cigarette smoking is more likely to be a causal factor for lung cancer than for pancreatic cancer.

If the association makes sense in terms of known biological mechanisms or other epidemiologic knowledge, it becomes more plausible as a cause-and-effect relationship. Part of the attractiveness of the hypothesis that a high-saturated fat, high-cholesterol diet predisposes to atherosclerosis is the fact that a biologic mechanism can be invoked. Such a diet increases blood lipids, which may in turn be deposited in arterial walls. A correlation between the number of telephone poles in a country and its coronary heart disease mortality rate lacks plausibility as a cause-and-effect relationship partly because it is difficult to imagine a biologic mechanism whereby telephone poles result in atherosclerosis. [Friedman, *supra*, at 183-84]

The "attributable risk," by comparison, is the proportion of the disease that is statistically attributable to the factor. Black & Lilienfeld, supra, 52 Fordham L. Review at 761. It "is a composite measure that takes into account both the relative risk of disease if exposed and the proportion of the population so exposed." Ibid....

Turning to the experts in this case, plaintiff's medical expert was Dr. Sokolowski. Initially, he explained that he had examined certain literature on colon cancer, including the landmark study by Dr. Irving Selikoff. See Irving Selikoff, et al., Mortality Experience of Insulation Workers in the United States and Canada, 330 Annals N.Y. Acad. Sci. 91 (1979). The study indicated a relative risk of colon cancer from the exposure to asbestos of 1.55. The attributable risk, which would vary according to the extent and intensity of the exposure, was approximately thirty-five percent. Thus, assuming a causal relationship, the Selikoff study indicates that thirty-five percent of the cases of colon cancer in the population exposed to asbestos can be attributed to that exposure.

Dr. Sokolowski had never treated or examined decedent, but he had reviewed decedent's medical records and plaintiff's answers to interrogatories. Those materials indicated that decedent had been exposed to asbestos in his work. They also indicated the absence of other risk factors such as a family history of colon cancer, a high-fat diet, and the undue consumption of alcohol. Dr. Sokolowski acknowledged that "many studies...show no statistically significant increase in colon cancer in workers exposed to asbestos." Finally, he relied on the results of animal and in vitro studies.

The trial court rejected Dr. Sokolowski's testimony as a "net opinion" unsupported by any facts. Specifically, the court stated that "[e]pidemiological evidence can only be used to show that a defendant's conduct increased a plaintiff's risk of injury to some measurable extent but it cannot be used to answer the critical question did the asbestos cause Mr. Landrigan's colon cancer."

The Appellate Division agreed with that assessment, explaining that Dr. Sokolowski had failed to account for other factors that may have caused decedent's cancer. Although it accepted the validity of the Selikoff study, the court stated that the 1.55 relative risk was insufficient to support Dr. Sokolowski's opinion that decedent's exposure had caused the cancer. Without expressly adopting a specific standard, the court cited with approval several cases that adopted a requirement that an epidemiological study show a relative risk in excess of 2.0 to prove that causation in a specific individual was more probable than not. The significance of a relative risk greater than 2.0 representing a true causal relationship is that the ratio evidences an attributable risk of more than fifty percent, which means that more than half of the cases of the studied disease in a comparable population exposed to the substance are attributable to that exposure. This finding could support an inference that the exposure was the probable cause of the disease in a specific member of the exposed population.

Defense counsel urges that the Appellate Division opinion may be read as requiring that an expert may not rely on an epidemiological study to support a finding of individual causation unless the relative risk is greater than 2.0. At oral argument before us, they agreed that such a requirement may be unnecessary. Counsel acknowledged that under certain circumstances a study with a relative risk of less than 2.0 could support a finding of specific causation. Those circumstances would include, for example, individual clinical data, such as asbestos in or near the tumor or a documented history of extensive asbestos exposure. So viewed, a relative risk of 2.0 is not so much a password to a finding of causation as one piece of evidence, among others, for the court to consider in determining whether the expert has employed a sound methodology in reaching his or her conclusion. ...

The court must also examine the manner in which experts reason from the studies and other information to a conclusion. As previously indicated, that conclusion must derive from a sound methodology that is supported by some consensus of experts in the field.

In the present case, Dr. Sokolowski began by reviewing the scientific literature to establish both the ability of asbestos to cause colon cancer and the magnitude of the risk that it would cause that result. Next, he assumed that decedent was exposed to asbestos and that his exposure, in both intensity and duration, was comparable to that of the study populations described in the literature. He then assumed that other known risk factors for colon cancer did not apply to decedent. After considering decedent's exposure and the absence of those factors, Dr. Sokolowski concluded that decedent's exposure more likely than not had been the cause of his colon cancer.

Without limiting the trial court on remand, its assessment of Dr. Sokolowski's testimony should include an evaluation of the validity both of the studies on which he relied and of his assumption that the decedent's asbestos exposure was like that of the members of the study populations. The court should also verify Dr. Sokolowski's assumption concerning the absence of other risk factors. Finally, the court should ascertain if the relevant scientific community accepts the process by which Dr. Sokolowski reasoned to the conclusion that the decedent's asbestos exposure had caused his cancer. Thus, to determine the admissibility of the witness's opinion, the court, without substituting its judgment for that of the expert, should examine each step in Dr. Sokolowski's reasoning.

Our decision does not necessarily mean that on remand the trial court must reach a different result. Although the diagnosis of decedent's disease and the cause of his death are not in dispute, the parties vigorously contest the probability that decedent's colon cancer was caused by asbestos exposure. The issue posed to both Dr. Wagoner and Dr. Sokolowski was the likelihood that decedent's colon cancer was caused by asbestos exposure. Dr. Wagoner did not rely exclusively on epidemiological studies in addressing that issue. In addition to relying on such studies, he, like Dr. Sokolowski, reviewed specific evidence about decedent's medical and occupational histories. Both witnesses also excluded certain known risk factors for colon cancer, such as excessive alcohol consumption, a high-fat diet, and a positive family history. From statistical population studies to the conclusion of causation in an individual, however, is a broad leap, particularly for a witness whose training, unlike that of a physician, is oriented toward the study of groups and not of individuals. Nonetheless, proof of causation in toxic-tort cases depends largely on inferences derived from statistics about groups. Gold, supra, 96 Yale L.J. at 401. ...

[Reversed and remanded.]

COMMENTARY AND QUESTIONS

1. Relative risk and attributable risk. Although the Landrigan opinion is not very explicit on this point, relative risk (RR) and attributable risk (AR) are, in a sense, reciprocal measures. When the relative risk is 2.0 (sometimes expressed as 2:1), the attributable risk is 50% (.5). What this relative risk of 2.0 or 2:1 means in popular parlance is that a person with that risk factor is twice as likely as someone without the factor to have the correlated harm occur. The precise equation that relates the two values is RR-1/RR=AR. So, for example, in the cigarette smoking to lung cancer example, where the relative risk is 10, the attributable risk is 90% (.9), i.e., nine of the ten lung cancers that befall smokers are attributable to smoking cigarettes rather than other factors. In the Selikoff study, the relative risk is 1.55 so the attributable risk is (1.55-1)/1.55=.35, or 35%

2. Legal causation and statistical proof: comparing apples and pears. What makes a relative risk value of 2.0 appear to be particularly important in the legal arena? The apparent significance of a relative risk value in excess of 2.0 is that it makes it appear more likely than not that the risk factor is the operative cause of the injury. This linguistic formulation tracks the standard that the plaintiff must meet to carry the burden of proof on the issue of causation-in-fact. That is, the plaintiff has the burden of persuading the trier of fact that defendant's action is more likely than not the cause of plaintiff's injury. Using the term attributable risk makes this linguistically even clearer, when the risk attributable to defendant is more than half (>50%) of the total risk it is easy to conclude that the defendant's act is more likely than not the cause of the plaintiff's injury.

The court in *Landrigan*, makes it very clear that failure to establish a relative risk value in excess of 2.0 is not fatal to a plaintiff's case. Why shouldn't it be? The court's answer is that other factors could be proved in the case that would make it more likely that in this particular case that the risk factor for which the defendant is responsible is the operative cause of the particular plaintiff's injury. Examples include specific clinical evidence, or proof of extraordinary exposures. What about the flip side of the issue — will proof of a relative risk in excess of 2.0 always result in a decision in plaintiff's favor on the issue of cause-in-fact? It should be obvious that the same type of individualized proof that can allow a plaintiff to win despite a relative risk that does not exceed 2.0, can also allow a defendant to prevail in a case of relative risk higher than 2.0.

3. Legal causation and statistical significance: comparing apples and pear melba. When the term significant appears in legal discourse, it usually has its lay meanings that speak to the importance of a factor, or that contrast the central with the peripheral. In relation to scientific studies that find a correlation significant (as between an exposure and the subsequent onset of disease), the word "significant" is a term of art that describes the reliability of the linkage. To be more precise, the significance of a correlation is the likelihood that the data observed are not the product of mere random chance. In a case of radiation exposure, one judge explained statistical significance in the following way:

> Where there is an increase of observed cases of a particular cancer or leukemia over the number statistically "expected" to normally appear, the question arises whether it may be rationally inferred that the increase is causally connected to specific human activity. The scientific papers and reports will often speak of whether a deviation from the expected numbers of cases is "statistically significant," supporting a hypothesis of causation, or whether the perceived increase is attributable to random variation in the studied population, i.e., to chance. The mathematical tests of significance commonly used in research tend to be stringent; for an increase to be considered "statistically significant," the probability that it can be attributed to random chance usually must be five percent or less (p=.05). In other words, if the level of significance chosen by the researcher is p=.05, than an observed correlation is "significant" if there is 1 chance in 20 - or less - that the increase resulted from chance. In scientific practice, levels of significance of .01 or .001 are used providing an even more stringent test of a chosen hypothetical relationship. (Allen v. United States, 588 F.Supp. 247 (D. Utah 1984).

That opinion made the further point, that even causal hypothesis that narrowly failed to satisfy a .05 level of significance is not, from the legal viewpoint, insignificant. For instance, data for which there is only a 1 in 19 chance of its being random fails a .05 significance test, but nevertheless evidences a relationship for which "the probability is 94.73 percent or 18 chances out of 19 that the observed relationship is not a random event ... [and] the certainty that the observed increase is related to its hypothetical cause rather than mere chance is still far more likely than not." *Id.*

What does all this mean for the trial of toxic tort cases? First, even causal hypotheses that are not statistically significant at traditional p-values used in scientific research may be significant proof that helps establish legal causation.

4. The plaintiff's dilemma. Under the *Landrigan* standard for proving causation, how often can plaintiffs win exposure-induced cancer cases where the epidemiological studies do not evidence a relative risk value in excess of 2.0? What will be the usual impact on available proof of the long latency periods between exposure and the onset of disease? Most likely the delay will make it difficult for plaintiffs to obtain reliable proof of exposure levels and introduce, in the course of living, many confounding variables, such as other exposures, or life-style choices.

5. The pitfalls of probabilistic proof. A hot debate in the legal literature surrounds the advisability of allowing proof of probabilities to establish causation in fact. There are numerous good articles on this subject, two of the classics are Lawrence Tribe, Trial by Mathematics: Precision and Ritual in the Legal Process, 84 Harv. L. Rev. 1329 (1971) and Charles Nesson, Agent Orange Meet the Blue Bus: Factfinding at the Frontier of Knowledge, 66 B. U. L. Rev. 521 (1986).

Consider the following hypotheticals:[30] following ingestion of defendant's toxic waste that was spilled into an aquifer, the cancer rate in a community rises from 10 per year to 19 per year (hypo 1) or 21 per year (hypo 2) and all other possible causes have been ruled out by undisputed expert testimony. If probability is translated uncritically into plaintiffs' failure or success in carrying the burden of proof on the cause in fact issue, then in hypo 1 defendant goes free of liability to any of the 19 victims and in hypo 2 defendant must compensate all 21 victims.. Is such a result absurd? Do the hypotheticals make it clear why the *Landrigan* court is chary of making a relative risk of 2.0 a litmus for recovery? Compare with that approach, the treatment given to a similar issue in Potter v. Firestone Tire Co., which appear later in this supplement.

Should plaintiffs be relieved of their usual burden of proof because of these proof problems? In Allen v. United States, noted above for its discussion of statistical significance, the court fashioned a more lenient standard that adapts the substantial factor doctrine that was developed in the joint and several liability context to allow for proof of cause-in-fact in toxic exposure cases.[31] *Allen* involved very compelling facts: the unannounced atmospheric testing of atomic weapons that resulted in mass exposure of the general public to ionizing radiation from the fallout released by the test. The government's lack of warning and haphazard monitoring of fallout levels made it impossible for citizens to avoid the exposure and likewise impossible for them to reliably prove their level of exposure. Still, the relative risk levels (a term not used in the *Allen* litigation) were far lower than 2.0. Although its precise ruling is elusive and not easy to summarize, the court allowed the plaintiffs to shift the burden of proof on the cause-in-fact issue (which the *Allen* court prefers to refer to as the factual connection issue) to the defendant by proving that

---

30. The hypotheticals are adapted from Richard Delgado, Beyond *Sindell*, 70 Calif. L. Rev. 881, 885 (1982).
31. The case was later reversed on the grounds that the United States was immune to suit.

the defendant's conduct was a substantial risk increasing factor. Once plaintiff makes that showing, the defendant is to come forward with evidence that tries to weaken the factual connection between its acts and the plaintiff's injuries. In the end, no fixed rule is announced: "Whether any of these factual connections will lead to liability is, as Professor Thode reminds us, 'an issue involving *the scope of the legal system's protection afforded to plaintiff* and not an issue of factual causation.' Thode, Tort Analysis: Duty-Risk v. Proximate Cause and the Rational Allocation of Functions Between Judge and Jury, 1977 Utah L. Rev. 1, 6." (emphasis by the court.) In short, the key issue becomes one of policy regarding the extent of protection offered by the legal system, the very essence of the proximate cause inquiry.

Are there other ways of relaxing the plaintiff's burden on cause in fact that are not fraught with unfairness to defendants? Professor Delgado suggests allowing full recovery for the harms caused by defendant (9 in hypo 1, 11 in hypo 2) to be shared by the entire class of 20 plaintiffs. This forces defendant to bear its costs and "[P]robabilities are not used ... to establish a causal link between conduct of a certain type and a particular injury. Richard Delgado, Beyond *Sindell*, 70 Calif. L. Rev. 881, 905 (1982).

PAGE196   **Additional text on Expert Testimony**

Section 1A.   EXPERT TESTIMONY IN TOXIC TORT CASES

Cases such as *Allen* and *Ferebee* pose the distinction between legal and scientific proof. The dilemma confronting courts arises because cases involving claims of toxic exposure-caused injury must frequently be decided before the scientific community has accumulated sufficient data to establish scientific causation. If courts adopt a scientific standard of causation, then plaintiffs will invariably lose where the cases involve matters" at the frontier of current medical and epidemiological inquiry." If, on the other hand, courts impose no limits on plaintiffs' ability to place a particular theory of causation before the trier of fact (almost always a lay jury in toxic tort cases), then quackery, coincidence, or the sympathy of jurors with injured parties could lead to findings of causation where the preponderance of credible evidence favors the defendant.

Courts have responded to this dilemma by developing rules governing the admissibility of evidence. In matters of a scientific or technical nature, for example, virtually all courts require that testimony be given only by experts having appropriate qualifications. Although this requirement provides a safeguard of sorts, plaintiffs' and defendants' bars both have developed cadres of qualified expert witnesses skilled in presenting their respective opposing views on toxic injury causation. A growing number of courts are demanding more than mere expertise, and are increasingly sophisticated about the difference between legal and scientific proof.

The case that follows, Daubert v. Merrill Dow Pharmaceuticals Inc., addresses the appropriate standard of admissibility for expert scientific evidence. In it the United States Supreme Court is reviewing a 1991 decision by the U.S. Court of Appeals for the Ninth Circuit (951 F.2d 1128) that affirmed summary judgment against two families who had alleged the morning sickness drug Bendectin caused their children's limb reduction birth defects. The Ninth Circuit opinion had ruled that the plaintiffs' expert proof was inadmissible because it was not based on methodologies generally accepted in the relevant scientific disciplines. Without peer-reviewed epidemiological evidence, the court said, the plaintiffs could not prove causation. This position is generally referred to as the *Frye* rule. It derives from an old criminal prosecution for murder in which the defendant attempted to have an expert witness testify to the results of a systolic blood pressure deception (lie detector) test, at that time a relatively novel scientific test. Frye v. United States, 293 F. 1013 (D.C. Cir. 1923). The appeals court there said:

> Just when a scientific principle or discovery crosses the line between the experimental and demonstrable stages is difficult to define. Somewhere in this twilight zone the evidential force of the principle must be recognized, and while courts will go a long way in admitting expert testimony deduced from a well-recognized scientific principle or discovery, the thing from which the deduction is made must be sufficiently established to have gained general acceptance in the particular field in which it belongs. We think the systolic blood pressure deception test has not yet gained such standing and scientific recognition among physiological and psychological authorities as would justify the courts in admitting expert testimony deduced from the discovery, development, and experiments thus far made.

Frye has come under attack on a number of grounds, some having to do with the problem of scientific advancement. Expert testimony founded on new, but not yet recognized general principles is not admissible under *Frye*. As the argument goes, this either stymies science, or at least those who deserve the right to have their cases considered on the basis of new lines of scientific inquiry. By the time of *Daubert*, a third of jurisdictions, federal and state, had repudiated or recanted *Frye*. See, Edward Imwinkelreid, *Science Takes the Stand: The Growing Misuse of Expert Testimony*, The Sciences 20, 22 (Nov./Dec. 1986).

In *Daubert*, the plaintiffs (petitioners) claimed that the Federal Rules of Evidence controlled the case and would permit their evidence on causation to be heard. As you will see, the Supreme Court agreed and then went on to offer some indication of how it viewed the meaning of the governing evidentiary rules. The key Rules in the case are as follows:

RULE 702. TESTIMONY BY EXPERTS

If scientific, technical, or other specialized knowledge will assist the trier of fact to understand the evidence or to determine a fact in issue, a witness qualified as an expert by knowledge, skill, experience, training, or education, may testify thereto in the form of an opinion or otherwise.

RULE 703. BASES OF OPINION TESTIMONY BY EXPERTS

The facts or data in the particular case upon which an expert bases an opinion or inference may be those perceived by or made known to the expert at or before the hearing. If of a type reasonably relied upon by experts in the particular field in forming opinions or inferences upon the subject, the facts or data need not be admissible in evidence.

Daubert v. Merrell Dow Pharmaceuticals, Inc.
United States Supreme Court
61 USLW 4805, 1993 WL 224478

BLACKMUN, J., delivered the opinion for a unanimous Court.[32]

In this case we are called upon to determine the standard for admitting expert scientific testimony in a federal trial.

I.   Petitioners Jason Daubert and Eric Schuller are minor children born with serious birth defects.   They and their parents sued respondent in California state court, alleging that the birth defects had been caused by the mothers' ingestion of Bendectin, a prescription anti-nausea drug marketed by respondent.   Respondent removed the suits to federal court on diversity grounds.

After extensive discovery, respondent moved for summary judgment, contending that Bendectin does not cause birth defects in humans and that petitioners would be unable to come forward with any admissible evidence that it does.   In support of its motion, respondent submitted an affidavit of Steven H. Lamm, physician and epidemiologist, who is a well-credentialed expert on the risks from exposure to various chemical substances.   Doctor Lamm stated that he had reviewed all the literature on Bendectin and human birth defects — more than 30 published studies involving over 130,000 patients.   No study had found Bendectin to be a human teratogen (i.e., a substance capable of causing malformations in fetuses).   On the basis of this review, Doctor Lamm concluded that maternal use of Bendectin during the first trimester of pregnancy has not been shown to be a risk factor for human birth defects.

Petitioners did not (and do not) contest this characterization of the published record regarding Bendectin.   Instead, they responded to respondent's motion with the testimony of eight experts of their own, each of whom also possessed impressive credentials.   These experts had concluded that Bendectin can cause birth defects.   Their conclusions were based upon "in vitro" (test tube) and "in vivo" (live) animal studies that found a link between Bendectin and malformations; pharmacological studies of the chemical structure of Bendectin that purported to show similarities between the structure of the drug and that of other substances known to cause birth defects; and the "reanalysis" of previously published epidemiological (human statistical) studies.

The District Court granted respondent's motion for summary judgment. The court stated that scientific evidence is admissible only if the principle upon which it is based is " 'sufficiently established to have general acceptance in the field to which it belongs.' "   The court concluded that petitioners' evidence did not meet this standard.   Given the vast body of epidemiological data concerning Bendectin, the court held, expert opinion which is not based on epidemiological evidence is not admissible to establish causation.   Thus, the animal-cell studies, live-animal studies, and chemical-structure analyses on which petitioners had relied could not raise by themselves a reasonably disputable jury issue regarding causation.   Petitioners' epidemiological analyses, based as they were on

---

32. Rehnquist, joined by Stevens, joined in Parts I and II-A, but dissented from the latter portions of the opinion finding that they answered abstract questions that were not presented by the *Daubert* case in its present posture.

recalculations of data in previously published studies that had found no causal link between the drug and birth defects, were ruled to be inadmissible because they had not been published or subjected to peer review. ... [Citing Frye v. United States, the United States Court of Appeals for the Ninth Circuit affirmed.]

The Court of Appeals emphasized that other Courts of Appeals considering the risks of Bendectin had refused to admit reanalyses of epidemiological studies that had been neither published nor subjected to peer review. Those courts had found unpublished reanalyses "particularly problematic in light of the massive weight of the original published studies supporting [respondent's] position, all of which had undergone full scrutiny from the scientific community." Contending that reanalysis is generally accepted by the scientific community only when it is subjected to verification and scrutiny by others in the field, the Court of Appeals rejected petitioners' reanalyses as "unpublished, not subjected to the normal peer review process and generated solely for use in litigation." The court concluded that petitioners' evidence provided an insufficient foundation to allow admission of expert testimony that Bendectin caused their injuries and, accordingly, that petitioners could not satisfy their burden of proving causation at trial. ...

II. A. In the 70 years since its formulation in the *Frye* case, the "general acceptance" test has been the dominant standard for determining the admissibility of novel scientific evidence at trial. Although under increasing attack of late, the rule continues to be followed by a majority of courts, including the Ninth Circuit. ...

The merits of the *Frye* test have been much debated, and scholarship on its proper scope and application is legion. Petitioners' primary attack, however, is not on the content but on the continuing authority of the rule. They contend that the *Frye* test was superseded by the adoption of the Federal Rules of Evidence. We agree.

We interpret the legislatively-enacted Federal Rules of Evidence as we would any statute. Rule 402 provides the baseline: "All relevant evidence is admissible, except as otherwise provided by the Constitution of the United States, by Act of Congress, by these rules, or by other rules prescribed by the Supreme Court pursuant to statutory authority. Evidence which is not relevant is not admissible." "Relevant evidence" is defined as that which has "any tendency to make the existence of any fact that is of consequence to the determination of the action more probable or less probable than it would be without the evidence." Rule 401. The Rule's basic standard of relevance thus is a liberal one. ...

Here there is a specific Rule [702] that speaks to the contested issue. [See text above]. Nothing in the text of this Rule establishes "general acceptance" as an absolute prerequisite to admissibility. Nor does respondent present any clear indication that Rule 702 or the Rules as a whole were intended to incorporate a "general acceptance" standard. The drafting history makes no mention of *Frye*, and a rigid "general acceptance" requirement would be at odds with the "liberal thrust" of the Federal Rules and their "general approach of relaxing the traditional barriers to 'opinion' testimony.". Given the Rules' permissive backdrop and their inclusion of a specific rule on expert testimony that does not mention "general acceptance," the assertion that the Rules somehow assimilated *Frye* is unconvincing. *Frye* made 'general acceptance' the exclusive test for admitting expert scientific testimony. That austere standard, absent from and incompatible with the Federal Rules of Evidence, should not be applied in federal trials.

B. That the *Frye* test was displaced by the Rules of Evidence does not mean, however, that the Rules themselves place no limits on the admissibility of purportedly scientific evidence. Nor is the trial judge disabled from screening such evidence. To the contrary, under the Rules the trial judge must ensure that any and all scientific testimony or evidence admitted is not only relevant, but reliable.

The primary locus of this obligation is Rule 702, which clearly contemplates some degree of regulation of the subjects and theories about which an expert may testify. "If scientific, technical, or other specialized knowledge will assist the trier of fact to understand the evidence or to determine a fact in issue" an expert "may testify thereto." The subject of an expert's testimony must be "scientific ... knowledge." The adjective "scientific" implies a grounding in the methods and procedures of science. Similarly, the word "knowledge" connotes more than subjective belief or unsupported speculation. The term "applies to any body of known facts or to any body of ideas inferred from such facts or accepted as truths on good grounds." Webster's Third New International Dictionary 1252 (1986). Of course, it would be unreasonable to conclude that the subject of scientific testimony must be "known" to a certainty; arguably, there are no certainties in science. But, in order to qualify as "scientific knowledge," an inference or assertion must be derived by the scientific method. Proposed testimony must be supported by appropriate validation — i.e., "good grounds," based on what is known. In short, the requirement that an expert's testimony pertain to "scientific knowledge" establishes a standard of evidentiary reliability.

Rule 702 further requires that the evidence or testimony "assist the trier of fact to understand the evidence or to determine a fact in issue." This condition goes primarily to relevance. ...

That these requirements are embodied in Rule 702 is not surprising. Unlike an ordinary witness an expert is permitted wide latitude to offer opinions, including those that are not based on first-hand knowledge or observation. Presumably, this relaxation of the usual requirement of first-hand knowledge — a rule which represents "a 'most pervasive manifestation' of the common law insistence upon 'the most reliable sources of information,' " Advisory Committee's Notes on Fed.Rule Evid. 602 (citation omitted) — is premised on an assumption that the expert's opinion will have a reliable basis in the knowledge and experience of his discipline.

C. Faced with a proffer of expert scientific testimony, then, the trial judge must determine at the outset, pursuant to Rule 104(a), whether the expert is proposing to testify to (1) scientific knowledge that (2) will assist the trier of fact to understand or determine a fact in issue. This entails a preliminary assessment of whether the reasoning or methodology underlying the testimony is scientifically valid and of whether that reasoning or methodology properly can be applied to the facts in issue. We are confident that federal judges possess the capacity to undertake this review. Many factors will bear on the inquiry, and we do not presume to set out a definitive checklist or test. But some general observations are appropriate.

Ordinarily, a key question to be answered in determining whether a theory or technique is scientific knowledge that will assist the trier of fact will be whether it can be (and has been) tested. "Scientific methodology today is based on generating hypotheses and testing them to see if they can be falsified; indeed, this methodology is what distinguishes science from other fields of human inquiry."

Another pertinent consideration is whether the theory or technique has been subjected to peer review and publication. Publication (which is but one element of peer review) is not a sine qua non of admissibility; it does not necessarily correlate with reliability, and in some instances well-grounded but innovative theories will not have been published. Some propositions, moreover, are too particular, too new, or of too limited interest to be published. But submission to the scrutiny of the scientific community is a component of "good science," in part because it increases the likelihood that substantive flaws in methodology will be detected. The fact of publication (or lack thereof) in a peer-reviewed journal thus will be a relevant, though not dispositive, consideration in assessing the scientific validity of a particular technique or methodology on which an opinion is premised.

Additionally, in the case of a particular scientific technique, the court ordinarily should consider the known or potential rate of error, and the existence and maintenance of standards controlling the technique's operation.

Finally, "general acceptance" can yet have a bearing on the inquiry. A "reliability assessment does not require, although it does permit, explicit identification of a relevant scientific community and an express determination of a particular degree of acceptance within that community." Widespread acceptance can be an important factor in ruling particular evidence admissible, and "a known technique that has been able to attract only minimal support within the community," may properly be viewed with skepticism.

The inquiry envisioned by Rule 702 is, we emphasize, a flexible one. Its overarching subject is the scientific validity — and thus the evidentiary relevance and reliability — of the principles that underlie a proposed submission. The focus, of course, must be solely on principles and methodology, not on the conclusions that they generate.

Throughout, a judge assessing a proffer of expert scientific testimony under Rule 702 should also be mindful of other applicable rules. Rule 703 provides that expert opinions based on otherwise inadmissible hearsay are to be admitted only if the facts or data are "of a type reasonably relied upon by experts in the particular field in forming opinions or inferences upon the subject." Rule 706 allows the court at its discretion to procure the assistance of an expert of its own choosing. Finally, Rule 403 permits the exclusion of relevant evidence "if its probative value is substantially outweighed by the danger of unfair prejudice, confusion of the issues, or misleading the jury...." Judge Weinstein has explained: "Expert evidence can be both powerful and quite misleading because of the difficulty in evaluating it. Because of this risk, the judge in weighing possible prejudice against probative force under Rule 403 of the present rules exercises more control over experts than over lay witnesses."

III. We conclude by briefly addressing what appear to be two underlying concerns of the parties and amici in this case. Respondent expresses apprehension that abandonment of "general acceptance" as the exclusive requirement for admission will result in a "free-for-all" in which befuddled juries are confounded by absurd and irrational pseudoscientific assertions. In this regard respondent seems to us to be overly pessimistic about the capabilities of the jury, and of the adversary system generally. Vigorous cross-examination, presentation of contrary evidence, and careful instruction on the burden of proof are the traditional and appropriate means of attacking shaky but admissible evidence. ... These conventional devices, rather than wholesale exclusion under an uncompromising "general acceptance" test, are the appropriate safeguards where the basis of scientific testimony meets the standards of Rule 702.

Petitioners and, to a greater extent, their amici exhibit a different concern. They suggest that recognition of a screening role for the judge that allows for the exclusion of "invalid" evidence will sanction a stifling and repressive scientific orthodoxy and will be inimical to the search for truth. It is true that open debate is an essential part of both legal and scientific analyses. Yet there are important differences between the quest for truth in the courtroom and the quest for truth in the laboratory. Scientific conclusions are subject to perpetual revision. Law, on the other hand, must resolve disputes finally and quickly. The scientific project is advanced by broad and wide-ranging consideration of a multitude of hypotheses, for those that are incorrect will eventually be shown to be so, and that in itself is an advance. Conjectures that are probably wrong are of little use, however, in the project of reaching a quick, final, and binding legal judgment — often of great consequence — about a particular set of events in the past. We recognize that in practice, a gatekeeping role for the judge, no matter how flexible, inevitably on occasion will prevent the jury from learning of authentic insights and innovations. That, nevertheless, is the balance that is struck by Rules of Evidence designed not for the exhaustive search for cosmic understanding but for the particularized resolution of legal disputes.

IV.   To summarize: "general acceptance" is not a necessary precondition to the admissibility of scientific evidence under the Federal Rules of Evidence, but the Rules of Evidence — especially Rule 702 — do assign to the trial judge the task of ensuring that an expert's testimony both rests on a reliable foundation and is relevant to the task at hand. Pertinent evidence based on scientifically valid principles will satisfy those demands.

The inquiries of the District Court and the Court of Appeals focused almost exclusively on "general acceptance," as gauged by publication and the decisions of other courts. Accordingly, the judgment of the Court of Appeals is vacated and the case is remanded for further proceedings consistent with this opinion. It is so ordered.

COMMENTARY & QUESTIONS

1. What did *Daubert* decide?   Apart from holding that *Frye* is not controlling in the wake of Evidence Rule 702, can you isolate the meaning of *Daubert*?   What seems to emerge is a requirement that the judge must employ discretion to insure that scientific evidence is sufficiently reliable, and that there are a number of non-exclusive factors to be considered in making that decision, but the factors, including general acceptance, certainly do resemble the *Frye* rule. *Daubert* does not confront the basic problem that civil suits are based on preponderance and science is based on something very different like criminal laws "beyond a reasonable doubt."

2. Is *Daubert* a plaintiff's victory?   On remand, what outcome would you predict?   The plaintiffs' eight experts were characterized by the Supreme Court as being possessed of "impressive credentials," yet their reanalysis of the epidemiological data was unpublished and did not fit the orthodox interpretation given to that by the defendant's expert and the literature in the field.   Even if the remand does not result in admission of the proffered testimony in *Daubert*, isn't it fairly clear that toxic tort plaintiffs, in general, are far better off having the *Frye* "generally accepted" test declared dead and buried, at least in litigation conducted in federal court?   To answer this question, it is good to recall the role played by summary judgment in the litigation process.

The standard for the grant of summary judgment requires that there be no genuine issue of material fact and that the party seeking summary judgment is entitled to judgment as a matter of law.   See generally, Federal Rule of Civil Procedure 56.   At least in theory, it would seem that the basic idea is that cases where there is not a honestly debatable issue of fact to be determined should not be tried.   Berry v. Armstrong Rubber Co., discussed in the next note, fits this mold.   In that case plaintiffs' experts' testimony was ruled inadmissible.   As a result, there remained no credible evidence to support plaintiffs' affirmative case on causation and damage, so the court ruled that there was no genuine issue of material fact that could be tried to a jury and granted the motion for summary judgment, thereby preventing a jury from hearing the case at all.

Preventing jury consideration is widely thought to have a major influence on outcomes.   Tactically, once a toxic tort case is permitted to be decided by the jury, (i.e., where the judge allows the jury to hear and evaluate the weight of the testimony offered by the plaintiffs' experts on the liability and causation issues) the frequently sympathetic nature of the cases (innocent and badly injured victim suing a target corporate defendant) makes them very problematic for the defendant and ripe for settlement.

3. *Daubert* and bad expert testimony.   Will *Daubert* change the result in cases where the testimony of plaintiffs' experts is unconvincing?   Cases that rely on bad expert testimony should, and do, and probably will continue to lose.   One recent example of this is Berry v. Armstrong Rubber Co., 989 F.2d 822 (5th Cir. 1993).   In consolidated cases plaintiffs sought recoveries for reduced property values traceable to defendant's long term waste disposal practices as well as for personal injuries caused by exposure to contaminated drinking water.   The Fifth Circuit upheld defendant's summary judgment because of the inadequacy of plaintiff's expert testimony. More specifically, the exclusion of expert testimony under Federal Rule of Evidence 703 was held proper where the experts testified in areas in which they were not qualified, offering opinions that were not based on tests that they had performed, or using data and methodology not recognized by other experts in the field. For example, significant portions of the testimony were based on data developed at locations other than the plaintiffs' property; the plaintiffs' property was not itself tested. Another expert's testimony (that of Nolan Augenbaugh of the *Wilsonville* case) was held properly rejected because it rested on an assumption that groundwater flowed toward plaintiffs' land, despite the lack of any testing by plaintiffs to substantiate that claim and the presence of EPA testing that showed the groundwater flowed in the opposite direction. Correspondingly, medical experts' testimony that relied on Augenbaugh's conclusions about the level of contaminants present at the plaintiffs' property, were likewise unfounded.

4. Distinguishing innovative explanations of causation from junk science. Peter Huber, the author of the Chapter 2 excerpt advocating increased acceptance of public risk, has also written a major article on this subject, Medical Experts and the Ghost of Galileo, 54 Law & Contemporary Problems 119 (1991). In that article he argues that there are virtually no "Galileos" serving as experts in toxic tort and product liability litigation. The credible scientific discoveries, the ones that identify "real risks," were not ones made and brought to light in the crucible of litigation. Rather, Huber traces the history of asbestos, the Ford Pinto, the Dalkon Shield, Rely tampons, DES, and thalidomide to typical sources within the accepted scientific community — traditional epidemiological research and inquiries prompted and followed up on by administrative agencies concerned with public safety. In contrast, Huber tells the story of incorrect conclusions reached by researchers into traumatic cancer (claims that traumatic injury causes cancer) and cerebral palsy, as cautionary vignettes. He uses these examples to urge the legal system to be wary of the "post hoc fallacy" that arises when researchers seek to identify causes after first observing the result. He criticizes the effort of researchers who observed cancers and thereafter linked them to histories of trauma. He makes his point by repeating one scientist's pithy observation, "Because toads appear after a rain it is not necessary to assume that it has rained toads."[33] Surely, this criticism cuts too broadly, but it should sound a cautionary note. Is Huber correct in asserting that the legal system functions best when it follows scientific discovery rather than getting out ahead of it?

5. Rubanick v. Witco Chemical: a methodologically—based admissibility test. [see coursebook, page 196, comment 6.]

PAGE 221   **Update on statutes of limitation**

6. A note on statutes of limitation. Toxic tort cases raise a number of difficult statute of limitations problems. As an initial matter, the discovery

---

33. 54 Law & Contemp. Probs. at 160, quoting Fred W. Stewart, Occupational and Post-Traumatic Cancer, 23 Bull. New York Academy of Medicine 145 (1947).

by plaintiffs that they are victims of a tort is seldom concurrent with the defendant's tortious conduct. Even in *Ferebee* (the paraquat spraying case) the plaintiff's decedent was unaware of the harm caused to him by the exposures until sometime significantly after the initial exposure occurred. Likewise in *Ayers* and *Anderson* the groundwater contamination and plaintiffs' subsequent ingestion of it began well in advance of plaintiffs' learning that contamination had occurred, and perhaps years in advance of plaintiffs suffering any physical injury from having ingested the water.

The courts have adopted two devices for dealing with statutes of limitations problems. The first doctrine relates to defining when a cause of action accrues. A lawsuit cannot be brought by a plaintiff to vindicate a cause of action before the cause of action has accrued to the plaintiff. To do otherwise defies logic, asking plaintiff to act on a legal right not yet in existence. The doctrine is intended to protect the courts themselves from the burden of adjudicating unripe controversies. In fairness to plaintiffs refused access to courts by the accrual rule, it is universally held that statutes of limitations only begin to run from the time a cause of action has accrued to the plaintiff. Most courts have held that accrual occurs only when all of the elements necessary for successful prosecution of the claim have occurred, and a central element of any tort claim is the injury to the plaintiff.

The second major development in limitation of actions law that operates to protect plaintiffs in toxic tort cases is the so-called "discovery rule." It too helps to define when a cause of action accrues. In that portion of the *Anderson* opinion addressing the effect of the statute of limitations on wrongful death claims being pressed on behalf of area children who had died of leukemia after drinking water from the polluted wells, the court stated the general discovery rule:

> The discovery rule is a method of defining when a cause of action accrues. The principle behind the rule is that "a plaintiff should be put on notice before his or her claim is barred by the passage of time." The notice required by the rule includes knowledge of both the injury and its cause — that plaintiff "has been harmed as a result of defendant's conduct." 628 F. Supp. at 1224 (citations omitted).[18]

It should be clear that the discovery rule addresses the problem of long latency periods intervening between tortious exposure and the onset of disease. If the statute of limitations has not yet begun to run until the disease is manifest, then plaintiffs will have ample opportunity to bring suit after the onset of the disease. There may be some proof difficulties in reconstructing the events surrounding exposure, but it is at least reasonable to consider these the lesser of evils. The principal alternatives to the discovery rule are requiring defendants to compensate all exposure victims as if they have developed the disease, or abandoning the discovery rule, and thereby limiting plaintiffs to damages that became manifest within a short time of exposure.

Ayers recognizes the existence of an additional potential discovery rule problem, the operation of the rules of res judicata (in particular merger and bar) that the New Jersey court labels "the single controversy rule." In most instances, in order to avoid duplicative and inefficient litigation of a case, all claims must be joined in a single suit. To the extent that claims have been omitted and not placed in issue, the single controversy rule deems them extinguished and "merged" into the original judgment. In cases like *Ayers* the pitfall of the single controversy rule is that later-initiated claims for matured illness will be allowed by the discovery rule, only to be barred by merger. The New Jersey approach to this problem is to recognize that the policies of the discovery rule would be set at naught if merger and bar were applied. The court points out that merger and bar only apply to cases that could have been brought at the time of the first suit, and here, technically speaking, the cause of action for bodily injury would not yet have come into existence.

6A.   Reopened statutes of limitation, statutes of repose. Beyond the typical questions associated with statutes of limitation in the environmental setting — notably discovery rule issues in cases of long-term latency toxic injuries — are other interesting issues, including statutes re-opening time-barred claims through new short term "windows" for filing on particular kinds of tort injury (e.g. asbestosis), and so-called "statutes of repose" which forbid all claims after a certain amount of time (e.g. ten years) regardless of applicable discovery rule circumstances. In defendants' view the former raise constitutional questions. From plaintiffs' perspective the latter represent legislative capitulations to industrial lobbyists, overriding the law's basic purpose of adjudicating private wrongs. For a case including both kinds of legislation see Concordia College v. W.R. Grace Co., et al., No. 92-1307, 8th Cir. July 14, 1993.

PAGE 223   **New material on compensation for toxic exposure**

Section 2A.   Compensation for fear, injury to individuals, and stigma. Victims of toxic exposures experience a welter of perceived losses. As the opinions in *Anderson* and *Ayers* should make clear, these losses cannot be neatly categorized as tangible and intangible, but more nearly form a spectrum that moves from more concrete and familiar items for which compensation in tort has traditionally been awarded, to items that are more ethereal and not traditionally the subject of recoveries. At the latter end of the scale are two items, fear of cancer and stigma that are perhaps the most contentious ones of all.

Fear of cancer in this context is to be distinguished from cancerphobia, which is increasingly being used in its more technical sense to denote a phobic reaction that is evidenced by recurrent dread in the absence of objective danger so substantial as to be indicative of mental illness.[34] Stigma in this context involves losses occasioned by how persons, such as potential buyers of realty, react to knowledge about contamination events that have not physically contaminated the parcel involved in the prospective transaction, not devaluation caused by the contamination of the parcel itself.

---

34. Note 3 on page 219 of the main text which addresses cancerphobia is (mea culpa) an example of lack of precision in using the term. It tends to lump the mental illness denotation of the term with broader usages that involve fear alone without disease.

Potter v. Firestone Tire and Rubber Co.
6 Cal. 4th 965, 25 Cal. Rptr. 2d 550
Supreme Court of California, 1993

Baxter, Justice.   We granted review in this case to consider whether emotional distress engendered by a fear of cancer or other serious physical illness or injury following exposure to a carcinogen or other toxic substance is an injury for which damages may be recovered in a negligence action in the absence of physical injury.[35] ...

Our analysis of existing case law and policy considerations relevant to the availability of damages for emotional distress leads us to conclude that, generally, in the absence of a present physical injury or illness, recovery of damages for fear of cancer in a negligence action should be allowed only if the plaintiff pleads and proves that the fear stems from a knowledge, corroborated by reliable medical and scientific opinion, that it is more likely than not that the feared cancer will develop in the future due to the toxic exposure.

We also conclude, however, that an exception to this general rule is warranted if the toxic exposure that has resulted in the fear of cancer is caused by conduct amounting to "oppression, fraud, or malice" as defined in Civil Code § 3294. In such cases, a plaintiff should be allowed to recover without having to show knowledge that it is more likely than not that the feared cancer will occur, so long as the plaintiff's fear is otherwise serious, genuine and reasonable. ...

This is a toxic exposure case brought by four landowners living adjacent to a landfill. As a result of defendant Firestone's practice of disposing of its toxic wastes at the landfill, the landowners were subjected to prolonged exposure to certain carcinogens. While none of the landowners currently suffers from any cancerous or precancerous condition, each faces an enhanced but unquantified risk of developing cancer in the future due to the exposure. ...

From 1963 until 1980, Firestone operated a tire manufacturing plant near Salinas. In 1967, Firestone contracted with Salinas Disposal Service and Rural Disposal (hereafter SDS), two refuse collection companies operating the Crazy Horse landfill (hereafter Crazy Horse), for disposal of its industrial waste. Firestone agreed to deposit its waste in dumpsters provided by SDS located at the plant site. SDS agreed to haul the waste to Crazy Horse and deposit it there.

Crazy Horse, a class II sanitary landfill owned by the City of Salinas, covers approximately 125 acres suitable for the disposal of household and commercial solid waste. Unlike dump sites that are classified class I, class II landfills such as Crazy Horse prohibit toxic substances and liquids because of the danger that they will leach into the groundwater and cause contamination. At the outset of their contractual relationship, SDS informed Firestone that no solvents, cleaning fluids, oils or liquids were permitted at Crazy Horse. Firestone provided assurances that these types of waste would not be sent to the landfill. Notwithstanding its assurances, Firestone sent large quantities of liquid waste to Crazy Horse, including

---

35. Eds.: The *Potter* case addressed several other salient issues that are canvassed in the Commentary and Questions that follow the excerpts from the court's opinion.

banbury drippings (a by-product of the tire manufacturing process) containing a combination of semiliquid toxic chemicals. Firestone also sent liquid waste oils, liquid tread end cements, and solvents to the landfill.

In May 1977, Firestone's plant engineer, who was in charge of all environmental matters, sent a memorandum to Firestone's plant managers and department heads. The memorandum, reflecting official plant policy, explained liquid waste disposal procedures and described the particular waste materials involved and the proper method of handling them. In order to comply with this policy, Firestone initially made efforts to take the waste materials to a class I dump site. However, Firestone accumulated more waste than had been anticipated and disposing of the waste proved costly. When noncompliance with the policy became widespread, the plant engineer sent another memorandum to plant management complaining about the lack of compliance and pointing out that the policy was required by California law.

During this time, the Salinas plant operated under a production manager who had been sent from Firestone's company headquarters in Akron, Ohio for the purpose of "turning the plant around" and making it more profitable. This manager became angered over the costs of the waste disposal program and decided to discontinue it. As a consequence, Firestone's hazardous waste materials were once again deposited at Crazy Horse.

Frank and Shirley Potter owned property and lived adjacent to Crazy Horse. Joe and Linda Plescia were their neighbors. In 1984, the Potters and the Plescias (hereafter plaintiffs) discovered that toxic chemicals had contaminated their domestic water wells. The chemicals included benzene; toluene; chloroform; 1,1- dichloroethene; methylene chloride; tetrachloroethene; 1,1,1- trichloroethane; trichloroethene; and vinyl chloride. Of these, both benzene and vinyl chloride are known to be human carcinogens. Many of the others are strongly suspected to be carcinogens.

In 1985, plaintiffs filed separate suits against Firestone for damages and declaratory relief. Their complaints against Firestone stated causes of action for, inter alia, negligence, negligent and intentional infliction of emotional distress, and strict liability/ultrahazardous activity. The two cases were tried together in a court trial. After considering all the evidence, the court found that Firestone was negligent; that negligent and intentional infliction of emotional distress were established; and that Firestone's conduct was an ultrahazardous activity that would subject Firestone to strict liability for resulting damages. Judgment was entered in favor of plaintiffs.

In its statement of decision, the trial court concluded that Firestone's waste disposal practices from 1967 until 1974 constituted actionable negligence. In particular, it determined that Firestone's dumping of liquid and semiliquid wastes at Crazy Horse, despite having been told that such dumping was prohibited, fell below the appropriate standard of care. In rejecting Firestone's argument that it was not negligent because the dangers posed by toxins were not widely known until the mid-1970's, the trial court concluded that: (1) Firestone had been informed by SDS that no solvents, cleaning fluids, oils or liquids were permitted at Crazy Horse; (2) it fell below the standard of care for a large, international corporation with scientific and legal experts in its employ, having been alerted to the impropriety of disposing of these wastes at the landfill, to violate these regulations without at least making reasonable inquiry into the reasons for the restrictions; and (3) if Firestone had made a minimal inquiry, it would have discovered, among other things, the dangers to groundwater from landfill leachates and the potential for contaminating domestic wells. [The trial court also found Firestone liable for intentional infliction of emotional distress and for strict liability for engaging in an ultrahazardous activity.]

In finding liability, the trial court determined that the toxic chemicals in plaintiffs' drinking water were the same chemicals or "daughter" chemicals as those used at the Firestone plant. Firestone was the heaviest single contributor of waste at Crazy Horse and the only contributor with the identical "suite" of chemicals to those found in the water. The court also noted the expert testimony established that the chemicals that migrated off the Firestone plant site so closely resembled those in the water that the comparison constituted a virtual "fingerprint" identifying Firestone as the source of the contaminants.

The court did not attribute any item of damage to any one specific theory of recovery. After noting that plaintiffs' likelihood of harm due to their toxic exposure was the subject of conflicting medical opinions at trial, the court concluded there was convincing evidence that the prolonged nature of the exposure had "enhanced" plaintiffs' risk of developing cancer and other maladies, and that this enhanced susceptibility was a "presently existing physical condition." The court observed that although there was no way to quantify this risk, the risk was nevertheless very real. In its view, reliable scientific opinion and common sense both supported the conclusion that a prolonged period of exposure substantially increased the susceptibility to disease.

The court also stated that although plaintiffs testified to a constellation of physical symptoms which they attributed to the toxic chemicals, it was "not possible to demonstrate with sufficient certainty a causal connection between these symptoms and the well water contamination. Nevertheless, plaintiffs will always fear, and reasonably so, that physical impairments they experience are the result of the well water and are the precursors of life threatening disease. Their fears are not merely subjective but are corroborated by substantial medical and scientific opinion." Based on these findings, plaintiffs were awarded damages totaling $800,000 for their lifelong fear of cancer and resultant emotional distress. [The court also awarded $142,975 as the present value of the costs of medical monitoring, based on plaintiffs' life expectancies.]

The court also awarded plaintiffs damages totaling $269,500 for psychiatric illness and the cost of treating such illness,[36] as well as damages totaling $108,100 for the general disruption of their lives and the invasion of their privacy.[37] Finally, the court awarded punitive damages totaling $2.6 million based on Firestone's conscious disregard for the

---

36. The court determined that these damages were separate and distinct from plaintiffs' basic fear of developing cancer or other serious physical illnesses in the future.

37. This award reflected the necessity for plaintiffs to shower elsewhere, use bottled water, and submit to intrusions by numerous agencies involved in testing water and soil.

rights and safety of others in dumping its toxic wastes at the landfill after 1977.

Firestone appealed [and] claimed[38] that the award for "fear of cancer" in the absence of physical injury was an unwarranted extension of liability for negligent infliction of emotional distress, that if such fear is compensable it should not be so where the plaintiff cannot establish that he or she has a "probability" of developing cancer, and that the amount of damages awarded each plaintiff was not based on proof of individualized injury. The award for "psychiatric injury" was challenged on the ground that the injury was indistinguishable from fear of cancer and was not supported by the evidence.

The Court of Appeal [in regard to the claims relating to fear of cancer] affirmed the judgment. The court held that, given the circumstances in which plaintiffs ingested the carcinogens, it was unnecessary for them to establish a present physical injury in order to recover for their fear of cancer. It further held it was unnecessary for plaintiffs to prove they were likely to develop cancer, noting their fear was certain, definite and real, and not contingent on whether they in fact develop the disease. Plaintiffs had proven the elements of a negligence cause of action and had demonstrated, under an objective standard, that their emotional distress was serious.... The court affirmed the amount of the compensatory damages award and found the punitive damage award proper.

A. NEGLIGENCE: FEAR OF CANCER

"Fear of cancer" is a term generally used to describe a present anxiety over developing cancer in the future.[39] Claims for fear of cancer have been increasingly asserted in toxic tort cases as more and more substances have been linked with cancer. Typically, a person's likelihood of developing cancer as a result of a toxic exposure is difficult to predict because many forms of cancer are characterized by long latency periods (anywhere from 20 to 30 years), and presentation is dependent upon the interrelation of myriad factors.

The availability of damages for fear of cancer as a result of exposure to carcinogens or other toxins in negligence actions is a relatively novel issue for California courts....

---

38. Eds: ... among numerous other things ...

39. Some commentators and courts have referred to claims for "fear of cancer" as "cancerphobia" claims. (See Sterling v. Velsicol Chemical Corp. (6th Cir.1988) 855 F.2d 1188, 1206, fn. 24 [hereafter Sterling]; Gale & Goyer, Recovery for Cancerphobia and Increased Risk of Cancer (1985) 15 Cumb.L.Rev. 723, 724-725.) Strictly speaking, however, there is a distinction between fear of cancer and cancerphobia. Cancerphobia, as a "phobic reaction," is a mental illness that is the recurrent experience of dread of a cancer in the absence of objective danger. In contrast, the fear of cancer is a claimed anxiety caused by the fear of developing cancer and is not a mental illness. (See ibid.) This opinion is concerned only with fear of cancer as a form of emotional distress and not with cancerphobia. Furthermore, while plaintiffs identified fear of cancer as the principal basis for the emotional distress claim at issue, our discussion is equally relevant to emotional distress engendered by fear that other types of serious physical illness or injury may result from toxic exposure.

1. Parasitic Recovery: Immune System Impairment and/or Cellular Damage as Physical Injury

Because it initially appeared plaintiffs might have suffered damage to their immune systems, we solicited the views of the parties on whether such damage constitutes physical injury. We did so because it is settled in California that in ordinary negligence actions for physical injury, recovery for emotional distress caused by that injury is available as an item of parasitic damages. Where a plaintiff can demonstrate a physical injury caused by the defendant's negligence, anxiety specifically due to a reasonable fear of a future harm attributable to the injury may also constitute a proper element of damages. [In the end, however, the court found that the *Potter* case, as litigated, did not present "an appropriate factual record for resolving whether impairment to the immune response system or cellular damage constitutes a physical injury for which parasitic damages for emotional distress ought to be available."]

2. Nonparasitic Fear of Cancer Recovery

We next determine whether the absence of a present physical injury precludes recovery for emotional distress engendered by fear of cancer. Firestone argues that California should not recognize a duty to avoid negligently causing emotional distress to another, but, if such a duty is recognized, recovery should be permitted in the absence of physical injury only on proof that the plaintiff's emotional distress or fear is caused by knowledge that future physical injury or illness is more likely than not to occur as a direct result of the defendant's conduct. Amici curiae, many of whom represent organizations of manufacturers and their insurers, would preclude all recovery for emotional distress in the absence of physical injury.

a. Independent Duty

Firestone first asks the court to expressly adopt the rule recently applied by the Supreme Court of Texas in Boyles v. Kerr (1993) 855 S.W.2d 593. There the court held that there is no duty to avoid negligently causing emotional distress to another, and that damages for emotional distress are recoverable only if the defendant has breached some other duty to the plaintiff.

That is already the law in California. Indeed, the Texas court relied on recent decisions of this court in which we recognized that there is no independent tort of negligent infliction of emotional distress... [U]nless the defendant has assumed a duty to plaintiff in which the emotional condition of the plaintiff is an object, recovery is available only if the emotional distress arises out of the defendant's breach of some other legal duty and the emotional distress is proximately caused by that breach of duty. Even then, with rare exceptions, a breach of the duty must threaten physical injury, not simply damage to property or financial interests.

Those limits on recovery for emotional distress caused by the negligent conduct of another do not aid Firestone here, however. Firestone did violate a duty imposed on it by law and regulation to dispose of toxic waste only in a class I landfill and to avoid contamination of underground water.[40] The violation led directly to plaintiffs' ingestion of various known and suspected carcinogens, and thus to their fear of suffering the very harm which the Legislature sought by statute to avoid. Their fear of cancer was proximately caused by Firestone's unlawful conduct which threatened serious physical injury. This is not a case in which a negligence cause of action is predicated only on a claim that the defendant breached a duty to avoid causing emotional distress.

b. Absence of Physical Injury

Amici curiae argue that no recovery for emotional distress arising from fear of cancer should be allowed in any case unless the plaintiff can establish a present physical injury such as a clinically verifiable cancerous or precancerous condition. Amici curiae advance several legal and policy arguments to support this position. None is persuasive....

Significantly, we recently reaffirmed the principle that in California, "damages for negligently inflicted emotional distress may be recovered in the absence of physical injury or impact...." (Burgess v. Superior Court, 2 Cal.4th 1064, 1074, 9 Cal.Rptr.2d 615, 831 P.2d 1197.) We held that "physical injury is not a prerequisite for recovering damages for serious emotional distress," especially where "there exists a 'guarantee of genuineness in the circumstances of the case.' [Citation.]" (Id., at p. 1079, 9 Cal.Rptr.2d 615, 831 P.2d 1197.) ...

Amici curiae next contend that substantial policy reasons nevertheless support a physical injury requirement for recovery of fear of cancer damages where no preexisting relationship exists. They suggest that allowing recovery in the absence of a physical injury would create limitless liability and would result in a flood of litigation which thereby would impose onerous burdens on courts, corporations, insurers and society in general. Allowing such recovery would promote fraud and artful pleading, and would also encourage plaintiffs to seek damages based on a subjective fear of cancer. In amici curiae's view, a physical injury requirement is thus essential to provide meaningful limits on the class of potential plaintiffs and clear guidelines for resolving disputes over liability without the necessity for trial.

This argument overlooks the reasons for our decision to discard the requirement of physical injury. As we observed more than a decade ago, "[t]he primary justification for the requirement of physical injury appears to be that it serves as a screening device to minimize a presumed risk of feigned injuries and false claims. [Citations.]" (Molien v. Kaiser Foundation Hospitals (1980) 27 Cal.3d 916, 925-926, 167 Cal.Rptr. 831, 616 P.2d 813 [hereafter *Molien*], disapproved on other grounds, Burgess, supra, 2 Cal.4th at p. 1074, 9 Cal.Rptr.2d 615, 831 P.2d 1197.) Such harm was "believed to be susceptible of objective ascertainment and hence to corroborate the authenticity of the claim." (*Molien*, supra, 27 Cal.3d at p. 926, 167 Cal.Rptr. 831, 616 P.2d 813.) ...

Our reasons for discarding the physical injury requirement in *Molien* remain valid today and are equally applicable in a toxic exposure case.

---

40. ...The substances sent to Crazy Horse by Firestone were prohibited under the classification established by the Department of Water Resources in 1966. Among the purposes for the classification was minimizing migration of leachates from Crazy Horse toward the groundwater basin and degrading nearby domestic wells.

That is, the physical injury requirement is a hopelessly imprecise screening device--it would allow recovery for fear of cancer whenever such distress accompanies or results in any physical injury, no matter how trivial, yet would disallow recovery in all cases where the fear is both serious and genuine but no physical injury has yet manifested itself. While we agree with amici curiae that meaningful limits on the class of potential plaintiffs and clear guidelines for resolving disputes in advance of trial are necessary, imposing a physical injury requirement represents an inherently flawed and inferior means of attempting to achieve these goals.

c. Likelihood of Cancer in the Future

We next consider whether recovery of damages for emotional distress caused by fear of cancer should depend upon a showing that the plaintiff's fears stem from a knowledge that there is a probable likelihood of developing cancer in the future due to the toxic exposure. This is a matter of hot debate among the parties and amici curiae. Firestone and numerous amici curiae argue that because fear of cancer claims are linked to a future harm which may or may not materialize, such claims raise concerns about speculation and uncertainty and therefore warrant a requirement that the plaintiff show the feared cancer is more likely than not to occur. Plaintiffs and other amici curiae respond that such a requirement is inappropriate in the context of a mental distress claim, and that there are viable methods, apart from requiring quantification of the cancer risk, to screen claims and determine the reasonableness and genuineness of a plaintiff's fears.

Plaintiffs favor the approach adopted by the Court of Appeal, which requires the following showing. The toxic exposure plaintiff must first prove the elements of a negligence cause of action. The plaintiff must then establish that his or her fear of cancer is serious, and that the seriousness meets an objective standard (i.e., the distress must be reasonable under the circumstances). Although a plaintiff is not required to establish that the cancer is likely to occur, the finder of fact should consider evidence regarding the likelihood that cancer will occur (i.e., evidence that the disease is only a remote possibility could lead a trier of fact to conclude that a plaintiff's fears were unreasonable). Finally, the finder of fact should test the genuineness of the plaintiff's fear under the factors discussed in *Molien*, supra, 27 Cal.3d 916, 167 Cal.Rptr. 831, 616 P.2d 813, including expert testimony, a juror's own experience, and the particular circumstances of the case....

We decline to adopt the Court of Appeal's approach.... A carcinogenic or other toxic ingestion or exposure, without more, does not provide a basis for fearing future physical injury or illness which the law is prepared to recognize as reasonable. The fact that one is aware that he or she has ingested or been otherwise exposed to a carcinogen or other toxin, without any regard to the nature, magnitude and proportion of the exposure or its likely consequences, provides no meaningful basis upon which to evaluate the reasonableness of one's fear. For example, nearly everybody is exposed to carcinogens which appear naturally in all types of foods. Yet ordinary consumption of such foods is not substantially likely to result in cancer. Nor is the knowledge of such consumption likely to result in a reasonable fear of cancer.

Moreover, permitting recovery for fear of cancer damages based solely upon a plaintiff's knowledge that his or her risk of cancer has been significantly increased by a toxic exposure, without requiring any further showing of the actual likelihood of the feared cancer due to the exposure, provides no protection against unreasonable claims based upon wholly speculative fears. For example, a plaintiff's risk of contracting cancer might be significantly increased by 100 or more percent due to a particular toxic exposure, yet the actual risk of the feared cancer might itself be insignificant and no more than a mere possibility. As even plaintiffs appear to concede, evidence of knowledge that cancer is only a remote possibility could lead a trier of fact to conclude that a claimed fear is objectively unreasonable. This concession only proves the point--the way to avoid damage awards for unreasonable fear, i.e., in those cases where the feared cancer is at best only remotely possible, is to require a showing of the actual likelihood of the feared cancer to establish its significance....

We turn now to Firestone's argument that fear of cancer should be compensable only where the fear is based upon knowledge that cancer is probable, i.e., that it is more likely than not that cancer will develop. In evaluating this argument, we first consider whether it is reasonable for a person to genuinely and seriously fear a disease that is not probable, and if so, whether the emotional distress engendered by such fear warrants recognition as a compensable harm.

We cannot say that it would never be reasonable for a person who has ingested toxic substances to harbor a genuine and serious fear of cancer where reliable medical or scientific opinion indicates that such ingestion has significantly increased his or her risk of cancer, but not to a probable likelihood. Indeed, we would be very hard pressed to find that, as a matter of law, a plaintiff faced with a 20 percent or 30 percent chance of developing cancer cannot genuinely, seriously and reasonably fear the prospect of cancer. Nonetheless, we conclude, for the public policy reasons identified below, that emotional distress caused by the fear of a cancer that is not probable should generally not be compensable in a negligence action.

As a starting point in our analysis, we recognize the indisputable fact that all of us are exposed to carcinogens every day. As one commentator has observed, "[i]t is difficult to go a week without news of toxic exposure. Virtually everyone in society is conscious of the fact that the air they breathe, water, food and drugs they ingest, land on which they live, or products to which they are exposed are potential health hazards. Although few are exposed to all, few also can escape exposure to any." (Dworkin, Fear Of Disease And Delayed Manifestation Injuries: A Solution Or A Pandora's Box? (1984) 53 Fordham L.Rev. 527, 576, fns. omitted.)

Thus, all of us are potential fear of cancer plaintiffs, provided we are sufficiently aware of and worried about the possibility of developing cancer from exposure to or ingestion of a carcinogenic substance. The enormity of the class of potential plaintiffs cannot be overstated; indeed, a single class action may easily involve hundreds, if not thousands, of fear of cancer claims.

With this consideration in mind, we believe the tremendous societal cost of otherwise allowing emotional distress compensation to a potentially unrestricted plaintiff class demonstrates the necessity of imposing some limit on the class. Proliferation of fear of cancer claims in California in the absence of meaningful restrictions might compromise the availability and affordability of liability insurance for toxic liability risks. "Should [fear of cancer] liability continue to grow, and thereby lead to a substantial increase in toxic tort litigation, such liability insurance will become even more scarce and prohibitively expensive." (Willmore, In Fear of Cancerphobia (Sept. 28, 1988) 3 Toxics L.Rptr. (Bur.Nat. Affairs) 559, 563 [hereafter Willmore].) In the end, the burden of payment of awards for fear of cancer in the absence of a more likely than not restriction will inevitably be borne by the public generally in substantially increased insurance premiums or, alternatively, in the enhanced danger that accrues from the greater number of residents and businesses that may choose to go without any insurance.

A second policy concern that weighs in favor of a more likely than not threshold is the unduly detrimental impact that unrestricted fear liability would have in the health care field. As amicus curiae California Medical Association points out, access to prescription drugs is likely to be impeded by allowing recovery of fear of cancer damages in negligence cases without the imposition of a heightened threshold. To wit, thousands of drugs having no known harmful effects are currently being prescribed and utilized. New data about potentially harmful effects may not develop for years. If and when negative data are discovered and made public, however, one can expect numerous lawsuits to be filed by patients who currently have no physical injury or illness but who nonetheless fear the risk of adverse effects from the drugs they used. Unless meaningful restrictions are placed on this potential plaintiff class, the threat of numerous large, adverse monetary awards, coupled with the added cost of insuring against such liability (assuming insurance would be available), could diminish the availability of new, beneficial prescription drugs or increase their price beyond the reach of those who need them most....

A third policy concern to consider is that allowing recovery to all victims who have a fear of cancer may work to the detriment of those who sustain actual physical injury and those who ultimately develop cancer as a result of toxic exposure. That is, to allow compensation to all plaintiffs with objectively reasonable cancer fears, even where the threatened cancer is not probable, raises the very significant concern that defendants and their insurers will be unable to ensure adequate compensation for those victims who actually develop cancer or other physical injuries. Consider, for instance, that in this case damages totaling $800,000 for fear of cancer were awarded to four plaintiffs. If the same recovery were to be allowed in large class actions, liability for this one type of injury alone would be staggering. As one commentator astutely noted: "It would be a regrettable irony if in the rush to compensate the physically injured we make it impossible to compensate those suffering of permanent and serious physical injuries." (Willmore, supra, 3 Toxics L.Rptr. at p. 563.)

A fourth reason supporting the imposition of a more likely than not limitation is to establish a sufficiently definite and predictable threshold for recovery to permit consistent application from case to case. Indeed, without such a threshold, the likelihood of inconsistent results increases since juries may differ over the point at which a plaintiff's fear is a genuine and reasonable fear, i.e., one jury might deem knowledge of a 2 or 5 percent likelihood of future illness or injury to be sufficient (cf. Heider v.

Employers Mutual Liability Ins. Co. (La.Ct.App.1970) 231 So.2d 438, 442 (affirming award for plaintiff's fear of becoming epileptic where experts estimated likelihood at 2 to 5 percent)), while another jury might not. A more definite threshold will avoid inconsistent results and may contribute to early resolution or settlement of claims.

Finally, while a more likely than not limitation may foreclose compensation to many persons with genuine and objectively reasonable fears, it is sometimes necessary to "limit the class of potential plaintiffs if emotional injury absent physical harm is to continue to be a recoverable item of damages in a negligence action." We have recognized, in analogous contexts, that restricting the liability of a negligent tortfeasor for emotional loss may be warranted in consideration of the following factors: the intangible nature of the loss, the inadequacy of monetary damages to make whole the loss, the difficulty of measuring the damage, and the societal cost of attempting to compensate the plaintiff. These considerations are equally relevant to fear of cancer claims in toxic exposure cases....

3. Oppressive, Fraudulent or Malicious Conduct

Plaintiffs argue that if damages for fear of cancer in the absence of physical injury are limited to cases in which the cancer will more likely than not occur, the court should distinguish intentional conduct. We agree that certain aggravated conduct may warrant different treatment. In this part, we recognize an exception to the general rule set out above.

Plaintiffs suggest that the more likely than not threshold should not be applied where a defendant intentionally violates a statute or regulation prohibiting the disposal of toxins. Plaintiffs are quick to point out that the policy concerns for limiting liability in ordinary negligence cases are not triggered in cases involving such defendants. Although an exception to the general rule appears appropriate, we do not believe it should focus on intentional violators of the law. For one thing, while a defendant may be aware that its conduct is wrong and potentially dangerous, it may not have knowledge of a particular statute or regulation proscribing it. There may be times where a defendant does not specifically intend to violate the law, yet the defendant proceeds to act egregiously in conscious disregard of others.

With these considerations in mind, we conclude it preferable to recognize an exception that focuses on the totality of circumstances in evaluating a defendant's conduct. Accordingly, we hold that a toxic exposure plaintiff need not meet the more likely than not threshold for fear of cancer recovery in a negligence action if the plaintiff pleads and proves that the defendant's conduct in causing the exposure amounts to "oppression, fraud, or malice" as defined in Civil Code section 3294, which authorizes the imposition of punitive damages. Thus, for instance, fear of cancer damages may be recovered without demonstrating that cancer is probable where it is shown that the defendant is guilty of "despicable conduct which is carried on by the defendant with a willful and conscious disregard of the rights or safety of others." (Civ.Code, s 3294, subd. (c)(1) (defining one type of "malice").) "A person acts with conscious disregard of the rights or safety of others when [he] [she] is aware of the probable dangerous consequences of [his] [her] conduct and willfully and deliberately fails to avoid those consequences." (BAJI No. 14.71 (1992 rev.) (7th ed. pocket pt.) (defining "malice").)

When a defendant acts with oppression, fraud or malice, no reason, policy or otherwise, justifies application of the more likely than not threshold. Any burden or consequence to society from imposing liability is offset by the deterrent impact of holding morally blameworthy defendants fully responsible for the damages they cause, including damage in the form of emotional distress suffered by victims of the misconduct who reasonably fear future cancer.

Under such circumstances, the potential liability of a defendant is not disproportionate to culpability. While the imposition of liability for emotional distress resulting from negligent handling of toxic substances may result in costs out of proportion to the culpability of the negligent actor, this concern is diminished or nonexistent when the conduct is despicable and undertaken in conscious disregard of the danger to the health or interests of others. The significance of the size of the potential class of plaintiffs is similarly diminished and the moral blame heightened since the defendant is aware of the danger posed by its conduct and acts in conscious disregard of the known risk....

Once the plaintiff establishes that the defendant has acted with oppression, fraud or malice, the plaintiff must still demonstrate that his or her fear of cancer is reasonable, genuine and serious in order to recover damages. In determining what constitutes reasonable fear, we refer to our previous discussion ... in which we observed that it is not enough for a plaintiff to show simply an ingestion of a carcinogen or a significant increase in the risk of cancer. In addition, the plaintiff must show that his or her actual risk of cancer is significant before recovery will be allowed. Under this reasoning, a plaintiff's fear is not compensable when the risk of cancer is significantly increased, but remains a remote possibility.

To reiterate, in the absence of a physical injury or illness, a plaintiff may recover damages for negligently inflicted emotional distress engendered by a fear of cancer without meeting the more likely than not threshold if the plaintiff pleads and proves that: (1) as a result of the defendant's negligent breach of a duty owed to the plaintiff, he or she is exposed to a toxic substance which threatens cancer; (2) the defendant, in breaching its duty to the plaintiff, acted with oppression, fraud or malice as defined in Civil Code section 3294; and (3) the plaintiff's fear of cancer stems from a knowledge, corroborated by reliable medical or scientific opinion, that the toxic exposure caused by the defendant's breach of duty has significantly increased the plaintiff's risk of cancer and has resulted in an actual risk of cancer that is significant.

In our view, Firestone's conduct brings this case within the "oppression, fraud or malice" exception for recovery of fear of cancer damages. The trial court determined that in May of 1977, officials in key management positions at Firestone's Salinas plant had increased knowledge regarding the dangers involved with the careless disposal of hazardous wastes, and had a specific, written policy for hazardous waste disposal. However, these officials, while professing support for the policy in written distributions, in actuality largely ignored the policy. The court found especially reprehensible the fact that Firestone, through its plant production manager, actively discouraged compliance with its internal policies and California law solely for the sake of reducing corporate costs.

Under these circumstances, we believe there are sufficient facts supporting the trial court's conclusion that such conduct displayed a conscious disregard of the rights and safety of others.[41] ...

COMMENTARY AND QUESTIONS

1. Dissenting from "more likely than not." Justice George, with the agreement of Justice Mosk, dissented from the imposition of the more–likely–than–not element of the majority's holding on the negligent infliction of cancer fear cause of action. That dissent built upon the majority's concession that –

> a reasonable person who has consumed, cooked with, and bathed in water that has been contaminated by toxic waste is likely to sustain serious emotional distress relating to fear of developing a serious illness in the future, not only when the person's chances of developing an illness is more than 50 percent, but also when his or her chance of developing the illness is considerably lower, for example, "only" 25 or 30 percent. In denying recovery to such a victim, despite the circumstance that--because of the risk of personal harm engendered by the defendant's negligent conduct--a person of ordinary sensibilities in the victim's position reasonably would suffer serious emotional distress, the majority opinion eliminates an important legal protection to which all persons, including victims of toxic waste exposure, long have been entitled. 6 Cal 4th at 1019, 25 Cal. Rptr.2d at 587.

Instead, Justice George would allow recovery for negligently inflicted emotional distress in toxic exposure cases where in addition to proof of serious emotional distress the plaintiff also proves that —

> (1) the level of toxic substances to which he or she was exposed posed a significant risk that the plaintiff will develop the feared disease or illness (i.e., a risk that is sufficiently substantial that it would result in serious emotional distress in a reasonable, rather than an unusually sensitive, person), and (2) the defendant's negligence substantially increased plaintiff's risk of contracting the disease or illness (so that the plaintiff's serious emotional distress is a condition for which the defendant appropriately should be held responsible.) 6 Cal 4th at 1025, 25 Cal. Rptr.2d at 591.

How persuasive are the majority's arguments in favor of using the "more likely than not" proviso as a limit on fear of cancer recoveries? To the extent that four of the five arguments in the opinion seem to be "a parade of horribles," they merit close inspection to see if they are really likely to come about in the absence of the prudential limit on recoveries.

2. Intentional infliction of emotional distress. The *Potter* case, in addition to its elaborate consideration of cancer fear recoveries, also set forth

---

41. Although this case falls within the oppression, fraud or malice exception announced above, any award of fear of cancer damages will still depend on whether plaintiffs' fears are reasonable with reference to the actual likelihood of cancer due to the toxic exposure.

standards for recovery where plaintiffs rely on intentional infliction of emotional distress rather than negligence as the basis for their claim. The court ruled that the intentional infliction of emotional distress claim against Firestone should fail unless the plaintiff proves (1) extreme and outrageous conduct, (2) directed at plaintiffs or undertaken with knowledge of their consumption of groundwater, and (3) with knowledge that plaintiffs would suffer severe emotional distress when the truth became known to them. See 6 Cal. 4th at 1002-03. The court explained that the fear of cancer giving rise to plaintiffs severe emotional distress must itself be established by plaintiff to be "reasonable, that is, that the fear is based on medically or scientifically corroborated knowledge that the defendant's conduct has significantly increased the plaintiff's risk of cancer and that plaintiff's actual risk of the threatened cancer is significant." *Id.* at 1004.[42]

How, if at all, does the intentional infliction of emotional distress claim vary from the "oppression, fraud, or malice" exception to the more likely than not rule being applied to recovering for fear of cancer in negligence cases? There are, to be sure slight variations in the proof required, but the similarities seem to outweigh the differences. First, the "bad actor" aspect of the conduct of defendant is roughly the same: conduct that is extreme and outrageous is also likely to be the same kind of conduct that satisfies the oppression, fraud, or malice standard, with its similarity to the standard used in awarding punitive damages. Second, the risk/fear calculus is quite similar. In both settings there has to be a "real" (scientifically supportable) and "significant" (not more likely than not, but not minuscule) risk before plaintiff can recover. The main difference seems to lie in the area of foreseeability. In the intentional tort, plaintiff needs to establish defendants knowledge that the plaintiffs will be exposed in the toxin, whereas in the "oppression, fraud or malice" cases, the key is conscious disregard for the safety of others.

Is this whole set of nice distinctions and differing proofs of the likelihood of subsequent harm all a fancy way of saying culpability counts in the law's willingness to require defendants to compensate plaintiffs for this particular item of intangible damage? The worse the defendant's behavior, the more extensive the recoveries. This understanding of the court's attitude would answer one of the questions that was not addressed by the appellate courts in the *Potter* litigation, the question of whether fear of cancer would be compensable on a claim that Firestone was strictly liable to plaintiffs because it was engaged in an ultrahazardous activity. Strict liability is not premised on the defendant's culpability, thus, the standard of proof of consequent harm would, presumably, be at least as high as in the negligence setting (more likely than not), or even higher. Owing to the irrelevance of culpability in strict liability cases, would it be good policy to prohibit recovery of damages for fear alone?

3. Optimal deterrence. Ever since the Learned Hand's famous opinion in the *Carroll Towing* case, tort theory, especially negligence actions, tries to use the damage function to encourage utility by deterring accidents that can be avoided by the use of care that costs less than the costs of the

---

42. It is important to contrast this somewhat lower standard of probability of subsequent onset of disease with that established in the excerpted part of the case for claims seeking recovery for fear of cancer standing on its own.

harms that are avoided. How does that approach work in toxic tort cases like *Potter*? Avoiding small risks does not warrant large expenditures on additional preventive measures, so no liability need be imposed. This tends to support the majority in *Potter* when it insists that for compensation to be awarded, the risk involved, a function of both severity and probability, be substantial. (Recall the definitions of risk and safety set forth on page 79 of the main text.) Does relying so heavily on the level of cancer risk measure the only relevant item in trying to determine the social costs of defendant's conduct, or is that like a risk manager's tendency to measure only hazard and probability without reference to outrage?

4. Double recovery for fear cancer and cancer itself. Assume that a plaintiff who meets the *Potter* test for recovering for fear of cancer subsequently develops cancer and again sues the defendant for damages. Should defendant get a set-off for any fear of cancer damages already paid? The two injuries are analytically distinguishable, being suffered in different temporal periods and one involving psychic distress and the other physical impairment. How do these two items of damage relate to "latency compensation" (a term that was coined in note 4 on page 220 of the main volume)?

5. Medical monitoring damages. On the medical monitoring issue, *Potter* takes a far more lenient approach, allowing recovery where reliable and competent medical testimony demonstrates that medical monitoring (beyond ordinary prudent preventive care) is needed in consequence of the toxic exposure. The court elaborated by listing five factors that should be considered: (1) the significance and extent of the exposure, (2) the toxicity of the chemicals, (3) the relative increase in risk of the onset of disease, (4) the seriousness of the diseases involved, and (5) the clinical value of early detection and diagnosis. *Id.* at 1009.

6. Comparative fault. The defense in *Potter* sought to reduce any emotional distress award that the plaintiffs might recover using comparative fault principles. The alleged faulty conduct of plaintiffs consisted in voluntary encounters with cancer risk factors, most notably the long-term cigarette smoking habits of the four named plaintiffs. On an evidentiary level, the defendant made the point that plaintiffs' benzene exposure through cigarette smoking was on the order of 40,000 to 60,000 ppb, an exposure that was more than 2,500 times as great as the exposure to benzene in the contaminated well water.

How should this defense figure into the tort calculus? As its name implies, fault on the part of plaintiffs is a part of the defense, so the smoking (or other risk increasing behavior) would have to be negligent or in some other way faulty. Thereafter, as the court in *Potter* pointed out, it is important to isolate the harm for which damages are being sought and the contribution of the plaintiff's conduct to that harm. In *Potter* the damages awarded were not damages for actually developing cancer, nor were they damages for the increased risk of developing cancer, the damages were instead being awarded for emotional distress suffered when the plaintiffs learned they had ingested contaminated water. Thus, to defend using comparative fault the defendant must show the causal link between plaintiffs' smoking and the emotional harm they incurred, something that Firestone had not addressed at trial.

The *Potter* ruling may seem a bit problematic for the future because plaintiffs can sidestep the defense by testifying that their distress was linked solely to the exposure for which defendant was responsible, that their own smoking (or whatever) didn't upset them. Such a claim by a plaintiff may not be as disingenuous as it may seem, recall the role of outrage factors in risk perception. Proof of long-time smoking might undercut other elements of plaintiffs case. In *Potter*, for example, the court seemed to think that the smoking evidence might undermine the plaintiffs' ability to claim that their fear of cancer was legitimate after they had seemingly ignored other events (their smoking) that could have prompted such fears for decades.

PAGE 223   b. COMMUNITY REACTIONS, AND INJURY TO LAND VALUES

Stigma and the new tort of "ToxiProx." Owners of land situated in close proximity to hazardous materials sites frequently find that the market value of their land has been adversely affected as a result of the nearby presence of the hazardous materials. This is particularly true in the case of sites at which toxic materials have been released into the environment, but is true to a lesser extent where a nearby facility is used for the proper treatment or disposal of hazardous materials, or even where the facility is simply one at which hazardous materials are known to be in use. Would-be-buyers discount the value of the parcel in consequence of the proximity of the hazardous materials, often without reference to whether those materials pose even a scintilla of risk of harm to the parcel being offered for sale Compensation increasingly is being sought for losses that are consequent upon toxic proximity alone. Consider the following cases that are in the process of working their way through the courts—

> A New Jersey trial court judge has certified a class action lawsuit brought by owners of parcels located in close proximity to an infamous hazardous waste site. The principal claim of the suit is that the affected homes are either unsaleable or seriously devalued by their proximity to the contaminated site. See, In re GEMS Landfill Superior Court Litigation, N.J. Super. Ct., Camden County, No. L-068199-85 (Feb. 2, 1994) as reported at 8 Toxics Law Reporter 1035-36 (Feb. 16, 1994).[43] See also, Exxon Corp. v. Yarema, 516 A2d. 990 (Md. 1986) (allowing recovery for decreased property value caused by groundwater contamination that did not reach the affected parcel); but see, Adkins v. Thomas Solvent, 440 Mich. 293, 487 N.W.2d 715 (1992) holding that diminished property values caused by negative publicity affecting parcels proximate to, but not themselves subject to, hazardous waste contamination, is a loss without legal injury.

---

43. The article describing the case indicates that plaintiffs will have to prove that the contaminants from the site have or will migrate and contaminate the individual plaintiffs' parcels. Counsel for plaintiffs, in a phone conversation, contends that he will need prove only a cause-in-fact link between the contamination at the GEMS Landfill and the decrease in each owners' property value.

> A California jury awarded $826,500 to a property owner whose site had been contaminated but later remediated to compensate for post-cleanup stigmatization of the property. The parties responsible for the contamination were also found liable for an additional $400,000 in lost rents incurred during the period of the contamination. See, Bixby Ranch Co. v. Spectrol Electronic Corp., Cal. Super. Ct., Los Angeles County, No. BC052566 (Dec. 13, 1993) (as reported at 8 Toxics Law Reporter 955-56, Jan. 26, 1994).

What is the legal theory supporting recovery in these cases? As these claims proliferate and more judicial opinions address the issue, it will be possible to determine whether these cases comprise a new unique toxic tort cause of action or are instead an additional element of damage (similar to fear of cancer claims) being asserted under existing rubrics of negligence, nuisance and/or strict liability.

Whatever the theory, there are also a panoply of cases growing up on the periphery of this issue. For example, New York's highest court, in determining how much compensation is due to owners of property condemned for high voltage lines, has recognized a compensable interest in favor of property owners who can prove that fear of EMF (electromagnetic field) emissions from high voltage power lines will cause a reduction in the value of their real property. See, Criscuola v. Power Authority of the State of New York, 81 N.Y.2d 649, 621 N.E.2d 1195, 602 N.Y.S.2d 588 (1993). Contemporary cases involving parcel valuation for tax assessment purposes are also beginning to take toxic contamination and its effect on market price into account in valuing the subject parcel. See, Westling v. County of Mille Lacs, 512 N.W.2d 863 (1994). Unlike the "toxiprox" example, in *Westling* the parcel being valued was itself contaminated. The court's language is broad enough to reach the toxiprox situation. In particular, the court approves an assessment that "included a deduction for the claimed stigma attached to the property because of the pollution." 512 N.W.2d at 866. Similarly, in Strawn v. Incollingo, N.J. Super. Ct. App. Div., No. A-4764-91T3 (Feb. 22, 1994) purchasers of homes in a new development were held to have a cause of action against the builder and brokers who sold them houses without disclosing the proximity to a closed landfill suspected of containing toxic waste.

COMMENTARY AND QUESTIONS

1. Distinguishing "community fears" from "rational fears." In an article entitled, "Arguing Public Policy as a Defense to Environmental Toxic Tort Claims," 8 Toxics Law Reporter 505 (1993), Martha Churchill[44] contrasts a community fear standard that relies on "popular anxiety, and even hysteria," with a rationally based fear standard that requires a plaintiff to "prove some objective danger which serves as a basis for the fear." She proposes this distinction as a means to prevent recovery in many fear of cancer cases. She views the extent of available compensation to be a matter of policy, and as an initial matter she castigates the legislative

---

44. In a note Ms. Churchill is described as being the president of Mid-America Legal Foundation, "a non-profit advocacy center devoted to products liability and environmental issues which affect the economy."

branch for not settling the dispute by enacting legislation requiring a rationally-based fear standard.

As for the judicial branch, acting in a vacuum of legislative inaction, she suggests that the toxic fear and stigma (toxiprox) cases decided thus far can be grouped into two camps according to which of those two standards a court adopts. The danger, in her view, of using the community fear standard to judge the reasonableness of a claimed toxic fear is that "a community exhibiting irrational or hysterical behavior may be considered "reasonable" simply on the grounds that its phobia is widely shared." (*Id.* at 506.) For her, the paradigmatic positions are those taken by the courts in Exxon Corp. v. Yarema and Adkins v. Thomas Solvent Co., two of the toxiprox cases noted above. The former allows recovery for community fear that resulted in devaluation of the parcel that was not itself contaminated, the latter refuses compensation without actual contamination of the plaintiff's own parcel. Ms. Churchill argues that the better public policy is for courts to insist that the fears be rationally based. She states that it is wrong for courts to allow "the reality of the market place [to prevail] over the reality in the groundwater." From the affected owners' point of view, the loss in the market place is still a very real loss even if the groundwater is still clean. Is there any compelling reason why this externality should be treated differently than most?

Page 223   The role of judges in settlements

Section 3. JUDICIAL CONTROL OF TOXIC TORT SETTLEMENTS

By now it should be apparent that toxic tort cases are not as simple to litigate as many other types of lawsuits. Their complex nature places them in the realm of cases where judges tend to maintain greater control over the litigation than is the norm in simpler cases. To some extent this can be explained as an inevitable concomitant of judges' concern with maintaining control over their docket, with being sure that cases proceed in an orderly and efficient fashion. There are some instances, however, where heightened judicial control is called for by the court rules and/or the nature of the cases as class actions, or inherently class action-like. In particular, settlements of class action lawsuits are typically made subject to judicial approval. For example, Federal Rule of Civil Procedure (FRCP) 23(e) provides, "A class action shall not be dismissed or compromised without the approval of the court, and notice of the proposed dismissal or compromise shall be given to all members of the class in such manner as the court directs."

The reason for expanding the judge's role in class action litigation stems from the possibility that the interests of the active litigants, most typically in the toxic tort setting the class representative and the defendant, are not always those of the class as a whole. For example, the terms of a settlement may benefit the named class representative more than other class members. Even more often, a settlement may benefit the interest of class counsel more than it benefits the interests of the class members. Here, consider the interest of plaintiffs' class counsel in settling a case and obtaining a large award of attorney's fees without the uncertainty and burden of trial. Counsel may be tempted to negotiate away some issues in hopes of enhancing the short-term monetary relief granted to the class. FRCP 23(e) interposes the judge and the possibility of notice as a protection for class interests.

Judicial oversight of the settlement in Shults v. Champion International Corp., excerpted below, is an example of a judge taking seriously the FRCP 23(e) responsibility. That class action toxic tort lawsuit began with allegations of dioxin pollution by defendant's paper mill of downstream waters and riparian areas. The suit captured significant attention in the press as a result of the magnitude of the claim — plaintiffs originally sought $5 *billion* in damages when it was filed in January of 1991.[45] As trial neared, the plaintiffs' demand became more focused and less extravagant, though still sizable ($360 million). Relying on nuisance, trespass negligence and gross negligence, the plaintiffs sought damages for loss of property value and for non-economic loss that included personal discomfort, stress, annoyance and anxiety associated with the contamination of the water and their riparian property.

Following an October 1992 mistrial caused by the inability of a jury to reach a verdict, the incentives for settlement seemed to increase significantly. Although six of the eight jurors had favored defendant, the other two had steadfastly held out for a plaintiff's verdict. Defendant was surely encouraged by the 6-2 split in its favor and the plaintiffs now seemed to be in a weak bargaining position. For plaintiffs (and their counsel) the prospect of a second trial further increased their sunk costs and the first trial had showed that there was a strong possibility that there would be a finding for defendants, meaning that there might be no winnings from which to pay a contingent fee to class counsel. A settlement agreement was reached within two months and lodged with the court for approval.

SHULTS v. CHAMPION INTERNATIONAL CORP.
36 ERC 1414, 1993 WL 145701
United States District Court for the Eastern District of Tennessee 1993

Hull, J. This is a class action for interference with property rights brought by riparian landowners on the Pigeon River and Douglas Lake in Cocke, Jefferson and Sevier Counties of Tennessee. The attorneys for the parties have negotiated a settlement agreement which has been submitted to the Court for approval. On January 19, 1993, after notice of the proposed settlement had issued to class members, the Court conducted a fairness hearing. Based upon the written objections signed by sixty-one (61) class members, the testimony at the fairness hearing, and the Court's personal assessment of the proposed agreement, the Court has decided not to approve the settlement.

The plaintiff class, composed of approximately two thousand, six hundred (2,600) riparian landowners and lessees, claimed that Champion's pulp and paper mill in Canton, North Carolina, discharges waste water into the Pigeon River which contains many toxic chemicals; that its paper-making process also discolors the river's water and makes it foul-smelling; that Champion's use of the river constitutes a private nuisance that unreasonably interferes with their rights as riparian property owners; and

---

45. The suit was originally commenced in state court in Tennessee and was removed to federal court by defendants on the basis of diversity of citizenship.

that this use is also a trespass contaminating their land and usable water. The plaintiffs sought damages to compensate for the diminution in the market value, rental value and/or use value of their realty, including compensation for the personal discomfort, stress, annoyance, and anxiety associated with this contamination of the river and lake water and their riparian properties. They also sought punitive damages and injunctive relief which would prohibit Champion from using lead, cadmium, cyanide, arsenic, elemental chlorine and chlorinated compounds in its mill processes.[46]

The proposed settlement provides for Champion to pay Six and One-Half ($6.5) Million Dollars into an interest bearing account which, after payment of the plaintiffs' litigation fees and expenses, will be used to establish a charitable fund to benefit the landowners and their communities, through environmental, educational, or other charitable activities. No compensatory or punitive damages are to be paid directly to any of the class members and no injunctive relief is to be imposed upon Champion.

The agreement not only settles the class action claims against Champion but would release Champion from liability for,

> all future claims, demands, rights of action and causes of
> action of every kind and character, whether arising in law or
> equity, both against the Settling Defendant and all other
> persons and entities, which each Class member, his, her or its
> heirs, executors, administrators, successors, and assigns, ever
> had, now have or hereafter may acquire, by reason of, arising
> out of, or in any way relating to Champion's Discharge [of
> waste water from its pulp and paper mill in Canton, North
> Carolina, into the Pigeon River and Douglas Lake].

The agreement entails the creation of The Pigeon River Endowment Fund which would be managed, invested, and administered by the already-existing East Tennessee Corporation, a tax exempt, nonprofit corporation organized ... to benefit, through environmental, educational, or other charitable activities including community or industrial development, not only those landowners who chose to be class members in this lawsuit but all landowners along the river and lake and their communities in Cocke, Sevier and Jefferson Counties. The Foundation is to establish a Board of Advisors of the Pigeon River Endowment Fund from the Pigeon River and Douglas Lake communities (not necessarily composed of class members), but is to retain control over the distribution of the funds. The document establishing the endowment specifically states its intention that the fund be continued in perpetuity. Presumably, disbursements to class members would be made only from the net income of the fund.

The objections raised by class members fall into several broad categories. Many members voiced disapproval of the fact that the

---

46. There were other tort theories raised in the original complaint, such as fear of cancer, but these were dismissed early in the proceedings. The pretrial order, which supplanted the pleadings, limited the action to one sounding in trespass and nuisance. At no time was any claim raised for a physical injury such as cancer based on exposure to toxic chemicals in the waters of the river or the lake.

settlement would allow for payment of the plaintiffs' attorneys but would not put any money directly into the pockets of the landowners.

Other objections focused on the fact that Champion accepts no blame for its long-term pollution of the river and is not being enjoined from polluting it in the future. Not surprisingly, many thought the settlement would give Champion a license to pollute in the future, free from any objection by those living downstream.

Even more serious objections focused on the fact that the lawsuit was tried as one for trespass and nuisance, but the settlement would settle any claim for personal injuries which class members may now have or may learn about in the future. Several people pointed out that they only recently learned of the possible dioxin contamination of their properties and speculated that there might be other toxic agents in the river or the lake about which they still know nothing. In addition, despite assurances to the contrary by the attorneys for both parties, the agreement precludes lawsuits based on possible future misconduct on Champion's part, rather than just barring claims based on conduct prior to the effective date of the agreement.

In evaluating the fairness, reasonableness, and adequacy of the proposed settlement, the Court has considered 1) the complexity, expense, and likely duration of the litigation; 2) the factual and legal obstacles to a verdict in favor of the class; 3) the possible range of recovery and certainty of damages; 4) the number of objectors to the settlement and the nature of their objections; and 5) the impact the settlement might have on the community.

Because the proof in this lawsuit had to be presented through numerous expert witnesses, the litigation was both lengthy and expensive. In addition, the many complicated legal issues and evidentiary questions raised in this action guarantee that any verdict would have to be appealed. Nevertheless, retrial is not impossible. All of the expert testimony in this case was videotaped and could be used in a second trial to minimize expert witness fees. Further, all evidentiary questions have already been resolved and attorneys for both sides of the case know exactly what evidence will be admitted into trial. A retrial would likely be shorter and less costly than the first trial. Finally, other law firms have expressed interest in the lawsuit and may be able to contribute money and expertise to a retrial. The Court does not find the length, complexity, or expense of this case prohibitive.

The Court is aware of no legal obstacles to a plaintiffs' verdict. In the first trial of this case, none of the representative plaintiffs demonstrated evidence of substantial property damage. However, they did have credible proof of stress, annoyance, and anxiety caused by the contamination of their water. It was obvious to the Court that any hope the class might have had of obtaining a sizable verdict depended on the availability of punitive damages. Unfortunately for the plaintiffs' case, most of the evidence of reprehensible conduct on Champion's part fell outside the statute of limitations. In the three-year period which preceded the filing of this lawsuit, the evidence showed that Champion not only stopped discharging dioxin into the Pigeon River, but embarked upon a major effort to redesign its manufacturing procedures to greatly reduce the odor and color pollution of the river. There was evidence that the water which borders the plaintiffs' properties was much more polluted when they acquired their land than it is today. Moreover, the evidence showed that Champion's discharges used to be regulated by the State of North Carolina (apparently with little concern for the people downstream in Tennessee), but are now monitored more evenhandedly by the federal Environmental Protection Agency. All these factors decrease the likelihood of a large punitive damages award. Nonetheless, the plaintiffs' case had moral strength. The undisputed evidence was that, for a great many years, Champion used the Pigeon River as its private sewer. The color contamination, which limited the depth to which light could penetrate the waters and greatly impaired normal aquatic life, and the smell associated with Champion's discharge, were obvious to even the most casual observer. Less obvious and more sinister was the fact that, historically, many toxic chemicals were released into the river with no warning to persons living downstream and no concern for possible damage to the ecosystem. The plaintiffs' outrage at this insult is justifiable and, in the Court's opinion, could support an award of punitive damages even though Champion's conduct today appears to be reasonable, and even though there is reason to believe that future contamination of the river will be held to a legal minimum.

As indicated earlier, the number of objectors is not great, but it is by no means insignificant. The objections they raise are serious ones.

Naturally, some class members objected to the fact that the only people getting any direct financial advantage from the settlement were the attorneys for the plaintiffs. However, this is not necessarily inappropriate. Only the attorneys for the plaintiffs advanced personal funds to finance the lawsuit. It is not unreasonable that some of the settlement funds be used to pay for the costs of this litigation.

In addition, while the class members may not know this, it is typical of settlement agreements that no liability be admitted by any party. This language does not disturb the Court. The Court agrees with the class members that the language of the settlement appears to give Champion a license to pollute the Pigeon River. However, the only real license given to Champion is the NPDES permit which controls and limits its waste water discharges. The Court believes that the Environmental Protection Agency will monitor Champion's activities and protect the interests of the class.

The objection which is of the gravest concern to the Court has to do with the language of the release. In the original notice of the class action sent out to all riparian property owners, the potential class members were advised:

> The class action seeks damages both for loss of value of the
> land and for other incidental damages attributable to the land
> use If you do not ask to be excluded, you will continue to be a
> part of the class, and will be bound by the Court's final
> decision whether Plaintiff wins or loses.

The Court is satisfied that, as of the date the class closed, those who had not opted out could be precluded from bringing a separate cause of action, such as a personal injury claim, about any condition known to them at that time. However, the Court is confidant that those who passively remained in the class had no idea that any outcome of the lawsuit could possibly preclude them (and their children and grandchildren), from ever bringing a lawsuit against Champion that "in any way related" to

Champion's discharges. This release language used in the proposed settlement is peculiarly suited to lawsuits arising out of discrete events such as accidental spills of toxic material. It does not strike the Court as appropriate in a lawsuit concerning continuing conduct that might well vary in its intensity or degree. Moreover, the toxic chemicals to which the class members where exposed were not made known to them in a timely fashion. Fears that, at some future date, we may discover additional harm from agents in the water, do not seem unfounded. No settlement that precludes future, unknown causes of action can be considered fair, reasonable, or in the best interests of the class as a whole.

The final factor which the Court considered is the impact this settlement would have upon the community. There is no question that a trust fund, which could be drawn upon by all members of the community, could be highly beneficial. If it did nothing more than make a college education available to all the youth of this area, the long term salutary impact on the community would be impressive. However, this benefit has to be weighed against the disheartening and even demoralizing effect upon the community of the knowledge that its only lawsuit to redress over eighty years of harm (and possible future harm) to an important environmental asset ended with the impaired parties receiving no direct compensation for the loss they have sustained.

When all of these factors are carefully weighed, the Court must reject the settlement as now proposed.

This does not mean that the parties are forced to retry this action. The Court would, in fact, welcome a settlement agreement if one could be fashioned that met the concerns expressed in this Order. The parties are advised that, based on the meager evidence of actual damages presented at the first trial, the fact that Champion's conduct in recent years has been much more responsible to its downstream neighbors, and the fact that Champion's discharges are now subject to federal regulation, a settlement in the amount of Six and One-Half ($6.5) Million Dollars would be approved.

The Court would also approve release language that barred all trespass and nuisance claims based on known conduct prior to the effective date of the settlement and barred any class member's personal injury claim arising prior to the date the class was closed.

The Court would allow twenty percent (20%) of the settlement monies to be used for attorneys' fees and, in addition, would reimburse the plaintiffs' out-of-pocket litigation expenses from the fund.

The balance of the settlement fund would be distributed directly, to the class members. The Court does not think placing the money in an endowment fund would be fair to the class for several reasons. For one thing, it is difficult to envision ways to spend the monies that would proportionately benefit all the members of the class. For another, the class members entered into this litigation with the idea that they would recover money damages for the "loss of value of the land and for incidental damages attributable to land use." They should not have their modest recovery involuntarily placed in a charity even if the charity would be beneficial to the community.

In the event that a settlement is reached, the Court would appoint a Master, pursuant to Rule 53, Federal Rules of Civil Procedure, to devise an equitable formula for distribution of the monies and to handle the actual disbursements to the class members.

If no acceptable settlement proposal is offered to the Court by August 1, 1993, the case will be reset for trial on September 7, 1993.

COMMENTARY & QUESTIONS

1. The revised settlement. The parties promptly negotiated a revised settlement that retained the $6.5 million figure and narrowed the scope of the release given to Champion vis-a-vis future claims for personal injury. The trust fund idea was abandoned, so that, in the judge's words, "This case that was tried for money damages for trespass and nuisance ... will end with a disbursement of money to those who suffered this harm." 17 BNA Chemical Regulation Reporter 303 (May 14, 1993).

2. Not so neutral judges. Senior Judge Hull made clear his predilections as to what he considered a fair and appropriate outcome for the *Shults* litigation and the parties crafted their ultimate settlement in those terms. Does the ability to reject settlements as "unfair," a very vague term, give the judge too much power over the outcome of litigation? Here it may be hard to complain with the judge's insistence that the very nature of a trespass/nuisance suit calls for a settlement that reflects that nature, i.e., a result that includes a payment to the plaintiffs that compensates for their alleged losses. Even so, an unfairness standard does little to constrain judges having a more wide-ranging conception of appropriate outcomes

3. Toting up the settlement's winners and losers. And the envelope please .... Plaintiffs' class counsel are the big winners. They get one-fifth of $6,500,000 ($1.3 million) off the top and are also repaid for the costs of the litigation, including such big ticket items such as expert witness fees. The remaining amount will be divided among the 2,600 class members, leading to an average recovery of under $2,000. Champion can also be considered a winner by avoiding all risk of the case being retried and setting a disastrous adverse precedent. Moreover, they may have won a deterrent to parallel suits if the mistrial demonstrated to other possible plaintiff groups the difficulty of winning this type of suit. This benefit is quite speculative in light of the Judge's commentary on the liability issues in the opinion. $6.5 million is, for Champion, a relatively small investment in avoiding this potential liability and others like it, and they get the benefit of paying with pre-tax dollars as a cost of doing business. Is it clear that the plaintiff class members lost? At least some commentators would say that they should have recovered nothing so their recoveries are a windfall to them extorted from the defendant by the use of the class action device that magnified the risk of an adverse precedent to the point where the defendant was better advised to settle than to litigate what was likely to be a winning defense. And the judge did not have to retry the case.

Chapter 5,   Environmental Remedies Drawn From Other Fields of Law

---

PAGE 228   **More on Maxxam and redwood clearcutting**

1A. The Pacific Lumber saga continued. Charles Hurwitz has floated another innovation on the shell of the old Pacific Lumber Co. In March 1993, Hurwitz's MAXXAM completed a novel sale of $385 million in "timber-secured bonds," which unlike junk bonds are directly secured by 179,000 acres of Pacific Lumber forests. Along with $235 million in new high yield bonds, the offering allows Hurwitz to retire $510 million of the original junk bond offering while extending the due dates to ten years or more from two -three years, and taking a quick $25 million dividend.

Left out of the deal are 6000 acres of the most fragile and wild redwood acreage, the so-called "Headwaters Forest," which is the subject of the most fervent environmental protection efforts. This acreage too Hurwitz would like to clearcut, but in lieu of harvesting he will entertain offers to buy it at around $600 million. A congressional bill introduced on August 4, 1993 by California Representatives Hamburg and Stark would authorize such purchase of the Headwaters Forest and 38000 acres of surrounding timberland. MAXXAM spokespersons made it clear they did not want to sell: "The economic impact of such a purchase would be crippling to Humboldt County tax rolls, to timber workers, and to the local economy.... Rep. Hamburg's disregard of this potential impact makes us wonder if his constituents are trees or people." San F. Chronicle, Aug. 5, 1993.

Rep. Stark also has responded to the novel timber-backed bonds, introducing a bill imposing a 75% severance tax on trees that secure such bond offerings.

To add to Maxxam's annoyances, environmentalists in California recently filed an endangered species lawsuit against Pacific Lumber's redwood clearcutting, on behalf of the marbled murrelet, a sea bird dependent upon old growth forests for its nesting habitat. Marbled Murrelet, et al. v. Pacific Lumber, C-93-1400-FMS, U.S. Dist. Ct. for the Northern District of California (1993).

PAGE 229   **"Socially-responsible corporations" and CERES**

1A. The CERES principles. The Valdez Principles for socially responsible corporate management have been updated into the "CERES Principles." CERES, a coalition of more than 100 environmental organizations involved in social investments has promulgated the CERES Principles, a more detailed set of socially-conscious corporate commitments. With the Interfaith Center on Corporate Responsibility CERES has advocated the corporate adoption of a Responsible Care program implementing their standards. Sun Oil Company was the first Fortune 500 company to commit itself to the CERES Principles, in its own 10-point HES (Health, Environment, Safety) program. The American Petroleum Institute has adopted its own STEP program, and the National Petroleum Refiners Association a BEST program (acronym translations unavailable). Sun's HES principles cover: Protection of the biosphere, Sustainable use of natural resources, Reduction and disposal of wastes, Energy conservation, Risk reduction, Safe products and service, Environmental restoration, Informing the public, Management commitment, and Audits and reports. See Wood, "Responsible Care," Chemical Week, July 7, 1993.

In early 1994 General Motors announced that it would be adopting the principles which possibly sets the stage for more large companies to follow suit.

It should be noted that many are suspicious of GM's motives due to the fact that while accepting the principles they continue to "lobby against higher fuel efficiency standards and zero-emissions vehicles."[47] There has also been a willingness to amend the principles in order to encourage acceptance. For example, notice that rather than requiring an environmentalist to sit on a company's board of directors as was the original requirement, now the demand is simply that companies simply "consider demonstrated environmental commitment as a factor" in choosing directors.

Coalition for Environmentally Responsible Economies, THE CERES PRINCIPLES (1992)

[The pledge taken by corporations adopting the CERES principles:]

Introduction

By adopting these Principles, we publicly affirm our belief that corporations have a responsibility for the environment, and must conduct all aspects of their business as responsible stewards of the environment by operating in a manner that protects the Earth. We believe that corporations must not compromise the ability of future generations to sustain themselves.

We will update our practices continually in light of advances in technology and new understandings in health and environmental science. In collaboration with CERES, we will promote a dynamic process to ensure that the Principles are interpreted in a way that accommodates changing technologies and environmental realities. We intend to make consistent, measurable progress in implementing these Principles and to apply them in all aspects of our operations through-out the world.

The Principles

1. *Protection of the Biosphere*

We will reduce and make continual progress toward eliminating any substance that may cause environmental damage to the air, water, or the earth or its inhabitants. We will safeguard all habitats affected by our operations and will protect open spaces and wilderness, while preserving biodiversity.

2. *Sustainable Use of Natural Resources*

---

47. Bill Magavern, director of energy projects for Public Citizen. From L.A. Times 2/4/94.

We will make sustainable use of renewable natural resources such as water, soils and forests. We will conserve nonrenewable natural resources through efficient use and careful planning.

3. Reduction and Disposal of Wastes

We will reduce and where possible eliminate waste through source reduction and recycling. All waste will be handled and disposed of through safe and responsible methods.

4. Energy Conservation

We will conserve energy and improve the energy efficiency of our internal operations and of the goods and services we sell. We will make every effort to use environmentally safe and sustainable energy sources.

5. Risk Reduction

We will strive to minimize the environmental, health and safety risks to our employees and the communities in which we operate through safe technologies and operating procedures, safe facilities and by being prepared for emergencies.

6. Safe Products and Services

We will reduce and where possible eliminate the use, manufacture and sale of products or services that cause environmental damage or health or safety hazards. We will inform our customers of the environmental impacts of our products or services and try to correct unsafe use.

7. Environmental Restoration

We will promptly and responsibly correct conditions we have caused that endanger health, safety or the environment. To the extent feasible, we will redress injuries we have caused to persons or damage we have caused to the environment and will restore the environment.

8. Informing the Public

We will inform in a timely manner everyone who may be affected by conditions caused by our company that might endanger health, safety or the environment. We will regularly seek advice and counsel through dialogue with persons in communities near our facilities. We will not take any action against employees for reporting dangerous incidents or conditions to management or to appropriate authorities.

9. Management Commitment

We will implement these Principles and sustain a process that ensures that the Board of Directors and Chief Executive Officer are fully informed about pertinent environmental issues and are fully responsible for environmental policy. In selecting our Board of Directors, we will consider demonstrated environmental commitment as a factor.

10. Audits and Reports

We will conduct an annual self-evaluation of our progress in implementing these Principles. We will support the timely creation of generally accepted environmental audit procedures. We will annually complete the CERES Report, which will be made available to the public.

Disclaimer

These Principles establish an environmental ethic with criteria by which investors and others can assess the environmental performance of companies. Companies that sign these Principles pledge to go voluntarily beyond the requirements of the law. These Principles are not intended to create new legal liabilities, expand existing rights or obligations, waive legal defenses, or otherwise affect the legal position of any signatory company, and are not intended to be used against a signatory in any legal proceeding for any purpose.

•

A recent district court case shows an infrequent example of a corporate law initiative concerning environmental issues. In United Paperworkers International Union v. International Paper Company, 801 F.Supp. 1134 (S.D.N.Y.,1992), the court overturned a corporate shareholder vote rejecting a proposal that the company adopt the CERES/Valdez Principles. The proposal had been submitted by the Presbyterian Church (U.S.A.), an institutional stockholder, and was included in the company's proxy materials for its annual meeting, but was accompanied by a strong negative statement from the Board of Trustees. The Board recommended a vote against the proposal, claiming that the company's own environmental code "in fact is both more stringent and more industry specific than the Valdez Principles," and stressing the company's purported exemplary performance and commitment to protecting the environment. The proposal lost, receiving only 5.9% of the votes cast at the company's annual meeting. The plaintiff union, also a shareholder, alleged that the Trustees' statement was false and misleading.

The Southern District ruled that the Board of Trustees was under no obligation to discuss its environmental record at all, and "could simply have stated that it opposed the proposal," but "since the Board chose to offer specific representations about the Company's environmental record and policies, it was obligated to portray that record fairly.... This it did not do." The court found that International Paper Company was not a model of environmental rectitude, with a number of serious ongoing environmental violation complaints and enforcement proceedings. Because of this environmental record and the misstatements in the Board's response to the shareholder proposal, the Court found that "the undisputed evidence compels a finding that the Board acted with a requisite knowledge and intent in making the misstatements and omissions," and voided the shareholders' rejection of the proposal. The Valdez Principles will be resubmitted to a vote at the Company's next annual meeting.

It is hard to make much of this case, since it may result merely in chastening Boards of Trustees from issuing overly-editorialized advisories to shareholders, but the point of Chapter 5 is nevertheless echoed: environmental law is where you find it.

PAGE 239   **Property cases and environmental law**

5A. Toxic land sales.

As to the question raised in Comment 5 of the coursebook text, whether the presence of toxics constitutes a breach of the warranty of marketability of title so that a buyer under contract can refuse to perform, most cases seem to say no, holding that toxics on the land are not a cloud on the title itself unless an administrative or judicial lien has been filed. See, e.g., Chic. Title Ins. Co. v. Kumar, 506 NE2d 154 (Mass. App. 1987); VSH Realty, Inc. v. Texaco, Inc., (Civ. 84-1531, 1st Cir., 1985); Harbeson, Toxic Clouds on Titles: Hazardous Waste and the Doctrine of Marketable Title, 19 B.C. Envtl L. Rev. 355 (1992).

In dealing with hazardous landfills and landsales, New Jersey and other states have moved away from the traditional notion of caveat emptor. In Strawn, et. al. v. Canuso, 638 A.2d. 141 (1994), a New Jersey appeals court found a real estate broker liable for failure to disclose the existence of a hazardous landfill. The court held the broker to a duty to disclose because:

> existence of such off-site conditions, which (1) are unknown to the buyers, (2) are known or should have been known to the seller and/or its broker, and (3) based on reasonable foreseeability, might materially affect the value or the desirability of the property involved in the transaction.

The court also rejected the defendant's argument that the buyers had constructive notice of the landfill's existence. See also the note in Chapter 4 on land sale stigma.

Chapter 6, The Interplay of Common Law and Statutes

Page 260   **Statutory interpretation**

1. The practical art of statutory interpretation. It is well understood that the United States has a long history of constitutional interpretation and that there are competing schools of academic thought regarding the proper way to interpret the constitution. At the poles, some scholars favor interpretation that stresses the static intent of the framers ("originalists") and others favor viewing the document with modern circumstances in mind ("interpretivists").

Statutory interpretation is also an extremely interesting area, of greater daily importance in the practice of law, with competing schools of academic thought regarding what is the proper approach to the task. Statutory interpretation addresses the process of giving meaning to regulations and other subsidiary(legislation as well as statutes themselves. The debate about approaches to interpretation begins primarily in the twentieth century with the advent of a heavier reliance on statutory governance and the rise of legal realism. See generally, William N. Eskridge, Jr. & Philip P Frickey, Cases and Materials on Legislation: Statutes and the Creation of Public Policy 569-635 (1988), for an exposition and critique of the leading theories of statutory interpretation. The lists and character of the various theories can be arrayed in several different ways. There are three rather traditional approaches — attempting to determine the inherent meaning of the words of the text itself; seeking the intent of the legislature at the time it acted; or defining special legislative intent on a provision , to reflect the larger purpose that was forwarded by enacting the legislation.[48] There are also calls for more varied forms of interpretation. See, e.g., William N. Eskridge, Jr., Dynamic Statutory Interpretation, 135 U. Pa. L. Rev. 1479 (1987); William D. Popkin, The Collaborative Model of Statutory Interpretation, 61 S. Cal. L. Rev. 541 (1988); Richard A. Posner, Legal Formalism, Legal Realism, and the Interpretation of Statutes and the Constitution, 37 Case W. Res. L. Rev. 179 (1986-87). Even though most environmental legislation is of recent origin that minimizes some of the questions about applying a statute that was passed under far different operative conditions than those now obtaining, it will affect outcomes in cases brought under the various statutes.

PAGE 277   **Liability of "arrangers" and "operators"**

5A. More on individual liability for corporate officers. Two competing lines of authority have developed for allowing individual corporate officers to be held liable as "operators" of toxic disposal facilities or persons "arranging for disposal" (and also for parent corporations to be held

---

48. Most of the commentary provided by the editors of this volume adopts on of these more traditional approaches to statutory interpretation.

liable for the actions of their subsidiaries) when hazardous substances are released into the environment: The first line of cases is characterized by findings of liability where the individual merely has the ability to prevent the action. The competing line of cases requires actual participation in the activity before liability will attach. Compare, e.g., United States v. Carolina Transformer Co., 978 F.2d 832 (4th Cir. 1993), with FMC Corp. v. United States Dep't of Commerce, 10 F.3d 987 (3d Cir. 1993).

PAGE 279   **Update on CERCLA amendments.**

1A. The Superfund Reform Act of 1994 and major changes in the liability scheme.   Congress has engaged in periodic review of the major environmental statutes. With CERCLA, this process was first undertaken in 1986 when the Superfund Amendment and Reauthorization Act (SARA) was passed.

The second major set of revisions to CERCLA were underway as this Supplement went to press. These newest statutory changes, labeled the Superfund Reform Act of 1994, make significant changes in the way portions of Superfund operate and are discussed in this chapter and in Chapter 21. In regard to the liability scheme these amendments serve an array of purposes, but their thrust lies in three principal areas—getting small players out of the liability net, creating a safe haven for new purchasers of contaminated parcels who cooperate in good faith with the agency and have not contributed to the release, and limiting liability for municipal solid waste and sewage sludge collection and disposal. The statutory language bears careful reading. The following was added to CERCLA § 107, 42 U.S.C.A. § 9607:

> Notwithstanding paragraphs (1) through (4) of this subsection, a person who does not impede the performance of response actions or natural resource restoration shall not be liable —
>
> (A) to the extent liability is based solely on subsection107(a)(3) or 107(a)(4) of this Act, and the arrangement for disposal, treatment, or transport for disposal or treatment, or the acceptance for transport for disposal or treatment, involved less than five hundred (500) pounds of municipal solid waste (MSW) or sewage sludge as defined in sections 101(41) and 101(44) of this Act, respectively, or such greater or lesser amount as the Administrator may determine by regulation;
>
> (B) to the extent liability is based solely on subsection 107(a)(3) or 107(a)(4) of this Act, and the arrangement for disposal, treatment, or disposal or treatment, involved less than ten (10) pounds or liters of materials containing hazardous substances or pollutants or contaminants of such greater or lesser amount as the Administrator may determine by regulation, except where-
>
>> i) the Administrator has determined that such material contributed significantly or could contribute to the costs of response at the facility; or
>>
>> ii) the person has failed to respond fully and completely to information requests by the United States, or has

failed to certify that, on the basis of information within its possession, it qualifies for this exception;

(C) to the extent liability is based solely on subsection107(a)(1) of this Act, for a release or threat of release from a facility, and the person is a bona fide prospective purchaser of the facility as defined in section 101(39);

(F) For more than 10 percent of total response costs at the facility, in aggregate, for all persons to the extent their liability is based solely on subsections 107(a)(3) or 107(a)(4) of this Act, and the arrangement for disposal, treatment, or transport for disposal or treatment, or the acceptance for transport for disposal or treatment involved only municipal solid waste (MSW) or sewage sludge as defined in sections 101(41) and 101(44), respectively, of this Act. Such limitation on liability shall apply only-

> i) where either the acts or omissions giving rise to liability occurred before the date thirty-six (36) months after enactment of this paragraph....

The idea of limiting the liabilities of municipalities for the garbage they collect and send to landfills that subsequently become CERCLA sites has a good bit of history behind it. Municipalities have long claimed that they deserve gentler treatment than ordinary generator PRPs.[49] In urging this view, they point to their not-for-profit orientation, their lack of resources with which to pay, and the fact that municipal solid waste (MSW) is, by and large, not hazardous. Their calls for special treatment did not fall on politically deaf ears. EPA has, from the start, had a policy of not suing MSW generators if there are other solvent PRPs at a site.[50]

EPA's policy of overlooking municipal contributors to CERCLA sites, however, gave little comfort to MSW generators who frequently were brought in as third party defendants sued for contribution by the PRPs whom EPA had sued. In what is probably the leading case, a number towns and cities (as well as individual MSW generators) tried to argue that the EPA policy established a binding statutory interpretation that MSW generators should not be held liable under CERCLA. The PRP third party plaintiffs countered that assertion by pointing to the ambiguous language of CERCLA and its failure to provide such an exemption. The PRPs also introduced expert testimony that as a "generic" matter, MSW includes hazardous waste. In an initial opinion, B.F. Goodrich v. Murtha, 815 F.Supp. 539 (D.Conn. 1993), the court rendered a split decision. The testimony of the expert was sufficient to state a CERCLA claim against the cities and towns, but not against the more than one thousand individual MSW generators. Later that same year, however, the court dismissed the claims against the municipalities. 840 F.Supp. 180 (D.Conn. 1993). The court found that plaintiffs had failed to produce any specific proof that MSW sent to the sites by the various municipalities contained hazardous

---

49. They also claim that they deserve gentler treatment than other PRPs even when they are owner/operators of a site. This claim is less compelling unless the hazardous materials at the site were introduced by fraud or other illegal acts.
50. Eventually, EPA formally adopted this position. See, "Interim Municipal Settlement Policy," 54 Fed. Reg. 51071 (1989).

wastes. Congress, in the Reform Act of 1994, has clarified the issue and, as a "compromise", has granted municipalities limited liability.

PAGE 277   Text update on CERCLA "disposal" *Aceto*

Section 1A. The Classes of Transactions That Constitute Disposal of Hazardous Materials

U.S. v. Aceto Agricultural Chemicals Corp.
United States Court of Appeals for the Eighth Circuit, 1989
872 F.2d 1373

Larson, J. This case arises from efforts by the Environmental Protection Agency (EPA) and the State of Iowa to recover over $10 million dollars in response costs incurred in the clean up of a pesticide formulation facility operated by the Aidex Corporation in Mills County, Iowa. Aidex operated the facility from 1974 through 1981, when it was declared bankrupt. Investigations by the EPA in the early 1980s revealed a highly contaminated site. Hazardous substances were found in deteriorating containers, in the surface soil, in fauna samples, an in the shallow zone of the groundwater, threatening the source of irrigation and drinking water for area residents. Using funds from the "Hazardous Substance Superfund," *see* 26 U.S.C. § 9507, the EPA, in cooperation with the State of Iowa, undertook various remedial actions to clean up the site.

The EPA now seeks to recover its response costs from eight pesticide manufacturers who did business with Aidex, in particular, who hired Aidex to formulate their technical grade pesticides into commercial grade pesticides. The complaint challenges it is a common practice in the pesticide industry for manufacturers of active pesticide ingredients to contract with formulators such as Aidex to produce a commercial grade product which may then be sold to farmers and other consumers. Formulators mix the manufacturer's active ingredients with inert materials using the specifications provided by manufacturer. The resulting commercial grade product is then packaged by the formulator and either shipped back to the manufacturer or shipped directly to customers of the manufacturer.

The complaint alleges that although Aidex performed the actual mixing or formulation process, the defendants owned the technical grade pesticide, the work in process, and the commercial grade pesticide while the pesticide was in Aidex's possession. The complaint also alleges the generation of pesticide-containing wastes through spills, cleaning of equipment, mixing and grinding operations, and production of batches which do not meet specifications is an "inherent" part of the formulation process.

The United States and the State of Iowa allege all eight defendants are liable for the response costs incurred at the Aidex site pursuant to section 7003 of the Resource Conservation and Recovery At (RCRA) because by virtue of their relationships with Aidex they "contributed to" the handling, storage, treatment, or disposal of hazardous wastes. *See* 42 U.S.C. § 6973 (a). Plaintiffs further allege that six of the eight companies are liable under section 9607 (a)(3) of the Comprehensive Environmental Response, Compensation, and Liability Act (CERCLA), because by virtue of their relationships with Aidex they "arranged for" the disposal of hazardous substances. *See* 42 U.S.C. § 9607 (a)(3).

LIABILITY UNDER CERCLA

To establish a prima facie case of liability under CERCLA, plaintiffs must establish

(1)   The Aidex site is a "facility;"

(2)   A "release" or "threatened release" of a "hazardous substance" from the Aidex site has occurred;

(3)   The release or threatened release has caused the United States to incur response costs; and

(4)   The defendants fall within at least one of the four classes of responsible persons described in section 9607(a).

The complaint adequately alleges facts which would establish the first three elements, and defendants do not challenge these allegations for purposes of this appeal. At issue in this appeal in whether the defendants "arranged for" the disposal of hazardous substances under the act, and thus fall within the class of responsible persons described in section 9607(a)(3). In findings plaintiffs' allegations sufficient to hold defendants liable as responsible persons, the district court relied on the principle that CERCLA should be broadly interpreted and took guidance from common law rules regarding vicarious liability. In particular, the district court found that defendants could be liable under common law for the abnormally dangerous activities of Aidex acting as an independent contractor, *see Restatement (Second) of Torts* §427A (1965), holding that the common law was an appropriate source of guidance when the statutory language and legislative history of CERCLA prove inconclusive.

The six CERCLA defendants challenge the district court's decision on appeal, arguing the court's decision on appeal, arguing the court's "hazardous activity" analogy is inapplicable to the facts of this case, and that Aidex, not they, "owned the hazardous waste and made the crucial decision how it would be disposed of or treated, and by whom." *United States v. A & F Materials Co.,* 582 F. Supp. 842, 845 [20 ERC 1957] (S.D. Ill. 1984). They argue Aidex was hired "to formulate, not to dispose," and that imposition of liability under CERCLA on these facts would lead to "limitless" liability. Finally, defendants assert the plain meaning of the statute requires an intent to dispose of some waste, or, at the very least, the authority to control the disposal process, and that neither are alleged by plaintiffs here.

The plaintiffs counter that defendants' ownership of the technical grade pesticide, the work in process, and the commercial grade product establishes the requisite authority to control Aidex's operations. Plaintiffs argue that because the generation of pesticide-containing wastes is *inherent* in the pesticide formulation process, Aidex could not formulate defendants' pesticides without wasting and disposing of some portion of them. Thus, plaintiffs argue, defendants could not have hired Aidex to formulate their pesticides without also "arranging for" the disposal of the waste...

Citing dictionary definitions of the word "arrange," defendants argue they can be liable under section 9607(a)(3) only if they intended to dispose of a waste. Defendants argue further the complaint alleges only an intent to arrange for formulation of a valuable product, and no intent to arrange for the disposal of a waste can be inferred from these allegations. We reject defendants' narrow reading of both the complaint and the statute.

Congress used broad language in providing for liability for persons who "by contract, agreement, *or otherwise arranged for*" the disposal of hazardous substances. *See A & F Materials*, 582 F. Supp. at 84. While the legislative history of CERCLA shreds little light on the intended meaning of this phrase, courts have concluded that a liberal judicial interpretation is consistent with CERCLA's "overwhelmingly remedial" statutory scheme...

While defendants characterize their relationship with Aidex as pertaining solely to formulation of a useful product, courts have not hesitated to look beyond defendants' characterizations to determine whether a transaction in fact involves an arrangement for the disposal of a hazardous substance. In *United States v. Conservation Chemical Co.*, 619 F. Supp. 162, 198 (W.D. Mo. 1985), for example, the court found defendants' sale of lime slurry and fly ash byproducts to neutralize and treat other hazardous substances at a hazardous waste site could constitute "arranging for disposal" of the lime slurry and fly ash. 619 F. Supp. at 237-41. Denying defendants' motions for summary judgment, the court reasoned that defendants contracted with the owner of the site "for deposit or placement" of their hazardous substances on the site, and thus could be bound liable under the statute. *Id.* at 241.

Other courts have imposed CERCLA liability where defendants sought to characterize their arrangement with another party who disposed of their hazardous substances as a "sale" rather than a "disposal" See New York v. General Electric Co., ___ F. Supp. 291, 297 [21 ERC 1097] (N.O.N.Y. 1984; A & F Materials, 582 F. Supp. at 845. In the G.E. case, General Electric had sold used transformer oil to a dragstrip, which used the oil for dust control. The oil contained PCBs and other hazardous substances, and the State of New York sought to recover costs for clean up of the site from G.E. G.E. , 592 F. Supp. at 293-94. In denying G.E.'s motion to dismiss, the court emphasized G.E. allegedly arranged for the dragstrip to take away its used transformer oil with "knowledge or imputed knowledge" that the oil would be deposited on the land surrounding the dragstrip. *Id.* at 297. Stating that CERCLA liability could not be "facially circumvented" by characterizing arrangements as "sales," the *G.E.* Court cited CERCLA's legislative history: "[P]ersons cannot escape liability by 'contracting away' their responsibility or alleging that the incident was caused by the act or omission of a third party." *Id.* at 297 (and authorities cited therein). *See A & F Materials*, 582 F. Supp. at 845.

Courts have also held defendants "arranged for" disposal of wastes at a particular site even when defendants did not know the substances would be deposited at that site or in fact believed they would be deposited elsewhere. *See State of Missouri v. Independent Petrochemical Corp..*, 610 F. Supp. 4, 5 [23 ERC 1109] (E.D. Mo. 1985); *United States v. Wade*, 577 F. Supp. 1326, 1333 n.3 (E.D. Pa. 1983).

Courts have, however, refused to impose liability where a "useful" substance is sold to another party, who then incorporates it into a product, which is later disposed of. *E.g., Florida Power & Light Co. v. Allis Chalmers Corp.,* 27 Env't Rep. Cas.(BNA) 1558 (S.D. Fla. 1988); *United States v. Westinghouse Electric Corp.,* 22 Env't Rep. Cas. 1230 (BNA) (S.D. Ind. 1983). *See also Edward Hines Lumber Co. v. Vulcan Materials Co.,* 685 F. Supp. 651, 654-657 [27 ERC 1904] (N.D. Ill.), *aff'd on other grounds,* 861 F.2d 155 [28 ERC 1457] (7th Cir. 1988). Defendants attempt to analogize the present case to those cited above, but the analogy fails. Not only is there no transfer of ownership of the hazardous substances in this case (defendants retain ownership throughout), but the activity undertaken by Aidex is significantly different from the activity undertaken by, for example, Florida Power & Light. Aidex is performing a process on products owned by defendants for defendants' benefit and at their direction; waste is generated and disposed of contemporaneously with the process. Florida Power & Light, on the other hand, purchased electrical transformers containing mineral oil with PCBs from defendant Allis Chalmers, used the transformers for approximately 40 years, and then made the decision to dispose of them at the site in question. *Florida Power & Light,* 27 Env't Rep. Cas. (BNA) at 1558-60. Allis Chalmers was thus far more removed from the disposal than the defendants are in this case.

Defendants nonetheless contend they should escape liability because they had no authority to control Aidex's operations, and our *NEPACCO* decision states "[i]t is the authority to control the handling and disposal of hazardous substances that is critical under the statutory scheme." *NEPACCO,* 810 F.2d at 743. In *NEPACCO,* we were confronted with the argument that only individuals who *owned* or *possessed* hazardous substances could be liable under CERCLA. We rejected that notion and imposed liability, in addition, on those who had the authority to control the disposal, even without ownership or possession. *Id.* at 743-44. Defendants in this case, of course, actually owned the hazardous substances, as well as the work in process. *NEPACCO* does not mandate dismissal of plaintiffs' complaint under these circumstances.

Finally, defendants' contention that the district court erred in looking to the common law must also be rejected. As the Seventh Circuit has recently held, the sponsors of CERCLA anticipated that the common law would provide guidance in interpreting CERCLA...

For all of the reasons discussed above, accepting plaintiffs' allegations in this case as true and giving them the benefit of all reasonable inferences therefrom, we agree with the district court that the complaint states a claim upon which relief can be granted under CERCLA. Any other decision, under the circumstances of this case, would allow defendants to simply "close their eyes" to the method of disposal of their hazardous substances, a result contrary to the policies underlying CERCLA. Accordingly, we affirm the court's judgment denying defendants' motion to dismiss for failure to state a claim upon which relief can be granted.

CONCLUSION

Plaintiffs alleged defendants contracted with Aidex for the formulation of their hazardous substances — technical grade pesticides — into commercial grade pesticides. Plaintiffs further alleged that inherent in the formulation process was the generation and disposal of wastes containing defendants' hazardous substances. Finally, plaintiffs alleged that defendants retained ownership of their hazardous substances throughout the formulation process. We hold these allegations are sufficient to establish — for purposes of defeating defendants' motion to dismiss — that defendants "arranged for" the disposal of hazardous substances under CERCLA, 42 U.S.C. § 9706 (a)(3), and "contributed to" the disposal of hazardous wastes under RCRA, 42 U.S.C. § 6973 (a).

COMMENTARY AND QUESTIONS

1. Who will win at trial? This decision denied defendants' motion to dismiss the complaint for failure to state a cause of action. In deciding a motion to dismiss, a court will assume that all allegations of the complaint are true. At trial, plaintiff will have to prove its allegations by a preponderance of the evidence. How would the plaintiff governments prove that generation of pesticide-containing waste is *inherent* in the pesticide formulation process? Would it require a showing that best available technology economically achievable will not eliminate the pollution? That no precautions will eliminate hazardous waste? (This would be similar to a common law showing of abnormally dangerous activity.) Would defendant be compelled to counter with proof that Aidex, long since bankrupt, was operating in a sloppy fashion?

Aceto has been adopted and led to liability in subsequent cases. Of particular note, in FMC Corp. v. United States, 10 F.3d 987 (3d Cir. 1993), the court initially adopted a three-pronged test for *Aceto* type liability and held that a party will be liable where it "(1) supplied raw materials to another and (2) owned or controlled the work done at the site, where (3) the generation of the hazardous substances was inherent in the production process." 10 F.3d at 997. The court found those three elements satisfied and imposed liability on the federal government for its role in the production of rayon at the site.[51] On somewhat similar facts, however, the federal government was not held liable for the contamination associated with the production of Agent Orange. See, United States v. Vertac Chemical Corp., 841 F.Supp. 884 (E.D. Ark. 1993).

2. Recycling. Where on the continuum between sale of a useful product and arranging for disposal does recycling fall? The short answer is that in most cases conventional recycling, even where the recycler pays for the used product, renders the seller of the used product liable as an arranger. The typical case of this sort might involve sellers of lead-acid batteries to lead reclaimers. See, e.g., Chesapeake and Potomac Telephone Co. of Va. v. Peck Iron & Metal Co., Inc., 814 F.Supp. 1269 (E.D. Va. 1992); but see Catellus Development Corp. v. United States, 828 F.Supp. 764 (N.D.Cal. 1993) (holding auto parts company not liable for sale of spent batteries to lead reclamation firm that caused release). Another case of this genre is California v. Summer Del Caribe, Inc., 821 F.Supp. 574 (N.D.Cal. 1993), where the sale to a recycler of solder dross left over after the defendant's manufacturing process resulted in liability when the solder dross was released into the environment at the recycling facility. The court's approach stressed the practical non-pecuniary benefit of these types of transactions to the seller by attaching liability as an arranger where the transfer allows the party to "get rid of or treat the by-product of [a] manufacturing process." A similar result of seller liability obtained

---

51. Early in 1994, however, the Third Circuit granted rehearing in the case, its decision had not been announced when this Supplement went to press..

when a smelter released hazardous reside from the plastic insulation on copper wire that the defendant had sold to the smelter for use in its recycling business. See, Courtaulds Aerospace, Inc. v. Huffman, 826 F.Supp. 345 (E.D.Cal. 1993). Will the imposition of arranger liability in the recycling context work at cross purposes with the desirability of recycling when compared to the use of virgin raw materials?

3.   U.S. v. Aceto and the Kepone case.   Refer to the Kepone case described in chapters 2 and 7. The Kepone criminal trial was a pre-CERCLA "tolling" case in which a federal district court refused to find Allied Chemical Corporation criminally responsible for the illegal activities of its formulator, Life Sciences Products Company (LSP). Under the *U.S. v. Aceto* rule, it is clear that if the LSP site was listed on the NPL, Allied would be liable, under CERCLA, for the costs of cleaning up the LSP site. In the Kepone situation, Allied exercised a greater degree of control over the waste management aspects of LSP's formulation process than defendants exercised over Aidex's. For example, Allied frequently sampled LSP's effluent, purchased LSP's pollution control equipment, and participated in negotiations between LSP and state pollution control officials.

PAGE 280   **CERCLA Liability of lenders.**

2A.   The Fleet Factors saga, updated.   In April 1991, EPA issued a new lender liability rule, see 40 CFR 300.1100, that responded to the maelstrom of criticism raised in protest of the 11th Circuit's *Fleet Factors* ruling. Subsequently, the *Fleet Factors* case itself returned to the trial court where the trial court on February 5, 1993, denied cross motions for summary judgment of EPA and Fleet Factors. What this means is that the court found that there was a genuine issue of material fact that needed to be decided in order to determine whether Fleet Factors was a PRP. The court, consistent with the EPA rule, considered Fleet's pre- and post-foreclosure actions separately. In the pre-foreclosure period, the test of the rule is that a lender will be deemed a PRP if it exercises decisionmaking control over hazardous substance handling and disposal practices, or if it exercises control akin to that of a general manager. The court found Fleet was clearly involved in the "goings-on" at the facility, but whether that involvement rose to a sufficient level to impose liability still needed to be adduced at trial. The post-foreclosure standard of the EPA rule gives the foreclosing lender significant leeway in winding up the business affairs of the debtor without incurring liability. Even though there was relatively little in the record at this stage to indicate that Fleet was not acting to wind up the business when it prepared the assets for sale, the judge held that issue for trial as well. A further issue remains as to whether Fleet, by selling assets that were themselves contaminated with hazardous substances, may have become an arranger under 107(a)(3). For a summary of developments in lender and trustee liability, see Hathaway, Recent Rulings on Envt'l Liability: Big Wins for Lenders, Big Losses for Trustees, 7 TXLR 1097 (1993).

Developments on the lender liability front have continued apace. The lender liability rule substantially clarified what steps a lender could take to protect collateral and after foreclosing without becoming so involved in management of the debtor as to stand in its shoes as either an owner/operator or arranger. Basically, the rule makes liable lenders who take control of the borrower's environmental compliance decisionmaking or who take responsibility for the overall management of the borrower as to all of its operations. Participation in financial and administrative affairs of the debtor, without these other elements, does not give rise to CERCLA liability. After EPA's promulgation of its lender liability rule , a series of decisions favoring lenders began to appear. In Michigan v. Tiscornia, 810 F.Supp. 901 (W.D.Mich. 1993), for example, conditioning continued financing on selection of a new CEO was characterized as exercising influence over general management operations that did not amount to sufficient control to result in lender liability.

While EPA and the lending community were generally satisfied with EPA's lender liability rule, some others were not. Specifically, some states and non-financial institution PRPs challenged the rule claiming it to be (1) an improper interpretation of the law and (2) beyond EPA's authority to promulgate such a rule that defines the scope of liability. Ultimately, in Kelley v. EPA, 15 F.3d 1100 (D.C.Cir. 1994), the rule was held invalid. The court said that "EPA must demonstrate either explicit or implicit evidence of congressional intent to delegate interpretive authority." This was not found in the various authorities granted to EPA under CERCLA, such as the power to promulgate the National Contingency Plan, the power to contract for cleanups, the power to enforce § 107 liability against PRPs, or the § 106 power to seek reimbursement for expenditures made by the Fund. Having found that the interpretive power was not given to EPA in this regard, the court further decided that even the normally extended judicial "deference to the agency's interpretation is inappropriate."

Into this valley of death rode the 400, or more accurately the 435 and the 100 (representatives and senators). As part of the Superfund Reform Act of 1994 Congress, while giving EPA a general express rulemaking authority, also took out the *Kelley* decision by "confirm[ing] without limitation, authority to promulgate regulations to define the terms of the Act as they apply to lenders and other financial services providers, and property custodians, trustees, and other fiduciaries." So, despite a temporary setback, EPA's lender liability rule lives on.

PAGE 283   **Corporate Succession — Choice of Law**

4A.   Choice of law, a common concern.   In regard to corporate successors, dissolved corporations, trusteeships, and many other potential relationships of parties to one another, there is frequently a choice of law problem that must be decided before the legal ramifications of the proven facts can be measured — what law applies, federal law or state law. The cases fall all over the map, with some choosing federal law to govern and some choosing state law. The variation in results is found without regard to the specific context (e.g., successorship, corporate dissolution, etc.). The cases choosing federal law emphasize the need for (or at least the desirability of) uniformity in the operation of a federal statute. Also, at times, particularly when the federal law would operate to bring in a PRP that state law would not, the ensuing discussion often mentions CERCLA's policy favoring an inclusive set of liable parties. The cases favoring state law note that Congress normally defers to the states in the regulation of these types of relationships and if Congress had wished to displace the operation of such things as state corporation law, it surely would have done so explicitly.

PAGE 284   **"Would you buy this land ?" update.**

Under the 1994 CERCLA Reform act, a new class of bona fide purchasers is defined by §101(39) as follows:

> The term "bona fide purchaser" means a person who acquires ownership of a facility after enactment of this provision, and who can establish by a preponderance of the evidence that-

>> (A) all active disposal of hazardous substances at the facility occurred before that person acquired the facility;

>> (B) the person conducted a site audit of the facility in accordance with commercially reasonable and generally accepted standards and practices. The Administrator shall have authority to develop standards by guidance or regulation, or to designate standards promulgated or developed by others, that satisfy this subparagraph. In the case of property for residential or other similar use, a site inspection and title search that reveal no basis for further investigation satisfy the requirements of this subparagraph;

>> (C) the person provided all legally required notices with respect to the discovery or release of any hazardous substances at the facility;

>> (D) the person exercised due care with respect to hazardous substances found at the facility and took reasonably necessary steps to address any release or threat of release of hazardous substances and to protect human health and the environment. The requirements of due care and reasonably necessary steps with respect to hazardous substances discovered at the facility shall be conclusively established where the person successfully completes a response action pursuant to a State voluntary response program, as defined in section 127 of this title; and

>> (E) the person provides full cooperation, assistance, and facility access to those responsible for response actions at the facility, including the cooperation and access necessary for the installation, integrity, operation, and maintenance of any complete or partial response action at the facility; and

>> (F) the person is not affiliated with any other person liable for response costs at the facility, through any direct or indirect familial relationship, or any contractual, corporate, or financial relationship other than that created by the instruments by which title to the facility is conveyed or financed.

The new exemption for bona fide purchasers is, of course, a direct statutory response to the problem of contaminated parcels becoming pariah parcels. In seeking to add solvent PRPs, CERCLA had the unintended effect of driving new development into previously undeveloped areas ("green fields"), leaving behind a series of unused industrial parcels burdened by the knowledge that any new owners would be stuck with CERCLA liability ("brown fields"). What would it take to induce a prospective purchaser of industrial property to select a brown field site in preference to a green field site? Brown field sites will often have industrial infrastructure advantages and may be more proximate to the needed workforce. Brown field sites may also meet with less vigorous NIMBY opposition.[52] Still, the key issues would be placing an upper bound on (1) potential CERCLA liability and (2) the cost of parcel cleanup that the new owner will have to bear.

On its face, amended § 107 grants to bona fide purchasers (BFPs) protection against CERCLA liability. That is only half of the battle. The cap on cleanup costs, to the extent that it is endorsed by the 1994 reforms, is achieved by bargaining with the responsible governmental officials, EPA and/or the states. Under the reform legislation, BFPs accept a variety of obligations to obtain that status. Some of the obligations are monetary in nature, others are more in the nature of cooperation requirements. A quid pro quo concept is at work here whereby the BFPs are to introduce an agreed upon quantum of new resources (i.e., money or cleanup work) to a site in exchange for their non-liable status.[53]

PAGE 292   CERCLA's Joint and several liability

4. Emerging cracks in EPA's joint and several armor. In United States v. Alcan Aluminum Corp., 990 F.2d 711 (2d Cir. 1993) and a separate case also entitled United States v. Alcan Aluminum Corp., 964 F.2d 252 (3d Cir. 1992), some modest inroads were made in the unrelenting stream of decisions imposing strict joint and several liability on all of the PRPs involved in the litigation. More significantly of the two, the Third Circuit *Alcan* case ordered the lower court to hear evidence of divisibility of harm. Relying heavily on the Restatement (Second) of Torts 433A, the court set the test for divisibility as follows:

> In sum, on remand, the district court must permit Alcan to
> attempt to prove that the harm is divisible and that the damages
> are capable of some reasonable apportionment. We note that
> the Government need not prove that Alcan's emulsion caused
> the release or the response costs. On the other hand, if Alcan
> proves that the emulsion did not or could not, *when mixed with
> other hazardous wastes*, contribute to the release and the

---

52. This advantage is speculative at best. It may be undercut by the increased militancy of minority communities that are often proximate to brown field sites and it is surely lessened by the new, legally required, consideration by governmental agencies of environmental justice issues.
53. One major contribution of the reform legislation to this process is that BFPs who work out agreements with state officials at sites where there is not yet federal involvement can rely on those arrangements if the state has in place an acceptable "voluntary response program."

resultant response costs, then Alcan should not be responsible for any response costs. In this sense, our result thus injects causation into the equation but, as we have already pointed out, places the burden of proof on the defendant instead of the plaintiff. We think that this result is consistent with the statutory scheme and yet recognizes that there must be some reason for the imposition of CERCLA liability. Our result seems particularly appropriate in light of the expansive meaning of "hazardous substance." Of course, if Alcan cannot prove that it should not be liable for any response costs or cannot prove that the harm is divisible and that the damages are capable of some reasonable apportionment, it will be liable for the full claim...964 F.2d at 270-71.

The Second Circuit took a similar tack:

Having rejected Alcan's proffered defenses to liability, one would suppose there is no limit to the scope of CERCLA liability. To avoid such a harsh result courts have added a common law gloss onto the statutory framework. They have at once adopted a scheme of joint and several liability but at the same time have limited somewhat the availability of such liability against multiple defendants charged with adding hazardous substances to a Superfund site. The Restatement (Second) of Torts 433A (1965) has been relied upon in determining whether a party should be held jointly and severally liable, for the entire cost of remediating environmental harm at the site. Under 433A of the Restatement where two or more joint tortfeasors act independently and cause a distinct or single harm, for which there is a reasonable basis for division according to the contribution of each, then each is liable for damages only for its own portion of the harm. In other words, the damages are apportioned. But where each tortfeasor causes a single indivisible harm, then damages are not apportioned and each is liable in damages for the entire harm.

Based on these common law principles, Alcan may escape any liability for response costs if it either succeeds in proving that its oil emulsion, when mixed with other hazardous wastes, did not contribute to the release and the clean-up costs that followed, or contributed at most to only a divisible portion of the harm. Alcan as the polluter bears the ultimate burden of establishing a reasonable basis for apportioning liability. The government has no burden of proof with respect to what caused the release of hazardous waste and triggered response costs. It is the defendant that bears that burden. To defeat the government's motion for summary judgment on the issue of divisibility, Alcan need only show that there are genuine issues of material fact regarding a reasonable basis for apportionment of liability. As other courts have noted, apportionment itself is an intensely factual determination.

In so ruling we candidly admit that causation is being brought back into the case — through the backdoor, after being denied entry at the front door — at the apportionment stage. We hasten to add nonetheless that causation — with the burden on defendant — is reintroduced only to permit a defendant to escape payment where its pollutants did not contribute more than background contamination and also cannot concentrate. To state this standard in other words, we adopt a special exception to the usual absence of a causation requirement, but the exception is applicable only to claims, like Alcan's, where background levels are not exceeded. And, we recognize this limited exception only in the absence of any EPA thresholds. 990 F.2d at 721-722. [emphasis in original]

Is there now an *Alcan* defense? How many PRPs will be in a position to carry the burden of proof on divisibility and basis for apportionment? One preliminary commentary on these developments suggests that only deep pocket, technically sophisticated PRPs will benefit from *Alcan*. See Daniel P. Harris & David M. Milan, Avoiding Joint and Several Liability Under CERCLA, 23 BNA Environment Reporter 1726 (1992).

A subsequent case, *Bell Petroleum*, may go even further than the *Alcans* in supporting the belief of some defense counsel that their clients can escape CERCLA joint and several liability. In Bell Petroleum Services Inc. v. Sequa Corp., 3 F.3d 899 (5th Cir. 1993), Sequa, one of three successive operators of a chromium plating facility, offered evidence of comparative sales, chrome flake purchases, and electric utility bills, in an effort to show the relative contribution of the three PRPs. The records offered were incomplete and relied on a variety of assumptions in projecting the amount of contamination attributable to each PRP, and the trial court initially ruled that Sequa was jointly and severally liable with the other PRPs. Because the government had previously settled with the other PRPs for $1.1 million out of a total of $1.7 million spent cleaning the site, this left Sequa with a judgment that would require it to pay $600,000.

On appeal, the Fifth Circuit, engaging in *de novo* review of the lower court's divisibility ruling, found that Sequa's evidence provided a reasonable basis for apportionment, rendering the imposition of joint and several liability inappropriate, and remanded the case for a determination of Sequa's share of the liability. The trial court interpreted the remand order as requiring obedience not only to the divisibility ruling, but also to a particular apportionment of only 4%, entered judgment against Sequa for $68,000. The trial court expressed its view that it could not take into account the full gamut of what it felt were relevant considerations saying it was "convinced that further evidence ... would demonstrate Sequa's share of the contamination is much higher." United States v. Bell Petroleum Services Inc., MO-88-CA-005 (W.D.Tex. March 11, 1994), discussed at 8 Toxics Law Reporter 1191 (March 23, 1994).

PAGE 295   Update on CERCLA contribution

3A. More on contribution. What are the differences between a government initiated § 107 suit and a contribution action? Should a party who was held liable to the government in a §107 action, automatically be held liable for contribution at the behest of a private party? At least one court has decided this question in the negative. In Farmland Industries, Inc. v. Morrison-Quirk Grain Co., 987 F.2d 1335 (8th Cir. 1993), a party seeking contribution moved for summary judgment against a party that had previously been held liable to the government in a § 107 suit. The thrust of the motion was that the prior finding of liability was conclusive against that party under the principles of collateral estoppel. The appellate court stated, "Liability [to the government] is not dependent on any showing of causation or fault...[Thus,] a private party cannot predicate a claim for contribution or indemnity solely on liability to the government, but must also prove causation." 987 F.2d at 1339-40. Is comparative causation the sole relevant inquiry in the contribution case, or must the inquiry be broader, trying to attempt an equitable allocation, an inquiry that includes causation, but also relative culpability and other factors as well?

PAGE 295   CERCLA attorneys fees

5. Attorney's fees awards in CERCLA cases. As with so many CERCLA issues, the recoverability of attorney's fees as a part of 107(a)(4)(b) response costs is an issue not answered by the statute or its legislative history. The general argument in favor of allowing fee recovery looks at the statutory language as indicating a desire that all costs of remediation are covered, even those that are incurred in obtaining the remedy. At a policy level, the argument stresses that the remedial nature of the statute evidences congressional intent that plaintiffs who have incurred costs of any kind should be made whole. Standing in opposition to these arguments are more traditional notions grounded in the American rule against fee shifting. The courts have not had an easy time reaching consensus. As an example, two 1993 decisions issued less than a week apart reach different conclusions. *Compare*, Stanton Road Associates v. Lahrey Enterprises, 984 F.2d 1015 (9th Cir. 1993) (fees not recoverable) *with* Chesapeake and Potomac Telephone Co. of Va. v. Peck Iron & Metal, 814 F.Supp. 1281 (E.D. Va. 1993) (fees recoverable). For a concordance of the numerous cases on this issue, see John M. Barkett, The CERCLA Attorney Fee Debate Heats Up, 7 TXLR 1448 (1993) (listing all decisions as of March 1993).

Eventually, this issue found its way to the United States Supreme Court. In Key Tronic Corp. v. United States, 1994 WL 237635 (U.S.), the Court ruled that CERCLA §107 does not provide for the award of private litigants' attorney's fees associated with bringing a cost recovery action. Interestingly, even before the Court rendered its decision, the current Congress had begun the process of amending CERCLA to make its desired result, no fee shifting as part of recovery of response costs, an explicit part of the Superfund Reform Act of 1994.[54]

PAGE 295   Update: CERCLA, insolvent PRPs and insurance

The transaction costs consumed by litigation over CGL policies has become one of the "black holes" of CERCLA. One of the reasons for this

---

54. At the same time, Congress, hoping to reduce ill-conceived contribution litigation, put in an express fee shifting provision that would operate to penalize parties who filed "spurious" contribution claims.

is that precedents are almost all of limited value and seem only to encourage additional litigation and intransigency. There are reasons for this. First, the sums involved are sufficiently large that the issue is "worth" litigating, particularly for the insurance companies who are facing multiple exposure to all of their policyholders in a given jurisdiction should they lose a major case. Moreover, given the effect of the contamination on the value of the site, in many cases the insurance coverage is the only real asset of a thinly capitalized site owner. Second, because the interpretation of insurance contracts is a state law issue, precedents from one state are not binding in another, so in states where the issue is not yet decided, each new decision in another state is that much more cannon fodder for the legal grist mill. Third, insurers are often of diverse citizenship from their insureds and are able to remove the litigation to federal court which results in decisions that attempt to predict how state courts would rule, but are not conclusive of the issue in subsequent cases brought in the state court system.

Congress, in the 1994 Reform Act, attempted to rectify this situation, but in a rather oblique way. Congress cannot simply legislate results for cases based on past activities.[55] Instead, Congress tried to prompt insureds to accept settlements offered by a new entity, the Environmental Insurance Resolution Fund (EIRF), in lieu of their insurance coverage.

The basic operative principle of the EIRF is a universal offer by the insurance industry (paid through the EIRF that they fund through a special tax) to pay a percentage of the possibly owing insurance claims in exchange for having PRP policyholders forego enforcement of their contractual rights under the insurance policy through litigation or otherwise.[56] The offer of payment to policyholders is varied by state depending on how the law of the state of the site has developed. In states where the law is more favorable than most to the insurers, the offer is only 20%, in states where the law is more favorable to insureds than most, the offer is 60%, in all other states the offer is 40%.

Perhaps for political reasons, the details of the tax needed to fund the insurance proposal was announced separately, after committee action on the bill itself. Even then, the proposal covered the funding of only the first five years (a total pf $2.17B) of the proposed ten-year period. The basics involve a two-prong approach. Roughly two-thirds of that amount will be raised by a retrospective tax (ranging from .2% to .27%) on commercial premiums collected between 1971 and 1985, and the remainder will be

---

55. The subject matter of these disputes involve previously consummated private contracts that are governed by state law raising questions about the authority of Congress to alter the relationships. Even if that hurdle is overcome, any effort of Congress to retroactively change the contractual obligations of the parties would almost certainly be a taking of property rights for which compensation would be owed (either to policy holders deprived of their policy benefits, or to companies required to pay when their contract would not have required such payment). These takings claims would reinvent the coverage litigation in a new disguise.
56. The scheme has a backward looking intent, limiting eligibility to claims relating to hazardous substances for which disposal took place on or before December 31, 1985. After that time, the language of virtually every insurance policy was sufficiently clear in regard to environmental claims coverage that there would be no need for something like EIRF.

raised by a tax on commercial multiple peril, fire and products liability policies (ranging from .34% to .44%) in the coming five years.

Whether the EIRF program will succeed in abating the litigation over CGL and similar insurance coverage is anyone's guess. Insureds may reject EIRF offers of settlement with only the small threat of having to pay 20% of the insurers "reasonable costs and legal fees...in connection with such [coverage] litigation after the resolution was offered to the eligible person," but only in the event that their final judgment is less favorable than the amount offered EIRF. The insurance industry has its "out" in a "poison pill" clause inserted into the legislation that abrogates the whole scheme if more than 15% of the EIRF offers are rejected by policyholders. Presumably, this option will come into play if policyholders are consistently rejecting EIRF offers and winning more than that in some jurisdictions, while accepting EIRF offers in other jurisdictions (where recoveries were likely to be less than EIRF offers).

PAGE 299   **Update on CERCLA and bankruptcy**

1A. CERCLA and Bankruptcy. In the welter of cases at the intersection of CERCLA and bankruptcy law that have arisen in the lower courts, there are several sets of issues of recurring interest and importance. It is helpful to recount a sampling of these issues to give a fuller flavor of the difficulties that arise when a PRP becomes insolvent.

One set of issues revolve around what would seem to be the simple prospect of making a CERCLA claim part of the bankruptcy proceeding. At this juncture, some explanation of bankruptcy proceedings may be helpful for the uninitiated. At a very simplified level, the basic format of bankruptcy proceedings follows a script that begins with the trustee in bankruptcy gathering all of the debtor's non-exempt assets and giving notice of the proceeding to all parties having claims against the debtor. Each potential claimant is then put into a contest with the other claimants to establish the validity and magnitude of the claim. Since relief in bankruptcy is premised on the debtor's insolvency (liabilities in excess of assets), the claims that are properly filed and validated ("allowed") in the process are thereafter awarded shares of the debtor's marshaled assets in proportion to the amount of their claim in relation to the total amount of allowed claims and the debtor is discharged form further liability on those claims.[57]

Looking now at some varieties of CERCLA claims against bankrupt debtors, a series of problems can be anticipated. First, if the contamination that would be the subject of CERCLA liability is undiscovered at the time of the bankruptcy proceeding, the trustee cannot give notice to the would-be claimants who, in turn, have no reason to be aware of the tendency of the bankruptcy and the need to file a claim. The long-standing legal rule in this situation, one having its moorings in the constitutional concept of due process of law, is that a person cannot be

---

57. This description ignores the fact that some creditors may have a preferred status that give them a special right to receive payment ahead of other creditors. Litigation about preferred status of government liens for cleanup expenditures is one such issue.

bound by the results of litigation who had no notice and opportunity to be heard. See Reliable Electrical Co. v. Olston Construction Co., 726 F.2d 620 (10th Cir. 1984). This means that "unknown" CERCLA claims would not be extinguished by bankruptcy.

Next, consider the case in which the contamination has been discovered at the time of the bankruptcy, but the magnitude of the anticipated cleanup cost chargeable to the debtor is not yet ascertained, or the debtor's liability for the contamination (i.e., status as a PRP) has not yet been established. Here, bankruptcy law, 11 U.S. C. § 502(c), provides the general rule that calls for the bankruptcy court to estimate the amount of "contingent claim" if ascertaining the amount of the claim by trial-like efforts would "unduly" delay the administration of the bankruptcy proceeding.

Finally, there has been some further development of the law in regard to establishing the precise point in time at which an environmental "claim" arises. Recall that Kovacs held that many environmental claims, such as CERCLA liability, are dischargeable debts in bankruptcy. As one commentator notes, however, "If the liability does not become a "claim" before the PRP enters bankruptcy, the EPA will not participate in the distribution of the debtor's bankruptcy estate, will not have its interest cut off by the debtor's discharge, and may assert its claims for liability after the conclusion of the debtor's bankruptcy case.[58] Particularly in cases where the debtor is a corporation that is reorganized (rather than liquidated) and comes out of the bankruptcy as a functioning entity, the non-dischargeability of CERCLA liability that had not arisen prior to the initiation of bankruptcy is significant. The leading case on determining when a CERCLA claim arises has become In re Chateaugay Corp., 944 F.2d 997 (2d Cir. 1991). That case held that a bankruptcy claim arises when there has been a release or threatened release of hazardous materials and that unincurred response costs of EPA are dischargeable claims. 944 F.2d at 1006. Thus, EPA and other potential CERCLA claimants were required to employ §502(c) allowing for the filing of contingent and unliquidated claims on the same basis as other general unsecured creditors. By the same token, the Chatequgay opinion also discussed when a CERCLA claim is property characterized as arising after the initiation of the bankruptcy ("post-petition") and thereby entitled to be treated as an expense of administration of the estate under §503(b). Recall that costs of administration are paid 100 cents on the dollar prior to the distribution to claimants of the debtor's remaining assets.

PAGE 304   **Update on statutory pre-emption defenses**

4A. Attempted statutory pre–emption's of common law actions. An underlying strategy of many environmental defendants can be seen in efforts to imply preemption against common law claims based on the existence of state or federal statutes and regulations that apply to a defendant's activity. That attempt to circumvent the common law is part of the backdrop of the *Silkwood* case.

---

58. Note, Discharging CERCLA Liability in Bankruptcy: When Does a Claim Arise?, 76 Minn. L. Rev. 327, 328 (1991), citing 11 U.S.C. §§727, 1141 (1988).

An interesting example of this strategy comes from recent efforts by industry in the Alaska legislature to override tort actions through *explicit* statutory preemption. House bill #282 was filed in the Alaska legislature providing that:

> § 09.45.330b is repealed and reenacted to read:
> b) "a person may not maintain an action [for private nuisance] if the occupation, structure, or act, including an emission or discharge, that is the subject of the action is authorized by:
>> 1) a statute or regulation;
>> 2) a license, permit, or order issued by the state or federal government;
>> 3) a court order or decision.

The Senate passed a similar bill, but the conference committee failed to approve a common version. Nevertheless it is remarkable that a sovereign state came so close to overriding a fundamental pillar of its common law system. Alaska may be a special case, where industry has an almost unfettered control over the legislative process. Alaska has been called "the world's northernmost banana republic." See also J. Frohnmeyer, Extreme Conditions: Big Oil and the Transformation of Alaska (1993). Students can be invited to see how this proposed amendment fails to accomplish what its lobbyist sponsors thought they were doing, by focusing its terms upon private nuisance.

A recent Maryland case raised the interesting question whether a sewage disposal plant that created noxious odors in a neighborhood could claim preemptive override against common law because it was specifically ordered to be constructed at that place by a series of federal court orders. The state court found that the federal authorities had directly mandated that the plant be built, but not how it should be built, so there remained open an area of conduct subject to nuisance liability. The court so held even though there was no evidence of negligence in construction of the plant, basing the defendant's liability upon the mere fact that it had caused unreasonable burden to the neighbors. (Washington Sanitary Commission v. CAE-link Corp, 622 A2d 745 at I(B) (Ct. App. MD, 1993).

Chapter 7,   The Force of Criminal Law in Environmental Cases

PAGE 335   Federal sentencing guidelines, *U.S. v. Rutana*

4A. Environmental prosecutions and sentencing guidelines. In the following case, an earlier appeal of which is noted in the coursebook at 335, the Court of Appeals has once again sent an environmental conviction back to the trial court for tougher sentencing under the federal guidelines. The opinion illustrates the tense process of applying a generic sentencing formula under the guidelines, in an area that always before had been in the realm of the trial judges' discretion.

United States v. John W. Rutana
United States Court of Appeals for the Sixth Circuit, 1994
18 F.3d 363

Kennedy, Circuit Judge. For the second time, the United States appeals the sentence of defendant John W. Rutana, who pled guilty to eighteen counts of knowingly discharging pollutants into a public sewer system in violation of the Clean Water Act. This Court vacated defendant's original sentence and remanded the case to the District Court for resentencing. United States v. Rutana, 932 F.2d 1155 (6th Cir.) ("Rutana I "), cert. denied, 112 S.Ct. 300 (1991). The United States appeals defendant's second sentence on the grounds that the District Court erred in declining to increase defendant's offense level as provided under United States Sentencing Guidelines §2Q1.2(b)(3) for the disruption of a public utility. For the reasons that follow, we again vacate defendant's sentence and remand the case to the District Court for resentencing....

Defendant was part owner and chief executive officer of Finishing Corporation of America ("FCA"), a now-bankrupt corporation. In 1985, FCA opened a plant in Campbell, Ohio that anodized aluminum. This process produced large quantities of highly acidic and highly alkaline wastewater. FCA discharged these hazardous pollutants into a city sewer line that led directly to the Campbell Waste Water Treatment Plant ("CWWTP"). The CWWTP discharges its effluent into the Mahoning River, which supplies drinking water to some downstream communities.

In January, February, March and April of 1987, four major bacteria kills occurred at the treatment plant. The CWWTP uses bacteria to treat waste before it discharges its effluent. The bacteria kills were attributed to FCA's discharges. FCA was notified after each kill of its involvement in the kills, but the company continued its discharges despite these warnings. A Federal Environmental Protection Agency ("EPA") investigation uncovered the fact that FCA had failed to obtain any permit that would allow any discharges, let alone discharges of the materials involved here.

On April 9, 1988, a CWWTP employee was burned while attempting to sample FCA's discharges. On May 15, 1988, the Ohio EPA sent a letter to the City of Campbell telling them that the treatment plant had violated its clean water permit. The City sent a copy of this letter to FCA. In July, 1988, after an investigation by the FBI, defendant agreed to voluntarily close the plant. However, FCA's discharges continued through 1988 and the treatment plant experienced additional bacteria kills. A second CWWTP employee was burned on December 16, 1988 while sampling a discharge from FCA.

Defendant was subsequently indicted for the following crimes: eighteen counts of knowingly discharging pollutants into a public sewer system, and thereby into the CWWTP in violation of national pretreatment standards, in violation of 33 U.S.C. §§1317(d) and 1319(c)(2)(A); two counts of knowingly placing people in imminent danger of death or serious bodily injury, in violation of 33 U.S.C. §§1317(d) and 1319(c)(3); and two counts of making a false statement in violation of 18 U.S.C. §1001. Defendant pled guilty to the first eighteen counts of the indictment and the remaining counts were dismissed.

A. The First Sentence. In the first sentencing proceeding, the pre-sentence report ("PSR1") calculated defendant's offense level of eighteen (18) as follows:

> (1) Base offense level of eight (8) for mishandling of hazardous or toxic substances, under U.S.S.G. §2Q1.2(a).
>
> (2) Increase of six (6) levels for repetitive discharge, under U.S.S.G. §2Q1.2(b)(1)(A).
>
> (3) Increase of four (4) levels for disruption of a public utility, under U.S.S.G. §2Q1.2(b)(3).
>
> (4) Increase of two (2) levels for playing a leadership role in the activity, under U.S.S.G. §3B1.1(c).
>
> (5) Decrease of two (2) levels for acceptance of responsibility, under U.S.S.G. §3E1.1(a).
>
> [8+6+4+2-2 = 18; for this the guidelines indicate a term of imprisonment of 27 to 33 months, based upon an offense level of 18 and a criminal history category I (Rutana had no prior offenses).]

While the court accepted the facts and findings of PSR1, it nevertheless departed downward from level 18 to level 6, and sentenced defendant to five years of probation, combined with 1,000 hours of community service. The court also imposed a $90,000 fine, which represented $5,000 per violation, and a special assessment of $950.

In granting the departure, the District Court had relied upon defendant's ownership of another company, which might fail if defendant were incarcerated, which in turn would cause the loss of jobs; and upon its belief that the minimum fine, which it believed to be mandatory, was too harsh. On appeal, this Court reversed...[and] the case was remanded for resentencing.

B. The Second Sentence. Upon remand, a different district judge ordered the preparation of a second pre-sentence report ("PSR2"). PSR2 recommended an offense level of 17; the calculations were identical to PSR1, except that PSR2 recommended a three-point reduction for acceptance of responsibility, provided for in a 1992 amendment to the Guidelines which had not been available at the time PSR1 was prepared. Defendant objected to the increases for his role in the offense and requested an additional two-level reduction under the disruption-of-a-public-utility guideline, U.S.S.G. §2Q1.2(b)(3), comment (n. 7).

The District Court did not accept the calculations in PSR2 and did not increase the offense level for disruption of a public utility, U.S.S.G. §2Q1.2(b)(3). The court sentenced defendant to four months of home confinement without an electronic monitoring device, three years of probation and imposed a fine of $30,000.

The United States raises just one issue on appeal: whether the District Court erred when it refused to increase defendant's offense level for disruption of a public utility under U.S.S.G. §2Q1.2(b)(3). This section provides: If the offense resulted in disruption of public utilities or evacuation of a community, or if cleanup required a substantial expenditure, increase by 4 levels. There is nothing in the Guidelines themselves or in the commentary thereto that discusses what the phrase "disruption of public utilities" encompasses. There is scant case law on this question. In United States v. Wells Metal Finishing, Inc., 922 F.2d 54 (1st Cir.1991), the First Circuit discussed the applicability of section 2Q1.2(b)(3) under circumstances very similar to the facts of this case. In Wells, the defendant discharged wastewater containing zinc and cyanide into the city sewer system. The defendant's discharges caused bacteria kills at the city's sewage treatment plant, which meant that waste was inadequately treated before it was discharged into a river, which served as a drinking water source. There was evidence that the city spent $1,000 to $10,000 per month over and above normal expenses to compensate for the defendant's discharges and resulting bacteria kills. The Wells court considered this evidence and affirmed the lower court's holding that the defendant's activities disrupted a public utility.

In the present case, defense counsel agreed with the United States that defendant's activities caused a disruption of a public utility: "What I would state to the Court is that the disruption, if there was any, and I agree with Mr. Sasse [government counsel] in his representation to the Court, that the disruption that took place was the killing of bacterias [sic]." The court drew a distinction between a "disruption" and an "impact" and found that defendant's activities had impacted a public utility but had not disrupted it and declined to apply the increase. It believed that to do so would be an overly technical interpretation and application of the Guidelines....

We find, however, that what occurred in this case was a disruption of public utility. The undisputed evidence shows that defendant's discharges caused several bacteria kills at the CWWTP and burned two CWWTP employees. Most importantly, defendant's discharges caused the CWWTP to violate its clean water permit.... We hold that the District Court erred in failing to apply section 2Q1.2(b)(3).

COMMENTARY AND QUESTIONS

1. **The mechanics of a sentencing formula.** The first sentencing report gives a good idea of how the guidelines work. Normally the trial judge cross references the final level number with the defendant's criminal history category. (See chart below) This produces a range of possible sentences within which the trial judge has wide discretion. Note that the first trial judge in *Rutana*, giving no rationale, rounded the offense level down to six. On the first remand, however, the second trial judge likewise

lowered the guidelines' level 17 downward on several grounds and the government chose only to take up on appeal the public utility disruption item. As a result the decision is vacated, and on remand the sentencing begins again on a clean slate. As of July, 1994, the case is again before the trial court. Why did the offense level and the sentencing drop so dramatically? Perhaps the particular ambiance and mitigating factors of the case justified a departure from the guidelines, but normally a judge departing from the guidelines must support a decision not to follow them. In any event it is clear that trial court discretion has not been eliminated by the guidelines. Should it be, given the subjectivities and disparities that otherwise arise in the multiplicity of trial courts?

SENTENCING TABLE
(in months of imprisonment)

Offense Level	Criminal History Category (Criminal History Points)					
	I (0 or 1)	II (2 or 3)	III (4, 5, 6)	IV (7, 8, 9)	V (10, 11, 12)	VI (13 or more)
Zone A 1	0 - 6	0 - 6	0 - 6	0 - 6	0 - 6	0 - 6
2	0 - 6	0 - 6	0 - 6	0 - 6	0 - 6	1 - 7
3	0 - 6	0 - 6	0 - 6	0 - 6	2 - 8	3 - 9
4	0 - 6	0 - 6	0 - 6	2 - 8	4 - 10	6 - 12
5	0 - 6	0 - 6	1 - 7	4 - 10	6 - 12	9 - 15
6	0 - 6	1 - 7	2 - 8	6 - 12	9 - 15	12 - 18
7	0 - 6	2 - 8	4 - 10	8 - 14	12 - 18	15 - 21
8	0 - 6	4 - 10	6 - 12	10 - 16	15 - 21	18 - 24
Zone B 9	4 - 10	6 - 12	8 - 14	12 - 18	18 - 24	21 - 27
Zone C 10	6 - 12	8 - 14	10 - 16	15 - 21	21 - 27	24 - 30
11	8 - 14	10 - 16	12 - 18	18 - 24	24 - 30	27 - 33
12	10 - 16	12 - 18	15 - 21	21 - 27	27 - 33	30 - 37
13	12 - 18	15 - 21	18 - 24	24 - 30	30 - 37	33 - 41
14	15 - 21	18 - 24	21 - 27	27 - 33	33 - 41	37 - 46
15	18 - 24	21 - 27	24 - 30	30 - 37	37 - 46	41 - 51
16	21 - 27	24 - 30	27 - 33	33 - 41	41 - 51	46 - 57
17	24 - 30	27 - 33	30 - 37	37 - 46	46 - 57	51 - 63
18	27 - 33	30 - 37	33 - 41	41 - 51	51 - 63	57 - 71
19	30 - 37	33 - 41	37 - 46	46 - 57	57 - 71	63 - 78
20	33 - 41	37 - 46	41 - 51	51 - 63	63 - 78	70 - 87
21	37 - 46	41 - 51	46 - 57	57 - 71	70 - 87	77 - 96
22	41 - 51	46 - 57	51 - 63	63 - 78	77 - 96	84 - 105
23	46 - 57	51 - 63	57 - 71	70 - 87	84 - 105	92 - 115
Zone D 24	51 - 63	57 - 71	63 - 78	77 - 96	92 - 115	100 - 125
25	57 - 71	63 - 78	70 - 87	84 - 105	100 - 125	110 - 137
26	63 - 78	70 - 87	78 - 97	92 - 115	110 - 137	120 - 150
27	70 - 87	78 - 97	87 - 108	100 - 125	120 - 150	130 - 162
28	78 - 97	87 - 108	97 - 121	110 - 137	130 - 162	140 - 175
29	87 - 108	97 - 121	108 - 135	121 - 151	140 - 175	151 - 188
30	97 - 121	108 - 135	121 - 151	135 - 168	151 - 188	168 - 210
31	108 - 135	121 - 151	135 - 168	151 - 188	168 - 210	188 - 235
32	121 - 151	135 - 168	151 - 188	168 - 210	188 - 235	210 - 262
33	135 - 168	151 - 188	168 - 210	188 - 235	210 - 262	235 - 293
34	151 - 188	168 - 210	188 - 235	210 - 262	235 - 293	262 - 327
35	168 - 210	188 - 235	210 - 262	235 - 293	262 - 327	292 - 365
36	188 - 235	210 - 262	235 - 293	262 - 327	292 - 365	324 - 405
37	210 - 262	235 - 293	262 - 327	292 - 365	324 - 405	360 - life
38	235 - 293	262 - 327	292 - 365	324 - 405	360 - life	360 - life
39	262 - 327	292 - 365	324 - 405	360 - life	360 - life	360 - life
40	292 - 365	324 - 405	360 - life	360 - life	360 - life	360 - life
41	324 - 405	360 - life	360 - life	360 - life	360 - life	360 - life
42	360 - life	360 - life	360 - life	360 - life	360 - life	360 - life
43	life	life	life	life	life	life

5. Corporate sentencing guidelines. Special sentencing guidelines for corporations convicted of criminal violations have been in the works for several years. These guidelines set a series of sentencing levels which increase or decrease depending upon the nature of the offense. For example, knowingly discharging a pollutant will increase the number of levels and voluntary disclosure serves to reduce the levels. There is great debate over the substance of these rules and as a result their acceptance and implementation has been delayed. The draft guidelines were not submitted by the statutory May 1 1994 deadline, and therefore the earliest that they may become law is November 1, 1995. It is expected that this extra time will provide industry representatives the opportunity to fight for changes in these rules. Industry representatives want more emphasis placed on whether or not there was actual criminal "intent" on the part of the corporation.

PAGE 347   **Liability of corporate officials**

4a. Executive liability and intent. In order to show intent the government is only required to show that the defendants knew what they were doing and not that they were aware that their conduct was unlawful. See U.S. v. Weitzenhoff, 1 F.3d 1523 (9th Cir. 1993). The more difficult question involves whether or not a corporate officer may be held responsible for environmental damages caused by their subordinates. For example, could Lee Iacoca be prosecuted for environmental crimes committed by employees in Washington? This is an area of the law which is as of yet unsettled and has become especially important as the new corporate sentencing guidelines, noted above, are being drafted.

Additionally, can a corporation be held responsible for the actions of subsidiary? For a discussion of this issue and the role it played in the Exxon oil spill see the article entitled, Raising the Stakes for Environmental Polluters: The Exxon Valdez Criminal Prosecution, 19 Ecol. L.Q. 147. See also the note on page 277 of the coursebook regarding CERCLA liability.

Chapter 8,   Fundamental Environmental Rights: Federal and State Constitutions, and the Public Trust Doctrine

PAGE 405   **A new form of public trust mechanism**

7. Federal public trusteeship and federal Trustees Councils. A new phenomenon in federal administrative law offers interesting possibilities for examining both the federal governments responsibilities under the public trust doctrine and what trusteeship duties may include for federal trustee's.

Under the provisions of three recent statutes, — the Clean Water Act Amendments, 33 U.S.C.A. § 1321(f)(5)(1977), the 1980 CERCLA Amendments, 42 U.S.C.A. § 9607(f)(1980), and the Oil Pollution Act of 1990, 33 U.S.C.A. § 2706(b)(1990) — Congress authorized the creation of state and federal "natural resources trustees" who have the power and responsibility to "restore, rehabilitate, or acquire the equivalent of...[injured public] natural resources" that are injured or destroyed, and to litigate for damages to recover for injuries to those resources. After the Exxon-Valdez oil spill of 1989, for example, a Trustee Council was created, based in Washington, D.C. with operations in Alaska.

The membership of the council consisted of the following:

Federal Trustees:
        Secretary of the US Dept. of Interior
        [Fish and Wildlife Service, National Park Service, Bureau of Land Management]
        Secretary of the US Dept. of Agriculture
        [Forest Service]
        Administrator of the National Oceanic and Atmospheric Administration, Dept. of Commerce

State of Alaska:
        Commissioner of Dept. of Environmental Conservation
        Commissioner of Dept. of Fish and Game
        Alaska Attorney-General

It is not at all clear what a Trustee Council is, much less how it will work over time. In part, Trustee Councils may have been invented mainly to overcome problems of citizen standing. See Fred Anderson's article "Natural Resource Damages, Superfund, and the Courts," 16 B.C. Envtl. Aff. L. Rev. 405, 411 (1989). In Alaska the Trustee Council apparently was created primarily as an entity for funding investigations into the oil spill's ecological consequences upon the Gulf of Alaska and Prince William Sound. It held its data under tight security, not responding to Freedom of Information Act requests for what it was finding, and in general seems to have acted primarily as an intra-governmental classified research task force. After federal and state settlements with defendants were reached, much of this information was released, but that required three years. It was never clear whether the trust that the Council was stewarding was the ecosystem of the Gulf of Alaska, or rather was focused only on statutory enforcement. Like most government agencies, the Trustee Council appeared to take its authority and guidance only from the terms of statutes and regulations, without any foundation in public trust law or the equity-based jurisdiction that underlies other trusts. The internal governance of the Trustee Council appeared to be by unanimous agreement, in consultation with EPA, rather than as a matter of individual trustee responsibility to a court-supervised mission, as in court-based trusts.

This new category of governmental trusteeship deserves observation and academic analysis. See Comment, "National Resource Damages: Trusting the Trustees," 27 San Diego L. Rev. 407 (1990); Martinuzzi, "The Exxon-Valdez Oil Spill Trustee Council: Probing its Legal Form and Responsibilities," (unpublished research paper, Boston College Law School, 1992).

Chapter 9, Public Powers and Private Property Rights: Constitutional Authority and Limitations

PAGE 442   EMF radiation as inverse condemnation?

3. Beyond tort — inverse condemnation where tort liability cannot be shown. Faced with the difficulty of making successful tort claims for the newly discovered potential threats posed by high tension electrical transmission lines, (see notes for Chapter 3 at 442), some legal analysis has been devoted to the question whether inverse condemnation offers an alternative remedy: In virtually every case the source of EMF radiation is a public utility company or other entity that possesses the power of eminent domain. Accordingly, are these entities arguably "taking an easement of EMF transmission" through property owners' land close to transmission facilities? In a recent California case the court decided no, although the reasoning may have turned on the particularly narrow claim made by the particular property owners. Zuidema v. San Diego Gas Electric Company, Cal. Super. Ct., San Diego Cty. (April 30, 1993). See Brown, "The Powerline Plaintiff and the Inverse Condemnation Alternative," 19 B.C. Envt'l. L. Rev. 655 (1992). Although analytically the inverse condemnation claim makes basic sense, since there is clearly an imposition of some trespassory invasion into propertyowners' territory, the argument may prove too much, since radio waves and other accepted electronic invasions constantly pass through our homes and bodies in modern life.

PAGE 449   The geography of Maine v. Johnson

This section from the city map of Wells, Maine shows the site layout of the takings challenge in Maine v. Johnson, coursebook at 449. The boundaries of the original Johnson parcel are highlighted. The litigation overturned restrictions on undeveloped lots #9-1 and #15.

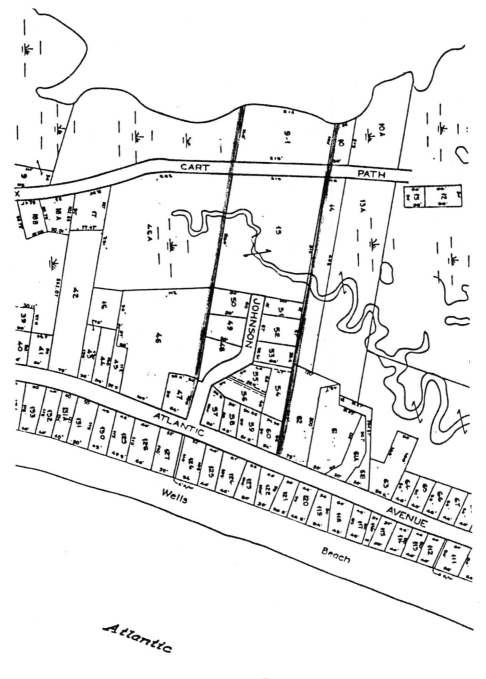

TOWN OF WELLS
York County, Maine

PAGE 473   **More on amortization, and extending baselines back in time to the time of investment**

b.1 What is the time baseline in takings?

Amortization is a fascinating area of takings law which has received limited serious academic analysis. The *Naegele* case noted above, after *Lucas* in Comment 4, F. Supp. 1068 (DMD N.C., 1992), discusses at some length the judicial considerations involved in judging the constitutional validity of an amortization clause.

The presence of an amortization does not establish the validity of the ordinance as a matter of law, nor does the absence of such a provision render such an ordinance an unconstitutional taking. For an amortization period to be reasonable it must give the property owner a reasonable opportunity to recoup or minimize the loss of use of his property by the end of the amortization period.

This leaves several questions unanswered. For instance: recoupment starting when? Is amortization just part of a general constitutional weighing process? If so, amortization periods of three or four or five years cannot be uniformly valid or invalid, but rather must be weighed in the particular circumstances of each particular amortized property. This appears to be the approach of the *Naegele* court. If the time period reviewed by the court to see whether property value has been recouped begins at the time *of the investment*, — rather than the start of the regulation — that emphasizes that the temporal baseline for amortization (and a fortiorari for all takings) is set by the time of the investment-backed expectation rather than the post-regulation period. The span of time over which a propertyowner is constitutionally supposed to make a reasonable economic return, in other words, is not some fixed period after a regulation has passed. Suppose, for example, that a purchaser of land for $500,000 may subsequently have made profits of many millions of dollars prior to the date of regulation. It would seem quixotic to insist that one has a constitutional right to continue any activity until the entire investment is *again* recouped post-regulation. Amortization analysis, viewing the economic returns on property throughout a propertyowner's time of ownership, thus indicates that investment-backed expectations may be used to strengthen the case for valid government regulations by establishing a baseline that extends back as well as forward in time.

PAGE 468   *Lucas* **and regulatory takings**

SECTION 4. THE REHNQUIST SUPREME COURT AND JUSTICE SCALIA'S REGULATORY TAKINGS MISSILE

After years of avoiding the difficult task of trying to define the line of "too far" beyond which regulation cannot go without compensating private landowners — a fundamental question of justice within a democracy that can only naïvely be given a simple answer — in the late '70's the Supreme Court began to take on such cases, notably in *Penn Central*, in the coursebook at 459, and *Keystone Bituminous Coal*, at 461.

These cases typically established the validity of regulatory burdens imposed upon propertyowners so long as they were left with "a reasonable beneficial" or "economically viable" use.[59]   This language is slippery and subjective, and certainly not a categorical rule. It only transposes the test to a review of the individual facts of each case. As noted in the text, constitutionally-permissible "reasonable" effects upon property value will be very different in cases where property uses pollute a river, say, and on the other hand where they impose no clear public harms.

The decisions did not consider what would happen in cases where protective regulation would reduce property value to a profitless level, but the properties caused great public harm, like polluting toxic dump operations. See coursebook at pages 465-68. Does the constitution require governments to pay off such owners, or else accord them a constitutional right to pollute?

Several Supreme Court majorities have recently attempted to address these questions and to define some overall categorical rules, in a series of decisions that echoes property rights initiatives elsewhere in the political arena. In the balance between public and private rights, it appears that these decisions have begun to erode the traditional presumption of validity and increase the burden of proof necessary to uphold governmental regulations.

The following case is a battle in that juridical-political war. It may be exceptional — a case where the trial court purported to find a total wipeout, a 100% loss of value — but it clearly signals antiregulatory arguments to come in a wider range of cases.

David H. Lucas v. South Carolina Coastal Council
United States Supreme Court, 1992
112 S.Ct. 2886

[In December 1986, petitioner Lucas bought two nonadjacent residential lots, #22 and #24, the last two unbuilt lots in a South Carolina barrier beach development, intending to build single-family homes. At that time, Lucas's lots were not subject to the state's coastal zone building permit requirements. In 1988, however, the state legislature enacted the Beachfront Management Act, which barred construction seaward of a coastal erosion line to be set by defendant Council after hydrological analysis of the barrier beach locations. The Council determined that Lucas's lots had been within the surf zone 50% of the time since 1949, and that they were well within the restricted 40-year erosion cycle area. Accordingly Lucas was prohibited from erecting any permanent habitable structures on his parcels.[60] He filed suit, arguing that the ban deprived him of all "economically viable use" of his property and therefore effected a "taking." The state trial court agreed, finding that the ban

---

[59].Penn Central, 438 U.S. at 138. In that decision, Justice Brennan said **triad, a phrasing that in part repeats the tests of substantive due process validity, see coursebook at 426-428, and introduces an ambiguous concept of investment-backed expectations (if one did not invest in buying property, but inherited it, is the takings test different?).

[60]The Act did allow the construction of certain nonhabitable improvements, e.g., "wooden walkways no larger in width than six feet," and "small wooden decks no larger than one hundred forty-four square feet."

rendered Lucas's parcels "valueless," and entered an award exceeding $1.2 million. In reversing, 404 S.E.2d 895, citing the *Mugler*-type noxious use cases, the state supreme court held itself bound, in light of Lucas's failure to attack the Act's general validity, to accept the legislature's "uncontested...findings" that new construction in the coastal zone threatened a valuable public resource, and that when a regulation is designed to prevent "harmful or noxious uses" of property akin to public nuisances, no compensation is owing under the Takings Clause regardless of the regulation's effect on the property's value.]

Scalia, J. ...Our decision in [Pennsylvania Coal v.] Mahon offered little insight into when, and under what circumstances, a given regulation would be seen as going "too far" for purposes of the Fifth Amendment. In 70-odd years of succeeding "regulatory takings" jurisprudence, we have generally eschewed any " 'set formula' for determining how far is too far, preferring to "engag[e] in...essentially ad hoc, factual inquiries...." We have, however, described at least two discrete categories of regulatory action as compensable without case-specific inquiry into the public interest advanced in support of the restraint. The first encompasses regulations that compel the property owner to suffer a physical "invasion" of his property....

The second situation in which we have found categorical treatment appropriate is where regulation denies all economically beneficial or productive use of land. [citing:] Agins, 447 U.S., at 260; see also Nollan v. California Coastal Comm'n, 483 U.S. 825, 834 (1987); Keystone Bituminous Coal Assn. v. DeBenedictis, 480 U.S. 470, 495 (1987); Hodel v. Virginia Surface Mining & Reclamation Assn., Inc., 452 U.S. 264, 295-296 (1981).[61] As we have said on numerous occasions, the Fifth Amendment is violated when land-use regulation "does not substantially advance

---

[61] [Original fn 6] We will not attempt to respond to all of Justice Blackmun's mistaken citation of case precedent. Characteristic of its nature is his assertion that the cases we discuss here stand merely for the proposition "that proof that a regulation does not deny an owner economic use of his property is sufficient to defeat a facial taking challenge" and not for the point that "denial of such use is sufficient to establish a taking claim regardless of any other consideration." Post, at 15, n. 11. The cases say, repeatedly and unmistakably, that " '[t]he test to be applied in considering [a] facial [takings] challenge is fairly straightforward. A statute regulating the uses that can be made of property effects a taking if it "denies an owner economically viable use of his land."' " Keystone, 480 U.S., at 495 (quoting Hodel, 452 U.S., at 295-296 (quoting Agins, 447 U.S., at 260)) (emphasis added). Justice Blackmun describes that rule (which we do not invent but merely apply today) as "alter[ing] the long-settled rules of review" by foisting on the State "the burden of showing [its] regulation is not a taking." Post, at 11, 12. This is of course wrong. Lucas had to do more than simply file a lawsuit to establish his constitutional entitlement; he had to show that the Beachfront Management Act denied him economically beneficial use of his land. Our analysis presumes the unconstitutionality of state land-use regulation only in the sense that any rule-with- exceptions presumes the invalidity of a law that violates it.... Justice Blackmun's realquarrel is with the substantive standard of liability we apply in this case, a long-established standard we see no need to repudiate.

legitimate state interests *or denies an owner economically viable use of his land.*" Agins, supra, at 260 (emphasis added). [62]

We have never set forth the justification for this rule. Perhaps it is simply, as Justice Brennan suggested, that total deprivation of beneficial use is, from the landowner's point of view, the equivalent of a physical appropriation. See San Diego Gas & Electric Co. v. San Diego, 450 U.S., at 652 (Brennan, J., dissenting). "[F]or what is the land but the profits thereof [?]" 1 E. Coke, Institutes ch. 1, §1 (1st Am. ed. 1812). Surely, at least, in the extraordinary circumstance when no productive or economically beneficial use of land is permitted, it is less realistic to indulge our usual assumption that the legislature is simply "adjusting the benefits and burdens of economic life," *Penn Central*, 438 U.S., at 124, in a manner that secures an "average reciprocity of advantage" to everyone concerned. *Pennsylvania Coal*, 260 U.S., at 415. And the functional basis for permitting the government, by regulation, to affect property values without compensation– that "Government hardly could go on if to some extent values incident to property could not be diminished without paying for every such change in the general law," id., at 413 – does not apply to the relatively rare situations where the government has deprived a landowner of all economically beneficial uses.

On the other side of the balance, affirmatively supporting a compensation requirement, is the fact that regulations that leave the owner of land without economically beneficial or productive options for its use – typically, as here, by requiring land to be left substantially in its natural state – carry with them a heightened risk that private property is being pressed into some form of public service under the guise of mitigating serious public harm.... We think, in short, that there are good reasons for our frequently expressed belief that when the owner of real property has been called upon to sacrifice all economically beneficial uses in the

---

62 [Original fn 7] Regrettably, the rhetorical force of our "deprivation of all economically feasible use" rule is greater than its precision, since the rule does not make clear the "property interest" against which the loss of value is to be measured. When, for example, a regulation requires a developer to leave 90% of a rural tract in its natural state, it is unclear whether we would analyze the situation as one in which the owner has been deprived of all economically beneficial use of the burdened portion of the tract, or as one in which the owner has suffered a mere diminution in value of the tract as a whole.... Unsurprisingly, this uncertainty regarding the composition of the denominator in our "deprivation" fraction has produced inconsistent pronouncements by the Court. Compare Pennsylvania Coal ...Keystone Bituminous.... The answer to this difficult question may lie in how the owner's reasonable expectations have been shaped by the State's law of property-i. e., whether and to what degree the State's law has accorded legal recognition and protection to the particular interest in land with respect to which the takings claimant alleges a diminution in (or elimination of) value. In any event, we avoid this difficulty in the present case, since the "interest in land" that Lucas has pleaded (a fee simple interest) is an estate with a rich tradition of protection at common law, and since the South Carolina Court of Common Pleas found that the Beachfront Management Act left each of Lucas's beachfront lots without economic value.

name of the common good, that is, to leave his property economically idle, he has suffered a taking.[63]

B ...It is correct that many of our prior opinions have suggested that "harmful or noxious uses" of property may be proscribed by government regulation without the requirement of compensation. For a number of reasons, however, we think the South Carolina Supreme Court was too quick to conclude that that principle decides the present case. The "harmful or noxious uses" principle was the Court's early attempt to describe in theoretical terms why government may, consistent with the Takings Clause, affect property values by regulation without incurring an obligation to compensate – a reality we nowadays acknowledge explicitly with respect to the full scope of the State's police power.... "Harmful or noxious use" analysis was, in other words, simply the progenitor of our more contemporary statements that "land-use regulation does not effect a taking if it 'substantially advance[s] legitimate state interests'...." Nollan, supra, at 834 (quoting Agins v. Tiburon, 447 U.S., at 260); see also Penn Central Transportation Co., supra, at 127; Euclid v. Ambler Realty Co., 272 U.S. 365, 387-388 (1926).

The transition from our early focus on control of "noxious" uses to our contemporary understanding of the broad realm within which government may regulate without compensation was an easy one, since the distinction between "harm-preventing" and "benefit-conferring" regulation is often in the eye of the beholder. It is quite possible, for example, to describe in either fashion the ecological, economic, and aesthetic concerns that inspired the South Carolina legislature in the present case. One could say that imposing a servitude on Lucas's land is necessary in order to prevent his use of it from "harming" South Carolina's ecological resources; or, instead, in order to achieve the "benefits" of an ecological preserve.[64] ...A

---

63 [Original fn 8] Justice Stevens criticizes the "deprivation of all economicallybeneficial use" rule as "wholly arbitrary", in that "[the] landowner whose property is diminished in value 95% recovers nothing," while the landowner who suffers a complete elimination of value "recovers the land's full value." Post, at 4. This analysis errs in its assumption that the landowner whose deprivation is one step short of complete is not entitled to compensation. Such an owner might not be able to claim the benefit of our categorical formulation, but, as we have acknowledged time and again, "[t]he economic impact of the regulation on the claimant and ... the extent to which the regulation has interfered with distinct investment- backed expectations" are keenly relevant to takings analysis generally. Penn Central Transportation Co. v. New York City, 438 U.S. 104, 124 (1978). It is true that in at least some cases the landowner with 95% loss will get nothing, while the landowner with total loss will recover in full. But that occasional result is no more strange than the gross disparity between the landowner whose premises are taken for a highway (who recovers in full) and the landowner whose property is reduced to 5% of its former value by the highway (who recovers nothing). Takings law is full of these "all-or-nothing" situations....

64 [Original fn 10, 11] The legislature's express findings include the following: "The General Assembly finds that: "(1) The beach/dune system along the coast of South Carolina is extremely important to the people of this State and serves the following functions: "(a) protects life and property by serving as a storm barrier which dissipates wave energy and contributes to shoreline stability in an economical and effective manner; "(b) provides the basis for a tourism industry

that generates approximately two-thirds of South Carolina's annual tourism industry revenue which constitutes a significant portion of the state's economy. The tourists who come to the South Carolina coast to enjoy the ocean and dry sand beach contribute significantly to state and local tax revenues; "(c) provides habitat for numerous species of plants and animals, several of which are threatened or endangered. Waters adjacent to the beach/dune system also provide habitat for many other marine species; "(d) provides a natural health environment for the citizens of South Carolina to spend leisure time which serves their physical and mental well- being. "(2) Beach/dune system vegetation is unique and extremely important to the vitality and preservation of the system. "(3) Many miles of South Carolina's beaches have been identified as critically eroding. " (4) ... [D]evelopment unwisely has been sited too close to the [beach/dune] system. This type of development has jeopardized the stability of the beach/dune system, accelerated erosion, and endangered adjacent property. It is in both the public and private interests to protect the system from this unwise development. "(5) The use of armoring in the form of hard erosion control devices such as seawalls, bulkheads, and rip-rap to protect erosion-threatened structures adjacent to the beach has not proven effective. These armoring devices have given a false sense of security to beachfront property owners. In reality, these hard structures, in many instances, have increased the vulnerability of beachfront property to damage from wind and waves while contributing to the deterioration and loss of the dry sand beach which is so important to the tourism industry. "(6) Erosion is a natural process which becomes a significant problem for man only when structures are erected in close proximity to the beach/dune system. It is in both the public and private interests to afford the beach/dune system space to accrete and erode in its natural cycle. This space can be provided only by discouraging new construction in close proximity to the beach/dune system and encouraging those who have erected structures too close to the system to retreat from it. ..... . "(8) It is in the state's best interest to protect and to promote increased public access to South Carolina's beaches for out-of-state tourists and South Carolina residents alike." S. C. Code s 48-39-250 (Supp. 1991).
[11] In the present case, in fact, some of the "[South Carolina] legislature's 'findings' ' to which the South Carolina Supreme Court purported to defer in characterizing the purpose of the Act as "harmpreventing," 304 S. C. 376, 385, 404 S. E. 2d 895, 900 (1991), seem to us phrased in "benefit-conferring" language instead. For example, they describe the importance of a construction ban in enhancing "South Carolina's annual tourism industry revenue," S. C. Code s 48-39250(1)(b) (Supp. 1991), in "provid[ing] habitat for numerous species of plants and animals, several of which are threatened or endangered," s 48- 39-250(1)(c), and in "provid[ing] a natural healthy environment for the citizens of South Carolina to spend leisure time which serves their physical and mental well-being." s 48-39-250(1)(d). It would be pointless to make the outcome of this case hang upon this terminology, since the same interests could readily be described in "harm-preventing" fashion. Justice Blackmun, however, apparently insists that we must make the outcome hinge (exclusively) upon the South Carolina Legislature's other, "harm- preventing" characterizations, focusing on the declaration that "prohibitions on building in front of the setback line are necessary to protect people and property from storms, high tides, and beach erosion." Post, at 6. He says "[n]othing in the record undermines [this] assessment," ibid., apparently seeing no significance in the fact that the statute permits owners of existing structures to remain (and even to rebuild if their structures are not "destroyed beyond repair," S. C. Code Ann. s 48- 39-290(B)), and in the fact that the 1990

given restraint will be seen as mitigating "harm" to the adjacent parcels or securing a "benefit" for them, depending upon the observer's evaluation of the relative importance of the use that the restraint favors. See Sax, Takings and the Police Power, 74 Yale L. J. 36, 49 (1964)....
Whether Lucas's construction of single-family residences on his parcels should be described as bringing "harm" to South Carolina's adjacent ecological resources thus depends principally upon whether the describer believes that the State's use interest in nurturing those resources is so important that any competing adjacent use must yield.... [65]

Noxious-use logic cannot serve as a touchstone to distinguish regulatory "takings" — which require compensation — from regulatory deprivations that do not require compensation. A fortiori the legislature's recitation of a noxious-use justification cannot be the basis for departing from our categorical rule that total regulatory takings must be compensated. If it were, departure would virtually always be allowed. The South Carolina Supreme Court's approach would essentially nullify Mahon's affirmation of limits to the noncompensable exercise of the police power. Our cases provide no support for this: None of them that employed the logic of "harmful use" prevention to sustain a regulation involved an allegation that the regulation wholly eliminated the value of the claimant's land. See Keystone Bituminous, 480 U.S. at 513-514 (Rehnquist, C.J., dissenting).

Where the State seeks to sustain regulation that deprives land of all economically beneficial use, we think it may resist compensation only if the logically antecedent inquiry into the nature of the owner's estate shows that the proscribed use interests were not part of his title to begin with. This accords, we think, with our "takings" juris prudence, which has traditionally been guided by the understandings of our citizens regarding the content of, and the State's power over, the "bundle of rights" that they acquire when they obtain title to property. It seems to us that the property owner necessarily expects the uses of his property to be restricted, from time to time, by various measures newly enacted by the State in legitimate exercise of its police powers; "[a]s long recognized, some values are enjoyed under an implied limitation and must yield to the police power." Pennsylvania Coal, 260 U.S.,at 413. And in the case of personal property, by reason of the State's traditionally high degree of control over commercial dealings, he ought to be aware of the possibility that new regulation might even render his property economically worthless (at least if the property's only economically productive use is sale or manufacture for sale), see Andrus v. Allard, 444 U.S. 51, 66-67 (1979)(prohibition on sale of eagle feathers). In the case of land, however, we think the notion pressed by the Council that title is somehow held subject to the "implied limitation" that the State may subsequently eliminate all economically

---

amendment authorizes the Council to issue permits for new construction in violation of the uniform prohibition.

[65] [Original fn 12] In Justice Blackmun's view, even with respect to regulations that deprive an owner of all developmental or economically beneficial land uses, the test for required compensation is whether the legislature has recited a harm-preventing justification for its action. See post, at 5, 13-17. Since such a justification can be formulated in practically every case, this amounts to a test of whether the legislature has a stupid staff....

valuable use is inconsistent with the historical compact recorded in the Takings Clause that has become part of our constitutional culture. [66][

Where "permanent physical occupation" of land is concerned, we have refused to allow the government to decree it anew (without compensation), no matter how weighty the asserted "public interests" involved.... We believe similar treatment must be accorded confiscatory regulations, i. e., regulations that prohibit all economically beneficial use of land: Any limitation so severe cannot be newly legislated or decreed (without compensation), but must inhere in the title itself, in the restrictions that background principles of the State's law of property and nuisance already place upon land ownership. A law or decree with such an effect must, in other words, do no more than duplicate the result that could have been achieved in the courts-by adjacent landowners (or other uniquely affected persons) under the State's law of private nuisance, or by the State under its complementary power to abate nuisances that affect the public generally, or otherwise.[67]

On this analysis, the owner of a lake bed, for example, would not be entitled to compensation when he is denied the requisite permit to engage in a landfilling operation that would have the effect of flooding others' land. Nor the corporate owner of a nuclear generating plant, when it is directed to remove all improvements from its land upon discovery that the plant sits astride an earthquake fault. Such regulatory action may well have the effect of eliminating the land's only economically productive use, but it does not proscribe a productive use that was previously permissible under relevant property and nuisance principles. The use of these properties for what are now expressly prohibited purposes was always

---

[66] [Original fn 15] After accusing us of "launch[ing] a missile to kill a mouse," post, at 1, Justice Blackmun expends a good deal of throw-weight of his own upon a noncombatant, arguing that our description of the "understanding" of land ownership that informs the Takings Clause is not supported by early American experience. That is largely true, but entirely irrelevant. The practices of the States prior to incorporation of the Takings and Just Compensation Clauses, see Chicago, B. & Q. R. Co. v. Chicago, 166 U.S. 226 (1897)-which, as Justice Blackmun acknowledges, occasionally included outright physical appropriation of land without compensation, see post, at 22-were out of accord with any plausible interpretation of those provisions. Justice Blackmun is correct that early constitutional theorists did not believe the Takings Clause embraced regulations of property at all, see post, at 23, and n. 23, but even he does not suggest (explicitly, at least) that we renounce the Court's contrary conclusion in Mahon. Since the text of the Clause can be read to encompass regulatory as well as physical deprivations (in contrast to the text originally proposed by Madison, see Speech Proposing Bill of Rights (June 8, 1789), in 12 J. Madison, The Papers of James Madison 201 (C. Hobson, R. Rutland, W. Rachal, & J. Sisson ed. 1979) ("No person shall be ... obliged to relinquish his property, where it may be necessary for public use, without a just compensation"), we decline to do so as well.

[67] [Original fn 16] The principal "otherwise" that we have in mind is litigation absolving the State (or private parties) of liability for the destruction of "real and personal property, in cases of actual necessity, to prevent the spreading of a fire" or to forestall other grave threats to the lives and property of others. Bowditch v. Boston, 101 U.S. 16, 18-19 (1880); see United States v. Pacific Railroad, 120 U.S. 227, 238-239 (1887).

unlawful, and (subject to other constitutional limitations) it was open to the State at any point to make the implication of those background principles of nuisance and property law explicit. See Michelman, Property, Utility, and Fairness, Comments on the Ethical Foundations of "Just Compensation" Law, 80 Harv. L. Rev. 1165, 1239- 1241 (1967). In light of our traditional resort to "existing rules or understandings that stem from an independent source such as state law" to define the range of interests that qualify for protection as "property" under the Fifth (and Fourteenth) amendments [citations omitted], this recognition that the Takings Clause does not require compensation when an owner is barred from putting land to a use that is proscribed by those "existing rules or understandings" is surely unexceptional. When, however, a regulation that declares "off-limits" all economically productive or beneficial uses of land goes beyond what the relevant background principles would dictate, compensation must be paid to sustain it. [68]

The "total taking" inquiry we require today will ordinarily entail (as the application of state nuisance law ordinarily entails) analysis of, among other things, the degree of harm to public lands and resources, or adjacent private property, posed by the claimant's proposed activities, see, e.g., Restatement (Second) of Torts §§826, 827, the social value of the claimant's activities and their suitability to the locality in question, see, e.g., id., §§828(a) and (b), 831, and the relative ease with which the alleged harm can be avoided through measures taken by the claimant and the government (or adjacent private landowners) alike, see, e.g., id., §§827(e), 828(c), 830. The fact that a particular use has long been engaged in by similarly situated owners ordinarily imports a lack of any common-law prohibition (though changed circumstances or new knowledge may make what was previously permissible no longer so, see Restatement (Second) of Torts, supra, §827, comment g. So also does the fact that other landowners, similarly situated, are permitted to continue the use denied to the claimant.

It seems unlikely that common-law principles would have prevented the erection of any habitable or productive improvements on petitioner's land; they rarely support prohibition of the "essential use" of land, Curtin v. Benson, 222 U.S. 78, 86 (1911). The question, however, is one of state law to be dealt with on remand. We emphasize that to win its case South Carolina must do more than proffer the legislature's declaration that the uses Lucas desires are inconsistent with the public interest, or the conclusory assertion that they violate a common-law maxim such as sic utere tuo ut alienum non laedas. As we have said, a "State, by ipse dixit, may not transform private property into public property without compensation...." Webb's Fabulous Pharmacies, Inc. v. Beckwith, 449 U.S. 155, 164 (1980). Instead, as it would be required to do if it sought to restrain Lucas in a common-law action for public nuisance, South Carolina must identify background principles of nuisance and property law that prohibit the uses he now intends in the circumstances in which the

---

[68] [Original fn 17] Of course, the State may elect to rescind its regulation and thereby avoid having to pay compensation for a permanent deprivation. See First English Evangelical Lutheran Church, 482 U.S., at 321. But "where the [regulation has] already worked a taking of all use of property, no subsequent action by the government can relieve it of the duty to provide compensation for the period during which the taking was effective." Ibid.

property is presently found. Only on this showing can the State fairly claim that, in proscribing all such beneficial uses, the Beachfront Management Act is taking nothing.[69] The judgment is reversed and the cause remanded....

JUSTICE KENNEDY, CONCURRING IN THE JUDGMENT.

...The South Carolina Court of Common Pleas found that petitioner's real property has been rendered valueless by the State's regulation.... This is a curious finding, and I share the reservations of some of my colleagues about a finding that a beach front lot loses all value because of a development restriction....

The finding of no value must be considered under the Takings Clause by reference to the owner's reasonable, investment-backed expectations. Kaiser Aetna v. United States, 444 U.S. 164, 175 (1979); Penn Central Transportation Co. v. New York City, 438 U.S. 104, 124 (1978); see also W. B. Worthen Co. v. Kavanaugh, 295 U.S. 56 (1935)....

In my view, reasonable expectations must be understood in light of the whole of our legal tradition. The common law of nuisance is too narrow a confine for the exercise of regulatory power in a complex and interdependent society. Goldblatt v. Hempstead, 369 U.S. 590, 593 (1962). The State should not be prevented from enacting new regulatory initiatives in response to changing conditions, and courts must consider all reasonable expectations whatever their source. The Takings Clause does not require a static body of state property law; it protects private expectations to ensure private investment. I agree with the Court that nuisance prevention accords with the most common expectations of property owners who face regulation, but I do not believe this can be the sole source of state authority to impose severe restrictions. Coastal property may present such unique concerns for a fragile land system that the State can go further in regulating its development and use than the common law of nuisance might otherwise permit.

The Supreme Court of South Carolina erred, in my view, by reciting the general purposes for which the state regulations were enacted without a determination that they were in accord with the owner's reasonable expectations and therefore sufficient to support a severe restriction on specific parcels of property.... With these observations, I concur in the judgment of the Court.

JUSTICE BLACKMUN, DISSENTING.

Today the Court launches a missile to kill a mouse.

The State of South Carolina prohibited petitioner Lucas from building a permanent structure on his property from 1988 to 1990. Relying on an

---

[69] [Original fn 18] Justice Blackmun decries our reliance on background nuisance principles at least in part because he believes those principles to be as manipulable as we find the "harm prevention"/"benefit conferral" dichotomy, see post, at 20-21. There is no doubt some leeway in a court's interpretation of what existing state law permits-but not remotely as much, we think, as in a legislative crafting of the reasons for its confiscatory regulation. We stress that an affirmative decree eliminating all economically beneficial uses may be defended only if an objectively reasonable application of relevant precedents would exclude those beneficial uses in the circumstances in which the land is presently found.

unreviewed (and implausible) state trial court finding that this restriction left Lucas' property valueless, this Court granted review to determine whether compensation must be paid in cases where the State prohibits all economic use of real estate. According to the Court, such an occasion never has arisen in any of our prior cases, and the Court imagines that it will arise "relatively rarely" or only in "extraordinary circumstances." Almost certainly it did not happen in this case.

Nonetheless, the Court presses on to decide the issue, and as it does, it ignores its jurisdictional limits, remakes its traditional rules of review, and creates simultaneously a new categorical rule and an exception (neither of which is rooted in our prior case law, common law, or common sense). I protest not only the Court's decision, but each step taken to reach it. More fundamentally, I question the Court's wisdom in issuing sweeping new rules to decide such a narrow case. Surely, as Justice Kennedy demonstrates, the Court could have reached the result it wanted without inflicting this damage upon our Taking Clause jurisprudence.

My fear is that the Court's new policies will spread beyond the narrow confines of the present case. For that reason, I, like the Court, will give far greater attention to this case than its narrow scope suggests-not because I can intercept the Court's missile, or save the targeted mouse, but because I hope perhaps to limit the collateral damage....

I B. Petitioner Lucas is a contractor, manager, and part owner of the Wild Dune development on the Isle of Palms. He has lived there since 1978. In December 1986, he purchased two of the last four pieces of vacant property in the development.[70] The area is notoriously unstable. In roughly half of the last 40 years, all or part of petitioner's property was part of the beach or flooded twice daily by the ebb and flow of the tide. See Transcript, 84-102. Between 1957 and 1963, petitioner's property was under water. Between 1963 and 1973 the shoreline was 100 to 150 feet onto petitioner's property. In 1973 the first line of stable vegetation was about halfway through the property. Between 1981 and 1983, the Isle of Palms issued 12 emergency orders for sandbagging to protect property in the Wild Dune development....

The Beachfront Management Act includes a finding by the South Carolina General Assembly that the beach/dune system serves the purpose of "protect[ing] life and property by serving as a storm barrier which dissipates wave energy and contributes to shoreline stability in an economical and effective manner." §48-39-250(1)(a). The General Assembly also found that "development unwisely has been sited too close to the [beach/dune] system. This type of development has jeopardized the stability of the beach/dune system, accelerated erosion, and endangered adjacent property." §48-39-250(4); see also §48-39- 250(6) (discussing the need to "afford the beach/dune system space to accrete and erode").

---

[70] The properties were sold frequently at rapidly escalating prices before Lucas purchased them. Lot 22 was first sold in 1979 for $96,660, sold in 1984 for $187,500, then in 1985 for $260,000, and, finally, to Lucas in 1986 for $475,000. He estimated its worth in 1991 at $650,000. Lot 24 had a similar past. The record does not indicate who purchased the properties prior to Lucas, or why none of the purchasers held on to the lots and built on them.

If the state legislature is correct that the prohibition on building in front of the setback line prevents serious harm, then, under this Court's prior cases, the Act is constitutional.... The Court consistently has upheld regulations imposed to arrest a significant threat to the common welfare, whatever their economic effect on the owner....

Nothing in the record undermines the General Assembly's assessment that prohibitions on building in front of the setback line are necessary to protect people and property from storms, high tides, and beach erosion. Because that legislative determination cannot be disregarded in the absence of such evidence, see, e.g., Euclid, 272 U.S., at 388; O'Gorman & Young v. Hartford Fire Ins. Co, 282 U.S. 251, 257-258 (1931) (Brandeis, J.), and because its determination of harm to life and property from building is sufficient to prohibit that use under this Court's cases, the South Carolina Supreme Court correctly found no taking....

The trial court...found the property "valueless." The court accepted no evidence from the State on the property's value without a home, and petitioner's appraiser testified that he never had considered what the value would be absent a residence. The appraiser's value was based on the fact that the "highest and best use of these lots...[is] luxury single family detached dwellings." The trial court appeared to believe that the property could be considered "valueless" if it was not available for its most profitable use....

Clearly, [this] Court was eager to decide this case. But eagerness, in the absence of proper jurisdiction, must-and in this case should have been-met with restraint.

III The Court's willingness to dispense with precedent in its haste to reach a result is not limited to its initial jurisdictional decision. The Court also alters the long-settled rules of review.

The South Carolina Supreme Court's decision to defer to legislative judgments in the absence of a challenge from petitioner comports with one of this Court's oldest maxims: "the existence of facts supporting the legislative judgment is to be presumed." United States v. Carolene Products Co., 304 U.S. 144, 152 (1938). Indeed, we have said the legislature's judgment is "well-nigh conclusive." Berman v. Parker, 348 U.S. 26, 32 (1954). ...

IV The Court does not reject the South Carolina Supreme Court's decision simply on the basis of its disbelief and distrust of the legislature's findings. It also takes the opportunity to create a new scheme for regulations that eliminate all economic value. From now on, there is a categorical rule finding these regulations to be a taking unless the use they prohibit is a background common-law nuisance or property principle.

A. I first question the Court's rationale in creating a category that obviates a "case-specific inquiry into the public interest advanced," if all economic value has been lost. If one fact about the Court's taking jurisprudence can be stated without contradiction, it is that "the particular circumstances of each case" determine whether a specific restriction will be rendered invalid by the government's failure to pay compensation....

This Court repeatedly has recognized the ability of government, in certain circumstances, to regulate property without compensation no matter how adverse the financial effect on the owner may be.... In Keystone

Bituminous Coal, the Court summarized over 100 years of precedent: "the Court has repeatedly upheld regulations that destroy or adversely affect real property interests."[71] The Court recognizes that "our prior opinions have suggested that 'harmful or noxious uses' of property may be proscribed by government regulation without the requirement of compensation," ante, at 17, but seeks to reconcile them with its categorical rule by claiming that the Court never has upheld a regulation when the owner alleged the loss of all economic value. Even if the Court's factual premise were correct, its understanding of the Court's cases is distorted. In none of the cases did the Court suggest that the right of a State to prohibit certain activities without paying compensation turned on the availability of some residual valuable use. Instead, the cases depended on whether the government interest was sufficient to prohibit the activity, given the significant private cost.

These cases rest on the principle that the State has full power to prohibit an owner's use of property if it is harmful to the public. "[S]ince no individual has a right to use his property so as to create a nuisance or otherwise harm others, the State has not 'taken' anything when it asserts its power to enjoin the nuisance-like activity." Keystone Bituminous Coal, 480 U.S., at 491, n. 20. It would make no sense under this theory to suggest that an owner has a constitutionally protected right to harm others, if only he makes the proper showing of economic loss....[72] Ultimately even the Court cannot embrace the full implications of its per se rule: it eventually agrees that there cannot be a categorical rule for a taking based on economic value that wholly disregards the public need asserted. Instead, the Court decides that it will permit a State to regulate

---

[71] [Dissent fn 10, 11] [In the First English Evangelica case,] on remand, the California court found no taking in part because the zoning regulation "involves this highest of public interests – the prevention of death and injury." First Lutheran Church v. Los Angeles, 210 Cal. App. 3d 1353, 1370, 258 Cal. Rptr. 893, (1989), cert. denied, 493 U.S. 1056 (1990). [11] The Court's suggestion that Agins v. Tiburon, 447 U.S. 255 (1980), a unanimous opinion, created a new per se rule, only now discovered, is unpersuasive. In Agins, the Court stated that "no precise rule determines when property has been taken" but instead that "the question necessarily requires a weighing of public and private interest." Id., at 260-262. The other cases cited by the Court, ante, at 9, repeat the Agins sentence, but in no way suggest that the public interest is irrelevant if total value has been taken. The Court has indicated that proof that a regulation does not deny an owner economic use of his property is sufficient to defeat a facial taking challenge. See Hodel v. Virginia Surface Mining & Reclamation Assn., Inc., 452 U.S. 264, 295-297 (1981). But the conclusion that a regulation is not on its face a taking because it allows the landowner some economic use of property is a far cry from the proposition that denial of such use is sufficient to establish a taking claim regardless of any other consideration. The Court never has accepted the latter proposition. The Court relies today on dicta in Agins, Hodel, Nollan v. California Coastal Comm'n, 483 U.S. 825 (1987), and Keystone Bituminous Coal v. DeBenedictis, 480 U.S. 470 (1987), for its new categorical rule. Ante, at 10.

[72] "Indeed, it would be extraordinary to construe the Constitution to require a government to compensate private landowners because it denied them 'the right' to use property which cannot be used without risking injury and death." First Lutheran Church, 210 Cal. App. 3d, at 1366

all economic value only if the State prohibits uses that would not be permitted under "background principles of nuisance and property law."[73]

Until today, the Court explicitly had rejected the contention that the government's power to act without paying compensation turns on whether the prohibited activity is a common-law nuisance.[74] The brewery closed in Mugler itself was not a common-law nuisance, and the Court specifically stated that it was the role of the legislature to determine what measures would be appropriate for the protection of public health and safety....

The Court rejects the notion that the State always can prohibit uses it deems a harm to the public without granting compensation because "the distinction between 'harm-preventing' and 'benefit-conferring' regulation is often in the eye of the beholder."...The Court, however, fails to explain how its proposed common law alternative escapes the same trap.

The threshold inquiry for imposition of the Court's new rule, "deprivation of all economically valuable use," itself cannot be determined objectively. As the Court admits, whether the owner has been deprived of all economic value of his property will depend on how "property" is defined....

The Court's decision in Keystone Bituminous Coal illustrates this principle perfectly. In Keystone, the Court determined that the "support estate" was "merely a part of the entire bundle of rights possessed by the owner." 480 U.S., at 501. Thus, the Court concluded that the support estate's destruction merely eliminated one segment of the total property. Ibid. The dissent, however, characterized the support estate as a distinct property interest that was wholly destroyed. Id., at 519. The Court could agree on no "value-free basis" to resolve this dispute.

Even more perplexing, however, is the Court's reliance on common-law principles of nuisance in its quest for a value-free taking jurisprudence. In determining what is a nuisance at common law, state courts make exactly

---

[73] Although it refers to state nuisance and property law, the Court apparently does not mean just any state nuisance and property law. Public nuisance was first a common-law creation, see Newark, The Boundaries of Nuisance, 65 L. Q. Rev. 480, 482 (1949) (attributing development of nuisance to 1535), but by the 1800s in both the United States and England, legislatures had the power to define what is a public nuisance, and particular uses often have been selectively targeted. See Prosser, Private Action for Public Nuisance, 52 Va. L. Rev. 997, 999-1000 (1966); J.F. Stephen, A General View of the Criminal Law of England 105-107 (2d ed. 1890). The Court's references to "common-law" background principles, however, indicate that legislative determinations do not constitute "state nuisance and property law" for the Court.

[74] Also, until today the fact that the regulation prohibited uses that were lawful at the time the owner purchased did not determine the constitutional question. The brewery, the brickyard, the cedar trees, and the gravel pit were all perfectly legitimate uses prior to the passage of the regulation. See Mugler v. Kansas, 123 U.S. 623, 654 (1887); Hadacheck v. Los Angeles, 239 U.S. 394 (1915); Miller, 276 U.S., at 272; Goldblatt v. Hempstead, 369 U.S. 590 (1962). This Court explicitly acknowledged in Hadacheck that "[a] vested interest cannot be asserted against [the police power] because of conditions once obtaining. To so hold would preclude development and fix a city forever in its primitive conditions." 239 U.S., at 410.

the decision that the Court finds so troubling when made by the South Carolina General Assembly today: they determine whether the use is harmful. Common-law public and private nuisance law is simply a determination whether a particular use causes harm. See Prosser, Private Action for Public Nuisance, 52 Va. L. Rev. 997, 997 (1966) ("Nuisance is a French word which means nothing more than harm"). There is nothing magical in the reasoning of judges long dead. They determined a harm in the same way as state judges and legislatures do today. If judges in the 18th and 19th centuries can distinguish a harm from a benefit, why not judges in the 20th century, and if judges can, why not legislators? There simply is no reason to believe that new interpretations of the hoary common law nuisance doctrine will be particularly "objective" or "value-free." Once one abandons the level of generality of sic utere tuo ut alienum non laedas, ante, at 26, one searches in vain, I think, for anything resembling a principle in the common law of nuisance.

C...The principle that the State should compensate individuals for property taken for public use was not widely established in America at the time of the Revolution. "The colonists...inherited...a concept of property which permitted extensive regulation of the use of that property for the public benefit- regulation that could even go so far as to deny all productive use of the property to the owner if, as Coke himself stated, the regulation 'extends to the public benefit...for this is for the public, and every one hath benefit by it." ' F. Bosselman, D. Callies & J. Banta, The Taking Issue 80-81 (1973)....

Although, prior to the adoption of the Bill of Rights, America was replete with land use regulations,... the Fifth Amendment's Taking Clause originally did not extend to regulations of property, whatever the effect.[75] Most state courts agreed with this narrow interpretation of a taking. "Until the end of the nineteenth century...jurists held that the constitution protected possession only, and not value." Siegel, Understanding the Nineteenth Century Contract Clause: The Role of the Property-Privilege Distinction and "Takings" Clause Jurisprudence, 60 S. Cal. L. Rev. 1, 76 (1986); Bosselman 106....

In short, I find no clear and accepted "historical compact" or "understanding of our citizens" justifying the Court's new taking doctrine. Instead, the Court seems to treat history as a grab-bag of principles, to be adopted where they support the Court's theory, and ignored where they do not....What makes the Court's analysis unworkable is its attempt to package the law of two incompatible eras and peddle it as historical fact.

The Court makes sweeping and, in my view, misguided and unsupported changes in our taking doctrine. While it limits these changes to the most narrow subset of government regulation-those that eliminate all economic value from land- these changes go far beyond what is necessary to secure

---

[75] James Madison, author of the Taking Clause, apparently intended it to apply only to direct, physical takings of property by the Federal Government. See Treanor, The Origins and Original Significance of the Just Compensation Clause of the Fifth Amendment, 94 Yale L.J., 694, 711 (1985). Professor Sax argues that although "contemporaneous commentary upon the meaning of the compensation clause is in very short supply," 74 Yale L.J., at 58, the "few authorities that are available" indicate that the clause was "designed to prevent arbitrary government action," not to protect economic value. Id., at 58-60.

petitioner Lucas' private benefit. One hopes they do not go beyond the narrow confines the Court assigns them to today. I dissent.

JUSTICE STEVENS, DISSENTING.

...II. In its analysis of the merits, the Court starts from the premise that this Court has adopted a "categorical rule that total regulatory takings must be compensated," and then sets itself to the task of identifying the exceptional cases in which a State may be relieved of this categorical obligation. The test the Court announces is that the regulation must do no more than duplicate the result that could have been achieved under a State's nuisance law. Ante, at 24. Under this test the categorical rule will apply unless the regulation merely makes explicit what was otherwise an implicit limitation on the owner's property rights.

In my opinion, the Court is doubly in error. The categorical rule the Court establishes is an unsound and unwise addition to the law and the Court's formulation of the exception to that rule is too rigid and too narrow.

THE CATEGORICAL RULE

As the Court recognizes, Pennsylvania Coal Co. v. Mahon, 260 U.S. 393 (1922), provides no support for its-or, indeed, any-categorical rule. To the contrary, Justice Holmes recognized that such absolute rules ill fit the inquiry into "regulatory takings." Thus, in the paragraph that contains his famous observation that a regulation may go "too far" and thereby constitute a taking, the Justice wrote: "As we already have said, this is a question of degree-and therefore cannot be disposed of by general propositions." Id. at 416. What he had "already...said" made perfectly clear that Justice Holmes regarded economic injury to be merely one factor to be weighed: "One fact for consideration in determining such limits is the extent of the diminution [of value.] So the question depends upon the particular facts." Id. at 413.

Nor does the Court's new categorical rule find support in decisions following Mahon. Although in dicta we have sometimes recited that a law "effects a taking if [it]...denies an owner economically viable use of his land," Agins v. Tiburon, 447 U.S. 255, 260 (1980), our rulings have rejected such an absolute position. We have frequently and recently-held that, in some circumstances, a law that renders property valueless may nonetheless not constitute a taking. See, e.g., First English Evangelical Lutheran Church of Glendale v. County of Los Angeles, 482 U.S. 304, 313 (1987); Goldblatt v. Hempstead, 369 U.S. 590, 596 (1962); United States v. Caltex, 344 U.S. 149, 155 (1952); Miller v. Schoene, 276 U.S. 272 (1928); Hadachek v. Sebastian, 239 U.S. 394, 405 (1915); Mugler v. Kansas, 123 U.S. 623, 657 (1887); cf. Ruckelshaus v. Monsanto Co., 467 U.S. 986, 1011 (1984); Connolly v. Pension Benefit Guaranty Corporation, 475 U.S. 211, 225 (1986). In short, as we stated in Keystone Bituminous Coal Assn. v. DeBenedictis, 480 U.S. 470, 490 (1987), " 'Although a comparison of values before and after' a regulatory action 'is relevant,...it is by no means conclusive." '

In addition to lacking support in past decisions, the Court's new rule is wholly arbitrary. A landowner whose property is diminished in value 95% recovers nothing, while an owner whose property is diminished 100% recovers the land's full value. The case at hand illustrates this arbitrariness well. The Beachfront Management Act not only prohibited the building of new dwellings in certain areas, it also prohibited the rebuilding of houses that were "destroyed beyond repair by natural causes or by fire." 1988 S. C. Acts 634, §3; see also Esposito v. South Carolina Coastal Council, 939 F. 2d 165, 167 (CA4 1991). Thus, if the homes adjacent to Lucas' lot were destroyed by a hurricane one day after the Act took effect, the owners would not be able to rebuild, nor would they be assured recovery. Under the Court's categorical approach, Lucas (who has lost the opportunity to build) recovers, while his neighbors (who have lost both the opportunity to build and their homes) do not recover. The arbitrariness of such a rule is palpable....

Moreover, because of the elastic nature of property rights, the Court's new rule will also prove unsound in practice. In response to the rule, courts may define "property" broadly and only rarely find regulations to effect total takings. This is the approach the Court itself adopts in its revisionist reading of venerable precedents. We are told that-notwithstanding the Court's findings to the contrary in each case-the brewery in Mugler, the brickyard in Hadacheck, and the gravel pit in Goldblatt all could be put to "other uses" and that, therefore, those cases did not involve total regulatory takings.

On the other hand, developers and investors may market specialized estates to take advantage of the Court's new rule. The smaller the estate, the more likely that a regulatory change will effect a total taking. Thus, an investor may, for example, purchase the right to build a multi-family home on a specific lot, with the result that a zoning regulation that allows only single-family homes would render the investor's property interest "valueless." In short, the categorical rule will likely have one of two effects: Either courts will alter the definition of the "denominator" in the takings "fraction," rendering the Court's categorical rule meaningless, or investors will manipulate the relevant property interests, giving the Court's rule sweeping effect. To my mind, neither of these results is desirable or appropriate, and both are distortions of our takings jurisprudence.

Finally, the Court's justification for its new categorical rule is remarkably thin. The Court mentions in passing three arguments in support of its rule; none is convincing. First, the Court suggests that "total deprivation of feasible use is, from the landowner's point of view, the equivalent of a physical appropriation." Ante, at 12. This argument proves too much. From the "landowner's point of view," a regulation that diminishes a lot's value by 50% is as well "the equivalent" of the condemnation of half of the lot. Yet, it is well established that a 50% diminution in value does not by itself constitute a taking. See Euclid v. Ambler Realty Co., 272 U.S. 365, 384 (1926) (75% diminution in value). Thus, the landowner's perception of the regulation cannot justify the Court's new rule....

In short, the Court's new rule is unsupported by prior decisions, arbitrary and unsound in practice, and theoretically unjustified. In my opinion, a categorical rule as important as the one established by the Court today should be supported by more history or more reason than has yet been provided.

THE NUISANCE EXCEPTION

Like many bright-line rules, the categorical rule established in this case is only "categorical" for a case or two in the U.S. Reports. No sooner does the Court state that "total regulatory takings must be compensated," ante, at 21, than it quickly establishes an exception to that rule.

The exception provides that a regulation that renders property valueless is not a taking if it prohibits uses of property that were not "previously permissible under relevant property and nuisance principles." Ante, at 24. The Court thus rejects the basic holding in Mugler v. Kansas, 123 U.S. 623 (1887). There we held that a state-wide statute that prohibited the owner of a brewery from making alcoholic beverages did not effect a taking, even though the use of the property had been perfectly lawful and caused no public harm before the statute was enacted....

The Court's holding today effectively freezes the State's common law, denying the legislature much of its traditional power to revise the law governing the rights and uses of property. Until today, I had thought that we had long abandoned this approach to constitutional law. More than a century ago we recognized that "the great office of statutes is to remedy defects in the common law as they are developed, and to adapt it to the changes of time and circumstances." Munn v. Illinois, 94 U.S. 113, 134 (1877). As Justice Marshall observed about a position similar to that adopted by the Court today: "If accepted, that claim would represent a return to the era of Lochner v. New York, 198 U.S. 45 (1905), when common-law rights were also found immune from revision by State or Federal Government. Such an approach would freeze the common law as it has been constructed by the courts, perhaps at its 19th- century state of development. It would allow no room for change in response to changes in circumstance. The Due Process Clause does not require such a result." PruneYard Shopping Center v. Robins, 447 U.S. 74, 93 (1980) (concurring opinion).

Arresting the development of the common law is not only a departure from our prior decisions; it is also profoundly unwise. The human condition is one of constant learning and evolution-both moral and practical. Legislatures implement that new learning; in doing so they must often revise the definition of property and the rights of property owners. Thus, when the Nation came to understand that slavery was morally wrong and mandated the emancipation of all slaves, it, in effect, redefined "property." On a lesser scale, our ongoing self-education produces similar changes in the rights of property owners: New appreciation of the significance of endangered species, see, e.g., Andrus v. Allard, 444 U.S. 51 (1979); the importance of wetlands, see, e.g., 16 U.S. C. §3801 et seq.; and the vulnerability of coastal lands, see, e.g., 16 U.S. C. §1451 et seq., shapes our evolving understandings of property rights.

Of course, some legislative redefinitions of property will effect a taking and must be compensated – but it certainly cannot be the case that every movement away from common law does so. There is no reason, and less sense, in such an absolute rule. We live in a world in which changes in the economy and the environment occur with increasing frequency and importance. If it was wise a century ago to allow Government " 'the largest legislative discretion" ' to deal with " 'the special exigencies of the moment," ' Mugler, 123 U.S., at 669, it is imperative to do so today. The rule that should govern a decision in a case of this kind should focus on the future, not the past. [76]The Court's categorical approach rule will, I fear, greatly hamper the efforts of local officials and planners who must deal with increasingly complex problems in land-use and environmental regulation. As this case-in which the claims of an individual property owner exceed $1 million-well demonstrates, these officials face both substantial uncertainty because of the ad hoc nature of takings law and unacceptable penalties if they guess incorrectly about that law....

III. It is well established that a takings case "entails inquiry into [several factors:] the character of the governmental action, its economic impact, and its interference with reasonable investment-backed expectations." PruneYard, 447 U.S., at 83. The Court's analysis today focuses on the last two of these three factors: the categorical rule addresses a regulation's "economic impact," while the nuisance exception recognizes that ownership brings with it only certain "expectations." Neglected by the Court today is the first, and in some ways, the most important factor in takings analysis: the character of the regulatory action....

In analyzing takings claims, courts have long recognized the difference between a regulation that targets one or two parcels of land and a regulation that enforces a state-wide policy....

The impact of the ban on developmental uses must also be viewed in light of the purposes of the Act. The legislature stated the purposes of the Act as "protect[ing], preserv[ing], restor[ing] and enhanc[ing] the beach/dune system" of the State not only for recreational and ecological purposes, but also to "protec[t] life and property." S. C. Code §48-39-260(1)(a) (Supp. 1990). The State, with much science on its side, believes that the "beach/dune system [acts] as a buffer from high tides, storm surge, [and] hurricanes." This is a traditional and important exercise of the State's police power, as demonstrated by Hurricane Hugo, which in 1989, caused 29 deaths and more than $6 billion in property damage in South Carolina alone.

In view of all of these factors, even assuming that petitioner's property was rendered valueless, the risk inherent in investments of the sort made by petitioner, the generality of the Act, and the compelling purpose motivating the South Carolina Legislature persuade me that the Act did not effect a taking of petitioner's property. Accordingly, I respectfully dissent.-

STATEMENT OF JUSTICE SOUTER. I would dismiss the writ of certiorari in this case as having been granted improvidently. After briefing and argument it is abundantly clear that an unreviewable assumption on which this case comes to us is both questionable as a conclusion of Fifth Amendment law and sufficient to frustrate the Court's ability to render certain the legal premises on which its holding rests.

---

[76] Even measured in terms of efficiency, the Court's rule is unsound. The Court today effectively establishes a form of insurance against certain changes in land-use regulations. Like other forms of insurance, the Court's rule creates a "moral hazard" and inefficiencies: In the face of uncertainty about changes in the law, developers will overinvest, safe in the knowledge that if the law changes adversely, they will be entitled to compensation. See generally Farber, Economic Analysis and Just Compensation, 12 Int'l Rev. of Law & Econ. 125 (1992).

The petition for review was granted on the assumption that the state by regulation had deprived the owner of his entire economic interest in the subject property. Such was the state trial court's conclusion, which the state supreme court did not review. It is apparent now that in light of our prior cases,... the trial court's conclusion is highly questionable....

Because the questionable conclusion of total deprivation cannot be reviewed, the Court is precluded from attempting to clarify the concept of total (and, in the Court's view, categorically compensable) taking on which it rests, a concept which the Court describes, see ante, at 11 n. 6, as so uncertain under existing law as to have fostered inconsistent pronouncements by the Court itself. Because that concept is left uncertain, so is the significance of the exceptions to the compensation requirement that the Court proceeds to recognize. This alone is enough to show that there is little utility in attempting to deal with this case on the merits....

The Court will be understood to suggest...that there are in fact circumstances in which state-law nuisance abatement may amount to a denial of all beneficial land use as that concept is to be employed in our takings jurisprudence under the Fifth and Fourteenth Amendments. The nature of nuisance law, however, indicates that application of a regulation defensible on grounds of nuisance prevention or abatement will quite probably not amount to a complete deprivation in fact. The nuisance enquiry focuses on conduct, not on the character of the property on which that conduct is performed.... Under these circumstances, I believe it proper for me to vote to dismiss the writ....

COMMENTARY AND QUESTIONS

1. Environmental policy: back off from challenging the sea.

> Everyone who hears these words of mine and does not put
> them into practice is like a foolish man who builds his house on
> sand. The rains come down, the streams rise, and the winds
> blow, and it falls with a great crash. *Matthew 7:26-27*

The modern real estate market's drive to develop prime residential housing on the barrier beaches of the U.S. has led to a series of disasters but no diminution of the building boom. The rate of building on our coastal beaches is five times greater than on inland locations. The threat of hurricane wipeouts is blunted by federally-subsidized flood hazard insurance that provides a base for mortgage financing that otherwise would not exist. (The insurance requires that localities be zoned with storm and erosion setback regulations, but the model regulations provide for variances where enforcement would impose economic burdens.) The obvious wise policy in confronting the inevitable onslaughts of coastal storms is not to stake out private property development lines at the shifting fragile edge of the seacoast, but to manage a measured retreat from the confrontation with nature. See Hearings on H.R. 5981 to establish a Barrier Islands Protection System, Before the Subcommittee on National Parks and Insular Affairs, 96th Cong. 2d Sess., March 1980.

And in eco-economic terms, what would the commercial market value of Mr. Lucas's million-dollar property be if it were not for the massive public subsidies that the real estate industry lobbied for and now takes for granted? Subtract from market value the amounts attributable to subsidized flood insurance; highway, causeway, and bridge construction and reconstruction; linear barrier beach extension of sewer and utilities; beach re-nourishment and beach protection; rescue operations; disaster aid; reconstruction financing; and the like, and the willingness of banks to finance and buyers to pay for risky barrier beach locations would drop to very little. See Siffin, Bureaucracy, Entrepreneurship, and Natural Resources: Witless Policy and the Barrier Islands, 1 Cato Journal (1981)(cataloguing the remarkable list of federal subsidies obtained by barrier beach developers). But the constitutional calculus apparently cannot offset public elements in private property value, and must use full market value as the constitutional starting point. The political process could cut the subsidies, or require that they be weighed in the procedures proposed in various Wise Use property rights bills but the political forces involved in subsidies make this highly unlikely.

2. On reading *Lucas*. The *Lucas* case is a vast, rich accumulation of takings jurisprudence that by itself will undoubtedly be the basis of semester-long law school seminars. The full, unedited text of the various *Lucas* opinions totals 75 pages.

Behind the pitched arguments about what substantive takings tests should apply to property value wipeouts – and subsidiary questions like whether this action was truly "ripe" for review, whether the land was truly valueless, and how much a federal court should defer to the findings of state legislatures and supreme courts – lie a concatenation of judicial politics. Has this majority overthrown the *Keystone Bituminous* majority? Is *Lucas* an assertion of the prior decade's Meese-Sununu judicial agenda? Why was certiorari granted in this case and not to *First English* after the California court had upheld that wipeout on remand? Does the majority decide this case as an extraordinary exception, where there is a total wipeout, or is it setting a test to encourage wider invalidations of regulatory restrictions? Would the votes have been quite different if it had not be such an extreme case? Does the harsh rhetoric of some of the exchanges evidence a breakdown in the Rehnquist Court's erstwhile attempts to maintain collegial respect?

Like many legal cases, this one could also support several screenplays.

3. The Takings Test after *Lucas*. What if anything has changed after *Lucas*? If it is quite clear that there was no categorical "bright line" test for regulatory takings before *Lucas* (is it?[77]), is there one now? ["categorical" means "admitting of no exceptions."] A major caveat was built into the test by Justice Scalia at the paragraph ending with original footnote 16 –

---

[77]. Justice Scalia says the Court had previously found categorical treatment appropriate in two situations, where there is "physical invasion" and "where regulation denies all economically beneficial or productive use of land." But even some physical invasions have been held noncompensable, U.S. v. Caltex, 344 U.S. 149, 155 (1994), and no case had ever held that denials of all economic value were categorically void. When Scalia cites *Agins*, "As we have said on numerous occasions, the Fifth Amendment is violated when land-use regulation '...denies an owner economically viable use of his land,'" he leaves off the modifier in *Agins* that applies this dictum only to zoning, where public harms are not measurable, rather than to land use regulations generally.

> Any limitation [for which a wipeout is nevertheless valid]
> cannot be newly legislated or decreed without compensation,
> but must inhere in the title itself, in the restrictions that
> background principles of the State's law of property and
> nuisance already place upon land ownership...[as] could have
> been achieved in the courts...under the State's law of private
> nuisance, or [a state's] complementary power to abate
> nuisances that affect the public generally, or otherwise.

But what does this mean? Are the common law precedents existing as of the date of this opinion the limit? What's this "otherwise," beyond the extreme examples given inthe footnote?

Here is a way to test what *Lucas* means: Would Justice Scalia, based on his *Lucas* reasoning, have held that Los Angeles County had to pay the First English corporation full market value for the flood hazard restrictions in *First English*, coursebook at 467, if it wanted to prevent the plaintiff from lodging 200 handicapped children in cabins in a floodway that had been completely destroyed by flashfloods several years before? Or what about regulations restricting construction on earthquake faults? (See Scalia in *Lucas* after fn 16, and coursebook at 466-467.) It would appear that the majority would not require compensation in such ludicrous cases, but why? The common law does not recognize flood jeopardy or earthquake location as a tort, so the Court must be adopting a flexible modern view of what constitutes "nuisance-like" restraints.

This re-imports judicial harm-weighing judgments into takings jurisprudence, and goes far beyond traditional common law. The only possible shift is of the burden of proof, but even this is not clear. If defining the property rights in the context of public harms is the basis of Scalia's test, then the state's public harm argument is not an exception to the new rule but an element of the takings challenge formula. Or if the state must prove the substantial existence of (a risk of) harm, how is that to be weighed in order to know whether it shifts the burden back to plaintiff? This is not a bright line test.

4. More baseline games. Does footnote 7 now re-open the baseline games? If I have a 100-acre parcel of land, two acres of which are restricted from any development because they are wetlands, have I suffered a 100% loss of those 2 acres or a 2% loss of the whole value? In Concrete Pipe & Products, Inc. v. Construction Laborers Pension Trust, 508 U. S.__(1993) the Supreme Court again held that "a claimant's parcel of property [cannot] first be divided into what was taken and what was left" in order to demonstrate a compensable taking. See also Tull v. Virginia, U.S. Supp. Ct. No. 92-122 (cert. denied, 1992). In Pennell v. San Jose, 108 S. Ct. 849 (1988) (saying that a rent control ordinance that makes one particular apartment in a larger complex uneconomic is not thereby shown to be a taking), Justice Rehnquist adopted, at least for that case, the view that an alleged taking loss is to be viewed over the entire property holding. The Court of Claims and the Federal Circuit, however, have tended to follow the Rehnquist dissent's baseline argument, narrowing the takings baseline to the regulated portion of the property. See Loveladies Harbor v. U.S., __F.3d__, 1994 WL 259489 (Fed. Cir. 1994). In *Loveladies*, the developer had sold off most of a parcel of more than 300 acres for a substantial profit in the years immediately prior to the regulation. The Federal Circuit decided that the baseline was the remaining 12 regulated wetlands acres alone, and thus the regulation was an invalid takings.

Another interesting post-*Lucas* case, applying the *Keystone Bituminous* holding that diminution is to be viewed across the entire relevant property, not just the regulated portion, injects a new market share twist. In Naegele Outdoor Advertising, Inc. v. City of Durham, 803 F. Supp. 1068 (DMD N.C., 1992), the court held that where an advertising company would lose all use of 106 of its 232 billboards in the city of Durham because of a sign regulation ordinance, the proper baseline was not each individual billboard, but the larger market share of Naegele's billboard business in the city of Durham. The court found that the plaintiff had lost only 46% of its billboards in the relevant market viewed as a whole, and that of that 46%, amortization provisions would allow substantial recoupment of some of the value over time. (Thus *Naegele* is not a total wipeout case.) Losses from the regulation would reduce Naegele's revenue by about 30% in the overall market area, and on careful balance that was held to be no taking. If the "relevant" property had been defined on the other hand as individual billboards, it is quite clear that many if not all of the regulated billboards, would have been found to have suffered unconstitutional taking, so the baseline definition game continues to be a fundamental element under the traditional diminution tests.

And what about the *time* baseline? In *Keystone Bituminous*, for example, assume the company had bought the land for $500,000 twenty years before the regulation, and made $200 million profit from the coal over that time, during which time most of the coal had been excavated except for the final "pillars," removal of which would destroy homes and resources on the surface: Is the constitutional "reasonable beneficial use" or "economically viable use" to be measured only by profits earnable *after* the regulation that is passed in order to prevent incipient harm? Does each parcel of property have a perpetual right to profit in the face of regulation? See the note on amortization at the end of this Supplement chapter. As in *Loveladies*, noted above, doesn't the concept of "investment-backed expectations" act to define the time baseline in terms of economic recovery of the original investment, not just post-regulation profits?

5. What's a wipeout? Among the questions that *Lucas* stirs up but doesn't resolve is the question "when is property value wiped out?" In fact, although the Court chose to accept the trial judge's finding that the land was "valueless," it is almost impossible to believe that Lucas's seafront lots, and any other parcel in the land for that matter, had absolutely no market value remaining.

In future cases, when will courts be able to find that there has been a total wipeout so as to apply *Lucas*, or will that never be possible? In original footnote 7, Justice Scalia says—

> When...a regulation requires a developer to leave 90% of a rural tract in its natural state, it is unclear whether we would analyze the situation as one in which the owner has been deprived of all economically beneficial use of the burdened portion of the tract, or as one in which the owner has suffered a mere diminution in value of the tract as a whole.

Thus the definition of the term "valueless" is more expansive than "having no value," and Scalia may have opened the door for subjective extensions of his categorical rule by the federal judiciary to property restriction cases far less pronounced than *Lucas*.

And does footnote 7 now re-open the baseline games? If I have a 150-acre parcel of land, two acres of which are restricted against any development because they are wetlands, haven't I suffered a 100% loss of those two acres? See Tull v. Virginia, US SupCt, No. 92-112.

6. Plant a seed... Notice also the offhand comment early in the Scalia opinion that, whereas most regulations are presumed valid, this case is an exception to

> our usual assumption that the legislature is simply "adjusting
> the benefits and burdens of economic life" *Penn Central*, 438
> U.S., at 124, in a manner that secures an "average reciprocity
> of advantage" to everyone concerned. *Pennsylvania Coal*, 260
> U.S., at 415.

Does this formulation imply that regulations are presumed valid *because they are presumed to give regulatees roughly as much benefit as burden*, and if they *don't*, they will be void? This tactic was tried by Justice Rehnquist in dissent in Keystone Bituminous, and would eliminate virtually all government regulation, which by definition enforces public policy by laying rule burdens on selected regulated interests. The cases he cites use the concept as further support for validity, not as a test of invalidity. See coursebook at 464.

7. The story behind the story. Do you detect an attempt by Justice Blackmun to raise skepticism about Mr. Lucas's bona fides? Lucas was portrayed in the media as just like any other private citizen who wanted to build a home for himself and his family and another for resale and got steamrolled by government. Lucas plunked down almost a million bucks for the two lots. This apparently was the highest price ever paid for lots in the Beachwood subdivision of the Wild Dunes development. Yet Lucas had been intimately associated with that development since 1979, having served as a contractor, a realtor, and as an assistant in planning to the Wild Dunes developer. (see trial transcript at 24, 33-34.) Is it likely that such insiders normally wait until the last, so as to be able to pay top dollar for a lot? And then for 19 months, from December 1986 until passage of the new act in June 1988, Lucas did nothing with the land, except, presumptively, paying approximately $10,000 a month in payments of interest charges and principal. (In media interviews, Lucas complained about his payments for taxes and insurance, but did not mention that he was paying any carrying charges on his property.) Was the case a put-up job, trying to create a good test case for the privateering "wise-use" movement? Does it matter?

Lucas on Remand

On remand to the Supreme Court of South Carolina there was a five-month hiatus as the parties waited for the court to hold a preliminary hearing defining the issues to be addressed on remand. When the hearing was finally held in October, however, the court moved to immediate oral argument to consider the merits without briefs. The court's major inquiry appears to have been whether there was any South Carolina nuisance case directly on point, on the issue of beach construction, and otherwise how damages should be assessed. Shortly after the oral hearing, in November 1992, the court released the following decision.

David H. Lucas v. South Carolina Coastal Council
Supreme Court of South Carolina, 1992
424 S.E.2d 484

... The United States Supreme Court reversed our opinion on June 29, 1992... rul[ing] that Coastal Council had advanced no State interest sufficient to justify the total regulatory taking of Lucas's land, and that, in fact, "where the State seeks to sustain regulation that deprives land of all economically beneficial use, ...it may resist compensation only if the logically antecedent inquiry into the nature of the owner's estate shows that the proscribed use interests were not part of his title to begin with. The Court remanded this issue to allow Coastal Council the opportunity to "identify background principles of nuisance and property law" by which Lucas could be restrained from constructing a habitable structure on his land.

The inquiry does not end here. The Court also noted that, pursuant to the 1990 Act, Lucas may apply for a special permit to build seaward of the baseline. Clearly, Lucas has been only temporarily deprived of the use of his land if he can obtain a special permit to construct habitable structures on his lots. The Court discerned, however, that our decision to dispose of the case on its merits "practically and legally" had precluded Lucas from asserting a claim with respect to his having been temporarily deprived of the right to build prior to the 1990 Act. Indeed, absent the Court's intervention and reversal, Lucas would have been unable to obtain further state-court adjudication with respect to a temporary taking. Accordingly, the remand of this case from the United States Supreme Court has created for Lucas a cause of action for the temporary deprivation of the use of his property, unless Coastal Council can demonstrate that Lucas's intended use of his land was not part of the bundle of rights inhering in his title.

We have reviewed the record and heard arguments from the parties regarding whether Coastal Council possesses the ability under the common law to prohibit Lucas from constructing a habitable structure on his land. Coastal Council has not persuaded us that any common law basis exists by which it could restrain Lucas's desired use of his land; nor has our research uncovered any such common law principle. We hold that the sole issue on remand from this Court to the circuit level is a determination of the actual damages Lucas has sustained as the result of his being temporarily deprived of the use of his property.

In this regard, we grant leave to the parties to amend their pleadings and present evidence of the actual damages Lucas has sustained as a result of the State's temporary nonacquisitory taking of his property without just compensation. We direct the trial judge to make specific findings of damages appropriate to compensate Lucas for his temporary deprivation of the use of his property. To this end, we do not dictate any specific method of calculating the damages for the temporary nonacquisitory taking. We do find, however, that because Lucas was unable to assert a temporary taking claim until the United States Supreme Court overturned our prior disposition of the case, and because Lucas has been unable to act pending our order on remand, that Lucas has suffered a temporary taking deserving of compensation commencing with the enactment of the 1988 Act and continuing through the date of this Order.

We are aware that, once Lucas applies for a special permit pursuant to the 1990 Act, Coastal Council could deny the special permit or place such restrictions on the permit that Lucas might contend a subsequent unconstitutional taking has occurred. We emphasize that this Order is made without prejudice to the right of the parties to litigate any subsequent deprivations which may arise as the result of Coastal Council's actions in regard to the granting or non-granting of a special permit for future construction.

COMMENTARY AND QUESTIONS

1. *Lucas* on Remand. The Supreme Court required a balance considering "background principles of the State's law of property and nuisance." The South Carolina Court holds that "Coastal Council has not persuaded us that any common law basis exists by which it could restrain *Lucas's* desired use of his land...." Coastal Council had argued that there were injuries in the nature of public and private nuisance on which it wished to go to trial or have further hearings. By refusing councils request, the South Carolina Court apparently was interpreting Justice Scalia command as requiring pre-existing defined nuisances in the state of South Carolina's caselaw dealing with barrier beaches. Such a truncated review would, of course, similarly reveal that most states caselaws did not have nuclear power plant nuisance cases on the books, nor flood plain construction as a nuisance and abatable nuisance, both examples that Justice Scalia gave of situations where nuisance like principles would justify wipe out regulations. The Coastal Council obviously wishes it had the opportunity to present evidence of the natural functions fulfilled by barrier beaches uncluttered by human structures, as Professor Sax would argue is part of the traditional balance as well as the new balance he advocates.

Is it strange that the South Carolina court explicitly recognized that *Lucas* dealt with the pre-1990 statute, and that there would have to be a new judicial hearing for any denial under the 1990 act? Presumptively wouldn't their conclusion that no South Carolina precedents were available to support regulation in the first case foreclose a defense of regulatory validity in the latter?

Notice also that the South Carolina court ignored the word "property" in Scalia's crucial caveat quoted above. Considering state concepts of property law would presumptively have allowed the court to weigh public trust rights as part of the balance of property rights in the Atlantic barrier beach foreshore. Justice Scalia's opinion invites continued definition of public trust rights as an integral part of the balance he calls for in *Lucas*.

2. Other readings of *Lucas* . Beyond South Carolina, other state supreme courts post- *Lucas* have not generally reflected dramatic shifts in the takings balance. In New Hampshire, where septic field regulation was used to substantially reduce the developability of the property owners

lakefront subdivided lots, eliminating one of them completely from development, the court held that–

> This regulation is rationally related to the protection of public health, and deprived land owners of no reasonable uses of their land. We find no constitutional defect in a regulation that seeks to prevent development which poses an "exceptional danger to health." Such a regulation would not exceed tort and property law restrictions even if it were applied to deprive an owner of all economically viable use of his or her land [citing *Lucas*].... Even in the absence of state regulation, no land owner has the right to use his or her property so as to injure others." Smith et al. v. Town of Wolfeboro, 615 A. 2d 1252 (N.H., 1992).

3. On the beach. Almost immediately after the remand decision, David Lucas applied for permission to develop his lots under the amended act. The request was quickly granted by the Council, in effect acknowledging that although theoretically a whole new review was possible, this case had been won by Lucas. Shortly thereafter, on July 7, to forestall Lucas's claims for attorneys fees and temporary takings damages, the Council negotiated a lump sum settlement, including purchase of Lucas's two lots, for a total payout of $1.575 million, apportioned at $425 thousand per lot and $725 thousand for "interim interest, attorney's fees, and costs."

Adding to the intimations of disingenuity abounding in this case, it has been reported that the state, having been forced in effect to buy the two Lucas lots, has thereafter felt financially-impelled to re-sell them at market value, for residential construction.

PAGE 468   **Article, Professor Sax on *Lucas* and Nature**

Sax, Property Rights and the Economy of Nature: Understanding Lucas v. South Carolina Coastal Council
45 Stanford Law Review 1433, 1993[78]

I. INTRODUCTION A. THE SETTING OF *LUCAS* IN THE SUPREME COURT

There was every reason to expect 1992 to be a year of dramatic change in the constitutional law of takings, ...[but] in the end, out of four potentially significant takings cases[granted certiorari, the Court wrote an extensive and doctrinally significant opinion in only one: Lucas v. South Carolina Coastal Council.

I suspect that the Court is frustrated with the takings issue. It wants to affirm the importance of property, but it cannot find a standard that will control regulatory excess without threatening to bring down the whole regulatory apparatus of the modern state. This difficulty may explain the fate of most of the 1992 takings cases. The same problem may explain Justice Scalia's taste for a "categorical" approach, seizing on clear (if

---

[78] © 1993 by the Board of Trustees of Leland Stanford Junior University. Reprinted by permission of the copyright holder and the author.

formalistic) measures, such as physicial invasion or diminution of value, before providing compensation. However inadequate such standards may be, they do provide the Court with some means to address property claims and to respond to the most extreme state intrusions – interference with possession or total loss of value and only dealing with those that seem to involve excess, it conveys a message to regulators to withdraw from the frontiers and follow more conventional modes of regulation....

If I am correct in suggesting that the current Court intends to play a restrained role in the property area, how is Justice Scalia's aggressive opinion in *Lucas* to be understood? The case is not as far reaching as its rhetoruc suggests. It does not protect all who suffer a complete loss in their property's value, for the categorical 100 percent diminution rule itself is sharply limited. Regulation that would be sustained under established common law "principles" of nuisance and property law is not affected. Presumably, states will have substantial latitude in determining the extent to which their existing legal principles limit property rights. Moreover, Justice Scalia is careful to provide assurance that *Lucas* is not a threat to conventional industrial regulation, including environmental laws such as those dealing with pollution or toxicx disposal. Thus, despite its tone, *Lucas* appears consistent with the restraint the Court has generally exercised in taking cases....

What, then, is the majority's agenda in the *Lucas* case? I believe Justice Scalia felt that the case presented a new, fundamental issue in property law, and that he had a clear message which he sought to convey: States may not regulate land use solely by requiring landowners to maintain their property in its natural state as part of a functioning ecosystem, even though those natural functions may be important to the ecosystem. In this sense, while the *Lucas* majority recognizes the emerging view of land as a part of an ecosystem, rather than as purely private property, the Court seeks to limit the legal foundation for such a conception....

The target of *Lucas* is broader than its immediate concern of coastal dune maintenance; the opinion encompasses such matters as wetlands regulation, which recently has generated a great deal of controversial litigation. *Lucas* also anticipates cases that will be brought under section nine of the Endangered Species Act, under which private landowners may be required to leave theur land undisturbed as habitat. In general, *Lucas* addresses legislation imposed to maintain ecological services performed by land in its natural state. The Court correctly perceives that an ecological worldview presents a fundamental challenge to established property rights, but the Court incorrectly rejects that challenge....

To appreciate the significance of *Lucas*, it is necessary to understand how the majority interpeted the intent of the South Carolina law. The statutes was so broadly drawn that it could be viewed as having a number of purposes. South Carolina might have intended to prohibit construction in a hazardous zone because of the resulting dangers to others and the inevitable burden which would be imposed on the state in the event of a catastrophic event such as a hurricane or an earthquake. Although the Court doubts that this was the actual purpose of the South Carolina law, the *Lucas* opinion makes clear that such a purpose could be implemented through noncompensable regulation.

Alternatively, South Carolina may have designed the statute to ensure that beaches were left undeveloped in order to preserve a visual amenity for tourists. If so, the Court would surely have viewed the case as the compensable taking of a visual easement, similar to a nondevelopment easement alongside a scenic highway. the majority implies that it thinks that this was probably the actual purpose of the regulation.....

If the Beachfront Management Act's puspose were only one of the above two alternatives, *Lucas* would be of little consequence. Instead, a third possible interpretation exists, and the Court's response to it invests the decision with fundamental importance. This interpretation also clarifies Justice Scalia's otherwise perplexing majority opinion. The regulation might have arisen from a determination that Lucas' property – coastal dune land – was performing an important ecological service to uplands by functioning as a storm and erosion barrier. Therefor, maintenance of the land in its natural condition might have been ecologically necessary....

Justice Scalia viewed *Lucas* as a potential precedent for cases where regulations premised on maintenance of natural function diminished the value of private property. If the South Carolina regulation had been sustained, the decision would have constitutionalized a broad panoply of laws requiring landowners to leave their property in its natural condition. The opinion recognizes that, in the name of environmental protection, an entirely new sort of regulation could be imposed. To prevent such a resuly, the Court repudiates the conclusion.

The *Lucas* majority may have designed the seemingly odd ruling to isolate the ecological regulations which Justice Scalia seeks to illegitimate, without heoaprdizing mainstream regulations. The majority's nuisance exception illustrates this point. Justice Scalia surely knows that nuisance law is a slippery legal concept – it has been applied to everything from brothels to bowling on Sundays. His use of nuisance law, however, is neither stupid nor careless. He invokes nuisance principles to emphasize the difference between regulations which are designed to maintain land in its natural condition and regulations which embrace conventional police power. Rather than describe how property may be used – which is the traditional function of nuisance law – this new sort of environmental regulation effectively determines whether property may be used at all. Traditional nuisance law, however broadly construed, limited use. Its protection was wide-ranging, but it did not characterize property as having inherent public attributes which always trump the landowner's rights....

The peculiar distinction drawn between land and what the Court calls personal property seems to have the same goal.... Justice Scalia's view of traditional private property principles also explains his rejection of a harm/benefit distinction and his recognition that landowners have positive development rights....

Read this way, Justice Scalia's opinion emphasizes four points: (1) leaving land in its natural condition is in fundamental tension with the traditional goals of private property law; (2) once natural conditions are considered the baseline, any departure from them can be viewed as "harmful," since the essence of human use of land is interrupting the land's natural state; (3) if any disruption of natural conditions can be viewed as harmful (as surely they can), then natural conditions generally could be viewed as normal and could be demanded by the state; and (4) with that predicate, states could exercise their police power to maintain natural conditions, thereby eliminating the economic value of private property to it owner.

Justice Scalia's opinion raises two important questions.   Are environmental regulations that require maintenance of natural conditions significantly new and different from traditional regulations? If so, how should the law respond?

III.   There are two fundamentally different views of property rights to which I shall refer as land in the "transformative economy" and land in the "economy of nature." The conventional perspective of private property, the transformative economy, builds on the image of property as a discrete entity that can be made one's own by working it and transforming it into a human artifact. A piece of iron becomes an anvil, a tree becomes lumber, and a forest becomes a farm. Traditional property law treats undeveloped land as essentially inert. The land is there, it may have things on or in it (e.g., timber or coal), but it is in a passive state, waiting to be put to use. Insofar as land is "doing" something -- for example, harboring wild animals -- property law considers such functions expendable. Indeed, getting rid of the natural, or at least domesticating it, was a primary task of the European settlers of North America.

An ecological view of property, the economy of nature, is fundamentally different. Land is not a passive entity waiting to be transformed by its landowner. Nor is the world comprised of distinct tracts of land, separate pieces independent of each other. Rather, an ecological perspective views land as consisting of systems defined by their function, not by man-made boundaries. Land is already at work, performing important services in its unaltered state. For example, forests regulate the global climate, marshes sustain marine fisheries, and prairie grass holds the soil in place. Transformation diminishes the functioning of this economy and, in fact, is at odds with it.

The ecological perspective is founded on an economy of nature, while the transformative economy has a technological perspective of land as the product of human effort....

For most of the modern era, the technological use of land has operated to end "the existence of nature." Land has been fenced, excluding wildlife so that it could instead support domesticated grazing animals, agriculture, and human settlements.... The settlers' property system invested proprietors with the right to sever natural systems to turn land to "productive" use. Thus, the transformative economy was built on the eradication of the economy of nature.

Even when people acknowledged the toll of development on natural resources, giving birth to the conservation movement in the nineteenth century, there was virtually no impact on the precepts of property law. The concerns of conservation were then largely aesthetic, and ecological understanding was limited....

The burst of concern for controlling industrial pollution also failed to propel nature's economy onto the legal agenda. Conventional pollution laws do not challenge the traditional property system. They do not demand that adjacent land be treated as part of a river's riparian zone nor that it be left to perform natural functions supportive of the river as a marine ecosystem. On the contrary, such laws assume that a river and its adjacent tracts of land are separate entities and that the essential purpose of property law is to maintain their separateness.... Benefits that adjacent lands and waters confer upon each other can, with rare exceptions, be terminated at the will of the landowner, because the ecological contributions of adjacent properties are generally disregarded in defining legal rights....

Viewing land through the lens of nature's economy reduces the significance of property lines. Thus a wetland would be an adjunct of a river, in service to the river as a natural resource. Beach dune land would be the frontal region of a coastal ecosystem extending far beyond the beach itself. A forest would be a habitat for birds and wildlife, rather than simply a discrete tract of land containing the commodity timber. Under such a view the landowner cannot justify development by simply internalizing the effect of such development on other properties. Rather, the landowner's desire to do anything at all creates a problem, because any development affects the delicate ecosystem which the untouched land supports. In an economy of nature the landowner's role is perforce custodial at the outset, before the owner ever transforms the land. Moreover, the object of the custody generally extends beyond the owner's legally defined dominion. The notion that land is solely the owner's property, to develop as the owner pleases, is unacceptable.

This emerging ecological view generates not only a different sense of the appropriate level of development, but also a different attitude towards land and the nature of land ownership itself. The differences might be summarized as follows:

TRANSFORMATIVE ECONOMY	ECONOMY OF NATURE
Tracts are separate. Boundary lines are crucial.	Connections dominate. Ecological services determine land units.
Land is inert/waiting it is a subject of its owner's dominion.	Land is in service; it is part of a community where single ownership of an ecological service unit is rare.
Land use is governed by private will; any tract can be made into anything. All land is equal in use rights (Blackacre is any tract anywhere).	Land use is governed by ecological needs; land has a destiny, a role to play. Use rights are determined by physical nature (wetland, coastal barrier, wildlife habitat).
Landowners have no obligations	Landowners have a custodial, affirmative protective role for ecological functions.
Land has a single (transformative) purpose.	Land has a dual purpose, both transformative and ecological.
The line between public and private is clear.	The line between public and private is blurred where maintenance of ecological service is viewed as an owner's responsibility.

No matter whether these differences are characterized as qualitative or quantitative, the economy of nature greatly affects conceptions of owner entitlement -- an issue that Justice Scalia correctly discerned beneath the surface of *Lucas* .

Although the majority opinion recognizes the differences between a transformative economy and an economy of nature, it rejects the demands of the economy of nature as legitimate obligations of land and of landowners. As suggested above, all the seeming oddities of the opinion -- the distinction between land and personal property, the total loss requirement, the novel nuisance test, the elimination of the harm/benefit distinction, the focus on historical use, and the requirement that restrictions be in the "title to begin with" -- can best be viewed as doctrinal devices which separate the demands of the transformational economy from those of the economy of nature.

The majority opinion correctly recognizes that a fundamental redefinition of property was possible in *Lucas* . In this light, *Lucas* represents the Court's rejection of pleas to engraft the values of the economy of nature onto traditional notions of the rights of land ownership. Justice Scalia assumes that redefinition of property rights to accommodate ecosystem demands is not possible. The Court treats claims that land be left in its natural condition as unacceptable impositions on landowners. By characterizing the demands of the economy of nature as pressing "private property into some form of public service," the Court fails to recognize that lands in a state of nature are already in public service but to a purpose that the Court is unwilling to acknowledge.

Given that the economy of nature is emerging as a prominent viewpoint, the Court should have asked whether notions of property law could be reformulated to accommodate ecological needs without impairing the necessary functions of the transformational economy.

Historically, property definitions have continuously adjusted to reflect new economic and social structures, often to the disadvantage of existing owners....

[Professor Sax then discusses the process by which the legal system can continue to integrate changing public conceptions of rights, continuing arguments in the coursebook text at 406ff.]

COMMENTARY AND QUESTIONS

1. Professor Sax's views of *Lucas*. In Professor Sax's article, the Court's agenda in *Lucas* is viewed as an attempt to forestall a necessary, naturally-evolving trend in the definition of private and public rights in property. Justice Scalia, on the other hand, would probably regard the idea of shifting the property paradigm toward an economy of nature as a fluffy-headed abandonment of the major premise of the American economy. As to Sax's analysis of the fundamental differences between "economy of nature" characterizations of land rights and the "transformative economy" perspective (which might be more ascerbically termed the "short-term developmentalist" or "free-standing-property-rights-in-a-vacuum" view), it is likely that the current federal judiciary will be in no hurry to acknowledge such a shift in existing conventional wisdom. Sax emphasizes, however, that the doctrinal distinctions that Justice Scalia attempts to establish – an inelastic nuisance definition, avoidance of harm/benefit analyses, and the inappositeness of personal property analogies – can not achieve clear categorical lines. Scalia's complex escape clauses invite and require further articulation whenever they are to be applied. If the values that a legislature is attempting to implement through environmental regulations can be made tangible through nuisance, public trust, or other concepts relevant to public rights, Professor Sax's description of where the law is likely to go may indeed be part of the continuing caselaw, especially if, as he implicitly argues, the functions of nature are undeniably real and inescapable to the health and progress of the ecosystem in which human species presently play such a dominant role.

2. A functional economy of nature, and public trust doctrines. Remarkably, in his analysis of public rights to functioning natural systems Professor Sax virtually fails to mention the public trust doctrines that he was so instrumental in bringing to our collective jurisprudential consciousness. Cf. 45 Stan. L. Rev. 1452 n. 90.

Note, however, how public trust precedents can provide rationale and support for public regulations that effectively hold land in a nondeveloped state. The public trust cases apparently developed out of concepts of utilitarian societal necessity, and it would be surprising, especially in light of the Supreme Court's re-emphasis in weighing regulations' validity in *Lucas* (in Chapter 9) upon "background principles of *property* and tort law..." which presumably include public trust law.

PAGE 474   **Update: exactions in the Supreme Court — Text replacement for §(c) Exactions**

Section C.   Exactions in the Supreme Court: *Nollan* and *Dolan*

Physical appropriations by the public, as opposed to mere regulatory prohibitions, are virtually always a taking. See Loretto v. Teleprompter, 458 U.S. 419 (1982). In many so-called "exaction" cases, however, government regulations have been upheld when they required regulated landowners to provide free property for public parks, or public schools, or roadways, and the like, for public ownership and use, in return for getting development permits, as in subdivision regulation and urban "linkage" programs.

In Nollan v. California Coastal Comm'n, 483 U.S. 825 (1987), the California Coastal Commission had denied the owners of a 1/10th acre lot permission to expand their seashore cabin into a three-bedroom home unless they allowed members of the public using the beach to walk alongside the Nollan's' seawall. The Commission said it needed this right-of-way easement for pedestrian passage along the rocky coastline, because without it beachgoers would not have a "visual access" visibly linking public sandy beaches north and south of the Nollan's property.[79]

79.. This is as hard to visualize as it was to litigate. Apparently the state commission argued that, lacking a declared easement, beachgoers looking along the shore to the next beach would see only private cabins, seawalls, and rocks coming down to the edge of the sea, and would not realize that there was actually an existing narrow path through the rocks on public property (below the high water mark) along the shore linking the two beaches. By opening up a declared easement, the implied visual barrier would be eliminated.

In *Nollan*, the Supreme Court struck down the exaction, but held that exactions in general are valid if they (a) occur in a case where the government could constitutionally have denied the entire permit application outright,[80] and (b) if there is a sufficient relationship between the exaction and the regulation — in effect to assure that the exaction is not arbitrary extortion. The definition of this latter "sufficient relationship" was and is the difficult part.

Writing for the Court, Justice Scalia did not question the first step. The Commission apparently could validly have prohibited the application outright because the Nollans had a reasonable remaining use of the cabin as it was. But he rejected the second step:

> The evident constitutional propriety disappears...if the condition substituted for the prohibition utterly fails to further the end advanced as the justification for the prohibition. When that essential nexus is eliminated, [the exaction is void].... Unless the permit condition serves the same governmental purpose as the development ban, the building restriction is not a valid regulation of land use but "an out-and-out plan of extortion...." It is quite impossible to understand how a requirement that people already on public beaches be able to walk across the Nollans' property reduces any obstacles to viewing the beach created by the new house.... 483 U.S. at 837-38. [Police power restrictions on property rights must constitute] a "'*substantial* advanc[e]'of a legitimate state interest." Id. at 841, (emph. in original).

In *Nollan*, Scalia found there was not a sufficient relationship between the purpose of the regulation (regulation of coastal density, access to the ocean, etc.) and the required lateral easement. He indicated that if the exaction had been to require an easement of visual access across Nollan's property *to* the beach from the shore road, that might well have been sufficiently related and OK. Id. at 836.

Notice the ambiguity in Scalia's different phrasings. What is the "essential nexus"? Must the exaction —

- just relate to the *purpose* of the police power regulation,

- relate to burdens that would be directly created and imposed upon the public by the proposed development,

- or both,

and must there be a finding that the benefit of the exaction is "substantial," or even more?

In the 1994 *Dolan* case, the Supreme Court seized the opportunity to tighten the terms of how much nexus had to be shown in exactions:

---

80. "The Commission argues that a permit condition that serves the same legitimate police-power purpose as a refusal to issue the permit should not be found to be a taking if the refusal to issue the permit would not constitute a taking. We agree." 483 U.S. at 836.

Florence Dolan v. City Of Tigard
Supreme Court of the United States, 1994
__ U.S. __, No. 93-518, 1994 WL 276693

[The city, acting through its Land Use Board of Appeals (LUBA), gave petitioners a permit to double the size of their electric and plumbing supply store and to expand their parking lot, but required as exaction conditions that they dedicate roughly 10% of their land within the 100-year floodplain for a recreational low-density "greenway" flood area and improvement of storm drainage and, further, that they dedicate an additional 15-foot strip of land adjacent to the floodplain as a pedestrian/bicycle pathway. LUBA found a reasonable relationship between (1) the development and the requirement to dedicate land for a greenway, since the larger building and paved lot would increase the impervious surfaces and thus the runoff into the creek, and (2) the impact of increased traffic from the development and facilitating a bikeway as an alternative means of transportation.

The Oregon Supreme Court had discussed the "relationship" or "nexus" definition. Citing a parade of exaction cases, the court held that "there is agreement among the states 'that the dedication should have some reasonable relationship to the needs created by the [proposed development].'" The court found that the two exactions were "reasonably related" because they served the purpose of the zoning ordinance, and they addressed burdens created or aggravated by the proposed development.]

Rehnquist, C.J. ...Under the well-settled doctrine of "unconstitutional conditions," the government may not require a person to give up a constitutional right — here the right to receive just compensation when property is taken for a public use — in exchange for a discretionary benefit conferred by the government where the property sought has little or no relationship to the benefit. See Perry v. Sindermann, 408 U. S. 593 (1972); Pickering v. Board of Ed. of Township High School Dist., 391 U. S. 563, 568 (1968).

Petitioner contends that the city has forced her to choose between the building permit and her right under the Fifth Amendment to just compensation for the public easements. Petitioner does not quarrel with the city's authority to exact some forms of dedication as a condition for the grant of a building permit, but challenges the showing made by the city to justify these exactions. She argues that the city has identified "no special benefits" conferred on her, and has not identified any "special quantifiable burdens" created by her new store that would justify the particular dedications required from her which are not required from the public at large.

In evaluating petitioner's claim, we must first determine whether the "essential nexus" exists between the "legitimate state interest" and the permit condition exacted by the city. Nollan, 483 U. S. at 837. If we find that a nexus exists, we must then decide the required degree of connection between the exactions and the projected impact of the proposed development....

Undoubtedly, the prevention of flooding along Fanno Creek and the reduction of traffic congestion in the Central Business District qualify as the type of legitimate public purposes we have upheld. It seems equally obvious that a nexus exists between preventing flooding along Fanno Creek and limiting development within the creek's 100-year floodplain. Petitioner proposes to double the size of her retail store and to pave her now-gravel parking lot, thereby expanding the impervious surface on the property and increasing the amount of stormwater run-off into Fanno Creek.

The same may be said for the city's attempt to reduce traffic congestion by providing for alternative means of transportation. In theory, a pedestrian/bicycle pathway provides a useful alternative means of transportation for workers and shoppers: "Pedestrians and bicyclists occupying dedicated spaces for walking and/or bicycling...remove potential vehicles from streets, resulting in an overall improvement in total transportation system flow." A. Nelson, Public Provision of Pedestrian and Bicycle Access Ways, Center for Planning Development, Georgia Institute of Technology, (1994). See also, Intermodal Surface Transportation Efficiency Act of 1991, Pub. L. 102-240 (recognizing pedestrian and bicycle facilities as necessary components of any strategy to reduce traffic congestion).

The second part of our analysis requires us to determine whether the degree of the exactions demanded by the city's permit conditions bear the required relationship to the projected impact of petitioner's proposed development. *Nollan*, supra, at 834, quoting *Penn Central*, 438 U. S. 104, 127 (1978) ("'[A] use restriction may constitute a taking if not reasonably necessary to the effectuation of a substantial government purpose'")....

The city required that petitioner dedicate "to the city as Greenway all portions of the site that fall within the existing 100-year floodplain [of Fanno Creek] ... and all property 15 feet above [the floodplain] boundary." In addition, the city demanded that the retail store be designed so as not to intrude into the greenway area. The city relies on the Commission's rather tentative findings that increased stormwater flow from petitioner's property "can only add to the public need to manage the [floodplain] for drainage purposes"....

The city made the following specific findings relevant to the pedestrian/bicycle pathway: "In addition, the proposed expanded use of this site is anticipated to generate additional vehicular traffic thereby increasing congestion on nearby collector and arterial streets. Creation of a convenient, safe pedestrian/bicycle pathway system as an alternative means of transportation could offset some of the traffic demand on these nearby streets and lessen the increase in traffic congestion."

The question for us is whether these findings are constitutionally sufficient to justify the conditions imposed by the city on petitioner's building permit. Since state courts have been dealing with this question a good deal longer than we have, we turn to representative decisions made by them.

In some States, very generalized statements as to the necessary connection between the required dedication and the proposed development seem to suffice. See, e.g., Billings Properties, Inc. v. Yellowstone County, 144 Mont. 25, 394 P. 2d 182 (1964); Jenad, Inc. v. Scarsdale, 18 N. Y. 2d 78, 218 N. E. 2d 673 (1966). We think this standard is too lax to adequately protect petitioner's right to just compensation if her property is taken for a public purpose.

Other state courts require a very exacting correspondence, described as the "specifi[c] and uniquely attributable" test. The Supreme Court of Illinois first developed this test in Pioneer Trust & Savings Bank v. Mount Prospect, 22 Ill. 2d 375, 380, 176 N. E. 2d 799, 802 (1961).[81] Under this standard, if the local government cannot demonstrate that its exaction is directly proportional to the specifically created need, the exaction becomes "a veiled exercise of the power of eminent domain and a confiscation of private property behind the defense of police regulations." Id., at 381, 176 N.E. 2d, at 802. We do not think the Federal Constitution requires such exacting scrutiny, given the nature of the interests involved.

A number of state courts have taken an intermediate position, requiring the municipality to show a "reasonable relationship" between the required dedication and the impact of the proposed development. Typical is the Supreme Court of Nebraska's opinion in Simpson v. North Platte, 292 N. W. 2d 297, 301 (1980), where that court stated: "The distinction, therefore, which must be made between an appropriate exercise of the police power and an improper exercise of eminent domain is whether the requirement has some reasonable relationship or nexus to the use to which the property is being made or is merely being used as an excuse for taking property simply because at that particular moment the landowner is asking the city for some license or permit."...

We think the "reasonable relationship" test adopted by a majority of the state courts is closer to the federal constitutional norm than either of those previously discussed. But we do not adopt it as such, partly because the term "reasonable relationship" seems confusingly similar to the term "rational basis" which describes the minimal level of scrutiny under the Equal Protection Clause of the Fourteenth Amendment. We think a term such as "rough proportionality" best encapsulates what we hold to be the requirement of the Fifth Amendment. No precise mathematical calculation is required, but the city must make some sort of individualized determination that the required dedication is related both in nature and extent to the impact of the proposed development....[82]

---

81. The "specifically and uniquely attributable" test has now been adopted by a minority of other courts. See, e.g., J. E. D. Associates., Inc. v. Atkinson, 121 N. H. 581, 585, 432 A. 2d 12, 15 (1981); Divan Builders, Inc. v. Planning Bd. of Twp. of Wayne, 66 N. J. 582, 600-601, 334 A. 2d 30, 40 (1975); McKain v. Toledo City Plan Comm'n, 26 Ohio App. 2d 171, 176, 270 N. E. 2d 370, 374 (1971); Frank Ansuini, Inc. v. Cranston, 107 R. I. 63, 69, 264 A. 2d 910, 913 (1970).

82. Justice Stevens' dissent takes us to task for placing the burden on the city to justify the required dedication. He is correct in arguing that in evaluating most generally applicable zoning regulations, the burden properly rests on the party challenging the regulation to prove that it constitutes an arbitrary regulation of property rights. See, e.g., Euclid v. Ambler Realty Co., 272 U. S. 365 (1926). Here, by contrast, the city made an adjudicative decision to condition petitioner's application for a building permit on an individual parcel. In this situation, the burden properly rests on the city. See Nollan, 483 U. S., at 836. This conclusion is not, as he suggests, undermined by our decision in Moore v. East Cleveland, 431 U. S.494 (1977), in which we struck down a housing ordinance that limited occupancy of a dwelling unit to members of a single family as violating the Due

We turn now to analysis of whether the findings relied upon by the city here, first with respect to the floodplain easement, and second with respect to the pedestrian/bicycle path, satisfied these requirements.

It is axiomatic that increasing the amount of impervious surface will increase the quantity and rate of storm-water flow from petitioner's property. Therefore, keeping the floodplain open and free from development would likely confine the pressures on Fanno Creek created by petitioner's development.... But the city demanded more — it not only wanted petitioner not to build in the floodplain, but it also wanted petitioner's property along Fanno Creek for its Greenway system. The city has never said why a public greenway, as opposed to a private one, was required in the interest of flood control.

The difference to petitioner, of course, is the loss of her ability to exclude others. As we have noted, this right to exclude others is "one of the most essential sticks in the bundle of rights that are commonly characterized as property." Kaiser Aetna, 444 U. S. at 176. It is difficult to see why recreational visitors trampling along petitioner's floodplain easement are sufficiently related to the city's legitimate interest in reducing flooding problems along Fanno Creek, and the city has not attempted to make any individualized determination to support this part of its request.... Petitioner would lose all rights to regulate the time in which the public entered onto the Greenway, regardless of any interference it might pose with her retail store. Her right to exclude would not be regulated, it would be eviscerated.

If petitioner's proposed development had somehow encroached on existing greenway space in the city, it would have been reasonable to require petitioner to provide some alternative greenway space for the public either on her property or elsewhere. See Nollan, 483 U. S. at 836 ("Although such a requirement, constituting a permanent grant of continuous access to the property, would have to be considered a taking if it were not attached to a development permit, the Commission's assumed power to forbid construction of the house in order to protect the public's view of the beach must surely include the power to condition construction upon some concession by the owner, even a concession of property rights, that serves the same end"). But that is not the case here. We conclude that the findings upon which the city relies do not show the required reasonable relationship between the floodplain easement and the petitioner's proposed new building.

With respect to the pedestrian/bicycle pathway, we have no doubt that the city was correct in finding that the larger retail sales facility proposed by petitioner will increase traffic on the streets of the Central Business District. The city estimates that the proposed development would generate roughly 435 additional trips per day. Dedications for streets, sidewalks, and other public ways are generally reasonable exactions to avoid excessive congestion from a proposed property use. But on the record before us, the city has not met its burden of demonstrating that the additional number of vehicle and bicycle trips generated by the petitioner's development reasonably relate to the city's requirement for a

---

Process Clause of the Fourteenth Amendment. The ordinance at issue in Moore intruded on choices concerning family living arrangements, an area in which the usual deference to the legislature was found to be inappropriate.

dedication of the pedestrian/bicycle pathway easement. The city simply found that the creation of the pathway "could offset some of the traffic demand ... and lessen the increase in traffic congestion."... No precise mathematical calculation is required, but the city must make some effort to quantify its findings in support of the dedication for the pedestrian/bicycle pathway beyond the conclusory statement that it could offset some of the traffic demand generated.

IV

Cities have long engaged in the commendable task of land use planning, made necessary by increasing urbanization particularly in metropolitan areas such as Portland. The city's goals of reducing flooding hazards and traffic congestion, and providing for public greenways, are laudable, but there are outer limits to how this may be done. "A strong public desire to improve the public condition [will not] warrant achieving the desire by a shorter cut than the constitutional way of paying for the change." Pennsylvania Coal, 260 U. S. at 416.

The judgment of the Supreme Court of Oregon is reversed....

JUSTICE STEVENS, WITH WHOM JUSTICE BLACKMUN AND JUSTICE GINSBURG JOIN, DISSENTING.

...The Court is correct in concluding that the city may not attach arbitrary conditions to a building permit or to a variance even when it can rightfully deny the application outright.... Yet the Court's description of the doctrinal underpinnings of its decision, the phrasing of its fledgling test of "rough proportionality," and the application of that test to this case run contrary to the traditional treatment of these cases and break considerable and unpropitious new ground.

Candidly acknowledging the lack of federal precedent for its exercise in rulemaking, the Court purports to find guidance in 12 "representative" state court decisions. To do so is certainly appropriate. The state cases the Court consults, however, either fail to support or decidedly undermine the Court's conclusions....

First,... the test on which the Court settles is not naturally derived from those courts' decisions. The Court recognizes as an initial matter that the city's conditions satisfy the "essential nexus" requirement announced in *Nollan* because they serve the legitimate interests in minimizing floods and traffic congestions. The Court goes on, however, to erect a new constitutional hurdle in the path of these conditions. In addition to showing a rational nexus to a public purpose that would justify an outright denial of the permit, the city must also demonstrate "rough proportionality" between the harm caused by the new land use and the benefit obtained by the condition. The Court also decides for the first time that the city has the burden of establishing the constitutionality of its conditions by making an "individualized determination" that the condition in question satisfies the proportionality requirement.

Not one of the state cases cited by the Court announces anything akin to a "rough proportionality" requirement.... One case purporting to apply the strict "specifically and uniquely attributable" test...nevertheless found that test was satisfied because the legislature had decided that the subdivision at issue created the need for a park or parks. Billings Properties, Inc. v. Yellowstone County, 394 P. 2d 182, 187-188 (1964).... Thus, although these state cases do lend support to the Court's reaffirmance of Nollan's reasonable nexus requirement, the role the Court accords them in the announcement of its newly minted second phase of the constitutional inquiry is remarkably inventive.

In addition, the Court ignores the state courts' willingness to consider what the property owner gains from the exchange in question. The Supreme Court of Wisconsin, for example, found it significant that the village's approval of a proposed subdivision plat "enables the subdivider to profit financially by selling the subdivision lots as home-building sites and thus realizing a greater price than could have been obtained if he had sold his property as unplatted lands." Jordan v. Village of Menomonee Falls, 137 N. W. 2d 442, 448 (Wisc. 1965).... In this case, moreover, Dolan's acceptance of the permit, with its attached conditions, would provide her with benefits that may well go beyond any advantage she gets from expanding her business. As the United States pointed out at oral argument, the improvement that the city's drainage plan contemplates would widen the channel and reinforce the slopes to increase the carrying capacity during serious floods, "confer[ring] considerable benefits on the property owners immediately adjacent to the creek."

The state court decisions also are enlightening in the extent to which they required that the entire parcel be given controlling importance.... None of the decisions identified the surrender of the fee owner's "power to exclude" as having any special significance. Instead, the courts uniformly examined the character of the entire economic transaction.

It is not merely state cases, but our own cases as well, that require the analysis to focus on the impact of the city's action on the entire parcel of private property. In Penn Central Transportation Co. v. New York City, 438 U. S. 104 (1978), we stated that takings jurisprudence "does not divide a single parcel into discrete segments and attempt to determine whether rights in a particular segment have been entirely abrogated." Id. at 130-131. Instead, this Court focuses "both on the character of the action and on the nature and extent of the interference with rights in the parcel as a whole." Andrus v. Allard, 444 U. S. 51, 65-66 (1979), reaffirmed the nondivisibility principle outlined in Penn Central, stating that "[a]t least where an owner possesses a full 'bundle' of property rights, the destruction of one 'strand' of the bundle is not a taking, because the aggregate must be viewed in its entirety." As recently as last Term, we approved the principle again. See Concrete Pipe & Products, Inc. v. Construction Laborers Pension Trust, 508 U. S. , (1993) (explaining that "a claimant's parcel of property [cannot] first be divided into what was taken and what was left" to demonstrate a compensable taking). Although limitation of the right to exclude others undoubtedly constitutes a significant infringement upon property ownership, Kaiser Aetna v. United States, 444 U. S. 164, 179- 180 (1979), restrictions on that right do not alone constitute a taking, and do not do so in any event unless they "unreasonably impair the value or use" of the property. Pruneyard Shopping Center v. Robbins, 447 U. S. 74, 82-84 (1980).

The Court's narrow focus on one strand in the property owner's bundle of rights is particularly misguided in a case involving the development of commercial property. As Professor Johnston has noted: "The subdivider is a manufacturer, processor, and marketer of a product; land is but one of his raw materials. In subdivision control disputes, the developer is not defending hearth and home against the king's intrusion, but simply attempting to maximize his profits from the sale of a finished product. As applied to him, subdivision control exactions are actually business regulations." Johnston, Constitutionality of Subdivision Control Exactions: The Quest for A Rationale, 52 Cornell L. Q. 871, 923 (1967)....

The Court's assurances that its "rough proportionality" test leaves ample room for cities to pursue the "commendable task of land use planning," even twice avowing that "[n]o precise mathematical calculation is required," are wanting, given the result that test compels here. Under the Court's approach, a city must not only "quantify its findings," and make "individualized determination[s]" with respect to the nature and the extent of the relationship between the conditions and the impact, ante, but also demonstrate "proportionality." The correct inquiry should instead concentrate on whether the required nexus is present and venture beyond considerations of a condition's nature or germaneness only if the developer establishes that a concededly germane condition is so grossly disproportionate to the proposed development's adverse effects that it manifests motives other than land use regulation on the part of the city....

Applying its new standard, the Court finds two defects in the city's case.... Even under the Court's new rule, both defects are, at most, nothing more than harmless error.

In her objections to the floodplain condition, Dolan made no effort to demonstrate that the dedication of that portion of her property would be any more onerous than a simple prohibition against any development on that portion of her property....

The Court's rejection of the bike path condition amounts to nothing more than a play on words. Everyone agrees that the bike path "could" offset some of the increased traffic flow that the larger store will generate, but the findings do not unequivocally state that it will do so, or tell us just how many cyclists will replace motorists. Predictions on such matters are inherently nothing more than estimates. Certainly the assumption that there will be an offsetting benefit here is entirely reasonable and should suffice whether it amounts to 100 percent, 35 percent, or only 5 percent of the increase in automobile traffic that would otherwise occur. If the Court proposes to have the federal judiciary micromanage state decisions of this kind, it is indeed extending its welcome mat to a significant new class of litigants. Although there is no reason to believe that state courts have failed to rise to the task, property owners have surely found a new friend today.

The Court has made a serious error by abandoning the traditional presumption of constitutionality and imposing a novel burden of proof on a city implementing an admittedly valid comprehensive land use plan. Even more consequential than its incorrect disposition of this case, however, is the Court's resurrection of a species of substantive due process analysis that it firmly rejected decades ago.... See Lochner v. New York, 198 U. S. 45 (1905).... The so-called "regulatory takings" doctrine that the Holmes dictum [in *Penn Coal*] kindled has an obvious kinship with the line of substantive due process cases that Lochner exemplified. Besides having similar ancestry, both doctrines are potentially open-ended sources of judicial power to invalidate state economic regulations that Members of this Court view as unwise or unfair....

Today's majority should heed the words of Justice Sutherland [upholding zoning in Euclid v. Ambler, the first Supreme Court zoning case]: "Such regulations are sustained, under the complex conditions of our day, for reasons analogous to those which justify traffic regulations, which, before the advent of automobiles and rapid transit street railways, would have been condemned as fatally arbitrary and unreasonable. And in this there is no inconsistency, for while the meaning of constitutional guaranties never varies, the scope of their application must expand or contract to meet the new and different conditions which are constantly coming within the field of their operation. In a changing world, it is impossible that it should be otherwise." 272 U. S. 365, 387 (1926).

In our changing world one thing is certain: uncertainty will characterize predictions about the impact of new urban developments on the risks of floods, earthquakes, traffic congestion, or environmental harms. When there is doubt concerning the magnitude of those impacts, the public interest in averting them must outweigh the private interest of the commercial entrepreneur. If the government can demonstrate that the conditions it has imposed in a land-use permit are rational, impartial and conducive to fulfilling the aims of a valid land-use plan, a strong presumption of validity should attach to those conditions. The burden of demonstrating that those conditions have unreasonably impaired the economic value of the proposed improvement belongs squarely on the shoulders of the party challenging the state action's constitutionality. That allocation of burdens has served us well in the past. The Court has stumbled badly today by reversing it.

I respectfully dissent.

JUSTICE SOUTER, dissenting.

...The Court treats this case as raising a further question [beyond *Nollan*], not about the nature, but about the degree, of connection required between such an exaction and the adverse effects of development. The Court's opinion announces a test to address this question, but as I read the opinion, the Court does not apply that test to these facts, which do not raise the question the Court addresses.

First, as to the floodplain and Greenway, the Court acknowledges that an easement of this land for open space (and presumably including the five feet required for needed creek channel improvements) is reasonably related to flood control, but argues that the "permanent recreational easement" for the public on the Greenway is not so related. If that is so, it is not because of any lack of proportionality between permit condition and adverse effect, but because of a lack of any rational connection at all between exaction of a public recreational area and the governmental interest in providing for the effect of increased water runoff. That is merely an application of *Nollan's* nexus analysis.... It seems to me such incidental recreational use can stand or fall with the bicycle path, which the city justified by reference to traffic congestion. As to the relationship the Court examines, between the recreational easement and a purpose never put forth as a justification by the city, the Court unsurprisingly finds a recreation area to be unrelated to flood control.

Second, as to the bicycle path, the Court...only faults the city for saying that the bicycle path "could" rather than "would" offset the increased traffic from the store. That again, as far as I can tell, is an application of *Nollan*, for the Court holds that the stated connection ("could offset") between traffic congestion and bicycle paths is too tenuous; only if the bicycle path "would" offset the increased traffic by some amount, could the bicycle path be said to be related to the city's legitimate interest in reducing traffic congestion.

I cannot agree that the application of *Nollan* is a sound one here, since it appears that the Court has placed the burden of producing evidence of relationship on the city, despite the usual rule in cases involving the police power that the government is presumed to have acted constitutionally. Having thus assigned the burden, the Court concludes that the City loses based on one word ("could" instead of "would"), and despite the fact that this record shows the connection the Court looks for. Dolan has put forward no evidence that the burden of granting a dedication for the bicycle path is unrelated in kind to the anticipated increase in traffic congestion, nor, if there exists a requirement that the relationship be related in degree, has Dolan shown that the exaction fails any such test. The city, by contrast, calculated the increased traffic flow that would result from Dolan's proposed development to be 435 trips per day, and its Comprehensive Plan, applied here, relied on studies showing the link between alternative modes of transportation, including bicycle paths, and reduced street traffic congestion.... *Nollan*, therefore, is satisfied, and on that assumption the city's conditions should not be held to fail a further rough proportionality test or any other....

COMMENTARY AND QUESTIONS

1. The battles of *Dolan*: a new essential nexus. The shadow of the property rights movement looms behind the pitched battles in the *Dolan* opinions. Although all the justices assumed the necessity of a nexus between the exaction and the *burdens imposed* by the proposed development (by no means previously a foregone concession), the strategic question was "how *much* nexus?" The Rehnquist opinion seems to say "a lot, more than ever before," but as the four dissenters note the quantum required and the lack thereof are not defined. Lacking federal precedents, the majority cited state cases, but adopted a test that had been applied in very few state cases. As the discussion between the justices reflects, it is not even clear that the new nexus test was applied, since the recreational entry character of the floodway easement lies at the core of the majority's rejection of this exaction.

"Rough proportionality" is a concept that will require a good deal of further judicial elaboration. If the floodplain portion of a proposed housing subdivision could be sold to buyers ignoring flood hazards for $200,000 a lot, would an exaction of a flowage easement preventing home construction have to demonstrate that each built lot would cause roughly $200,000 in discounted risk of death and destruction?

2. Presumption of validity/burden of proof. A strategic issue looming even larger than the heightened nexus requirement is who has the burden of proving their case. Previously the presumption of validity was presumed to cast the burden on the private party attacking government. As the dissenters note, the majority placed that burden squarely on government to show that there "would" be serious effects. While not directly saying they were doing so, the majority justified the shift by saying the city's decision was "adjudicative," for which more evidence was necessary. In a footnote to his dissent, Justice Souter said, "the adjudication here was of Dolan's requested variance from the permit conditions otherwise required to be imposed by the Code. This case raises no question about..."reverse spot" zoning, which singles out a particular parcel for different, less favorable treatment than the neighboring ones."

If indeed this case marks a shift toward putting the burden of proof of validity upon regulatory government, its consequences will change the administrative state as we know it. The *Dolan* majority, however, is far more likely to apply such a shift selectively against environmental regulations than generally, say, against regulations managing securities markets, or ordinances regulating speech or demonstrations.

3. Other worms in the can. Several issues less clearly debated deserve notice. In presenting Ms. Dolan's case, and noting that "the city has identified 'no special benefits' conferred on her," is Justice Rehnquist setting up a future assertion of his dissenting arguments in *Keystone Bituminous* that a regulation is void if it does not give the regulatees a "reciprocity of advantage" roughly proportional to the burdens imposed? (As opposed to the precedents which used reciprocity only to show validity; see coursebook at 464 Comment 6.)

A judicial review of necessity? In reusing a quotation from *Penn Central* about the basic due process requirements of valid regulation "'[A] use restriction may constitute a taking if not *reasonably necessary* to the effectuation of a substantial government purpose'" (emphasis added), is the majority opening up a general inquiry by judges into the wisdom of legislative judgments about how social problems should best be addressed? The temptation toward an activist judiciary is not restricted to the progressive sector.

And the initially-pronounced principle against "unconstitutional conditions" is not drawn from exactions cases or regulatory precedents. The cases cited for the phrase are cases of administrative due process. Courts regularly have held that you do not yield your constitutional procedural rights by taking benefits that come with built-in limitations on procedure, despite Justice Rehnquist's vehement arguments in that situation that citizens "must take the bitter with the sweet." See Cleveland Bd. of Educ. v. Loudermill, 470 U.S. 532 (1985, Rehnquist, J., dissenting).

4. Predicting the future. What will be the future effect of *Dolan* on exactions? Faced with the difficulties of negotiating conditions that can be practically defended against *Dolan* challenges, will local governments just deny permits outright, forswearing the flexibility and adjustments previously available under prior exactions law?

Will the rough proportionality concept be expanded further, so that local governments will have to bear the burden of convincing a judge that the private property burdens of regulatory decisions are justified in each case by public harms imposed, even where reasonable, economically viable uses remain? The politics and law of this debate will continue to be interesting.

E. WISE USERS AND THE ANTI-REGULATION TAKINGS AGENDA

As part of the anti-regulatory initiatives currently focusing on the national political arena, regulatory takings challenges have been leveled in all three branches of government. In court there have been cases like *Lucas* and many others, often filed in the federal Claims Court which had an influx of anti-regulatory judges appointed in the 1980s. One notable case that is pending is the *Hage* case in which a Nevada rancher grazing cattle at subsidized rates on public lands has argued that a restriction on the number of head he could graze is a taking. See Williams, The Compensation Game, Wilderness Magazine, Sept. 22, 1993.

In Washington D.C. a variety of legislative attempts have been underway to limit public policies that restrict private property interests, reflecting the "Wise Users'" political drives against property-regulating restrictions (see Chapter 1 in this Supplement) and the judicial initiatives noted above in the Federal Circuit and the Supreme Court.

Consider one of the several similar amendments promoted by Rep. Billy Tauzin of Louisiana for attachment to environmental statutes:

> Sec. 8(a) A private property owner that as a consequence of a final qualified agency action of an agency head, is deprived of 50 percent or more of the fair market value, or the economically viable use, of the affected portion of the property, as determined by a qualified appraisal expert, is entitled to receive compensation.... H.R. 3875, 103d Cong. 1st Sess. (1993).

One of these provisions was successfully added to a Senate version of the Safe Drinking Water Act Reauthorization. The property rights advocates have argued that they just codify existing constitutional law tests of takings. Do they? How difficult would it be to demand compensation for restrictions on factory units burdened with various pollution regulations under the terms of such a provision? What would be the overall effect? As of July 1994, President Clinton had not clarified his Administration's views on takings, and was apparently trying to negotiate some sort of compromise position.

There is no mention of SUBSIDIES in the political rhetoric of the anti-regulationists. Consider, says the jaundiced envirnmentalist, the rancher Hage, or the grazing, timber, real estate, and mining lobbying groups that have been promoting the onrushing property rights movement as rugged individualism. Do "property rights" get created by programs to transfer public resources for $1.86 per acre per grazing cow, or for below- market value public timber, or for the taxpayer-financed flood insurance program, or for the mountain of federal gold deposits given away for $5 an acre under the mining acts?[83] Does a legislatively-created (as opposed to

---

83. The major contributors to "People for the American West!" are mining companies – more than sixty companies in the mineral extraction business have

judicial) analysis of regulatory burdens on business make sense if it does not consider the private wealth created by subsidies?

What would be the property rights reception for an amendment to the Wise Users takings amendments saying —

> "In any review and application of this compensation provision, comprehensive accounting shall be made of values attributable to public economic and regulatory subsidies, and all values so attributable shall be offset against purported regulatory burdens." ?

---

contributed in some cases more than $100,000 to this one Wise Use populist group.

Chapter 10, Environmental Issues in the Division of Authority Between Federal and State Governments

Section 5. THE TENTH AMENDMENT AND STATE SOVEREIGNTY AS A LIMIT ON FEDERAL POWER

There has long been debate as to whether the tenth amendment to the United States Constitution alters, in any way, the power relation between the states and the federal government established by the supremacy clause. The tenth amendment, in relevant part, declares that "powers not delegated to the United States by the Constitution, nor prohibited by it to the States, are reserved to the States ... ." The claim made for giving the tenth amendment some bite in the matter of federal-state relations, is that somehow the amendment erects an area of inviolate state sovereignty that cannot be encroached upon by the federal government.

The conventional wisdom and the vast majority of cases reject that claim. The rejection is captured in a phrase, often repeated in cases raising the issue:" [the tenth amendment] states but a truism that all is retained which has not been surrendered." United States v. Darby, 312 U.S. 100, 124 (1941). The "truism" confirms federal supremacy (within the sphere of the federal government's enumerated powers) and some abdication of elements of state sovereignty as being surrendered on nationhood, but notes the fact that the remainder of state sovereignty was unaffected. Nevertheless, the idea of state sovereignty is an important one in the federal system, and there are occasional cases in which the Supreme Court has been willing to restrict the federal government's encroachment on the states, even when the federal government is pursuing national objectives that are within its sphere of constitutional competence. Importantly for the study of environmental law, the tenth amendment argument is, at times, made in environmental cases.

In one recent case, the tenth amendment argument was successful in limiting one facet of Low-Level Radioactive Waste Policy Amendments Act of 1985, Pub.L. 99-240, 99 Stat. 1842, 42 U.S.C. 2021b et seq. That litigation grew out of Congress' attempt to respond to the declining number of low-level radioactive waste disposal sites nationwide and the threat of a total absence of such sites in the future. Congress sought to spur the siting by the states of low-level radioactive waste facilities, preferably on a collaborative basis, where several states would send their waste to a regional facility. To insure action by the states, Congress used a mix of incentives and penalties, three of which were challenged by the State of New York on tenth amendment and other grounds. The challenged provisions included what the Court characterized as "monetary incentives," "access incentives," and the "take title provision." The monetary incentives revolved around a series of federal disposal surcharges on wastes generated outside of the disposal state. The surcharges would create a fund that would be used to reward states that achieved specific milestones in the process of establishing disposal facilities. The access incentives potentially limited disposal to wastes generated in states participating in the programs that Congress sought to encourage. Finally, the take title provision, as a sort of last resort, required states that were not participating in the programs to take title to the waste involved.

New York v. United States
___ U.S. ___, 112 S.Ct. 2408, 120 L.Ed.2d 120 (1992),

O'CONNOR, J.   This case implicates one of our Nation's newest problems of public policy and perhaps our oldest question of constitutional law. The public policy issue involves the disposal of radioactive waste.... The constitutional question is as old as the Constitution: it consists of discerning the proper division of authority between the Federal Government and the States. We conclude that while Congress has substantial power under the Constitution to encourage the States to provide for the disposal of the radioactive waste generated within their borders, the Constitution does not confer upon Congress the ability simply to compel the States to do so. ...

II. A. ... These questions [of state and federal authority] can be viewed in either of two ways. In some cases the Court has inquired whether an Act of Congress is authorized by one of the powers delegated to Congress in Article I of the Constitution. In other cases the Court has sought to determine whether an Act of Congress invades the province of state sovereignty reserved by the Tenth Amendment. In a case like this one, involving the division of authority between federal and state governments, the two inquiries are mirror images of each other. If a power is delegated to Congress in the Constitution, the Tenth Amendment expressly disclaims any reservation of that power to the States; if a power is an attribute of state sovereignty reserved by the Tenth Amendment, it is necessarily a power the Constitution has not conferred on Congress.

It is in this sense that the Tenth Amendment "states but a truism that all is retained which has not been surrendered." As Justice Story put it, "[t]his amendment is a mere affirmation of what, upon any just reasoning, is a necessary rule of interpreting the constitution. Being an instrument of limited and enumerated powers, it follows irresistibly, that what is not conferred, is withheld, and belongs to the state authorities." 3 J. Story, Commentaries on the Constitution of the United States 752 (1833). This has been the Court's consistent understanding: "The States unquestionably do retai[n] a significant measure of sovereign authority ... to the extent that the Constitution has not divested them of their original powers and transferred those powers to the Federal Government."

Congress exercises its conferred powers subject to the limitations contained in the Constitution. Thus, for example, under the Commerce Clause Congress may regulate publishers engaged in interstate commerce, but Congress is constrained in the exercise of that power by the First Amendment. The Tenth Amendment likewise restrains the power of Congress, but this limit is not derived from the text of the Tenth Amendment itself, which, as we have discussed, is essentially a tautology. Instead, the Tenth Amendment confirms that the power of the Federal Government is subject to limits that may, in a given instance, reserve power to the States. The Tenth Amendment thus directs us to determine, as in this case, whether an incident of state sovereignty is protected by a limitation on an Article I power. ...

II. B. Petitioners do not contend that Congress lacks the power to regulate the disposal of low level radioactive waste. Space in radioactive waste disposal sites is frequently sold by residents of one State to residents of another. Regulation of the resulting interstate market in waste disposal is therefore well within Congress' authority under the Commerce Clause. Petitioners likewise do not dispute that under the Supremacy Clause Congress could, if it wished, pre-empt state radioactive waste regulation. Petitioners contend only that the Tenth Amendment limits the power of Congress to regulate in the way it has chosen. Rather than addressing the problem of waste disposal by directly regulating the generators and disposers of waste, petitioners argue, Congress has impermissibly directed the States to regulate in this field. ...

1. As an initial matter, Congress may not simply "commandee[r] the legislative processes of the States by directly compelling them to enact and enforce a federal regulatory program." Hodel v. Virginia Surface Mining & Reclamation Assn., Inc., 452 U.S. 264, 288, 101 S.Ct. 2352, 2366, 69 L.Ed.2d 1 (1981). In Hodel, the Court upheld the Surface Mining Control and Reclamation Act of 1977 precisely because it did not "commandeer" the States into regulating mining. The Court found that "the States are not compelled to enforce the steep-slope standards, to expend any state funds, or to participate in the federal regulatory program in any manner whatsoever. If a State does not wish to submit a proposed permanent program that complies with the Act and implementing regulations, the full regulatory burden will be borne by the Federal Government." ...

2. This is not to say that Congress lacks the ability to encourage a State to regulate in a particular way, or that Congress may not hold out incentives to the States as a method of influencing a State's policy choices. Our cases have identified a variety of methods, short of outright coercion, by which Congress may urge a State to adopt a legislative program consistent with federal interests. Two of these methods are of particular relevance here.

First, under Congress' spending power, "Congress may attach conditions on the receipt of federal funds." ...

Second, where Congress has the authority to regulate private activity under the Commerce Clause, we have recognized Congress' power to offer States the choice of regulating that activity according to federal standards or having state law pre-empted by federal regulation. ...

With these principles in mind, we turn to the three challenged provisions of the Low-Level Radioactive Waste Policy Amendments Act of 1985.

III. [The opinion had little difficulty in concluding that monetary and access incentives in the legislation passed muster as rather straightforward examples of the federal power to tax and spend and the direct regulation of interstate commerce.]

C. The take title provision is of a different character. This third so-called "incentive" offers States, as an alternative to regulating pursuant to Congress' direction, the option of taking title to and possession of the low level radioactive waste generated within their borders and becoming liable for all damages waste generators suffer as a result of the States' failure to do so promptly. In this provision, Congress has crossed the line distinguishing encouragement from coercion. ...

The take title provision offers state governments a "choice" of either accepting ownership of waste or regulating according to the instructions of Congress. Respondents do not claim that the Constitution would authorize Congress to impose either option as a freestanding requirement. On one hand, the Constitution would not permit Congress simply to transfer radioactive waste from generators to state governments. Such a forced transfer, standing alone, would in principle be no different than a congressionally compelled subsidy from state governments to radioactive waste producers. The same is true of the provision requiring the States to become liable for the generators' damages. Standing alone, this provision would be indistinguishable from an Act of Congress directing the States to assume the liabilities of certain state residents. Either type of federal action would "commandeer" state governments into the service of federal regulatory purposes, and would for this reason be inconsistent with the Constitution's division of authority between federal and state governments. On the other hand, the second alternative held out to state governments — regulating pursuant to Congress' direction — would, standing alone, present a simple command to state governments to implement legislation enacted by Congress. As we have seen, the Constitution does not empower Congress to subject state governments to this type of instruction.

Because an instruction to state governments to take title to waste, standing alone, would be beyond the authority of Congress, and because a direct order to regulate, standing alone, would also be beyond the authority of Congress, it follows that Congress lacks the power to offer the States a choice between the two. ...

VII ... States are not mere political subdivisions of the United States. State governments are neither regional offices nor administrative agencies of the Federal Government. The positions occupied by state officials appear nowhere on the Federal Government's most detailed organizational chart. The Constitution instead "leaves to the several States a residuary and inviolable sovereignty," The Federalist No. 39, p. 245 (C. Rossiter ed. 1961), reserved explicitly to the States by the Tenth Amendment.

Whatever the outer limits of that sovereignty may be, one thing is clear: The Federal Government may not compel the States to enact or administer a federal regulatory program. The Constitution permits both the Federal Government and the States to enact legislation regarding the disposal of low level radioactive waste. The Constitution enables the Federal Government to pre-empt state regulation contrary to federal interests, and it permits the Federal Government to hold out incentives to the States as a means of encouraging them to adopt suggested regulatory schemes. It does not, however, authorize Congress simply to direct the States to provide for the disposal of the radioactive waste generated within their borders. While there may be many constitutional methods of achieving regional self-sufficiency in radioactive waste disposal, the method Congress has chosen is not one of them. The judgment of the Court of Appeals is accordingly affirmed in part and reversed in part.

COMMENTARY & QUESTIONS

1. The lines of dissent. Justices White, Blackmun, and Stevens dissented from the invalidation of the take title provision. The thrust of their objection was based on estoppel (New York had reaped benefits of the law) and the view that the precedents cited by the majority did not establish so great a limitation on congressional choice of means.

2. The new "truism." Has the old "truism" taken on a new meaning? Historically, the issue in tenth amendment cases was that of federal competence, was the action within federal power. What Chief Justice Rehnquist and others had been lobbying for in various opinions in recent years was a concept of independent limitation of federal power derived from a notion of inviolable state sovereignty that survived the framing of the United States Constitution. A phrase that had come to be associated with this idea was a claim that the federal government was disabled from legislation that sought to regulate the "states qua states." To what extent is that view established as a general principle in Part II of the opinion and then applied to strike down the take title provision?

3. Incentives and the dormant commerce clause. Interestingly, for federalism purposes, among the incentives that Congress used (and the Court upheld) to spur the siting of regional facilities were granting those facilities the right to exclude waste from states not a party to the agreement governing the regional facility and the right to charge differential waste disposal fees. The power of exclusion and charging differential fees for disposal, absent congressional authorization, would violate the dormant commerce clause.

PAGE 503   **Text Replacement for pages 503-508, environmental "dormant commerce clause" cases.**

B. THE "DORMANT COMMERCE CLAUSE" — INVALIDATING STATE LAWS THAT EXCESSIVELY BURDEN INTERSTATE COMMERCE

As pointed out in the introductory segment of this Chapter, the states voluntarily surrendered a portion of their sovereignty in order to form an effective nation. One area of substantial constitutional concern was the need for the states to integrate their economies in order to obtain the benefits of relatively free movement of goods among them and in foreign commerce. The national government was thus granted jurisdiction over interstate and international commerce.

Although the commerce clause is written as a grant of legislative authority to Congress, it has long been interpreted as at least partially self-executing. Even in advance of congressional action on a matter, courts have been willing to invalidate state laws that unduly burden or restrict the interstate movement of goods in commerce on the ground that they are inconsistent with the surrender of the commerce power to the national government. The fact that the courts may activate and use the commerce clause in cases where Congress has let its regulatory authority under the clause, lie dormant gives rise to the label "dormant commerce clause" for this branch of constitutional analysis.

Action by the judiciary in dormant commerce clause cases in no degree reduces the plenary authority of Congress and the principle of legislative supremacy. Congress can always act to permit state action that courts have invalidated on this basis, or Congress can act to forbid state regulation of interstate commerce that courts have found to be constitutionally permissible. Dormant commerce clause issues frequently arise in the environmental protection context.

Section 1. The Basics of Dormant Commerce Clause Adjudication

For contemporary purposes, for almost a decade and one-half the leading Supreme Court decision in the dormant commerce clause area has been City of Philadelphia v. New Jersey, 437 U.S. 617 (1978). In that case an effort by New Jersey to forbid out-of-state garbage from its landfill sites was struck down as unconstitutional. The Court there explained succinctly the logic justifying the judicial activism inherent in striking down state laws in advance of congressional action and established a methodology by which it would review challenged state enactment's:

> Although the Constitution gives Congress the power to regulate commerce among the States, many subjects of potential federal regulation under that power inevitably escape congressional attention "because of their local character and their number and diversity." South Carolina State Highway Dept. v. Barnwell Bros., Inc., 303 U.S. 177, 185. In the absence of federal-legislation, these subjects are open to control by the States so long as they act within the restraints imposed by the Commerce Clause itself. The bounds of these restraints appear nowhere in the words of the Commerce Clause, but have emerged gradually in the decisions of this Court giving effect to its basic purpose. That broad purpose was well expressed by Mr. Justice Jackson in his opinion for the Court in H.P. Hood & Sons, Inc. v. DuMond, 336 U.S. 525, 537-538: "This principle that our economic unit is the Nation, which alone has the gamut of powers necessary to control of the economy, including the vital power of erecting customs barriers against foreign competition, has as its corollary that the states are not separable economic units." As the Court said in Baldwin v. Seelig, 294 U.S. 511, 527, "what is ultimate is the principle that one state in its dealings with another may not place itself in a position of economic isolation."

> The opinions of the Court through the years have reflected an alertness to the evils of "economic isolation" and protectionism, while at the same time recognizing that incidental burdens on interstate commerce may be unavoidable when a State legislates to safeguard the health and safety of its people. Thus, where simple economic protectionism is effected by state legislation, a virtually per se rule of invalidity has been erected. The clearest example of such legislation is a law that overtly blocks the flow of interstate commerce at a State's borders. But where other legislative

> objectives are credibly advanced and there is no patent
> discrimination against interstate trade, the Court has adopted a
> much more flexible approach, the general contours of which
> were outlined in Pike v. Bruce Church, Inc., 397 U.S. 137, 142:
> "Where the statute regulates evenhandedly to effectuate a
> legitimate local public interest, and its effects on interstate
> commerce are only incidental, it will be upheld unless the
> burden imposed on such commerce is clearly excessive in
> relation to the putative local benefits.... If a legitimate local
> purpose is found, then the question becomes one of degree.
> And the extent of the burden that will be tolerated will of
> course depend on the nature of the local interest involved, and
> on whether it could be promoted as well with a lesser impact on
> interstate activities..."Philadelphia v. New Jersey, 437 U.S. at
> 623-624.

More recently, with the NIMBY phenomenon in full flower, states have renewed their efforts to bar the importation of out-of-waste. In the case that follows, the United States Supreme Court was faced wit a taxing scheme that applied an additional tax to out-of-state hazardous waste sent to Alabama for disposal. As in Philadelphia v. New Jersey, the discrimination against interstate commerce violated the constitution.

Chemical Waste Management, Inc. v. Guy Hunt, Governor of Alabama
United States Supreme Court, 1992
60 USLW 4433, 1992 WL 112337

JUSTICE WHITE delivered the opinion of the Court.

Alabama imposes a hazardous waste disposal fee on hazardous wastes generated outside the State and disposed of at a commercial facility in Alabama. The fee does not apply to such waste having a source in Alabama. The Alabama Supreme Court held that this differential treatment does not violate the Commerce Clause. We reverse.

I. Petitioner, Chemical Waste Management, Inc., a Delaware corporation with its principal place of business in Oak Brook, Illinois, owns and operates one of the Nation's oldest commercial hazardous waste land disposal facilities, located in Emelle, Alabama. Opened in 1977 and acquired by petitioner 1978, the Emelle facility is a hazardous waste treatment, storage, and disposal facility operating pursuant to permits issued by the Environmental Protection Agency (EPA) under the Resource Conservation and Recovery Act of 1976 (RCRA), and the Toxic Substances Control Act, and by the State of Alabama under Ala. Code § 22-30-12(i)(1990). Alabama is 1 of only 16 States that have commercial hazardous waste landfills, and the Emelle facility is the largest of the 21 landfills of this kind of located in these 16 States.

The parties do not dispute that the waste and substances being landfilled at the Emelle facility "include substances that are inherently dangerous to human health and safety and to the environment. Such waste consists of ignitable, corrosive, toxic and reactive wastes which contain poisonous and cancer causing chemicals and which can cause birth defects, genetic damage, blindness, crippling and death." 584 So.2d 1367, 1373 (1991). Increasing amounts of out-of-state hazardous wastes are shipped to the

Emelle facility for permanent storage each year. From 1985 through 1989, the tonnage of hazardous waste received every year has more than doubled, increasing from 341,000 tons in 1985 to 788,000 tons by 1989. Of this, up to 90% of the tonnage permanently buried each year is shipped in from other States.

Against this backdrop Alabama enacted Act No. 90-326 (the Act). Ala. Code §§ 22-30B-1 to 22-30B-18 (1990 and Supp. 1991). Among other provisions, the Act includes a "cap" that generally limits the amount of hazardous wastes or substances that may be disposed of in any 1-year period, and the amount of hazardous waste disposal of during the first year under the Act's new fees becomes the permanent ceiling in subsequent years. Ala. Code § 22-30B-2.3 (1990). The cap applies to commercial facilities that dispose of over 100,000 tons of hazardous wastes or substances per year, but only the Emelle facility, as the only commercial facility operating within Alabama, meets this description. The Act also imposes a "base fee" of $25.60 per ton on all hazardous wastes and substances disposed of at commercial facilities, to be paid by the operator of the facility. Ala. Code § 22-30B-2(a) (Supp. 1991). Finally, the Act imposes the "additional fee" at issue here, which states in full:

> For waste and substances which are generated outside of Alabama and disposed of at a commercial site for the disposal of hazardous waste or hazardous substances in Alabama, an additional fee shall be levied at the rate of $72.00 per ton. § 22-30B-2(b)....

II. No State may attempt to isolate itself from a problem common to the several States by raising barriers to the free flow of interstate trade.[84] Today, in Fort Gratiot Sanitary Landfill, Inc. v. Michigan Dept. of Natural Resources, 60 USLW 4438 (1992), we have also considered a Commerce Clause challenge to a Michigan law prohibiting private landfill operators from accepting solid waste from outside that State to amount to economic protectionism barred by the Commerce Clause:

> [T]he evil of protection can reside in legislative means as well as legislative ends. Thus, it does not matter whether the ultimate aim of ch. 363 is to reduce the waste disposal costs of

---

84. The Alabama Supreme Court Assumed that the disposal of hazardous waste constituted an article of commerce, and the State does not explicitly argue here to the contrary. In Fort Gratiot Sanitary Landfill, Inc. v. Michigan Dept. of Natural Resources, we have reaffirmed the idea that "[s]olid waste, even if it has no value, is an article of commerce." As stated in Philadelphia v. New Jersey, 437 U.S. 617, 622-623 (1978): "All objects of interstate trade merit Commerce Clause protection; none is excluded by definition at the outset.... Just as Congress has power to regulate the interstate movement of these wastes, States are not free from constitutional scrutiny when they restrict that movement." The definition of "hazardous waste" makes clear that it is simply a grade of solid waste, albeit one of particularly noxious and dangerous propensities, but whether the business arrangements between out of state generators of hazardous waste and the Alabama operator of a hazardous waste landfill are viewed as "sales" of hazardous waste or "purchases" of transportation and disposal services, "the commercial transactions unquestionably have an interstate character. The Commerce Claus thus imposes some constraints on [Alabama's] ability to regulate these transaction." Fort Gratiot Sanitary Landfill, 60 USLW at 4440.

New Jersey residents or to save remaining open lands from pollution, for we assume New Jersey has every right to protect it residents' pocketbooks as well as their environment. And it may be assumed as well that New Jersey may pursue those ends by slowing the flow of all waste into the State's remaining landfills, even though interstate commerce may incidentally be affected. But whatever New Jersey's ultimate purpose, it may not be accompanied by discriminating against articles of commerce coming from outside the State unless there is some reason, apart from their origin, to treat them differently. Both on its face and in its plain effect, ch. 363 violates this principle of nondiscrimination.... Fort Gratiot Sanitary Landfill, at 4440 (Quoting Philadelphia v. New Jersey, supra, at 626-627).

The Act's additional fee facially discriminates against hazardous waste generated in States other than Alabama, and the Act overall has plainly discouraged the full operation of the Emelle facility.[85] Such burdensome taxes imposed on interstate commerce alone are generally forbidden...

The State, however, argues that the additional fee imposed on out-of-state hazardous waste serves legitimate local purposes related to its citizens' health and safety. Because the additional fee discriminates both on its face and in practical effect, the burden falls on the State "to justify it both in terms of the local benefits flowing from the statute and the unavailability of nondiscriminatory alternatives adequate to preserve the local interests at stake." Hunt v. Washington Apple Advertising Comm'n, 432 U.S. 333, 353 (1977). "At a minimum such facial discrimination invokes the strictest scrutiny of any purported legitimate local purpose and of the absence of nondiscriminatory alternatives." Hughes v. Oklahoma, 441 U.S. 322, 337 (1979).[86]

The State's argument here does not significantly differ from the Alabama Supreme Court's conclusions on the legitimate local purposes of the additional fee imposed, which were:

> The Additional Fee serves these legitimate local purposes that cannot be adequately served by reasonable nondiscriminatory alternatives: (1) protection of the health and safety of the citizens of Alabama from toxic substances; (2) conservation of the environment and the state's natural resources; (3) provision for compensatory revenue for the costs and burdens that out-

---

85. The Act went into effect July 15, 1990. The volume of hazardous waste buried at the Emelle facility fell dramatically from 791,000 tons in 1989 to 290,000 tons in 1991.

86. To some extent the State attempts to avail itself of the more flexible approach outlined in, e.g., Brown-Forman Distillers Corp. v. New York State Liquor Auth., 476 U.S. 573, 579 (1986), and Pike v. Bruce Church, Inc., 397 U.S. 137, 142 (1970), but this lesser scrutiny is only available "where other legislative objectives are credibly advanced *and* there is *no* patent discrimination against interstate trade." Philadelphia v. New Jersey, 437 U.S. 617, 624 (1978) (emphasis added). We find no room here to say that the Act presents "effects upon interstate commerce that are only incidental," ibid., for the Act's additional fee on its face targets only out-of-state hazardous waste. While no "clear line" separates close cases on which scrutiny should apply, "this is not a close case." Wyoming v. Oklahoma, 502 U.S.__, n. 12 (1992).

of-state waste generators impose by dumping their hazardous waste in Alabama; (4) reduction of the overall flow of wastes traveling on the state's highways, which flow creates a great risk to the health and safety of the state's citizens. 584 So.2d, at 1389.

These may all be legitimate local interests, and the petitioner has not attacked them. But only rhetoric, and not explanation, emerges as to why Alabama targets *only* interstate hazardous waste to meet these goals. As found by the Trial Court, "[a]lthough the Legislature imposed an additional fee of $72.00 per ton on waste generated outside Alabama, there is absolutely no evidence before this Court that waste generated outside Alabama is more dangerous than waste generated in Alabama. The Court finds under the facts of this case that the only basis for the additional fee is the origin of the waste." App. to Pet. for Cert. 83a-84a. In the face of such findings, invalidity under the Commerce Clause necessarily follows, for "whatever [Alabama's] ultimate purpose, it may not be accomplished by discriminating against articles of commerce coming from outside the State unless there is some reason, apart from their origin, to treat them differently." Philadelphia v. New Jersey, 437 U.S., at 626-627. The burden is on the State show that "the discrimination is demonstrably justified by a valid factor unrelated to economic protectionism," Wyoming v. Oklahoma, 502 U.S. -, -(slip op., at 16) (1992) (emphasis added), and it has not carried this burden.

Ultimately, the State's concern focuses on the volume of the waste entering the Emelle facility. Less discriminatory alternatives, however, are available to alleviate this concern, not the least of which are a generally applicable per-ton additional fee on all hazardous waste disposed of within Alabama, or a per-mile tax on all vehicles transporting hazardous waste across Alabama roads, or an evenhanded cap on the total tonnage landfilled at Emelle which would curtail volume from all sources. To the extent Alabama's concern touches environmental conservation and the health and safety of its citizens, such concern does not vary with the point of origin of the waste, and it remains within the State's power to monitor and regulate more closely the transportation and disposal of all hazardous waste within its bordered. Even with the possible future financial and environmental risks to be borne by Alabama, such risks likewise do not vary with the waste's State of origin in a way allowing foreign, but not local, waste to be burdened. In sum, we find the additional fee to be "an obvious effort to saddle those outside the State" with most of the burden of slowing the flow of waste into the Emelle facility. Philadelphia v. New Jersey, 437 U.S., at 629. "That legislative effort is clearly impermissible under the Commerce Clause of the Constitution."

Our decisions regarding quarantine laws do not counsel a different conclusion. The Act's additional fee may not legitimately be deemed a quarantine law because Alabama permits both the generation and landfilling of hazardous waste within its borders and the importation of still more hazardous waste subject to payment of the additional fee. In any event, while it is true that certain quarantine laws have not been considered forbidden protectionist measures, even though directed against out-of-state commerce, those laws "did not discriminate against interstate commerce as such, but simply prevented traffic in noxious articles, whatever their origin." Philadelphia v. New Jersey, supra, at 629....

The law struck down in Philadelphia v. New Jersey left local waste untouched, although no basis existed by which to distinguish interstate waste. But "[i]f one is inherently harmful, so is the other. Yet New Jersey has banned the former while leaving its landfill sites open to the latter." 437 U.S. at 629. Here, the additional fee applies only to interstate hazardous waste, but at all points from its entrance into Alabama until it is landfilled at the Emelle facility, every concern related to quarantine applies perforce to local hazardous waste, which pays no additional fee. For this reason, the additional fee does not survive the appropriate scrutiny applicable to discriminations against interstate commerce.

Maine v. Taylor, 477 U.S. 131 (1986), provides no additional justification. Maine there demonstrated that the out-of-state baitfish were subject to parasites foreign to in-state baitfish. This difference posed a threat to the State's Natural resources, and absent a less discriminatory means of protecting the environment-and none was available-the importation of baitfish could properly be banned. To the contrary, the record establishes that the hazardous waste at issue in this case is the same regardless of its point of origin. As noted in Fort Gratiot Sanitary Landfill, "our conclusion would be different is the important waste raised health or other concerns not presented by [Alabama] waste." 60 USLW at 442. Because no unique threat is posed, and because adequate means other than overt discrimination meet Alabama's concerns, Maine v. Taylor provides the State no respite.

III. The decision of the Alabama Supreme Court is reversed, and the cause remanded for proceedings not inconsistent with this opinion, including consideration of the appropriate relief to petitioner.

[The dissenting opinion of Chief Justice Rehnquist is omitted.]

COMMENTARY AND QUESTIONS

1. Discriminatory legislation. The threshold inquiry in most dormant commerce clause cases is whether the challenged state law attempts to discriminate against interstate commerce. At least as a matter of the common language appearing in many of the cases, there is "a virtually *per se* rule of invalidity" for discriminatory legislation. As will be seen in Maine v. Taylor, 477 U.S. 131 (1986), main text at page 508, however, even discriminatory legislation, upon a proper showing, can be sustained against a dormant commerce clause attack.

2. Even-handed legislation, the *Pike* test, and burden weighing. Regulation that is not deemed discriminatory against interstate commerce is subjected to the test set forth in the quotation from Pike v. Bruce Church, Inc. that appeared in the *Philadelphia* case. The purpose of the legislation must be legitimate (in furtherance of local public interest) and the burden on interstate commerce must be only "incidental." Even then, the burden of interstate commerce must be weighed against the local benefits in a fairly complex calculus that seeks to account for the importance of the local benefit and the extent of the burden on interstate commerce. This line of analysis is more fully considered in conjunction with Proctor & Gamble Corp. v. Chicago, main text at page 512.

3. The potential breadth of the Philadelphia v. New Jersey and *Chemical Waste* rulings. It seems fair to characterize the holdings in *Philadelphia* and *Chemical Waste* as being that states may not, consistent with the dormant commerce clause, hoard their natural resources, such as landfill or hazardous waste disposal sites. It also seems fair to characterize those cases as having held that states cannot bar interstate movement, even of articles that are undesirable, such as refuse and other forms of waste. What would a quarantine law have to do to avoid similar invalidation?

4. Using proof to support imposing differential fees. Although favorable precedents upholding differential in-and out-of-state fees are rare, Baldwin v. Montana Fish & Game Commission, 436 U.S. 371 (1978), upheld a 300% out-of-state/in-state elk hunting license fee differential. Montana justified the fee differential by pointing out its substantial expenditures on management and support of the elk herd and other natural resources using funds raised from laying taxes on its residents. In effect, Montana argued that it was evening out the burden of managing the elk herd between its in-state hunters, who paid via general taxes and out-of-state hunters who were not subject to Montana's taxing authority. Although the challenges to the Montana fee schedule were not based on the dormant commerce clause,[87] the logic of the decision raises the possibility that a dormant commerce clause challenge likewise could be overcome by proofs linking the additional fee charged to out-of-state waste disposal to specific in-state expenditures made in relation to in-state waste. In a sense, this is the obverse of the Court's willingness to entertain proof that accepting out-of-state waste for disposal is in fact more expensive than accepting in-state waste.

Oregon tried to make such a showing in an effort to justify a $2.50/ton fee for out-of-state solid waste in contrast to an $0.85/ton fee charged for in-state solid waste. In a Oregon Waste Systems v. Department of Environmental Quality, 114 S.Ct 1345 (1994), the Supreme Court invalidated the fee differential. The Court rejected the claim that the differential was a "compensatory tax" that evened out the tax burden imposed by Oregon on in- and out-of-state disposal firms. Oregon pointed out that its in-state waste firms paid other Oregon taxes, such as income tax. The majority was unimpressed, finding that the taxes on income and taxes on waste disposal are not being imposed on substantially equivalent activities.

Is there any line of justification for differential tipping fees (waste disposal fees) that will survive the careful scrutiny the Court insists will be given in such cases? There needs to be some objective reason to impose the higher fees, and unless the depository state has engaged in some sort of pre-treatment of its wastes, it is hard to imagine what makes all in-state pile of garbage different from an out-of-state pile of garbage. Mandatory pre-treatment of in-state municipal solid waste, for example, could include segregation of waste streams, so that small volume hazardous materials such as household batteries and non-commercial volumes of paints and solvents are absent from the in-state materials being landfilled. A differential fee might be justified upon a showing that the non-pretreated out-of-state waste stream will, in the long run, require more expensive

---

87. Two constitutional challenges were presented, one claiming a denial of equal protection and the other claiming a denial of the privileges and immunities of citizenship.

remedial treatment by the depository state than would the safer in-state waste stream.

5. Alabama's options after the *Chemical Waste Management* decision. The Supreme Court decision in the principal case was limited to the invalidation of the "additional fee" charged to out-of-state waste. The Court left undisturbed both the basic fee charged to all waste regardless of state of origin and the cap on total volume of waste to be disposed in any given year. Can Alabama raise the basic fee to slow the volume of waste sent to Emelle facility? Can Alabama pick a limit on the total volume that Emelle can accept at a figure as low as 100,000 tons per year, or even lower? The Court expressly acknowledged these devices as being constitutionally permissible means of slowing the total volume of waste disposed of in Alabama. Can Alabama force the closure of the facility by legislation? In regard to this last suggestion consider not only the takings claim that will be made by the facility operator, but also the claim of federal licensure as preemptive of the state's right to forbid the operation of the facility. Can the state avoid the preemption problem by relying on the *Pacific Gas & Electric* case, main text at page 483?

6. The similarity of dormant commerce clause analysis to takings analysis. In Chapter 9, at page 426 of the main text, the analysis of private property-based takings challenges to environmental regulations employed four separate inquiries: (1) proper authority; (2) proper (and not poison) public purpose; (3) a sufficiently close means-ends rationality; and (4) avoidance of excessive burdens. Dormant commerce clause analysis follows that same analytical breakdown remarkably closely. As with takings, the first item, proper authority, is necessary but not usually controversial, and is seldom the inquiry that scuttles challenged state or local regulations.[88] The takings law inquiry into proper and poison purposes is plainly picked up in dormant commerce clause cases in the disparate intensity of judicial review given to "discriminatory" as opposed to "even-handed" legislation. The inquiries into means-end rationality and balancing of burdens also appear in dormant commerce clause cases. See *Proctor & Gamble*, main text at page 512. In cases identified as discriminatory and protectionist, a far stricter means-ends fit and an absence of alternatives is required. In cases falling on the proper purpose side of the line, only basic rationality need to shown. Finally, as to the fourth inquiry, the avoidance of excessive burdens on the individual in the takings context finds a direct analog in the avoidance of excessive burdens on interstate commerce in the dormant commerce clause cases. If the burden on interstate commerce is disproportionate in comparison to other law's benefits, the law will be invalidated.

---

88. The treatment of the environmental altruism issue in *Proctor & Gamble* at page 512 of the main text, may reflect a concern on the authority issue, however. Another way the authority question is raised, of course, is where a defendant argues that the state or local power is eliminated by pre-emption.

PAGES 520-523   **Text replacement for pages 520-533, Scrutiny of protectionist environmental regulation under dormant commerce clause.**

Section 3. AVOIDING DORMANT COMMERCE CLAUSE SCRUTINY OF REGULATORY ACTIONS FAVORING IN-STATE INTERESTS

Remembering, Philadelphia v. New Jersey and Chemical Waste Management v. Hunt and their bans on reserving in-state waste disposal capacity for in-state users, it is easy to see how such parochial legislation gets enacted. It is very popular to legislate preferences that provide local benefits at the expense of out-of-state third parties who are not part of the voting electorate. In a post-Love Canal, NIMBY world, moreover, holding threats posed by dumpsites to a minimum is a very popular position. As one waste disposal official said in a federal hearing on the subject, "Everyone wants us to pick up the trash, but no one wants us to put it down."

After the Supreme Court's decision in Philadelphia, but before its June, 1992 decisions in Chemical Waste and Fort Gratiot Sanitary Landfill Inc. v. Michigan Department of Natural Resources, 60 USLW 4438, the states engaged in an array of devices to try to forbid out-of-state waste importation without violating the dormant commerce clause. This section will sample a number of statutes that have sought to discriminate against out-of-state waste while avoiding constitutional invalidation. Simultaneously, this survey also will provide a vehicle for reviewing some aspects of dormant commerce clause jurisprudence and exploring a number of additional doctrinal wrinkles.

a. THE MARKET PARTICIPANT DOCTRINE

Swin Resource Systems Inc. v. Lycoming County

United States Circuit Court of Appeals for the Third Circuit 1989
883 F.2d 245, certiorari denied, 110 S.Ct. 1127

BECKER, Circuit Judge.

[The operator of a solid waste processing facility brought suit against a county which operated a landfill, challenging on dormant commerce clause grounds regulations giving the county residents preference in use of the landfill.]

THE MARKET PARTICIPANT DOCTRINE

Swin contends that Lycoming's attempt to preserve its landfill's capacity for local residents by charging a higher price to dispose of distant waste in the landfill (and limiting the volume of distant waste accepted by the landfilled) constitutes an impermissible interference with and discrimination against interstate commerce in violation of the commerce clause. The district court granted the defendants' motion to dismiss the commerce clause claim on the ground that Lycoming had acted as a "market participant." Under the market participant doctrine, a state or state subdivision that acts as a market participant rather than a market regulator "is not subject to the restraints of the Commerce Clause." White v. Massachusetts Council of Construction Employers, Inc., 460 U.S. 204, 208 (1983)....

For the reasons explained below, we hold that Lycoming County acted as a market participant rather than a market regulator in deciding the conditions under which Swin could use its landfill. It is useful to begin our analysis with a review of the four principal market participant cases.

In Alexandria Scrap Corp. v. Hughes, 426 U.S. 794 (1976) the Supreme Court upheld Maryland's statutory scheme to rid the state of derelict automobiles, even though the scheme entailed two types of discrimination: (1) Maryland paid bounties to in-state scrap auto hulk processors while refusing to pay bounties to out-of-state processors on the same terms; and (2) Maryland paid bounties only for vehicles formerly titled in Maryland. The Court held that the statutory scheme was consistent with the commerce clause on the ground that Maryland was participating in the market rather than regulating it. As the majority put it, "[n]othing in the purposes animating the Commerce Clause prohibits a State, in the absence of congressional action, from participating in the market and exercising the right to favor its own citizens over others." 426 U.S. at 810.

In Reeves, Inc. v. Stake, 447 U.S. 429 (1980), the Court upheld a South Dakota policy of confining the sale of cement by a state-operated cement plant to residents of South Dakota in order to meet their demand during a "serious cement shortage." The Court affirmed "[t]he basic distinction drawn in *Alexandria Scrap* between States as market participants and States as market regulators" and concluded that "South Dakota, as a seller of cement, unquestionably fits the 'market participant' label." 447 U.S. at 436. The Court upheld the South Dakota policy even though Reeves, a Wyoming corporation that had purchased about 95% of its cement from South Dakota's state-operated plant for over twenty years, was forced to cut production by over 75% as a result of the policy.

In *White*, the Court, deeming the case "well within the scope of *Alexandria Scrap* and *Reeves*," upheld an executive order of the Mayor of Boston requiring all construction projects funded in whole or in part either by city funds or city-administered federal funds to be performed by a work force of at least 50% city residents. 460 U.S. at 211 n.7....

In South-Central Timber Development Co. v. Wunnicke, 467 U.S. 82 (1984), however, a plurality struck down Alaska's requirement that timber taken from state lands be processed in-state prior to export. Adhering to the distinction suggested in *White*, the plurality held that "[t]he limit of the market-participant doctrine must be that it allows a State to impose burdens on commerce within the market in which it is a participant, but [does not] allow [ ] it to ... impose conditions, whether by statute, regulation, or contract, that have a substantial regulatory effect outside of that particular market." 467 U.S. at 97. The Alaska policy crossed the line distinguishing participation from regulation because the conditions it attached to its timber sales amounted to "downstream regulation of the timber-processing market in which it is not a participant." 467 U.S. at 99....

No court, to our knowledge, has ever suggested that the commerce clause requires city-operated garbage trucks to cross state lines in order to pick up the garbage generated by residents of other states. If a city may constitutionally limit its trucks to collecting garbage generated by city residents, we see no constitutional reason why a city cannot also limit a city-operated dump to garbage generated by city residents. With respect to municipal garbage trucks and municipal garbage dumps, application of the market participant doctrine enables "the people [acting through their local government] to determine as conditions demand ... what services and functions the public welfare requires." *Reeves*, 447 U.S. at 438 n.11. The residents who reside within the jurisdiction of a county or municipality are unlikely to pay for local government services if they must bear the cost but the entire nation may receive the benefit....

DOES A "NATURAL RESOURCE" EXCEPTION APPLY HERE?

Swin's vigorous argument that Lycoming has attempted to harbor a scarce natural resource for its own residents brings us to the potential caveat we mentioned. While the harboring of a scarce manufactured product or human service does not preclude the invocation of the market participant doctrine because it is scarce (in *Reeves* the Supreme Court applied the doctrine to South Dakota's effort to harbor cement for its own residents despite a serious cement shortage) applied to a state's effort to harbor a scarce natural resource. Unlike a manufactured product or the provision of a human service, a state does not have the ability to develop a *natural* resource if it has not had the fortuity to be favored with such a resource. While it may seem fair for South Dakota to favor its citizens in the sale of cement from a state-owned cement plant, for a state to favor its own citizens in selling right to mine coal or limestone on state-owned lands, for example, or in selling state-owned coal or limestone, would seem less fair, especially if the state happened to be endowed with the bulk of our nation's coal or limestone reserves and the other states were dependent upon it....

Whether there is a natural resource exception to the market participation doctrine is a difficult question, but, fortunately, one which we need not answer at this level of abstraction. First, land, the natural resource at issue here, cannot be used for a landfill without the expenditure of at least some money to prepare it for that purpose. The Lycoming landfill is therefore "not simply happenstance," Sporhase v. Nebraska, 458 U.S. 941, 957 (1982), but is at least to some extent like South Dakota's cement plant in that government funds were needed to construct it. Moreover, since the land upon which the landfill was constructed has to be leased in this case, the land, even prior to development, bore some resemblance to South Dakota's cement plant in that is devotion to public use required the disbursement or promise of future disbursement of government resources....

COMMENTARY & QUESTIONS

1. The economic unreality of the market participant doctrine. The majority opinion in *Swin* raised a vigorous dissent by Chief Judge Gibbons. He argued that the market participant doctrine itself arose out of a "peculiar eruption of Dixieism" and is undercut by later Supreme Court decisions.[89] He also attacked the application of the market participant doctrine as premised on economic unreality:

> The present appeal provides a typical case in point. However much their market might be regulated, private landfill operators still desire to turn a profit. Few, if any, would give a second thought to the origin of the waste filling the space sold. Nor is it likely that any would long stay in business even assuming some highly unusual public commitment to the preservation of that space by locals. Under any realistic view, the Lycoming landfill in private hands would never have hindered its ability to sell space to the highest bidder by erecting a differential rate structure that discriminated against waste the further its point of origin. If anything, it would have created a fee structure that did precisely the opposite. A vendor of landfill space hoping to attract business, as do genuine market participants, would logically attempt to lure large volume purchasers concerned with transportation costs through a discount, especially when it appeared that customers dealing in local waste could not themselves provide sufficient business. As an exercise toward the political end of saving space for county waste, Lycoming County's price structure makes good regulatory sense. As an essay in market participation, it is aberrant and the majority's application of the label "market participant" to Lycoming County is an economic jest. 883 F.2d at 262.

There can be little doubt that Chief Judge Gibbons has correctly analyzed the economically irrational nature of the local preference aspect of Lycoming County's fee schedule, but is the market participant doctrine bottomed on the expectation that governmental entities will act in an economically rational fashion? Isn't a more plausible basis for the doctrine captured in the phrase that the state has "put its money where its mouth is." That is, the state has entered the market to buy the privilege of running a business irrationally. The state when it spends its money has not merely commanded via regulation that someone else, whose assets the state did not purchase in the marketplace, run her business in an irrational way that favors the state's residents and discriminates against interstate commerce.

2. A second strike for flow control. In C & A Carbone, Inc. v. Town of Clarkstown, __ S.Ct. __, 62 U.S.L.W. 4315 (1994), the Supreme Court struck down another effort at what is increasingly being referred to as the "flow control" process, by which state and local governments seek to plan where and how their waste streams will be transported, treated, and disposed of. In this case, the town of Clarkstown, New York, under a state order to close its existing municipal landfill and open a new solid waste

---

89. Eds.: His intent in this phrase was to attack decisions of the Court that challenged the accepted workings of federal supremacy and left the states some small range of operation in which to act contrary to federal directives. The principal object of his venom was National League of Cities v. Usery, 426 U.S. 833 (1976) which was decided on the same day and espousing some of the same ideas as *Alexandria Scrap*. *National League of Cities* has since been expressly overruled, thereby undercutting the conceptualization of states' rights that it shared with *Alexandria Scrap*.

transfer facility on that site, used a flow control ordinance to help secure the financing of the $1.4 million project. In order to induce a private firm to construct the needed facility, run it for a five year period, and then when it had made back the original investment plus a set profit, sell it to the town for one dollar, the town agreed to guarantee a minimum waste flow of 120,000 tons per year at a tipping fee of $81/ton. That fee exceeded the disposal cost of unsorted waste on the open market. To insure that the guaranteed tonnage would be sent to the facility, the town enacted an ordinance requiring all solid waste found within its borders to be brought to the facility (and be charged the $81/ton tipping fee). Carbone, a recycler of solid waste, violated the ordinance by sending the non-recyclable waste it collected out of state. Litigation ensued in which the New York state courts upheld the ordinance, finding that the ordinance did not discriminate against interstate commerce because it "applies evenhandedly to all solid waste processed within the Town, regardless of point of origin."[90] Writing for the Supreme Court majority Justice Kennedy was unsympathetic:

> We [here] consider a so-called flow control ordinance, which requires all solid waste to be processed at a designated transfer station before leaving the municipality. The avowed purpose of the ordinance is to retain the processing fees charged at the transfer station to amortize the cost of the facility. Because it attains this goal by depriving competitors, including out-of-state firms, of access to a local market, we hold that the flow control ordinance violates the Commerce Clause....

> At the outset we confirm that the flow control ordinance does regulate interstate commerce, despite the town's position to the contrary. The town says that its ordinance reaches only waste within its jurisdiction and is in practical effect a quarantine: It prevents garbage from entering the stream of interstate commerce until it is made safe. This reasoning is premised, however, on an outdated and mistaken concept of what constitutes interstate commerce.

> While the immediate effect of the ordinance is to direct local transport of solid waste to a designated site within the local jurisdiction, its economic effects are interstate in reach. The Carbone facility in Clarkstown receives and processes waste from places other than Clarkstown, including from out of State. By requiring Carbone to send the non-recyclable portion of this waste to the Route 303 transfer station at an additional cost, the flow control ordinance drives up the cost for out-of-state interests to dispose of their solid waste. Furthermore, even as to waste originant in Clarkstown, the ordinance prevents everyone except the favored local operator from performing the initial processing step. The ordinance thus deprives out-of-state businesses of access to a local market. These economic effects are more than enough to

---

90. Town of Clarkstown v. C.A. Carbone, Inc., 182 App. Div. 2d 213, 587 N. Y. S. 2d 681 (2d Dept. 1992).. The New York Court of Appeals denied petitioners' motion for leave to appeal. 80 N. Y. 2d 760, 605 N. E. 2d 874 (1992).

bring the Clarkstown ordinance within the purview of the Commerce Clause. It is well settled that actions are within the domain of the Commerce Clause if they burden interstate commerce or impede its free flow....

Clarkstown maintains that special financing is necessary to ensure the long-term survival of the designated facility. If so, the town may subsidize the facility through general taxes or municipal bonds. But having elected to use the open market to earn revenues for its project, the town may not employ discriminatory regulation to give that project an advantage over rival businesses from out of State....

State and local governments may not use their regulatory power to favor local enterprise by prohibiting patronage of out-of-state competitors or their facilities.

Three dissenters, Justices Souter, Blackmun, and Rehnquist, writing for himself, noted that the economic burden of the monopoly granted to the transit facility fell on the Clarkstown citizenry. The dissent concluded:

The Commerce Clause was not passed to save the citizens of Clarkstown from themselves. It should not be wielded to prevent them from attacking their local garbage problems with an ordinance that does not discriminate between local and out-of-town participants in the private market for trash disposal services and that is not protectionist in its purpose or effect. Local Law 9 conveys a privilege on the municipal government alone, the only market participant that bears responsibility for ensuring that adequate trash processing services continue to be available to Clarkstown residents. Because the Court's decision today is neither compelled by our local processing cases nor consistent with this Court's reason for inferring a dormant or negative aspect to the Commerce Clause in the first place, I respectfully dissent.

The *Carbone* case may have an impact on a significant number of trash-to-energy facilities that rely on similar flow controls to insure that sufficient amounts of waste will be brought in to serve them as fuel.

b.   THE CONGRESSIONAL AUTHORIZATION DOCTRINE

Dormant commerce clause jurisprudence exists in the vacuum created by congressional inaction. Nothing in the doctrine impairs the plenary power of Congress to override the judicially defined dormant commerce clause principles by expressly authorizing what courts would otherwise disallow. Congress has occasionally expressly done so. At least a few environmental and natural resource cases have argued that Congress, by the scheme of its legislation, has impliedly immunized state action from commerce clause scrutiny. Courts have demanded that the evidence of such a congressional intent be clear and the attempts in the environmental area have been unsuccessful. See South-Central Timber Development Co. v. Wunnicke, 467 U.S. 82 (1984).

In regard to limiting waste importation, at least one state, Alabama (before attempting the differential fee system involved in *Chemical Waste*

Management), tried (unsuccessfully) an argument paralleling the congressional authorization approach. The Emelle facility received more than 85% of its waste from outside of Alabama, with materials coming from all but two of the other states. In an inventive twist, attempting to limit the flow of hazardous materials into the Emelle facility, Alabama Code §22-30-11 forbade acceptance of out-of-state wastes from any state of origin that had not met certain *federal* compliance requirements for hazardous waste management within its own borders.

In setting its exclusionary conditions, Alabama borrowed the substance of §104(c)(9) of CERCLA as amended by SARA, 42 U.S.C.A. §9604(c)(9). The crux of §104(c)(9) is that it requires all states to have an EPA-approved Assurance of Hazardous Waste Capacity. These assurances amount to having a plan for disposing of at least as much hazardous waste as the state generates. Acceptable plans for disposal include having in-state disposal capacity for all such waste, or formal agreements with states that have excess disposal capacity. Under federal law, the burden of this provision falls on the states that will need to export some portion of their waste. There is no requirement in federal statutory law that a state agree to accept wastes generated elsewhere.

The Alabama law was challenged by the owner of the Emelle facility and a waste industry association. A district court decision upholding the law, National Solid Waste Management Association v. Alabama Department of Environmental Management, 729 F.Supp. 792 (N.D.Ala. 1990), was reversed on appeal. 910 F.2d 713 (11th Cir. 1990).[91] After finding that the Alabama law was a "protectionist measure" to be scrutinized strictly, the court addressed the congressional authorization argument:

> Defendants contend that SARA's section 104(c)(9) effected a redistribution of power over interstate commerce. According to defendants, the SARA amendments to CERCLA gave the states more responsibility for hazardous waste management, including an obligation to develop increased treatment and disposal capacity. But nothing in SARA evidences congressional authorization for each state to close its borders to wastes generated in other states to force those other states to meet federally mandated hazardous waste management requirements. SARA places the burden of making capacity assurances for future hazardous waste management on the generating state and imposes a sanction on that state for failure to satisfy its obligation.[92] Congress has not, in our opinion, authorized Alabama to restrict the free movement of hazardous wastes across Alabama's borders. See State of Alabama v. United States EPA, 871 F.2d at 1555 n. 3 ("Although Congress may override the commerce clause by express statutory language, it has not done so in enacting CERCLA." If Congress intended to allow the states to restrict

---

91. This decision was later modified in ways not relevant to the congressional authorization doctrine. 924 F.2d 1001 (1990) and thereafter certiorari was denied, 111 S.Ct. 2800 (1991).

92. The sanction, withholding of funds for remedial cleanups of Superfund sites on the National Priorities List, seems effective because, in March 1989, almost every state had at least one site on this list. See 40 C.F.R. Part 300, App. B (1989).

the interstate movement of hazardous wastes as Alabama has tried to do, Congress could (and still can) plainly say so.[93] 910 F.2d 713, 721-22.

c. FACIALLY EVEN-HANDED REGULATORY SYSTEMS

As a matter of doctrine, it is patent that even-handed state environmental regulation that does not discriminate against interstate commerce has a good chance of being upheld against a dormant commerce clause challenge. The more intriguing problem in the area of blocking the importation of out-of-state waste, is how to accomplish a discriminatory result using regulations that are even-handed. The even-handed laws may still be struck down if their burden on interstate commerce is excessive, but at least they survive to that last stage of constitutional inquiry and may be upheld if heir impact on interstate commerce is not too significant.

The most obviously even-handed laws are ones that treat in-state and out-of-state wastes identically. Michigan enacted a law that it thought was sufficiently interstate commerce neutral by authorizing its counties to discriminate on the basis of the origin of wastes as either in-county or out-of-county. More specifically, the Michigan Solid Waste Management Act (MSWMA) provided for a state-wide regulatory scheme for disposal of solid waste that delegated much of the responsibility for planning to the individual counties:

> A person shall not accept for disposal solid waste ... that is not generated in the county in which the disposal area is located unless the acceptance of solid waste ... that is not generated in the county is explicitly authorized in the approved county solid waste management plan.[94]

If a county wants to serve out-of-county disposers of waste it could do so only as part of a state-approved county waste management plan. A dormant commerce clause challenge to the statute was mounted by a landfill operator whose request to his county waste planning agency for authorization to accept out-of-state waste was denied. The law was upheld by the United States Circuit Court of Appeals:

> Further, we find no error in the district court's ultimate conclusion that "MSWMA imposes only incidental effects upon interstate commerce, and may therefore be upheld" unless clearly excessive as compared to local benefits under *Pike*. MSWMA does, indeed, as found by Michigan courts and by the district court, provide a "comprehensive plan for waste disposal, through which appropriate planning for such disposal

---

93. For example, under the Low-level Radioactive Waste Policy Act, 42 U.S.C. §§ 2021b-2021j (1982 & Supp. V 1987), states are encouraged to enter into regional compacts to provide for teh establishment and operation of regional compacts to provide for the establishment and operation of regional disposal facilities for low-level radioactive waste. 42 U.S.C. § 2021d. In this Act, which predates SARA, Congress expressly authorized states that enter into such compacts to ban waste shipments form states that neither enter into a compact nor meet federal deadlines for establishing their own facilities. 42 U.S.C. § 2021e(e)(2), (f)(2)(1).

94. Mich. Stat. Ann. § 13.29(13a); Mich. Comp. Laws Ann. § 299.413a.

can result." Thus, we conclude that the attack on the facial
constitutionality of the Michigan statute in question must fail.

The Supreme Court, however, disagreed with the premise that the
legislation was sufficiently even-handed to be tested by the Pike v. Bruce
Church standard. Writing for a seven majority, Justice Stevens stated,
"our prior cases teach that a State (or one of its political subdivisions) may
not avoid the strictures of the Commerce Clause by curtailing the
movement of articles of commerce through subdivisions of the State,
rather than through the State itself." Fort Gratiot Sanitary Landfill, Inc. v.
Michigan Department of Natural Resources, 60 USLW 4438, 4440 (June
1, 1992). The Court, in accord with its typical dormant commerce clause
jurisprudence, required the state to bear the burden of justification for its
discrimination. The Court almost peremptorily found all of the proffered
justifications wanting and invalidated the ban.

COMMENTARY & QUESTIONS

1. Localization as a device. The in-county rule adopted by Michigan is
not the only form of localization of waste requirement that can be
imagined. Citing the dangers of long distance transport of materials, for
example, a state could place a twenty mile limit on transport of waste for
landfilling. Such a law will wall out most interstate wastes, but it also
means that there must be a significant number of in-state sites. Will such
a law survive after *Fort Gratiot*?

Chapter 11,   Environmental Administrative Law

PAGE 539   **Diagramming government**

The diagram on the following page is an attempt to provide a schematic chart for the political and functional structure of government as it works day to day in reality. Because operative reality is a great deal more complex than the models learned in eighth grade civics, the chart shows more than the traditional three branches of government.

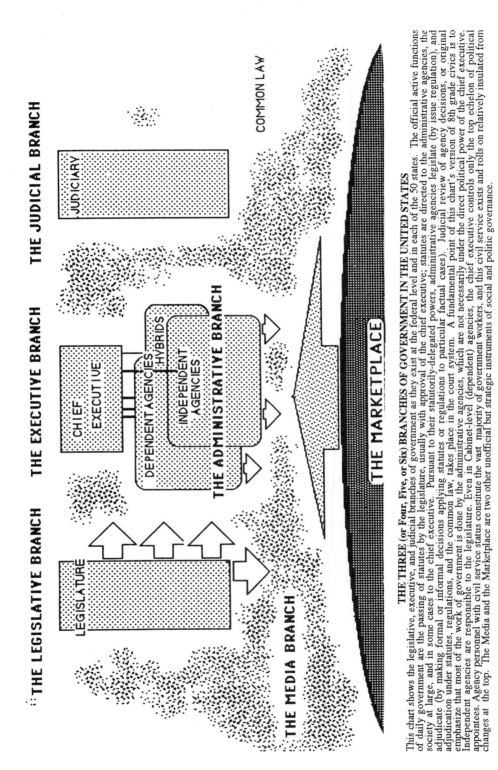

THE THREE (or Four, Five, or Six) BRANCHES OF GOVERNMENT IN THE UNITED STATES

This chart shows the legislative, executive, and judicial branches of government as they exist at the federal level and in each of the 50 states. The official active functions of daily government are the passing of statutes by the legislature, usually with approval of the chief executive; statutes are directed to the administrative agencies, the society at large, and in some cases to the chief executive. Pursuant to their statutorily-delegated powers, administrative agencies legislate (by issue regulation), and adjudicate (by making formal or informal decisions applying statutes or regulations to particular factual cases). Judicial review of agency decisions, or original adjudication under statutes, regulations, and the common law, takes place in the court system. A fundamental point of this chart's version of 8th grade civics is to emphasize that most of the work of government is done by the administrative agencies, which are not necessarily under the direct political power of the chief executive. Independent agencies are responsible to the legislature. Even in Cabinet-level (dependent) agencies, the chief executive controls only the top echelon of political appointees. Agency personnel with civil service status constitute the vast majority of government workers, and this civil service exists and rolls on relatively insulated from changes at the top. The Media and the Marketplace are two other unofficial but strategic instruments of social and politic governance.

PAGE 569   Citizens oversight councils

Faced with the conclusion that official regulatory oversight and enforcement before the Alaska oil spill had been lax and complacent in the face of industry corner-cutting, three models of citizen oversight councils were initiated: a private contractually-negotiated model, a state legislated council, and a federal model written into law in OPA '90. As noted in the coursebook, 570, the first model was subsumed into the third. The state council, after its research began to produce embarrassing evidence of state non-enforcement of pollution laws, was defunded and shut down by an effort led by industry lobbyists in the legislature.

The federal oversight councils authorized in the statutory provisions below will be far harder to neutralize. The terms of this innovative administrative experiment are interesting and potentially important far beyond the waters of the Gulf of Alaska.

Oil Po llution Act of 1994, 33 U.S.C.A. §2732
Subchapter II— Prince William Sound Provisions

§2732. Terminal and tanker oversight and monitoring

This section may be cited as the "Oil Terminal and Oil Tanker Environmental Oversight and Monitoring Act of 1990".

(2) The Congress finds that —

(A) the March 24, 1989, grounding and rupture of the fully loaded oil tanker, the EXXON VALDEZ, spilled 11 million gallons of crude oil in Prince William Sound, an environmentally sensitive area;

(B) many people believe that complacency on the part of the industry and government personnel responsible for monitoring the operation of the Valdez terminal and vessel traffic in Prince William Sound was one of the contributing factors to the EXXON VALDEZ oil spill;

(C) one way to combat this complacency is to involve local citizens in the process of preparing, adopting, and revising oil spill contingency plans;

(D) a mechanism should be established which fosters the long-term partnership of industry, government, and local communities in overseeing compliance with environmental concerns in the operation of crude oil terminals;

(E) such a mechanism presently exists at the Sullom Voe terminal in the Shetland Islands and this terminal should serve as a model for others;

(F) because of the effective partnership that has developed at Sullom Voe, Sullom Voe is considered the safest terminal in Europe;

(G) the present system of regulation and oversight of crude oil terminals in the United States has degenerated into a process of continual mistrust and confrontation;

(H) only when local citizens are involved in the process will the trust develop that is necessary to change the present system from confrontation to consensus;

(I) a pilot program patterned after Sullom Voe should be established in Alaska to further refine the concepts and relationships involved; and

(J) similar programs should eventually be established in other major crude oil terminals in the United States because the recent oil spills in Texas, Delaware, and Rhode Island indicate that the safe transportation of crude oil is a national problem.

(b) Demonstration Programs

(1) Establishment. There are established two Oil Terminal and Oil Tanker Environmental Oversight and Monitoring Demonstration Programs (hereinafter referred to as "Programs") to be carried out in the State of Alaska.

(2) Advisory function

The function of these Programs shall be advisory only.

(3) Purpose

The Prince William Sound Program shall be responsible for environmental monitoring of the terminal facilities in Prince William Sound and the crude oil tankers operating in Prince William Sound. The Cook Inlet Program shall be responsible for environmental monitoring of the terminal facilities and crude oil tankers operating in Cook Inlet located South of the latitude at Point Possession and North of the latitude at Amatuli Island, including offshore facilities in Cook Inlet.

(4) Suits barred

No program, association, council, committee or other organization created by this section may sue any person or entity, public or private, concerning any matter arising under this section except for the performance of contracts.

(c) Oil Terminal Facilities and Oil Tanker Operations Association

(1) Establishment

There is established an Oil Terminal Facilities and Oil Tanker Operations Association (hereinafter in this section referred to as the "Association") for each of the Programs established under subsection (b) of this section.

(2) Membership

Each Association shall be comprised of 4 individuals as follows:

(A) One individual shall be designated by the owners and operators of the terminal facilities and shall represent those owners and operators.

(B) One individual shall be designated by the owners and operators of the crude oil tankers calling at the terminal facilities and shall represent those owners and operators.

(C) One individual shall be an employee of the State of Alaska, shall be designated by the Governor of the State of Alaska, and shall represent the State government.

(D) One individual shall be an employee of the Federal Government, shall be designated by the President, and shall represent the Federal Government.

(3) Responsibilities

Each Association shall be responsible for reviewing policies relating to the operation and maintenance of the oil terminal facilities and crude oil tankers which affect or may affect the environment in the vicinity of their respective terminals....

(d) Regional Citizens' Advisory Councils

(1) Membership

There is established a Regional Citizens' Advisory Council (hereinafter in this section referred to as the "Council") for each of the programs established by subsection (b) of this section.

(2) Membership

Each Council shall be composed of voting members and nonvoting members, as follows:

(A) Voting members

Voting members shall be Alaska residents and, except as provided in clause (vii) of this paragraph, shall be appointed by the Governor of the State of Alaska from a list of nominees provided by each of the following interests, with one representative appointed to represent each of the following interests, taking into consideration the need for regional balance on the Council:

(i) Local commercial fishing industry organizations, the members of which depend on the fisheries resources of the waters in the vicinity of the terminal facilities.

(ii) Aquaculture associations in the vicinity of the terminal facilities.

(iii) Alaska Native Corporations and other Alaska Native organizations the members of which reside in the vicinity of the terminal facilities.

(iv) Environmental organizations the members of which reside in the vicinity of the terminal facilities.

(v) Recreational organizations the members of which reside in or use the vicinity of the terminal facilities.

(vi) The Alaska State Chamber of Commerce, to represent the locally based tourist industry.

(vii)(I) For the Prince William Sound Terminal Facilities Council, one representative selected by each of the following municipalities: Cordova, Whittier, Seward, Valdez, Kodiak, the Kodiak Island Borough, and the Kenai Peninsula Borough.

(II) For the Cook Inlet Terminal Facilities Council, one representative selected by each of the following municipalities: Homer, Seldovia, Anchorage, Kenai, Kodiak, the Kodiak Island Borough, and the Kenai Peninsula Borough.

(B) Nonvoting members

One ex-officio, nonvoting representative shall be designated by, and represent, each of the following:

(i) The Environmental Protection Agency.

(ii) The Coast Guard.

(iii) The National Oceanic and Atmospheric Administration.

(iv) The United States Forest Service.

(v) The Bureau of Land Management.

(vi) The Alaska Department of Environmental Conservation.

(vii) The Alaska Department of Fish and Game.

(viii) The Alaska Department of Natural Resources.

(ix) The Division of Emergency Services, Alaska Department of Military and Veterans Affairs.

(3) Terms

(A) Duration of Councils

The term of the Councils shall continue throughout the life of the operation of the Trans-Alaska Pipeline System and so long as oil is transported to or from Cook Inlet.

(B) Three years

The voting members of each Council shall be appointed for a term of 3 years...

(4) Self-governing

Each Council shall elect its own chairperson, select its own staff, and make policies with regard to its internal operating procedures. After the initial organizational meeting called by the Secretary under subsection (i) of this section, each Council shall be self-governing.

(5) Dual membership and conflicts of interest prohibited....

Each Council shall —

(A) provide advice and recommendations to the Association on policies, permits, and site-specific regulations relating to the operation and maintenance of terminal facilities and crude oil tankers which affect or may affect the environment in the vicinity of the terminal facilities;

(B) monitor through the committee established under subsection (e) of this section, the environmental impacts of the operation of the terminal facilities and crude oil tankers;

(C) monitor those aspects of terminal facilities' and crude oil tankers' operations and maintenance which affect or may affect the environment in the vicinity of the terminal facilities;

(D) review through the committee established under subsection (f) of this section, the adequacy of oil spill prevention and contingency plans for the terminal facilities and the adequacy of oil spill prevention and contingency plans for crude oil tankers, operating in Prince William Sound or in Cook Inlet;

(E) provide advice and recommendations to the Association on port operations, policies and practices;

(F) recommend to the Association —

(i) standards and stipulations for permits and site-specific regulations intended to minimize the impact of the terminal facilities' and crude oil tankers' operations in the vicinity of the terminal facilities;

(ii) modifications of terminal facility operations and maintenance intended to minimize the risk and mitigate the impact of terminal facilities, operations in the vicinity of the terminal facilities and to minimize the risk of oil spills;

(iii) modifications of crude oil tanker operations and maintenance in Prince William Sound and Cook Inlet intended to minimize the risk and mitigate the impact of oil spills; and

(iv) modifications to the oil spill prevention and contingency plans for terminal facilities and for crude oil tankers in Prince William Sound and Cook Inlet intended to enhance the ability to prevent and respond to an oil spill; and

(G) create additional committees of the Council as necessary to carry out the above functions, including a scientific and technical advisory committee to the Prince William Sound Council.

(7) No estoppel

No Council shall be held liable under State or Federal law for costs or damages as a result of rendering advice under this section. Nor shall any advice given by a voting member of a Council, or program representative or agent, be grounds for estopping the interests represented by the voting Council members from seeking damages or other appropriate relief.

(8) Scientific work

In carrying out its research, development and monitoring functions, each Council is authorized to conduct its own scientific research and shall review the scientific work undertaken by or on behalf of the terminal operators or crude oil tanker operators as a result of a legal requirement to undertake that work. Each Council shall also review the relevant scientific work undertaken by or on behalf of any government entity relating to the terminal facilities or crude oil tankers. To the extent possible, to avoid unnecessary duplication, each Council shall coordinate its independent scientific work with the scientific work performed by or on behalf of the terminal operators and with the scientific work performed by or on behalf of the operators of the crude oil tankers.

(e) Committee for Terminal and Oil Tanker Operations and Environmental Monitoring

(1) Monitoring Committee

Each Council shall establish standing Terminal and Oil Tanker Operations and Environmental Monitoring Committee (hereinafter in this section referred to as the "Monitoring Committee") to devise and manage a comprehensive program of monitoring the environmental impacts of the operations of terminal facilities and of crude oil tankers while operating in Prince William Sound and Cook Inlet. The membership of the Monitoring Committee shall be made up of members of the Council, citizens, and recognized scientific experts selected by the Council.

(2) Duties

In fulfilling its responsibilities, the Monitoring Committee shall —

(A) advise the Council on a monitoring strategy that will permit early detection of environmental impacts of terminal facility operations and crude oil tanker operations while in Prince William Sound and Cook Inlet;

(B) develop monitoring programs and make recommendations to the Council on the implementation of those programs;

(C) at its discretion, select and contract with universities and other scientific institutions to carry out specific monitoring projects authorized by the Council pursuant to an approved monitoring strategy;

(D) complete any other tasks assigned by the Council; and

(E) provide written reports to the Council which interpret and assess the results of all monitoring programs.

(f) Committee for Oil Spill Prevention, Safety, and Emergency Response

(1) Technical Oil Spill Committee

Each Council shall establish a standing technical committee (hereinafter referred to as "Oil Spill Committee") to review and assess measures designed to prevent oil spills and the planning and preparedness for responding to, containing, cleaning up, and mitigating impacts of oil spills. The membership of the Oil Spill Committee shall be made up of members of the Council, citizens, and recognized technical experts selected by the Council.

(2) Duties

In fulfilling its responsibilities, the Oil Spill Committee shall —

(A) periodically review the respective oil spill prevention and contingency plans for the terminal facilities and for the crude oil tankers while in Prince William Sound or Cook Inlet, in light of new technological developments and changed circumstances;

(B) monitor periodic drills and testing of the oil spill contingency plans for the terminal facilities and for crude oil tankers while in Prince William Sound and Cook Inlet;

(C) study wind and water currents and other environmental factors in the vicinity of the terminal facilities which may affect the ability to prevent, respond to, contain, and clean up an oil spill;

(D) identify highly sensitive areas which may require specific protective measures in the event of a spill in Prince William Sound or Cook Inlet;

(E) monitor developments in oil spill prevention, containment, response, and cleanup technology;

(F) periodically review port organization, operations, incidents, and the adequacy and maintenance of vessel traffic service systems designed to assure safe transit of crude oil tankers pertinent to terminal operations;

(G) periodically review the standards for tankers bound for, loading at, exiting from, or otherwise using the terminal facilities;

(H) complete any other tasks assigned by the Council; and

(I) provide written reports to the Council outlining its findings and recommendations.

(g) Agency cooperation

...Each Federal department, agency, or other instrumentality shall, with respect to all permits, site-specific regulations, and other matters governing the activities and actions of the terminal facilities which affect or may affect the vicinity of the terminal facilities, consult with the appropriate Council prior to taking substantive action with respect to the permit, site-specific regulation, or other matter. This consultation shall be carried out with a view to enabling the appropriate Association and Council to review the permit, site-specific regulation, or other matters and make appropriate recommendations regarding operations, policy or agency actions. Prior consultation shall not be required if an authorized Federal agency representative reasonably believes that an emergency exists requiring action without delay.

(h) Recommendations of the Council

In the event that the Association does not adopt, or significantly modifies before adoption, any recommendation of the Council made pursuant to the authority granted to the Council in subsection (d) of this section, the Association shall provide to the Council, in writing, within 5 days of its decision, notice of its decision and a written statement of reasons for its rejection or significant modification of the recommendation.

(i) Administrative actions....

(2) Compensation

No member of an Association or Council shall be compensated for the member's services as a member of the Association or Council, but shall be allowed travel expenses, including per diem in lieu of subsistence, at a rate established by the Association or Council not to exceed the rates authorized for employees of agencies under sections 5702 and 5703 of Title 5. However, each Council may enter into contracts to provide compensation and expenses to members of the committees created under subsections (d), (e), and (f) of this section.

(k) Funding

(1) Requirement

Approval of the contingency plans required of owners and operators of the Cook Inlet and Prince William Sound terminal facilities and crude oil tankers while operating in Alaskan waters in commerce with those terminal facilities shall be effective only so long as the respective Association and Council for a facility are funded pursuant to paragraph (2).

(2) Prince William Sound program

The owners or operators of terminal facilities or crude oil tankers operating in Prince William Sound shall provide, on an annual basis, an aggregate amount of not more than $2,000,000, as determined by the Secretary. Such amount —

(A) shall provide for the establishment and operation on the environmental oversight and monitoring program in Prince William Sound....

(3) Cook Inlet program

The owners or operators of terminal facilities, offshore facilities, or crude oil tankers operating in Cook Inlet shall provide, on an annual basis, an aggregate amount of not more than $1,000,000....

(1) Regulatory authority

Nothing in this section shall be construed as modifying, repealing, superseding, or preempting any municipal, State or Federal law or regulation, or in any way affecting litigation arising from oil spills or the rights and responsibilities of the United States or the State of Alaska, or municipalities thereof, to preserve and protect the environment through regulation of land, air, and water uses, of safety, and of related development. The monitoring provided for by this section shall be designed to help assure compliance with applicable laws and regulations and shall only extend to activities —

(A) that would affect or have the potential to affect the vicinity of the terminal facilities and the area of crude oil tanker operations included in the Programs; and

(B) are subject to the United States or State of Alaska, or municipality thereof, law, regulation, or other legal requirement.

(2) Recommendations

This subsection is not intended to prevent the Association or Council from recommending to appropriate authorities that existing legal requirements should be modified or that new legal requirements should be adopted.

(o) Alternative voluntary advisory group in lieu of Council [This provision was used to certify the privately negotiated Prince William Sound Regional Citizens Advisory Council, PWS RCAC, as the federally-recognized Council under OPA]....

The requirements of subsections (c) through (l) of this section...are deemed to have been satisfied so long as the following conditions are met:

(1) Prince William Sound

With respect to the Prince William Sound Program, the Alyeska Pipeline Service Company or any of its owner companies enters into a contract for the duration of the operation of the Trans-Alaska Pipeline System with the Alyeska Citizens Advisory Committee in existence on August 18, 1990, or a successor organization, to fund that Committee or organization on an annual basis in the amount provided for by subsection (k)(2)(A) of this section and the President annually certifies that the Committee or organization fosters the general goals and purposes of this section and is broadly representative of the communities and interests in the vicinity of the terminal facilities and Prince William Sound....

PAGE 570   **Citizen enforcement attorneys fees and the Supreme Court: *Dague***

One of the dramatic changes in environmental administrative law has been the congressional decision to put the possibility of attorneys fee recoveries into regulatory statutes to encourage citizens to take on the onerous burdens of trying to enforce federal laws. Prevailing plaintiffs, however, have often found courts responsive to defendants' attempts to restrict such awards, in some cases finding that public interest plaintiffs — since they are supposed to be motivated by civic impulse rather than commercial incentive — should be given less-than-commercial fee rates.

In this case the Supreme Court faced another situation: whether a citizen enforcement fee should be able to claim an enhancement over normal hourly rates to take account of the fact that attorneys take a gamble on a zero-recovery when they represent citizen plaintiffs enforcing federal law.

City of Burlington, v. Ernest Dague, Sr., et al.

Supreme Court of the United States, 1992

__U.S. __, 112 S. Ct. 2638

Scalia, J.   Respondent Dague owns land in Vermont adjacent to a landfill that was owned and operated by petitioner City of Burlington. Represented by attorneys retained on a contingent-fee basis, he sued Burlington over its operation of the landfill. The District Court ruled, inter alia, that Burlington had violated provisions of the SWDA and the CWA, and ordered Burlington to close the landfill by January 1, 1990. It also determined that Dague was a "substantially prevailing party" entitled to an award of attorney's fees under the Acts, see 42 U.S.C. § 6972(e); 33 U.S.C. § 1365(d), 732 F. Supp. 458 (Vt. 1989).

In calculating the attorney's fees award, the District Court first found reasonable the figures advanced by Dague for his attorneys' hourly rates and for the number of hours expended by them, producing a resulting "lodestar" attorney's fee of $198,027.50. (What our cases have termed the "lodestar" is "the product of reasonable hours times a reasonable rate," Pennsylvania v. Delaware Valley Citizens' Council for Clean Air, 478 U.S. 546, 565 (1986) (Delaware Valley I.) Addressing Dague's request for a contingency enhancement, the court looked to Circuit precedent, which provided that "the rationale that should guide the court's discretion is whether" without the possibility of a fee enhancement...competent counsel might refuse to represent [environmental] clients thereby denying them effective access to the courts. (quoting Friends of the Earth v. Eastman Kodak Co., 834 F. 2d 295, 298 (CA2 1987). Following this guidance, the court declared that Dague's "risk of not prevailing was substantial" and that "absent an opportunity for enhancement, [Dague] would have faced substantial difficulty in obtaining counsel of reasonable skill and competence in this complicated field of law." It concluded that "a 25% enhancement is appropriate, but anything more would be a windfall to the attorney's." It therefore enhanced the lodestar amount by 25%—$49,506.87. The Court of Appeals affirmed...

[The Supreme Court reversed holding that contingency settings should not receive enhancements.] An enhancement for contingency would likely duplicate in substantial part factors already subsumed in the lodestar. The risk of loss in a particular case (and therefore, the attorney's contingent risk) is the product of two factors: (1) the legal and factual merits of the claim, and (2) the difficulty of establishing those merits. The second factor, however, is ordinarily reflected in the lodestar—either in the higher number of hours expended to overcome the difficulty, or in the higher hourly rate of the attorney skilled and experienced enough to do so. Blum v. Stenson, 465 U.S. 886, 898 (1984). Taking account of it again through lodestar enhancement amounts to double-counting. Delaware Valley II, 483 U.S., at 726-727 (plurality opinion).

The first factor (relative merits of the claim) is not reflected in the lodestar, but there are good reasons why it should play no part in the calculation of the award... The consequence of awarding contingency enhancement to take account of this "merits" factor would be to provide attorneys with the same incentive to bring relatively meritless claims as relatively meritorious ones.

BLACKMUN and STEVENS , JJ, dissenting.   In language typical of most federal fee-shifting provisions, the statutes involved in this case authorize courts to award the prevailing party a "reasonable" attorney's fee. Two principles, in my view, require the conclusion that the "enhanced" fee awarded to respondents was reasonable. First, this Court consistently has recognized that a "reasonable" fee is to be a "fully compensatory fee," *Hensley v. Eckerhart*, 461 U.S. 424, 435 (1983), and is to be "calculated on the basis of rates and practices prevailing in the relevant market." *Missouri v. Jenkins*, 491 U.S. 274, 286 (1989). Second, it is a fact of the market that an attorney who is paid only when his client prevails will tend to charge a higher fee than one who is paid regardless of outcome, and relevant professional standards long have recognized that this practice is reasonable.

O'CONNOR, J., dissenting. I continue to be of the view that in certain circumstances a "reasonable" attorney's fee should not be computed by the purely retrospective lodestar figure, but also must incorporate a reasonable incentive to an attorney contemplating whether or not to take a case in the first place. See Pennsylvania v. Delaware Valley Citizens' Council for Clean Air, 483 U.S. 711, 731-734 (1987) (Delaware Valley II) (O'CONNOR, J., concurring in part and concurring in judgment). As JUSTICE BLACKMUN cogently explains, when an attorney must choose between two cases—one with a client who will pay the attorney's fees win or lose and the other who can only promise the statutory compensation if the case is successful—the attorney will choose the fee-paying client, unless the contingency-client can promise an enhancement of sufficient magnitude to justify the extra risk of nonpayment. Thus, a reasonable fee should be one that would "attract competent counsel," Delaware Valley II, supra, at 733 (O'CONNOR, J., concurring in part and concurring in judgment), and in some markets this must include the assurance of a contingency enhancement if the plaintiff should prevail. I therefore dissent from the Court's holding that a "reasonable" attorney's fee can never include an enhancement for cases taken on contingency.

COMMENTARY AND QUESTIONS

1. Does the lodestar capture the disincentives against contingency public suits? The debate in *Dague* comes down to a question of practical logic. Does an award of normal rates for hours worked take account of the burdens implicit in public interest contingency cases to level the balance, so that attorneys are encouraged to take on these cases rather than regular commercial clients? Putting yourself in the situation of an attorney who must make such a choice, is your personal benefit-cost ratio the same in either case? Does Justice Scalia's logic incorporate the practical calculus that inclines attorneys in public enforcement actions to hold back on massive investments of time and resources in cases that may not pay?

On the other hand, does Congress's mandate for "reasonable attorney and expert witness fees" necessarily mean that attorneys should have a level choice between citizen enforcement and commercial clients. Isn't there something to the argument of the pro bono civic nature of the undertaking that is in part its own reward?

For an analysis of *Dague*, see Axline, "Decreasing Incentives to Enforce Environmental Laws," 43 J. Urb. & Contemp. Law 257 (1993).

PAGE 574   **More restrictions on standing: *Lujan v. Defenders of Wildlife***

[Text replacement for 574-580]

b. The courts' ability to constrict standing

The evolution of standing, making the administrative and judicial forums open to citizen participation, was noted earlier as an important part of the 1960s' pluralistic expansion of the legal system. When Congress began to attach provisions authorizing citizen enforcement lawsuits to major environmental statutes, see coursebook at 565-66, it made a dramatic practical difference in whether federal laws would be obeyed, and a dramatic indication of the fact that in the absence of active citizens, government agencies could not or would not do a sufficient job of enforcing federal law. The standing doctrine continues to be a threshold question in all litigation, and is not subject to clear objective standards.

Standing is ultimately a judicial doctrine. It is courts that determine when citizens can claim standing and when they cannot, even under statutory grants of standing. Standing principles can be broadened to permit litigation on issues for which judges want to have dispositive determinations, and conversely can be narrowed to nip off challenges that courts would rather not have to decide. In the federal courts, standing turns on several different inquiries: on personal injury-in-fact, which has been held necessary to establish Article III "case or controversy" standing; on the "zone of interests" test, a court-made rule drawn from the APA's §702, requiring that plaintiffs must be within a class that Congress intended to benefit when it passed the law that they are attempting to enforce;[95] and several judge-made "prudential principles" by which

---

95. This is a test that the Supreme Court has often interpreted broadly. See Clarke v. Securities Industry Ass'n, 479 U.S. 388 (1987):
The [APA] should be construed "not grudgingly but as serving a broad remedial purpose" [citations]....The "zone of interest" formula [in *Data Processing*, 397 U.S. 153 (1970)] has not proved self-explanatory, but significant guidance can be drawn from that opinion. First, the Court interpreted the phrase "a relevant statute" in §702 quite broadly (indeed even using a different statute from the one sued under).... Second, the Court approved the "trend...toward [the] enlargement of the class of people who may protest administrative action".... The test is not meant to be especially demanding; in particular there need be no indication of congressional purpose to benefit the would-be plaintiff. 479 U.S. at 395-400.

courts have denied standing — where plaintiffs attempt to argue the claims of third parties, where the judicial remedy would not relieve the particular injury claimed, etc.[96]

In many cases the premise of the case is that the government agency has violated the law, but there will be no enforcement unless the courts grant a citizen group standing. Many such cases recently have denied standing. Lujan v. National Wildlife Federation, 110 S.Ct. 3177 (1990), coursebook at 575.

In the following case the Bush Administration decided to make a frontal assault on Congress's authorization of citizen enforcement actions by arguing for a tightened Art. III constitutional standing test in cases where citizens were granted enforcement standing by statute.

Manuel Lujan, Jr., Secretary of the Interior, v. Defenders of Wildlife
United States Supreme Court, 1992
112 S.Ct. 2130

Justice Scalia delivered the opinion of the court with respect to Parts I, II, III-A, and IV, and an opinion with respect to Part III-B in which Chief Justice Rehnquist, Justice White, and Justice Thomas join.

I. The Endangered Species Act, 87 Stat. 884, as amended, 16 U.S.C. §1531 et seq., seeks to protect species of animals against threats to their continuing existence caused by man. See generally TVA v. Hill, 437 U.S. 153 (1978).... Section 7(a)(2) of the Act then provides, in pertinent part: "Each Federal agency shall, in consultation with and with the assistance of the Secretary [of the Interior], insure that any action authorized, funded, or carried out by such agency...is not likely to jeopardize the continued existence of any endangered species or threatened species or result in the destruction or adverse modification of habitat of such species which is determined by the Secretary, after consultation as appropriate with affected States, to be critical." 16 U.S.C. §1536(a)(2).

BACKGROUND

In 1978, the Fish and Wildlife Service (FWS) and the National Marine Fisheries Service (NMFS), on behalf of the Secretary of the Interior and the Secretary of Commerce respectively, promulgated a joint regulation stating that the obligations imposed by §7(a)(2) extend to actions taken in foreign nations. 43 Fed.Reg. 874 (1978).... A revised joint regulation, reinterpreting §7(a)(2) to require consultation only for actions taken in the United States or on the high seas, was proposed in 1983, 48 Fed.Reg. 29990 (1983), and promulgated in 1986, 51 Fed.Reg. 19926 (1986); 50 C.F.R. 402.01 (1991).

Shortly thereafter, respondents, organizations dedicated to wildlife conservation and other environmental causes, filed this action against the Secretary of the Interior, seeking a declaratory judgment that the new regulation is in error as to the geographic scope of §7(a)(2), and an injunction requiring the Secretary to promulgate a new regulation restoring the initial interpretation. The District Court granted the Secretary's motion to dismiss for lack of standing. Defenders of Wildlife v.

---

96. See, e.g., Valley Forge Christian College v. Americans United, 454 U.S. 464 (1982).

Hodel, 658 F.Supp. 43, 47-48 (Minn.1987). The Court of Appeals for the Eighth Circuit reversed by a divided vote. Defenders of Wildlife v. Hodel, 851 F.2d 1035 (1988). On remand, the Secretary moved for summary judgment on the standing issue, and respondents moved for summary judgment on the merits. The District Court denied the Secretary's motion, on the ground that the Eighth Circuit had already determined the standing question in this case; it granted respondents' merits motion, and ordered the Secretary to publish a revised regulation. Defenders of Wildlife v. Hodel, 707 F.Supp. 1082 (Minn.1989). The Eighth Circuit affirmed. 911 F.2d 117 (1990). .

II. ...When the suit is one challenging the legality of government action or inaction, the nature and extent of facts that must be averred (at the summary judgment stage) or proved (at the trial stage) in order to establish standing depends considerably upon whether the plaintiff is himself an object of the action (or forgone action) at issue. If he is, there is ordinarily little question that the action or inaction has caused him injury, and that a judgment preventing or requiring the action will redress it. When, however, as in this case, a plaintiff's asserted injury arises from the government's allegedly unlawful regulation (or lack of regulation) of someone else, much more is needed. In that circumstance, causation and redressability ordinarily hinge on the response of the regulated (or regulable) third party to the government action or inaction — and perhaps on the response of others as well. The existence of one or more of the essential elements of standing "depends on the unfettered choices made by independent actors not before the courts and whose exercise of broad and legitimate discretion the courts cannot presume either to control or to predict," ASARCO Inc. v. Kadish, 490 U.S. 605, 615 (1989) (opinion of Kennedy, J.); see also Simon, supra, 426 U.S., at 41-42 and it becomes the burden of the plaintiff to adduce facts showing that those choices have been or will be made in such manner as to produce causation and permit redressability of injury. E.g., Warth, supra, 422 U.S., at 505. Thus, when the plaintiff is not himself the object of the government action or inaction he challenges, standing is not precluded, but it is ordinarily "substantially more difficult" to establish. Allen, supra, 468 U.S., at 758; Simon, supra; 426 U.S., at 44-45, Warth, supra, 422 U.S., at 505,.

III. We think the Court of Appeals failed to apply the foregoing principles in denying the Secretary's motion for summary judgment. Respondents had not made the requisite demonstration of (at least) injury and redressability.

A. Respondents' claim to injury is that the lack of consultation with respect to certain funded activities abroad "increas[es] the rate of extinction of endangered and threatened species." Complaint P 5, App. 13. Of course, the desire to use or observe an animal species, even for purely aesthetic purposes, is undeniably a cognizable interest for purpose of standing. See, e.g., Sierra Club v. Morton, 405 U.S., at 734. "But the 'injury in fact' test requires more than an injury to a cognizable interest. It requires that the party seeking review be himself among the injured." Id., at 734-735. To survive the Secretary's summary judgment motion, respondents had to submit affidavits or other evidence showing, through specific facts, not only that listed species were in fact being threatened by funded activities abroad, but also that one or more of respondents' members would thereby be "directly" affected apart from their " 'special interest' in th[e] subject."

Id., at 735, 739. See generally Hunt v. Washington State Apple Advertising Comm'n, 432 U.S. 333, 343 (1977).

With respect to this aspect of the case, the Court of Appeals focused on the affidavits of two Defenders' members — Joyce Kelly and Amy Skilbred. Ms. Kelly stated that she traveled to Egypt in 1986 and "observed the traditional habitat of the endangered Nile crocodile there and intend[s] to do so again, and hope[s] to observe the crocodile directly," and that she "will suffer harm in fact as a result of [the] American...role...in overseeing the rehabilitation of the Aswan High Dam on the Nile...and [in] develop[ing]...Egypt's...Master Water Plan." App. 101. Ms. Skilbred averred that she traveled to Sri Lanka in 1981 and "observed th[e] habitat" of "endangered species such as the Asian elephant and the leopard" at what is now the site of the Mahaweli Project funded by the Agency for International Development (AID), although she "was unable to see any of the endangered species;" "this development project," she continued, "will seriously reduce endangered, threatened, and endemic species habitat including areas that I visited...[, which] may severely shorten the future of these species;" that threat, she concluded, harmed her because she "intend[s] to return to Sri Lanka in the future and hope[s] to be more fortunate in spotting at least the endangered elephant and leopard." Id., at 145-146. When Ms. Skilbred was asked at a subsequent deposition if and when she had any plans to return to Sri Lanka, she reiterated that "I intend to go back to Sri Lanka," but confessed that she had no current plans: "I don't know [when]. There is a civil war going on right now. I don't know. Not next year, I will say. In the future." Id., at 318.

We shall assume for the sake of argument that these affidavits contain facts showing that certain agency-funded projects threaten listed species — though that is questionable. They plainly contain no facts, however, showing how damage to the species will produce "imminent" injury to Mss. Kelly and Skilbred. That the women "had visited" the areas of the projects before the projects commenced proves nothing. As we have said in a related context, " '[p]ast exposure to illegal conduct does not in itself show a present case or controversy regarding injunctive relief...if unaccompanied by any continuing, present adverse effects.' " Lyons, 461 U.S., at 102 (quoting O'Shea v. Littleton, 414 U.S. 488, 495-496 (1974)). And the affiants' profession of an "inten[t]" to return to the places they had visited before — where they will presumably, this time, be deprived of the opportunity to observe animals of the endangered species — is simply not enough. Such "some day" intentions — without any description of concrete plans, or indeed even any specification of when the some day will be — do not support a finding of the "actual or imminent" injury that our cases require.

Besides relying upon the Kelly and Skilbred affidavits, respondents propose a series of novel standing theories. The first, inelegantly styled "ecosystem nexus," proposes that any person who uses any part of a "contiguous ecosystem" adversely affected by a funded activity has standing even if the activity is located a great distance away. This approach, as the Court of Appeals correctly observed, is inconsistent with our opinion in National Wildlife Federation, which held that a plaintiff claiming injury from environmental damage must use the area affected by the challenged activity and not an area roughly "in the vicinity" of it. 497 U.S., at 887-889, 110 S.Ct., at — ; see also Sierra Club, 405 U.S., at 735,

92 S.Ct., at 1366. It makes no difference that the general-purpose section of the ESA states that the Act was intended in part "to provide a means whereby the ecosystems upon which endangered species and threatened species depend may be conserved," 16 U.S.C. §1531(b). To say that the Act protects ecosystems is not to say that the Act creates (if it were possible) rights of action in persons who have not been injured in fact, that is, persons who use portions of an ecosystem not perceptibly affected by the unlawful action in question.

Respondents' other theories are called, alas, the "animal nexus" approach, whereby anyone who has an interest in studying or seeing the endangered animals anywhere on the globe has standing; and the "vocational nexus" approach, under which anyone with a professional interest in such animals can sue. Under these theories, anyone who goes to see Asian elephants in the Bronx Zoo, and anyone who is a keeper of Asian elephants in the Bronx Zoo, has standing to sue because the Director of AID did not consult with the Secretary regarding the AID-funded project in Sri Lanka. This is beyond all reason. Standing is not "an ingenious academic exercise in the conceivable," United States v. Students Challenging Regulatory Agency Procedures (SCRAP), 412 U.S. 669, 688 (1973), but as we have said requires, at the summary judgment stage, a factual showing of perceptible harm. It is clear that the person who observes or works with a particular animal threatened by a federal decision is facing perceptible harm, since the very subject of his interest will no longer exist. It is even plausible — though it goes to the outermost limit of plausibility — to think that a person who observes or works with animals of a particular species in the very area of the world where that species is threatened by a federal decision is facing such harm, since some animals that might have been the subject of his interest will no longer exist, see Japan Whaling Assn. v. American Cetacean Soc., 478 U.S. 221, 231, n. 4 (1986). It goes beyond the limit, however, and into pure speculation and fantasy, to say that anyone who observes or works with an endangered species, anywhere in the world, is appreciably harmed by a single project affecting some portion of that species with which he has no more specific connection.

B. Besides failing to show injury, respondents failed to demonstrate redressability.... Since the agencies funding the projects were not parties to the case, the District Court could accord relief only against the Secretary: He could be ordered to revise his regulation to require consultation for foreign projects. But this would not remedy respondents' alleged injury unless the funding agencies were bound by the Secretary's regulation, which is very much an open question...

IV. The Court of Appeals found that respondents had standing for an additional reason: because they had suffered a "procedural injury." The so-called "citizen-suit" provision of the ESA provides, in pertinent part, that "any person may commence a civil suit on his own behalf (A) to enjoin any person, including the United States and any other governmental instrumentality or agency...who is alleged to be in violation of any provision of this chapter." 16 U.S.C. §1540(g). The court held that, because §7(a)(2) requires interagency consultation, the citizen-suit provision creates a "procedural righ[t]" to consultation in all "persons" — so that anyone can file suit in federal court to challenge the Secretary's (or presumably any other official's) failure to follow the assertedly correct consultative procedure, notwithstanding their inability to allege any discrete injury flowing from that failure. 911 F.2d, at 121-122. To understand the remarkable nature of this holding one must be clear about what it does not rest upon: This is not a case where plaintiffs are seeking to enforce a procedural requirement the disregard of which could impair a separate concrete interest of theirs (e.g., the procedural requirement for a hearing prior to denial of their license application, or the procedural requirement for an environmental impact statement before a federal facility is constructed next door to them). Nor is it simply a case where concrete injury has been suffered by many persons, as in mass fraud or mass tort situations. Nor, finally, is it the unusual case in which Congress has created a concrete private interest in the outcome of a suit against a private party for the government's benefit, by providing a cash bounty for the victorious plaintiff. Rather, the court held that the injury-in-fact requirement had been satisfied by congressional conferral upon all persons of an abstract, self-contained, noninstrumental "right" to have the Executive observe the procedures required by law. We reject this view.

We have consistently held that a plaintiff raising only a generally available grievance about government — claiming only harm to his and every citizen's interest in proper application of the Constitution and laws, and seeking relief that no more directly and tangibly benefits him than it does the public at large — does not state an Article III case or controversy...

Since Schlesinger v. Reservists Against the War, 418 U.S. 208 (1974), we have on two occasions held that an injury amounting only to the alleged violation of a right to have the Government act in accordance with law was not judicially cognizable because "assertion of a right to a particular kind of Government conduct, which the Government has violated by acting differently, cannot alone satisfy the requirements of Art. III without draining those requirements of meaning." Allen, 468 U.S., at 754; Valley Forge Christian College v. Americans United for Separation of Church and State, Inc., 454 U.S. 464, 483 (1982)....

To be sure, our generalized-grievance cases have typically involved Government violation of procedures assertedly ordained by the Constitution rather than the Congress. But there is absolutely no basis for making the Article III inquiry turn on the source of the asserted right. Whether the courts were to act on their own, or at the invitation of Congress, in ignoring the concrete injury requirement described in our cases, they would be discarding a principle fundamental to the separate and distinct constitutional role of the Third Branch — one of the essential elements that identifies those "Cases" and "Controversies" that are the business of the courts rather than of the political branches. "The province of the court," as Chief Justice Marshall said in Marbury v. Madison, 5 U.S. (1 Cranch) 137, 170, 2 L.Ed. 60 (1803) "is, solely, to decide on the rights of individuals." Vindicating the public interest (including the public interest in government observance of the Constitution and laws) is the function of Congress and the Chief Executive. The question presented here is whether the public interest in proper administration of the laws (specifically, in agencies' observance of a particular, statutorily prescribed procedure) can be converted into an individual right by a statute that denominates it as such, and that permits all citizens (or, for that matter, a subclass of citizens who suffer no distinctive concrete harm) to sue. If the concrete injury requirement has the separation-of-powers significance we have always said, the answer must be obvious: To permit

Congress to convert the undifferentiated public interest in executive officers' compliance with the law into an "individual right" vindicable in the courts is to permit Congress to transfer from the President to the courts the Chief Executive's most important constitutional duty, to "take Care that the Laws be faithfully executed," Art. II, §3. It would enable the courts, with the permission of Congress, "to assume a position of authority over the governmental acts of another and co-equal department," Frothingham v. Mellon, 262 U.S., at 489, 43 S.Ct., at 601, and to become " 'virtually continuing monitors of the wisdom and soundness of Executive action.' " Allen, 468 U.S., at 760 (quoting Laird v. Tatum, 408 U.S. 1, (1972)). We have always rejected that vision of our role: "When Congress passes an Act empowering administrative agencies to carry on governmental activities, the power of those agencies is circumscribed by the authority granted. This permits the courts to participate in law enforcement entrusted to administrative bodies only to the extent necessary to protect justiciable individual rights against administrative action fairly beyond the granted powers.... This is very far from assuming that the courts are charged more than administrators or legislators with the protection of the rights of the people. Congress and the Executive supervise the acts of administrative agents.... But under Article III, Congress established courts to adjudicate cases and controversies as to claims of infringement of individual rights whether by unlawful action of private persons or by the exertion of unauthorized administrative power." Stark v. Wickard, 321 U.S. 288, 309-310 (1944). "Individual rights," within the meaning of this passage, do not mean public rights that have been legislatively pronounced to belong to each individual who forms part of the public....

It is clear that in suits against the government, at least, the concrete injury requirement must remain.

We hold that respondents lack standing to bring this action and that the Court of Appeals erred in denying the summary judgment motion filed by the United States.

JUSTICE KENNEDY, with whom JUSTICE SOUTER joins, concurring in part and concurring in the judgment.

I agree with the Court's conclusion in Part III-A that, on the record before us, respondents have failed to demonstrate that they themselves are "among the injured." Sierra Club v. Morton, 405 U.S. 727, 735 (1972)....

While it may seem trivial to require that Mss. Kelly and Skilbred acquire airline tickets to the project sites or announce a date certain upon which they will return, this is not a case where it is reasonable to assume that the affiants will be using the sites on a regular basis, see Sierra Club v. Morton, supra, 405 U.S., at 735, nor do the affiants claim to have visited the sites since the projects commenced. With respect to the Court's discussion of respondents' "ecosystem nexus," "animal nexus," and "vocational nexus" theories, I agree that on this record respondents' showing is insufficient to establish standing on any of these bases. I am not willing to foreclose the possibility, however, that in different circumstances a nexus theory similar to those proffered here might support a claim to standing. See Japan Whaling Assn. v. American Cetacean Soc., 478 U.S. 221, 231, n. 4 (1986) ("respondents...undoubtedly have alleged a sufficient 'injury in fact' in that the whale watching and studying of their members will be adversely affected by continued whale harvesting").

In light of the conclusion that respondents have not demonstrated a concrete injury here sufficient to support standing under our precedents, I would not reach the issue of redressability that is discussed by the plurality in Part III-B.

I also join Part IV of the Court's opinion with the following observations. As government programs and policies become more complex and far-reaching, we must be sensitive to the articulation of new rights of action that do not have clear analogs in our common-law tradition. Modern litigation has progressed far from the paradigm of Marbury suing Madison to get his commission, Marbury v. Madison, 5 U.S. (1 Cranch) 137, 2 L.Ed. 60 (1803), or Ogden seeking an injunction to halt Gibbons' steamboat operations. Gibbons v. Ogden, 22 U.S. (9 Wheat.) 1, 6 L.Ed. 23 (1824). In my view, Congress has the power to define injuries and articulate chains of causation that will give rise to a case or controversy where none existed before, and I do not read the Court's opinion to suggest a contrary view. See Warth v. Seldin, 422 U.S. 490, 500 (1975); In exercising this power, however, Congress must at the very least identify the injury it seeks to vindicate and relate the injury to the class of persons entitled to bring suit. The citizen-suit provision of the Endangered Species Act does not meet these minimal requirements, because while the statute purports to confer a right on "any person...to enjoin...the United States and any other governmental instrumentality or agency...who is alleged to be in violation of any provision of this chapter," it does not of its own force establish that there is an injury in "any person" by virtue of any "violation." 16 U.S.C. §1540(g)(1)(A).

The Court's holding that there is an outer limit to the power of Congress to confer rights of action is a direct and necessary consequence of the case and controversy limitations found in Article III. I agree that it would exceed those limitations if, at the behest of Congress and in the absence of any showing of concrete injury, we were to entertain citizen-suits to vindicate the public's nonconcrete interest in the proper administration of the laws...

An independent judiciary is held to account through its open proceedings and its reasoned judgments. In this process it is essential for the public to know what persons or groups are invoking the judicial power, the reasons that they have brought suit, and whether their claims are vindicated or denied. The concrete injury requirement helps assure that there can be an answer to these questions; and, as the Court's opinion is careful to show, that is part of the constitutional design.

With these observations, I concur in Parts I, II, III-A, and IV of the Court's opinion and in the judgment of the Court.

JUSTICE STEVENS, concurring in the judgment.

Because I am not persuaded that Congress intended the consultation requirement in §7(a)(2) of the Endangered Species Act of 1973 (ESA), 16 U.S.C. §1536(a)(2), to apply to activities in foreign countries, I concur in the judgment of reversal. I do not, however, agree with the Court's conclusion that respondents lack standing because the threatened injury to their interest in protecting the environment and studying endangered species is not "imminent." Nor do I agree with the plurality's additional conclusion that respondents' injury is not "redressable" in this litigation.

I. In my opinion a person who has visited the critical habitat of an endangered species, has a professional interest in preserving the species and its habitat, and intends to revisit them in the future has standing to challenge agency action that threatens their destruction. Congress has found that a wide variety of endangered species of fish, wildlife, and plants are of "aesthetic, ecological, educational, historical, recreational, and scientific value to the Nation and its people." 16 U.S.C. §1531(a)(3). Given that finding, we have no license to demean the importance of the interest that particular individuals may have in observing any species or its habitat, whether those individuals are motivated by aesthetic enjoyment, an interest in professional research, or an economic interest in preservation of the species. Indeed, this Court has often held that injuries to such interests are sufficient to confer standing, and the Court reiterates that holding today.

The Court nevertheless concludes that respondents have not suffered "injury in fact" because they have not shown that the harm to the endangered species will produce "imminent" injury to them. I disagree. An injury to an individual's interest in studying or enjoying a species and its natural habitat occurs when someone (whether it be the government or a private party) takes action that harms that species and habitat. In my judgment, therefore, the "imminence" of such an injury should be measured by the timing and likelihood of the threatened environmental harm, rather than — as the Court seems to suggest — by the time that might elapse between the present and the time when the individuals would visit the area if no such injury should occur.

...In this case, however, the likelihood that respondents will be injured by the destruction of the endangered species is not speculative. If respondents are genuinely interested in the preservation of the endangered species and intend to study or observe these animals in the future, their injury will occur as soon as the animals are destroyed. Thus the only potential source of "speculation" in this case is whether respondents' intent to study or observe the animals is genuine. In my view, Joyce Kelly and Amy Skilbred have introduced sufficient evidence to negate petitioner's contention that their claims of injury are "speculative" or "conjectural." As Justice Blackmun explains, a reasonable finder of fact could conclude, from their past visits, their professional backgrounds, and their affidavits and deposition testimony, that Ms. Kelly and Ms. Skilbred will return to the project sites and, consequently, will be injured by the destruction of the endangered species and critical habitat...

II. Although I believe that respondents have standing,... a reading of the entire statute persuades me that Congress did not intend the consultation requirement in §7(a)(2) to apply to activities in foreign countries. Accordingly, notwithstanding my disagreement with the Court's disposition of the standing question, I concur in its judgment.

JUSTICE BLACKMUN, with whom JUSTICE O'CONNOR joins, dissenting.

I part company with the Court in this case in two respects. First, I believe that respondents have raised genuine issues of fact — sufficient to survive summary judgment — both as to injury and as to redressability. Second, I question the Court's breadth of language in rejecting standing for "procedural" injuries. I fear the Court seeks to impose fresh limitations on the constitutional authority of Congress to allow citizen-suits in the federal courts for injuries deemed "procedural" in nature. I dissent...

I.A.1. Were the Court to apply the proper standard for summary judgment, I believe it would conclude that the sworn affidavits and deposition testimony of Joyce Kelly and Amy Skilbred advance sufficient facts to create a genuine issue for trial concerning whether one or both would be imminently harmed by the Aswan and Mahaweli projects. In the first instance, as the Court itself concedes, the affidavits contained facts making it at least "questionable" (and therefore within the province of the factfinder) that certain agency-funded projects threaten listed species. The only remaining issue, then, is whether Kelly and Skilbred have shown that they personally would suffer imminent harm.

I think a reasonable finder of fact could conclude from the information in the affidavits and deposition testimony that either Kelly or Skilbred will soon return to the project sites, thereby satisfying the "actual or imminent" injury standard. The Court dismisses Kelly's and Skilbred's general statements that they intended to revisit the project sites as "simply not enough." But those statements did not stand alone. A reasonable finder of fact could conclude, based not only upon their statements of intent to return, but upon their past visits to the project sites, as well as their professional backgrounds, that it was likely that Kelly and Skilbred would make a return trip to the project areas. Contrary to the Court's contention that Kelly's and Skilbred's past visits "proves nothing," the fact of their past visits could demonstrate to a reasonable factfinder that Kelly and Skilbred have the requisite resources and personal interest in the preservation of the species endangered by the Aswan and Mahaweli projects to make good on their intention to return again. Cf. Los Angeles v. Lyons, 461 U.S. 95, 102 (1983) ("Past wrongs were evidence bearing on whether there is a real and immediate threat of repeated injury") (internal quotations omitted). Similarly, Kelly's and Skilbred's professional backgrounds in wildlife preservation, see App. 100, 144, 309-310, also make it likely — at least far more likely than for the average citizen — that they would choose to visit these areas of the world where species are vanishing.

By requiring a "description of concrete plans" or "specification of when the some day [for a return visit] will be," the Court, in my view, demands what is likely an empty formality. No substantial barriers prevent Kelly or Skilbred from simply purchasing plane tickets to return to the Aswan and Mahaweli projects. This case differs from other cases in which the imminence of harm turned largely on the affirmative actions of third parties beyond a plaintiff's control.... To be sure, a plaintiff's unilateral control over his or her exposure to harm does not necessarily render the harm non-speculative. Nevertheless, it suggests that a finder of fact would be far more likely to conclude the harm is actual or imminent, especially if given an opportunity to hear testimony and determine credibility.

I fear the Court's demand for detailed descriptions of future conduct will do little to weed out those who are genuinely harmed from those who are not. More likely, it will resurrect a code-pleading formalism in federal court summary judgment practice, as federal courts, newly doubting their jurisdiction, will demand more and more particularized showings of future harm....

2. The Court also concludes that injury is lacking, because respondents' allegations of "ecosystem nexus" failed to demonstrate sufficient proximity to the site of the environmental harm. To support that conclusion, the Court mischaracterizes our decision in Lujan v. National Wildlife Federation, 497 U.S. 871 (1990), as establishing a general rule that "a plaintiff claiming injury from environmental damage must use the area affected by the challenged activity." In National Wildlife Federation, the Court required specific geographical proximity because of the particular type of harm alleged in that case: harm to the plaintiff's visual enjoyment of nature from mining activities. One cannot suffer from the sight of a ruined landscape without being close enough to see the sites actually being mined. Many environmental injuries, however, cause harm distant from the area immediately affected by the challenged action. Environmental destruction may affect animals traveling over vast geographical ranges, see, e.g., Japan Whaling Assn. v. American Cetacean Soc., 478 U.S. 221 (1986) (harm to American whale watchers from Japanese whaling activities), or rivers running long geographical courses, see, e.g., Arkansas v. Oklahoma, 112 S.Ct. 1046, (1992) (harm to Oklahoma residents from wastewater treatment plant 39 miles from border). It cannot seriously be contended that a litigant's failure to use the precise or exact site where animals are slaughtered or where toxic waste is dumped into a river means he or she cannot show injury...

I have difficulty imagining this Court applying its rigid principles of geographic formalism anywhere outside the context of environmental claims. As I understand it, environmental plaintiffs are under no special constitutional standing disabilities. Like other plaintiffs, they need show only that the action they challenge has injured them, without necessarily showing they happened to be physically near the location of the alleged wrong. The Court's decision today should not be interpreted "to foreclose the possibility...that in different circumstances a nexus theory similar to those proffered here might support a claim to standing." (Kennedy, J., concurring in part and concurring in the judgment).

B.   ...I find myself unable to agree with the plurality's analysis of redressability, based as it is on its invitation of executive lawlessness, ignorance of principles of collateral estoppel, unfounded assumptions about causation, and erroneous conclusions about what the record does not say. In my view, respondents have satisfactorily shown a genuine issue of fact as to whether their injury would likely be redressed by a decision in their favor.

II. The Court concludes that any "procedural injury" suffered by respondents is insufficient to confer standing. It rejects the view that the "injury-in-fact requirement...[is] satisfied by congressional conferral upon all person of an abstract, self-contained, noninstrumental 'right' to have the Executive observe the procedures required by law." Whatever the Court might mean with that very broad language, it cannot be saying that "procedural injuries" as a class are necessarily insufficient for purposes of Article III standing.

Most governmental conduct can be classified as "procedural." Many injuries caused by governmental conduct, therefore, are categorizable at some level of generality as "procedural" injuries. Yet, these injuries are not categorically beyond the pale of redress by the federal courts. When the Government, for example, "procedurally" issues a pollution permit, those affected by the permittee's pollutants are not without standing to sue. Only later cases will tell just what the Court means by its intimation that "procedural" injuries are not constitutionally cognizable injuries. In the meantime, I have the greatest of sympathy for the courts across the country that will struggle to understand the Court's standardless exposition of this concept today.

The Court expresses concern that allowing judicial enforcement of "agencies' observance of a particular, statutorily prescribed procedure" would "transfer from the President to the courts the Chief Executive's most important constitutional duty, to 'take Care that the Laws be faithfully executed,' Art. II, sec. 3." In fact, the principal effect of foreclosing judicial enforcement of such procedures is to transfer power into the hands of the Executive at the expense — not of the courts — but of Congress, from which that power originates and emanates.

Under the Court's anachronistically formal view of the separation of powers, Congress legislates pure, substantive mandates and has no business structuring the procedural manner in which the Executive implements these mandates. To be sure, in the ordinary course, Congress does legislate in black-and-white terms of affirmative commands or negative prohibitions on the conduct of officers of the Executive Branch. In complex regulatory areas, however, Congress often legislates, as it were, in procedural shades of gray. That is, it sets forth substantive policy goals and provides for their attainment by requiring Executive Branch officials to follow certain procedures, for example, in the form of reporting, consultation, and certification requirements...

The consultation requirement of §7 of the Endangered Species Act is a similar, action-forcing statute. Consultation is designed as an integral check on federal agency action, ensuring that such action does not go forward without full consideration of its effects on listed species. Once consultation is initiated, the Secretary is under a duty to provide to the action agency "a written statement setting forth the Secretary's opinion, and a summary of the information on which the opinion is based, detailing how the agency action affects the species or its critical habitat." 16 U.S.C. §1536(b)(3)(A). The Secretary is also obligated to suggest "reasonable and prudent alternatives" to prevent jeopardy to listed species. Ibid. The action agency must undertake as well its own "biological assessment for the purpose of identifying any endangered species or threatened species" likely to be affected by agency action. §1536(c)(1). After the initiation of consultation, the action agency "shall not make any irreversible or irretrievable commitment of resources" which would foreclose the "formulation or implementation of any reasonable and prudent alternative measures" to avoid jeopardizing listed species. §1536(d). These action-forcing procedures are "designed to protect some threatened concrete interest," of persons who observe and work with endangered or threatened species. That is why I am mystified by the Court's unsupported conclusion that "[t]his is not a case where plaintiffs are seeking to enforce a procedural requirement the disregard of which could impair a separate concrete interest of theirs."

Congress legislates in procedural shades of gray not to aggrandize its own power but to allow maximum executive discretion in the attainment of

Congress' legislative goals. Congress could simply impose a substantive prohibition on executive conduct; it could say that no agency action shall result in the loss of more than 5% of any listed species. Instead, Congress sets forth substantive guidelines and allows the Executive, within certain procedural constraints, to decide how best to effectuate the ultimate goal. See American Power & Light Co. v. SEC, 329 U.S. 90, 105 (1946). The Court never has questioned Congress' authority to impose such procedural constraints on executive power. Just as Congress does not violate separation of powers by structuring the procedural manner in which the Executive shall carry out the laws, surely the federal courts do not violate separation of powers when, at the very instruction and command of Congress, they enforce these procedures.

To prevent Congress from conferring standing for "procedural injuries" is another way of saying that Congress may not delegate to the courts authority deemed "executive" in nature..... [But] here Congress seeks not to delegate "executive" power, but only to strengthen the procedures it has legislatively mandated. "We have long recognized that the nondelegation doctrine does not prevent Congress from seeking assistance, within proper limits, from its coordinate Branches." Touby v. United States,111 S.Ct. 1752, 1756 (1991). "Congress does not violate the Constitution merely because it legislates in broad terms, leaving a certain degree of discretion to executive or judicial actors " (emphasis added).

Ironically, this Court has previously justified a relaxed review of congressional delegation to the Executive on grounds that Congress, in turn, has subjected the exercise of that power to judicial review. INS v. Chadha, 462 U.S. 919, 953-954, n. 16 (1983); American Power & Light Co. v. SEC, 329 U.S., at 105-106. The Court's intimation today that procedural injuries are not constitutionally cognizable threatens this understanding upon which Congress has undoubtedly relied. In no sense is the Court's suggestion compelled by our "common understanding of what activities are appropriate to legislatures, to executives, and to courts." In my view, it reflects an unseemly solicitude for an expansion of power of the Executive Branch.

It is to be hoped that over time the Court will acknowledge that some classes of procedural duties are so enmeshed with the prevention of a substantive, concrete harm that an individual plaintiff may be able to demonstrate a sufficient likelihood of injury just through the breach of that procedural duty. For example, in the context of the NEPA requirement of environmental impact statements, this Court has acknowledged "it is now well settled that NEPA itself does not mandate particular results [and] simply prescribes the necessary process," but "these procedures are almost certain to affect the agency's substantive decision." Robertson v. Methow Valley Citizens Council, 490 U.S., 332, 350 (1989) (emphasis added). See also Andrus v. Sierra Club, 442 U.S. 347, 350- 351 (1979) ("If environmental concerns are not interwoven into the fabric of agency planning, the 'action-forcing' characteristics of [the environmental-impact statement requirement] would be lost"). This acknowledgment of an inextricable link between procedural and substantive harm does not reflect improper appellate factfinding. It reflects nothing more than the proper deference owed to the judgment of a coordinate branch — Congress — that certain procedures are directly tied to protection against a substantive harm.

In short, determining "injury" for Article III standing purposes is a fact-specific inquiry. "Typically...the standing inquiry requires careful judicial examination of a complaint's allegations to ascertain whether the particular plaintiff is entitled to an adjudication of the particular claims asserted." Allen v. Wright, 468 U.S., at 752. There may be factual circumstances in which a congressionally imposed procedural requirement is so insubstantially connected to the prevention of a substantive harm that it cannot be said to work any conceivable injury to an individual litigant. But, as a general matter, the courts owe substantial deference to Congress' substantive purpose in imposing a certain procedural requirement. In all events, "[o]ur separation-of-powers analysis does not turn on the labeling of an activity as 'substantive' as opposed to 'procedural.' " Mistretta v. United States, 488 U.S. 361, 393, (1989). There is no room for a per se rule or presumption excluding injuries labeled "procedural" in nature.

In conclusion, I cannot join the Court on what amounts to a slash-and-burn expedition through the law of environmental standing. In my view, "[t]he very essence of civil liberty certainly consists in the right of every individual to claim the protection of the laws, whenever he receives an injury." Marbury v. Madison, 1 Cranch 137, 163, 2 L.Ed. 60 (1803). I dissent.

COMMENTARY AND QUESTIONS

1. After *Lujan v. Defenders*, how much harm is needed to find sufficient injury for standing, a $5 bounty? The Supreme Court as a whole apparently agrees that if the two individual plaintiffs had plane tickets in hand, they would have actionable injuries. Is the difference between having and not having plane tickets a serious distinction or a ridiculous technicality when determining standing?

The majority also says that constitutional standing would exist "[where] Congress has created a concrete private interest in the outcome of a suit[97]...for the government's benefit, by providing a cash bounty for the victorious plaintiff." So if Congress authorized payment of a $5 pecuniary reward for successful law enforcement, even Scalia would admit there was standing — which makes the Court's test seem rather superficial and disingenuous.

If a small money bounty would be sufficient to give a citizen Art. III standing in the *Lujan* terms, then why not likewise the authorizations for attorneys and expert witness fees for prevailing parties, see coursebook at 571, which already exist on the books in the statutory standing provisions? Especially where plaintiffs are public interest attorneys groups, the prospect of recovering tens of thousand dollars for their labors enforcing the law would seem to be a tangible interest.

And a final braintickler. We all assume that when Congress passes a statute and gives a federal agency the authority to prosecute it — e.g. the FTC is given authority to prosecute antitrust violations — the agency has Art. III standing. Why? What's the FTC's constitutional injury or

---

97. The quote says "a suit against a private party," but it is difficult to see any Art. III difference between suits against private and public defendants.

interest,[98] if it is not the enforcement standing created by Congress' delegation to the agency? If Congress can delegate statutory enforcement authority to the FTC, then why can't it also delegate that authority to private organizations similarly dedicated to enforcing public law? (In administrative law there is no bar preventing delegations to private parties, so that is not the distinction.) Could Scalia be wrong in asserting that a congressionally-created procedural interest is not sufficient for standing?

2. "Nexus" approaches to the standing hurdle? Which, if any, of the nexus approaches offers a workable doctrine from which to generate standing? In assessing these possible innovative claims for environmental standing, it is useful to note that the Court regularly uses the term "interest" interchangeably with "injury" in defining what is required for Art. III standing.

3. Restricted standing for developers, too? Judicial restrictions on standing can sometimes hurt developers as well as environmentalists. In a recent case, for example, a court held that timber companies and an industry trade association lacked standing to seek recovery for alleged damages resulting from the U.S. Forest Service's actions to protect the red-cockaded woodpecker. The court found that since "no right is conferred on the companies to harvest a set amount of timber each year and there is no substantial likelihood that this injury will be redressed by the relief that plaintiffs seek" no claims can be brought for alleged reduction in timber harvested, quality of life injuries from layoffs, income reduction, decreased tax base, or a loss in public services because each of these claims fails to meet the injury-in fact required for standing. Region of Forest Service Timber Purchasers Council v. Alcock. 23 ELR 21051 (11th Cir., June 21, 1993).

4. Redressability. Redressability — considering whether the harms claimed by plaintiffs as a basis for standing are likely to be resolved by a judicial remedy — has previously been considered one of the court-made "prudential principles" subject to being overridden by congressional mandates expanding standing, not an Art. III requirement that must be met even if a statute purports to grant standing without it. By trying to shift redressability into a basic *Art. III* requirement, Justice Scalia launches an attempt to limit Congress' ability to authorize citizen enforcement.

5. Ongoing scrutiny of standing law theory. One of the best explorations of standing doctrine stimulated by the Supreme Court's recent efforts to constrain standing has been Professor Cass Sunstein's article "What's Standing after *Lujan*? — Of Citizen Suits, 'Injuries,' and Article III," 91 Mich. L. Rev. 163 (1992).

Sunstein reviews the history and foundational logic of the Art. III case or controversy requirement. He calls into question the recent Supreme Court caselaw establishing "injury" as the necessary and sufficient threshold test for standing and coupling it with further "prudential principles" like requirements for showing a causal nexus and a showing of redressability. "At least in general," the article concludes, "standing

---

98.. The FTC is an independent agency, and thus would seem not to have constitutional standing as an executive subordinate of the President who has the constitutional duty to see that the laws are faithfully executed.

depends on whether any source of law has created a cause of action." If Congress can create new causes of action, it would seem that it generally could also "create standing [for enforcing them] as it chooses and...deny standing when it likes."

1A. Obstacles in the quest for regulatory efficiency

A. AN EXPERIMENT IN ADMINISTRATIVE INNOVATION: "OMNIBUS," OR CONSOLIDATED, GENERIC RULEMAKING. *AFL-CIO v. OSHA*

A recent example of a regulatory agency's procedural innovation occurred recently when the Occupational Health and Safety Administration (OSHA) desperately decided to forego the traditional unending treadmill of regulating contaminants in the workplace one-by-one — a process by which the agency was constantly falling farther and farther behind — and instead make an omnibus rule that would simultaneously regulate more than 400 substances. The experiment went to court in a consolidated appeal, in a lawsuit filed for different reasons by both industrial management and labor:

AFL-CIO, et al. v. OSHA
965 F.2d 962
United States Court of Appeal for the 11th Circuit, 1992

Fay C.J.   ...On June 7, 1988, OSHA published a Notice of Proposed Rulemaking for its Air Contaminants Standard. 53 Fed. Reg. 20960-21393. In this single rulemaking, OSHA proposed to issue new or revised PELs (Permittable Exposure Limits) for over 400 substances.

Unlike most of the OSHA standards previously reviewed by the courts, the Air Contaminants Standard regulates not a single toxic substance, but 428 different substances. The agency explained its decision to issue such an omnibus standard in its Notice of Proposed Rulemaking:

> OSHA has issued only 24 substance-specific health regulations since its creation It has not been able to review the many thousands of currently unregulated chemicals in the workplace nor to keep up with reviewing the several thousand new chemicals introduced since its creation. It has not been able to fully review the literature to determine if lower limits are needed for many of the approximately 400 substances it now regulates.

> Using past approaches and practices, OSHA could continue to regulate a small number of the high priority substances and those of greatest public interest. However, it would take decades to review currently used chemicals and OSHA would never be able to keep up with the many chemicals which will be newly introduced in the future. 53 Fed.Reg. at 20963.

For this reason, OSHA "determined that it was necessary to modify this approach through the use of *generic* rulemaking, which would simultaneously cover many substances." 54 Fed. Reg. at 2333. "Generic" means something "common to or characteristic of a whole group or class...." Previous "generic" rulemakings by OSHA have all dealt with requirements that, once promulgated, could be applied to numerous different situations.[99]... By contrast, the new Air Contaminants Standard is an amalgamation of 428 unrelated substance exposure limits. There is little common to this group of diverse substances except the fact that OSHA considers them toxic and in need of regulation. In fact, this rulemaking is the antithesis of a "generic" rulemaking; it is a set of 428 specific and individual substance exposure limits. Therefore, OSHA's characterization of this as a "generic" rulemaking is somewhat misleading.

Nonetheless we find nothing in the OSH Act that would prevent OSHA from addressing multiple substances in a single rulemaking. Moreover, because the statute leaves this point open, [however,] and because OSHA's interpretation of the statute is reasonable, it is appropriate for us to defer to OSHA's interpretation. See *Chevron*....

However, we believe the PEL for each substance must be able to stand independently, i.e., that each PEL must be supported by substantial evidence in the record considered as a whole and accompanied by adequate explanation. OSHA may not, by using such multi-substance rulemaking, ignore the requirements of the OSH Act. Both the industry petitioners and the union argue that such disregard was what, in essence, occurred. Regretfully, we agree....

[The Court held that:

> (1) the evidence presented by OSHA failed to establish that the prior-existing exposure limits for the workplace presented significant risks of material health impairment, or that the new proposed standards eliminated or substantially lessened the risk;
>
> (2) OSHA did not sufficiently establish that the new PELs were economically or technologically feasible; and
>
> (3) OSHA had not sufficiently explained why it had allowed an across-the-board four-year delay before implementation of the new rule was required.

The rule was remanded to OSHA to try again, leaving open the practical question whether such omnibus rulemaking experiments offer a feasible prescription for resolving regulatory gridlock.]

COMMENTARY AND QUESTIONS

1. The quest for efficiency. OSHA's attempt to cope with the vast number of rulemakings Congress had required of it foundered on the rocks of judicial review. The court's requirement of voluminous individual data bases for each proposed new standard proved quite simply to be

---

99. The three "generic" rulemakings were: Cancer Policy, 29 C.F.R. Part 1990; Access to Employee Exposure and Medical Records Regulation, 29 C.F.R. §1910.20; Hazard Communication Standard, 29 C.F.R. §1910.1200.

impossible. One of the dirty little secrets of American government is that no one is given the economic or political capital needed to enforce all the laws on the books. But a will to enforce coupled with innovative administrative planning can improve upon the situation. Will OSHA keep trying? Based on informal communications with OSHA, the agency is giving up the attempt to do consolidated rulemaking, although Labor Secretary Reich gamely said he was " encouraged for the future" despite the court decision.

EPA, on the other hand, is reportedly proceeding with major new "cluster rulemaking" under the Clean Water Act, treating classes of industry in the same business in an omnibus process. (EPA's job is easier than OSHA's because its statutory standards under the CWA are based on industry-wide "best available technology" rather than the individual safety of each substance standard as with OSHA.)

B. ANTI-REGULATORY INITIATIVES: "THE UNHOLY TRINITY" IN ADMINISTRATIVE POLICY DEBATES

Ongoing political initiatives in three areas — regulatory takings, unfunded mandates (i.e. where federal laws require state and local implementation but don't pay for it), and "cost-benefit risk assessment" — have been termed "the unholy trinity" by environmentalists who have been facing arguments on the three themes being used to frustrate environmental legislation on a broad range of political issues. "Wise Use" movement groups, in calling for their balance between economic and environmental interests, have sometimes added the latter two to their central property rights theme.

In environmentalists' jaundiced view, the initiatives are often designed less on the merits of administrative reform — to improve the efficiency and rationality of necessary governmental actions protecting public interests — than to create obstacles to the passage of updated protective laws, and, once passed, to create procedural logjams retarding the ability of agencies to issue regulations.

Takings. Here is an example of the language of a regulatory takings amendment sought to be added to current legislation:

> Sec. 2(a)(2) A number of Federal environmental programs, specifically the Endangered Species Act of 1973 and section 404 of the Federal Water Pollution Control Act have been implemented by employees, agents, and representatives of the Federal Government in a manner that deprives private property owners of the use and control of their property.

> Sec. 8(a) A private property owner that as a consequence of a final qualified agency action of an agency head, is deprived of 50 percent or more of the fair market value, or the economically viable use, of the affected portion of the property, as determined by a qualified appraisal expert, is entitled to receive compensation.... H.R. 3875, 103d. Cong. 1st Sess. (1993)("The Property Owners Bill of Rights." sponsored by Rep. Billy Tauzin of Louisiana).

Unfunded Mandates. State and local governments understandably resist the substantial legal duties dropped in their laps, particularly with the Reagan Administration's New Federalism attempts to lower federal expenditures. Here is a provision attempting to limit unfunded federal mandates:

> Sec. 3(a) Not withstanding any other provision of law, any requirement under a federal statute or regulation that state or local government conduct an activity (including a requirement that a government meet national standards in providing a service) shall apply to the government only if all funds necessary to pay the direct costs incurred by the government in conducting the activity are provided by the federal government. H.R. 140, 103d Cong., 1st Sess. (1993) (Rep. Condit of California).

Cost-Benefit/Risk Assessment. As noted in Chapter 2 of this Supplement, some amendment proposals seek to require procedural review or even substantive application of cost-benefit and risk assessment accounting in all regulatory actions. The ostensible idea is that bureaucratic tunnel vision and pointless expenditures of public and private funds can be avoided, and a "scientific" basis for regulatory action can dictate who gets regulated and how. Here is a sample bill:

> Sec. 1 In promulgating any final regulation relating to public health and safety or the environment...the administrator of the Environmental Protection Agency shall publish each of the following in the Federal Register:
>
> > (1) An estimate, performed with as much specificity as practicable, of the risk of the health and safety of individual members of the public addressed by the regulation and its effect on human health or the environment and the costs associated with implementation of, and compliance with, the regulation.
> >
> > (2) A comparative analysis of the risk addressed by the regulation relative to other risks to which the public is exposed.
> >
> > (3) The administrator's certification that —
> >
> > > (A) The estimate under paragraph (1) and the analysis under paragraph (2) are based upon a scientific evaluation of the risk to the health and safety of individual members of the public and to human health or the environment and are supported by the best available scientific data;
> > >
> > > (B) The regulation will substantially advance the purpose of protecting the public health and safety or the environment against the specified identified risk; and
> > >
> > > (C) The regulation will produce benefits to the public health and safety or the environment that will justify the cost to the government and the public of

implementation of and compliance with the regulation.
H.R. 3395, 103d. Cong. 1st Sess. (1993)(Rep. Tauzin)

There is a difference between cost-benefit analysis and risk assessment, the latter often acting primarily as an information process rather than an accurately quantified numerical input into a cost-benefit analysis. EPA and many resource economists resist the blanket imposition of procedural or substantive requirements. As Karl A. Hausker, EPA deputy assistant administrator for policy, planning, and evaluation, recently said, on risk assessments EPA opposed the addition of a blanket risk/cost-benefit requirement in the EPA Cabinet bill, but was more comfortable with risk ranking and estimating requirements, such as those contained in a proposal by Sen. Daniel Patrick Moynihan (D-NY) and one by Sen. Max S. Baucus (D-Mont) for risks from radon in air and water.

Environmentalists argue that such requirements cripple government's ability to regulate effectively in protecting the public interest. This, they claim, is exactly what the wise use movement and its allies are trying to do. Antiregulation legislators have attempted to create gridlock in Congress by adding "unholy trinity" amendments to a number of bills reauthorizing important environmental provisions like the Safe Drinking Water Act.

When the bill to elevate the EPA to cabinet level status was recently before the Congress, opponents attached riders to the bill which requiring detailed risk-assessment and cost-benefit analysis before any agency actions could be taken.[100] As a result, efforts to elevate the EPA were stalled. Similar efforts have obstructed attempts to re authorize the Endangered Species and Clean Water Acts.

If such bills pass, moreover, the environmentalists' criticism has been that they are crafted so as to create "paralysis by analysis," so that nothing will be done by agencies until reams of paperwork have been completed, and have survived extended judicial review challenges.

Executive Orders

In response to Unholy Trinity issues, the Clinton Administration has drafted or issued executive orders touching on all three areas, revisiting and revising prior executive orders from the Reagan and Bush Administrations.

Regulatory takings. President Reagan issued an executive order, **E O 12630**, that received little implementation requiring takings issues to be factored into agency rulemaking using tests that were inclined toward the insulation of regulatees.

President Clinton's staff has been working on a new executive order that reportedly emphasizes the identification and weighing of public rights and public harms in the public/private balance.

Unfunded Mandates. E.O. 12875. In early 1994 President Clinton issued an executive order concerning unfunded mandates. In his order the President expressed his desire for better understanding between federal

---

100. See Peter A.A. Berle, Safeguarding Environmental Protection, *Audubon magazine* , May, 1994.

and local government.   Clinton emphasized what he felt was a need to lessen the strain on local governments created by unfunded federal mandates by "enhancing...Intergovernmental Partnership."   E.O. 12875.

Under E.O. 12,875 guidelines issued by the Office of Management and Budget, before a rule that contains an unfunded mandate can be issued, agencies must tell the Office for Information and Regulatory Affairs:

> 1.) What the unfunded mandate is;
>
> 2.) What legislation requires the unfunded mandate;
>
> 3.) How much it will cost state, local, and tribal governments;
>
> 4.) Which state and local officials have been consulted by the agencies about the unfunded mandate, and what their actions and concerns were; and
>
> 5.) Why the agencies support "the need to issue the regulation containing the mandate."

Cost-benefit/ risk assessment. The Reagan Administration had attempted to require overall cost-benefit analyses, policed by his Office of Management and Budget, before any federal rule could be issued, an initiative that was not widely implemented.   EO 12,291.   See Sunstein, Cost-Benefit Analysis and the Separation of Powers, 23 Ariz. L.Rev. 1267 (1981).

President Clinton issued EO 12,866 repealing the Reagan regulatory orders and substituting a less formal review process.

Chapter 12,   The National Environmental Policy Act

PAGE 596   A current overview on NEPA

NEPA continues to be a paradox, a bit like the Tarbaby, seemingly innocuous, taking punches, but hanging in there, often gumming up the internal agency and external political processes of questionable projects and programs, despite attempts in some sectors of the federal judiciary to melt it away. A good concise overview of NEPA's quixotic progress is Blumm, NEPA at Twenty, 20 Envt'l Law 447 (1991).

PAGE 600   Adoptions of NEPA-model acts

International adoption of NEPA-model statutes. The NEPA model has been greeted and adapted as a welcome rationality mechanism by a variety of countries and multi-lateral organizations in Europe and the third world. Outside of the US, national environmental impact assessment schemes are used by more than 50 nations. Unlike the US, these nations "rarely rely upon courts to oversee the accuracy of an EIS or the procedures used to prepare it," but rather rely upon public disclosure and comment upon EISs.   In addition, those entities that prepare environmental impact statements are usually independent of project proponents.   Multi-national EIS schemes are used by vairous organizations, including the European Community, Association of South East Asian Nations (ASEAN), various UN organizations, OECD and the World Bank.   Nicholas A. Robinson, "International Trends in Envt'l Impact Assessment," 19 B.C. Envt'l Aff. L. R. 591, 597-98, 611-619 (1991).

State governments' adoption of NEPA-model statutes. "Little NEPA" laws are in use in 16 states, the District of Columbia and Puerto Rico. Some directly follow the federal statute, others differ significantly:

• Some state NEPAs are more substantive than the federal model (among them, California, Minnesota and New York); others (e.g., Virginia) primarily enforce the procedural requirements.

• Some of the laws, explicit or as interpreted by courts, apply only to *state* action. States where the law applies to action taken by *counties and municipalities* as well include California, Hawaii, Massachusetts, Minnesota, New York and Washington.

• Some states have a lower threshold (action that *"may* affect the environment") than NEPA, including California, Hawaii and Wisconsin.

• State courts are more likely to declare an EIS sufficient. States typically employ a more summary hearing (under state administrative procedures act) without discovery. State courts are typically more deferential to agency findings than their federal counterparts. The EIS process used now by states is more developed and refined than under earlier (1970s) federal NEPA suits. "CEQ Annual Report," 22 *Envt'l Quality* 373, 373-377 (1992); David Sive, "Little NEPAs and the Environmental Impact Process," C806 A.L.I. 1, 1-4, 6-7 (1992). *See* Nicholas A. Robinson,

"SEQRA's Siblings: Precedents from Little NEPAs in the Sister States," 46 Alb. L. Rev. 1155, 1156-62 (1982) (Little NEPA development from 1970-1982).

PAGE 644   **What is a final action triggering NEPA? The *NAFTA* case**

In Public Citizen v. Office of the U.S. Trade Representative, the district court required that an EIS be prepared on the environmental impact of the North American Free Trade Agreement before NAFTA could be submitted to Congress for ratification. 822 F.Supp. 21 (D.D.C. 1993). The court held that NEPA requires that an EIS be prepared for "every recommendation or report on proposals for legislation...significantly affecting the quality of the human environment." This reawakened the debate about which – if not all – proposals for legislation require EISs, and also about when in a proposal's life an EIS is required —.only when it is final, or when it is being processed in preparatory stages? It also fell into a firestorm of political pressures attempting to consummate the trilateral agreement on a fast track. The Clinton Administration quickly appealed the trial court's decision.

United States Trade Representative v. Public Citizen; Friends of the Earth, Inc.; Sierra Club, et al.
U.S. Court of Appeals for the D.C. Circuit, 1993
5 F.3d 549

MIKVA, Chief Judge: Appellees sued the Office of the United States Trade Representative, claiming that an environmental impact statement was required for the North American Free Trade Agreement ("NAFTA").... In its appeal of that ruling, the government contends that the Trade Representative's preparation of NAFTA without an impact statement is not "final agency action" under the Administrative Procedure Act ("APA") and therefore is not reviewable by this court.... We conclude that NAFTA is not "final agency action" under the APA,... and express no view on the government's other contentions.

I. BACKGROUND

In 1990, the United States, Mexico, and Canada initiated negotiations on the North American Free Trade Agreement. NAFTA creates a "free trade zone" encompassing the three countries by eliminating or reducing tariffs and "non- tariff" barriers to trade on thousands of items of commerce. After two years of negotiations, the leaders of the three countries signed the agreement on December 17, 1992. NAFTA has not yet been transmitted to Congress.[101] If approved by Congress, NAFTA is scheduled to take effect on January 1, 1994.

Negotiations on behalf of the United States were conducted primarily by the Office of the United States Trade Representative ("OTR"). OTR, located "within the Executive Office of the President," is the United States' chief negotiator for trade matters. OTR "report[s] directly to the

---

[101]. [This case was argued Aug. 24, 1993, and decided Sept. 24, 1993.]

President and the Congress, and [is] responsible to the President and the Congress for the administration of trade agreements ..."

Under the Trade Acts and congressional rules, NAFTA is entitled to "fast-track" enactment procedures which provide that Congress must vote on the agreement, without amendment, within ninety legislative days after transmittal by the President. The current version of NAFTA, once submitted, will therefore be identical to the version on which Congress will vote. President Clinton has indicated, however, that he will not submit NAFTA to Congress until negotiations have been completed on several side agreements regarding, among other things, compliance with environmental laws.

Public Citizen first sought to compel OTR to prepare an environmental impact statement for NAFTA in a suit filed on August 1, 1991. 782 F.Supp. 139 (D.D.C.), aff'd on other grounds, Public Citizen v. Office of the United States Trade Representative, 970 F.2d 916 (D.C.Cir.1992) (Public Citizen I). The district court dismissed Public Citizen's claim for lack of standing. This court affirmed but did not reach the standing issue. Instead, we ruled that because NAFTA was still in the negotiating stages, there was no final action upon which to base jurisdiction under the APA. Public Citizen's current challenge is essentially identical, except that the President has now signed and released a final draft of NAFTA....

II. ...In drafting NEPA,... Congress did not create a private right of action. Accordingly, Public Citizen must rest its claim for judicial review on the Administrative Procedure Act. Section 702 of the APA confers an action for injunctive relief on persons "adversely affected or aggrieved by agency action within the meaning of a relevant statute." 5 U.S.C. A. §702. Section 704, however, allows review only of *final* agency action." 5 U.S.C.A. §704 (emphasis added). The central question in this appeal then is whether Public Citizen has identified some agency action that is final upon which to base APA review.

In support of its argument that NAFTA does not constitute "final agency action" within the meaning of the APA, the government relies heavily on Franklin v. Massachusetts, 112 S.Ct. 2767 (1992). *Franklin* involved a challenge to the method used by the Secretary of Commerce to calculate the 1990 census...pursuant to a reapportionment statute requiring that she report the "tabulation of total population by States ... to the President." After receiving the Secretary's report, the President must transmit to Congress the number of Representatives to which each state is entitled under the method of equal proportions. 2 U.S.C.A. §2a(a). The Supreme Court held that APA review was unavailable because the final action under the reapportionment statute (transmittal of the apportionment to Congress) was that of the President, and the President is not an agency.

To determine whether an agency action is final, "[t]he core question is whether the agency has completed its decisionmaking process, and whether the result of that process is one that will directly affect the parties." *Franklin*,112 S.Ct. at 2773. The *Franklin* Court found that although the Secretary had completed her decisionmaking process, the action that would directly affect the plaintiffs was the President's calculation and transmittal of the apportionment to Congress, not the Secretary's report to the President.

This logic applies with equal force to NAFTA. Even though the OTR has completed negotiations on NAFTA, the agreement will have no effect on Public Citizen's members unless and until the President submits it to Congress. Like the reapportionment statute in *Franklin*, the Trade Acts involve the President at the final stage of the process by providing for him to submit to Congress the final legal text of the agreement, a draft of the implementing legislation, and supporting information. 19 U.S.C.A. §2903(a)(1)(B). The President is not obligated to submit any agreement to Congress, and until he does there is no final action. If and when the agreement is submitted to Congress, it will be the result of action by the President, action clearly not reviewable under the APA.

The district court attempts to distinguish *Franklin* by noting that unlike the census report (which the President was authorized to amend before submitting to Congress), NAFTA is no longer a "moving target" because the "final product ... will not be changed before submission to Congress." The district court goes on to say that NAFTA "shall" be submitted to Congress. This distinction is unpersuasive. NAFTA is just as much a "moving target" as the census report in *Franklin* because in both cases the President has statutory discretion to exercise supervisory power over the agency's action. It is completely within the President's discretion, for example, to renegotiate portions of NAFTA before submitting it to Congress or to refuse to submit the agreement at all. In fact, President Clinton has conditioned the submission of NAFTA on the successful negotiation of side agreements on the environment, labor, and import surges....

Public Citizen seeks to distinguish *Franklin* by arguing that the EIS requirement is an independent statutory obligation for the OTR and thus the agency's failure to prepare an EIS is reviewable final agency action. But the preparation of the census report in *Franklin* was also an "independent statutory obligation" for the Secretary of Commerce.... Furthermore, although the argument that the absence of an EIS "directly affects" Public Citizen's ability to lobby Congress and disseminate information seems persuasive on its face, this court has stated that an agency's failure to prepare an EIS, by itself, is not sufficient to trigger APA review in the absence of identifiable substantive agency action putting the parties at risk. Foundation on Economic Trends v. Lyng, 943 F.2d 79, 85 (D.C.Cir.1991).

Finally, Public Citizen argues that applying *Franklin* in this case would effectively nullify NEPA's EIS requirement because often "some other step must be taken before" otherwise final agency actions will result in environmental harm. In support of this position, it catalogs a number of cases in which courts have reviewed NEPA challenges to agency actions that require the involvement of some other governmental or private entity before becoming final. Although we acknowledge the stringency of *Franklin's* "direct effect" requirement, we disagree that it represents the death knell of the legislative EIS. *Franklin* is limited to those cases in which the President has final constitutional or statutory responsibility for the final step necessary for the agency action directly to affect the parties.... The requirement that the President, and not OTR, initiate trade negotiations and submit trade agreements and their implementing legislation to Congress indicates that Congress deemed the President's involvement essential to the integrity of international trade negotiations. When the President's role is not essential to the integrity of the process, however, APA review of otherwise final agency actions may well be available.

The government advances many other arguments opposing the preparation of an EIS, including weighty constitutional positions on the separation of powers and Public Citizen's lack of standing, as well as the inapplicability of NEPA to agreements executed pursuant to the Trade Acts in general, and NAFTA in particular. It also suggests that the judicial branch should avoid any conflict with the President's power by exercising the "equitable discretion" given it by §702 of the APA. We need not and do not consider such arguments in light of the clear applicability of the *Franklin* precedent.

The ultimate destiny of NAFTA has yet to be determined. Recently negotiated side agreements may well change the dimensions of the conflict that Public Citizen sought to have resolved by the courts. More importantly, the political debate over NAFTA in Congress has yet to play out. Whatever the ultimate result, however, NAFTA's fate now rests in the hands of the political branches. The judiciary has no role to play.

RANDOLPH, Circuit Judge, concurring. ...The majority holds that with respect to the North American Free Trade Agreement, there has been no "final" action because the President has not even transmitted NAFTA to Congress for its approval; and that if and when the President does submit the agreement and its implementing legislation, this would not qualify because...the President is not an "agency."

I do not quarrel with either one of these rationales. But I get a bit concerned when the opinion announces that it is too early to toll the bell for judicial review in a "legislative EIS" case and then starts trying to limit *Franklin*. The idea behind this is that proposing legislation to Congress can constitute "final ... action," and that when an "agency" rather than the President does the proposing, §704 of the APA will be satisfied. I am not so sure. *Franklin* held not only that the President is outside the APA's definition of "agency," but also that "action" cannot be considered "final" under the APA unless it "will directly affect the parties." 112 S.Ct. at 2773. When the alleged "action" consists of a proposal for legislation, how can this condition for judicial review be satisfied?... In general...it is difficult to see how the act of proposing legislation could generate direct effects on parties, or anyone else for that matter. The head of an independent agency, a member of the President's Cabinet, or the President himself may send a letter to the Speaker of the House and the President of the Senate transmitting a draft of proposed legislation. Such "executive communications" are commonplace. Yet only a Member of Congress may introduce a bill embodying the proposal, and even then no one will be affected, directly or otherwise, unless and until Congress passes the bill and the President signs it into law. If one takes *Franklin* at its word, a legislative proposal's lack of any direct effects would seem to mean that [regarding *any* agency proposals for legislation] there can be no final action sufficient to permit judicial review under the APA. Of course, there is a big difference between saying that APA review is unavailable and saying that officials do not have to comply with NEPA when they suggest legislation. If Congress believed an agency had not lived up to its obligation to prepare an impact statement, it could always refuse to consider the agency's proposal. Or, if Congress wanted to evaluate environmental impacts before putting the measure to a vote, congressional committees could hold hearings on the subject....

I am therefore not prepared to say whether in NEPA cases, the act of [an agency] proposing legislation constitutes final action under §704 of the APA, as *Franklin* has interpreted that provision. This is a troublesome question, bound to arise in future cases, and we should not stake out a position on it here. The nub of the problem is that judicial review under the APA demands "final agency action" whereas the duty to prepare an impact statement arises earlier. The main objective of an impact statement is to ensure that the decisionmaker considers environmental effects prior to taking action. This is why in Kleppe v. Sierra Club, 427 U.S. 390, 406 n. 15, the Court — without mentioning §704 of the APA — identified the "time at which a court enters the process" to be "when the report or recommendation on the proposal is made, and someone protests either the absence or the adequacy of the final impact statement." *Franklin* 's direct-effects-on-the-parties test, as applied to NEPA suits, may have to be reconciled with the portion of Kleppe v. Sierra Club just quoted. But there is no need to make the attempt in this case. It is enough to hold that regardless of whether the President's submission of NAFTA to Congress would be final action, there is no "final" action that can be attributed to an "agency."

COMMENTARY AND QUESTIONS

1. New loopholes in NEPA? There are several grounds on which NEPA is held not to apply to NAFTA in this case:

> • This is not a *final* agency action, because it is still in the process of being finalized, which will be done by the President and Congress.
> • This is not a final *agency* action, because it is the President and Congress who will take the final action.
> • This is not a final agency *reviewable action* under the terms of APA §704, because it is not an action that itself "directly affects" the plaintiffs.

As Judge Randolph's concurrence indicates, isn't NEPA's mandate of EISs on "agency...proposals for legislation" quite nullified by this logic? Could any agency proposal for legislation ever be subject to judicial review, or are the terms of NEPA now left up to voluntary enforcement by the executive branch and Congress, who have not enforced NEPA in the past?

Beyond agency proposals for legislation, do parts of the majority opinion also imply that an EIS will not be challengeable whenever an agency can say "we are just taking preparatory steps"? By its terms NEPA seeks to shape ongoing government decisional processes, so that even more than most government actions challenged under the APA, NEPA violations consider the preparatory stages of a program.

The "direct effect" element imported from *Franklin* sounds like a heightened standing inquiry — plaintiffs have to claim a direct injury deriving from the challenged action. If this *USTR* case means that an agency gets a good defense against NEPA suits by saying that other actors will have to act before the harm can occur, that would open up a large loophole indeed.

Chapter 13,   Roadblock Statutes; Endangered Species

The Endangered Species Act's prohibition on "taking" species by harming them: the *Sweet Home* case

13A. Narrowing the §9 harm definition? Beyond §7's direct prohibition against harmful agency actions, a basic part of the Act's protective structure since the passage of the ESA in 1973 has been the provision of ESA §9 that prohibits "taking" endangered species by "harming" or "harassing" them. These prohibitions were interpreted by a long succession of regulations to include acts that cause "significant habitat modification or degradation" or alter endangered species' breeding, feeding, or sheltering patterns. See coursebook at 673, Comment 13.

This statutory definition has meant that government species-protection strategies can address actions like destruction of nests, and other actions not directly causing physical injury to the animals themselves, and moreover address habitat destruction, the number one cause of species extinctions.

A recent D.C. Circuit panel, however, produced a revised opinion on re-hearing that seems to say that "harm" and "harass" only occur when a person causes direct immediate physical injury or death to an individual animal:

In Sweet Home Chapter Of Communities for a Great Oregon, v. Babbitt, 17 F.3d 1463 (D.C. Cir. 1994),   17 F.3d 1463, writing for the majority, Judge Williams said —

> the Act states that "take" means to "harass, harm, pursue, hunt, shoot, wound, kill, trap, capture, or collect, or to attempt to engage in any such conduct." 16 U.S.C. §1532(19). The Fish & Wildlife Service (FWS) has in turn defined the component term "harm" in such a way as to encompass any "significant" habitat modification that leads to an injury to an endangered species of wildlife: Harm in the definition of "take" in the Act means an act which actually kills or injures wildlife. Such act may include significant habitat modification or degradation where it actually kills or injures wildlife by significantly impairing essential behavioral patterns, including breeding, feeding or sheltering. 50 CFR § 17.3....
>
> The potential breadth of the word "harm" is indisputable.... The immediate context of the word, however, argues strongly against any such broad reading. With the single exception of the word "harm," the words of the definition contemplate the perpetrator's direct application of force against the animal taken: "harass, harm, pursue, hunt, shoot, wound, kill, trap, capture, or collect". The forbidden acts fit, in ordinary language, the basic model "A hit B."...

Thus the gulf between the Service's habitat modification concept of "harm" and the other words of the statutory definition, and the implications in terms of the resulting extinction of private rights, counsel application of the maxim noscitur a sociis — that a word is known by the company it keeps.... The structure and history of the Act confirm this reading. The ESA pursues its conservation purposes through three basic mechanisms: (1) a federal land acquisition program, ESA § 5; (2) the imposition of strict obligations on federal agencies to avoid adverse impacts on endangered species, ESA § 7; and (3) a prohibition on the taking of endangered species by anybody, ESA § 9. The Act addresses habitat preservation in two ways — the federal land acquisition program and the directive to federal agencies to avoid adverse impacts. The latter frames the duty in terms that the Service has now transposed to the private anti-"take" provision: every such agency is to "insure that any action authorized, funded, or carried out by such agency ... is not likely to jeopardize the continued existence of any endangered species or threatened species or result in the destruction or adverse modification of habitat of such species which is determined ... to be critical", unless an exemption is granted. 16 U.S.C. § 1536(a)(2). Thus, on a specific segment of society, the federal government, the Act imposes very broad burdens, including the avoidance of adverse habitat modifications; on a broad segment, every person, it imposes relatively narrow ones....

Congress's deliberate deletion of habitat modification from the definition of "take" strengthens our conclusion. As introduced before the Senate Commerce Committee, S. 1983 defined "take" as including "the destruction, modification, or curtailment of [a species'] habitat or range."... But the "take" definition of the version of S. 1983 submitted to the Senate omitted any reference to habitat modification, defining "take" to mean "harass, pursue, hunt, shoot, wound, kill, trap, capture, or collect, or to attempt to engage in any such conduct." In rejecting the Service's understanding of "take" to encompass habitat modification, "we are mindful that Congress had before it, but failed to pass, just such a scheme."...

 Congress amended the Act in 1982, with two possible implications. First, one might argue that one of the amendments so altered the context of the definition of "take" as to render the Service's interpretation reasonable, or even, conceivably, to reflect express congressional adoption of that view. Second, one might argue that the process of amendment, which brought the Service's regulation and a judicial endorsement to the attention of a congressional subcommittee, constituted a ratification of the regulation. We reject both theories....

Judge Mikva, in dissent, argued that

Chevron does not place the burden on the responsible agency to show that its interpretation is clearly authorized or reasonable. On the contrary, the burden is on the party

seeking to overturn such an interpretation to show that
Congress has clearly spoken to the contrary, or that the
agency's interpretation is unreasonable.... And a fair reading
allows for no other conclusion than that the agency's
interpretation is reasonable....

The [statutory] definition of "take" includes several words that
might be read as broadly, or nearly as broadly, as "harm":
especially "harass," "wound," and "kill." Indeed, as the
regulation at issue defines "harm" as an act (including habitat
modification) that "actually kills or injures wildlife," the FWS
might as easily have derived a proscription of habitat
modification from the words "kill," "wound," and "harass," as
from the word "harm."

In fact, the House Report specifically comments upon the
breadth of the ESA's prohibition of "harassment," stating:
["Take"] includes harassment, whether intentional or not. This
would allow, for example, the Secretary to regulate or prohibit
the activities of birdwatchers where the effect of those activities
might disturb the birds and make it difficult for them to hatch or
raise their young. H.R. Rep. No. 93-412 at 11 (1973).
Accordingly, FWS has defined the term "harass" nearly as
broadly as the term "harm": Harass in the definition of "take"
in the Act means an intentional or negligent act or omission
which creates the likelihood of injury to wildlife by annoying it
to such an extent as to significantly disrupt normal behavioral
patterns which include, but are not limited to, breeding, feeding
or sheltering. 50 C.F.R. § 17.3. Appellants have not
challenged this definition....

"Harm" is not a single elastic word among many ironclad ones
but an ambiguous term surrounded by other ambiguous terms.
Consequently, even if it is ever appropriate to measure an
agency's construction of a statute against a seldom-used and
indeterminate principle of statutory construction, this is not the
place for *noscitur a sociis*.... There is no reasonable definition
of the word "harm" (or, for that matter, the word "harass") that
would not render superfluous some of the other defined terms.
For example, one cannot "kill" or "wound" an animal without
also "harming" it, even under the narrowest conceivable
interpretation of "harm." Does that mean we must read
"harm" out of the statute altogether? That would hardly be
faithful to Congress's intent, which was to define takings "in the
broadest possible manner to include any conceivable way in
which a person can "take' or attempt to "take' any fish or
wildlife." S. Rep. No. 93-307 at 7 (1973)....

It is true that the Senate Committee chose not to use the S.
1983 definition of "take," which specifically encompassed
habitat modification. Instead, the Committee adopted a
definition from the other bill under consideration, S. 1592,
which did not explicitly include habitat modification. But as
the district court noted, there is no indication in the legislative
history as to why the Committee selected one definition over
the other. And, in any event, the crucial word "harm" was

never voted on by the Committee but was added later on the floor of the Senate. It might well have been intended to cover the entire landscape originally contemplated by the S. 1983 definition....

In sum, the majority has found nothing in the language, structure, purpose, or legislative history that unambiguously shows that "harm" does not encompass habitat modification. Under *Chevron*, that should dispose of the case: the FWS's gap-filling measure is a permissible exercise of its discretion as delegated by Congress.... The majority may believe it is making good policy — but that is not our job. I dissent.

Under the *Sweet Home* majority's interpretation, would it now be legal, in the D.C. Circuit at least, if endangered eagles lived there, to burn an eagle's nest unless there was an eagle or eaglet in it?

Note both the importance of the mysterious arts of statutory interpretation, and the role of judicial deference to agencies articulated in *Chevron*, see coursebook at 589. Normally courts defer to statutory interpretations made by the agencies charged with their enforcement, and especially so when the interpretations have been long-held over a succession of administrations. Beyond deference, as a matter of overall statutory interpretation, if one looks at the statute from the perspective of asking what it "does," what does "harm" mean?

The federal government has asked for a rehearing en banc. Wise Use groups have been advancing the *Sweet Home* precedent in cases around the country. (Note the references in both opinions to the background issue of private property rights. Cf. coursebook at 441, Comment 2. The battle over this fundamental shift in definitions will be interesting.

PAGE 680   **Update on the old-growth forest/ Spotted Owl controversy**

Upon application by the Bureau of Land Management (BLM) for exemption from the provisions of the Endangered Species Act for 44 timber sales from its FY 1991 timber sales program, the Endangered Species Committee ("God Squad") impaneled by the Bush Administration exempted 13 of 44 timber sales in spotted owl habitat, subject to some mitigation and enhancement measures to be undertaken by the BLM.

The God Committee decision of May 14, 1992 did not immediately lead to reopened timber cutting in the owl's prime habitat. Timber sales were still under a variety of injunctions under other statutes, like Judge Dwyer's decision in the coursebook at 674. The Committee decision was appealed by environmentalists, especially because of comments by one of the Administration delegates voting for the exemption that the standards of the Act in his mind had not been met. Portland Audubon Society v. Endangered Species Committee, 1993 U.S. App. LEXIS 6678 (9th Cir., 1993).

Timber Summit

The "jobs vs. owls" controversy played through the 1992 presidential campaign, and President Clinton tried to make good on his campaign promise to forge a solution to what appeared to be an intractable standoff. In spring 1993, the President held a "timber summit" with administration officials, logging interests, and environmentalists. Labor Secretary Robert Reich said that 20,000 jobs in the timber industry have been lost in the last two years, but the contribution of the owl-protection standoff to this loss of jobs was unclear, with environmentalists asserting that most of the job loss was due to automation at US mills and the export of raw logs for milling abroad. Other groups asserted that any timber industry job losses resulting from conservation of old growth forests would pale compared to the loss of the thousands of jobs in the salmon industry which could result from continued clear-cutting. That message got through to the President. "If we destroy our old-growth forest, we'll lose jobs in salmon fishing and tourism, and eventually, in the timber industry as well," he said. Spawning habitats for salmon have been harmed by sedimentation that results from timber harvesting.

Later in 1993, Clinton released a plan for the old growth forests of the Northwest. The Forest Plan called for the following:

> LOGGING LIMITS: Allows for logging of about 12 billion board feet of timber over 10 years, or about 1.2 billion annually on federal lands in the region that produced more than 4 billion a year during peak harvests in the late 1980s.

> PROTECTIVE RESERVES: Establishes a 6.7 million-acre network of protective reserves for the threatened northern spotted owl and other species, where limited logging of dead and dying trees and thinning of some live trees would be allowed.

> EXPERIMENTAL AREA: Sets up special management areas where experimental harvesting techniques would be used.

> BUFFER ZONE: Establishes no-logging buffer zones around sensitive streams and protects watersheds in an attempt to head off future endangered species listings of salmon and other wildlife.

> ECONOMIC ASSISTANCE: Asks Congress for $1.2 billion over five years, including $270 million in the coming year, to assist the region's economy. It includes economic development grants, small business zones, job training money and funds to put displaced loggers to work restoring rivers damaged by excessive logging

> TAX CHANGE: Asks Congress to encourage more domestic milling by eliminating a tax subsidy for the export of raw logs from private lands.[102]

The administration submitted the plan, now designated as "ROD (Rule of Decision), Option 9," as an EIS as required by court order in Seattle

---

102. See Elliot Diringer, "Clinton Reveals Northwest Timber Plan," *San Francisco Chronicle*, July 2, 1993 at A1. In addition, the President supports a bill which would restore a ban on the export of raw logs from public lands, saving 6,000 jobs in Washington state alone. Kathy Lewis, "Logging Proposal Offered; Clinton Seeks End to Northwest Fight," *Dallas Morning News*, July 2, 1993 at 1A.

Audubon v. Robertson, coursebook at 674, 1991 WL 180099, (W.D. Wash. 1991). In early June, 1994, Judge Dwyer lifted the injunction in that case.

Dwyer said the Clinton plan corrected the problems in the federal protection of the northern spotted owl and other wildlife that triggered his 1991 injunction, but he stressed that all parties are free to challenge the legality of the president's new blueprint.   More than a dozen environmental groups have brought five lawsuits against the Clinton proposal since it was sent to Dwyer in April. The timber industry has filed two more lawsuits against the plan in Washington, D.C.

PAGE 683   **Under-enforcement of the ESA?**

5A.   Managing species for extinction? A recent article in Science magazine concluded that because of political pressures and other constraints, the federal agencies with jurisdiction over endangered species, Interior's Fish and Wildlife Service and Commerce's National Oceanic and Atmospheric Administration, were under-protecting species in their recovery planning under the ESA. The researchers began their study to determine whether federal recovery efforts attempt to save too much, as some critics of the ESA charge.

> "Our analysis does not show that recovery plans attempt to save too much, but instead that recovery goals have often been set that risk extinction rather than ensure survival," they said. Few species have actually recovered from the brink of extinction because of the Endangered Species Act, said the authors, who reviewed the 314 recovery plans approved by federal agencies as of August 1991. The researchers reported they found that many recovery plans set "goals for population size and number of populations at or below what exist in the wild" when the plan was written.
>
> In an analysis of recovery goals versus current population size in the recovery plans surveyed, the researchers found that between 28 percent and 37 percent of all threatened or endangered species are "managed for extinction."
>
> The ESA requires recovery plans with measurable criteria that if met, would result in the species being downlisted from endangered to threatened and eventually removed from the threatened list. But the researchers said they found that recovery goals have not included "biologically defensible estimates,... suggest[ing] that political, social, or economic considerations may have been operating that reduced recovery goals so that they were below what might have been set if they had been developed strictly on biologically based estimates," the researchers wrote. "We suggest this occurs more often than previously believed and represents a fundamental problem in recovery efforts." Timothy H. Tear; Michael J. Scott; Patricia H. Hayward; Brad Griffith, "Status and Prospects for Success of the endangered Species Act: A Look at Recovery Plans," SCIENCE, November 1993 at 976; see BNA Nat'l Env't Daily, Nov. 15, 1993.

Given the dramatic goals of the ESA and the widespread human-based character of species endangerment, it is inevitable that major political conflicts arise in ESA enforcement. It is probably equally inevitable that agency biologists and policy officials will tend to avoid strong enforcement of their statutory mandate in order to avoid exacerbating the political context. Is this an indictment?

PAGE 683   **Environmental protectors versus environmental protectors; and §7(d) and the strategy of "sunk costs"**

Sometimes the efforts of one group of environmental protectors can clash with the efforts and goals of another, a situation which invites enlightened negotiation but doesn't always get it.

A recent controversy involved the Boston Harbor cleanup. The Conservation Law Foundation, an eminent environmental law citizens group had successfully sued the EPA and state environmental agencies in federal district court in 1985 and won a $4 billion cleanup order. Energized by the order, the defendant agencies forged a complex and difficult program of sewage treatment facilities to achieve the required water quality for the Harbor, and began to build. Part of the plan included the discharge of treated wastes nine miles offshore through a giant outfall pipe.

Although the environmental agencies were generally aware that a significant number of endangered species were in the area, in their fervor to comply with the water pollution order virtually no thought was given to following the requirements of the Endangered Species Act. The formal biological assessment required of any project in an area known to contain listed species was not done. Even more troubling, in spite of the evidence of risk of harm the agencies did not undertake consultation with the National Marine Fisheries Service.

In 1991, faced with political opposition to the Pipe and evidence that the world's most endangered whale — the North Atlantic Right Whale which had Massachusetts and Cape Cod Bays as critically important parts of its migratory life cycle — might be impacted by construction activities and nutrient-rich discharges into its prime habitat, the agencies belatedly decided that a formal assessment and formal consultation were necessary, though work had already begun and continued unabated.

In a hearing for a preliminary injunction against continued construction, pro-whale environmentalists argued that ESA had been violated by commencement of construction without a biological assessment (ESA §7(c)), by continuing heavy construction which forecloses possible alternative designs despite the fact that consultation with NMFS has not concluded (ESA §7(d)), and by jeopardizing the species' survival (§7(a)).

In a scenario reminiscent of very different old-boy porkbarrel cases, the defendants persuaded the judge to dismiss the entire case without an evidentiary hearing. They persuaded the judge (a jurist with a strong environmental consciousness who had originally ordered the pollution cleanup) (1) that an SEIS filed in 1988 that touched upon endangered species "counted" as the substantial equivalent of a biological assessment, and if it didn't the procedural violation was not sufficient to require judicial sanction, (2) that continued construction of multi-million dollar works did not foreclose alternatives because the ongoing works could be abandoned or redesigned later, and (3) that absent further scientific evidence of potential harm, plaintiffs had not proved jeopardy. The Bays Legal Fund, and Greenworld, Inc. v. Browner, et al., 93-10883 and 10623-MA, (D. Mass. July 1993).

Among the interesting features of such cases — beyond the irony of switched roles played by environmental protectors — are their potential erosions of important environmental law principles. The ESA, for instance, is designed to embody "institutionalized caution" as Justice Burger declared in the *TVA v. Hill* case, with the burden of proving safety incumbent upon defendants, rather than requiring plaintiffs to prove harm as well as risk. See Houck, "The 'Institutionalization of Caution' Under §7 of the Endangered Species Act: What Do You Do When You Don't Know?" 12 ELR 15001 (1982). Ruling on the factual merits without permitting an evidentiary hearing so that factual evidence can be adduced it similarly troubling.

Such cases raise a further fascinating problem: the common practical defense tactic of "sunk costs." In the *Overton Park* case, for instance, the agencies had attempted to build so much of the Interstate highway up to the boundaries of the Park that there would be no alternative left but to go through despite the protective law. Up until the last moment they could say that the law was not yet being violated, though all park preservation alternatives were being foreclosed. Coursebook at page 553, note 16. With the Tellico Dam and a host of other major cases, especially those dealing with public works projects, defendants have rushed construction along in the face of potential statutory constraints, pouring so much concrete or cutting so many trees before a citizen group can finally get to a court hearing that they can say the questions of preservation and statutory compliance have regrettably become moot.

But ESA §7(d) was written to prevent just such official disingenuity. It declares that after formal consultation with the wildlife agency has begun, and until a final biological opinion is produced in that consultation, a federal agency –

> shall not make any irreversible or irretrievable commitment of resources with respect to...agency action which has the effect of foreclosing the formulation or implementation of any reasonable or prudent alternative measures.

This extraordinary provision is intended to undercut the "sunk cost" strategy. In practical terms it seemed that the outfall pipe construction expenditures were hardly reversible, much less retrievable. To say that one can write off millions of dollars later if necessary, is to indulge in a spendthrift premise in a climate where taxpayer ire effectively will forestall future large expenditures for a retrofit. In the Boston case, moreover, extensive evidence of practical alternatives foregone was available for a hearing on the merits, but the court's accelerated dismissal finessed that opportunity.

Full disclosure notice, if it is not already apparent: one of the authors was involved with the case, attempting to facilitate the submission of amicus curiae scientific evidence at trial, and was sorely disappointed that neither the factual evidence nor the law of §7 received a full hearing on the merits.

Page 684   ESA reauthorization

The ESA is up for reauthorization, and as usual plays the role of a political football. (Sunset provisions attached to much recent public interest legislation effectively guarantees that environmental protections passed into law have to be defended against assault every five years.) There are currently four proposed ESA reauthorization bills; two on the House side and two on the Senate side. The two House bills were introduced in the Environment and Natural Resources Subcommittee of the Merchant Marine and Fisheries Committee by Chairman Gerry E. Studds (D MA)(H.R. 2043, the "environmentally friendly" reauthorization bill) and Representative W.J. "Billy" Tauzin (D LA)(H.R. 1490, the development-oriented bill, which in part attempts to restrict enforcement by authorizing compensation for affected private propertyowners). The two Senate bills were introduced in the Clean Water, Fisheries and Wildlife Subcommittee of the Environment and Public Works Committee by Chairman Max S. Baucus (D MT)(S. 921, much like Studds') and Senator Howard M. Metzenbaum (D OH)(S. 74, a limited attempt to override *Lujan II).*

As of June 1994 there have been no substantive hearings on any of the bills. Currently the House Subcommittee is holding hearings to establish the basic ESA reauthorization issues on the House side. Staff members predict that the action on ESA reauthorization will begin on the House side, followed by Subcommittee mark-up, and after the House vote, to the Senate side.

There is already some emerging consensus on what the primary reauthorization issues are. Each competing bill focuses on encouraging private landowners to participate in formal cooperative agreements to promote habitat preservation. The bills provide for consideration of the economic impact of listing decisions and development of recovery plans, a process that currently is effectively restricted to the process of designating critical habitat. They also include proactive approaches to protecting potentially endangered species through ecosystem and habitat protection, an initiative supported by Secretary of Interior Bruce Babbitt.

Because Rep. Studds is the chairman of the Merchant Marine and Fisheries Committee, his bill is considered the most likely to succeed and has over ninety sponsors.

PAGE 685   A statutory roadblock comparison: *Les v. Reilly*

C. THE DELANEY CLAUSE AS A CONTRASTING EXAMPLE OF THE ROADBLOCK APPROACH

In terms of subject matter, this chapter has focused on the declared congressional goal of preserving endangered species. In terms of its taxonomic perspective, however, the chapter considers the approach of stark statutory prohibitions. Their relative inflexibility can be both an asset and a liability for effective enforcement of national policy. (In this regard, Chapter 17's consideration of Congress's stark statutory 90% rollback in auto emissions offers a similar taxonomic case study.)

The following case reflects the national debate on risk, the practical virtues of a clear unambiguous draconian statutory standard, and political distrust of agency ability to stand up to regulated interests.

Kathleen Les et al. v. William K. Reilly
United States Court of Appeals for the Ninth Circuit, 1992
968 F.2d 985

Schroeder, C.J. Petitioners seek review of a final order of the Environmental Protection Agency permitting the use of four pesticides as food additives although they have been found to induce cancer. Petitioners challenge the final order on the ground that it violates the provisions of the Delaney clause, 21 U.S.C. §348(c)(3), which prohibits the use of any food additive that is found to induce cancer.

Prior to 1988, EPA regulations promulgated in the absence of evidence of carcinogenicity permitted use of the four pesticides at issue here as food additives. In 1988, however, the EPA found these pesticides to be carcinogens. Notwithstanding the Delaney clause, the EPA refused to revoke the earlier regulations, reasoning that, although the chemicals posed a measurable risk of causing cancer, that risk was "de minimis."

We set aside the EPA's order because we agree with the petitioners that the language of the Delaney clause, its history and purpose all reflect that Congress intended the EPA to prohibit all additives that are carcinogens, regardless of the degree of risk involved.

Background

The Federal Food, Drug, and Cosmetic Act (FFDCA), 21 U.S.C. §§301-394 (West 1972 & Supp. 1992), is designed to ensure the safety of the food we eat by prohibiting the sale of food that is "adulterated." 21 U.S.C. §331(a). Adulterated food is in turn defined as food containing any unsafe food "additive." 21 U.S.C. §342(a)(2)(C). A food "additive" is defined broadly as "any substance the intended use of which results or may reasonably be expected to result ... in its becoming a component ... of any food." 21 U.S.C. §321(s). A food additive is considered unsafe unless there is a specific exemption for the substance or a regulation prescribing the conditions under which it may be used safely. 21 U.S.C. §348(a).

Before 1988, the four pesticide chemicals with which we are here concerned- benomyl, mancozeb, phosmet and trifluralin-were all the subject of regulations issued by the EPA permitting their use. In October 1988, however, the EPA published a list of substances, including the pesticides at issue here, that had been found to induce cancer. Regulation of Pesticides in Food: Addressing the Delaney Paradox Policy Statement, 53 Fed. Reg. 41,104, 41,119 (Oct. 19, 1988). As known carcinogens, the four pesticides ran afoul of a special provision of the FFDCA known as the Delaney clause, which prescribes that additives found to induce cancer can never be deemed "safe" for purposes of the FFDCA. The Delaney clause is found in FFDCA section 409, 21 U.S.C. §348. That section limits the conditions under which the Secretary may issue regulations allowing a substance to be used as a food additive: No such regulation shall issue if a fair evaluation of the data before the Secretary-(A) fails to establish that the proposed use of the food additive, under the conditions of use to be specified in the regulation, will be safe: Provided, That no additive shall be deemed to be safe if it is found to induce cancer when ingested by man or animal, or if it is found, after tests which are appropriate for the evaluation of the safety of food additives, to induce cancer in man or animal.... 21 U.S.C. §348(c)(3).

The FFDCA also contains special provisions which regulate the occurrence of pesticide residues on raw agricultural commodities. Section 402 of the FFDCA, 21 U.S.C. §342(a)(2)(B), provides that a raw food containing a pesticide residue is deemed adulterated unless the residue is authorized under §408 of the FFDCA, 21 U.S.C. §346a, which allows tolerance regulations setting maximum permissible levels and also provides for exemption from tolerances under certain circumstances. When a tolerance or an exemption has been established for use of a pesticide on a raw agricultural commodity, then the FFDCA allows for the "flow-through" of such pesticide residue to processed foods, even when the pesticide may be a carcinogen. This flow- through is allowed, however, only to the extent that the concentration of the pesticide in the processed food does not exceed the concentration allowed in the raw food....It is undisputed that the EPA regulations at issue in this case allow for the concentration of cancer-causing pesticides during processing to levels in excess of those permitted in the raw foods.

The proceedings in this case had their genesis in October 1988 when the EPA published a list of substances, including these pesticides, that were found to induce cancer. 53 Fed. Reg. 41,104, App. B. Simultaneously, the EPA announced a new interpretation of the Delaney clause: the EPA proposed to permit concentrations of cancer-causing pesticide residues greater than that tolerated for raw foods so long as the particular substances posed only a "de minimis" risk of actually causing cancer. 53 Fed. Reg. at 41,110. Finding that benomyl, mancozeb, phosmet and trifluralin (among others) posed only such a de minimis risk, the Agency announced that it would not immediately revoke its previous regulations authorizing use of these substances as food additives.

Petitioners filed an administrative petition in May 1989 requesting the EPA to revoke those food additive regulations. Following public comment, the EPA issued a Notice of Response refusing to revoke the regulations. After the petitioners filed objections to that response, the EPA published its final order denying the petition to revoke the food additive regulations. This petition for review...followed.

The issue before us is whether the EPA has violated §409 of the FFDCA, the Delaney clause, by permitting the use of carcinogenic food additives which it finds to present only a de minimis or negligible risk of causing cancer. The Agency acknowledges that its interpretation of the law is a new and changed one. From the initial enactment of the Delaney clause in 1958 to the time of the rulings here in issue, the statute had been strictly and literally enforced. 56 Fed. Reg. at 7751-52. The EPA also acknowledges that the language of the statute itself appears, at first glance, to be clear on its face. Id. at 7751 ("[S]ection 409 mandates a zero risk standard for carcinogenic pesticides in processed foods in those instances where the pesticide concentrates during processing or is applied during or after processing.").

The language is clear and mandatory. The Delaney clause provides that no additive shall be deemed safe if it induces cancer. 21 U.S.C.A.

§348(c)(3). The EPA states in its final order that appropriate tests have established that the pesticides at issue here induce cancer in humans or animals. 56 Fed. Reg. at 7774-75. The statute provides that once the finding of carcinogenicity is made, the EPA has no discretion. As a leading work on food and drug regulation notes:

> [T]he Delaney Clause leaves the FDA room for scientific judgment in deciding whether its conditions are met by a food additive. But the clause affords no flexibility once FDA scientists determine that these conditions are satisfied. A food additive that has been found in an appropriate test to induce cancer in laboratory animals may not be approved for use in food for any purpose, at any level, regardless of any "benefits" that it might provide. Richard A. Merrill and Peter B. Hutt, Food and Drug Law 78 (1980).

This issue was litigated before the D.C. Circuit in connection with the virtually identical "color additive" prohibition of 21 U.S.C. §376(b)(5)(B). The D.C. Circuit concluded that "[t]he natural — almost inescapable — reading of this language is that if the Secretary finds the additive to induce cancer in animals, he must deny listing." Public Citizen v. Young, 831 F.2d 1108, 1112 (D.C. Cir. 1987), cert. denied, 485 U.S. 1006 (1988). The court concluded that the EPA's de minimis interpretation of the Delaney clause in 21 U.S.C. §376 was "contrary to law." 831 F.2d at 1123. The *Public Citizen* decision reserved comment on whether the result would be the same under the food additive provisions as it was under the food color provisions, 831 F.2d at 1120, but its reasoning with respect to the language of the statute is equally applicable to both.

The Agency asks us to look behind the language of the Delaney clause to the overall statutory scheme governing pesticides, which permits the use of carcinogenic pesticides on raw food without regard to the Delaney clause. Yet section 402 of the FFDCA, 21 U.S.C. §342(a)(2)(C), expressly harmonizes that scheme with the Delaney clause by providing that residues on processed foods may not exceed the tolerance level established for the raw food. The statute unambiguously provides that pesticides which concentrate in processed food are to be treated as food additives, and these are governed by the Delaney food additive provision contained in §409. If pesticides which concentrate in processed foods induce cancer in humans or animals, they render the food adulterated and must be prohibited.

The legislative history, too, reflects that Congress intended the very rigidity that the language it chose commands. The food additive Delaney clause was enacted in response to increasing public concern about cancer. It was initially part of a bill, introduced in the House of Representatives in 1958 by Congressman Delaney, to amend the FFDCA. H.R. 7798, 85th Cong., 1st Sess. (1957), reprinted in XIV A Legislative History of the Federal Food, Drug, and Cosmetic Act and its Amendments 91 (1979) (hereinafter, "Legislative History"). The bill, intended to ensure that no carcinogens, no matter how small the amount, would be introduced into food, was at least in part a response to a decision by the FDA to allow a known carcinogen, the pesticide Aramite, as an approved food additive. Food Additives: Hearings Before a Subcommittee of the House Committee on Interstate and Foreign Commerce, 85th Cong., 1st and 2d Sess. 171 (1958), reprinted in XIV Legislative History 163, 336. Of the FDA's approval for sale of foods containing small quantities of Aramite, Congressman Delaney stated: The part that chemical additives play in the cancer picture may not yet be completely understood, but enough is known to put us on our guard. The safety of the public health demands that chemical additives should be specifically pretested for carcinogenicity, and this should be spelled out in the law. The precedent established by the Aramite decision has opened the door, even if only a little, to the use of carcinogens in our foods. That door should be slammed shut and locked. That is the purpose of my anticarcinogen provision. Id. at 498, reprinted in XIV Legislative History at 660. The scientific witnesses who testified before Congress stressed that because current scientific techniques could not determine a safe level for carcinogens, all carcinogens should be prohibited. See 56 Fed. Reg. at 7769. While Congressman Delaney's bill was not ultimately passed, the crucial anticancer language from the bill was incorporated into the Food Additives Amendment of 1958 which enacted section 409 of the FFDCA into law. H.R. 13254, 85th Cong., 2d Sess. (1958), reprinted in XIV Legislative History 880, 887. Thus, the legislative history supports the conclusion that Congress intended to ban all carcinogenic food additives, regardless of amount or significance of risk, as the only safe alternative.

Throughout its 30-year history, the Delaney clause has been interpreted as an absolute bar to all carcinogenic food additives. See 53 Fed. Reg. at 41,104 (announcing a shift in the EPA's position, away from reading section 409's Delaney clause "literally")...

The EPA contends that the legislative history shows that Congress never intended to regulate pesticides, as opposed to other additives, with extraordinary rigidity under the food additives provision. The Agency is indeed correct that the legislative history of the food additive provision does not focus on pesticides, and that pesticides are regulated more comprehensively under the Federal Insecticide, Fungicide, and Rodenticide Act (FIFRA), 7 U.S.C. §136-136y (West 1980 & Supp. 1992). Nevertheless, the EPA's contention that Congress never intended the food additive provision to encompass pesticide residues is belied by the events prompting passage of the provision into law: FDA approval of Aramite was the principal impetus for the food additive Delaney clause and Aramite was itself a regulated pesticide. Thus, Congress intended to regulate pesticides as food additives under §409 of the FFDCA, at least to the extent that pesticide residues concentrate in processed foods and exceed the tolerances for raw foods.

Finally, the EPA argues that a de minimis exception to the Delaney clause is necessary in order to bring about a more sensible application of the regulatory scheme. It relies particularly on a recent study suggesting that the criterion of concentration level in processed foods may bear little or no relation to actual risk of cancer, and that some pesticides might be barred by rigid enforcement of the Delaney clause while others, with greater cancer-causing risk, may be permitted through the flow-through provisions because they do not concentrate in processed foods. See National Academy of Sciences, Regulating Pesticides in Food: The Delaney Paradox (1987). The EPA in effect asks us to approve what it deems to be a more enlightened system than that which Congress established. The EPA is not alone in criticizing the scheme established by the Delaney clause. See, e.g., Richard A. Merrill, FDA's Implementation of the Delaney Clause: Repudiation of Congressional Choice or

Reasoned Adaptation to Scientific Progress, 5 Yale J. on Reg. 1, 87 (1988) (concluding that the Delaney clause is both unambiguous and unwise: "at once an explicit and imprudent expression of legislative will"). Revising the existing statutory scheme, however, is neither our function nor the function of the EPA. There are currently bills pending before the House and the Senate which would amend the food additive provision to allow the Secretary to establish tolerance levels for carcinogens, including pesticide residues in processed foods, which impose a negligible risk. H.R. 2342, 102d Cong., 1st Sess. (1991); S. 1074, 102d Cong., 1st Sess. (1991). If there is to be a change, it is for Congress to direct.

The EPA's refusal to revoke regulations permitting the use of benomyl, mancozeb, phosmet and trifluralin as food additives on the ground the cancer risk they pose is de minimis is contrary to the provisions of the Delaney clause prohibiting food additives that induce cancer. The EPA's final order is set aside.

COMMENTARY AND QUESTIONS

1. Zero risk or reasonable risk? The court's reasoning goes even further than the court itself appears to perceive. If the Delaney Clause must be interpreted literally, then EPA not only must prohibit the sale of agricultural products under the normal safety standards "to the extent that pesticide residues concentrate in processed foods and exceed the tolerances for raw foods," but practically speaking EPA also cannot set any tolerance levels for pesticides in food, other than zero tolerance, for pesticides found to cause cancer in laboratory animals. Thus we have the anomalous result that EPA can register for use, under FIFRA, a pesticide that has been found to be weakly carcinogenic in test animals — but that has important social and economic benefits and cannot feasibly be replaced by substitute pest control methods — however, EPA must, at the same time, interdict the sale of raw agricultural products or processed foods containing any trace of this pesticide. Congress must obviously clear this pesticide policy logjam. Should Congress adopt a zero risk approach, a reasonable risk approach, or some combination of both? For example, should Congress mandate a zero risk approach for strong carcinogens (e.g., for those causing a higher than one in a million risk of cancer) and a reasonable risk approach for weaker carcinogens? This is another chapter in the long debate over how to incorporate risk analysis into regulatory policy. (Here, and in the following notes, see Chapter 2 in the coursebook and this Supplement).

2. What's an agency to do? Is an agency ever justified in not reading a clear statutory mandate literally? The Delaney Clause, enacted in 1958, is a crude regulatory device that makes a number of questionable toxicological assumptions, including (1) that high-dose, relatively small group animals tests can accurately predict low-dose, large group human responses, and (2) that substances causing cancer in animals also invariably cause cancer in human beings. (See coursebook Chapter 2). The atmosphere in Congress during hearings on the Delaney Clause was one of pervasive "cancer phobia." But isn't an unambiguous legislative directive to be followed to the letter, regardless of its scientific or policy merits? Sometimes the whole point of a stark statutory command is to avoid the delay, dilution, and political vulnerability of the normal administrative process where agencies study conditions, make and remake tentative draft standards, negotiate with every squeaking wheel about adjusting terms, defend the final standards in court challenges, and then undertake a similar odyssey in designing and applying an enforcement scheme. A clear statutory command efficiently sidesteps much of this administrative process morass.

The same dilemma arises in this area as in the case of the ESA. Clear stark statutory commands don't leave much wiggle room, and subject an agencies and regulatees to a tougher level of judicial superintendence. For that reason, such commands are more likely to be obeyed by regulatees and regulators alike. The agency that considers whether to inject a little flexibility or slack into statutory enforcement — recognizing that strict enforcement of all statutes is practically impossible, politically problematic, and sometimes not necessarily rational — runs the risk of overstepping its constitutional role, being accused of abdicating its public service obligations, and sabotaging declared national policy, as indeed it may be. Perhaps that is why so many important administrative issues are ultimately shifted to courts and Congress.

3. What's a public interest environmental advocacy group to do, in balancing the virtues and shortcomings of crude blunt roadblocks? Here's the dilemma: Assume that a stark statutory provision like the Delaney Clause has been on the books since 1958, and it starts to look a bit outdated in the minds of many fair-minded observers. Or assume that a new environmental protection provision is being proposed that would be a decisive, readily-enforceable crude blunt instrument,... but in a number of cases its terms would be overinclusive, and undersensitive to the rational public policy sensitivities of the issue. Assume further that an environmental advocacy group knows that the agency that would enforce a more subjective, flexible, discretionary standard is extremely vulnerable to political pressure from the regulated industry — as for instance with the Forest Service and the timber industry, the Federal Highway Administration and the highway construction industry.

What is an environmental group to do then, especially in cases like the chemical risk field where many rational policy analysts and resource economists outside the industry establishment affirm that a stark prohibition may be logically inconsistent and poor public policy, and that a measured balancing process would be a far better way to set standards? An intricate, complex, expert balancing process for setting standards for a wide array of substances, however, cannot be done case-by-case in Congress. Such standard setting inevitably must be delegated to an administrative agency, and there the whole statutory mandate can be lost to the cupidity of the political marketplace within the agency process.

This is a dilemma regularly faced by public interest groups, including the Natural Resources Defense Council, which brought the *Les* case, but also has many experts on its staff who understand and would be happy to have a legal standard that accurately reflected the complex subtleties of the issue. On one hand is the argument of seeking to put into law the optimal balanced rational policy. On the other is the political reality that subtle protective standards can turn out to be no standard at all in agency practice. It is a dilemma between optimal substantive theory and tactical realities, and its resolution requires acknowledgment that often both sides are right.

4. Les v. Reilly update. The Supreme Court denied certiorari for Les v. Reilly *sub nom.* National Agricultural Chemicals Association v. Les, 61 USLW 3568 (1993). The bills noted in the Circuit Court's opinion did not leave their committees in the 102nd Congress and have been reintroduced by Senator Kennedy (D, MA) and Congressman Waxman (R, CA) as S. 331, 103rd Cong., 1st Sess. (1993) and H.R. 872, 103rd Cong., 1st Sess. (1993), respectively.

Chapter 14,   Public Resource Management Statutes

One theme of this chapter is an examination of the three most popular public resource management philosophies: 1) multiple use, sustained yield; 2) dominant use; and 3) single use. These management strategies are responses to the tragedy of commons that is so frequently played out with regard to public resources.   Multiple use, sustained yield (MUSY), discussed at pages 693-694 of the main volume, is the statutory standard that applies to the BLM lands and national forests. National wildlife refuges, wilderness areas, water rights, and hardrock mining and mineral leasing on federal lands are administered according to dominant use principles, discussed on pages 694-700 of the main volume. Dominant use is also the way the BLM lands and national forests have traditionally been managed. In recent years, the de facto dominant use management of these federal lands has been in defiance of Congress' MUSY mandate. The major difference between MUSY and dominant use is that, in most instances, MUSY emphasizes long-term sustainable mixtures of appropriate compatible uses, while dominant use stresses shorter term maximization of a primary use and other secondary uses that are compatible with it. The chief advantage of MUSY is its flexibility, while the major advantage of dominant use is its predictability. MUSY suffers from vagueness and manipulability by a politically inspired agency, while dominant use can "lock up" a resource permanently because once having declared a dominant use, Congress would be unlikely to change it.

Single use is not separately discussed in the main chapter. This management system involves the dedication of a natural resource to a use for which it is uniquely suited. For example, the National Park System has been set aside for recreational uses. (See pages 698-699 of the main volume.) Marine fisheries under federal jurisdiction (beyond the three-mile limit) are assigned to commercial exploitation. (See Fisheries Conservation and Management Act, 16 U.S.C.A. sec. 1801 et seq. (1988).)

Single use management, however, does not preclude conflicts over resource allocation. The ambiguity of the National Park Service Act (quoted at page 699 of the main volume) forces the National Park Service to choose or mediate between users contending for incompatible high and low-intensity recreational opportunities. This conflict is often reflected in lawsuits contesting "over commercialization" of national parks (see page 699 of the main volume). The decline of marine fishery stocks has prompted the imposition of management measures of two types:

1) gear restrictions, minimum size limits, closed seasons, trip-length restrictions, and quotas contained in permits required of all comers; and 2) exclusion of newcomers to the field by restricting catch quotas to existing captains or boats engaged in a particular fishery. This latter mechanism is a form of market access restriction (see Chapter 16).

PUBLIC RESOURCES PLANNING

To an increasing degree, MUSY, dominant use, and single use approaches are defined, refined and applied in the context of mandatory public resource planning. Professor Coggins, referring to federal public lands, has observed that "(f)ederal land use planning threatens to become the most critical stage in the overall process for allocating public natural resources."[103] FLPMA and the Natural Forest Management Act (NFMA) require formal, participatory land use planning, and the resulting plans are legally binding because on-the-ground management decisions must be consistent with the adopted plans. Under NFMA, for example, the Forest Service must prepare Land Resource Management Plans (LRMPs) for all national forests:

> The LRMP defines the "management direction" for the forest. 36 C.F.R. sections 219.1(b), 219.3. It constitutes a program for all natural resource management activities and establishes management requirements to be employed in implementing the plan. It identifies the resource management practices, the projected levels of production of goods and services, and the location where various types of resource management may occur. Implementation of the LRMP is achieved through individual site-specific projects and all projects must be consistent with the LRMP. 16 U.S.C.A. section 1604(i); 36 C.F.R. section 219.10(e).[104]

PAGE 700   **The National Forests Planning Case**

Land use planning is the battleground on which most current conflicts over National Forest management are decided. The following case illustrates how courts become involved in the public resource planning process.

Citizens for Environmental Quality v. United States [Forest Service]
United States District Court for the District of Colorado, 1989
731 F. Supp. 970

FINESILVER, C.J.   This case involves broad attacks by environmental groups on governmental plans for the management of a large forest in Colorado.[105]   In effect, the groups seek to nullify management plans which have been under study and development since 1981...

The present litigation centers on the issue of whether the National Forests should be used or preserved, and reflects the need for balancing the nation's legitimate economic needs with its limited natural resources. Congress addressed this problem in 1976 by passing the National Forest

---

103. The Developing Law Of Land Use Planning On The Federal Lands, 61 U. Colo. L. Rev. 307 (1990).
104. Citizens for Environmental Quality v. United States, infra., chapter 14.
105 The area covered by the Plan, the Rio Grande National Forest, is located in South Central Colorado and contains 1,851,792 acres of National Forest System lands.

Management Act which directed the Secretary to develop, maintain, and revise LRMPs for units of the National Forest System ("NFS"). The task of satisfying the nation's need for timber and other forest products while preserving forest lands for the use of future generations is a complex one. Nonetheless, the NFMA contemplates that through careful planning and management, both economic and aesthetic needs will be met.

The potential impact of the NFMA planning process on the nation poses important environmental and economic issues. Of the 191 million acres included in the National Forest System, 108.1 million acres have been developed for recreation, logging and other uses; 32.5 million are protected as official wilderness, and an additional 50.4 million acres remain roadless with 5.5 million of them recommended for classification as wilderness.

In 1985, cash receipts from NFS activities amounted to $1.1 billion dollars in revenue, $225 million of which was returned to county governments for support of schools and roads. In the same year, recreational use amounted to 225 million visitor-days with an estimated assigned monetary value of about $ 2.2 billion. Forest plans average about $ 2.5 million each to develop.

Pursuant to NFMA mandate, the U.S. Forest Service is in the final stages of developing LRMPs for all national forests. Because of the financial value of the resources at stake and the cost of producing plans, sixty-two final plans have been the subject of formal administrative appeals within the Forest Service. These appeals have reflected an intense concern that the plans resolve resource use issues, meet requirements of the NFMA, are financially feasible, and are politically supported by the people most affected. This case is among the first requesting broad judicial review of Forest Service decisions regarding forest land management plans. Additional litigation is anticipated as more of these plans reach the implementation stage.

[The court then reviewed, in extensive detail, the planning provisions of the National Forest Management Act and the Forest Service's implementing regulations, all of which operate within a framework of multiple use, sustained yield management.

Nine alternative plans with differing emphases were considered in the planning process including a "no action" alternative, a "market output" alternative, a "non-market" alternative, a "reduced budget" alternative, an "improved area economy" alternative, and a "low expenditure, high present value" alternative. Alternative A[106] was chosen as the Plan because it "... (seems) to satisfy all the broad public policy goals ... [and] better serves pressing public needs for commercial products."

The ROD [Record of Decision] describes the selected alternative as follows:

> The proposed action [emphasizes] opportunities to better serve community needs in the San Luis Valley. It provides opportunities to improve the condition of the Forest by

---

106 Alternative A is entitled "Moderate Market Opportunities" and is designed to produce moderate increases in water, fuelwood and forage supplies available in the Forest and increases commercial sawtimber production by 50%.

regenerating overmature spruce, aspen and lodgepole pine stands and by improving winter ranges. This alternative would produce an increase in the amount of water available in the Rio Grande and Conejos Rivers, provide increasing volumes of timber for the Nation, provide greater amounts of fuelwood for surrounding communities, increase livestock grazing over time, and increase developed recreation, including downhill skiing.

On February 19, 1985, Plaintiff filed an administrative appeal of the decision to adopt the Plan with the Chief of the Forest Service.... On May 28, 1987 the Chief issued his decision denying the appeal which the Secretary did not review. The decision constitutes final agency action....

AGENCY PRECEDENT/ECONOMICALLY SUITABLE LANDS

Intervenors [several national environmental groups] claim that Defendants failed to follow Agency precedent as set forth in the Secretary's decision on the San Juan and Grande Mesa, Uncompahgre, and Gunnison National Forests. Intervenors assert that the Secretary's decision in that case requires the Forest Service to conduct a particularly rigorous analysis when it contemplates an unprofitable timber sale program and attempts to justify that program on the basis that it will benefit other, non-timber aspects of forest management....[107]

An agency must abide by established norms and policies unless it provides a convincing reason why a departure from its policies is justified. Grace Petroleum Corp. v. F.E.R.C., 815 F.2d 589, 591 (10th Cir. 1987). Agencies must also treat similar cases in a like fashion. Squaw Transit Co. v. United States, 574 F.2d 492, 496 (10th Cir. 1978).

The San Juan/GMUG decision is set forth in a Memorandum from Deputy Assistant Secretary of Agriculture Douglas MacCleery to Forest Service Chief Max Peterson ("MacCleery Decision")....

In arguing that the San Juan/GMUG decision does not apply to the Rio Grande Plan, Defendants contend that it applies only to Forests which (1) propose an expansion of a timber program in which projected timber sale revenues would fall short of projected timber costs for the entire planning horizon, and (2) projects that the bulk of the costs would be for road construction and timber management activities while the bulk of the benefits would be nontimber and nonmarket benefits resulting from the vegetation management effects of the timber program.

The MacCleery decision should not be read so restrictively. The MacCleery Decision was based on the fact that:

> [The] selected alternatives for both national forests would permit an increase in timber sales from recently experienced

---

107 Timber expenditures exceed timber receipts in 76 of 119 national forests: These sales occur because the minimum acceptable bid is based on lumber prices and milling costs, rather than on the seller's costs of supplying timber. These latter costs include timber appraisal, environmental impact assessment, logging and transportation planning, reforestation, and administration of the sale. Daniels, Rethinking Dominant Use Management in the Forest-Planning Era, 17 Envtl. L. 483, 491 (1987).

levels ... and therefore, the planning documents must discuss and rationalize this possibility.

The alternative selected for the Rio Grande Plan permits an increase in timber sales from recently experienced sales. The decision further states:

> A particularly strong obligation is imposed on the Forest Service to explain the economic, social and environmental tradeoffs which are likely to occur when resource objectives or responses to public issues are proposed which would reduce economic efficiency (reduce present net value).

The alternative adopted for the Rio Grande Forest significantly reduces present net value ("PNV") from the Current Program. Nowhere does the Deputy Secretary specifically limit his evaluation of the San Juan and GMUG National Forests to those forests. The present case is sufficiently similar to the San Juan/GMUG forests for the MacCleery guidelines to apply... .

... The Alternative selected for the Plan was ranked seventh in PNV (Present Net Value), yet no rationale for this was set forth as required by agency precedent. Until these issues...are addressed, the planning process is procedurally deficient... .

BROAD RANGE OF REASONABLE ALTERNATIVES

We agree with Plaintiff and Intervenors that the Rio Grande Forest Plan failed to formulate a broad range of alternatives in violation of Forest Service regulation 36 C.F.R. § 219.12(f).... This section requires that the Forest Service take a "hard look" at alternatives which not only emphasize differing factors, but lead to differing results. Consideration of alternatives which lead to similar results is not sufficient under NEPA and this section. State of California v. Block, 690 F.2d 753 (9th Cir. 1982).

The Forest Planners considered nine alternatives in arriving at the LRMP for the Rio Grande National Forest. Among the alternatives were a "no action alternative," a "market output" alternative, a "non-market" alternative, and a "reduced budget" alternative. Two of the alternatives... provide for a reduction in timber production from current levels. Intervenors claim that Defendant's use of harvest level constraints in its FORPLAN [forest planning computer model] skewed the formulation of alternatives analysis so that no alternative which harvested timber at an overall profitable level could be considered.[108] Intervenors allege that this failure prevented the agency from considering a broad range of alternatives...

From the record, it appears that the Forest Service first established production goals, and then formulated alternatives which would reach those goals through employing data constraints. The remaining lands were then declared to be unsuitable for timber production after the production goals had been satisfied. We have earlier held that production goals may be used in determining the suitable timber base for timber

---

108 Intervenors contend that the alternative with the lowest timber harvest level. . .was constrained by FORPLAN to harvest an amount equal to 80% of the amount harvested in recent years, an amount which is 35% below what Intervenors believe to be the profitable level.

harvesting. However, we also ruled that such goals may not control the suitability analysis absent adequate explanation. Similarly, Defendants provide no adequate justification for allowing production goals to control the formulation of alternatives.

We find that this result-biased decision making process prevented the Forest Service from establishing a legitimately broad range of reasonable alternatives as required by the statutory and regulatory scheme.... Defendants' range of alternatives cannot be said to reflect a wide range of goals since the proposed alternatives each contemplate timber production at a highly unprofitable level. A broad range of alternatives must also include an alternative which contemplates timber harvesting at a profitable level even if that level requires reducing current timber production levels.

We do not hold that an alternative which provides for profitable timber production must be selected. We merely hold that it must be considered in the same way as other alternatives... .

We are not persuaded that Defendants adequately considered each of the alternatives which were developed during the planning process. In its Evaluation of Alternatives, the Forest Service "readily dismissed" Alternatives E and I stating:

> Alternatives E, F and I [do not] provide commercial timber
> yields or make available forage and grazing lands in amounts
> necessary to satisfy pressing public needs. There are both
> local and nation (sic) needs for these materials and resources,
> but local needs for them are genuinely pressing and urgent.

No data is cited in support of the proposition that there are "pressing public needs" for an increase in timber production.

From its evaluation, it is clear that the Forest Service gave a "hard look" only to those alternatives which increased timber production. Alternatives which reduced timber production were "readily dismissed." The Forest Service thus considered only alternatives which led to a similar result – increased timber production. This does not constitute a consideration of a broad range of alternatives.... While nothing prevents the Forest Service from adopting an alternative which increases timber production, this does not permit the Forest Service to seriously consider only those alternatives which provide for increased timber production, to the exclusion of alternatives which do not have the same end result....

Defendants are ENJOINED from increasing current timber harvest levels in the Rio Grande National Forest Plan until compliance with this order and opinion is demonstrated.

COMMENTARY AND QUESTIONS

1. The *CEQ* case. In this opinion, the court accurately perceived FORPLAN to be a question-begging exercise in self-justification by the Forest Service. (Another Forest Service computer model had been criticized on the same basis in the *Block* case, cited by the court.) The *Citizens for Environmental Quality* court is seen taking a "hard look" at the Forest Service action and assuring that the agency itself took a hard and ostensibly unbiased look at the impacts and alternatives of the proposed action (see Chapters 11 and 12 of the main volume). But what will courts do when the Forest Service becomes more sophisticated in its planning?

This decision is a mixed bag in other respects. The court rejected plaintiffs' apparently cogent claims with regard to decision making with inadequate data, unsuitability of land for timber purposes, and the need for cumulative impact review under NEPA.

2. NEPA and public resource planning. Note how NEPA concepts (e.g., "reasonable alternatives" including a "no action alternative") inform the court's evaluation of planning process legality here. In fact, forest planning is subject to NEPA's requirements, and an EIS must accompany the LRMP. (See Chapter 12 of the main volume.) Is this a refutation of the accusation that NEPA is a "paper tiger"? Or does the fact that NEPA is "merely procedural" constrain judicial review of forest plans? What, for example, will the courts do when the Forest Service moves beyond its obviously question-begging FORPLAN and adopts a more sophisticated planning methodology? See Nevada Land Action Association v. U.S. Forest Service, 37 ERC 2131 (9th Cir.1993)(Forest Service was not arbitrary and capricious in preparing LRMP that reduced grazing levels). For an example of the BLM's cavalier attitude toward land-use planning, see Natural Resources Defense Council v. Hodel, 624 F. Supp. 1045 (D.Nev. 1985)(in which Judge Burns "resist(ed) the invitation to become western Nevada's rangemaster.")

3. The Consistency Clause. The consistency clause is a taxonomic device that is found in several environmental statutes, including FLPMA and the Coastal Zone Management Act. (See pp. 950-955 of main volume for a discussion of the CZMA consistency clause.) The function of a consistency clause is to assure that completed plans are actually implemented. But does it really accomplish this purpose? One of the authors drafted a consistency clause to implement the water quality planning provisions of a state water pollution control statute, only to see it circumvented by 1) plans that were intentionally so vague that there was nothing specific to be consistent with, and 2) ad hoc plan amendments made to conform to projects that were politically desirable. It appears that the Forest Service is systematically adopting the former strategy by including only general goals in LRMPs and postponing specific recommendations to the project proposal stage. See Sierra Club v. Robertson, 810 F. Supp. 1021 (W.D. Ark. 1992); Sierra Club v. Robertson, 845 F. Supp. 485 (S.D. Ohio, 1994); and Sierra Club v. Marita, 843 F.Supp. 1526 (E.D. Wis. 1994).

4. Below cost sales. The NFMA does not prohibit below-cost sales of timber on federal lands. Should public resources ever be allocated for less than it costs to manage them? Or should other factors, such as maintenance of stable timber communities and jobs in the timber industry, be considered? Should it depend on ability to pay? If not, should the substantial subsidy afforded to recreational users be eliminated?

5. Where will planning lead? Professor Coggins has speculated that the public resource land use planning process "could cause the demise of multiple use, sustained yield management":

> Planning is ultimately a form of zoning. Completed plans will specify areas more suited to some particular uses than others.

Thus, for example, a part of a national forest may be removed from the commercial timber base because it is marginal, is needed for endangered species protection, or is more valuable for another use, such as a campground.... Planning, coupled with allied "zoning" processes of the federal lands, eventually will result in de facto dominant use management regimes.[109]

Is this bad? Isn't the crux of multiple use-sustained yield management the possibility that even de facto dominant uses must be adaptable to changing social needs and therefore must not impair the sustainable use of the land for other potentially valuable purposes? Multiple use, sustained-yield may also survive because natural resource planning processes may come to diametrically opposed results in different planning areas. Contrast Sierra Club v. Espy, 822 F. Supp. 356 (E.D. Tex. 1993); reversed on other grounds, 18 F.3rd 1020 (5th Cir.1994)(even-aged logging in Texas enjoined because even-aged management techniques should be the exception rather than the rule), with Sierra Club v. Marita, 843 F. Supp. 1526 (E.D. Wis. 1994)(even-aged management for 80% of suitable forest land upheld).

6. Single use and dominant use planning. Planning is required for the National Park System by the National Parks and Recreation Act of 1978, 16 U.S.C.A. section 1a-1 et seq. "With the exception of the Alaska refuges, the [National Wildlife Refuge System] is the only federal land system for which formal planning is not statutorily required." Fink, The National Wildlife Refuges: Theory, Practice, and Prospect, 18 Harv. Env. L. Rev. 1, 46(1994)(recommending an organic act for the NWRS, based on the principles of conservation biology, that would include a formal planning process with a consistency clause).

7. Clinton Administration changes in federal land management policy. Secretary of the Interior Bruce Babbitt, while Governor of Arizona, declared that we:

> need a new western land ethic for non wilderness. The old concept of multiple use no longer fits the reality of the new west. It must be replaced by a concept of public use. From this day on, we must recognize the new reality that the highest and best, most productive use of western public land will usually be for public purposes — watershed, wildlife, and recreation....
>
> The multiple use concept is not adequate for public land management. Forest Service resources are devoted to accelerated logging while families search in vain for improved campsites in the National Forest. Frivolous and uneconomical mining claims disrupt forest administration and recreational uses. Elk herds are reduced to make way for cattle which provide fewer economic benefits to local communities. Mining, logging and other commercial uses are subsidized while wildlife and recreational uses are ignored.
>
> The time is at hand to go beyond multiple use. Mining entry must be regulated, timber cutting must be honestly subordinated to watershed and wildlife values, and grazing must be subordinated to regeneration and restoration of

109. Coggins, footnote 1, supra., at 352.

> grasslands. Many of the forest and BLM plans now being circulated ignore the primacy of public values. It is now time to replace neutral concepts of multiple use with a statutory mandate that public lands are to be administered primarily for public purposes. Coggins, Wilkinson, and Leshy, Federal Public Land and Resources Law (3rd. ed. 1993), 1080-1081.

Is this a new public lands management philosophy of "public use," or a reformulation of "dominant use"? Is logging in an environmentally sound manner any less a public use than camping?

As Secretary of the Interior, Babbitt has advocated amending the General Mining Law of 1872 to require royalty payments and mine reclamation, raising the grazing fee to reflect fair market value, and curtailing below-cost timber sales.

Amendment of the General Mining Law was bogged down in Congress as of summer 1994. The Forest Service has declared that it will administratively terminate below-cost timber sales. With regard to grazing fees, Secretary Babbitt's initial strategy was to support a bill in Congress to increase grazing fees from the current $1.86 per animal unit month to $4.28, to be phased in over a three year period. The current market value on private land of such grazing rights is between five dollars and $15, depending on the quality of grazing land. A coalition of Western senators defeated this measure by means of a filibuster. The Interior Department then proposed regulations to raise grazing fees to a somewhat lower figure than $4.28.

President Clinton appointed Jim Baca, former New Mexico Land Commissioner and member of the Wilderness Society's governing board, as Director of the BLM. Mr. Baca resigned his post after approximately one year in office. It is rumored that Mr. Baca had

become a political liability to President Clinton because Baca was too outspoken and impatient a conservationist.

The avowed philosophy of the Clinton Administration with regard to federal land management is to resolve conflict by a "new, consensus — building style."[110] Professor Coggins, on the other hand, charges "that the current Administration has backed and filled, waffled, reversed itself, and otherwise obfuscated on nearly every major federal land issue it has confronted — while ducking most of them."[111]

---

110. Bruce Babbitt, Remarks to The Society of Range Management, 22 Land and Water Law Review, 399, 402 (1994).
111. Coggins, Commentary: Overcoming the Unfortunate Legacies of Western Public Land Law, 22 Land and Water Law Review, 381, 398 (1994).

Chapter 15, Traditional Review-and-Permit Process, and a Survey of Modern Standard- Setting Approaches

Section E. CAUSE-BASED ENVIRONMENTAL STATUTES AND THE POLLUTION PREVENTION APPROACH

Environmental law is like Perseus in the Ancient Greek myth of Perseus and Medusa. Perseus, the young hero, was dispatched on a quest to bring back the head of Medusa, one of the Gorgons. The Gorgons were three baleful maidens who had wings, claws, and enormous teeth, and whose heads were covered with serpents instead of hair. Anyone looking directly at a Gorgon would immediately be turned to stone. Perseus killed Medusa — who alone of the three sisters was mortal — by surprising her while she was asleep and then performing his grisly task by thrusting his sword backwards while looking at her image mirrored in the back of his shield.

The causes of environmental degradation are excessive human population, unsustainable consumption patterns, and pollution externalities (see page 10 of main volume). Like Medusa's two immortal sisters, population and consumption have thus far been virtually invulnerable to regulatory intervention. Pollution, on the other hand, has been significantly curtailed since the dawn of the Environmental Movement, but only by indirect mechanisms such as harm-based or technology-based statutes (see Chapters 18 and 19) that limit the amount of pollution that can be discharged into the environment. Pollution prevention has only recently been articulated as the primary goal of pollution-control programs. (see pages 1036-1037 of the main volume).

Professor Donald Hornstein has detected a trend toward "cause-oriented reform" that would allow Perseus to attack the Medusa of pollution directly, and even, perhaps, make headway against Medusa's heretofore immortal sisters as well.

Donald T. Hornstein, Lessons from Federal Pesticide Regulation on the Paradigms and Politics of Environmental Law Reform
10 Yale Journal on Regulation 371, 380-388 (1993)

As a general matter, cause-oriented reforms focus on reducing human pressures on natural resources, often by encouraging "clean" technologies or changes in consumption and use patterns. Roughly speaking, this approach contrasts with the focus of risk-based reforms on managing environmental effects to some level of acceptable risk. For all the attention given to risk-based reform, cause-oriented approaches to policymaking may actually pack as much force in explaining many recent changes in environmental law. For example, there has been an increased tendency to build environmental protection directly into statutory programs governing production processes in transportation, energy, and agriculture, without any attempt to justify the programs in risk-reduction terms. Thus, the Intermodal Surface Transportation Efficiency Act of 1991[112] establishes programs for mass transit and transportation planning to address the "underlying causes" of many environmental problems. The 1992 National Energy Policy Act[113] creates programs to foster energy conservation and includes tax benefits to promote renewable energy sources, with explicit congressional references to addressing the "underlying causes" of pollution problems. The 1985 and 1990 Farm Bills[114] both contain provisions designed to encourage "alternative" agricultural production techniques in the name of their environmental benefits.[115]

Cause-oriented reforms also seem better able to explain recent legislative and regulatory efforts toward pollution prevention and source reduction. These efforts seek to shift policy away from the current regulatory emphasis on "pollution control," which often imposes relatively expensive after-the-fact cleanup requirements, toward more direct incentives for less pollution production processes or product design.... [S]uch measures as solid-waste recycling or packaging requirements, which have proliferated explosively at the state and local level over the past five years,[116] seem more likely to reflect the influence of cause-oriented policymaking. So, too, programs designed expressly to eliminate toxic chemicals in industrial and agricultural processes, without obsessive reliance on risk assessments..., seem best described as cause-oriented reforms. The increasing willingness to rely on zoning and other forms of land-use planning to effectuate environmental policy also fits better into a cause-based, rather than risk-based, approach to reform....

This Article makes the case for deliberate and careful experimentation in the near term with cause-oriented reforms without either jettisoning too soon existing regulatory structures or abandoning appropriate insights from quantitative risk assessments. Such a deliberate strategy of "probing" for measures that might ameliorate the underlying causes of environmental problems, despite the caution I believe is required in the undertaking, would represent a watershed in the development of environmental law. It would constitute a strategy best capable of experimenting with incentive-based rather than command-and-control regulation, best able to achieve a new round of environmental gains, and most likely to accommodate in a workable fashion the uncertainties and diverse values in environmental policymaking.

---

112. Pub. L. No. 102-240.

113. Pub. L. No. 102-486.

114. Pub. L. No. 99-198, and Pub. L. No. 101-624.

115. The major provisions of the 1985 Farm Bill deny federal subsidies, loans, or credits to farming operations that destroy wetlands or produce crops on highly erodible land. The 1990 Farm Bill places a greater emphasis than any earlier farm legislation on reducing agricultural runoff and nonpoint source pollution of surface water.

116. At least six states have enacted mandatory statewide recycling requirements, and twenty-three states have legislation or executive orders establishing a preference in state procurement practices for items made from recycled materials.

COMMENTARY AND QUESTIONS

1. Pollution prevention as a cause-based paradigm. Except for an executive order mandating pollution prevention planning for federal facilities,[117] pollution prevention at the federal level has been more hortatory than mandatory (see pages 1036-1037 of the main volume). Most of the pollution prevention lawmaking has taken place at the state level. A January 1994 report of the United States General Accounting Office[118] evaluated 105 state pollution prevention programs nationwide and found them to be seriously flawed:

> Both regulatory and non-regulatory programs exist: The former require pollution prevention planning by industry ; the latter promote voluntary prevention by offering technical assistance, education, and outreach activities to industry. However, GAO found that many state programs claiming to conduct pollution prevention activities were inordinately involved in waste recycling, treatment, and/or disposal. These programs obtain funding from EPA that rewards their after-the-fact strategies without looking into whether prevention was possible, which is inconsistent with the policy established by the Pollution Prevention Act. Specifically, the lack of emphasis on pollution prevention at the EPA regional offices may negatively affect the administration of EPA funding. GAO also found that many programs are dependent for their existence on EPA funding, even though this funding is not expected to be permanent. Thus, the state programs expected to implement pollution prevention were instead concentrating on other strategies and, in any case, do not appear likely to survive once federal resources are withdrawn. [20% of the programs] are regulatory, and the rest are non-regulatory.... Existing regulatory programs typically require each reporting facility to submit a toxics use-reduction plan that designates a target amount of waste reduction by a certain date. The target amount is left to the discretion of the facility.... In contrast, non-regulatory programs typically rely on widespread education of business and industry sectors to promote voluntary pollution prevention. These programs are often separated from the regulatory arm of state government and oriented toward providing technical assistance to companies.... Non-regulatory programs conduct more technical assistance and technology transfer than regulatory programs, but these non regulatory programs cannot require industry to conduct pollution prevention planning and take a somewhat passive and reactive approach to their customers rather than one of active outreach. As a result, those companies in need of pollution prevention assistance that fail to seek it out for themselves may not receive it.

---

117. E.O. 12856 (August 3, 1993), Federal Compliance with Right-To-Know Laws and Pollution Prevention Requirements.
118. Pollution Prevention: EPA Should Reexamine the Objectives and Sustainability of State Programs (GAO/PEMD-94-8).

Do these shortcomings of state pollution prevention legislation cast doubt on Professor Hornstein's approach emphasizing "deliberate and careful experimentation," or do they instead illustrate just how painstaking and political such a process will be? Will legislatures be inclined to perform the comprehensive analysis this approach entails without the stimulus of public outrage engendered by an environmental "horror story"? How would you draft a state pollution prevention statute so as to avoid the pitfalls described by the GAO report? Despite the pitfalls, the underlying rationale of the cause-based prevention approach obviously holds compelling logic and significant potential for improved longterm management of environmental quality.

BIBLIOGRAPHY ON POLLUTION PREVENTION

Commoner, Making Peace With the Planet, (1990).

EPA, Pollution Prevention Strategy, 56 FR 7849, Feb. 26, 1991.

EPA Office of Pollution Prevention, Pollution Prevention 1991 (EPA 21P-3003, October, 1991).

EPA Office of Research and Development, Facility Pollution Prevention Guide (EPA/600/R-92/088, May, 1992).

Heaton, Repetto & Sobin, Backs to the Future: U.S. Government Policy Toward Environmentally Critical Technology (World Resources Institute, 1992).

Heaton, Repetto & Sobin, Transforming Technology: An Agenda for Environmentally Sustainable Growth In the 21st Century (World Resources Institute, 1991).

Johnson, From Reaction to Proaction: The 1990 Pollution Prevention Act, 17 Colum. J. Env. L. 153 (1992).

Roy, Pollution Prevention, Organizational Culture, and Social Learning, 22 Environmental Law 189 (1991).

Schmidheiny, Changing Course (MIT Press, 1992).

Strasser, Review of Commoner, Making Peace With The Planet, 19 Ecology L.Q. 413 (1992).

Chapter 16, Regulatory Control of Market Access: Pesticides and Toxics

---

Section A(2). The Trouble with FIFRA

In the main volume, FIFRA was favorably contrasted with ToSCA. But FIFRA itself has not effectively protected public health and the environment against the adverse effects of toxic pesticides.

Well over one billion pounds of pesticides are applied annually in the United States, at least 50 million pounds in the Great Lakes Watershed alone.[119] Pesticides have been shown to cause significant environmental impacts, such as acute or chronic health effects among workers in the manufacturing process, on third parties due to accidents in manufacturing or transport, among applicators and farmworkers, and among consumers due to residues on food; contamination of groundwater due to leaching; contamination of surface waters from farm run-off; poisoning of wildlife; and contamination of the environment due to improper disposal of unused pesticides and their containers.[120] Pesticide contamination of groundwater, for example, is a potent threat to human health because nearly 50% of all Americans derive their potable water from groundwater. Many of these are homeowners on private wells who drink untreated groundwater directly from aquifers.

In 1991, the United States General Accounting Office evaluated EPA's efforts to deal with the problem of groundwater contamination by pesticides.[121] In testimony based on that study, a USGAO official concluded that

> EPA needs to take more initiative in ensuring that groundwater contamination by pesticides is minimized. Efforts are needed in three areas. First, EPA has been slow in reviewing the scientific studies needed to assess pesticides' potential to leach into groundwater. Therefore, detailed information on the factors that contribute to leaching is not available to pesticide applicators and the pace of reassessing older pesticides has been slowed. Second, while EPA has used the regulatory tools

---

119. USGAO, Issues Concerning Pesticides Used in the Great Lakes Watershed (June, 1993).
120. Hornstein, Lessons from Federal Pesticide Regulation on the Paradigms and Politics of Environmental Law Reform, 10 Yale J. Reg., 369, 394-95 (1993).
121. Pesticides: EPA Could Do More to Minimize Groundwater Contamination (April, 1991).

available[122] in some cases, the agency could do more to help prevent groundwater contamination from worsening. Third, when EPA assesses risks from pesticide residues in food — in order to set residue limits known as tolerances — the agency is not routinely considering the additional exposure that can result from pesticide-contaminated groundwater. As a result, the agency lacks assurance that tolerances for pesticides that leach into groundwater are set low enough to protect public health.[123]

Professor Hornstein attributes these problems, in great measure, to the centrality of risk assessment under FIFRA:

(R)isk analysis...serves as a procedural device that favors pesticide-using political constituencies in three ways. First, because EPA has no independent method of developing data, risk analysis makes EPA dependent on the data generated by pesticide manufacturers — raising opportunities for various types of bias. Information bias is not limited to cases of data falsification.... The more intractable problems are foot-dragging in submitting data to [EPA] and the ability of industry to shade the way data is presented (without falsification) simply by emphasizing the subtle but genuinely contestable "inference options" on which risk assessments depend. In the mid-70s, an internal EPA audit on the data underlying twenty-three randomly selected pesticides found that "all but one of the tests reviewed were unreliable and inadequate to demonstrate safety" —- a level of unreliability that, by 1992, continued for at least some pesticides.... In short, the risk assessment enterprise is so information intensive that it creates strategic incentives to avoid a serious scientific examination of "true" levels of public health and environmental risk.

Second, despite the burden of proof ostensibly shouldered by pesticide manufacturers under FIFRA, the informational demands of risk analysis doom the regulatory process to a perpetual state of slow motion. The General Accounting Office (GAO) reported in March 1992 that, "[a]fter some 20 years collecting data to reevaluate the health and environmental effects of 19,000 older pesticides, EPA...had reregistered only 2 products. Despite a congressional deadline of 1997 recently set for reregistration, GAO confirms EPA's own projections that the reregistration effort will extend "until early in the next century." Even when EPA chooses to act, the risk analyses required for Special Reviews or cancellation proceedings effectively inoculate manufacturers against timely action. Special Reviews, which were introduced in the mid-1970s to accelerate the cancellation process which then took an average of two years, now themselves average over seven

---

122. Such as prominent advisories on pesticide labels, prohibitions on use within a specified distance of wells (i.e., well setbacks), prohibitions on use in designated geographic areas, and restricting pesticides' use to certified applicators.
123. USGAO, EPA Should Act Promptly to Minimize Contamination of Groundwater by Pesticides (May, 1991).

years.... As a practical matter, the burdensomeness of risk analysis has tempered FIFRA's success in shifting the burden of proof to manufacturers.

Third, risk analysis offers the conceptual umbrella of "science" under which numerous non-scientific values can take shelter from public scrutiny and yet prolong the longevity of pesticides that may be neither desirable nor needed....[124]

Thus FIFRA, although it facially requires a manufacturer to bear a more demanding burden of proof than TosCA, has failed because, in practice, political pressures have caused the same "information bias" in FIFRA that has virtually disabled ToSCA.

Are proactive market access statutes inherently ineffectual in a nation that presumes the beneficence of an unregulated market system? Professor Hornstein does not directly ask this question, but he appears to imply a positive answer to it when he argues that FIFRA has "[been] one of the most colossal regulatory failures in Washington" because it does not get at the root causes of excessive pesticide use. American pesticide law "is not a body of law that addresses in any strategic way the underlying prevalence of pesticides in American agriculture, nor is it a body of law designed to minimize pesticide use."[125] He recommends a "cause-based approach" to pesticide regulation that "would emphasize pest control technologies that can reduce pesticide use without significantly decreasing crop yields or growers' profitability" and "address existing economic incentive structures that lead growers to forego improved technologies in favor of pesticide use which actually exceeds economically optimal levels."[126] Professor Hornstein advocates the exploration of various policy options, such as pesticide risk taxes and enhanced "extension" programs, to encourage low-input agriculture.

There is evidence that EPA is beginning to using its authority to prevent pesticide pollution of groundwater. For the first time, EPA has registered a pesticide (acetochlor) only on condition that it not be detected in groundwater. Production of acetochlor must immediately be suspended if it is detected in groundwater. The acetochlor registration also includes a ten-year "sunset" (termination of registration) provision. Water Policy Report, March 30, 1994, 30.

---

124. Hornstein, note 2, supra., 436-438.

125. Hornstein, note 2 supra., 392.

126. Id., 372. For a more thorough explication of Professor Hornstein's "cause-based" approach, see chapter 15 of this Update. For a brief discussion of the agricultural subsidy programs that encourage heavy pesticide use, see chapter 20 of this Update.

Chapter 17,   Direct Legislation of Specific Pollution Standards, and Technology-Forcing :   Automobile Air Pollution

Page 772   Overview of technology-forcing

C.   Any of the regulatory strategies analyzed in chapters 16-23, if sufficiently stringent, might act sufficiently drastically to force the development of new technology.[127] This chapter focuses on direct legislative or administrative setting of environmental protection standards that either ban some or all uses of a substance or limit releases of the target substance to amounts lower than can be achieved with technology currently available. Insofar as government seeks to achieve technology-forcing through a complete prohibition on manufacture or use (sometimes referred to as "sunsetting" a dangerous substance), technology-forcing acts as a "roadblock" to further commercial activity (see Chapter 13). Like roadblock statutes, product bans are crude, blunt instruments that frequently contain mitigating devices in order to gain acceptance by the regulated public. Some of these mechanisms are lead times for product phaseout, waivers, hardship variances, and sympathetic enforcement. (See the main volume for a discussion of mitigating devices in the context of motor vehicle emissions reductions.)

Crude, blunt regulatory devices may also cause unintended consequences. The "Delaney Clause" — banning residues on processed food of substances that have been found to cause cancer in laboratory animals — has led to the "Delaney Paradox": the introduction of less carcinogenic substitutes has been precluded. Similarly, the phase-down of lead in gasoline has led to increased use of toxic aromatics, including benzene, in the gasoline supply.[128]

Because the American legal system discourages potential curtailment of economic activity, technology-forcing is a last regulatory resort. In this sense, technology-forcing is as disfavored a regulatory strategy as a denial of market access (see Chapter 16). The following statement in the Fifth Circuit's *Corrosion Proof Fittings* decision[129] (see chapter 2 of this supplement) typifies the prevailing judicial skepticism regarding technology-forcing:

> As a general matter, we agree with the EPA that a product ban can lead to great innovation, and it is true that an agency, under ToSCA, as under other regulatory statutes, "is empowered to issue safety standards which require improvements in existing technology or which require the

---

127. Ashford, Ayers, and Stone, Using Regulation to Change the Market for Innovation, 9 Harv. Env. L. Rev. 419, 424, 429 (1985).
128. Waxman, Wetstone, and Barnett, Cars, Fuels, and Clean Air: A Review Of The Clean Air Act Amendments of 1990, 21 Env. L. 1947, 1968 (1991).
129. In this case, the court overturned EPA's ban on the use of asbestos in almost all products.

development of new technology." Chrysler Corp. v. Department of Transportation, 472 F.2d 659, 673 (6th Cir. 1972). As even the EPA acknowledges, however, when no adequate substitutes currently exist, the EPA cannot fail to consider this lack when formulating its own guidelines. Under ToSCA, therefore, the EPA must present a stronger case to justify the ban, as opposed to regulation, of products with no substitutes.

The Second Circuit Court of Appeals also resisted a product ban when it required EPA to list lead as a criteria pollutant over EPA's objection that 90% of airborne lead came from automobiles, and EPA had the statutory authority to force the removal of lead from gasoline (see page 783 of the main volume).

It would appear that technology-forcing will only be condoned where a regulatory agency has exhausted all other regulatory alternatives for controlling a demonstrably intolerable product.

See Ethyl Corp. v. EPA, 541 F.2d 1 (D.C.Cir.1976)(upholding EPA's phaseout of lead in gasoline).

In the relatively few situations where technology-forcing has been attempted, industry has been successful in developing innovative technology that has significantly reduced the environmental threat. In addition to the auto emissions case study presented in the main volume, Ashford et al. give the following regulatory efforts as examples of effective technology-forcing: EPA's prohibition of the commercial distribution and then the manufacture of PCBS; the Consumer Product Safety Commission's and EPA's ban on the use of CFCs from aerosol applications; EPA's phased reduction leading to a prohibition on the use of lead in gasoline; and OSHA's drastic reduction in the occupational exposure standard for lead.[130] It may be that technology-forcing has generally been successful because legislatures and regulatory agencies "hedge their bets" when forcing technology. For example, when Congress enacted the strict 1970 reductions in permissible tailpipe emissions, it was aware that the catalytic converter had been developed and subjected to limited testing.

In the Clean Air Act Amendments of 1990, Congress once again relied on technology-forcing to address the stubborn problem of ozone from automobile emissions:

Waxman, Wetstone, and Barnett, Cars, Fuels and Clean Air: A Review of Title II of the Clean Air Act Amendments of 1990

21 Environmental Law 1947, 1991-2004 (1991)

A major innovation in Title II is the clean-fuel vehicle program, contained in new part C. This program requires the use of a new generation of "clean fuel vehicles" in the most heavily polluted cities. These vehicles, which must meet emission standards eighty percent below today's standards, will often run on clean alternative fuels, such as natural gas, ethanol, or even electricity....

---

130. Ashford et al., note 1, supra., 432-443.

The clean-fuel requirements for light-duty vehicles and light-duty trucks in the final legislation have three central components. First, new sections 242 through 245 establish special emission standards for clean-fuel vehicles. Second, new section 246 establishes a program to require the use of clean-fuel vehicles in centrally fueled fleets in polluted cities. Finally, new section 249 establishes a large-scale program to introduce clean-fuel vehicles to the passenger car market in California.

Section 242 of the Act requires EPA to set emission standards for clean-fuel vehicles in two years. These standards ... mandate a [sixty and later an] eighty percent reduction in exhaust emissions of organic gasses and NOX [nitrogen oxides] from today's already controlled levels. They are intended to develop a new generation of clean vehicles, in a fuel-neutral manner.

The most heavily polluted cities must reduce aggregate emissions of VOCS [volatile organics] and NOX by sixty to eighty percent from today's levels — and keep them there notwithstanding future economic and population growth — to attain the federal health standard for ozone. This is an immense undertaking, made more immense by the fact that most polluted cities have already adopted most of the obvious control measures. It cannot be accomplished unless vehicle emissions are cut drastically. Indeed, Los Angeles, the most polluted city in the country, cannot achieve attainment by 2010 without the widespread use of zero-emission, electric vehicles.

The standards for clean-fuel vehicles reflect this imperative.... In percent terms, this [eighty percent reduction] is equivalent to the level of technology-forcing required by the 1970 amendments. Under the new clean-fuel standards, organic gas and NOX emissions will be reduced ninety-eight percent below uncontrolled levels.

Meeting these standards will necessitate major advances in vehicles and fuels. Unlike any standards previously established, the final standards appear unachievable by vehicles running on conventional gasoline. They probably can be met by vehicles that use reformulated gasoline, but only if manufacturers develop an additional "preheated" catalyst to capture the emissions that occur during the first seconds of operation. Vehicles built to run on alternative fuels like natural gas, ethanol, or methanol are also likely to meet the standards....

The 1990 amendments establish two programs to require the use of clean-fuel vehicles meeting the [emissions] standards.... One is for fleet vehicles and one is for passenger cars in California.

The fleet program...requires clean-fuel vehicles to be used by the owners of centrally fueled fleets of ten or more vehicles in serious, severe, and extreme ozone nonattainment areas. Examples of centrally fueled fleets are fleets of delivery vans, taxicabs, or school buses that regularly refuel at a common location. When the program is fully phased in, it is expected to cover 250,000 vehicles per year.... By model year 2000, seventy percent of the new vehicles purchased by covered fleet operators must be clean-fuel vehicles.... To ensure that the clean-fuel vehicles run on the clean fuels for which they are designed, the [fleet owners must] fuel the vehicles exclusively with clean fuels....

Ultimately, clean-fuel vehicles must penetrate the passenger-car market to achieve major reductions in air pollution. For this reason, the second clean-fuel program in part C establishes a mandatory pilot program in California that will introduce clean-fuel vehicles to the passenger-car market....

Developing a successful alternative fuels program is often said to pose a "chicken and egg" problem. Car makers argue that they should not be forced to make clean-fuel vehicles until clean fuels are widely available. Oil companies argue the converse: they should not be forced to make clean fuels until clean-fuel vehicles are widely available. Both sides argue that even if the vehicles and fuels are available, there is no guarantee that the consumer will buy them.

The fleet program...tackles this problem through a demand-side approach: it requires fleet operators to buy clean-fuel vehicles and to refuel them with clean fuels. These requirements create a built-in demand that overcomes the "chicken and egg" issue. In the case of the passenger car market, however, it is not practical to mandate that a certain percentage of consumers buy only clean-fuel vehicles. Instead, the California pilot program takes a supply-side approach to ensuring the use of both clean-fuel vehicles and clean fuels.

The California pilot program mandates that vehicle manufacturers produce and sell minimum volumes of clean-fuel vehicles in California. [The California Air Resources Board has determined that 2 percent of the cars offered for sale in the 1998 model year must be electric, rising to 5 percent in 2001 and 10 percent in 2003.]

The "production mandate" in the California program makes it the obligation of the vehicle manufacturer to ensure that the vehicles find their way into the consumer's garage. The program thus capitalizes on the enormous capacity of manufacturers to influence vehicle purchases. Car companies control the most important factors that affect consumer purchases: they determine how well the vehicle will perform, what its styling will look like, how the vehicle is advertised, and at what price the vehicle will sell. The production mandate forces manufacturers to develop and market a vehicle that consumers will want to buy — which is exactly the incentive that is needed to make the clean-fuel program a success.

COMMENTARY AND QUESTIONS

1. Will it work? In light of the case study in the main volume, how do you think the auto and fuel companies will react to part C? If you were the CEO of an American auto manufacturer, what percentage of your budget would you spend on lobbying against the implementation of part C? On R&D of cars that include new catalysts and run on reformulated gasoline? On R&D of cars that run on electricity and natural gas? Would it make a difference to you that the Japanese auto manufacturers are reportedly taking part C seriously and spending large sums on new fuel systems? Or that the Pentagon is promoting the development of electric military vehicles that elude enemy radar? Chrysler Corporation is manufacturing an electric mini-van for sale in California in 1998; but, at the same time, Chrysler is predicting that consumers will not purchase the electric van because of its high cost and limited range, and because of the absence of recharge facilities in California.[131]

The future of ZEVs [zero emission vehicles] in the United States also depends on whether other states choose to follow California's lead. New York and Massachusetts have elected to adhere to the California program, and ten other eastern states and the District of Columbia are considering such a move.

In the long run, forcing the development of a reliable, economically accessible electric vehicle will only succeed if new types of batteries are perfected in response to the potential market created by the Clean Air Act. Three promising technologies are in the offing: nickel-metal hydride batteries; sodium nickel-chloride batteries; and sodium-sulfur batteries. As you might imagine, none of these technologies has been pioneered by the auto industry.[132] Critics of electric vehicle mandates, like the auto industry, argue that the decrease in vehicle emissions brought about by the introduction of electric cars would be offset by increased power plant emissions caused by the recharge of electric vehicles; but this charge is hotly disputed by electric car advocates.

---

131. Chrysler, With Misgivings, Will Sell Electric Mini-Vans, New York Times, 5/6/94, D1.
132. Wald, California Regulators To Meet On Electric Cars, New York Times, 5/12/94, D2.

Chapter 18, Administrative Standard-Setting Statutes: The Clean Air Act's Harm-Based Ambient Standards

Page 773 **Introduction to the diverse personalities of the Federal Clean Air Act**

Prologue

Recall for a moment the children's story, *The Blind Men and the Elephant*. In that tale, several wise blind men each obtain a wholly different impression of the elephant by grasping a different portion of its anatomy, without having the benefit of an overview, which would reveal how all the parts fit together to form the whole beast. Over years of teaching, students have suffered from the same difficulty. Almost inevitably, what is studied is not the Clean Air Act as an integrated whole, but its trunk, tail, ears, legs, belly, and what-have-you. Thus, in the previous chapter, the CAA's direct legislation of technology-forcing performance standards for tailpipe emissions was studied as one particular regulatory technique. This chapter will look primarily at the CAA's harm-based ambient standards for the most common pollutants. The next (though focusing on the Clean Water Act) will look at technology-based regulation used in other sections of the CAA for regulating hazardous air pollutants, and Chapter 20 will look at market-based strategies in the 1990 CAA amendments, the most extensive use of market theories in the US air pollution control field.

This Prologue is intended to give a brief glimpse of the whole beast that is the Clean Air Act while adding a dimension not present in the story of the elephant — changes in the shape of the beast over time. It is not meant to be an exhaustive view, but it will provide a feeling of how the various major pieces of that Act work together.

Stage 1 — 1970. Begin with the assumption that some particular air pollutant is in need of reduction by some quantified amount.[133] The logical starting place in fashioning a pollution control strategy is to look at the sources emitting that pollutant into the atmosphere and measure the magnitude of their respective emissions. As an example, consider carbon monoxide (CO), a significant combustion by-product that is frequently found in harmful concentrations in many of the nation's urban areas. The survey of its sources finds that automobiles are emitting 64.2 million pounds per year nationally, and that large stationary sources of pollution that rely on fossil fuel combustion, such as power plants, foundries, etc., are also major contributors to the problem. Fortunately, the problem is thought to be largely a local one, for unlike some problem pollutants, such

---

133. This assumption is intended to finesse and leave for a more theoretical discussion the rationale that can be used to justify pollution control and the selection of a particular level of environmental (ambient air, in this case) quality as a goal.

as ozone in the lower atmosphere, CO does not tend to travel long distances after its emission.[134]

Having identified the major components of the CO emissions problem, the quest begins for a regulatory strategy that will sufficiently reduce emissions to achieve acceptable air quality. An array of strategies are possible, every source of emissions can be required to reduce their emissions by the same percentage (a "rollback" strategy) until the desired results are achieved, some sources can make all the reductions while others go unchanged, etc. There is also a question of the governmental level of regulation. Federal regulation that is uniformly applicable nationwide is one possibility, state-by-state regulation that addresses polluters on a localized, more particularized basis is also a possibility. And, of course, the strategies don't have to be uniform — any mix and match is OK as long as it works. The goal, hopefully, is to come up with a mix that works, and does so in a generally fair and efficient manner.

One major strategic decision made by Congress was that of deciding on how clean the air should be. In 1970 Congress chose a "harm-based" approach to this question. For a series of pollutants of especial concern, those widely emitted and posing dangers to public health and welfare (the so-called "criteria pollutants," one of which is CO), national ambient air quality standards (NAAQS) were to be established by the Environmental Protection Agency.[135] The primary concern was that the NAAQS be strict enough "to protect the public health" after "allowing an adequate margin of safety." A secondary, more protective, NAAQS was also called for with the goal of protecting public welfare.

Looking at the 1970 Clean Air Act, Congress made a number of additional fundamental strategy decisions by dividing the universe of sources of pollution into two major categories, mobile sources and stationary sources, with the former subject to direct federal regulation that applied nationwide and the latter subject to state-by-state control. In some ways the dichotomy is an obvious one. Even though there are millions of mobile sources, there are only a handful of producers of motor vehicles and the design of a car or truck calls for an integrated pollution control system that is best built into every vehicle at the time of manufacture. Moreover, there are tremendous economies of scale in the mass production of motor vehicles and to allow each of the fifty states (or smaller governmental units within the states) to each set their own standards for motor vehicles threatened to play havoc with that industry. With an exception for California, where the control of motor vehicle pollution was already underway and was recognized as requiring more stringent regulation than elsewhere in the nation, there was to be a single

---

134. Emissions of CO in one region tend not to affect ambient air quality in another region. This makes regulation simpler because there is no need to account for spillover effects. The Clean Air Act, of course, does regulate other pollutants with propensities to travel. This facet of regulation is explored both in this chapter and in regard to the operation of the Clean Water Act on interstate streams.

135. Hazardous air pollutants were the subject of separate regulation that is discussed in this chapter and, given the change in direction marked by the 1990 amendments, in Chapter 19.

national standard for motor vehicle emissions. California could adopt a second, more stringent standard.[136]

Stationary sources, on the other hand, were often custom built installations, and a one regulation fits all approach promised tremendous inefficiencies. For example, a nationwide 20% CO emissions rollback for stationary sources would mean that plants that could easily trim a far greater proportion of their CO pollution would not need to do so, while plants that could reduce CO pollution only by drastic and expensive measures would be forced to undertake such measures. Here, the Clean Air Act made a different choice, let the states, who are in far better touch with the economic and pollution control realities of their stationary sources, make the choice about how to get the needed reductions in emissions. The statutory mechanism that Congress chose was to require the states to adopt state implementation plans (SIPs) that were, in effect, a prescription for how the state would regulate its stationary sources in order to control pollution sufficiently to attain the NAAQS. The federal government, working through the Environmental Protection Agency (EPA), would superintend the process. EPA would review each SIP, for each of the criteria pollutants, to determine if the SIP would work. If EPA disapproved of a SIP, the state would have to redraft it until EPA approved. If the states refused to draft an adequate SIP, EPA was authorized to impose a federal implementation plan (FIP), a fate most of the states felt would be the worst of all possible regulatory worlds. Apart from reflexive opposition to yielding control to the national government, the states feared that EPA would be insensitive to the particular problems of their industries and ways of life.

In yet another aspect of the original Clean Air Act, Congress did make one national rule for stationary sources, it adopted a third distinctive approach for new pollution sources. These new source performance standards (NSPS) required all new stationary sources to employ the best available technology for a facility of its kind.[137] In this way, Congress eliminated some facets of the race of laxity (of air pollution control) as a means by which relatively clean air areas could seek to attract new plants to locate there rather than in another state that would be forced to impose more costly air pollution control requirements to insure attainment of the air quality called for by the NAAQS.

With the NAAQS mandating certain levels of ambient air quality and this bifurcated design of federal mobile source regulation and state stationary source regulation and the congressional choice of a quality target, the basic outline of the beast, the Clean Air Act of 1970, comes into focus. Congress decided that the air must be safe to breathe and, toward that end, directly regulated car and truck emissions, leaving the states to do the rest.

---

136. The size of California market for motor vehicles was so large that the automakers could profitably design cars intended for sale in that market alone.
137. Technology-based standards are explored in Chapter 19, using the Clean Water Act as the primary example. Over time the Clean Air Act has increasingly employed technology-based forms of regulation, beginning in 1970 with the NSPS, expanding with technology based controls for non-attainment and PSD areas in 1977, and switching, in 1990, to technology-based controls as the primary approach to hazardous air pollutants.

The division of regulation has a profound effect on the states' efforts to draw up their plans for attainment of the mandated ambient air quality. As to pollutants such as CO, NO_x, ozone,[138] and lead, all of which were in 1970 (and, with the exception of lead, still are) significant by-products of motor vehicle use, the contribution to ambient pollution from mobile sources is, to some significant degree, beyond state control. Much of the allowable emissions of those pollutants will inevitably result from the operation of motor vehicles, whose emission characteristics the states are forbidden from regulating. This means that the states will have to regulate their stationary sources all the more stringently. Especially in urbanized air quality control regions (AQCRs),[139] where the number and concentration of automobiles is high, coming up with a state plan that will attain the mandated air quality for CO, NO_x, and ozone, will be difficult and impose unpopular and expensive burdens on the industries whose stationary source emissions are being regulated.

To ease some of this burden on stationary sources, the states do have authority to regulate mobile source *use* even though they cannot regulate design or emissions directly. States can regulate transportation, by encouraging carpooling and mass transit; states can insist that the federally required pollution controls installed on mobile sources be inspected and properly maintained (I&M), and so on. These types of controls are extraordinarily unpopular because they affect large numbers of citizens (i.e., all automobile users), but they do offer states an alternative to imposing all of the emission reduction burden on their stationary sources.

A series of four hypothetical examples (which we will label "SIP 1" through "SIP 4") will help clarify how the SIP process might work in this setting. The acute exposure[140] NAAQS for carbon monoxide is a maximum concentration of 40 micrograms of CO per liter of air for a 1 hour of human exposure.

SIP 1:

For a hypothetical AQCR assume that mobile sources, if no action is taken, will emit a sufficient amount of CO pollution so that the worst one hour ambient concentration of CO would be 30 micrograms per liter of air.[141] Under that scenario, which we will refer to as SIP 1, the stationary sources will have to be regulated in such a way that their contribution to

---

138. Ozone is, to be more accurate, not itself part of automobile emissions. Rather, NOx and volatile organic compounds (VOCs), two components of automobile emissions, are ozone precursors, meaning that they undergo chemical changes after their emission and become ozone.

139. Most states have chosen to subdivide their regulatory effort into a series of smaller geographic divisions, each of which must meet the NAAQS.

140. The NAAQS are usually expressed as a maximum allowable concentration of the pollutant that persists for a period of exposure. Some pollutants have more than one exposure period, such as an acute short term exposure, and a lower allowable concentration for longer term, or chronic exposures. Some of the NAAQS allow for their exceedance one or two times per year.

141. Some concentrations of pollutants are products of uncontrollable natural processes. Plainly the state SIP cannot affect these background amounts of the target pollutant. For the purposes of this example, the background amounts will be treated as insignificantly small.

the one hour worst CO pollution episode will be only 10 micrograms per liter.

Before going further, it is important to realize that these simple assumptions about how much these two types of sources will contribute to a one hour worst case scenario mask a welter of difficult calculations. Trying to predict ambient air quality, especially during acute episodes, is tricky business at best. Weather conditions contribute importantly, as does topography (as affected by human induced changes, such as buildings and land development patterns). Moreover, the inventory of emissions from the various sources is imperfect. There are few continuous real time emissions monitors that sample plant smokestacks or a car tailpipes. Formulas that are used to approximate diffusion and dilution of effluents are just that, formulaic approximations that imperfectly describe the complex fluid dynamics of air flow. Nevertheless, the way the Clean Air Act works, the idea of the SIP process is to try to write a recipe for emissions (regulation) that will result in the desired avoidance of unsafe pollutant concentrations.

Returning to the hypothetical AQCR, the SIP 1 option of making no effort to reduce mobile source emissions places heavy reliance on limiting the CO contribution of stationary sources. Owing to the fundamental division of regulatory authority, the states cannot insist on cleaner cars so under the SIP 1 scenario the state might have to require expensive combustion controls for existing plants, refuse to permit new sources, or even force closure of existing sources.

SIP 2:

The Clean Air Act does not, however, take away the ability of the states to lessen mobile source pollution indirectly. The states are allowed to insist that vehicles are inspected and maintained. Experience shows that I&M programs do succeed in reducing mobile source emissions because the pollution control equipment on cars is subject to failure and I&M results in repair and improved performance of those systems. In SIP 2, the state has adopted an I&M program that results in a reduction in the contribution of mobile sources to CO loadings.

SIP 3:

A further option, added by the state in SIP 3, is the retirement of old clunkers. Older vehicles, especially those built before 1977, even when properly maintained, produce far greater emissions than do newer vehicles. The disparity of emissions is so great, that a reduction in number of the old vehicles offers a useful reduction in CO loadings.

SIP 4:

A final strategy for the states is transportation controls. As the legislated standards for mobile sources make clear, by expressing their commands in pollutant grams per vehicle mile driven terms, pollution from motor vehicles is proportionate to the number of miles driven. Thus, reductions in vehicle use will lessen effluent loadings. Transportation planning may involve improving mass transit (new facilities, more convenient routes, more frequent service, bus lanes, lower fares, van pools, etc.) or penalizing individual automobile use (lane restrictions, parking taxes, eliminating parking at center city destinations served by mass transit, etc.). It may also involve larger land use controls, such as controlling new development patterns to minimize the usage of motor vehicles. Depending on how far a state is willing to go, transportation planning probably has the greatest potential to reduce mobile source emissions from what otherwise would occur. Based on numbers invented for this hypothetical, the following table and chart show the increased flexibility that a state could obtain in dealing with its stationary sources if it did more to regulate vehicle use.

Note: Chart comparing the effects of the hypotheticals

In reading the chart below, notice how much flexibility a state can obtain for its regulation of stationary sources by taking steps to insure cleaner vehicle performance, retire "dirty" vehicles. and reduce vehicle usage. Under the terms of the 1990 CAA amendments, as discussed later in this chapter, states with persistent attainment problems traceable to mobile source emissions can also choose to require that all new vehicles in the state meet the more stringent "California" auto emission standards.

Relating Mobile and Stationary Source Contributions to Pollution

Comparing State Implementation Plans (SIPs)	SIP 1	SIP 2	SIP 3	SIP 4
Projected Mobile Source Emissions (MSE)	30	30	30	30
Reductions in MSE from I & M	0	5	5	5
Reductions in MSE from retiring old vehicles	0	0	3	3
Reductions in MSE from altering vehicle use	0	0	0	7
Actual Mobile Source Emissions (MSE)	30	25	22	15
Allowable Stationary Source Emissions	10	15	18	25
Carbon monoxide (acute) NAAQS	40	40	40	40

All values in micrograms per liter

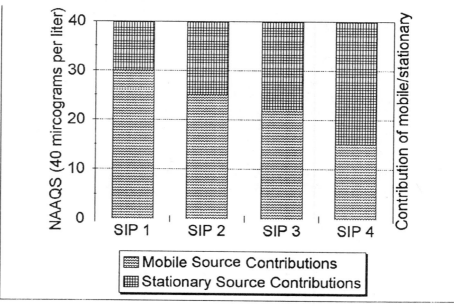

Stage 2 — 1977 Amendments. After seven years experience with the Clean Air Act, a few of its operative characteristics had become evident. The most important for understanding the basic building blocks of the regulatory system, was that some AQCRs were unable to satisfy the NAAQS and would be unable to do so in the short term without totally crippling the industrial (stationary source) economy of the region. A second major concern was that there was not sufficient regulation to protect clean air areas against degradation of air quality to the lowest legally mandated common denominator, air as dirty as the NAAQS allows. Both of these realizations prompted major additions to the Clean Air Act, one addressing the special concerns of non-attainment areas and one addressing the special concerns of prevention of significant deterioration (PSD) areas.

For non-attainment areas, which included most of the nation's industrial centers, their political power made it possible to force a retreat from the NAAQS as a rigid short-term requirement, to the NAAQS as a goal toward which "reasonable further progress" was required. This relaxation is significant, but because the NAAQS represent the point at which public health is at stake, even the economic imperatives of allowing economic development to occur in non-attainment areas was kept in check by increased requirements for stationary sources and inspection and maintenance of automobiles. All sources were subjected to a technology-based requirement, that they employ "reasonable available control technologies" (RACT). All major new sources were held to a process-based technology standard called "lowest achievable emissions rate" (LAER), and to assure further progress toward attainment of the NAAQS, major new sources had to "offset" their new pollution by an even greater reduction of old pollution.[142]

In PSD areas, the key regulatory initiative was the imposition of a lower ceiling for allowable pollution that, in effect, superseded the NAAQS as the federally mandated quality level. The new ceiling was calculated by measuring current air quality as a baseline, and then allowing only a relatively small incremental amount of pollution.

Stage 3 — 1990 Amendments. For more than a decade, the Clean Air Act seemed to muddle through in its 1977 configuration, making relatively little further progress toward attainment in non-attainment areas, and virtually no progress in the regulation of hazardous air pollutants. Additionally, the well-known, but largely unregulated, problem of long range transport of pollutants was attracting attention, particularly in regard to acid deposition that was poisoning the lakes of the northeastern states with pollution generated primarily by coal-burning power plants located in the Midwest. The statute was being criticized on all fronts, some claimed it was too expensive in achieving the results it did obtain, others claimed it was inadequate because the air in hundreds of localities inhabited by tens of millions of people was not yet safe, let alone clean. At this point Congress took extraordinary action, making major revisions on all of these fronts.

---

142. Offsets, together with bubbles and allied concepts that allow some emissions trading among sources, were the first forays of the Clean Air Act into the use of market devices and trading as a regulatory strategy. These concepts are studied in greater detail in Chapter 20.

As to the basic NAAQS attainment issue, Congress became far more insistent on compliance by a time certain and far more directive in regard to what states would be required to include in their SIPs. It also gave states burdened by persistent excessive automotive emissions the option of requiring the sale of low emission vehicles (LEVs), essentially on the same basis as California. As to hazardous air pollutants, Congress abandoned the harm-based approach in favor of a technology based approach that called for the installation of the maximum available control technology (MACT). In regard to long range deposition, Congress established an elaborate emissions trading scheme that should reduce SO_2 and NO_x emissions by 10 million tons in a decade, thereby almost halving the most important precursor emissions of acid rain.[143]

With this silhouette of the beast in mind, it should be easier to see why and how the harm-based ambient standards material in this chapter are part of a larger effort at air quality regulation.

PAGE 801   **U.S. primary ambient standards under the Clean Air Act**

On the following page is a chart from the *Cleveland Electric* case, showing the NAAQSs (national ambient air quality standards) for criteria air pollutants that were being applied in that case. 572 F.2d 1150 (6th Circ., 1978). A contemporary version of the standards would also contain lead. Note that the chart, like almost everyone else, ignores the nonmandatory secondary standards

---

143. This last development is studied in Chapter 20.

TABLE   EFFECTS THRESHOLD, BEST CHOICE SIGNIFICANT RISK LEVELS AND SAFETY MARGINS CONTAINED IN PRIMARY AMBIENT AIR QUALITY STANDARDS

Pollutant	Lowest best judgment estimate for effects threshold and best choice for significant risk levels			U.S. primary air quality standard	Margin of safety* (percent)
	Concentration	Averaging time	Adverse health effect		
Sulfur dioxide	300 to 400 ug/m³	24 hour	Mortality increase	365 ug/m³	None
	91 ug/m³	Annual	Increased frequency of acute respiratory disease	80 ug/m³	14
Total suspended particulates	250 to 300 ug/m³	24 hour	Mortality increase	260 ug/m³	None
	70 to 250 ug/m³	do.	Aggravation of respiratory disease	260 ug/m³	None
	100 ug/m³	Annual	Increased frequency of chronic bronchitis	75 ug/m³	33
Suspended sulfates	10 ug/m³	24 hour	Increased infections in asthmatics	None	None
	15 ug/m³	Annual	Increased lower respiratory infections in children	None	None
Nitrogen dioxide	140 ug/m³	do.	Increased severity of acute respiratory illness in children	100 ug/m³	40
Carbon monoxide	23 ug/m³	8 hour	Diminished exercise tolerance in heart patients	10 ug/m³	**130
	73 ug/m³	1 hour	Diminished exercise tolerance in heart patients	40 ug/m³	**82
Photochemical oxidants	200 ug/m³	do.	Increased susceptibility to infection	160 ug/m³	25

* Safety margin equals effects threshold minus standard divided by standard X 100.
** Safety margins based upon carboxyhemoglobin levels would be 100 percent for the 8 hour standard and 67 percent for the 1 hour standard.

TABLE 2.—THRESHOLD AND ILLUSTRATIVE HEALTH RISKS FOR SELECTED AMBIENT LEVELS OF SUSPENDED SULFATES

Adverse health effect	Threshold concentration and exposure duration	Illustrative health risk		
		Definition	Level	Sulfur dioxide equivalent
Increase in daily mortality	25 ug/m³ for 24 hr or longer	2½ percent increase in daily mortality	38 ug/m³ for 24 hr	600 ug/m³ for 24 hr.
Aggravation of heart and lung disease in the elderly	9 ug/m³ for 24 hr or longer	50 per cent increase in symptom aggravation	48 ug/m³ for 24 hr	750 ug/m³ for 24 hr.
Aggravation of asthma	6 to 10 ug/m³ for 24 hr	75 percent increase in frequency of asthma attacks	30 ug/m³ for 24 hr.	450 ug/m³ for 24 hr.
Excess acute lower respiratory disease in children	13 ug/m³ for several yr	50 percent increase in frequency	20 ug/m³ annual average	100 to 250 ug/m³ annual average.
Excess risk for chronic bronchitis	10 to 15 ug/m³ for up to 10 yr	50 percent increase in risk	15 to 20 ug/m³ annual average	100 to 250 ug/m³ annual average.

Chapter 19, Administrative Standards Based on Available Technology: The Federal Clean Water Act

PAGE 825   WQSs: they're back!

Although the major focus of the Clean Water Act and its enforcement prior to the 1990's was on technology-based regulatory standards, with the ambient water quality standards (WQS) process left in the background, in the last several years CWA enforcement has rediscovered water quality-based permitting. The 1987 amendments to the Clean Water Act formally encouraged a re-emphasis upon water quality-based permitting. EPA has incorporated the renewed WQS approach, so that today many large dischargers, especially in so-called "toxic hot spots," are now operating under water quality-based effluent limitations.

PAGE 829   Note on recent technology-forcing

2A. Technology-forcing from BAT. One example of how technology-based effluent limitations can encourage innovative technology is Louisiana-Pacific Corp's new pulp mill in British Columbia. Paper mills have come under increasing scrutiny because they discharge dioxin, a toxic pollutant that is caused by the use of chlorine to bleach paper. The new mill has no wastewater discharge because it uses a freeze crystallization technology to separate pollutants from water in the plant's effluent, and the bleaching agent used is hydrogen peroxide rather than chlorine. The cost of this new process is comparable to that of traditional pulping technology. According to a company spokesperson, tighter environmental standards were a key consideration in choosing the new technology. BNA Environmental Reporter Current Developments, 11/1/91, 1660. Another incentive to develop innovative pollution control technology is a growing, lucrative market abroad, especially in Asia, for pollution control equipment.

EPA has been hampered in its attempt to stimulate innovative technology through technology-based effluent limitations because the Clean Water Act does not give the agency explicit authority to consider pollution prevention when developing effluent limitations regulations. The Senate version of the Clean Water Act Reauthorization Bill (S6239) contains such an enabling provision, but industry has been sharply critical of it.

PAGE 830   Update: Does CWA cover groundwater?

3A. What waters are "navigable...waters of the United States"? Groundwater? Reservoirs? Noncontiguous wetlands? Two federal courts have recently disagreed about whether groundwater is within the ambit of the CWA. Contrast Sierra Club v. Colorado Refining Co., 838 F. Supp. 1428 (D. Colo. 1993)(tributary groundwater is covered), with Oconomowoc

Lake v. Dayton Hudson Corp., 1994 WL 192793 (7th Cir. 1994)("waters of the United States" do not include groundwater, even if the groundwater is hydrologically connected to surface water").

Can a mining company that cannot conveniently meet NPDES standards avoid the CWA point source rules by planning to build a dam across an existing trout stream, and calling the resulting reservoir a "waste treatment lagoon" and "collection pond" for acidic mine tailings? Treatment ponds are not "waters of the United States" for purposes of the CWA, so the mine would not need an NPDES discharge permit to discharge into the reservoir. The Bush Administration's EPA apparently concluded that such dammed waters would not be waters of the United States. A local environmental group made up of neighbors living near the trout stream has sued to try to overturn this administrative decision. Alaskans for Juneau v. EPA, D.C. Alaska, J93-019-CV(JWS). Does the rule that the CWA does not apply to artificial ponds unconnected to other surface waters (see Oconomowoc Lake, supra) also apply to the impoundment of natural waterbodies?

For a discussion of the extent of the CWA's coverage in the wetlands setting, see the note on Hoffman Homes v. EPA in Chapter 23 of this supplement.

PAGE 830   **Update on definition of "point source"**

4A. Can a human being be a point source? The United States Court of Appeals for the Second Circuit has held that an individual human being is not a point source within the meaning of the CWA. U.S. v. Villegas, 3 F.3rd 643 (1993). This was a criminal prosecution involving a co-owner of a blood-testing laboratory who threw vials containing blood contaminated with hepatitis-B virus into the Hudson River. Over a strong dissent by Judge Oakes, the majority concluded that "Congress [did not intend] the CWA to impose criminal liability on an individual for the myriad, random acts of human waste disposal, for example a passerby who flings a candy wrapper into the Hudson River, or a urinating swimmer." The federal government has requested the United States Supreme Court to review this decision (No. 93-1572, 4/4/94).

PAGE 831   **Update: federal facilities' compliance**

7A. What can federal polluters be made to pay? In Department of Energy v. Ohio, 112 S.Ct. 1627 (1992), the Supreme Court held that neither RCRA nor the CWA provides the unambiguous waiver of sovereign immunity that would entitle a state to recover civil penalties for past violations of environmental laws at a federal facility. The Court ruled that federal facilities could be made to pay coercive fines designed to promote future compliance, but not punitive fines for past violations. This decision was overruled by the Federal Facilities Compliance Act of 1992, P.L. 102-386, which amended RCRA but not the CWA. A number of bills have been introduced in Congress to similarly amend the CWA.

Cleanup of federal facilities, from former weapons plants to nuclear waste repositories, will be one of our top environmental priorities over the next

decade.   The following excerpt from the Conference Report on the
Federal Facilities Compliance Act makes it clear that states will be major
factors in achieving compliance by and cleanup of federal facilities:

> Sovereign immunity is expressly waived with respect to any
> substantive or procedural provision of law respecting control,
> abatement or management of solid waste or hazardous waste.
> In doing so the conferees reaffirm the original intent of
> Congress that each department, agency, and instrumentality of
> the United States be subject to all of the provisions of federal,
> state, interstate, and local solid waste and hazardous waste
> laws and regulations. By adding the word "management" to the
> first sentence of the waiver, we confirm the federal
> government's obligation to comply with all solid and hazardous
> waste provisions at all sites, without exceptions. This waiver
> subjects the federal government to the full range of available
> enforcement tools,...to penalize isolated, intermittent or
> continuing violations as well as to coerce future compliance
> (Conference Report, page 18).

PAGE 835   **EPA experiments with multimedia regulation**

2A. Multimedia Rulemaking? EPA is experimenting with its first set of
joint, multimedia rules for a single industry — the pulp and paper industry.
These rules will include all toxic air and water releases from paper plants.
BNA Environmental Reporter Current Developments, 11/5/93, 1227. EPA
is also restructuring its enforcement efforts to emphasize multimedia
enforcement integrating numerous federal environmental statutes. The
Agency hopes that multimedia enforcement will discourage the "toxic
shell game," in which pollutants are simply transferred from one receiving
medium to another depending upon the intensity of enforcement.

PAGE 843   **Schematic chart of various technology-based effluent
                      limitations (TBELs)**

The chart on the folowing page illustrates the classes of water pollutants
with their appropriate technology-based effluent limitations, compliance
dates, and available variances.

TBELS: Technology-Based Effluent Limitations

Pollutant Type	Eff. Limitation	Compliance Date	Variance
Conventionals	BCT	3 years from promulgation	FDF
Non-conventionals/ Nontoxics	BAT	same	FDF 301(c) and (g) variances based on economics and receiving water quality
Toxics	BAT	same	FDF 301(k) 2-year extension for adoption of innovative/ alternative technology
Heat	BAT	same	316(a) water quality-based variance 10-year grace period
New Source Discharges	BDT	on construction	none 10-year grace period

PAGE 845   Update on regulation of CSOs and industrial overflows

6A. Combined sewer overflows and industrial stormwater finally regulated. EPA's long-awaited CSO Control Policy, which was negotiated among governmental and environmental group representatives, was released on April 19, 1994. 59 Fed. Reg. 18688. It focuses on the immediate implementation of nine minimum controls, and the development of long-term CSO control plans targeting environmentally sensitive receiving waters. The nine minimum controls include improved maintenance of sewers, the use of collection systems to prevent overflows, improved pretreatment requirements, and prohibition of dry-weather overflows. The financial abilities of governmental units may be considered in developing a plan's long-term compliance schedule.

EPA's industrial point source stormwater control program is one of the most exciting current developments in water pollution control. It is a model of regulatory efficiency, and might well serve as a template for a nonpoint source control program. An industrial point source discharger of stormwater must comply with the terms of a general permit for its industrial sector. Each general permit requires the development and implementation of pollution prevention plans incorporating appropriate low-tech, reasonably inexpensive Best Management Practices (BMPs) such as planning, reporting, personnel training, preventive maintenance, and good housekeeping. For example, a discharger that experiences runoff from an uncovered outdoor pile of raw materials might either 1) build an enclosure for the pile, or 2) move it indoors. Stormwater pollution prevention plans must be reviewed and certified by a Registered Professional Engineer (PE). This systematic industrial stormwater control program replaces the case-by-case imposition of BMPS pursuant to CWA section 304(e)(see Note 3, supra.) that was utilized in *Rybachek*. See Proposed Multisector Storm Water Permit For 29 Industrial Sectors, 58 Fed. Reg. 61146 (Nov. 19, 1993).

PAGE 848   **New evidence of Professor Houck's incisive wisdom**

11A. Unregulated pollutant discharges. A recent report by the Comptroller General supports Professor Houck's conclusion that the priority pollutant list is unduly restrictive:

> We found that, for our sample of 236 facilities, approximately 77 of the pollution cases we identified were not controlled by permit limits. That is, approximately 77 percent of the discharge of all [toxic] pollutants across our sample was uncontrolled. Through further review of these uncontrolled discharges, we found that the vast majority were nonpriority pollutants (72 percent) as opposed to priority pollutants. This signifies that the pollutant category with the greatest number of toxic discharges (812 of 1217) was the least controlled. USGAO, Poor Quality Assurance and Limited Pollutant Coverage Undermine EPA's Control of Toxic Substances, GAO/PEMD-94-9, 55.

PAGE 848   **CWA reauthorization**

12A. Continuing delays in CWA reauthorization. As of mid-June, 1994, prospects for full formal reauthorization of the CWA during the current session of Congress appeared bleak. Proponents of the "unholy trinity" noted in chapter 11 of this supplement (industrial advocates of required benefit-cost analysis in EPA regulations, landowners and farmers demanding compensation for all diminution of value caused by regulation, and governmental units decrying "unfunded mandates") have thus far stymied all environmental legislation in this session. Moreover, there are acrimonious and apparently irresolvable disagreements in Congress over issues such as wetlands protection, nonpoint source control, watershed management, pollution prevention requirements, and funding for POTWs.

PAGE 852   **Nonpoint sources and CZMA**

1A. Nonpoint source controls from beyond the CWA. Congress took a small step toward nonpoint source control in section 6217 of the Coastal

Zone Act Reauthorization Amendments of 1990, P.L. 101-508 (see Chapter 23 for a discussion of the CZMA). Section 6217 provides that a state with an approved coastal zone management program must develop and submit to EPA and NOAA for approval a coastal nonpoint pollution control program. Failure to submit an approvable program by July, 1995, will result in the loss of federal grants under both the CZMA and CWA. State nonpoint pollution control programs must include enforceable policies and management mechanisms — which may be non- regulatory or voluntary — to address coastal nonpoint source pollution. Management mechanisms must reflect "best available nonpoint pollution control practices, technologies, processes, siting criteria, operating methods, or other alternatives." Section 6217 is weak not only because of the compromise inherent in "enforceable measures" that may be "non- regulatory," but also because Congress has provided meager funding for this program.

A promising method of reducing nonpoint source pollution is point- nonpoint source pollution trading. For example, a POTW located on a segment that is water quality limited for nutrients would currently be required to install costly tertiary treatment in order to meet water quality- based effluent limitations. Why not allow the POTW to obtain pollution credits by paying upstream farmers to reduce their nonpoint source discharges of nutrients (e.g., from fertilizer applications) through the installation of low-tech, inexpensive BMPs? EPA has funded a number of demonstration projects involving point-nonpoint source trading, but the CWA would have to be amended in order to authorize a nationwide program along these lines. See USGAO RCED-92-153, Pollutant Trading Could Reduce Compliance Costs If Uncertainties Are Resolved; Letson, Point/Nonpoint Source Pollution Reduction Trading: An Interpretive Survey, 32 Nat. Res. J. 219 (1992); and Bartfield, Point-Nonpoint Source Trading: Looking Beyond Potential Cost Savings, 23 Envtl. L. 43 (1993). See Chapter 20 for a discussion of trading pollution rights in the air pollution setting.

PAGE 852   **Update on water quality standard-setting**

2A. WQS enforcement. States and EPA have generally been reluctant to set "total maximum daily loads" (one of the necessary steps in setting water quality-based effluent limitations) until sued by citizen groups. See, e.g., Alaska Center for the Environment v. EPA, 20 F.3d 981 (9th Cir., 1994).

Nevertheless, the 1987 CWA amendments revived water quality- based permitting on water quality-limited stretches. See Ackels v. EPA, 7 F.3d 862 (9th Cir., 1993) (placer miners, including the Rybacheks, unsuccessfully sued to overturn water quality-based effluent limitations); NRDC v. EPA, 16 F.3rd 1395 (4th Cir., 1993)(upholding EPA's approval of Maryland's and Virginia's water quality standards for dioxin); American Paper Institute v. EPA, 966 F.2d 346 (D.C. Cir., 1993)(upholding EPA's use of "narrative criteria," such as "no toxics in toxic amounts," instead of chemical-specific criteria); Dioxin/Organochlorine Center v. EPA, 37 ERC 1845 (D.C.W.D.Wash.1993)(water quality-based effluent limitations may precede technology-based limitations where water quality warrants it).

PAGE 856   **Must upstream dischargers comply with pollution standards of downstream states? — *Arkansas v. Oklahoma***

6A. Arkansas v. Oklahoma. In Arkansas v. Oklahoma, 112 S.Ct. 1046 (1992), the Supreme Court appeal of Oklahoma v. EPA noted in the casebook at 856, note 6, the Supreme Court upheld EPA regulations that no EPA or state NPDES permit shall be issued "[w]hen the imposition of conditions cannot ensure compliance with the applicable water quality requirements of all affected states." 40 CFR §122.4(d), and §123.25 (1991). Distinguishing Ouellette, the Court stated that "[l]imits on an affected State's direct participation in permitting decisions, however, do not in any way constrain the EPA's authority to require a point source to comply with downstream water quality standards."

The Court of Appeals had interpreted the CWA as prohibiting any discharge of effluent in an upstream state that would reach downstream state waters that were already in violation of existing water quality standards — even though the upstream discharge would not lead to a detectable change in downstream water quality. The Supreme Court, in reversing the Court of Appeals, accepted EPA's interpretation that the downstream state's antidegradation standard would only be violated if the discharge caused an actually detectable or measurable change in water quality. EPA's construction of the CWA deserves extraordinary deference in this case, said the Court, because federally-approved water quality standards, when applied in an interstate context, become federal law.

The Supreme Court made it clear that the CWA does not ban new discharges(from new or existing discharges) into waterbodies that are in violation of applicable water quality standards. The section 303 process of translating water quality standards into water quality-based effluent limitations through modeling and wasteload allocations is the vehicle for "allocat[ing] the burden of reducing undesirable discharges between existing sources and new sources." This process is a less sophisticated version of the Clean Air Act's nonattainment provisions. On interstate wastes, EPA, with its authority to (1) reject state water quality standards and wasteload allocations and promulgate federal standards and allocations, and (2) veto state discharge permits, is the final arbiter of the load allocation process.

PAGE 858   **Recent citizen enforcement issues; integrated water resource management issues**

7A. CWA citizen enforcement. A study conducted by the U.S. Public Interest Research Group has concluded that approximately 15 percent of U.S. industrial facilities, 19 percent of municipal facilities, and 18 percent of federal facilities are in serious, chronic violation of the CWA. BNA Environmental Reporter Current Developments, 8/20/93, 733. In addition, neither states nor EPA have adequate controls to detect error or fraud in DMRs, which are the key to enforcement under the CWA. USGAO, EPA Cannot Ensure the Accuracy of Self- Reported Compliance Monitoring Data, GAO/RCED-93-21.

Can a citizen suit be brought against a discharger for discharging a pollutant that is not listed in its discharge permit? The U.S. Court of Appeals for the Second Circuit has held that the permit can serve as a shield against citizen suits: as long as the discharger discloses all discharged pollutants in its permit application, the CWA only authorizes citizen suits to be brought to enforce effluent limitations that are included in the permit. Atlantic States Legal Foundation v. Eastman Kodak Co., 12 F.3d 353 (1993), reh. den. No. 93-7091 (2/17/94). The citizen group has requested the United States Supreme Court to grant certiorari in this case.

One of the most difficult questions involving CWA citizen suits is whether a state administrative compliance action, as opposed to a state judicial proceeding, will bar a subsequent citizen suit. Contrast Washington Public Interest Research Group v. Pendleton Woolen Mills, 11 F.3d 883 (9th Cir., 1993)(CWA section 309(g) bars citizen suits only if agency is diligently pursuing administrative penalty action; compliance order does not bar citizen suit), with North & South Rivers Watershed Ass'n v. Scituate, 949 F.2d 552 (1st Cir., 1991)(compliance action bars citizen suit).

An interesting constitutional question involving citizen suits arose in Delaware Valley Toxics Coalition v. Kurz-Hastings, Inc., 813 F.Supp. 1132 (D.C.E.D.Penna.1993), a case arising under the citizen suit provisions of the Emergency Planning and Community Right-To-Know Act. Defendant manufacturer, in that case, argued that citizen suits are unconstitutional delegations of Executive power to the judiciary in violation of the separation of powers doctrine. The court rejected this argument on the following grounds: 1) the unlawful delegation of Executive power doctrine only applies to persons under congressional control, and "private litigants are not controlled by Congress"; 2) Congress itself provided for citizen suits, and is capable of determining how its statutes will be enforced; and 3) EPA may bar a citizen suit by commencing its own action with the 60-day notice period.

8. Water quality and water quantity; integrated resource management. The technology-based approach of the CWA has been instrumental in cleaning up and preventing significant amounts of industrial and municipal point source pollution since 1972. But the CWA is replete with omissions and loopholes that prevent it from achieving its goal of attaining and maintaining clean water: 1) lack of control over nonpoint source and groundwater pollution; 2) inadequate protection of wetlands, especially from dredging, filling, and draining (see Chapter 23); 3) limited coverage of toxic pollutants; 4) lack of safeguards against unwise coastal and riparian land use; 5) a cumbersome water quality-based permitting process exacerbated by an unworkable antidegradation policy; 6) lackluster enforcement; 7) lack of control over dams, navigation projects, and other "improvements," and 8) lack of jurisdiction over water allocation (water quantity), which is closely tied to water quality. For an excellent, albeit unduly pessimistic, analysis and evaluation of the CWA, see Adler et al., The Clean Water Act 20 Years Later (1993).

Water allocation is primarily a function of state law and supervening federal statutes such as the Federal Power Act, 16 U.S.C.A. sec. 791 et seq. The United States Supreme Court recently upheld a regulatory link between the CWA and water allocation through section 401 of the CWA, 33 U.S.C.A., sec. 1341, which requires a state to provide a certification that a proposed activity will not violate state water quality standards before a federal license or permit can be issued for that activity. The terms of a state §401 certification are binding on the federal agency granting the permit or license.

9. Water quantity/water quality: state authority vs. the Federal Energy Regulatory Commission. In Public Utility District No. 1 of Jefferson County and City of Tacoma v. Washington Department of Ecology, 1994 WL 223821 (May 31, 1994), petitioners city and a local utility district wanted to build a hydroelectric project on a high quality river. The project would have appreciably reduced the river's stream flow, and thus would have interfered with the excellent fishery in the river. In order to protect the fishery, respondent state environmental agency included a minimum flow requirement in its §401 certification to the Federal Energy Regulatory Commission, the federal agency that licenses hydroelectric works under the Federal Power Act. The Supreme Court, in a 7-2 decision, affirmed the Washington Supreme Court's finding that FERC had to honor the minimum flow certification. Justice O'Connor, writing for the majority, reasoned that the State agency had a legal right to protect its water quality standards, which included an antidegradation requirement for the particular river stretch involved. In response to petitioners' argument that the CWA is only concerned with "quality," not water "quantity," Justice O'Connor wrote:

> This is an artificial distinction. In may cases, water quantity is closely related to water quality; a sufficient lowering of the water quantity in a body of water could destroy all of its designated uses, be it for drinking water, recreation, navigation, or, as here, as a fishery. In any event, there is recognition in the Clean Water Act itself that reduced stream flow... can constitute water pollution.

The City of Tacoma decision endows state water quality standards with increasing importance because, through a 401 certification, these standards are binding on federal permitting agencies. For example, state agencies effectively possess a veto over section 404 dredge and fill permits issued by the Corps of Engineers (see Chapter 23). After this decision, a state might impose a minimum flow requirement in a certification for a 404 permit in order to prevent wetland draining. Is the 401 certification restricted to point source pollution? Must the BLM (see Chapter 14) request a state certification that a proposed grazing permit, allowing cattle to graze in riparian zones, will not violate state water quality standards?

Water quality and quantity are only two aspects of comprehensive, integrated water resources management. Hazardous waste disposal, air pollution, and transportation patterns are only a few of the other factors that bear upon water resources management. "Watershed management" is currently being proposed as a potential solution to the fragmentation of water resources management. We might manage water resources in a more systematic, integrated fashion by planning and regulating on a watershed basis, rather than waterbody-by-waterbody as we currently do. But although "watershed management" is a promising concept, it is also fraught with difficulties. See Goldfarb, Watershed Management: Slogan or Solution? 21 Environmental Affairs Law Review 483 (1994).

Exercise: The Average River and its Watershed

A Complex Hypothetical Overview

CLASS EXERCISE: THE AVERAGE RIVER STUDY PROBLEM

The Average River is just that, a typical river system that arises in the mountain highlands (Magic Mountain) and flows into the sea (Pedantic Ocean). As shown on the accompanying map, the Average River is also subject to typical threats to its water quality: (1) a second home development, with each home serviced by its own on-site septic system, is planned for the slopes of Magic Mountain, threatening to degrade the currently pristine water quality found in Riverview State Park; (2) Purview Farms, just downstream from the park, is a large, modern farming operation that causes fertilizer and pesticide residues to flow overland into the river during storm events, and also causes groundwater contamination at various times; (3) the Dratt Chemical Co. discharges biochemical oxygen demand, toxic organic chemicals, and phenols from its plant's production and sanitation facilities directly into the river, causing a violation of water quality standards downstream of the plant; Dratt also collects its stormwater, which is contaminated by runoff from uncovered raw material storage piles, and discharges it through a drainage ditch into the river; (4) below Dratt is a wetland area in which a residential subdivision is planned; (5) the City of Grossville, population 500,000 is serviced by a POTW that utilizes only primary treatment and is currently undersized, resulting in the overflow of polluted water from the city's combined sewers into streets and the Average River; (6) Grossville's POTW problems are exacerbated because the Nurd Auto Co. discharges heavy metals into the Grossville sewers, and these heavy metals contaminate the POTW's sewage sludge, which is currently being stored on concrete slabs on the POTW grounds because ocean dumping — which Grossville once used to dispose of sewage sludge — has been prohibited by federal law and the heavy metals in the sludge preclude incineration, composting, or land disposal. (7) The Zaaapp Power Company has applied to the Federal Energy Regulatory Commission for a license to construct a hydroelectric dam on the river between Riverview State Park and Purview Farms. If constructed, this facility will exacerbate existing pollution problems by raising water temperatures in the reservoir, causing eutrophication, and periodically dewatering the lower river.

Is the Clean Water Act capable of protecting the Average River from these threats? If it is, what can you do if government does not act effectively to protect the river?

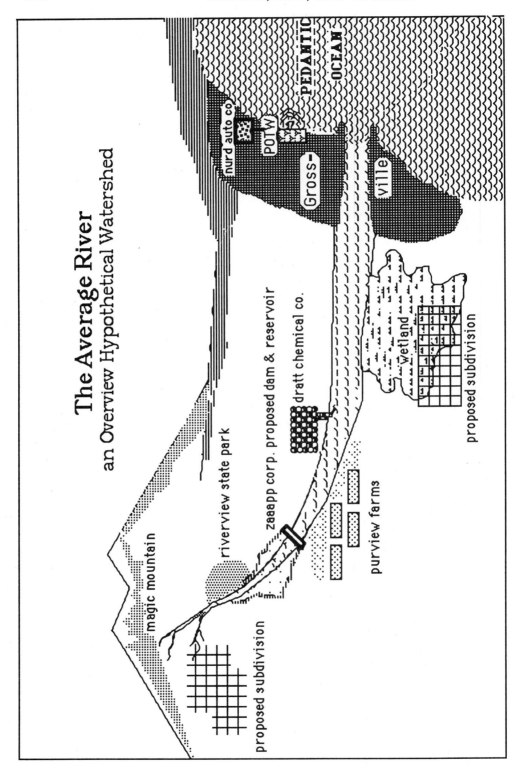

The Average River
an Overview Hypothetical Watershed

Chapter 20, Economic Incentive and Artificial Pollution Market Statutes

6. Subsidies. Just as imposing a charge on environmentally damaging behavior is a form of economic regulation, paying a bounty for environmentally favorable behavior creates an economic incentive that leads to improved environmental outcomes. Subsidies can take a number of forms. The most obvious, and therefore the politically most sensitive, are direct payments to the subsidized entities. Less obviously, government offers subsidies when it provides goods or services to entities at below-cost prices. See, e.g., coursebook at 681. Perhaps least obvious, government extends a subsidy when it provides special tax treatment to an activity. Subsidies falling into this last category are at times called "tax expenditures." A subsidy that helps corporations purchase pollution control equipment, for example, alters the cost function of the firm and makes the installation of that equipment a more likely choice,[144] especially when there are costs associated with continuing pollution at previous levels.

---

144. There is a subtle point to be noted here, Not all subsidies that seem to promote environmentally favorable outcomes are economic incentives as that term is used in this chapter. Subsidies that support behavior that is already required are not being used as economic incentives, they are simply wealth transfers that benefit the subsidized party. For example, when the Internal Revenue Service issued its June, 1994 ruling that CERCLA cleanup costs were tax deductible business expenses (rather than capital improvements to the underlying land), it reduced the cost of cleanups to profitable corporate PRPs. The PRPs still paid the same amount for the cleanup, but their profits were offset by the amount of the cleanup expense and, therefore, they paid less tax; possibly more than $50 billion less. Because there was already an enforceable legal obligation to clean up, however, the subsidy was not required to induce cleanup behavior.

Chapter 21,   A Statutory System For Managing and Funding Environmental Remediation: CERCLA

PAGE 897   More on the cost of cleanups

9A. How much will this cost? The Congressional Budget Office, in a February, 1994 report entitled, "The Total Cost of Cleaning Up Nonfederal Superfund Sites," offered a series of estimates of the total outlays likely to be spent at nonfederal Superfund sites. It made low-end, middle, and high-end projections as follows:

PROJECTION	# OF NPL SITES	COST (in 1992 $)	COMPLETED BY YEAR
Low-end	2,300	$ 42 billion	2047
Middle	4,500	$ 75 billion	2060
High-end	7,800	$ 120 billion	2075

If these figures are not sufficiently disconcerting, remember that they do not include cleanups at federal sites, such as the Rocky Mountain Arsenal, which appear to be multi-billion dollar problems in their own right. Also remember that the calculation in 1992 dollars means that future expenditures are inflation-adjusted and discounted, so, for example, the $75B mid-range figure represents the present discounted value of actual future outlays of $230B (also in 92 dollars). Perhaps in an effort to underscore the need for a change in Superfund policy, the report expressly states that it assumes no changes in present policy, and no limits on authorized spending. It also does not make any adjustment for technological changes that may improve cleanup efficiencies.

9B. And just who is paying? The staggering amounts of money that are needed for CERCLA cleanups has to come from somewhere, but where? For almost a decade and a half, the answer was that the polluter-pays principle was going to be invoked with a vengeance. Given the way CERCLA's liability scheme works, especially with the almost inescapable imposition of joint and several liability on PRPs, PRPs appear likely to pay almost all of the costs. For the most part, the Superfund itself will pay only in those cases where no financially solvent, jointly and severally liable PRPs can be identified.[145] Moreover, recall that the Superfund is funded primarily by a tax on chemical feedstocks, so the chemical industry takes a hit beyond its PRP, share and the public at large escapes the cost.

With a small administrative flick of the pen in June 1994, however, the public share has suddenly leaped to nearly one-third of the future expense. That major shift in financial burden occurred when the Internal Revenue Service (IRS) issued Revenue Ruling 94-38 concerning the deductibility of CERCLA cleanup costs. See Internal Revenue Bulletin

---

145. The Reform Act of 1994 makes some change in the arrangement that shifts the orphan share to the Superfund. See materials in Chapter 6 of this Supplement for the details of that change.

1994-25 (June 20, 1994). Up until that point, IRS had taken the position that cleanups were to be capitalized as part of the land — that is, the expense of cleanup was to be added to the taxpayer's basis in the asset, its cost of acquiring the land and maintaining its value for sale. Thus, under the previous IRS position, the only effect cleanup expenditures would have on the taxpayer's tax liability would come into play when the land was sold. The profit (if any) on the sale of the land would be less and therefore the tax liability then would be less. Under Revenue Ruling 94-38, however, cleanup costs, except those that are incurred for the construction of an ongoing treatment facility, are now fully deductible under §162 of the Internal Revenue Code as ordinary business expenses of the year in which the costs are incurred. This means that the immediate tax liability of the affected firm is greatly reduced. Consider this example: In 1994, profitable Major Corporation A spends $100,000 on CERCLA cleanup. The present level of the corporate tax is 35%. With the $100,000 now being deductible, A's 1994 net profit is now $100,000 less and its tax liability is $35,000 less. This is money that the federal treasury no longer receives for the benefit of the general public.

PAGE 898   **CERCLA'S continuing evolution**

12. Superfund's most recent scorecard. As part of recent congressional hearings, EPA Administrator Carol Browner was called upon to announce the Clinton Administration position on Superfund. Her statement of May 12, 1993 to a senate subcommittee was not overly revealing, but did sound a some new notes. She began with a barrage of statistics intended to demonstrate a pattern of increasing EPA activity and success in moving NPL sites through the several phases of the Superfund process. The roll call was impressive, including over 3000 removal actions at over 2600 sites including all 1200 currently on the NPL, RI/FSs "underway or completed at almost 1200 sites, remedies selected at 800 sites, remedial designs underway or completed at nearly 700 sites, and remedial actions underway or completed at nearly 500 sites." Beyond that, 54 sites had been delisted, that is, cleaned to the point that they merited removal from the Superfund system. On the money side, Browner emphasized EPA's recent success with what it euphemistically calls an "Enforcement First" policy. "Enforcement First," initiated in 1989, simply means that "EPA attempts to get responsible parties to perform cleanups before it uses taxpayer dollars to perform the cleanup itself." Over the life of Superfund, and especially in recent years, PRPs have committed to pay more than $7.4 billion. PRP-led work is now running at 72% of remedial action work, up from 32% in 1988. In somewhat less precise terms, Browner also explained that Superfund was influencing corporate and municipal behavior by inducing voluntary cleanup actions and waste minimization efforts. Further, she cited a significant degree of technological innovation in the cleanup industry as both improving the cost-effectiveness of cleanups and as a product that will be available for export to other nations.

Administrator Browner also identified areas in which the Clinton Administration is displeased with the Superfund program. Here she noted that:

> we are paying a high price in terms of administrative and
> cleanup costs incurred by EPA, and a high price in terms of the
> transaction and cleanup costs incurred by companies and
> state and local governments potentially liable for
> contamination. We are paying a high price in terms of
> uncertainty and wasted time. We are paying a high price in
> terms of basic fairness — or unfairness — of the program.
> Finally, we are paying a high price in terms of the anxiety and
> frustration of local communities concerned about delays in
> cleaning up contaminated sites.

In detailing the nature of the complaints about Superfund, Administrator
Browner highlighted transaction costs, municipal liability fairness
concerns, the possibility that cleanups in minority areas are being
handled differently (and less advantageously for the residents than
cleanups in majority areas), and the volatile question of "How clean is
clean?"

13. Is the Clinton Administration re-thinking Superfund? In the same
congressional testimony recounted above, Administrator Browner also
outlined EPA's efforts for responding to the perceived problems she had
just recounted. She outlined a four pronged strategy that included

> (1) a national advisory committee with broad public interest and
> private corporate (as well as governmental) membership,

> (2) an internal EPA workgroup charged with improving Superfund's
> operation (giving special attention to continuing initiatives such as
> accelerated cleanup models, presumptive remedies, and improved
> compliance monitoring and cost documentation and recovery)

> (3) improvements in data collection, and

> (4) EPA staff involvement in reviewing proposals for legislative
> alteration of Superfund.

Are there any bold new initiatives apparent on the face of this agenda?
The most significant hint of change is the apparent willingness to open up
the "How clean is clean?" issue with some willingness to listen to
benefit/cost concerns in setting new standards.

14. Documenting Superfund's inefficiency; a/k/a the high cost of lawyers.
A 1992 Rand Corporation study found very high transaction costs under
Superfund. See Jean Paul Acton & Lloyd S. Dixon, Superfund and
Transaction Costs (1992). For large private sector PRPs studied in their
report, transaction costs during the 1984-89 period were 21% of their
Superfund outlays, with the bulk of that money being spent on legal
representation. *Id.* at 56. For insurance companies, many of whom
seemed insistent on litigating every conceivable coverage issue to the
death, transaction costs were astronomical. Of an estimated $470 million
spent industrywide on claims related to inactive hazardous waste sites in
1989, Acton and Dixon found that 88% ($410 million) went to transaction
costs, of which $200 million was expended on coverage disputes with
policy holders and $175 million was spent on defending policy holders in
litigation, with the remaining $35 million going to internal insurance
company overhead. *Id.* at 24, 30-32.

How damning is this data? Is it simply an indication that insurance companies have made a living off of litigation in the past (i.e., reducing outlays by contesting them) and are doing so again in the hazardous waste liability area? The study offers some evidence of that. In other areas of general liability insurance, transaction costs tend to run high also, including areas having few coverage disputes. For example, Acton and Dixon note that a major insurance industry reporting service found industrywide transaction costs as high as 42% for medical malpractice liability claims and 32% for more general liability claims (such as homeowners). These costs occur in areas where there is seldom extended coverage litigation. This permits a comparison to hazardous waste claims. If the coverage dispute costs are deleted from the Superfund findings, they are still out of line: lawyers are still getting the lion's share of the money, by a ratio of almost 3:1 over indemnity payments actually made. The comparable ratios of transaction costs to indemnity payments are .7:1 and .5:1 for malpractice and general liability respectively.

Are the high transaction costs money well spent? The obvious answer would seem to be, "No, every dollar "wasted" on litigation costs is a dollar not available for cleanup." The expenditures may be even less useful than that. Normally, the dollars spent on defending against liability are viewed as likely to produce a net savings. Defendants (and their insurers) normally pay claims if the cost of those payments is likely (both in the short and long term) to be less than the sum of the cost of defending claims (sometimes successfully) and paying the losses that remain after litigation. In the Superfund defense context, however, defense of liability is almost always unavailing. Joint and several liability with relaxed standards of causation and broad definitions of who is a PRP make efforts at defending the liability issue very unlikely to result in any "savings" to the PRP. Realistically, in the vast majority of cases the only transaction costs that should be incurred in are ones expended on cost allocation issues. Are there reasons why the defense bar and insurance counsel have persisted so long in tilting against the windmill of PRP liability? One simple explanation is that the self interest of defense counsel and that of the insurance companies lies in *increasing* these costs. The counsel earn their livings by litigating and the insurance companies raise premiums and increase their gross intake in response to their increased costs. If they maintain the same margin of profitability, increased premiums result in increased profits. Presumably, the marketplace should limit this cost spiral, with more prudent insurers being able to offer their insureds lower premiums, thereby claiming a larger market share. It is not clear that this market discipline has been imposed yet.

In a sharp contrast to the more typical strategy, some attorneys who practice in the area are advocating more cooperative strategies for their defense clients. See, Bruce T. Wallace & William J. Stapleton, Environmental Litigation, (Chapter entitled "Initial Organizing Principles and Strategies," forthcoming 1994).

The Reform Act of 1994

Congress is in the process of enacting significant reforms to the Superfund law as this Supplement goes to press. As explained in Chapter

6, the final package seems likely to resemble closely a version of the bill that was unanimously adopted by the House Energy and Commerce Committee in May, 1994. The full text of that version of the bill can be found in the BNA, Daily Environment Report, Special Supplement of May 5, 1994. Many of the reforms targeted the remediation and cost allocation portions of Superfund that are highlighted in this chapter. What follows is an attempt to summarize the most salient reforms.

The big picture approach to the new Superfund amendments: Although it misses many details, the easiest way to conceive of the new amendments is in terms of criticisms of the existing law and responses to those criticisms, as noted on the following chart. It is important to remember that the criticisms come from a variety of quarters, not solely the waste generators and other usual members of the PRP class. Critics also include environmental groups, affected local communities, the states, and EPA itself. This array of critics, as well as the political process itself, tend to ensure that the bill's provisions represent a series of compromises.

ISSUE	CRITICISM	RESPONSES
Remedy Selection-Safety and Consistency	Too much variation in setting permissible exposure levels and cleanup requirements	EPA will set national cleanup goals for carcinogens at consistent levels (i.e., pick a specific acceptable risk) EPA will create a national risk assessment protocol that determines how conservative various risk assessment assumptions must be Abolishes the ARAR concept and replaces it with "applicable requirements" that are adopted explicitly by statute or rule
Remedy Selection — Practicality	Too little attention given to real cost and implementability in the remedy selection process	To be selected, remedies must be reasonably achievable and not unreasonably costly Remedy selection will take future land use into account EPA, with Fund bearing insolvents' share and part of the unallocated share, will be more cost sensitive in its decisionmaking Eliminate the preference for permanent remedies and treatment except as to "hot spots"
Remedy Selection — Complexity and Delay	RI/FS process takes too long and requires too much information	Expand the presumptive remedies program (this may also reduce cost in the RI/FS stage) Encourage voluntary cleanups

Remedy Selection — Process and evnviron-mental justice	Community interests often disregarded	New process includes 20-mewmber community work groups Expanded technical assistance to communities Modify HRS scoring of sites to reflect multiple sources of contamination
Cost Allocation-Cost	Transaction costs are unbelievably high	Reduce private party cost allocation litigation by forcing disputes into ADR [146] Make de minimis settlements more available for generators of up to 1% of volume of waste Make quick cash outs (settlements with contribution protection) available for most small PRPs, including $0 for those with less than a certain amount of waste and residential landowners Eliminate insurance coverage litigation with scheduled payments for PRP liabilities to all CGL policyholders from an insurance fund (see Chapter 6)
Cost Allocation-Fairness	Particularly with the use of joint and several liability and the strategic behavior of EPA and major PRPs, many parties' shares were not fairly related to their responsibly	Employ more precisely delineated factors in the allocation process Relieve parties of some portion of the liability by having Fund pay for share allocable to known but insolvent parties and the associated portion of the unallocated share, up to $300M per year
Cost Allocation-Fairness	Municipal solid waste disposal is treated the same as disposal of more hazardous waste	Explicitly limit municipal MSW generator and transporter liability to 10% of total cost, remainder of municipal liability at these sites to Fund Exempt small MSW contributors from liability
Federalism	State resentment of EPA actions and cost sharing formulas	States establishing qualifying programs can assume many EPA functions including remedy selection and oversight Standard 15% federal cost share of state capital expenditures and operation and maintenance costs

---

146. The ADR system is vital and its details are discussed in the text following the chart.

The ADR system. The ADR system for cost allocation is one of the central pillars of the Superfund reform. It replaces what may be viewed as a kind of litigator's free-for-all that is fostered by the present system. Under the post-SARA Superfund law, EPA's optimal strategy for obtaining prompt PRP action is to rely on joint and several liability and the fears of the PRP class to get some of the PRPs at the site to take a leadership role in either doing the cleanup work or paying for it. The PRPs who are thus "forced" to shoulder costs disproportional to their fair share thereafter seek to redistribute the loss to others in the PRP community. There are no clear rules for this allocation process and the amount of strategic behavior that has come to attend the process is legion.

The ADR process in the reform legislation has several features. It begins by staying existing cost allocation litigation or barring it from the time the ADR process is initiated until 60 days after it has reached its result. The ADR process kicks in early in the remedial history, no later than eighteen months after the RI process has begun. By that time EPA must have completed its search for responsible parties and it must then give them and the public notice of the initiation of the allocation ADR. A neutral allocator is chosen by selection of the parties from a list maintained by EPA. EPA then distributes the information it has collected and that opens a sixty-day period in which any interested party can make proposals for the inclusion of other PRPs Within 30 days after that, the allocator issues a final list of parties to the allocation.

Once the parties are identified, the allocator has broad powers to obtain information from them, similar to those of EPA under CERCLA § 104(e) and including a subpoena power for the compulsion of witnesses and delivery of documents. The allocator is authorized to convene the allocation parties to facilitate a settlement, but if no agreement is forthcoming, the allocator "shall prepare a written report, with a nonbinding equitable allocation of percentage shares for the facility ... ." The factors to be used in fashioning the allocation are the so-called "Gore factors," harkening back to an unenacted amendment to SARA offered by then-Senator Gore that sought to identify the factors to be considered in cost allocation under CERCLA. The factors are:

(A) the amount of hazardous substances contributed by each allocation party; (B) the degree of toxicity of those substances; (C) the mobility of the substances; (D) the degree of involvement of each allocation party in the generation, transportation, treatment, storage, or disposal of the hazardous substances; (E) the degree of care exercised by each of the parties with respect to the hazardous substances; (F) the cooperation of each allocation party in contributing to the response action and in providing complete and timely information during the allocation process; (G) and such other factors as EPA determines are appropriate by published regulation or guidance, including guidance with respect to the identification of orphan shares.

The allocator's report is required to identify a percentage share attributable to each allocation party and a share denominated the "orphan" share. This term has a precise meaning that is narrower than the meaning sometimes given to the term in more general Superfund parlance. As defined in the Reform Act, the orphan share has two types of components, one attributable to "specifically identified but insolvent or defunct responsible parties who are not affiliated with any allocation party," and the other attributable to limited ability to pay parties or municipalities whose allocation share exceeds the share actually assumed by those parties in settlements with the government.[147] What is excluded by that definition is shares attributable to unknown or unidentifiable parties, this share is referred to as the "unallocated."

Based on the factors and the information generated by EPA and the parties, the allocator prepares an allocation report that assigns shares to each of the PRPs, as well as identifying an orphan share and an unallocated share. EPA is then, in effect, given 60 days to decide that it is willing to settle with PRPs on the basis of the allocator's report. To refuse to settle on that basis, EPA, with the concurrence of the Attorney General, must find that such a settlement would "not be fair, reasonable, and in the public interest." Although not subject to judicial review, that finding is subject to a form of political review. If PRPs object to the EPA action, their objections are presented to "an official appointed by the President." Presumably, EPA will be under intense pressure to accept allocator's reports.

Once a report is issued, PRPs wishing to settle on the allocator's proposed terms must exercise the initiative and make an offer to do so.[148] The incentives to settle on the basis of shares assigned by the allocator[149] are significant. First, the allocation process, although not likely to be perceived as perfectly fair by all of the parties, should avoid gross injustice. The factors listed are those that have won general assent, and although their application leaves a great deal of room for flexibility, the allocators are likely to be sufficiently familiar with the way allocations have worked in the past to generate results that will not shock the parties. Perhaps more importantly, the assumption of the statutorily defined orphan share by the Fund reduces the allocation shares of the other parties making their liabilities correspond more closely to their "fair share." Settling parties also receive contribution protection and reimbursement from the Fund if they have already paid or expended services worth more than their allocated share. This means that parties accepting the allocator's assigned share will buy a peace that includes avoidance of all further litigation costs, whether defending contribution actions or seeking cost recovery for their "overpayments." EPA is left to deal with all of that in litigation with any non-settling PRPs. Finally, the unstated incentive to settle is the fate that awaits non-settling PRPs who face joint and several liability that will subject them to liability for (1) their own allocated share,

---

147. The legislation provisions specifically quantifies the liability of parties who fall into those categories.

148. Timing here is a bit murky. The issuance of the allocation report triggers a 60-day period in which a PRP cannot be sued by EPA as a "party who has not resolved its liability to United States following allocation." Elsewhere the legislation refers to EPA's obligation, in cases where EPA itself does not reject the allocation, to "accept a timely offer of settlement from a party based on the share determined by the allocator."

149. EPA is required to add a surcharge to the allocator's assigned share. The Reform Act calls for settlements based on the allocation report to include "a premium that compensates for the United States litigation risk with respect to potentially responsible parties who have not resolved their liability to the United States ... ."

(2) the orphan share, and (3) and excess previously paid by settling PRPs that the Fund was obliged to cover under the Reform Act.[150]

COMMENTARY AND QUESTIONS

1. **Promise and practice.** You may recall that CERCLA was previously the subject of sweeping amendatory improvements in 1986. It was thought that many of the innovations of those amendments, such as de minimis settlements, would greatly improve the functioning of CERCLA. They didn't. Will the Reform Act of 1994 fare any better? Which provisions seem ripe for de facto nullification by the real world actors who must carry the reforms into operation? The most obvious candidate for failure is the Environmental Insurance Resolution Fund (EIRF), discussed in Chapter 6, that will fail if too few insureds accept the offered payments in lieu of their right to litigate their insurance claims. EPA could frustrate the allocation system by refusing to accept allocations, or by insisting on outrageous premiums. If too many PRPs refuse their allocations, the burden on EPA of chasing the others may overload EPA's resources. On the remedial side, the needed revision of cleanup standards may take too long to accomplish, the new standards might offer little relief from the present ones, etc. Moreover, many of the transaction costs will continue, especially those costs incurred by PRPs in trying to produce evidence of the extent of contamination caused by other PRPs.

2. **The perils of good and bad recordkeeping.** In cost allocation litigation among generators, a key item is the waste in list that identifies the nature and volume of the waste attributable to the various PRPs. Especially at older sites, or at the more poorly operated sites, the owner and operator of the site has only sketchy records of what wastes were brought by whom. Generators who maintained and retained accurate business records that disclose their waste disposal practices are frequently penalized for the accuracy of their records. They are clearly identified as PRPs as is the volume and type of waste they contributed to the site. In contrast, generators without a present clue as to how their waste was disposed evade responsibility because no one can be found who can tell where their waste was sent. How might the law respond to this apparent inequity? The ADR system of the Reform Act expressly lists PRP cooperation, including "providing complete and timely information," as a factor to be weighed in the allocation. Does that solve the problem? Would an allocator be quick to infer that substantial amounts of a PRPs waste are present at a site from a good faith claim by that PRP that it has no records indicating that such disposal took place?

3. **Don't forget what you know about pre-amendment Superfund just yet.** One of the more perverse twists in working with the amended Superfund is that the pre-amendment practices continue, in most regards, at many sites. The new provisions will apply fully only at sites where the ROD is signed after the date of introduction of the legislation, which was February 4, 1994. This means that at roughly 1,500 sites where RODs were signed

---

150. The non-settlers cannot seek several liability based on the allocation report. It is not admissible evidence on the issue of allocation except in regard to equitably allocating response costs among a group of liable non-settling parties.

before that date, including most of the nation's worst sites, the new process has limited applicability. Consider in this regard the following:

> *Remedy Selection* — The new remedy selection provisions will not apply to remedy selection at the "old ROD sites." This might seem axiomatic, because the ROD embodies the remedy selection and, therefore, there is no need to revisit the decision already made. While that is true, few of the remedies have been implemented fully and the new remedy selection process is not only more streamlined, it is more flexible with regard to the preference for treatment over containment, the smaller set of requirements that will be deemed to be ARARs, and taking subsequent use into account. What this means is that reconsideration of "old ROD sites," were it allowed, might lead to the selection of less expensive remedies.

> *Orphan share payment, cost allocation and ADR procedures* — Parties at "old ROD sites" can invoke the newly provided ADR process to assist them in the cost allocation portion of the case. Thus, initiation of § 107 suits would be barred, or pending litigation stayed, during the statutory period allowed for the non-binding allocation. However, the allocation in those cases is not required to account for the orphan share, nor is the Superfund required to pay the orphan share at those sites. This means that the squabbling about how to allocate this sometimes significant orphan share (and the unallocated share) probably will continue unabated. Hopefully, when the allocation process is employed for "old ROD cases" the allocator's report will at least prove helpful to courts adjudicating cost recovery and contribution cases.

PAGE 909   **More on divisibility**

1a. Cross referencing chapter 6's divisibility cases. A smattering of cases are now being decided favoring defendants on this issue. These are described in this Supplement in the material that is to be added to the main text's page 292 as a new note 4. Even so, the facts of those cases are sufficiently atypical that, in most cases, divisibility cannot be established.

PAGE 909   **More on contribution**

1A. Who decides contribution cases? Although it has not given rise to extensive litigation, the question of whether a judge or jury is to decide CERCLA contribution cases has long been considered an open issue. One case supporting a jury right is United States v. Shaner, 23 Env. L. Rep. 20236, 1992 WL 154618 (E.D. Pa. 1992), while American Cyanamid Co. v. King, 814 F. Supp. 209, 36 ERC 1430 (1993), is typical of cases that rule against a jury right. In general, when Congress establishes a new cause of action, it can, with some limitations not relevant in this context, opt to create or deny a jury right. Here the statute and its legislative history are inconclusive, although the language of 113(f) does state that *"the court* may allocate response costs among liable parties *using such equitable factors* as the court determines are appropriate." Emphasis supplied. This offers some textual support for implying that Congress intended CERCLA contribution suits would not be tried to a jury. Moreover, as the *King* court noted, the 113(f) contribution claim "does not arise out of an allegation of defendants' negligence liability or a claim for damages. The underlying issues to be tried are whether defendants are liable for response costs under 107, and to what extent, if any, they are liable for their share of those costs to the plaintiffs. Logically, plaintiffs' right to recovery derives directly from the state and federal government's equitable right to hold defendants liable for response costs and to seek restitution." 36 ERC at 1434.

Page 919   Less than de minimus PRPs

2A. *De micromis* ? EPA has issued a guidance document that sets up a new category of PRPs, termed *"de micromis,"* whose contribution of hazardous materials to CERCLA sites is very small. The text of this guidance can be found at 8 Toxics Law Reporter 320 (August 18, 1993). One commentator offered this conclusion regarding the role of the guidance in EPA's overall strategy:

The de micromis settlement guidance basically gives the agency a streamlined approach to resolve the potential liability of contributors of minuscule amounts of hazardous substances at superfund sites. While the agency has not traditionally pursued these parties in the past, they increasingly have been subject to contribution actions by third parties. The de micromis settlement provides a way for these parties to quickly resolve their liability with the government, rather than being dragged into protracted litigation with third-party plaintiffs.

John W. Olmstead, Superfund Settlements with De Micromis Waste Contributors, 8 Toxics Law Reporter 1258, 1263 (April 6, 1994).

Page 923   CERCLA contribution litigation

8. As the judicial results come in. There is little reason to expect CERCLA contribution actions to be easy to litigate, after all, their central issue is cost allocation in a context where many factors are relevant, but where there is no consensus regarding the weights to be assigned to the various factors. Reading the judicial opinions confirms the gloomy prediction — contribution litigation is complex and resource intensive, generating case-specific results that offer little guidance for the proper determination of other cases. *Compare*, e.g., New York v. SCA Services, Inc, 1993 WL 59407, 36 ERC 1439 (S.D. N.Y. 1993) (refusing approval of proposed settlement as unfair and not in the public interest), *with* American Cyanamid Co. v. King, 814 F.Supp. 215, 36 ERC 1435 (D. R.I. 1993) (approving proposed settlement without conducting fairness hearing).

One typical pattern of litigation in these cases is that the plaintiff in the contribution action reaches some agreement on settlement with some, but not all, of the defendants. Recall that all of the parties in these 113(f) suits are PRPs, although the plaintiff has usually incurred a greater share (perhaps all) of the costs to date. The agreement calls for the settling parties to pay some specified amount to the plaintiff and in return the settling defendants are released from further liability, not only to the plaintiff, but to all of the other PRPs. Stated differently, if the court accepts the settlement, not only are the plaintiff's claims against the settling defendant dismissed, so are any cross claims lodged against the settling defendants by the non-settling defendants. In a sense, the settlement works in an analogous manner to the contribution protection that can be granted by the government to settling PRPs.

The ability of the plaintiff to "protect" settling defendants against cross claims may seem odd, but it is a necessary element of the law if settlements are to be encouraged in multi-party liability situations. This is a linchpin of the Uniform Comparative Fault Act (UCFA), 12 U.L.A. 44 (Supp. 1992). Why, for example, would anyone settle with the contribution suit plaintiff if all that settlement did was to extinguish liability to that one party without cutting off additional liability to other jointly and severally liable co-parties for the exact same conduct? In recognition of the policy of encouraging settlement, the UCFA gives the equivalent of contribution protection to settlers, but it protects non-settlers by reducing their liability by the amount of the share of the settling parties rather than by the amount that was actually paid in settlement. This is a subtle, but vital, distinction because it keeps the plaintiff interested in receiving full value in settlement. If the plaintiff receives too little from the settlers and the non-settlers are able to set off the settlers *"fair share"* the plaintiff will be unable to collect the full share that would have been paid by the settlers had there not been the settlement. The *King* court tried to explain this principle by example:

> A private party sues five defendants for contribution under 113(f)(1) of CERCLA. Plaintiff seeks recovery for $100,000 for response costs. One defendant settles for $5,000. At trial, it is determined that each of the five original defendants are liable for an equitable share equaling 10% of the $100,000 — or $10,000 per defendant. The plaintiff is found to be liable for 50% — or $50,000. The settling defendant is still responsible for only $5,000. The non-settling defendants, however, may reduce their collective share of liability by the amount of the settling defendant's equitable *share* — in this case, $10,000. Thus, the four non-settling defendants are responsible for $10,000 each, for a total of $40,000. The plaintiff bears the "loss" of $5,000 in contribution recovery as a result of compromising for less than the settling party's equitable share. Conversely, the plaintiff may reap any "windfall" from a settlement with one of the five defendants for more than $10,000, or more than the defendant's equitable share. That is the rub of the green. 814 F.Supp. at __, 36 ERC at 1437.

And now that should be perfectly clear!

Senior Judge Pettine, author of the *King* opinion goes so far as to say that applying the UCFA removes the need for courts to superintend the fairness of settlements. Do you agree? The problematic variable here is evaluating how the difficulty of proving what is an equitable apportionment affects the settlement process and the remaining litigation.

Recently, the United States Supreme Court has adopted a similar approach in a non-CERCLA case involving the liability of non-settling joint tortfeasors in a maritime action. See, McDermott, Inc. v. AmClyde, 114 S.Ct. 1461 (1994). That case involved the setting in which the plaintiff negotiated a more favorable settlement than that which would have obtained against the settling defendant in the litigation and recovered more than 100% of the total to be allocated.

9. Using the Gore factors to compare apples and oranges. How should the six Gore factors be applied when trying to allocate responsibility between different classes of PRPs, such as site owner/operators on the one hand and generators on the other? The first three factors, distinguishable waste contributions, volume of waste, and toxicity of waste, all seem directed toward an allocation among generator PRPs *inter sese*, but not in comparison to the site owners or operators. Accordingly a number of courts have placed principal reliance on the last three factors, degree of involvement, care, and cooperation, in the apples and oranges comparisons. See, e.g., Travelers Indemnity Co. v. Dingwell, 884 F.2d 629 (1st Cir. 1992).

Chapter 22, A Composite Approach to Preventing Releases of Hazardous Wastes: The Resource Conservation and Recovery Act

Page 940   More on hazardous waste statutory systems

9. RCRA and the waste disposal system. The following EPA Chart[151] depicts a selective overview of the hazardous waste regulatory system, including RCRA and CERCLA.

Simplified Waste System Chart

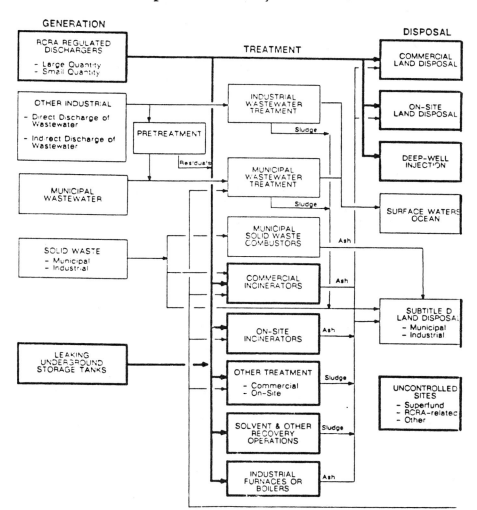

[Note: Bold lines refer to RCRA and Superfund hazardous waste system.]

---

151. From EPA, The Hazardous Waste System (1987).

Notice that the Chart does not deal with every source or possible
exposure route of hazardous wastes or toxic substances. For example,
hazardous air emissions (see Chapter 18), pesticide applications (see
Chapter 16), and "poison runoff' from farms, industries, and urban areas
(see Chapter 19) are not included in the Chart. Note also that direct
dischargers of wastewater may also be RCRA generators if the sludges
from their waste treatment processes (see the definition of "solid waste"
on page 929 of the main volume) qualify as RCRA hazardous wastes. Only
industrial wastes discharged into municipal treatment plants (POTWs) are
covered· under RCRA's "domestic sewage exclusion." RCRA's
Underground Storage Tank (UST) program is described in note 12 infra.
The Deep-Well Injection program is found in the Safe Drinking Water
Act, 42 U.S.C.A. sec. 1421 et seq. Several facilities in the south-central
United States have been licensed to dispose of hazardous wastes in deep,
confined geological strata, but deep-well injection is not permitted in other
areas of the country because of unfavorable hydrogeological conditions.

Finally, the Chart illustrates Barry Commoner's admonition that
"Everything Goes Somewhere." Every waste treatment process creates a
residual, which, because it is highly concentrated, is often more toxic
than the corresponding waste inputs. Sludge and ash residuals are "the
muck stops here" endpoints of the hazardous waste regulatory systems;
and, as you might imagine, their regulation has been highly contentious.
See Chapter 19 for a discussion of municipal sewage sludge
management, and Comment 12 below, for a reference to the incinerator
ash controversy.

10. A walk through RCRA. As the material in the main volume makes
clear, RCRA is a highly complex statute that integrates many taxonomic
regulatory mechanisms into a comprehensive (although not complete, as
pointed out in Note 9, supra.) hazardous waste management system. The
RCRA regulatory cycle is a three stage one: generator — transporter —
TSD. Most of RCRA's conceptual complexity is found at the "generator"
stage. The requirements that RCRA imposes on transporters and TSDs are
technically complex, but, as generally described in the main volume, are
relatively simple conceptually. The following exerpts from EPA's RCRA
Orientation Manual (1986) are intended to clarify the "front end" of the
RCRA process, which is also the stage that is of greatest interest to
students of environmental law and management because it is the
generator that initiates the statutory management process and is
ultimately responsible for the proper disposal of hazardous waste.

U.S. EPA, "What Is Hazardous Waste?" from RCRA Orientation Manual (1986)

[RCRA's Subtitle C program, the portion of RCRA's regulatory scheme
with real teeth in it, is triggered by the tricky process of identification and
listing of wastes as "hazardous."] All solid waste generators, from national
manufacturers to the corner drycleaners, must determine if their solid
waste is hazardous and thus subject to regulation under Subtitle C....

Although Congress defined the term "hazardous waste" in the Act [see
coursebook page 930], EPA was required to develop the regulatory

framework that would identify those solid wastes that must be managed as hazardous wastes under Subtitle C. This framework (40 CFR Part 261) specifies that a solid waste is hazardous if it meets one of four conditions:

1) exhibits, on analysis, any of the <u>characteristics</u> of a hazardous waste

2) Has been named as a hazardous waste and <u>listed</u>

3) Is a <u>mixture</u> containing a listed hazardous waste and a non-hazardous solid waste (unless the mixture is specifically excluded or no longer exhibits any of the characteristics of hazardous waste)

4) Is not <u>excluded</u> from regulation as a hazardous waste.

Furthermore, the by-products of [substances **"derived from"**] the treatment of any hazardous waste are also considered hazardous unless specifically excluded. [The derived-from rules have contributed greatly to the complexity of RCRA's administrative law.]

CHARACTERISTICS

EPA has identified four characteristics for hazardous waste. Any solid waste that exhibits one or more of them is classified as hazardous under RCRA. The characteristics are:

- Ignitability
- Corrosivity
- Reactivity
- [TCLP] Toxicity[152]

EPA used two criteria in selecting these characteristics. The first criterion was that the characteristics be capable of being defined in terms of physical, chemical, or other properties that cause the waste to meet the definition of hazardous waste in the Act. The second criterion was that the properties defining the characteristics be measurable by standardized and available testing protocols. The second criterion was adopted because the primary responsibility for determining whether a solid waste exhibits any of the characteristics rests with the generators. EPA believed that unless generators were provided with widely available and uncomplicated methods for determining whether their wastes exhibited the characteristics, the identification system would prove unworkable.... Largely due to this second criterion, EPA refrained from adding carcinogenicity, mutagenicity, bioaccumulation potential, and phytotoxicity to the set of proposed characteristics....

LISTING OF HAZARDOUS WASTE

A solid waste is also hazardous if it is named on one of three lists developed by EPA:

1) <u>Non-Specific source wastes</u> (40 CFR sec. 261.30) - These are generic wastes, commonly produced by manufacturing and industrial processes.

---

152. The TCLP (Toxicity Characteristic Leaching Procedure) is a test that simulates the potential of a waste to leach into groundwater if improperly stored or disposed of. Its harm-based criterion is drinking water standards established under the Safe Drinking Water Act.

Examples from this list include spent halogenated solvents used in degreasing, and wastewater treatment sludge from electroplating processes.

2) Specific source wastes (40 CFR Sec. 261.32) - This list consists of wastes from specifically identified industries such as wood preserving, petroleum refining and organic chemical manufacturing. These wastes typically include sludges, still bottoms, wastewaters, spent catalysts, and residues, e.g., wasteweater treatment sludge from the production of pigments.

3) Commercial chemical products (40 CFR Section 261.33(e) and (f) - The third list consists of specific commercial chemical products, or manufacturing chemical intermediates. This list includes chemicals such as chloroform and creosote, acids such as sulfuric acid and hydrocholoric acid, and pesticides such as DDT and Kepone.[153]

MIXTURES

One of the questions that faced EPA when setting the conditions for identifying hazardous wastes was how to classify a waste mixture that contains both a listed hazardous waste and a non-hazardous solid waste. EPA decided that any waste mixture containing a listed hazardous waste is considered a hazardous waste and must be managed accordingly. This applies regardless of what percentage of the waste mixture is composed of listed hazardous wastes. Without such a regulation, generators could evade Subtitle C simply by commingling listed wastes with non-hazardous solid waste. Most of these waste mixtures would not be caught by the four Subtitle C characteristics because they would contain wastes which were listed for other reasons than exhibiting the characteristics, e.g., they are acutely toxic. Allowing this situation would leave a major loophole in the Subtitle C management system and create inconsistencies in how wastes are managed under that system....

SPECIFICALLY EXCLUDED WASTES

Congress decided that certain types of solid waste should not be considered hazardous waste under Subtitle C. These include a number of common solid wastes that do not present a significant threat to human health or the environment or are currently managed under other programs in a way that minimizes any threat to human health or the environment.... [See the discussion of excluded wastes on pages 930-931 of the main volume].

SMALL QUANTITY GENERATORS

[Small quantity generators (SQGs) of between 100 kilograms per month and 1000 kgm may store hazardous wastes on site for longer periods of time than larger generators, but must comply with RCRA in virtually all other respects. Very small quantity generators of under 100 kgm are substantially exempt from RCRA.]

---

153. See the discussion of the Kepone case (United States v. Allied Chemical) in Chapters 2, 6, and 7 of the main volume. Had RCRA existed at the time, the Kepone wastes dumped by Life Sciences, Inc., on-site in pits, ponds, and lagoons would clearly have fallen within RCRA's ambit. See specifically page 252 of the main volume.

REGULATORY REQUIREMENTS FOR GENERATORS

Once a generator determines that all or part of the waste produced is hazardous he must comply with the regulatory requirements of Subtitle C. The regulatory requirements for hazardous waste generators include:

- •Obtaining an EPA ID number
- •Handling of hazardous waste before transport
- •Manifesting of hazardous waste
- •Recordkeeping and reporting.

EPA ID NUMBER

One way that EPA monitors and tracks generators is by assigning each generator a unique identification number. Without this number the generator is barred from treating, storing, disposing of, transporting, or offering for transportation any hazardous waste. Furthermore, the generator is forbidden from offering his hazardous waste to any transporter, or [TSD] that does not also have an EPA ID number.

PRE-TRANSPORT REGULATIONS

Pre-transport regulations are designed to ensure safe transportation of a hazardous waste from origin to ultimate disposal. In developing these regulations, EPA adopted those used by the Department of Transportation (DOT) for transporting hazardous wastes (49 CFR Parts 172, 173, 178, and 179). These DOT regulations require:

- •Proper packaging to prevent leakage of hazardous waste, during both normal transport conditions and in potentially dangerous situations, e.g., when a drum falls out of a truck.

- •Identification of the characteristics and dangers associated with the wastes being transported through labeling, marking and placarding of the packaged waste.

It is important to note that these pre-transport regulations only apply to generators shipping waste off-site.

In addition to adopting the DOT regulations outlined above, EPA also developed pre-transport regulations that cover the accumulation of waste prior to transport. A generator may acccumulate hazardous waste on-site for 90 days or less as long as the following requirements are met: [Proper storage; Emergency planning; and Personnel training].

If the generator accumulates hazardous waste on-site for more than 90 days he is considered an operator of a storage facility and must comply with the Subtitle C requirements for such facilities. [A generator of between 100 and 1000 kg/m of hazardous waste that ships its waste off-site may accumulate its hazardous waste for longer periods of time.] Under temporary, unforeseen and uncontrollable circumstances the 90-day period may be extended for up to 30 days....

THE MANIFEST

(T)he Subtitle C program was designed to manage hazardous waste from cradle to grave. The Uniform Hazardous Waste Manifest (the manifest) is the key to this objective. Through the use of a manifest, generators can track the movement of hazardous waste from the point of generation (the cradle) to the point of ultimate treatment, storage, or disposal (the grave). RCRA manifests contain a lot of information including the following:

- Name and EPA identification number of the generator, the transporter(s), and the facility where the waste is to be treated, stored, or disposed of

- U.S. DOT description of the waste being transported

- Quantities of the waste being transported

- Address of the treatment, storage, or disposal facility to which the generator is sending his waste....

It is especially important for the generator to prepare the manifest properly since he is responsible for the hazardous waste he produces and its ultimate disposal.

The manifest is part of a controlled tracking system. Each time the waste is transferred, e.g., from a transporter to a designated facility or from a transporter to another transporter, the manifest must be signed to acknowledge receipt of the waste. A copy of the manifest is retained by each link in the transportation chain. Once the waste is delivered to the designated facility the owner or operator of that facility must send a copy back to the generator....

If 35 days pass from the date on which the waste was accepted by the initial transporter and the generator has not received a copy of the manifest from the designated facility, the generator must contact the transporter and/or the designated facility to determine the whereabouts of the waste. If 45 days pass and the manifest still has not been received, the generator must submit [to the appropriate management agency, which in most cases is a state agency,] an exception report.

RECORDKEEPING AND REPORTING

[A generator must 1) file a biennial report describing all hazardous waste shipments and their dispositions, 2) submit an exception report when a signed manifest is not received from a TSD within 45 days, and 3) retain copies of all waste analyses, manifests, and reports for three years.]

INTERNATIONAL SHIPMENTS

[RCRA] directs the exporter to notify the Administrator [of EPA] of the nature of the shipment, e.g., dates, quantity, and description of the wastes, at least 4 weeks prior to shipment. Within 30 days of the receipt of this notification, the State Department, acting on behalf of the Administrator, must inform the receiving country about the export. The country, in turn, must consent (in writing) to accept the waste. If an international agreement exists between the United States and the receiving country, then notice and consent for each shipment are not required.[154]

---

154. The Clinton administration has recommended a ban on exports of hazardous waste to nations other than Canada and Mexico. The three North American countries routinely ship waste across borders for cheaper and more convenient disposal. The United States Senate has ratified the Basel Convention, which sharply limits international shipments of hazardous waste, but has not enacted legislation to put its provisions into effect. All told, the United States exports less than 1 percent of its hazardous wastes (approximately 145,000 tons per year).

11. What is a hazardous waste? Because classification as a hazardous waste under RCRA has such profound regulatory consequences for generators, there has been frequent litigation relating to whether particular wastes meet RCRA's statutory definition of "hazardous." A major blow to EPA's RCRA administration was struck when the D.C. Circuit vacated EPA's "mixture" and "derived-from" rules in Shell Oil Co. v. EPA, 950 F.2d 741 (1991). The ground for vacating the rules was a failure of EPA to properly allow for notice and comment, a defect that could be overcome by repeating the process with adequate procedural steps. EPA then re-enacted the rules on an interim basis until new rules could be promulgated with full notice and comment. The interim rules were also challenged in the D.C. Circuit. In response to this challenge, Congress enacted legislation stating that the interim mixture and derived-from rules "shall not be terminated or withdrawn until revisions are promulgated and become effective." Congress also set a deadline of October 4, 1994 for promulgation of the new rules. The meaning of this enactment, and the question of whether it renders the existing lawsuit moot, are currently before the D.C. Circuit. See BNA Environment Reptr. Curr. Dev. 3/11/94, 1917-1918.

•

12. When exempt household waste is incinerated, is its hazardous ash exempt too? Chicago v. EDF. The United States Supreme Court recently resolved a split between two of the nation's Circuit Courts of Appeal with regard to whether ash created by the incineration of municipal solid waste can be regulated as hazardous waste under RCRA Subtitle C. Items that would normally qualify as hazardous solid waste, such as discarded batteries, paint, garden care products, and many others, are mixed with other refuse in municipal garbage. Congress foresaw the burden municipalities would face if their entire waste streams had to be disposed of at Subtitle C facilities, and Congress therefore exempted municipal solid waste (MSW) from Subtitle C. However, when burned, as is common in trash-to-energy incinerators, the ash left after the combustion of MSW would often, depending on its characteristics, be considered a hazardous waste that required RCRA Subtitle C disposal. Perhaps displaying insufficient foresight, Congress did not specify if ash from incineration of MSW is also Subtitle C exempt. The Supreme Court held that the generation of toxic ash is not included within the activities covered by the exemption, and thus must be regulated under Subtitle C if the ash possesses the characteristics of hazardous waste. Chicago v. EDF, 114 S.Ct. 1588 (1994). Congress is considering whether to amend RCRA in order to clarify that municipal incinerator ash is to be treated as a "special waste," not a hazardous waste.

Other cases construing RCRA's definition of "hazardous waste" include American Mining Congress v. EPA, 824 F.2d 1177 (D.C. Cir., 1987)(EPA is not authorized to regulate in-process recycled materials because they are not "discarded materials"), Horsehead Resource Development Co., v. Browner, 16 F.3d 1246 (D.C. Cir., 1994)(EPA can regulate cement kiln dust and combustion residues when they are produced by boilers and industrial furnaces that burn fuel containing hazardous waste), and NRDC

Cushman, Clinton Seeks Ban on Export Of Most Hazardous Waste, New York Times, 2/28/94, p. 19.

v. Hazardous Waste Treatment Council, 1994 WL 220331 (D.C. Cir., 1994)(used oil need not be listed as a hazardous waste in all circumstances).

13.   Underground storage tank regulation.   Subtitle I of RCRA[155] establishes a comprehensive regulatory program for Underground Storage Tanks.[156] RCRA defines an UST as:

> Any one or combination of tanks (including underground pipes connected thereto) which is used to contain an accumulation of regulated substances [hazardous substances and petroleum, except for RCRA Subtitle C hazardous wastes], and the volume of which (including the volume of the underground pipes connected thereto) is 10 percent or more beneath the surface of the ground.[157]

The UST Program excludes (1) farm or home fuel tanks of less than 1,100 gallons; (2) take home heating oil tanks; (3) septic tanks; (4) pipelines regulated under other laws; (5) wastewater or stormwater collection and treatment systems; and (6) UST systems holding less than 110 gallons or *de minimis* amounts of hazardous materials.

The UST Program contains the following elements:

- Standards for design, construction, and installation of   new tanks;

- Requirements for retrofitting existing tanks with anti-corrosion, overfill prevention, and release detection systems (existing tanks must upgrade by December 1998 or close down);

- Operation, maintenance, and inspection requirements;

- Release detection, investigation, and reporting requirements;

- Corrective action obligations;

- Tank closure procedures; and

- Financial responsibility requirements.

A miniature Superfund (the Leaking Underground Storage Tank Trust Fund, financed by a tax on motor fuels) has been created to fund EPA or state cleanups of UST releases.

---

155. RCRA sections 9001 *et seq.*, 42 U.S.C.A. sections 6991 *et seq.*
156. Called the UST Program. It was originally referred to as the LUST (Leaking Underground Storage Tank) Program.
157. RCRA section 9000(1), 42 U.S.C.A. section 6991(1).

6. The "no migration" variance. RCRA authorizes variances to the land ban based on a harm-based review. In order to obtain a variance from BDAT standards, a petitioner must show "to a reasonable degree of certainty, that there will be no migration of hazardous constituents from the disposal unit or injection zone for as long as the wastes remain hazardous." EPA interprets this statutory language to mean that concentrations of hazardous constituents shall not exceed Agency-approved health-based or environmental-based levels, in any environmental medium, at the boundary of the unit or injection zone. EPA has set strict ambient standards for granting a "no migration" variance, and few variances have been granted thus far. See Proposed EPA Interpretation Of RCRA No Migration Variances, 57 FR 35940, August 11, 1992. The "no migration" variance is an interesting taxonomic device in that it places the burden of overcoming uncertainty on the applicant, who must show that the fundamental technology-based standard is unnecessary. This approach remedies one of the shortcomings of the harm-based approach — the heavy regulatory burden placed on a standard-setting agency to established harm-based standards under conditions of pervasive scientific uncertainty and political rancor (see Chapter 18 in the main volume).

Chapter 23,   Land Use-Based Environmental Control Statutes

PAGE 953   **More on "consistency" analysis**

3a. Consistency issues. The consistency clause is a feature of a number of federal natural resource management statutes, including the National Forest Management Act and the Federal Lands Policy and Management Act. See Sup.14 for a discussion of the consistency clause as a taxonomic device. Important questions to ask with regard to consistency clauses are: Who is the "consistencor" and who is the "consistencee"? Who determines consistency or inconsistency? Who has the last word? Which activities must be consistent with the plan? Is there enough specificity in the plan to allow for a rational consistency determination? What is the judicial role in reviewing a consistency finding? With regard to these issues, compare the CZMA consistency clause to those included in the Federal Lands Policy and Management Act and the National Forest Management Act (see Sup.14). Another set of consistency clauses is included in section 176(c) of the Clean Air Act Amendments of 1990 (42 U.S.C.A. sec. 7506(c). Before any federal agency supports, licenses, permits, approves, or in any way provides financial assistance for any activity, that agency must assure that such action conforms to the approved SIP (see main volume, Chapter 18). Moreover, all new transportation plans submitted for federal approval or funding must conform to the mobile source pollution cleanup elements of applicable state SIPs.

Under the CZMA, the federal agency proposing an activity directly affecting a state's coastal zone must prepare a consistency determination, which is reviewable by federal courts applying the arbitrary and capricious test. Louisiana v. Interior Department, 777 F.Supp. 486 (D.C.E.D.La. 1991).

PAGE 954   **The geographic scope of consistency analysis**

7. Interstate consistency? Does a coastal state have the right to review and object to a federally permitted activity conducted in an adjacent or upstream state? This issue has arisen through the state of North Carolina's objection to a proposal by Virginia Beach, Virginia, to withdrawn 60 million gallons of drinking water per day from the mutually shared Lake Gaston. North Carolina argues that this diversion would adversely impact Lake Gaston and the Roanoke River, which flows from Virginia through North Carolina to the Atlantic Ocean. The CZMA is silent on whether interstate consistency reviews are necessary, and both the Bush and Clinton administrations have waffled on this question, but the latest Clinton administration position is one of opposition to interstate consistency reviews such as North Carolina is seeking. Water Policy Report, May 25, 1994, 29-30.

6. When siting works. Professor Barry Rabe and his colleagues, after concluding that siting statutes have failed to site a single hazardous waste or low-level radioactive waste disposal facility in the United States, describe successful efforts to site hazardous waste disposal facilities in the Canadian provinces of Alberta and Manitoba.[158] This process stressed bottom-up (rather than top-down), voluntary, participatory, and cooperative decision-making; it was driven by "social" rather than "technical" criteria. First, a moratorium on siting proposals was accompanied by extensive public education as to the problems of hazardous waste management and the potential economic benefits for a host community. Those communities expressing interest were informed that they were free to opt out of the siting process at any time. Those that continued were encouraged to negotiate such factors as site selection and design (within broad site elimination guidelines), type of disposal technology, and impact management (mitigation, compensation, and contingency measures). It is not clear whether participating communities received grants to employ independent experts with regard to these issues. Although negotiations were conducted by local governments, a final plebiscite was held to determine community acceptance. Agreements were made with the eventual host community that committed the federal government to 1) restrict out-of-province waste imports to the new facility, 2) develop transfer and disposal facilities in other provinces, and 3) reduce the volume of wastes being generated and requiring disposal. Responding to fears that a private contractor operating the facility would be insufficiently reliable, a "crown corporation" was established to share facility management with private companies overseen by provincial regulatory authorities.

Would such a siting system — emphasizing public participation, burden sharing, and a substantial governmental role in facility management — work in the United States? Professor Rabe and his co-authors see no intrinsic reason why this process should not be transferable, but they do ask, "Are American communities likely to be receptive and willing to explore such deliberations, or are they so distrustful of any approach that conflict is inevitable"? How would you answer this question? The Clinton Administration has announced a "temporary capacity freeze" on hazardous waste incinerators until at least November 1994, pending a "national dialogue" on hazardous waste disposal. BNA Env. Reptr. Curr. Dev. 5-21-93, 131-132.

---

158. Rabe et al., NIMBY and Maybe: Conflict and Cooperation in the Siting of Low-Level Radioactive Waste Disposal Facilities in the United States and Canada, 24 Env. L. 67 (1994).

7. Does federal jurisdiction extend to isolated intra-state waters?   The
case of Hoffman Homes, Inc., v. Environmental Protection Agency, 1993
U.S. App. LEXIS 18186 (7th Cir., No. 90-3810, July 19, 1993) tested the
extent of the federal government's power to regulate wetlands under the
Commerce Clause. The tangled procedural background of this decision
should be understood in order to evaluate the decision's importance.

Hoffman Homes filled a one-acre site in Illinois without a permit under §
404 of the Clean Water Act. This site was not directly connected to any
body of water, either through surface or ground water, and lay
approximately 750 feet from the nearest surface waterbody. The Corps of
Engineers issued a cease and desist order and instructed Hoffman to
apply for an after-the-fact permit. When EPA interposed objections, the
Corps denied the permit and referred the matter to EPA.

EPA's Administrative Law Judge (ALJ) found that although the site was a
wetland, it was not subject to the CWA's permit requirements because it
was isolated from other waterbodies and because EPA had failed to show
that the site performed flood-control or sediment-trapping functions or that
it actually attracted or potentially could attract migratory birds. The ALJ
found only a "theoretical possibility" that the site would be used by
migratory birds.

EPA's Chief Judicial Officer (CJO) reversed the ALJ and levied a $50,000
penalty against Hoffman. The CJO held that EPA was only required to
"show some minimal, potential effect on interstate commerce," and that
EPA had done so by showing that a nearby wetland site (also illegally
filled by Hoffman) actually had provided habitat for migratory birds before
having been filled.

The Seventh Circuit Court of Appeals vacated the penalty, holding that
the Commerce Clause does not empower Congress to regulate isolated
wetlands (961 F.2d 1310, 1992). On rehearing, the court vacated its
opinion and order and remanded for settlement negotiations (975 F.2d
1554, 1992). These negotiations proved fruitless.

In its final determination of this matter, the Seventh Circuit agreed with
the CJO that EPA could legally regulate "waters whose connection to
interstate commerce may be potential rather than actual, minimal rather
than substantial," and that "it is reasonable to interpret ... migratory birds
to be that connection between a wetland and interstate commerce."
Nevertheless, the court upheld the ALJ and vacated the penalty because
EPA had not shown by substantial evidence that the site was suitable for
migratory bird habitat; in fact, EPA had not adduced any direct evidence
relating to that particular site. Its differences from the nearby site that did
harbor migratory birds rendered any analogy questionable. In reaching
this conclusion, the court remarked that:

> [t]he migratory birds are better judges of what is suitable for
> their welfare than are we, the ALJ or the CJO. Having avoided
> [this site] the migratory birds have thus spoken and submitted
> their own evidence. We see no need to argue with them. No
> justification whatsoever is seen from the evidence to interfere

with private ownership based on what appears to be no more than a well intentioned effort in these particular factual circumstances to expand governmental control beyond reasonable or practical limits. After April showers not every temporary wet spot necessarily becomes subject to government control.

The *Hoffman Homes* case thus ends up with a jurisdictional test—absent other connections with interstate commerce or navigable waters—focusing on whether there is substantial evidence of at least "minimal potential use" of an isolated wetland by interstate migratory waterfowl.

8. Section 404 reauthorization. The congressional reauthorization of section 404, as of summer 1994, is one of the most contentious aspects of the continuing Clean Water Act reauthorization process. Major section 404-related issues being debated in Congress are 1) exemptions for wetlands that were converted to farmland before 1972, 2) expansion of the scope of regulated activities to include draining, clearing, and excavating in wetlands and buffer areas, 3) codification of the "no net loss" of wetlands goal, 4) limitations on acceptable mitigation strategies, 5) exemptions for small non-commercial projects, 5) awards of partial compensation to any landowner whose property values decline as a result of section 404 regulation (see discussion of the "Wise Use Movement" in Sup.9), 6) categorization and prioritization of wetlands for regulatory purposes, and 7) termination of EPA's role as joint administrator of the section 404 program.

PAGE 971   **Attempts at comprehensive watershed management**

5. Watershed Management. An interesting development in regional environmental management is the recent emphasis on watershed management. Managing natural resources on a watershed basis has been attempted frequently over the past century, and its current incarnations take many forms. The watershed may not always be the optimum "problem-shed" for management purposes. Moreover, current watershed management proposals rarely confront the fundamental problem that land-use authority in the United States most often resides at the local level, whereas most environmental problems transcend municipal boundaries. It remains to be seen whether watershed management will be a misleading buzzword or a genuine innovation in land-use and natural resources management. See Goldfarb, Watershed Management: Slogan or Solution? 21 Env. Aff L. Rev. 483 (1994).

PAGE 978
Chapter 24A,[*] Environmental Justice — Race, Poverty, and the Environment

> Poor people and people of color bear the brunt of
> environmental dangers, from pesticides to air pollution to
> toxics to occupational hazards. At the same time, poor people
> and people of color also have the fewest resources to cope with
> these dangers, legally, medically or politically.[159]

Issues of environmental justice – the way race, low income, and political disenfranchisement are reflected in environmentalism – appear in a number of places in the coursebook and this Supplement. The *Poletown* case (pages 430-435) is an example, where a poor but stable mixed-race neighborhood was sacrificed in an official decisionmaking process that could avoid the merits of the controversy because of the community's relative powerlessness. The same kind of community (with an even higher ratio of people of color) was involved in the *Overton Park* fight (pages 545-557) and *Escamilla v. ASARCO* (Supplement Chapter 3), although those battles were won by the citizens. The *Tellico Dam* cases (pages 659-673) involved an Appalachian farming community and Native Americans. Some of the same issues arise in the Three-Mile Island cases (*PANE*, at pages 622-623), in the campaign to reduce airborne lead levels to protect the developmental health of urban children (pages 780-787), in *Boomer* (pages 103-116) where the cement company had selected a low-density, low-income area in which to build its polluting factory, and elsewhere. The coursebook, however, does not regularly take specific note of the income and political character of plaintiff groups, and of their racial compositions.

Yet it is increasingly clear that many environmental burdens are especially likely to be visited upon communities of color or communities marked by their low-level incomes and limited political clout. The burdens range from loss of critical urban amenities and quality of life issues to rat bites and pollution exposure effects.[160]

---

[*] For purposes of updating the coursebook without changing the basic chapter numbering scheme we are here incorporating environmental justice issues as new Chapter 24A, building upon materials prepared and circulated to teachers in 1992.

159. Taken from Luke W. Cole, Empowerment as the Key to Environmental Protection: The Need for Environmental Poverty Law, to be published by the Ecology Law Quarterly, 1992. This paper presents a thoroughly supported argument that environmental and poverty law must combine as disciplines id the systemic ills that lead to environmental racism are to be cured.

160. Among the catalogue of environmental justice settings:
• Physical taking of low-income and/or minority communities through eminent domain such as the *Poletown* and *Overton Park* cases
• The effects of pesticides on migrant workers in the California grape-growing regions

In the current discourse about environmental justice (or "environmental racism"), however, it is the field of toxic contamination that has provided the focusing images of the phenomenon.

Over the last several years, many people have begun to see a pattern in the distribution of toxic harms and the characteristics of the people who were most often exposed to them. The correlation was highlighted in Charles Lee's 1987 study "Toxic Wastes and Race in the United States," sponsored by the United Church of Christ Commission for Racial Justice. The exposure of racial minorities and low-income groups to environmental hazards appeared to be both quantitatively and qualitatively greater than that of the general public. The U.S. GAO reached tentative conclusions along the same line in its 1983 study "Siting of Hazardous Waste Landfills and Their Correlation with Racial and Economic Status of Surrounding Communities." The chart reprinted after the following case surveys some of the data that has emerged.

With increasing recognition of such patterns, there have been two major responsive reactions:

First, pointed criticisms of the established environmental groups as lily-white middle class enterprises have prompted serious soul-searching and extensive efforts to integrate more minority and low-income individuals and groups into the mainstream environmental organizations and alliances that built the successes of environmentalism in the U.S.[161]

Second, there have been serious attempts to mobilize the tools of environmental law to rectify the problems being chronicled. For some this has meant an attempt to depict race and poverty as the illegal motivators of many current discriminatory pollution management decisions. This avenue for approaching the problem tracks the Equal Protection analysis found in constitutional law. Whether because of the times, or the circumstances surrounding these attempts, this approach has not been highly successful in court. In recent months there have been attempts to mobilize Title VI of the 1964 Civil Rights Act, and administrative agency initiatives led by the Clinton Administration's EPA.

• Disproportionate environmental exportation of toxic and other wastes to Third World countries for disposal
• Discrimination against the indigenous peoples of an area, such as the HydroQuebec Power Project in James Bay, PQ.
• The physical location of hazardous-waste treatment, storage and disposal facilities
• The high frequency of heavy industry and hazardous waste facilities located in or near low-income/racial minority neighborhoods
• Accusations of racism within the environmental movement, including predominately white, middle and upper class membership in environmental organizations, hiring biases within environmental agencies and organizations, and claims that the environmental movement is a movement out of touch with the people it should be working with and for on a daily basis.
161. The "Group of Ten" that has built so much of environmental law are the Sierra Club, Sierra Club Legal Defense Fund, Friends of the Earth, Wilderness Society, National Audubon Society, Natural Resources Defense Council, Environmental Defense Fund, National Wildlife Federation, Izaak Walton League , and National; Parks and Conservation Association.

The following case is an example of one court's evaluation of the elements commonly found in environmental justice scenarios where a LULU (Locally Unwanted Land Use) is proposed for a community of low income and color, and the community's argument is cast in constitutional terms:

East Bibb Twiggs Nbhd. Assoc. v. Macon-Bibb County Planning & Zoning Comm.

United States District Court, M.D. Georgia, 1989
706 F.Supp. 880

OWENS, C.J. This case involves allegations that plaintiffs have been deprived of equal protection of the law by the Macon-Bibb County Planning & Zoning Commission ("Commission"). Specifically, plaintiffs allege that the Commission's decision to allow the creation of a private landfill in census tract No. 133.02 was motivated at least in part by considerations of race. Defendants vigorously contest that allegation. Following extensive discovery by the parties, this court conducted a non-jury trial on October 4-5, 1988. The parties were permitted to supplement the record following the conclusion of the trial. Based upon a thorough examination of the file and careful consideration of both the evidence submitted and arguments offered during the trial, the court now issues the following ruling.

On or about May 14, 1986, defendants Mullis Tree Service, Inc. and Robert Mullis ("petitioners") applied to the Commission for a conditional use to operate a non-putrescible[162] waste landfill at a site bounded at least in part by Davis and Donnan Davis Roads. The property in question is located in census tract No. 133.02, a tract containing five thousand five hundred twenty- seven (5,527) people, three thousand three hundred sixty-seven (3,367) of whom are black persons and two thousand one hundred forty-nine (2,149) of whom are white persons. The only other private landfill approved by the Commission is situated in the adjacent census tract No. 133.01, a tract having a population of one thousand three hundred sixty-nine (1,369) people, one thousand forty-five (1,045) of whom are white persons and three hundred twenty (320) of whom are black persons. That site was approved as a landfill in 1978. The proposed site for the landfill in census tract No. 133.02 is zoned A-Agricultural, and the parties are in agreement that property so zoned is eligible for the construction of and subsequent operation as a landfill of this type.

On May 27, 1986, the Commission conducted a hearing on petitioners' application for a conditional use. Evidence was presented by petitioners, and certain individuals expressed various concerns about the location of the landfill in this area. The Commission deferred the decision on petitioners' application pending input from the City of Macon and the County of Bibb regarding the location of a landfill on the proposed site.

By letters dated June 5, 1986, and June 10, 1986, respectively, the County and the City responded to invitations from the Commission to participate

---

162. Putrescible waste was described as waste such as household garbage which decomposes rapidly, thus requiring immediate cover. Non-putrescible waste was described as non-garbage waste, like wood, wood by-products, paper and corrugated products, packaging, metal goods, tires and refrigerators.

in the evaluation of the instant application and to participate in the development of a procedure by which the City and the County actively participate in the evaluation of future applications for landfills. The Bibb County Board of Commissioners, through its Chairman, Mr. Emory Green, while expressing its appreciation for and accepting the Commission's offer to participate, stated that the Commission had full authority to act on any such application and that any suggestion or recommendation offered by the County Commission would be for "informational" purposes only. The City, through Mayor George Israel, applauded the Commission's suggestion that a procedure be developed, but it had "no comment" regarding the specific project in question in that the project was located outside the Macon city limits. During this exchange of letters, the Environmental Protection Division ("EPD") of the Georgia Department of Natural Resources informed Mr. Mullis by letter dated May 30, 1986, that the proposed site was acceptable for disposal of non-putrescible waste.

The Commission reconvened on June 23, 1986, to consider petitioners' application. Petitioners were present and were represented by Mr. Charles Adams. Approximately one hundred fifty (150) individuals opposed to the landfill attended the Commission meeting. Numerous statements were made, and various opinions were offered. Included among those reasons offered in opposition to the landfill were the following: (1) threat to the residential character of the neighborhood; (2) devaluation of the residents' property; (3) danger to the ecological balance of the area; (4) concern regarding the possible expansion of the landfill into a public dump; (5) hazards to residents and children from increased truck traffic; and (6) dissatisfaction with the perceived inequitable burden borne by the East Bibb Area in terms of "unpleasant" and "undesirable" land uses.

Mr. Mullis and his representative, Mr. Adams, emphasized the need for an additional landfill and championed the free enterprise system as the appropriate developer and manager of such sites. They relied upon the reports supplied by Tribble & Richardson, Inc., an engineering concern with vast experience in examining proposed landfill sites, and upon the EPD's approval of the site. Petitioners further emphasized that the landfill would be managed pursuant to the existing regulations and under close supervision of the EPD.

After hearing the views of numerous individuals, the Commission voted to deny the application. The stated reasons were as follows: (1) the proposed landfill would be located adjacent to a predominantly residential area; (2) the increase in heavy truck traffic would increase noise in the area; and (3) the additional truck traffic was undesirable in a residential area.

Pursuant to a request from petitioners through both Tribble & Richardson and Mr. Charles Adams, the Commission voted on July 14, 1986, to rehear petitioners' application. The rehearing was conducted on July 28, 1986. Applicant Robert Mullis and his representatives addressed numerous concerns which had been previously raised by citizens opposed to the landfill and by members of the Commission. Specifically, Mr. Mullis informed those present that he had met all of the existing state, city, county and planning and zoning commission requirements for the approval of a permit to operate a landfill. He also reiterated that the site had been tested by engineers and that it had been found geologically suitable for a landfill. He explained that burning, scavenging, open dumping and disposal of hazardous wastes would be strictly prohibited, and he advised that this landfill would be regulated and inspected by the EPD. Mr. Mullis and Mr. Hodges of Tribble & Richardson pointed out that the site entrance would be selected by the EPD and that such selection would be subject to approval by the Commission. Mr. Mullis assured those present that the site would be supervised at all times. Finally, Mr. Mullis informed the Commission and the other participants that the buffer zone would be increased an additional fifty (50) feet, from one hundred (100) feet to one hundred fifty (150) feet, in those areas where the landfill site adjoined residences. Also included in the record was a letter dated July 15, 1986, in which Mr. Mullis stated that there existed only five residences contiguous to the proposed landfill site and only twenty-five houses within a one mile radius of the site.

The citizens opposing the landfill voiced doubts about the adequacy of the buffer zone and the potential health threats from vermin and insects. Concerns were expressed regarding the impact the landfill might have upon the water in the area in that many of the residents relied upon wells for their household water. Certain of the participants questioned whether the residents of this area were subject to the same considerations afforded residents in other areas of the city and county when decisions of this nature were made....

At the conclusion of the discussion, the Commission deliberated and voted.[163] The Commission approved the application subject to the following conditions: (1) approval by the county engineer; (2) approval or permits from all applicable state and federal agencies; (3) restriction on dumping of all but non-putrescible materials; and (4) review and approval by the Commission of the final site plan.

On November 10, 1986, the Commission approved the final site plan for the landfill. On November 20, 1986, the EPD issued a permit to Mullis Tree Service conditioned upon the permitee complying with the following conditions of operation:

1. No hazardous or putrescible waste shall be deposited at the landfill.

---

163. Each Commissioner articulated his or her position on the record. Each Commissioner noted the difficulty of the decision. Mr. Pippinger emphasized the forthright approach taken by petitioner and the approval given by the Environmental Protection Division for the proposed landfill. He stated that his decision to vote in favor of the application was based upon "all of the details [,] the use of the land and the facts and conclusions that I have gleamed (sic) out of this." Commissioner Ingram voted "no" on petitioners' application, citing the need for a comprehensive approach to the waste problem and the impropriety of reconsidering petitioners' application after initially denying same. Chairperson Cullinan voted in favor of petitioners' application, and he stated as follows: "We can't rule on sites until they are brought to use. This site was brought to us.... If others are brought to us in North Macon, South Macon, West Macon, we have to be as deliberative and as thoughtful and make an independent assessment there to see whether in fact the land use is adequate." The motion to approve petitioners' application carried three votes to one vote.

2. Materials placed in the landfill shall be spread in layers and compacted to the least practical volume.

3. A uniform compacted layer of clean earth cover not less than one (1) foot in depth shall be placed over all exposed waste material at least monthly or more frequently as may be determined by the division.

4. The disposal site shall be graded and drained to minimize runoff onto the landfill surface, to prevent erosion and to drain water from the surface of the landfill.

5. The landfill shall be operated in such manner as to prevent air, land, or water pollution, public health hazards or nuisances.

6. Access to the landfill shall be limited to authorized entrances which shall be closed when the site is not in operation.

7. Suitable means shall be provided to prevent and control fires. Stockpiled soil is considered to be the most satisfactory fire fighting material.

8. The Design and Operational Plan submitted by the permittee and approved by the Division for this landfill is hereby made a part of this permit and the landfill shall be operated in accordance with the plan.

9. This permit shall become null and void one year from the effective date if the permitted disposal operation has not commenced within one year from the effective date.

"To prove a claim of discrimination in violation of the Equal Protection Clause a plaintiff must show not only that the state action complained of had a disproportionate or discriminatory impact but also that the defendant acted with the intent to discriminate." United States v. Yonkers Board of Education, 837 F.2d 1181, 1216 (2nd Cir.1987); see Washington v. Davis, 426 U.S. 229 (1976); E & T Realty v. Strickland, 830 F.2d 1107 (11th Cir.1987). A plaintiff need not establish that "the challenged action rested solely on racially discriminatory purposes. Rarely can it be said that a legislature or administrative body operating under a broad mandate made a decision motivated solely by a single concern, or even that a particular purpose was the 'dominant' or 'primary' one." Village of Arlington Heights v. Metropolitan Housing Development Corp., 429 U.S. 252, 265 (1977). "Determining whether invidious discriminatory purpose was a motivating factor demands a sensitive inquiry into such circumstantial and direct evidence of intent as may be available." Considerations include the following: (1) the impact of the official action — whether it bears more heavily on one race than upon another; (2) the historical background of the decision; (3) the specific sequence of events leading up to the challenged decision; (4)[and (5)] any departures, substantive or procedural, from the normal decision-making process; and ([6]) the legislative or administrative history of the challenged decision. Id. at 266-268.

Having considered all of the evidence in light of the above-identified factors, this court is convinced that the Commission's decision to approve the conditional use in question was not motivated by the intent to discriminate against black persons. Regarding the discriminatory impact of the Commission's decision, the court observes the obvious — a decision to approve a landfill in any particular census tract impacts more heavily upon that census tract than upon any other. Since census tract No. 133.02 contains a majority black population equaling roughly sixty percent (60%) of the total population, the decision to approve the landfill in census tract No. 133.02 of necessity impacts greater upon that majority population.

However, the court notes that the only other Commission approved landfill is located within census tract No. 133.01, a census tract containing a majority white population of roughly seventy-six percent (76%) of the total population. This decision by the Commission and the existence of the landfill in a predominantly white census tract tend to undermine the development of a "clean pattern, unexplainable on grounds other than race...." Village of Arlington Heights, 429 U.S. at 266.

Plaintiffs hasten to point out that both census tracts, Nos. 133.01 and 133.02, are located within County Commission District No. 1, a district whose black residents compose roughly seventy percent (70%) of the total population. Based upon the above facts, the court finds that while the Commission's decision to approve the landfill for location in census tract No. 133.02 does of necessity impact to a somewhat larger degree upon the majority population therein, that decision fails to establish a clear pattern of racially motivated decisions.[164]

Plaintiffs contend that the Commission's decision to locate the landfill in census tract No. 133.02 must be viewed against an historical background of locating undesirable land uses in black neighborhoods. First, the above discussion regarding the two Commission approved landfills rebuts any contention that such activities are always located in direct proximity to majority black areas. Further, the court notes that the Commission did not and indeed may not actively solicit this or any other landfill application. The Commission reacts to applications from private landowners for permission to use their property in a particular manner. The Commissioners observed during the course of these proceedings the necessity for a comprehensive scheme for the management of waste and for the location of landfills. In that such a scheme has yet to be introduced, the Commission is left to consider each request on its individual merits. In such a situation, this court finds it difficult to understand plaintiffs' contentions that this Commission's decision to approve a landowner's application for a private landfill is part of any pattern to place "undesirable uses" in black neighborhoods. Second, a considerable portion of plaintiffs' evidence focused upon governmental decisions made by agencies other than the planning and zoning commission, evidence which sheds little if any light upon the alleged discriminatory intent of the Commission.

Finally, regarding the historical background of the Commission's decision, plaintiffs have submitted numerous exhibits consisting of newspaper articles reflecting various zoning decisions made by the Commission. The court has read each article, and it is unable to discern a series of official actions taken by the Commission for invidious purposes. See Village of Arlington Heights, 429 U.S. at 267. Of the more

---

164. The court further finds it clear that the Commissioner's decision to approve petitioners' application is not a "single invidiously discriminatory act" which makes the establishment of a clear pattern unnecessary. See Village of Arlington Heights, 429 U.S. at 266 n. 14.

recent articles,[165] the court notes that in many instances matters under consideration by the Commission attracted widespread attention and vocal opposition. The Commission oft times was responsive to the opposition and refused to permit the particular development under consideration, while on other occasions the Commission permitted the development to proceed in the face of opposition. Neither the articles nor the evidence presented during trial provides factual support for a determination of the underlying motivations, if any, of the Commission in making the decisions. In short, plaintiffs' evidence does not establish a background of discrimination in the Commission's decisions.

"The specific sequence of events leading up to the challenged decision also may shed some light on the decisionmaker's purpose." Village of Arlington Heights, 429 U.S. at 267, 97 S.Ct. at 564, 50 L.Ed.2d at 466. Plaintiff identifies as the key piece of evidence in this regard a statement contained in "Action Plan for Housing," a study of the status of housing in the Macon area conducted by the Macon-Bibb County Planning and Zoning Commission. The study states that "[r]acial and low income discrimination still exist in the community."[166] The study was issued in March of 1974, and it constitutes a recognition by the Commission that racial discrimination still existed in the Macon community in 1974. That recognition in no way implies that racial discrimination affected the decision-making process of the Commission itself. Rather, the statement indicates the Commission's awareness that certain individuals and/or groups in society had yet to come to grips with the concept of equality before the law. The Commission's recognition of the situation does not constitute its adoption. Indeed, such recognition probably encourages that Commission to exercise vigilance in guarding against such unprincipled influence. The statements of the various Commissioners during their deliberations indicates a real concern about both the desires of the opposing citizens and the needs of the community in general.

In terms of other specific antecedent events, plaintiffs have not produced evidence of any such events nor has the court discerned any such events from its thorough review of the record. No sudden changes in the zoning classifications have been brought to the court's attention. Plaintiffs have not produced evidence showing a relaxation or other change in the standards applicable to the granting of a conditional use. Thus, this court finds no specific antecedent events which support a determination that race was a motivating factor in the Commission's decision.

Plaintiffs contend that the Commission deviated from its "normal procedures" in several ways. First, plaintiffs point to the Commission's efforts to encourage input from the County and the City. These efforts do

---

165. Several of the articles date from the late 1950's and the early 1960's. At least one article dates from 1940, and another dates from 1950. Those articles printed in the past fifteen years or so received primary consideration by the court as more representative of the Commission's activity. However, the court read each article.

166. The court believes this evidence is more probative of the "historical background of discrimination" than it is indicative of the specific sequence of events leading up to the challenged decision. Even considered in the historical context, the statement neither admits nor indicates that such discrimination existed in the Commission itself.

not constitute evidence that "improper purposes are playing a role"[167] in the Commission's decision. The statements of the Commissioners make clear that such efforts had their genesis in the Commission's concerns about accountability to the public for certain controversial governmental decisions and about centralized planning for the area's present and future waste disposal problems....

The final factor identified in Village of Arlington Heights involves the legislative or administrative history, particularly the contemporary statements made by members of the Commission. Plaintiffs focus on the reasons offered by the Commission for the initial denial of petitioners' application, i.e., that the landfill was adjacent to a residential area and that the approval of the landfill in that area would result in increased traffic and noise, and they insist that those reasons are still valid. Thus, plaintiffs reason, some invidious racial purpose must have motivated the Commission to reconsider its decision and to approve that use which was at first denied. This court, having read the comments of the individual commissioners, cannot agree with plaintiffs' arguments.

Mr. Pippinger, who first opposed the approval of the conditional use, changed his position after examining the area in question and reviewing the data. He relied upon the EPD's approval of the site and upon his determination that the impact of the landfill on the area had been exaggerated. Mrs. Kearnes, who also inspected the site, agreed with Mr. Pippinger.

Dr. Cullinan also inspected the site. After such inspection and after hearing all of the evidence, he stated that, based "on the overriding need for us to meet our at large responsibilities to Bibb County I feel that [the site in question] is an adequate site and in my most difficult decision to date I will vote to support the resolution."

Both Dr. Cullinan and Mr. Pippinger were concerned with the problems of providing adequate buffers protecting the residential area from the landfill site and of developing an appropriate access to the site for the dumping vehicles. These concerns were in fact addressed by both the Commission and the EPD.

The voluminous transcript of the hearings before and the deliberations by the Commission portray the Commissioners as concerned citizens and effective public servants. At no time does it appear to this court that the Commission abdicated its responsibility either to the public at large, to the particular concerned citizens or to the petitioners. Rather, it appears to this court that the Commission carefully and thoughtfully addressed a serious problem and that it made a decision based upon the merits and not upon any improper racial animus.

For all the foregoing reasons, this court determines that plaintiffs have not been deprived of equal protection of the law. Judgment, therefore, shall be entered for defendants. SO ORDERED.

COMMENTARY AND QUESTIONS

1. Was the *East Bibb* court clearly wrong? Is it clear that racial or low-income discrimination was the basis of the siting decision in this case?

---

167. See Village of Arlington Heights, 429 U.S. at 267.

On one hand we do not agree with the court that the fact that the Commission does not plan its own siting choices but rather "reacts to [private] applications" disproves a discriminatory pattern. The history of environmental controversies is full of decisions that are made in a subtle interaction between private market tendencies and governmental procedures. The court also too-hastily avoids discussion of the plaintiffs' proffered proof on the "historical background" of discrimination in the area. And the court does not deal with the question of low-income discrimination, in large part because the plaintiffs' proof was largely focused on race.

But on the other hand, the facts of *East Bibb Twiggs* do not present an overwhelming case for proving invidious discriminatory intent. Plaintiffs' case would have been stronger if the disparate racial effects had been more pronounced. In R.I.S.E. v. Kay, 768 F. Supp. 1144 (E.D. Va. 1991), three prior landfills located in the contested area between 1969 and 1977 had been placed in sites where populations within a one-mile radius were between 95% and 100% black. (The population within a half-mile of the challenged site in *R.I.S.E.* was only 64% black, and the judge dismissed the discrimination claim.)

As to discrimination against low-income areas, is this likely to be conscious "classist" intent, or the logical result of a process in which economics and political circumstances dictate a choice of the cheapest, easiest solutions? The lack of litigation on the effects of toxic siting on low-income communities may show that the need to prove invidious intent in this realm is even tougher, or that it misses the point.

It may also be that discrimination is a thing of the past, that current procedures are race- and class-blind, and modern siting is not producing the disproportionate results of past procedures. Or perhaps it is increasingly tough to smoke out discriminatory intent in light of the players' increased sophistication. Determining the motivating reality of siting decisions under the *Arlington Heights* factors may require impractical psychosocial studies, or at least emphatic use of historical data, a step the *East Bibb Twiggs* court was unwilling to take.

Must legal arguments indeed be based on proof of *intent*? If so there does not seem to be much likelihood of widespread redress of existing patterns. If on the other hand courts could look to *effect itself* — not as evidence of intent but as a pejorative result on its own term — the prospects for rectification of environmental injustices would be improved.

The chart that follows is taken from the forthcoming book by Paul Mohai and Bunyan Bryant, Race and the Incidence of Environmental Hazards: A Time for Discourse, Westview Press, Boulder, CO., (1992).

TABLE 1:
Studies Providing Systematic Empirical Evidence
Regarding the Burden of Environmental Hazards
by Income and Race

Study	Hazard	Focus of of Study	Distribution Inequitable by Income	Distribution Inequitable by Race?	Income or Race More Important?
CEQ (1971)	Air Pollution	Urban areas	Yes	NA	NA*
Freeman (1972)	Air Pollution	Urban areas	Yes	Yes	Race
Harrison (1975)	Air Pollution	Urban areas	Yes	NA	NA
		Nation	No	NA	NA
Kruvant (1975)	Air Pollution	Urban area	Yes	Yes	Income
Zupan (1975)	Air Pollution	Urban area	Yes	NA	NA
Burch (1976)	Air Pollution	Urban area	Yes	No	Income
Berry, et al. (1977)	Air Pollution	Urban areas	Yes	Yes	NA
	Solid Waste	Urban areas	Yes	Yes	NA
	Noise	Urban areas	Yes	Yes	NA
	Pesticide Poisoning	Urban areas	Yes	Yes	NA
	Rat Bite Risk	Urban areas	Yes	Yes	NA
Handy (1977)	Air Pollution	Urban area	Yes	NA	NA
Asch & Seneca (1978)	Air Pollution	Urban areas	Yes	Yes	Income
Gianessi, et al. (1979)	Air Pollution	Nation	No	Yes	Race
Bullard (1983)	Solid Waste	Urban area	NA	Yes	NA
U.S. GAO (1983)	Hazardous Waste	Southern U.S.	Yes	Yes	NA
United Church of Christ (1987)	Hazardous Waste	Nation	Yes	Yes	Race
Gelobter (1988; 1992)	Air Pollution	Urban Areas	Yes	Yes	Race
		Nation	No	Yes	Race
West, et al. (1992)	Toxic Fish Consumption	State	No	Yes	Race
Mohai & Bryant (1992)	Haz. Waste	Urban area	Yes	Yes	Race

*Not applicable

2. Baseline games. As in regulatory takings, the choice of a baseline determines the scope of the examination, and has a huge impact on the determination of whether or not there is an excessive burden on a low-income or racial minority neighborhood. In making its determination of racial or low-income bias, should a court examine only the past siting decisions of the particular agency involved, or the actions of the municipal government as a whole? How far back in time should a court look — 5 years, 20 years, or 100 years? How should it define the membership boundary of the group alleging the discrimination? Which individuals should be included in a "minority" classification? Which minorities are most likely to be discriminated against, and most in need of heightened judicial scrutiny? What dollar amount defines "low-income"? What percentage of the families on a block must be below this amount for the block to be included within the class requesting heightened judicial scrutiny?

Finally, what should the baseline geographic unit be? City blocks? Neighborhoods? Census tracts? City quadrants? County lines? It seems to us that the most appropriate basis for ascertaining the degree of disparate impact upon populations is to assess demographics within a given radius distance from the challenged sites. The following chart does this in an urban setting; it is taken from the book by Paul Mohai and

Bunyan Bryant, Race and the Incidence of Environmental Hazards: A Time for Discourse, Westview Press, Boulder, CO., (1992) and was produced by the California Rural Legal Assistance Foundation's Environmental Justice Project.

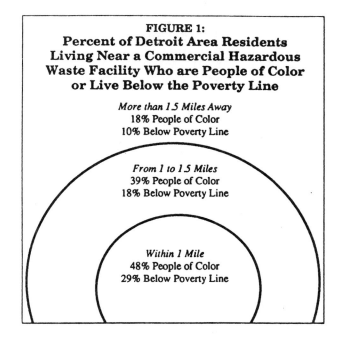

FIGURE 1:
Percent of Detroit Area Residents Living Near a Commercial Hazardous Waste Facility Who are People of Color or Live Below the Poverty Line

More than 15 Miles Away
18% People of Color
10% Below Poverty Line

From 1 to 15 Miles
39% People of Color
18% Below Poverty Line

Within 1 Mile
48% People of Color
29% Below Poverty Line

In Bean v. Southwestern Waste Management Corp., 482 F. Supp. 673 (S.D. Tex. 1979), a group of Houston residents brought suit against the Texas Department of Health (TDH) alleging that the site selection decision for two new solid waste disposal facilities was motivated in part by racial discrimination, in violation of 42 U.S.C.A. §1983. The plaintiffs attempted to show that TDH's approval of these permits was part of a longstanding pattern of racially discriminatory site selection. The court spent a good portion of its opinion comparing existing waste site locations with the demographics of both the target area and the city of Houston as a whole. The court found that almost 60% of the city -wide waste site permits were located in areas with 25% or less minority population. The court noted that although one of the two proposed target area sites was located within a 58.4% minority community, the community surrounding the other site had only a 18.4% minority population, and that such statistics did not imply any sort of systematic discrimination. Finally, the justices chose to examine city-wide waste site distribution on a "census tract" basis, rather than at the "city quadrant" level urged by the plaintiffs. This level of examination actually indicated that minority census tracts had a slightly *lower* concentration of waste sites than predominantly Anglo census tracts. In ruling against the neighborhood residents, the court acknowledged that more extensive demographic data illustrating discrimination might well have changed its ruling. In the absence of such data, however, or any evidence supporting the "supplemental factors" test suggested in *Arlington Heights*, it could find no evidence of a discriminatory pattern.

3. *Arlington Heights* and Beyond.   As mentioned in number one above, a conclusive inquiry into the subjective motivations behind a hazardous waste siting decision is inherently difficult. What weight of evidence must a plaintiff put forward to prove a defendant's motivations? The six factors of *Arlington Heights* aim to provide a measuring stick for defendant motivations, but how reliable are the factors? Does the court's seemingly circular use of the "impact" factor reveal its limitations as a measurement of motivation?   How complete must the historical background of discrimination be for the court to find a racial motivation based on this second factor?   Was the court correct in dismissing plaintiffs' evidence regarding the sequence of events because the evidence was more applicable to the "historical background" factor?   How could the court find no abnormalities in procedural due process when the Commission had initially denied the defendant's application, only to approve it four weeks later?   If the Commission was not motivated by "some invidious racial purpose" when it approved the application, are other motivations obvious?

In short, we must ask ourselves, are these six factors workable indicators of intent?   Do you agree with the court that the plaintiffs failed to meet their burden of proof under the six factors?

4. With purified siting decisions, would toxic environmental injustices still occur? In several provocative articles, Professor Vicki Been has examined the question whether the disproportionality of locally undesirable land uses (LULUs) in poor and minority communities can best be explained as a product of systematic racism and classism in the siting process, or rather as a result of the dynamics of the marketplace itself. Professor Been suggests that even in a scenario where the siting process is completely neutral, the dynamics of the market in subsequent years after a siting would tend to produce the same disproportionate conditions of toxic disposal site LULUs surrounded by poor and minority communities that we witness today. Poverty, housing discrimination, job locations, discretion exercised by those deciding whether or not to invest in a particular community, transportation and other public services — these are all factors which could, despite a fair siting process, lead communities around a toxic waste treatment site to become poorer and home to a greater percentage of minorities. Housing, for example, tends to become more affordable because property values decrease due to the presence of such facilities. Prof. Been concludes that it is not possible to determine, based on disparate impacts alone, that a siting process is flawed. The significant role that market dynamics play in distributing the burden of LULUs in poor and minority communities must also be analyzed. Been, "Locally Undesirable Land Uses in Minority Neighborhoods: Disproportionate Siting or Market Dynamics?" 103 Yale L.J. 1383 (1994).

Responses to Professor Been's theory on facility siting have questioned whether an either–or analysis is necessary. As plausible as Professor Been's suggestion about the significant role of the free market is, so too is that which identifies systematic racism or classism as important factors. As activist Dr. Robert Bullard says –

> given the political and economic climate of the time, unpopular
> polluting facilities such as hazardous waste landfills,

incinerators, garbage dumps, lead smelters, and paper mills
are likely to end up in somebody's backyard. But whose?
More often that not, polluting industries end up in communities
of color, rather that in the affluent white suburbs.... Zoning is
the chief device for regulating land use. However,
exclusionary zoning practices have provided benefits for
whites at the expense e of people of color....

Environmental and health risks are not randomly distributed
throughout the population. On close examination of the costs
and benefits derived from unpopular environmental decisions,
communities of color have borne and continue to bear a
disproportionate share of the burden of the nation's pollution
problems.... [R]ace continues to be a potent predictor of where
people live, which communities get dumped on, and which are
spared.

Some institutional arrangements between government and
industry have placed communities of color at greater risk than
the general population. For example, one unanticipated result
of more stringent federal environmental regulations has been
the increased vulnerability of communities of color to the siting
of unpopular industrial facilities such as municipal landfills,
toxic waste dumps, lead smelters, and incinerators. Robert
Bullard, Confronting Environmental Racism: Voices from the
Grassroots, 10-11 (1993).

The two perspectives do not necessarily contradict one another. It seems
likely that analysis of the causes of environmental injustices, and the
solutions for it, will have to take account of both skewing in the siting
processes and subsequent marketplace dynamics in response to siting

5. Beyond toxic sites and civil rights laws. The problem of toxic waste
siting was the first issue to give focus to environmental justice, and civil
rights theories have provided the initial basis for legal actions in the field.
The environmental problems faced by communities of color and low
income, however, as noted at the beginning of this Chapter of the
Supplement, extend far beyond toxics. The remedies of environmental
law, moreover, have always been characterized by the widest possible
range of theories deployable to achieve a rational environmental
accounting.

Thus it is not surprising that a second generation of environmental justice
cases is beginning, as attorneys target other environmental burdens faced
by these communities, using new theories of legal redress.

A case in point was recently filed in Washington , D.C. by the Sierra Club
Legal Defense Fund, Friends of the Earth, and American Rivers against
the Federal Highway Administration's plans to build a bridge and arterial
highways through the middle of a poor black community in the eastern
part of the city, disrupting the life of the community and the River corridor,
which has been the focus of a community-based cleanup project.
Because of these disruptions and the potential release of contaminated
river sediments and air pollutants, the lawsuit has been filed under NEPA,
the Clean Air Act, §4f of the Transportation Act, and other statutes.

Anacostia Watershed Society, et al. v. Pena, et al., Civ. No. 94-1051 (HHG) D.D.C. 1994. In addition plaintiffs are successfully enlisting administrative agency attention to their claims, at least within EPA, owing to the Clinton Administration's Executive Order on Environmental Justice and a recent special sensitivity within EPA, as noted in the next Comment.

In other settings, air pollution issues look as if they may open a second major front in environmental justice law. See Mank, What Comes after Technology: Using an "Exceptions Process" to Improve Residual Risk Regulation of Hazardous Air Pollutants, 13 Stanford Envtl Law J. 263 (1994).

6. A national political issue; executive branch policy. If existing judicial remedies do not seem likely to respond to the emerging data on disproportionate environmental exposures based on race and poverty, that will not end the debate. The issues of environmental justice continue to be media-accessible and to attract public attention. Some observers are calling for new legislative initiatives, or, more ambitiously, for the addition of anti-discrimination provisions to the various currently proposed environmental amendments to the U.S. Constitution. In recognition of the volatility of these issues, the Bush Administration's EPA produced a study, Environmental Equity (1992), that attempted to address them in federal policy, and concluded after a brief survey that there was no major problem. Environmental critics labeled this report mere public relations.

The Clinton Administration issued a substantial Executive Order, E.O. 12898 (1994, **see Appendix 3** of this Supplement) calling upon all federal agencies to integrate a concern and active consideration of environmental justice issues in their administration of federal laws. Subsequently the EPA under Carol Browner's direction has substantially increased its programmatic attention to the issue, and the Civil Rights Commission has opened investigations of state siting laws accused of disproportionate impacts.

Title VI of the 1964 Civil Rights Act was long thought not to offer serious remedies for the kinds of problems involved in environmental justice. Since 1993, however, the EPA's Office of Civil Rights has reversed that position, and opened investigatory files on twelve major cases alleging violations of Title VI. Title VI of the 1964 federal Civil Rights Act, 42 U.S.C.A. §2000d, reads—

> No person in the United States shall, on the ground of race, color, or national origin, be excluded from participation in, be denied the benefits of, or be subjected to discrimination under any program or activity receiving Federal financial assistance.

In three cases, the Clinton EPA has decided to begin formal enforcement proceedings under Title VI and its attendant regulations. **See Appendix 3.**

The seriousness with which EPA and other agencies seem to be taking the issue and the Executive Order may well change the balance of power in environmental cases previously proceeding only under difficult constitutional theories, as in *East Bibb*.

7. Bibliography, Appendix 4, and an Internet bulletin board. Because the environmental justice field is so recently developed as a field of active academic and litigative effort, a bibliography may be particularly helpful in providing a starting point for students interested in exploring the field. There is an extended environmental justice bibliography in Appendix 4.

An excellent periodical resource on issues of environmental justice is "Race, Poverty & the Environment," a quarterly newsletter published by the California Rural Legal Assistance Foundation and the Earth Island Institute Urban Habitat Program. For more information, write to RPE, c/o Earth Island, 300 Broadway, Suite 28, San Francisco, CA, 94133.

A group of environmental law professors has begun to organize an academic environmental justice network to coordinate and cooperate in the further development of the field. As part of this environmental justice network, a national on-line electronic bulletin board, based at the Boston College Law School's Internet Gopher, is scheduled to begin its trial run period in September 1994. The Internet service will be staffed by the school's Black American Law Students Association, by the Conservation Research Group, its environmental law society, and by Alternatives for Community and Environment, the environmental justice institute based at Boston College Law School. The network can be reached at —

lordca@bcvms.bc.edu.

A Role Playing Assignment: Race, Poverty and the Environment

Environmental Dispute Resolution (EDR) and Race, Poverty, & Environment / Environmental Justice role-playing assignment

ASSIGNMENT:
• Coursebook pages 954-959,
• This Chapter 24A — (focus on the *East Bibb Twiggs* case's *facts* rather than the law of the case)
• SKIM: Coursebook pages 980-996 (Chapter 24) — (skim for concepts and process in ADR, especially the Hudson River negotiation example)
• Read the following Simulation Prospectus and Hypothetical, *Mullis Toxics*

SIMULATION PROSPECTUS AND HYPOTHETICAL CASE

The negotiation simulation is based on the facts of *East Bibb Twiggs*, modified to emphasize toxics (see below).
1. The negotiation will go on for ____**[90 minutes]**____.
2. You will first each introduce yourselves, stating your role assignment identity and your most desired outcome.
3. You as a group may then want to summarize/stipulate the factual and procedural position of this controversy as it exists under the laws and conditions in your jurisdiction, so as to have a basis for subsequent discussion.
4. Facts: In each case you should presume that all of you have been invited (by public notice to all interested parties, issued by a local official) to meet on this day to see if a negotiated community decision can be reached on "MTS's" toxic landfill siting application.
Note: for this exercise, assume that it deals with an application by Mullis *Toxics* Service (not, as in reality, Mullis*Tree* Service) to locate a low-level

toxics solid waste disposal facility in East Bibb. MTS (**owns**)(**holds an option to buy**) the parcel of land proposed for the dump site.

The official agencies have undertaken extensive reviews of the MTS application. The time of this negotiation is (**before**)(**after**) the official decisional entity has decided to approve the application.

5. You should assume that all official players at a higher level than local government (perhaps excepting EPA) strongly prefer, all things being equal, locating the facility where MTS wants it.

6. In order to succeed, a negotiation must achieve the consensus agreement of all involved parties about what should be done, except that one citizen may remain off the wagon.

7. Operate in good faith, given your role, in attempting to resolve the controversy successfully.

8. Be realistic.

9. Use the facts of *East Bibb Twiggs*, adapted as directly as possible to your situation, as you stipulate them initially with your panel.

10. It can be realistically predicted that any possible court challenge would be messy and time consuming but (like the actual decision in *East Bibb Twiggs*) very unlikely to find an unconstitutional motivation under the *Arlington Heights* tests.

MULLIS TOXICS

Toxic Hypothetical Situation based on
East Bibb Twiggs Neighborhood Assn. v. Macon-Bibb County Planning &
Zoning Commission
706 F. Supp. 880 (M.D. Georgia 1989)

Assume that:

1.) On May 14, 1986, the **Mullis Toxics Service** ("Mullis") applied to the Macon-Bibb County Planning and Zoning Commission ("the Commission") for a conditional use permit to operate a toxic waste landfill in Macon, Georgia. Mullis sought to build the landfill in a census tract where 3,367 black residents and 2,149 white residents lived. On June 23, 1986, the Commission convened to consider Mullis's application. Approximately 150 opponents of the Mullis plan attended the meeting. The Commission denied Mullis's application. The stated reasons were as follows: (1) the proposed landfill would be located adjacent to a predominantly residential area; (2) the increase in heavy truck traffic would increase noise in the area; (3 the additional truck traffic was undesirable in a residential area; and (4) the possible toxic contamination was an uncertain and troubling public risk.

2.) In July, 1986, the Commission convened to reconsider Mullis's application. Mullis addressed numerous concerns which had been previously raised by citizens opposed to the landfill and by members of the Commission. Mullis informed those present that he had met all of the existing state, city, county and planning and zoning commission requirements for the approval of a permit to operate a landfill. Mullis assured those present that the site would be supervised at all times. He also informed the Commission and the citizens that the buffer zone would be increased an additional 50 feet, from 100 feet to 150 feet, in those areas where the landfill site adjoined residences. As to the toxic risk, he emphasized that the landfill would be held to federal RCRA compliance, and thus would be safe. After substantial deliberation, the Commission approved Mullis's application subject to four conditions: (1) approval by the county engineer; (2) approval by applicable state and federal agencies; (3) restrictions on dumping of the most highly volatile and toxic materials; and (4) Commission approval of a final site. In November, 1986, the Commission granted final approval for Mullis's conditional use permit.

3.) In *East Bibb Twiggs*, the plaintiffs, residents of Macon-Bibb County, challenged the county Planning and Zoning Commission's decision to permit the creation of a private landfill in a census tract in which sixty percent of the residents were black. The court admitted that the landfill would affect black citizens to a "somewhat larger degree" than whites in the predominantly black census tract. The court noted that the only other Commission-approved landfill was located in a predominantly white census tract and stated that this landfill placement undermined the "development of a 'clear pattern, unexplainable on grounds other than race.'" The court was not persuaded by the plaintiffs' contention that both census tracts were located within a County Commission District composed of roughly seventy percent blacks.

Chapter 24B,   Alternative Dispute Resolution

Page 985   Map of the Hudson River settlement negotiatons

The following map shows the major points of controversy and bargaining that were on the negotiating table in the case study reported in the coursebook at 984 and following:

MAP OF THE SITES OF CONTROVERSY ON THE HUDSON

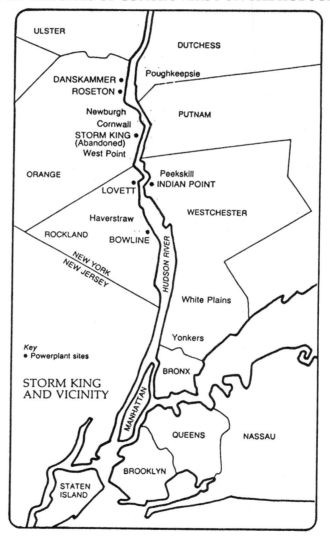

Chapter 25,   International Environmental Law

International environmental law is a huge and growing area. For further exploration of the field consult International Environmental Law and World Order: a Problem-Oriented Coursebook, by L. Guruswamy, G. Palmer, and B. Weston (West Publishing Company, 1994). For staying abreast of issues, we recommend BNA's International Environment Daily Reporter on-line service.

PAGE 1023   **"Extraterritoriality": domestic law with international effects – the *Antarctica* case, and *Lujan v. Defenders* excerpt**

The National Environmental Policy Act's §102 includes the following provision:

> §102(2). Congress authorizes and directs that, to the fullest extent possible...all agencies of the Federal Government shall—...
>
> (F) recognize the worldwide and long-range character of environmental problems and, where consistent with the foreign policy of the United States, lend appropriate support to initiatives, resolutions, and programs designed to maximize international cooperation in anticipating and preventing a decline in the quality of mankind's world environment.

This seems to imply that NEPA has a scope of action broader than the territory of the U.S. The overwhelming tendency of courts, however, has been to restrict U.S. laws to U.S. territory.

As noted in the NEPA chapter at 653, and at page 1023, there have been longstanding arguments that NEPA and other federal laws should be applicable to situations where persons and entities – especially federal agencies – make decisions while under the jurisdiction of the U.S. that have destructive consequences overseas. An example would be where a federal agency is, for instance, helping to build potentially destructive dams in Sri Lanka, as in *Lujan II* in the administrative standing materials. Extraterritorial impacts of the domestic laws of an environmentally-sophisticated nation like the U.S. could result in beneficial leverage upon international environmental conditions. On the other hand, critics argue that U.S. courts should stay at home and out of other sovereigns' business.

The following case is perhaps a dramatic step in the direction of extraterritorial leverage — although the court denies it — while the excerpt that follows it, from Justice Stevens' concurrence in *Lujan* (Chapter 11 of this Supplement) does not seem to encourage general theories of extraterritoriality.

Environmental Defense Fund v. Massey
United States Court of Appeals for the District of Columbia Circuit, 1993
986 F.2d 528

[EDF appealed the district court's order dismissing, for lack of subject matter jurisdiction, its action seeking declaratory and injunctive relief under NEPA for acts by the National Science Foundation at its bases in Antarctica. The district court, following the Supreme Court's decision in EEOC v. Arabian American Oil Co., 111 S. Ct. 1227 (1991)("Aramco"), had found that Congress had not given a clear expression of legislative intent in NEPA that the statute should apply extraterritorially, so it didn't.]

MIKVA, Chief Judge. We reverse the district court's decision, and hold that the presumption against the extraterritorial application of statutes described in *Aramco* does not apply where the conduct regulated by the statute occurs primarily, if not exclusively, in the United States, and the alleged extraterritorial effect of the statute will be felt in Antarctica—a continent without a sovereign, and an area over which the United States has a great measure of legislative control.

We therefore remand to the district court for a determination of whether NSF actually failed to comply with Section 102(2)(C) of NEPA, [by failing to prepare an EIS before proceeding with plans to incinerate waste at its McMurdo Station research facility in Antarctica] as EDF alleges in its complaint.

I. As both parties readily acknowledge, Antarctica is not only a unique continent, but somewhat of an international anomaly. Antarctica is the only continent on earth which has never been, and is not now, subject to the sovereign rule of any nation. Since entry into force of the Antarctic Treaty in 1961, the United States and 39 other nations have agreed not to assert any territorial claims to the continent or to establish rights of sovereignty there. Hence, Antarctica is generally considered to be a "global common" and frequently analogized to outer space.

...Following the passage of NEPA, NSF promulgated regulations applying the EIS requirement to its decisions regarding proposed actions in Antarctica. Since the issuance of Executive Order 12144, however, NSF has contended that proposed action affecting the environment in Antarctica is governed by the Executive Order, not NEPA. Executive Order 12144 declares that federal agencies are required to prepare environmental analyses for "major Federal actions significantly affecting the environment of the global commons outside the jurisdiction of any nation (e.g., the oceans or Antarctica)" [but explicitly denies a cause of action to plaintiffs seeking agency compliance]. ...Thus, what is at stake in this litigation is whether a federal agency may decide to take actions significantly affecting the human environment in Antarctica without complying with NEPA and without being subject to judicial review.

II. A. The Presumption Against Extraterritoriality

[The court discusses the general presumption against the extraterritorial application of statutes, which provides that "rules of the United States statutory law, whether prescribed by federal or state authority, apply only to conduct occurring within, or having effect within, the territory of the United States." The Supreme Court in *Aramco* stated that the doctrine's purpose is "to protect against unintended clashes between our laws and those of other nations which could result in international discord." The presumption against extraterritoriality does not apply in three categories of cases: 1) where there is "an affirmative intention of Congress clearly expressed" to apply the statute to conduct within other sovereign nations; 2) where failure to extend the statute extraterritorially will result in adverse effects within the US (e.g. Sherman Anti-Trust Act or Lanham Trade-mark Act); and 3) where the conduct occurs within the US (even if effects of regulation are felt beyond US borders).]

Despite these well-established exceptions to the presumption against extraterritoriality, the district court below by-passed the threshold question of whether the application of NEPA to agency actions in Antarctica presents an extraterritoriality problem at all. In particular, the court failed to determine whether the statute seeks to regulate conduct in the United States or in another sovereign country. It also declined to consider whether NEPA would create a potential for "clashes between our laws and those of other nations" if it was applied to the decisionmaking of federal agencies regarding proposed actions in Antarctica. After a thorough review of these relevant factors, we conclude that this case does not present an issue of extraterritoriality.

II. B. Regulated Conduct Under NEPA

[The court discusses NEPA's §102(2)(C) requirement that Federal agencies prepare an EIS for major Federal actions which have the potential to significantly affect the human environment, noting that NEPA does not proscribe action in foreign jurisdictions, but only ensures that environmental effects are included in agency decisionmaking.] ... Because the decisionmaking processes of federal agencies take place almost exclusively in this country and involve the workings of the United States government, they are uniquely domestic. ... Moreover, NEPA would never require enforcement in a foreign forum or involve "choice of law" dilemmas. This factor alone is powerful evidence of the statute's domestic nature....

In sum, since NEPA is designed to regulate conduct occurring within the territory of the United States, and imposes no substantive requirements which could be interpreted to govern conduct abroad, the presumption against extraterritoriality does not apply to this case.

II. C. The Unique Status of Antarctica

Antarctica's unique status in the international arena further supports our conclusion that this case does not implicate the presumption against extraterritoriality. ... Where the U.S. has some real measure of legislative control over the region at issue, the presumption against extraterritoriality is much weaker... and where there is no potential for conflict "between our laws and those of other nations," the purpose behind the presumption is eviscerated, and the presumption against extraterritoriality applies with significantly less force. ...

This Court...[has previously] conclude[d]...that the presumption against extraterritoriality should not apply ...[because] Antarctica is not a "country" at all, as it has no sovereign, and ... "to the extent that there is any assertion of governmental authority in Antarctica, it appears to be predominately that of the United States." ...The United States controls all air transportation to Antarctica and conducts all search and rescue operations there [and] has exclusive legislative control over ... research installations established there by the United States Antarctica Program. This legislative control, taken together with the status of Antarctica as a sovereignless continent, compels the conclusion that the presumption against extraterritoriality is particularly inappropriate under the circumstances presented in this case. As stated aptly by a State Department official in congressional testimony shortly following the enactment of NEPA, application of [NEPA] to actions occurring outside the jurisdiction of any State, including the United States, would not conflict with the primary purpose underlying this venerable rule of interpretation — to avoid ill-will and conflict between nations arising out of one nation's encroachments upon another's sovereignty.... There are at least three general areas: The high seas, outer space, and Antarctica.

... Thus, in a sovereignless region like Antarctica, where the United States has exercised a great measure of legislative control, the presumption against extraterritoriality has little relevance and a dubious basis for its application.

II. D. Foreign Policy Considerations

Although NSF concedes that NEPA only seeks to regulate the decisionmaking process of federal agencies, and that this case does not present a conflict between U.S. and foreign sovereign law, NSF still contends that the presumption against extraterritoriality controls this case. In particular, NSF argues that the EIS requirement will interfere with U.S. efforts to work cooperatively with other nations toward solutions to environmental problems in Antarctica. In NSF's view, joint research and cooperative environmental assessment would be "placed at risk of NEPA injunctions, making the U.S. a doubtful partner for future international cooperation in Antarctica."

...We are not convinced that NSF's ability to cooperate with other nations in Antarctica in accordance with U.S. foreign policy will be hampered by NEPA injunctions. ...[Case precedents] illustrate that the government may avoid the EIS requirement where U.S. foreign policy interests outweigh the benefits derived from preparing an EIS. Since NEPA imposes no substantive requirements, U.S. foreign policy interests in Antarctica will rarely be threatened, except perhaps where the time required to prepare an EIS would itself threaten international cooperation. Thus, contrary to NSF's assertions, where U.S. foreign policy interests outweigh the benefits of the EIS requirement, NSF's efforts to cooperate with foreign governments regarding environmental practices in Antarctica will not be frustrated by forced compliance with NEPA.

II. E. NEPA's Plain Language and Interpretation

NSF's final argument is that even if the presumption against extraterritoriality does not apply to this case, the plain language of Section 102(2)(C) precludes its application to NSF's decisionmaking regarding proposed agency action in Antarctica. We read the plain language differently.

Section 102(2)(C), on its face, is clearly not limited to actions of federal agencies that have significant environmental effects within U.S. borders. This Court has repeatedly taken note of the sweeping scope of NEPA and the EIS requirement. Far from employing limiting language, Section 2 states that NEPA is intended to "encourage productive and enjoyable harmony between man and his environment" as well as to "promote efforts which will prevent or eliminate damage to the environment and biosphere." Clearly, Congress painted with a far greater brush than NSF is willing to apply. ...

Section 102(2)(F) further supports the conclusion that Congress, when enacting NEPA, was concerned with worldwide as well as domestic problems facing the environment (federal agencies required to "recognize the worldwide and long-range character of environmental problems"). NSF acknowledges that Section 102(2)(F) clearly addresses international environmental problems, but argues that this section announces Congress' only requirement for agencies pursuing action in the international arena.

We find nothing in the statute which supports the construction of Section 102 urged by NSF. Apparently, NSF has chosen to ignore the clear interrelationship between the Section 102 subsections and the Section 102 mandate as a whole. Section 102 lists several requirements under NEPA for "all Federal agencies." Compliance with one of the subsections can hardly be construed to relieve the agency from its duty to fulfill the obligations articulated in other subsections. ...

We also note, that prior to the issuance of Executive Order 12144, the Council on Environment Quality ("CEQ") maintained that NEPA applies to the decisionmaking process of federal agencies regarding actions in Antarctica....

CONCLUSION

Applying the presumption against extraterritoriality here would result in a federal agency being allowed to undertake actions significantly affecting the human environment in Antarctica, an area over which the United States has substantial interest and authority, without ever being held accountable for its failure to comply with the decisionmaking procedures instituted by Congress—even though such accountability, if it was enforced, would result in no conflict with foreign law or threat to foreign policy. NSF has provided no support for its proposition that conduct occurring within the United States is rendered exempt from otherwise applicable statutes merely because the effects of its compliance would be felt in the global commons. We therefore reverse the district court's decision, and remand for a determination of whether the environmental analyses performed by NSF, prior to its decision to resume incineration, failed to comply with Section 102(2)(C) of NEPA.

We find it important to note, however, that we do not decide today how NEPA might apply to actions in a case involving an actual foreign sovereign or how other U.S. statutes might apply to Antarctica. We only hold that the alleged failure of NSF to comply with NEPA before resuming incineration in Antarctica does not implicate the presumption against extraterritoriality. Reversed and remanded.

COMMENTARY AND QUESTIONS

1. Beyond Antarctica? Note that this decision holds that the presumption against extraterritorial application of statutes does not apply because: [1] "the conduct [the administrative agency decision] regulated by the statute occurs primarily if not exclusively, in the United States, [2] the alleged extraterritorial effect of the statute would be felt in...[in a place] without a sovereign, and [3] it will be felt in an area over which the United States has a great measure of legislative control. If all three of these criteria are necessary in order to imply extraterritorial effect for a statute that does not clearly assert it, won't the rule of this case be limited to federal agency actions which play themselves out on the high seas or at the other Pole, or in outer space?

On the other hand, considering the way the court argues the *Aramco* holding, couldn't the presumption against extraterritorial effect be equally well circumvented by arguments under elements (1) and/or (3)? Thus where a statute is held to regulate operative decisions made within the United States, the presumption could be circumvented without regard to the other two questions? Or, a narrower argument would be that element (1) could be applied against Federal agencies, if not against private corporations making decisions within the United States. In *Aramco*, one of the main reasons the Supreme Court refused to apply the federal statute was the vast scope of petitioners' argument, "advancing a construction of [the statute] that would logically result in the statute's application to foreign as well as American employers..."

Especially where a statute is procedural, like NEPA, moreover, U.S. regulation of agency decisionmaking procedures is far less likely to create a contradiction with the laws of a foreign nation. This is doubly true in cases where statutes are being applied to regulate federal agencies that are *spending U.S. funds* in a foreign country rather than directly regulating conduct. It would seem less controversial to put strings on spending projects of, for example, U.S.A.I.D., the federal Agency for International Development.

The panel that decided this case, Mikva, Wald, and Edwards, may be notable for its alleged "liberal" cast, but represents a great deal of expertise in administrative law and statutory construction. Although the court goes out of its way to limit the scope of its assertions, the scope of the distinctions it draws between this NEPA case and *Aramco* may well lead to extended application of federal statutes to federal agency actions overseas.

Manuel Lujan, Jr., Secretary of the Interior, v. Defenders of Wildlife
United States Supreme Court, 1992
112 S.Ct. 2130

[The case turned on a denial of standing, as presented and discussed earlier, in Chapter 11 of this Supplement.]

JUSTICE STEVENS, concurring... Because I am not persuaded that Congress intended the consultation requirement in §7(a)(2) of the Endangered Species Act of 1973 (ESA), 16 U.S.C.A. §1536(a)(2), to apply to activities in foreign countries, I concur in the judgment of reversal....

I am persuaded that the Government is correct in its submission that §7(a)(2) does not apply to activities in foreign countries. As with all questions of statutory construction, the question whether a statute applies extraterritorially is one of congressional intent. Foley Bros., Inc. v. Filardo, 336 U.S. 281, 284-285 (1949). We normally assume that

"Congress is primarily concerned with domestic conditions," and therefore presume that " 'legislation of Congress, unless a contrary intent appears, is meant to apply only within the territorial jurisdiction of the United States.' " EEOC v. Arabian American Oil Co., 499 U.S.__, 111 S.Ct. 1227 (1991) (quoting *Foley Bros.*, 336 U.S., at 285).

Section 7(a)(2) provides, in relevant part: "Each Federal agency shall, in consultation with and with the assistance of the Secretary [of the Interior or Commerce, as appropriate, insure that any action authorized, funded, or carried out by such agency (hereinafter in this section referred to as an 'agency action') is not likely to jeopardize the continued existence of any endangered species or threatened species or result in the destruction or adverse modification of habitat of such species which is determined by the Secretary, after consultation as appropriate with affected States, to be critical, unless such agency has been granted an exemption for such action by the Committee pursuant to subsection (h) of this section...." 16 U.S.C.A. §1536(a)(2).

Nothing in this text indicates that the section applies in foreign countries. Indeed, the only geographic reference in the section is in the "critical habitat" clause, which mentions "affected States." The Secretary of the Interior and the Secretary of Commerce have consistently taken the position that they need not designate critical habitat in foreign countries.... Consequently, neither Secretary interprets §7(a)(2) to require federal agencies to engage in consultations to insure that their actions in foreign countries will not adversely affect the critical habitat of endangered or threatened species.

That interpretation is sound, and, in fact, the Court of Appeals did not question it. There is, moreover, no indication that Congress intended to give a different geographic scope to the two clauses in §7(a)(2). To the contrary, Congress recognized that one of the "major causes" of extinction of endangered species is the "destruction of natural habitat." S.Rep. No. 93-307, p. 2 (1973); see also, H.Rep. No. 93-412, p. 2 (1973); TVA v. Hill, 437 U.S. 153, 179(1978). It would thus be illogical to conclude that Congress required federal agencies to avoid jeopardy to endangered species abroad, but not destruction of critical habitat abroad.

The lack of an express indication that the consultation requirement applies extraterritorially is particularly significant because other sections of the ESA expressly deal with the problem of protecting endangered species abroad. Section 8, for example, authorizes the President to provide assistance to "any foreign country (with its consent) ... in the development and management of programs in that country which [are] ... necessary or useful for the conservation of any endangered species or threatened species listed by the Secretary pursuant to section 1533 of this title." 16 U.S.C.A. §1537(a). It also directs the Secretary of Interior, "through the Secretary of State," to "encourage" foreign countries to conserve fish and wildlife and to enter into bilateral or multilateral agreements. §1537(b). Section 9 makes it unlawful to import endangered species into (or export them from) the United States or to otherwise traffic in endangered species "in interstate or foreign commerce." §1538(a)(1)(A), (E), (F). Congress thus obviously thought about endangered species abroad and devised specific sections of the ESA to protect them. In this context, the absence of any explicit statement that the consultation requirement is applicable to agency actions in foreign countries suggests that Congress did not intend that §7(a)(2) apply extraterritorially.

Finally, the general purpose of the ESA does not evince a congressional intent that the consultation requirement be applicable to federal agency actions abroad. The congressional findings explaining the need for the ESA emphasize that "various species of fish, wildlife, and plants in the United States have been rendered extinct as a consequence of economic growth and development untempered by adequate concern and conservation," and that these species "are of aesthetic, ecological, educational, historical, recreational, and scientific value to the Nation and its people." §1531(1), (3). The lack of similar findings about the harm caused by development in other countries suggests that Congress was primarily concerned with balancing development and conservation goals in this country.

In short, a reading of the entire statute persuades me that Congress did not intend the consultation requirement in §7(a)(2) to apply to activities in foreign countries. Accordingly, notwithstanding my disagreement with the Court's disposition of the standing question, I concur in its judgment.

COMMENTARY AND QUESTIONS

1. **Reading Justice Stevens, and *Foley*: broad or narrow?** A restrictive reading of Justice Steven's opinion would focus on his narrow statutory interpretation of the Endangered Species Act, in which he concludes that Congress did not want the Act to apply overseas.

But what of the broader argument, that even if a statute is written so as to be applicable to actions overseas, courts should presume that Congress never wants to have the terms of its laws applied outside the national territory unless it specifically says so in a "clear statement." This is the way many courts interpret the so-called *Foley* rule.

Foley, however, involved application of a U.S. labor law (the Eight Hour Workday law) to a private contracting company working for U.S. funded construction projects in Iran and Iraq, not to the actions of a federal agency itself. Just as the policy of that labor law did not seem very relevant or appropriate to Iran or Iraq, the language of the statute gave no indication that Congress was thinking of anything but the U.S. labor market. The *Foley* court, moreover, did not apply an anti-extraterritorial presumption. Rather it did a careful job of statutory interpretation and concluded that Congress had not intended the law to apply overseas.[168]

Environmental circumstances and statutes tend to be different from *Foley* on both counts, applying in relevant situations involving federal agencies, usually with statutory language that is geographically expansive. It is well understood by all today that environmental conditions do not respect borders. As a result, especially in cases where requiring federal agencies acting overseas to obey U.S. law would not create active conflicts with the foreign state's laws, it is possible that the "clear statement" rule will be less applicable in international environmental cases, instead leaving *Foley* as, at most, a weak rebuttable presumption.

---

168. See Justice Marshall's dissenting opinion in *Aramco*, 111 S.Ct. at 1236.

PAGE 1024   Environmentalism and free trade

Joining the GATT controversies noted in the coursebook, the North American Free Trade Agreement (NAFTA) has again raised sweeping questions about the relationship between the environment and free trade. In the debates over the adoption of NAFTA a primary issue has been whether the economic incentives and energies incorporated in NAFTA would inevitably undermine environmental protection — particularly in Mexico, but by competitive effect in Canada and the United States as well. For a skeptical environmentalist's view, see Note, "Is This Land Really Our Land? – Impacts of Free Trade Agreements on U.S. Environmental Protection, 23 Envt'l. L. 635 (1993)). For a typically upbeat view of the "win-win" scenario for economic health and enhanced environmental protection, see "U.S. Trade Representative Sees No 'Downward Harmonization' under NAFTA," 15 International Environmental Reporter [Current Reports] 448-449 (July 1, 1992).

Canada and Mexico assented to side agreements on environmental protection to facilitate the approval of NAFTA by Congress. The provisions guaranteeing enforcement of the various environmental statutes of the three participant nations are critically important. Picking up on one of the major themes of the coursebook, it is notable that the Canadian agreement makes specific reference to enforcement in the federal courts of Canada, recognizing citizen initiative as a way of circumventing governmental hesitancy. The Mexican situation is more problematic, as the Mexican government strongly opposes judicial remedies for alleged violations of environmental statutes, and the gap between Mexican statutes on the books and their enforcement on the ground continues to be a very serious problem. Environmentalists predictably will be wrestling the political process in Washington trying to assure that the parties' theoretical assent to environmental protection does not ignore the practical requirements of achieving environmental protection.

An interesting article probing the technical requirements of a harmonization of different nations' legal standards – both product standards and process standards – reports the discussions of a Conference on Trade and the Environment in Pacific Rim Nations: Bousquet and Berlin, "Environment and Trade: The Question of Standards," 12 Environmental Law Newsletter of the ABA Standing Committee on Envt'l Law No. 2 at 1 (Spr.- Summer '93).

PAGES 1030-31   **UNCED, the United Nations Conference on Environment and Development – the Rio Earth Summit**

> Progress in many fields, too little progress in most fields, and no progress at all in some fields.... We will be held accountable...We are heading toward a crisis of uncontrollable dimensions unless we change course.
> —*Norwegian Prime Minister Gro Harlem Bruntland*

The United Nations Conference on Environment and Development took place in Rio de Janeiro, Brazil from June 3rd to June 14th, 1992. It took years of preparation, attracted worldwide attention, and generated controversy, hope, and a tremendous amount of paperwork 178 countries participated in the conference, which was also attended by 140 heads of state, the largest gathering of national chiefs of state in the history of the world. The Earth Summit produced five international law documents for signature by the official delegates:[169]

• **The Rio Declaration on Environment and Development**, U.N. Doc. A/CONF. 151/5, reprinted in 31 I.L.M. 874, 877 (1992)– A statement of 27 principles underlying the "Earth Summit," which was approved by all of the nations attending UNCED. It reaffirms the 1972 Stockholm Declaration on Human Environment, and proclaims the goal of UNCED to be the establishment of "a new and equitable global partnership." Principle 1 declares that "Human beings are at the center of concerns for sustainable development. They are entitled to a healthy and productive life in harmony with nature." The Declaration goes on to affirm "the right to development," and states that "eradicating poverty" is an "indispensable requirement for sustainable development." It goes on to encourage elimination of "unsustainable patterns of production and consumption," "right-to-know" provisions, and the development of environmental laws. It stresses the importance of internalizing the environmental costs of production, and concludes with a call for the "further development of international law in the field of sustainable development."

• **Convention on Biological Diversity**, June 5, 1992, reprinted in 31 I.L.M. 818 (1992) – This convention aims to lower the rate of global plant and animal extinction by establishing national conservation management systems. It also seeks to establish international standards for the biotechnology industry, including rules governing the commercial use of genetic resources. Under the terms of the convention, nations with natural resources valued by the biotechnology industry have an interest in both the direct sale of the natural resource, *and* in any patent or royalty arising from biotechnology derived from that resource. The accord between Merck Pharmaceutical and the government of Costa Rica is often used as an example. Signatories also agree to establish ecosystem inventories,

---

169. This text draws in part upon Nick Yost's "Rio and the Road Beyond," 11 Envt'l L.Q. (ABA, 1992). For further brief descriptions of these documents, see generally Edith Brown Weiss, Introductory Note, 31 I.L.M. 814-17 (1992).
The best recent update to orient the reader to Rio is the Winter 1993 Issue of 4 Colorado Journal of International Environmental Law and Policy, a symposium beginning with an overview essay by David Getches, "The Challenge of Rio," 4 Colo. J. Internat'l Envt'l. L, & Policy 1 (1993). Some participants in the symposium are bullish on what happened at Rio, others not. The whole symposium is interesting reading. See also Geoffrey Palmer, "The Earth Summit: what went wrong at Rio?," 70 Wash. U. L.Q.1005 (1992); Gardner, Richard N. Negotiating Survival: four priorities after Rio. New York: Council on Foreign Relations Press, 1992; and Rogers, Adam. The Earth Summit: a planetary reckoning. Los Angeles, Global View Press, 1993. An interesting symposium on environmental rights and international peace comprises the Summer 1992 issue of Volume 52 of the Tennessee Law Review, including an article by Professor Lee Breckenridge, "Protection of Biological and Cultural Diversity: Emerging Recognition of Local Community Rights and Ecosystems under International Environmental Law, 59 Tenn. L. Rev. 735 (1992).

and to develop national strategies and programs to implement the principles of the Biodiversity Convention. It was signed by 153 nations. The only delegation refusing to sign was that of the United States, citing concerns over "financing and protection of intellectual property rights." Thirty nations must ratify this convention for it to become a part of international law.

• **The Framework Convention on Climate Change**, U.N. Doc. A/AC. 237/18, reprinted in 31 I.L.M. 849 (1992) – Anthropogenic emission of greenhouse gases is the focus of this framework convention, specifically; how to stabilize global emissions of carbon dioxide, methane and chlorofluorocarbons while achieving "sustainable social and economic growth." Article 3 sets forth the principles that should guide this endeavor, urging the parties to "protect the climate system for the benefit of present and future generations," and to "take precautionary measures to anticipate, prevent or minimize...climate change." Article 4 outlines the commitments of the signatories, including the sponsorship and exchange of research findings, and the development of national programs designed to mitigate climate change. References to specific timetables and precise emission levels were deleted in order to gain the endorsement of the U.S. delegation. All attending nations signed this convention. It must be ratified by fifty nations to become international law.

• **Non-legally Binding Authoritative Statement of Principles for a Global Consensus of the Management, Conservation and Sustainable Development of all Types of Forests**, U.N. Doc. A/CONF. 151/6, reprinted in 31 I.L.M. 881 (1992) – This statement sets worldwide standards for good forestry practices, stressing the importance of "sustainable use" in developing management regimes. It also addresses the financial and ecological relationships between timber-importing and timber-exporting countries. It urges that total global forest cover be increased, but puts no special emphasis on old growth forests. Though it was finished during UNCED, the final wording is considerably weaker than the original version, a result of pronounced disagreements in point of view between "developed" and "developing" nations. The developed nations persisted in characterizing tropical forests as the world's "carbon sinks" or "carbon sponges," while the developing nations who control these forests saw them as sovereign national resources, to be dealt with as they saw fit. From this "Southern" perspective, the "Northern" countries were trying to buy the "right to pollute"; first generating the vast majority of the world's anthropogenic greenhouse gases, and then telling the South not to cut its forests so as to help soak up the excess carbon dioxide the Northern lifestyle required. This convention could lead to a binding treaty, but at this writing, no arrangements have been made to begin this process.

• **Agenda 21**, U.N. Doc. A/CONF. 15 1/4, reprinted in AGENDA 21 & The UNCED PROCEEDINGS 47-1057 (Nicholas A. Robinson ed. 1992) – This is an 800-page, 120-chapter guide to the implementation of the Conventions on Climate Change and Biodiversity, and of the "sustainable development" principles contained within the Rio Declaration. It is designed to serve as the foundation for international environmental law and cooperation into the next century. It addresses everything from marine pollution to desertification to population dynamics to patterns of consumption. There are chapters on management of resources, the roles of "subgroups" (women, children, indigenous peoples, NGO's, etc.) within the environmental context, the development of a body of environmental laws within existing legal systems, and the actual "Means of Implementation" required to achieve these goals. Agenda 21 creates a permanent United Nations Commission on Sustainable Development, which will oversee compliance with the provisions of the Conventions on Climate Change and Biodiversity by their signatories. It also establishes a Global Environmental Facility to work with the World Bank on coordinating aid transfer from richer to poorer countries, calls for increased levels of aid from richer countries, and suggests that a Convention on Desertification be held to address this growing environmental challenge.[170]

The Rio Declaration on Environment and Development

adopted June 14, 1992, at the final session of the
U.N. Conference on Environment and Development

The United Nations Conference on Environment and Development, Having met at Rio de Janeiro from 3 to 14 June 1992, Reaffirming the Declaration of the United Nations Conference on the Human Environment, adopted at Stockholm on 16 June 1972, and seeking to build upon it, With the goal of establishing a new and equitable global partnership through the creation of new levels of cooperation among States, key sectors of societies and people, Working towards international agreements which respect the interests of all and protect the integrity of the global environmental and developmental system, Recognizing the integral and interdependent nature of the Earth, our home, Proclaims that:

PRINCIPLE 1 Human beings are at the center of concerns for sustainable development. They are entitled to a healthy and productive life in harmony with nature.

PRINCIPLE 2 States have, in accordance with the Charter of the United Nations and the principles of international law, the sovereign right to exploit their own resources pursuant to their own environmental and developmental policies, and the responsibility to ensure that activities within their jurisdiction or control do not cause damage to the environment of other States or of areas beyond the limits of national jurisdiction.

PRINCIPLE 3 The right to development must be fulfilled so as to equitably meet developmental and environmental needs of present and future generations.

PRINCIPLE 4 In order to achieve sustainable development, environmental protection shall constitute an integral part of the development process and cannot be considered in isolation from it.

---

170. For copies of these documents, as well as other information on the UNCED Conference, sustainable development and international environmental law, the following organizations should prove helpful:
United Nations Publications Sales American Bar Association
2 United Nations Plaza 1800 M Street, NW, S-200
Room DC2-853 Dept. 416 Washington, D.C. 20036
New York, NY 10017
(Tel) (212) 963-8302 or (800) 253-9646

PRINCIPLE 5 All States and all people shall cooperate in the essential task of eradicating poverty as an indispensable requirement for sustainable development, in order to decrease the disparities in standards of living and better meet the needs of the majority of the people of the world.

PRINCIPLE 6 The special situation and needs of developing countries, particularly the least developed and those most environmentally vulnerable, shall be given special priority. International actions in the field of environment and development should also address the interests and needs of all countries.

PRINCIPLE 7 States shall cooperate in a spirit of global partnership to conserve, protect and restore the health and integrity of the Earth's ecosystem. In view of the different contributions to global environmental degradation, States have common but differentiated responsibilities. The developed countries acknowledge the responsibility that they bear in the international pursuit of sustainable development in view of the pressures their societies place on the global environment and the technologies and financial resources they command.

PRINCIPLE 8 To achieve sustainable development and a higher quality of life for all people, States should reduce and eliminate unsustainable patterns of production and consumption and promote appropriate demographic policies.

PRINCIPLE 9 States should cooperate to strengthen endogenous capacity-building for sustainable development by improving scientific understanding through exchanges of scientific and technological knowledge, and by enhancing the development, adaptation, diffusion and transfer of technologies, including new and innovative technologies.

PRINCIPLE 10 Environmental issues are best handled with the participation of all concerned citizens, at the relevant level. At the national level, each individual shall have appropriate access to information concerning the environment that is held by public authorities, including information on hazardous materials and activities in their communities, and the opportunity to participate in decision-making processes. States shall facilitate and encourage public awareness and participation by making information widely available. Effective access to judicial and administrative proceedings, including redress and remedy, shall be provided.

PRINCIPLE 11 States shall enact effective environmental legislation. Environmental standards, management objective and priorities should reflect the environmental and developmental context to which they apply. Standards applied by some countries may be inappropriate and of unwarranted economic and social cost to other countries, in particular developing countries.

PRINCIPLE 12 States should cooperate to promote a supportive and open international economic system that would lead to economic growth and sustainable development in all countries, to better address the problems of environmental degradation. Trade policy measures for environmental purposes should not constitute a means of arbitrary or unjustifiable discrimination or a disguised restriction on international trade. Unilateral actions to deal with environmental challenges outside the jurisdiction of the importing country should be avoided. Environmental measures addressing transboundary or global environmental problems should, as far as possible, be based on an international consensus.

PRINCIPLE 13 States shall develop national law regarding liability and compensation for the victims of pollution and other environmental damage. States shall also cooperate in an expeditious and more determined manner to develop further international law regarding liability and compensation for adverse effects of environmental damage caused by activities within their jurisdiction or control to areas beyond their jurisdiction.

PRINCIPLE 14 States should effectively cooperate to discourage or prevent the relocation and transfer to other States of any activities and substances that cause severe environmental degradation or are found to be harmful to human health.

PRINCIPLE 15 In order to protect the environment, the precautionary approach shall be widely applied by States according to their capabilities. Where there are threats of serious or irreversible damage, lack of full scientific certainty shall not be used as a reason for postponing cost-effective measures to prevent environmental degradation.

PRINCIPLE 16 National authorities should endeavor to promote the internalization of environmental costs and the use of economic instruments, taking into account the approach that the polluter should, in principle, bear the cost of pollution, with due regard to the public interest and without distorting international trade and investment.

PRINCIPLE 17 Environmental impact assessment, as a national instrument, shall be undertaken for proposed activities that are likely to have a significant adverse impact on the environment and are subject to a decision of a competent national authority.

PRINCIPLE 18 States shall immediately notify other States of any natural disasters or other emergencies that are likely to produce sudden harmful effects on the environment of those States. Every effort shall be made by the international community to help States so afflicted.

PRINCIPLE 19 States shall provide prior and timely notification and relevant information to potentially affected States on activities that may have a significant adverse transboundary environmental effect and shall consult with those States at an early stage and in good faith.

PRINCIPLE 20 Women have a vital role in environmental management and development. Their full participation is therefore essential to achieve sustainable development.

PRINCIPLE 21 The creativity, ideals and courage of the youth of the world should be mobilized to forge a global partnership in order to achieve sustainable development and ensure a better future for all.

PRINCIPLE 22 Indigenous people and their communities, and other local communities, have a vital role in environmental management and development because of their knowledge and traditional practices. States should recognize and duly support their identity, culture and interests and enable their effective participation in the achievement of sustainable development.

PRINCIPLE 23 The environment and natural resources of people under oppression, domination and occupation shall be protected.

PRINCIPLE 24 Warfare is inherently destructive of sustainable development. States shall therefore respect international law providing protection for the environment in times of armed conflict and cooperate in its further development, as necessary.

PRINCIPLE 25 Peace, development and environmental protection are interdependent and indivisible.

PRINCIPLE 26 States shall resolve all their environmental disputes peacefully and by appropriate means in accordance with the Charter of the United Nations.

PRINCIPLE 27 States and people shall cooperate in good faith and in a spirit of partnership in the fulfillment of the principles embodied in this Declaration and in the further development of international law in the field of sustainable development.

COMMENTARY AND QUESTIONS

1. The Rio Declaration.   Reviewing the terms of the Rio Declaration, which were agreed to by more than 140 countries at Rio but of course are not enforceable, do you note its vagueness and counter-balanced modifier clauses. Is such a document worth negotiating for its aspirational and hortatory effect, like the Universal Declaration of Human Rights?

Agenda 21

[AN OUTLINE OF TOPIC HEADINGS]

Because Agenda 21 is a massive multi-volume document, we here provide just an index of its chapters to give a sense of the approach and depth of the Agenda. Each of the chapters sets out detailed prescriptions for future action. Although like the Rio Declaration Agenda 21 is not enforceable, its specificity and expert foundation appears to many to give it potential force in the future management of global environmental conditions.

CHAPTER
  1. Preamble
SECTION I: SOCIAL AND ECONOMIC DIMENSIONS
  2.   International cooperation to accelerate sustainable development in developing countries and related domestic policies
  3.   Combating poverty
  4.   Changing consumption patterns
  5.   Demographic dynamics and sustainability
  6.   Protecting and promoting human health conditions
  7.   Promoting sustainable human settlement development

8.   Integrating environment and development in decision-making

SECTION II: CONSERVATION AND MANAGEMENT OF RESOURCES FOR DEVELOPMENT

9.   Protection of the atmosphere

10.   Integrated approach to the planning and management of land resources

11.   Combating deforestation

12.   Managing fragile ecosystems: combating desertification and drought

13.   Managing fragile ecosystems: sustainable mountain development

14.   Promoting sustainable agriculture and rural development

15.   Conservation of biological diversity

16.   Environmentally sound management of biotechnology

17.   Protection of the oceans, all kinds of seas, including enclosed and semi-enclosed seas, and coastal areas and the protection, rational use and development of their living resources

18.   Protection of the quality and supply of freshwater resources: application of integrated approaches to the development, management and use of water resources

19.   Environmentally sound management of toxic chemicals, including prevention of illegal international traffic in toxic and dangerous products

20.   Environmentally sound management of hazardous wastes, including prevention of illegal international traffic in hazardous wastes

21.   Environmentally sound management of solid wastes and sewage-related issues

22.   Safe and environmentally sound management of radioactive wastes

SECTION III: STRENGTHENING THE ROLE OF MAJOR GROUPS

23.   Preamble

24.   Global action for women towards sustainable and equitable development

25.   Children and youth in sustainable development

26.   Recognizing and strengthening the role of indigenous people and their communities

27   Strengthening the role of non-governmental organizations: partners for sustainable development

28.   Local authorities' initiatives in support of Agenda 21

29.   Strengthening the role of workers and their trade unions

30.   Strengthening the role of business and industry

31.   Scientific and technological community

32.   Strengthening the role of farmers
      SECTION IV: MEANS OF IMPLEMENTATION
33.   Financial resources and mechanisms
34.   [Environmentally sound technology: transfer, cooperation
      and capacity-building]
35.   Science for sustainable development
36.   Promoting education, public awareness and training
37.   National mechanisms and international cooperation for
      capacity-building in developing countries
38.   International institutional arrangements
39.   International legal instruments and mechanisms
40.   Information for decision-making

COMMENTARY AND QUESTIONS

1. Agenda 21 after Rio.[171] Since the adoption of Agenda 21, much debate
has arisen over the adequacy of the signatory nations' follow-up and
implementation of this blueprint for sustainable development.

Although 178 nations agreed to enact Agenda 21, the progress which has
been made has left some members of the international community
disheartened.[172] To oversee the implementation of Agenda 21, the United
Nations set up the Commission on Sustainable Development (CSD), a 53-
member group charged with monitoring each nation's progress in
implementing the Agenda. On this CSD the industrialized countries have
19 representatives, Africa and Asia each have 12, and Latin America has
10. In a recent address to the Commission on Sustainable Development,
Ambassador Ramtane Lamamra, Algeria's Representative to the U.N. said

> Nearly two years after the Rio Summit, the assessment of the
> implementation of Agenda 21 is, overall, rather disappointing,
> in spite of some limited achievements. The solemn
> commitments which were undertaken have since undergone a
> process of erosion; the Rio spirit itself seems to be fading. One
> of the elements which is indicative of these trends, and which
> deserves the attention of this Commission is the decline of the
> interest of major groups to the process. Another critical area
> for the follow-up to Agenda 21 is the issue of the transfer of
> environmentally-sound technologies, trade and consumption
> patterns and capacity-building. Earth Times, 5/17/94, page 8.

Integration of Agenda 21 into every aspect of society has proved to be a
complex undertaking. National governments remain the dominant actors
in the integration process. How and to what degree they choose to
implement Agenda 21 will ultimately determine the impact of the Earth
Summit.

---

171. Researched and drafted by Renita Ford, BCLS '96.
172   NRDC, "Keeping the Promises of the Earth Summit" A country by country
progress report one year after Rio (NRDC, eds., 1993 at ix,2.)

> Effective execution of Agenda 21 will require a profound reorientation of all human society, unlike anything the world has ever experienced–a major shift in the priorities of both governments and an unprecedented redeployment of human and financial resources. this shift will demand that a concern for the environmental consequences of every human action be integrated into individual and collective decision-making at every level. David Sitarz, "Understanding Agenda 21" in Agenda 21: The Earth Summit Strategy to Save Our Planet (Earthpress) at 1.

Lacking the ability to enforce the implementation of Agenda 21, the Commission will rely on publicity and international pressure to achieve its goal. A global commission that lacks the power of enforcement may seem powerless to encourage effective implementation of Agenda 21, but there is hope.

> It is said that the momentum of Rio is being dissipated. [Speaking at the opening session of the CSD] Nitin Desai, United Nations Undersecretary General for Policy Coordination and Sustainable Development, said that despite these problems, there has been "significant progress" on the international level.

> He mentioned work being done on the desertification convention, on the issue of straddling fish stocks and on the small islands. But he conceded that progress is not being made on the national level, adding that only one-third of member states have set up bodies to coordinate action on sustainable development issues. Earth Times, 5/17/94 at 3.

NEGOTIATING STRATEGIES OF THE NORTH AND SOUTH.

The South's negotiating strategy takes into account its interest in principles, standards, institutional and financial mechanisms, technology and compliance.

Through international institutions the nations of the South attempt to exert political pressure on industrial nations to uphold the commitments made at Rio to provide aid for maintaining higher environmental standards in developing countries. The aid would allow for cleaner technologies and the expansion of the World Bank known as the Global Environmental Facility (GEF). There was also a promise to double the annual share of aid from industrial countries to 7/10 of one percent of the industrial world's economic output. (NYTimes, Nov. 30, 1993).

There are two issues that define the South's approach to negotiations about its responsibilities in integrating environmental norms into development policies and practices. The first is a sort of pollution buffer:

> **Ensuring that the South has adequate environmental space for its future development.**

> Adequate environmental space is the space necessary to pollute in order to develop. The South feels that given the kind of technology they use for development, the developing countries will have to "pollute" to some extent in order to develop. Furthermore, if anyone has to put a curb on

development, it should be the North and not the South because
it has yet to develop and needs to grow. The basis for this idea
is that, in order to reverse the current state of deterioration of
the global environment, the world will have to take certain
drastic environmental protection measures. These measures
will include, for example, curbing emissions, evolving new
technologies and technological processes, and effecting
changes in lifestyles. These will require adjustments in global
production and consumption patterns and will involve low
costs. The South's primary concern [is] how the burden of
adjustment could be shared in a manner that would not
compromise its ability to alleviate the miserable economic and
social conditions of the developing countries. Believing,
perhaps correctly, that the North may not be willing to alter its
consumption patterns and mode of production because of the
economic implications to its people, the Group concluded that
if the burden of adjustment is to be shared in an equitable
manner, it is imperative that the developing countries claim "a
right" to adequate environmental space and strive for the
recognition of this right by the international community. Chris
Mensah, "The role of the Developing Countries" in The
Environment After Rio: International Law and Economics
(1994) at 38.

The second strategy is a shift of economic development elements from
North to South:

**Modify global relations in such a way that the South obtains
the required resources, technology, and access to markets
which would enable it to pursue a development process that is
both environmentally sound and rapid enough to meet the
needs and aspirations of its growing population.**

This objective links environment to development and calls for
equity within current international economic relations. The
premise for this issue is that the South can only achieve
environmentally sound protection development and lifestyle
through the attainment of economic growth and development.
Economic growth and development for the South is impossible,
given the serious resource constraints they are facing, and
also the current state of international economic relations,
namely, external debt, low commodity prices, cost of
technology for development and rising poverty. Any solution
to the environmental problem will have to begin by bridging the
current gap dictated by the current terms of trade between the
South and the North. "The role of the Developing Countries"
in The Environment After Rio: International Law and
Economics, at 39.

The North has also developed its own strategy for international
environmental negotiations. The European Community, in particular,
recently strengthened its program known as the 5th Environmental Action
Programme to encompass an eight -step program that enforces the key
issues of Agenda 21:

[T]he new program will mark a change of direction by defining
a comprehensive strategy intended to provide a clear sense of

purpose for future community action in the environmental field until the end of the present decade.

The Programme stresses that the achievement of long-term sustainability will require in some instances profound changes in consumption and production patterns and in lifestyles, with the aim of reducing wasteful practices and ensuring sustainable use of natural resources.

The U.S. on the other hand has not been as successful in implementing steps to uphold ing its part of the bargain in international environmental responsibility. After failing to take the lead in environmental negotiations at the Earth Summit, a commission known as the President's Commission on Sustainable Development was formed. The commission produced the following principles on sustainable development. The production of such vague and non-descript principles has been criticized by various members of the international community....

Principles of Sustainable Development (U.S.):

1. We must preserve and, where possible, restore the integrity of natural systems — soils, water, air, and biological diversity — which sustain both economic prosperity and life itself.

2. Economic growth, environmental protection, and social equity should be interdependent, mutually reinforcing national goals, and policies to achieve these should be integrated.

3. Along with appropriate protective measures, market strategies should be used to harness private energies and capital to protect and improve the environment.

4. Population must be stabilized at a level consistent with the capacity of the earth to support its inhabitants.

5. Protection of natural systems requires changed patterns of consumption consistent with a steady improvement in the efficiency with which society uses natural resources.

6. Progress toward the elimination of poverty is essential for economic progress, equity, and environmental quality.

7. All segments of society should equitably share environmental benefits and burdens.

8. All economic and environmental decision-making should consider the well-being of future generations, and preserve for them the widest possible range of choices.

9. Where public health may be adversely affected, or environmental damage may be serious or irreversible, prudent action is required even in the face of scientific uncertainty.

10.   Sustainable development requires fundamental changes in the conduct of government, private institutions, and individuals.

11.   Environmental and economic concerns are central to our national and global security.

12.   Sustainable development is best attained in a society in which free institutions flourish.

13.   Decisions affecting sustainable development should be open and permit informed participation by affected and interested parties, that requires a knowledgeable public, a free flow of information, and fair and equitable opportunities for review and redress.

14.   Advances in science and technology are beneficial, increasing both our understanding and range of choices about how man and the environment relate. We must seek constant improvements in both science and technology in order to achieve eco-efficiency, protect and restore natural systems and change consumption patterns.

15.   Sustainability in the United States is closely tied to global sustainability. Our policies for trade, economic development, aid, and environmental protection must be considered in the context of the international implications of these policies.

COMMENTARY AND QUESTIONS

1. Do these Principles accomplish anything? The carefully drafted language of these Principles, which undoubtedly reflect many hours of intergovernmental committee work, as well as the efforts of one of the national governments best positioned to make an attempt to implement the Rio policies, reflects all of the shortcomings of international environmental programatic reform. What will come of them?

2. Weighing the Earth Summit. The debate on what was accomplished at Rio continues. The international agreements reached there contained "brackets" by which countries softened their commitments, or provided loopholes from strict requirements, a traditional minuet in international lawmaking chronicled in Chapter 25 of the coursebook. Institutionally it will be interesting to see what happens in the U.N. Commission on Sustainable Development in carrying on the Rio mandate, and what comes of attempts to set up an "Environmental Enforcement Commission" to implement principles of international law emerging from past and future agreements on environmental protection.

Appendices...

Appendix 1, **Federal Environmental Statutes over 100+ Years**

Appendix 2, **Environmental On-Line Electronic Resources, and Periodical-Looseleaf Services**

Appendix 3, **Federal Environmental Justice Materials**

Appendix 4, **An Environmental Justice Bibliograpy**

Appendix 5, **EPA Chart: Distribution of Highway Salt through the Environment**

Appendix 1,   Federal Environmental Statutes over 100+ Years

For students who want to get an overview of the statutory field, and a sense of the legal history of federal environmental legislation, here is a chronological compilation of some representative federal acts over the past century, many of which are still with us in original or amended form.

1877

Dangerous Cargo Act (See 46 U.S.C.A. §2106), as amended

1891

Forest Reserve Act (general), Mar. 3 (16 U.S.C.A. §§471 et seq.; 26 Stat. 1103), as amended

1899

Refuse Act of 1899, Mar. 3 (33 U.S.C.A. §§407, 30 Stat. 1152)

1900

Lacey Act, May 25 (16 U.S.C.A. §§667e, 701; 31 Stat. 187; see also 18 U.S.C.A. §§42-44), as amended

1902

False Branding or Marking Act, Jul. 1 (21 U.S.C.A. §16-17; 32 Stat. 632)

1906

Federal Meat Inspection Act, Dec. 15 (19 U.S.C.A. §§1306 et seq.; 81 Stat. 584), as amended

Heyburn Act (Pure Food and Drugs), Jun. 30 (34 Stat. 768)

1910

Pickett Act of 1910, Jun. 25 (43 U.S.C.A. §§141-143; 36 Stat. 847)

1916

National Park Service Organic Act, Aug. 25 (16 U.S.C.A. §1-4, 22, 43; 39 Stat. 535), as amended

1918

Migratory Bird Treaty Act, Jul. 3 (16 U.S.C.A. §§703-711; 40 Stat. 755), as amended

1920

Mineral Leasing Act of 1920, Feb. 25 (30 U.S.C.A. §§22 et seq.; 41 Stat. 437), as amended

1924

Oil Pollution Act, Jun. 7 (33 U.S.C.A. §§431-437; 43 Stat. 604), as amended

1926

Black Bass Act, May 20 (16 U.S.C.A. §§851-852; 44 Stat. 576), as amended

1929

Migratory Bird Conservation Act, Feb. 18 (16 U.S.C.A. §§715-715r; 45 Stat. 1222), as amended

1931

Animal Damage Control Act, Mar. 2 (7 U.S.C.A. §426-426b; 46 Stat. 1468), as amended

1934

Fish and Wildlife Coordination Act, Mar. 10 (16 U.S.C.A. §§661-666c; 48 Stat. 401), as amended

Taylor Grazing Act, June 28 (43 U.S.C.A. § 315, 48 Stat. 1269), as amended

1935

Historic Sites, Buildings and Antiquities Act, Aug. 21 (16 U.S.C.A. §§461-467; 49 Stat. 666), as amended

Soil Conservation and Domestic Allotment Act of 1935, Apr. 27 (16 U.S.C.A. §§590a-590i, 590j-590q; 49 Stat. 163), as amended

1936

Game Management Supply Depots Act of June 24, 1936 (16 U.S.C.A. §667; 49 Stat. 1913)

1937

Flood Control Act of 1937, Aug. 28 (33 U.S.C.A. §§701b et seq.; 50 Stat. 877), as amended

Wildlife Restoration Act, Sep. 2 (16 U.S.C.A. §§669-669i; 50 Stat. 917), as amended

1938

Federal Food, Drug and Cosmetic Act [FDA], Jun. 25 (21 U.S.C.A. §§301-392; 52 Stat. 1040), as amended

Flood Control Act of 1938, Jun. 28 (33 U.S.C.A. §§701b et. seq.; 52 Stat. 1215-1226), as amended

1939

Federal Advisory Committee Act, 5 U.S.C.A. App. I

1940

Bald Eagle Protection Act, Jun. 8 (16 U.S.C.A. §§668-668d; 54 Stat. 250), as amended

1941

Flood Control Act of 1941, Aug. 18 (33 U.S.C.A. §§642a et seq.; 55 Stat. 638), as amended

1943

Columbia Basin Projects Act, Mar. 10 (16 U.S.C.A. §§835-835c5; 57 Stat. 14), as amended

1944

Flood Control Act of 1944, Dec. 22 (16 U.S.C.A. §§460d, 825s et seq.; 58 Stat. 887), as amended

1946

Administrative Procedure Act (judicial review provisions) [APA], Jun. 11 (5 U.S.C.A. §§551-559 et seq.; 60 Stat. 237), as amended

Atomic Energy Act of 1946 [AEA], Aug 1 (42 U.S.C.A. §§2011-2282; 60 Stat. 755), as amended

1947

Federal Insecticide, Fungicide and Rodenticide Act [FIFRA], Jun. 25 (7 U.S.C.A. §§135-135k; 61 Stat. 163), as amended

Mineral Leasing Act for Acquired Lands, Aug. 7 (30 U.S.C.A. §§351-359; 61 Stat. 913), as amended

1948

Federal Water Pollution Control Act, Jun. 30 (62 Stat. 1155; See 33 U.S.C.A. §§ 1251-1376), as amended

Refuge Trespass Act, Jun. 25 (18 U.S.C.A. §41; 62 Stat. 686)

1950

Fish Restoration and Management Projects Act, Aug. 9 (16 U.S.C.A. §§777-777k; 64 Stat. 430), as amended

Northwest Atlantic Fisheries Act of 1950, Sep. 27 (16 U.S.C.A. §§981-991; 64 Stat. 1067), as amended

1953

Outer Continental Shelf Lands Act, Aug. 7 (43 U.S.C.A. §§1331-1343; 67 Stat. 462; see also 10 U.S.C.A. §§7421-7426, 7428-7438), as amended

Submerged Lands Act, May 22 (43 U.S.C.A. §§1301-1315; 67 Stat. 29; see also 10 U.S.C.A. §§7421-7426, 7428-7438), as amended

1954

Atomic Energy Act of 1946 Amendments, Aug. 13 (68 Stat. 715)

Watershed Protection and Flood Prevention Act, Aug. 4 (16 U.S.C.A. §§1001-1007, 33 U.S.C.A. §701b; 68 Stat. 666), as amended

1955

Clean Air Act [CAA], Jul. 14 (42 U.S.C.A. §§7401-7642; 69 Stat. 322), as amended

1956

Colorado River Storage Project Act, Apr. 11 (43 U.S.C.A. §§620-620o, except certain sections classified to the Colorado River Basin Project Act; 70 Stat. 105), as amended

Fish and Wildlife Act of 1956, Aug. 8 (15 U.S.C.A. §§713c3 note-713c3; 70 Stat. 1119), as amended

Great Lakes Fishery Act of 1956, Jun. 4 (16 U.S.C.A. §§931-939c; 70 Stat. 242), as amended

Small Reclamation Projects Act of 1956, Aug. 6 (43 U.S.C.A. §§422a-422k; 70 Stat. 1044), as amended

Waterfowl Depredations Prevention Act, Ju;. 3 (7 U.S.C.A. §§442-445; 70 Stat. 492), as amended

1957

Poultry Products Inspection Act, Aug. 28 (21 U.S.C.A. §§451-469; Pub. L. 85-172; 71 Stat. 441), as amended

1958

Federal-Aid Highway Act of 1958, Apr. 16 (23 U.S.C.A. §§101 et seq.; Pub. L. 85-381; 72 Stat. 89), as amended

Federal Aviation Act of 1958, Aug. 23 (14 U.S.C.A. §§81 et seq.; Pub. L. 85-726; 72 Stat. 731), as amended

Fish-Rice Rotation Farming Program Act of March 15, 1958 (16 U.S.C.A. §§778-778c; Pub. L. 85-342,§1; 72 Stat. 35)

1960

Federal Hazardous Substances Act, Jul. 12 (15 U.S.C.A. §§1261-1273; Pub. L. 86-613; 74 Stat. 372), as amended

Mineral Leasing Act Revision of 1960, Sep. 2 (30 U.S.C.A. §§181 et seq.; Pub. L. 86-705; 74 Stat. 781)

Multiple-Use Sustained-Yield Act of 1960, Jun. 12 (16 U.S.C.A. §§528-531; Pub. L. 86-517; 74 Stat. 215), as amended

National Historic Preservation Act, Oct. 15 (16 U.S.C.A. §§470-470w6), as amended

Sikes Act (military reservation), Sep. 15 (16 U.S.C.A. §§670a-670o; Pub. L. 86-797,§§1-5; 74 Stat. 1052-1053), as amended

1961

Federal Water Pollution Control Act Amendments of 1961, Jul. 20 (See 33 U.S.C.A. §1151 et seq.; Pub. L. 87-88; 75 Stat. 204)

Oil Pollution Act, Aug. 30 (33 U.S.C.A. 1001-1015; Pub. L. 87-167; 75 Stat. 402), as amended

Wetlands Loan Act, Oct. 4 (16 U.S.C.A. §§715k3-715k5; Pub. L. 87-383; 75 Stat. 813), as amended

1962

Refuge Recreation Act, Sep. 28 (16 U.S.C.A. §§460k-460k4; Pub. L. 87-714; 76 Stat. 653), as amended

1963

Recreation Coordination and Development Act of May 28, 1963 (16 U.S.C.A. 4601; Pub. L. 88-29; 77 Stat. 49)

1964

Federal Transit Act, Jul. 9 (49 U.S.C.A. §§1601-1611; Pub. L. 88-365; 78 Stat. 302), as amended

National Wilderness Preservation System Acts — Statutes establishing areas in the National Wildlife Refuge System as part of the National Wilderness Preservation System pursuant to the Wilderness Preservation Act of 1964, Sep. 3 (16 U.S.C.A. 1131-1136; Pub. L. 88-577,§2; 78 Stat. 890)

Urban Mass Transportation Act of 1964, Jul. 9 (49 U.S.C.A. §1601-11; Pub. L. 88-365; 78 Stat. 30), as amended

Water Resources Research Act of 1964, Jul. 17 (42 U.S.C.A. §§1961-1961c6; Pub. L. 88-379; 78 Stat. 320), as amended

Wilderness Act of 1964, Sep. 3 (16 U.S.C.A. §§1131-1136; Pub. L. 88-577; 79 Stat. 890), as amended

1965

Act of October 9, 1965, authorizing public service facilities in national parks only where consistent with park purposes, Oct. 9 (16 U.S.C.A. §20; Pub. L. 89-249,§1; 79 Stat. 969)

Administrative Procedure Act Amendments, Nov. 8 (5 U.S.C.A. §§500-576; Pub. L. 89-332,§3; 79 Stat. 1281)

Anadromous Fish Conservation Act, Oct. 30 (16 U.S.C.A. §§757a-757f; Pub. L. 89-304; 79 Stat. 1125), as amended

Federal Water Project Recreation Act, Jul. 9 (16 U.S.C.A. §§4601-5 et seq.; Pub. L. 89-72; 79 Stat. 213), as amended

Freedom of Information Act, Jul. 4 (5 U.S.C.A. §552; Pub. L. 89-487; 80 Stat. 250), as amended

Clean Air Act Amendments of 1965, Oct. 20 (42 U.S.C.A. §7521; Pub. L. 89-272, Title I,§101(8); 79 Stat. 992)

Federal Water Project Recreation Act, Jul 9 (16 U.S.C.A. 4601-5 et. seq; Pub. L. 89-72; 79 Stat. 213), as amended.

Land and Water Conservation Fund Act of 1965, Jul. 9 (16 U.S.C.A. §§4601-5; Pub. L. 89-72; 79 Stat. 218), as amended

Shore Line Erosion Protection Act (Public Property), Oct. 27 (33 U.S.C.A. §426g; Pub. L. 89-298, Title III,§ 310(b); 79 Stat. 1095)

Solid Waste Disposal Act, Oct. 20 (42 U.S.C.A. §§3251-3259; Pub. L. 89-272, Title II; 79 Stat. 997), as amended

Water Resources Planning Act, Jul. 22 (42 U.S.C.A. 1962 et seq.; Pub. L. 89-80; 79 Stat. 244), as amended

1966

Clean Air Act Amendments of 1966, Oct. 15 (42 U.S.C.A. §§1857c, 18571; Pub. L. 89-675; 80 Stat. 954)

Department of Transportation Act [DOT], Oct. 15 (3 U.S.C.A. §19 et seq.; Pub. L. 89-670; 80 Stat. 931), as amended

Federal-Aid Highway Act of 1966, Sep. 13 (23 U.S.C.A. §§101 et seq.; Pub. L. 89-574; 80 Stat. 766), as amended

Fur Seal Act of 1966, Dec. 17 (16 U.S.C.A. §§1151, 1152; Pub. L. 103-199; 107 Stat. 2327)

National Wildlife Refuge System Administration Act of 1966, Dec. 5, 1969 (16 U.S.C.A. §§668dd-668ee; Pub. L. 91-135; 83 Stat. 283), as amended

1967

National Emission Standards Act, Nov. 21 (42 U.S.C.A. §§7401 et seq.; Pub. L. 90-148,§1; 81 Stat. 485)

Fisherman's Protective Act of 1967, Aug. 12, 1968 (22 U.S.C.A. §§1971 note et seq.; Pub. L. 90-482; 82 Stat. 729, 730), as amended

1968

Colorado River Basin Project Act, Sep. 30 (43 U.S.C.A. §§616aa-1 et seq.; Pub. L. 90-537; 82 Stat. 885), as amended

Estuary Protection Act, Aug. 3 (16 U.S.C.A. 1221-1226; Pub. L. 90-454 82 Stat. 625)

Great Lakes Basin Compact Act (Pub. L. 90-419; 82 Stat. 414)

National Trails Systems Act, Oct. 2 (16 U.S.C.A. §§1241-1249; Pub. L. 90-543; 82 Stat. 919), as amended

Wild and Scenic Rivers Act, Oct. 2 (16 U.S.C.A. §§1271-1287; Pub. L. 90-542; 82 Stat. 906), as amended

1969

Endangered Species Conservation Act of 1969, Dec. 5 (16 U.S.C.A. §§668aa-668cc-5; Pub. L. 91-135,§12(d); 83 Stat. 283), as amended

Federal Coal Mine Health and Safety Act, Dec. 30 (15 U.S.C.A. §§633 et seq.; Pub. L. 91-173; 83 Stat. 742), as amended

National Environmental Policy Act of 1969 [NEPA], Jan. 1, 1970 (42 U.S.C.A. §§4321 et seq.; Pub. L. 91-190; 83 Stat. 852), as amended

1970

Airport and Airway Development Act of 1970, May 21 (49 U.S.C.A. §§1701 et seq.; Pub. L. 91-258, Title I; 84 Stat. 219), as amended

Animal Welfare Act of 1970, Dec. 24 (7 U.S.C.A. 2131-2147 et seq.; Pub. L. 91-579; 84 Stat. 1560)

Clean Air Act Amendments of 1970, Dec. 31 (42 U.S.C.A. §§215 note et seq.; Pub. L. 91-604; 84 Stat. 1676)

Environmental Education Act, Oct. 30 (20 U.S.C.A. §§1531-1536; Pub. L. 91-516,§§1-7; 84 Stat. 1312-1315), as amended

Environmental Protection Agency, 5 U.S.C.A. App. II, Reorganization Plan No. 3 of 1970

Environmental Quality Improvement Act of 1970, Apr. 3 (42 U.S.C.A. §§4371-4374; Pub. L. 91-224, Title II,§§202-205; 84 Stat. 114), as amended

Government in the Sunshine Act, Sep. 13 (5 U.S.C.A.,§551 et seq.; Pub. L. 94-406; 90 Stat. 1241)

Mining and Minerals Policy Act of 1970, Dec. 31 (30 U.S.C.A. §21a; Pub. L. 91-631; 84 Stat. 1876)

National Oceanic and Atmospheric Administration, 5 U.S.C.A. App. II, Reorganization Plan No. 4 of 1970

Noise Pollution and Abatement Act of 1970, Dec. 31 (42 U.S.C.A. §§1858, 1858a; Pub. L. 91-604 s.14; 84 Stat. 1709)

Occupational Safety and Health Act of 1970 [OSHA], Dec. 29 (5 U.S.C.A. §§5108 et seq.; Pub. L. 91-596; 84 Stat. 1590), as amended

Poison Prevention Packaging Act of 1970, Dec. 30 (15 U.S.C.A. §§1471-1476 et seq.; Pub. L. 91-601; 84 Stat. 1670), as amended

Resource Recovery Act of 1970, Oct. 26 (42 U.S.C.A. 3251-3254f, 3256-3259; Pub. L. 91-512; 84 Stat. 1227)

Water Bank Act, Dec. 13 (16 U.S.C.A. 1301-1311; Pub. L. 91-559; 84 Stat. 1468), as amended

Watershed Protection and Flood Protection Act, (16 U.S.C.A. 100; Pub.L. 83-566)

1971

Alaska Native Claims Settlement Act, Dec. 18 (43 U.S.C.A. §§1601-1624; Pub. L. 92-203; 85 Stat. 688), as amended

Lead-Based Paint Poisoning Prevention Act, Jan. 13 (42 U.S.C.A. §§4801 et seq.; Pub. L. 91-695; 84 Stat. 2078), as amended

Wild Free-Roaming Horses and Burros Act, Dec. 15 (16 U.S.C.A. §§1331-1340; Pub. L. 92-195; 85 Stat. 649-651)

1972

Black Lung Benefits Act, May 19 (30 U.S.C.A. 901, 902 et seq.; Pub. L. 92-303; 86 Stat. 150), as amended

Coastal Zone Management Act of 1972, Oct. 27 (16 U.S.C.A. §§1451-1464; Pub. L. 92-583; 86 Stat. 1280), as amended

Consumer Product Safety Act, Oct. 27 (5 U.S.C.A. §§5314, 5315 et seq.; Pub. L. 92-573; 86 Stat. 1207), as amended

Federal Environmental Pesticide Control Act of 1972 [FEPCA], Oct. 21 (7 U.S.C.A. §§136-136y et seq.; Pub. L. 92-516; 86 Stat. 973), as amended

Federal Water Pollution Control Act Amendments of 1972, Oct. 18 (12 U.S.C.A. §24 et seq.; Pub. L. 92-500; 86 Stat. 816)

Marine Mammal Protection Act of 1972 [MMPA], Oct. 21 (16 U.S.C.A. §§1361-1362, 1371-1384, 1401-1407; Pub. L. 92-522; 86 Stat. 1027), as amended

Marine Protection, Research and Sanctuaries Act of 1972, Oct. 23 (16 U.S.C.A. §§1431-1434 et seq.; Pub. L. 92-532; 86 Stat. 1052), as amended

Noise Control Act of 1972, Oct. 27 (42 U.S.C.A. §§4901-4918 et seq.; Pub. L. 92-574; 86 Stat. 1234). as amended

Ports and Waterways Safety Act of 1972, Jul. 10 (33 U.S.C.A. §§1221-1227; Pub. L. 92-340; 86 Stat. 424), as amended

1973

Emergency Daylight Saving Time Energy Conservation Act of 1973, Dec. 15 (15 U.S.C.A. 260a note; Pub. L. 93-182; 87 Stat. 707), as amended.

Endangered Species Act of 1973 [ESA], Dec. 28 (7 U.S.C.A. §§136 et seq.; Pub. L. 93-205§§2-15; 87 Stat. 884), as amended

Flood Disaster Protection Act of 1973, Dec. 31 (12 U.S.C.A. §§24 et seq.; Pub. L. 93-234; 87 Stat. 975), as amended

Oil Pollution Act Amendments, Oct. 4 (33 U.S.C.A. 1001-1010; 87 Stat. 424)

Trans-Alaska Pipeline Authorization Act, Nov. 16 (43 U.S.C.A. §§1651-1655; Pub. L. 93-153, Title II,§§201-206; 87 Stat. 584), as amended

1974

Archeological and Historic Preservation Act, Jun. 27 (16 U.S.C.A. §§469-469c; Pub. L. 86-523§1; 74 Stat. 220)

Deepwater Port Act of 1974, Jan. 3, 1975 (33 U.S.C.A. §§1501-1524 et seq.; Pub. L. 93-627; 88 Stat. 2126), as amended

Energy Supply and Environmental Coordination Act of 1974, Jun. 22 (15 U.S.C.A. §§791-798 et seq.; Pub. L. 93-319; 88 Stat. 246), as amended

Environmental Education Amendments of 1974, May 10 (20 U.S.C.A. 1531, 1532, 1536; Pub. L. 94-278; 88 Stat. 121)

Forest and Rangeland Renewable Resources Planning Act of 1974, Aug. 17 (16 U.S.C.A. §§581h, 1601-1676; Pub. L. 93-378; 88 Stat. 476), as amended

Intervention on the High Seas Act, Feb. 5 (33 U.S.C.A. §§1471-1487; Pub. L. 93-248,§§2-18; 88 Stat. 8), as amended

National Wildlife Refuge System Administrative Act Amendments of 1974, Dec. 3 (16 U.S.C.A. §§668dd, 715s; Pub. L. 93-509; 88 Stat. 1603)

Safe Drinking Water Act, Dec. 16 (21 U.S.C.A. §§349 et seq.; Pub. L. 93-523; 88 Stat. 1660), as amended

Transportation Safety Act of 1974, Jan. 3, 1975 (45 U.S.C.A. §§39 et seq.; Pub. L. 93-633; 88 Stat. 2156), as amended

1975

Energy Policy and Conservation Act, Dec. 22 (12 U.S.C.A. §1904 note et seq.; Pub. L. 94-163; 89 Stat. 871), as amended

Federal Coal Leasing Amendments Act of 1975, Aug. 4, 1976 (30 U.S.C.A. §§181 note et seq.; Pub. L. 94-377; 90 Stat. 1083)

Federal Insecticide, Fungicide, and Rodenticide Act Amendments [FIFRA], Jul. 2 (7 U.S.C.A. §136y; Pub. L. 94-51; 89 Stat. 257)

1976

Airport and Airway Development Act Amendments of 1976, Jul. 12, (49 U.S.C.A. §§322 et seq.; Pub. L. 94-353; 90 Stat. 871), as amended

Alaska Natural Gas Transportation Act of 1976, Oct. 22 (15 U.S.C.A. §§719-719o et seq.; Pub. L. 94-586; 90 Stat. 2903), as amended

Animal Welfare Act Amendments of 1976, Apr. 22 (7 U.S.C.A. §§2131-2134 et seq.; Pub. L. 94-279; 90 Stat. 417)

Coastal Zone Management Act Amendments of 1976, Jul. 26 (5 U.S.C.A. §§5316 et seq.; Pub. L. 94-370; 90 Stat. 1013), as amended

Federal Coal Leasing Amendments Act of 1976, Oct. 30, 1978 (30 U.S.C.A. §181 note; Pub. L. 95-554; 92 Stat. 2075)

Federal Land Policy and Management Act of 1976 [FLPMA], Oct. 21 (7 U.S.C.A. §§1010-1012a et seq.; Pub. L. 94-579; 90 Stat. 2744), as amended

Magnuson Fishery Conservation and Management Act, Apr. 13 (16 U.S.C.A. §§971 et seq.; Pub. L. 94-265, 90 Stat. 331), as amended

National Forest Management Act of 1976, Oct. 22 (16 U.S.C.A. §§472a et seq; Pub. L. 94-588; 90 Stat. 2949), as amended

National Park System Mining Regulation Act, Sep. 28 (16 U.S.C.A. §§1901-1912; Pub. L. 94-429,§1; 90 Stat. 1342)

Resource Conservation and Recovery Act of 1976 [RCRA], Oct. 21 (42 U.S.C.A. §§6901-6987; Pub. L. 94-580; 90 Stat. 2795)

Solid Waste Disposal Act, as amended by RCRA, Oct. 21 (42 U.S.C.A. §§6901-6907 et seq.; Pub. L. 94-580,§2; 90 Stat. 2795-9839)

Toxic Substances Control Act, Oct. 11 (15 U.S.C.A. §§2601-2629; Pub. L. 94-469; 90 Stat. 2003), as amended

Wetlands Loan Extension Act of 1976, Feb. 17 (16 U.S.C.A. §§668dd et seq.; Pub. L. 94-215; 90 Stat. 189)

1977

Black Lung Reform Benefits Act of 1977, Mar. 1 (26 U.S.C.A. §§4121 note et seq.; Pub. L. 95-239; 92 Stat. 95)

Clean Air Act Amendments of 1977, Aug. 7 (15 U.S.C.A. §§792 note et seq.; Pub. L. 95-95; 91 Stat. 685), as amended

Clean Water Act of 1977 (amendment to FWPCA) [CWA], Dec. 27 (33 U.S.C.A. §§1251-1376; Pub. L. 95-247; 91 Stat. 1566), as amended

Federal Mine Safety and Health Act of 1977, Nov. 9 (5 U.S.C.A. §§5314 et seq.; Pub. L. 95-164; 91 Stat. 1290), as amended

Safe Drinking Water Amendments of 1977 [SDAW], Nov. 16 (5 U.S.C.A. §5108 et seq.; Pub. L. 95-190; 91 Stat. 1393)

Soil and Water Resources Conservation Act of 1977, Nov. 18 (16 U.S.C.A. §§2001-2009; Pub. L. 95-192; 91 Stat. 1407-1411), as amended

Surface Mining Control and Reclamation Act of 1977 [SMCRA], Aug. 3 (18 U.S.C.A. §1114 et seq.; Pub. L. 95-87; 91 Stat. 445), as amended

1978

Antarctic Conservation Act of 1978, Oct. 28 (16 U.S.C.A. §§2401-2412 et seq.; Pub. L. 95-541; 92 Stat. 2048)

Endangered Species Act Amendments of 1978, Nov. 10 (16 U.S.C.A. §§1531 note et seq.; Pub. L. 95-632; 92 Stat. 3751)

Environmental Education Act of 1978, Nov. 1 (20 U.S.C.A. §§3011-3018; Pub. L. 89-10, Title III,§§351-358, as added Pub. L. 95-561, Title III,§301(a); 92 Stat. 2217), as amended

Environmental Resources Extension Act of 1978, Jun. 30 (16 U.S.C.A. §§1671-1676; Pub. L. 95-306; 92 Stat. 349), as amended

Forest and Rangeland Renewable Resources Research Act of 1978, Jun. 30 (16 U.S.C.A. §§1600 note et seq.; Pub. L. 95-307; 92 Stat. 353), as amended

Federal Pesticide Act of 1978, Sep. 30 (7 U.S.C.A. §§136-136y; Pub. L. 95-396; 92 Stat. 819)

Outer Continental Shelf Lands Act Amendments of 1978, Sep. 18 (16 U.S.C.A. §§1456 et seq.; Pub. L. 95-372; 92 Stat. 629), as amended

National Ocean Pollution Planning Act of 1978, May 8 (33 U.S.C.A. §§1701-1708; Pub. L. 95-273; 92 Stat. 228), as amended

Port and Tanker Safety Act of 1978, Oct. 17 (33 U.S.C.A. §§1221-1232; Pub. L. 95-474; 92 Stat. 1471)

Public Rangelands Improvement Act of 1978, Oct. 25 (16 U.S.C.A. §§1332-1333, 43 U.S.C.A. §§1739 et seq.; Pub. L. 95-514; 92 Stat. 1803

Quiet Communities Act of 1978, Nov. 8 (42 U.S.C.A. §§4901 note et seq.; Pub. L. 95-609; 92 Stat. 3079)

Renewable Resource Extension Act of 1978, Jun. 30 (16 U.S.C.A. §§1671-1676; Pub. L. 95-306; 92 Stat. 349), as amended

Sikes Act Amendments of 1978, Oct. 5 (16 U.S.C.A. §§670a note et seq.; Pub. L. 95-420; 92 Stat. 921)

Uranium Mill Tailings Radiation Control Act of 1978, Nov. 8 (42 U.S.C.A. §§2014; Pub. L. 95-604; 92 Stat. 3021), as amended

1979

Archaeological Resources Protection Act of 1979, Oct. 31 (16 U.S.C.A. §§470aa et seq.; Pub. L. 96-95; 93 Stat. 721), as amended

Aviation Safety and Noise Abatement Act of 1979, Feb. 18, 1980 (49 U.S.C.A. §§1348 note et seq.; Pub. L. 96-193; 94 Stat. 50), as amended

Emergency Energy Conservation Act of 1979, Nov. 5 (42 U.S.C.A. 6261et seq.; Pub. L. 96-102; 93 Stat. 749), as amended.

Hazardous Liquid Pipeline Safety Act of 1979, Nov. 30 (49 U.S.C.A. §§1811, 2001-2014; Pub. L. 96-129, Title II; 93 Stat. 1003), as amended

1980

Act to Prevent Pollution from Ships, Oct. 21 (16 U.S.C.A. §742c, 33 U.S.C.A. §§1001-1011, 1013-1016, 1321, 1901-1911; Pub. L. 96-478; 94 Stat. 2297; See also 46 U.S.C.A. §§3301, 3702), as amended

Alaska National Interest Lands Conservation Act [ANILCA], Dec. 2 (16 U.S.C.A. §§410hh et seq.; Pub. L. 96-487; 94 Stat. 2371), as amended

Asbestos School Hazard Detection and Control Act of 1980, Jun. 14 (20 U.S.C.A. §§1411, 3601-3611; Pub. L. 96-270; 94 Stat. 487)

Comprehensive Environmental Response, Compensation and Liability Act of 1980 [CERCLA], Dec. 11 (42 U.S.C.A. §§9601-9657; Pub. L. 96-510; 94 Stat. 2767), as amended

Equal Access to Justice Act, Oct. 21 (5 U.S.C.A. §§504 et seq.; Pub. L. 96-481, Title II; 94 Stat. 2325), as amended

Fish and Wildlife Conservation Act of 1980, Sep. 29 (16 U.S.C.A. §§2901-2911; Pub. L. 96-366; 94 Stat. 1322), as amended

Hazardous Substance Response Revenue Act of 1980, Dec. 11 (26 U.S.C.A. §§4611-4682; Pub. L. 96-510, Title II; 94 Stat. 2796), as amended

Low-Level Radioactive Waste Policy Act, Dec. 22 (42 U.S.C.A. §2021b-2021d; Pub. L. 96-573; 94 Stat. 3347), as amended

National Historic Preservation Act Amendments of 1980, Dec. 12 (16 U.S.C.A. §§469c-2 et seq.; Pub. L. 96-515; 94 Stat. 2987)

Renewable Energy Resources Act of 1980, Jun. 30 (42 U.S.C.A. §§7371-7375; Pub. L. 96-294, Title IV; 94 Stat. 715)

Solar Energy and Energy Conservation Act of 1980, Jun. 30 (12 U.S.C.A. §1451 et seq.; Pub. L. 96-294; 94 Stat. 719)

Solid Waste Disposal Act Amendments of 1980, Oct. 21 (42 U.S.C.A. §§6901 note et seq.; Pub. L. 96-482; 94 Stat. 2334)

1981

Black Lung Benefits Amendments of 1981, Dec. 29 (30 U.S.C.A. §§801 note et seq.; Pub. L. 97-119; 95 Stat. 1643-1645)

Lacey Act Amendments of 1981, Nov. 16 (16 U.S.C.A. §§667e et seq.; Pub. L. 97-79; 95 Stat. 1073), as amended

1982

Coastal Barrier Resources Act, Oct. 15 (16 U.S.C.A. §§3501-3510, 42 U.S.C.A. §4028; Pub. L. 97-348; 96 Stat. 1653), as amended

Endangered Species Act Amendments of 1982, Oct. 13 (16 U.S.C.A. §§1531 et seq.; Pub. L. 97-304; 96 Stat. 1411)

Nuclear Waste Policy Act of 1982, Jan. 7, 1983 (42 U.S.C.A. §§10101-10108 et seq.; Pub. L. 97-425; 96 Stat. 2201), as amended

1983

Fur Seal Act Amendments of 1983, Oct. 14 (5 U.S.C.A. §§8332 et seq.; Pub. L. 98-129; 97 Stat. 835)

National Trails System Act Amendments of 1983, Mar. 28 (16 U.S.C.A. §§1241-1247, 1249-1251; Pub. L. 98-11, Title II; 97 Stat. 42)

1984

Atlantic Striped Bass Conservation Act, Oct. 31 (16 U.S.C.A. §§757g, 1851 note; Pub. L. 98-613; 98 Stat. 3187), as amended

Deepwater Port Act Amendments of 1984, Sep. 25 (33 U.S.C.A. §§1501 note et seq.; Pub. L. 98-419; 98 Stat. 1607)

Environmental Programs Assistance Act of 1984, Jun. 12, (42 U.S.C.A. §4368a, 4368a note; Pub. L. 98-313; 98 Stat. 235)

Water Resources Research Act of 1984, Mar. 22 (42 U.S.C.A. §§1959-1959h et seq.; Pub. L. 98-242; 98 Stat. 97), as amended

[Assorted wilderness designation bills]

1985

Low- Level Radioactive Waste Policy Amendments Act of 1985, Dec. 22 (42 U.S.C.A. §§2021b-2021d; Pub. L. 96-573; 94 Stat. 3347), as amended

Outer Continental Shelf Lands Act Amendments of 1985, Apr. 7, 1986 (43 U.S.C.A. §§1301 et seq.; Pub. L. 99-272, Title VIII; 100 Stat. 147)

1986

Asbestos Hazard Emergency Response Act of 1986, Oct. 22 (15 U.S.C.A. §§2601 note et seq.; Pub. L. 99-519; 100 Stat. 2970), as amended

Emergency Planning and Community Right-to-Know Act of 1986, Oct. 17 (42 U.S.C.A. §§ 11001 et seq.; Pub. L. 99-499; 100 Stat. 1728)

Freedom of Information Reform Act of 1986, Oct. 27 (5 U.S.C.A. §§552; Pub. L. 99-570, Title I,§§1801-1804; 100 Stat. 3204-48)

Radon Gas and Indoor Air Quality Research Act of 1986, Oct. 17 (42 U.S.C.A. §7401 note; Pub. L. 99-499, Title IV; 100 Stat. 1758)

Safe Drinking Water Act Amendments of 1986, Jun. 19 (15 U.S.C.A. §§1261 et seq.; Pub. L. 99-339; 100 Stat. 642), as amended

Superfund Amendment and Reauthorization Act of 1986 [SARA], Oct. 17 (10 U.S.C.A. §§2701 et seq.; Pub. L. 99-499; 100 Stat. 1613)

1987

Alaska Native Claims Settlement Act Amendments of 1987, Feb. 3, 1988 (15 U.S.C.A. §§78m et seq.; Pub. L. 100-241; 101 Stat. 1788)

Energy Conservation Act of 1987, (101 Stat. 103)

Environmental Resources Extension Act Amendments of 1987, Jan. 5, 1988 (16 U.S.C.A. §§1600 note et seq.; Pub. L. 100-231; 101 Stat. 1565)

Nuclear Waste Policy Amendments Act of 1987, Dec. 22 (42 U.S.C.A. §§ 5841 note et seq.; Pub. L. 100-203 Title V,§§5001-5065; 101 Stat. 1330-227)

Water Quality Act of 1987, Feb. 4 (33 U.S.C.A. §§1251 et seq.; Pub. L. 100-4; 100 Stat. 7)

1988

Asbestos Information Act of 1988, Oct. 31 (15 U.S.C.A. §2607 note; Pub. L. 100-577; 102 Stat. 2901)

Federal Insecticide, Fungicide, and Rodenticide Act Amendments of 1988, Oct. 25 (7 U.S.C.A. §§136 et seq.; Pub. L. 100-532; 102 Stat. 2654)

Marine Mammal Protection Act Amendments of 1988, Nov. 23 (16 U.S.C.A. §§1166 et seq.; Pub. L. 100-711; 102 Stat. 4755)

Medical Waste Tracking Act of 1988, Nov. 1 (18 U.S.C.A. §3063 et seq.; Pub. L. 100-582; 102 Stat. 2950)

National Wild and Scenic Rivers System Acts. Pursuant to the Wild and Scenic Rivers Act (16 U.S.C.A. 1271-1287; 82 Stat. 906)

Ocean Dumping Ban Act of 1988, Nov. 18 (33 U.S.C.A. §§ 1268 et seq.; Pub. L 100-688; 102 Stat. 4139)

Shore Protection Act of 1988, Nov. 18 (33 U.S.C.A. §§2601, 2602-2609; Pub. L. 100-688; 102 Stat. 4154)

1990

Antarctic Protection Act of 1990, Nov. 16 (16 U.S.C.A. §§2461, 2462-2466; Pub. L. 101-594; 104 Stat. 2975)

Asbestos School Hazard Abatement Reauthorization Act of 1990, Nov. 28 (Pub. L 101-637; 104 Stat. 4589)

Clean Air Act Amendments, Nov. 15 (42 U.S.C.A. §7521; Pub. L. 101-549, Title II,§§201-207, 227(b), 230(1)-(5); 104 Stat. 2472-2474, 2507, 2529)

Fish and Wildlife Conservation Act of 1990, Nov. 16 (16 U.S.C.A. §2910; Pub. L. 101-593, Title I,§106; 104 Stat. 2954)

Forest Resources Conservation and Shortage Relief Act of 1990, Aug. 20 (16 U.S.C.A. §§620 et. seq.; Pub. L. 101-382, Title IV; 104 Stat. 714), as amended

National Environmental Education Act, Nov. 16 (20 U.S.C.A. §§5501, 5502-5510; Pub. L. 101-619; 104 Stat. 3325)

National Forest Foundation Act, Nov. 16 (16 U.S.C.A. §§583j et seq.; Pub. L. 101-593, Title IV; 104 Stat. 2969), as amended

National Indian Forest Resources Management Act, Nov. 28 (25 U.S.C.A. §§3101 et seq.; Pub. L. 101-630, Title III; 104 Stat. 4532)

Oil Pollution Act of 1990, Aug. 18 (Pub. L. 101-380; 104 Stat. 484; See 33 U.S.C.A. §2761, 2735), as amended

Pollution Prevention Act of 1990, Nov. 5 (42 U.S.C.A. §§13101, 13101 note, 13102-13109; Pub. L. 101-508, Title VI, Subtitle F,§§6601-6610; 104 Stat. 1388-321)

Pollution Prosecution Act of 1990, Nov. 16 (42 U.S.C.A. §4321; Pub. L. 101-593; 104 Stat. 2962)

Ports and Waterways Safety Act, Aug. 18 (33 U.S.C.A. §§1223, 1228; Pub. L. 101-380, Title IV,§§4106(c), 4107(a); 104 Stat. 514)

Tongass Timber Reform Act, Nov. 28 (16 U.S.C.A. §§427a(i)(1) et seq.; Pub. L. 101-626; 104 Stat. 4426)

1991

Federal Transit Act Amendments of 1991, Dec. 18 (5 U.S.C.A. §§5314 et seq.; Pub. L. 102-240, Title III; 105 Stat. 2087)

Silvio O. Conte National Fish and Wildlife Refuge Act, Dec. 11 (16 U.S.C.A. §§668dd notes, 3954; Pub. L. 102-212; 105 Stat. 1655)

Striped Bass Act of 1991, Oct. 17 (16 U.S.C.A. §§757g et seq.; Pub. L. 102-130; 105 Stat.626)

1992

National Historic Preservation Act Amendments of 1992, Oct. 30 (16 U.S.C.A. §§461 notes et seq.; Pub. L. 102-575, Title XL; 106 Stat. 4753)

Wild Bird Conservation Act of 1992, Oct. 23 (16 U.S.C.A. §§943 et seq.; Pub. L. 102-440; 106 Stat. 2224)

1993

Forest Resources Conservation and Shortage Relief Amendments Act of 1993, Jul. 1 (16 U.S.C.A. §§620 et seq.; Pub. L. 103-45; 107 Stat. 223)

National Forest Foundation Act Amendment Act of 1993, Oct. 12 (16 U.S.C.A. §583j; Pub. L. 103-106; 107 Stat. 1031)

Appendix 2, (A) Environmental On-Line Electronic Resources, and

(B) Periodical-Looseleaf Services

A. Environmental On-Line Electronic Resources

　　　　1• Environment OnLine: The Internet and environmental research
　　　　2• The E-Law Network

•

1. ENVIRONMENT ONLINE: UPDATE '93
By Patricia Gayle Alston[173]
Agency for Toxic Substances and Disease Registry
U.S. Public Health Service

INFORMATION SOURCES ON THE INTERNET

The highest levels of the U.S. Government have begun using electronic mail services to encourage the exchange of ideas on the environment. The President, Vice President, and selected members of Congress all have addresses on the Internet:

　　　　president@whitehouse.gov

　　　　vice-president@whitehouse.gov

　　　　congress@hr.house.gov

On CompuServe, one of the largest and most popular subscriber services, a White House Forum is in place with an environment section.

In addition to incorporating key decision makers, existing online systems are expanding their linkages to each other and the environmental information they have available. For example, both CompuServe and EcoNet have added Internet electronic mail connections. Messages can

---

173. Gayle Alston is a Health Education Specialist, Agency for Toxic Substances and Disease Registry, Public Health Service, U.S. Department of Health and Human Services. She has a B.S. in library science from Appalachian State University and an M.L.S. from Emory University. She was formerly Library and Records Manager at the U.S. Environmental Protection Agency's Atlanta office. She is immediate past-chair of the Environmental and Resources Management Division of the Special Libraries Association (SLA) and is involved in the American Library Association's task Force on the Environment.
Communications to the author should be addressed to Gayle Alston, ATSDR, 1600 Clifton Road MS E33, Atlanta, GA 30333; 404/639-6205; Fax 404/639-6207; Internet — pgal@atsod3.vm.cdc.gov.

be posted from one online system to another or sent to another Internet user. On CompuServe, Network Earth has been renamed Earth Forum; Network Earth has moved to American Online. EcoNet has added RACHEL's Hazardous Waste News to its system.

Federal organizations are also increasing their accessibility over the Internet. For example, the reference section of the U.S. Department of Agriculture's National Agricultural Library (NAL) now accepts requests at the following Internet address: agref@nalusda.gov. NAL is also exploring the connection between its bulletin board (Agricultural Library Forum) and the Internet.

In addition, the Library of Congress is now accessible on the Internet through remote login: locis.loc.gov. The Federal Register, the publication of final and proposed federal regulations, is available by subscription through the Internet from the commercial vendor Counterpoint.

The Online Library System from EPA is now accessible through the Internet. The Internet address is epaibm.rtpnc.epa.gov. At the first menu, select "Public Access." At the second menu, select "OLS." Direct-dial access is also available (919/549-0720, 7-E-1/300-9600). At the first system prompt, type "IBMPSI." At the second prompt, type "OLS." Type "Q" or "QUIT" at the system prompt to logout. Printing is available only through telecommunications software.

Another group seeking to provide access to multiple files through the Internet and other electronic methods is the Consortium for International Earth Science Information Network (CIESIN). CIESIN is partially funded by the National Aeronautics and Space Administration (NASA). CIESIN is working to: identify major collections of socioeconomic and health data relevant to global environmental change research; provide mechanisms to access these data and information resources; and create a vehicle to stimulate the integration of health and social science data with natural science data.

CIESIN is developing a global environmental directory describing what and where data are, how they were collected, and how they can be acquired. the directory will also provide pointers to holders of data in various locations. The Green Pages system is currently available via the Internet or direct dial. For a quick reference guide on Green Pages or for more information on CIESIN, contact: CIESIN, 2250 Pierce Road, University Center, MI   48710; 517/797-2700; Fax 517/797-2622; Internet—ciesin.info@ciesin.org.

For example, CIESIN is working with the federal Agency for Toxic Substances and Disease Registry (ATSDR) to make portions of the Agency's HazDat database publicly accessible. HazDat (Hazardous Substance Release/Health Effects Database) contains information on National Priorities List (NPL) sites throughout the country. The information is abstracted from public health assessments, petitioned health assessments, health consultations, health studies, and *Toxicological Profiles* of hazardous substances. The database will provide information on contaminants and their locations at a site, type of health concerns, health recommendations, and toxicology information.

Other Internet developments include at AT&T Corporation agreement with the National Science Foundation (NSF) to provide directory and database services for NSF's national data network, which is part of the Internet. AT&T will develop and maintain a Directory of Directories of numerous resources, including servers, library catalogs, and file transfer protocol sites.

A more complete listing of environmental resources on the Internet is available for the U.S. EPA Office of Pollution Prevention and Toxics Library. The Office can be contacted at 401 M Street SW, TX-793, Washington, DC 20460; 202/260-3944; Internet — library.tsca@epamail.epa.gov.

BULLETIN BOARDS

Electronic bulletin boards are another environmental information resource available from many different organizations, including departments of the federal government. The Pollution Information Exchange System (PIES) bulletin board has established an Environmental Librarians Exchange. Bibliographies and other information will be posted to the board by environmental librarians. In addition, two United Nations programs based in France — the International Cleaner Production Information Clearinghouse — are now accessible via PIES.

The EPA's Office of Air Quality Planning and Standards Technology Transfer Network has added the National Air Toxics Information Clearinghouse (NATICH), which was previously available only through subscription. Information includes development and implementation of air toxics programs, agency names and contacts, and ongoing air toxic research. Fourteen bulletin boards are available by dialing the central number (919/541-5742). Recently, the bulletin board became available on the Internet: ttnbbs.rtpnc.epa.gov.

Other changes to EPA-sponsored bulletin boards include the addition of a toll-free number for the Office of Research and Development (800/258-9605). The Alternative Treatment Technology Information Center (ATTIC) has established a separate phone number for 9600 baud access (301/670-3813). A second number (301/670-3808) will support 1200 and 2400 baud.

The State Superfund Network bulletin board was developed by Clean Sites and the Environmental Law Institute with seed money from the EPA. Program information, administrative enforcement and judicial documents, policy and procedure documents, and Records of Decisions are available through the system. Access is restricted to state Superfund program staff. For more information, contact Clean Sites Inc., 1199 N. Fairfax Street, Alexandria, VA 22314; 703/683-1380.

The U.S. Department of Labor (DOL) bulletin board now provides toll-free access (800/597-1221). DOL's service includes information on job safety and health regulations from the Occupational Safety and Health Administration.

The U.S. Department of Energy (DOE) has begun offering an Electronic Publishing System bulletin board (202/586-2557). The service offers several of DOE's energy reports online, such as Electronic Power Monthly, Weekly Coal Production, Weekly Petroleum Status Report, and Natural Gas Monthly.

The Gulf Bulletin Board (800/235-4662) supports the Gulf of Mexico Initiative. In addition to information on this program, the system contains the national telephone locators for EPA and NOAA personnel, the Toxic Chemical Release Inventory and a list of environmental experts.

Localized bulletin boards are also expanding their environmental coverage. One example is the Boston Computer Society (BCS), Environmental Group. In addition to monthly meetings, the group posts information on environmental resources, environmental computer games, geographical information systems, and more. For additional information, contact Doug Seale (617/782-2347 or Internet — dseal@igc.apc.org). The BCS newsletter also covers environmental information topics.

ONLINE DATABASES

The number of online databases available to seekers of environmental information is also increasing. For example, Westlaw now has Superfund liability documents in the Environmental Data Resources, Inc.'s National Priorities List and superfund Enforcement Tracking System Database (EDR-NPLSETS). Information in this database include additional information on NP sites, such as potentially responsible parties (PRPs). Also available on Westlaw are the Clean Air Act 1990 Amendment Law and Practice and Hazardous Waste Law and Practice, which are published by John W. Wiley and Sons.

On ORBIT, PESTDOC has been renamed Derwent Crop Protection File, and Standard Pesticide File has been renamed Derwent Crop Protection Registry. Also available exclusively on ORBIT are TULSA (Petroleum Abstracts), which requires a licensing agreement and a subset, Environmental Resources Technology (ERTH), which does not require a licensing agreement. Both include data from 1965 to present. ERTH includes petroleum-related environmental information, such as oil spill technology. The TULSA subset is available under another name — Petroleum and Energy Products (PEP) — on DIALOG. However, only citations of articles are included and only those written from 1981 to the present. A licensing agreement is also needed for PEP>

New on DIALOG is the CHEMTOX database, formerly available only as a personal computer-based system. This database was discussed in Part II of this series in the October 1991 issue of *DATABASE*. Another DIALOG file, PTS Newsletter Database, has added several environmental newsletters, including Ohio Industry Environmental Advisor, Environmental Watch — Western Europe and Chemical Process Safety Reporter. No longer available on DIALOG are the files APTIC, Aquaculture, and Chemical Exposure.

This year, Chemical and Engineer News became available on STN. This database offers full text from 1991 to the present and contains more than 8,000 articles. Another database available on STN is the German-produced CHEMSAFE, which contains information on 1,500 substances and more than 40 properties. It is updated twice a year. STN has also added Material Safety Data Sheets (MSDSs) produced by the Canadian Center for Occupational Health and Safety. This database contains approximately 85,000 MSDSs from 550 suppliers, some international.

Other STN databases that provide chemical properties and suppliers and CSCHEM and CSCORP, produced by Chemical Sources International

Inc. in Clemson, South Carolina. CSCORP provides the addresses and contact information for companies supplying the chemical products in CSCHEM. The CHEMLIST file has been expanded to include substances on the European Inventory of Existing Commercial Chemical Substances (EINECS).

The Chemical Hazards Information Systems (ChemHazIs) from the Chemical Information System (CIS) contains approximately 2,270 records. The records are based on information compiled by the National Toxicology Program of the U.S. Department of Health and Human Services. While the information is contained in an MSDS format, it *cannot* be substituted for and MSDS. Information is provided on potential toxicity, exposures, and identifying existing data gaps.

CIS is also offering a database of more than 900 MSDSs covering information of insecticides, fungicides, and herbicides from 25 manufacturers. The information is updated quarterly. CROPPRO is also available on the National Pesticide Information Retrieval System (NPIRS).

The Emergency Response Notification System (ERNS) offers information from 1987 to the present. Data has been gathered from the EPA, the Department of Transportation (DOT), and the National Response Center. Subscribers can retrieve information related to reports of releases of oil and hazardous substances. Because the information is entered when the incident is reported, some records may not contain complete or accurate information. (One interesting note, in the emergency response arena, the word "event" is being used by some to replace the term "accidental spill." After all, how often would a hazardous substance be deliberately spilled? This discrepancy, however, could complicate searches later, if the word is widely substituted in the literature.)

The EPA Civil Enforcement Docket is also available on CIS. This database includes cases filed by the Department of Justice on behalf of EPA from 1971 to present.

Also available is the Regulated Materials Database (REGMAT), which summarizes substance-specific regulations pertaining to over fifteen laws from six agencies with environmental responsibilities.

DATABASES ON DISKETTE

Several diskette programs are also available. The National Environmental Health Association (NEHA) offers "Fundamental Toxicology and Risk Assessment." Contact NEHA at 303/756-9090 for more information.

In 1992, the EPA released the MIXTOX database containing summary information and literature citations on studies of toxicologic interactions and interactions of n environmental chemical with a pharmaceutical chemical. Drugs and drug mixtures are not included. The database contains information primarily on binary mixtures. Searches can be done on compound names and CAS numbers. For more information, contact Dr. Richard C. Hertzberg, Project Coordinator, U.S. EPA, 26 MLK jr. Drive, Cincinnati, OH; 513/569-7582.

Riskpro is a diskette program distributed by the American Chemical Society (202/872-4378). It contains information on recognized EPA standards and procedures and on complete environmental pollution monitoring systems. Information is also available on predicting the environmental impact of chemical release and estimating long-term effects of health-threatening situations.

The World Resources 1992-1993 Data Base Diskette ($119) contains data on global environmental conditions. For more information, contact the World Resources Institute at 800/822-0504.

CD-ROMS

Government agencies and intergovernmental organizations are taking an active role in disseminating environmental information on CD-ROM. For instance, the United Nations will soon be making available the complete text of the first Earth Summit, which was held in June 1992. The Earth Summit CD-ROM, available in English, Spanish, and French, contains preparatory conference papers, full and excerpted national and regional environmental reports, research papers, reports from participants and nongovernmental organizations from participants and nongovernmental organizations (NGOs), official statements, and the book, *The Global Partnership*. Also on this disc is *Agenda 21*, the action plan for the environment for the twenty-first century. Much of this information has not been previously published. For more information, contact United Nations Publications at 800/253-9646 or 212/963-8302; Fax 212/963-3489.

The Government Printing Office (GPO) offers the Air CHIEF CD-ROM (055-000-00398-0; $15) that contains air emissions data specific to types and quantities of pollutants. The Air CHIEF CD-ROM offers electronic data equivalent to approximately $900 worth of paper documents. Compilation of Air Pollutant Emission Factors, commonly referred to as AP-42, is one of the documents on this disc. Government agencies and nonprofit organizations can contact the EPA at 919/542-5285 to inquire about receiving a single copy free of charge.

Another CD-ROM available from the GPO contains regulations, documents, and technical information from the Occupational Safety and Health Administration (OSHA). This quarterly subscription provides full-text searching of OSHA documents, including all OSHA standards, Administrative directives, speeches, fact sheets, memorandums of understanding with other agencies, corporate-wide settlement agreements, Congressional testimony, and hazard information bulletins. The GPO document order number is 729-013-00000-5; quarterly updates are available for $88.

On the state level, Florida has developed a multimedia CD-ROM set called Florida Agricultural Information Retrieval System (FAIRS). More than 1,300 Florida publications on energy, pest control, waste management, and irrigation are available on two CD-ROMs. An updated CD-ROM is issued approximately three to four times a year. For more information, contact the University of Florida, P.O. Box 110340, Gainesville, FL 32611-0340; 904/392-7853; Fax 904/392-3856.

Commercial database vendors also have expanded the number of available environmental CD-ROMS. DIALOG is offering Environmental Chemistry, a health and safety CD-ROM that contains the entire contents of the Royal Society of Chemistry's Chemical Safety NewsBase and other products produced by RSC.

SilverPlatter Information, Inc. is now marketing all of the Cambridge Scientific Abstracts CD-ROMs. One of the new products is PolTox III from CAB, containing approximately 100,000 entries from the past ten years. Extensive information on environmental agrochemicals, groundwater contamination, toxicology, health hazards of pesticides, and heavy metals is included.

Another commercial vendor, Micromedex, has added the National Institute for Occupational Safety and Health's NIOSH Pocket Guide to Chemical Hazards on its TOMES PLUS CD-ROM. Information in the NIOSH Pocket Guide includes chemical structures or formulas, identification codes, synonyms, exposure limits, chemical and physical properties, signs and symptoms of exposure, and procedures for emergency treatment.

Micromedex also distributes the Environmental/Safety Library, an Information Handling Service (IHS) product. This set of CD-ROMs includes titles from the Code of Federal Regulations (CFR). The Environmental/Safety Library features all of Title 40 CFR EPA and portions of 29 CFR OSHA, 42 CFR Occupational Safety and Health research and Related Activity Regulations, 49 CFR DOT, pertinent Federal Register notices from 1990 to the present, and industry standards for both OSHA and EPA. The information is updated bimonthly.

Counterpoint, in addition to offering its weekly Federal Register CD-ROM, has compiled an archival Federal Register CD-ROM, containing all 1992 issues. This CD-ROM sells for $99. Counterpoint also has CD-ROMS available with a complete set of CFR titles (updated monthly) and a separate CD-ROM, Environmental Health and Safety, with CFR Titles 29, 40, and 49.

Occupational Health Services (OHS) now provides regulatory data on its Hazardline Plus CD-ROM. This information is supplied by ERMD Computer Services, Inc. The OHS Desktop Series features approximately 17,000 MSDSs summary information, and selected excerpts of the CFR. These MSDSs meet requirements of the following organizations: Chemical Manufacturers Association, ANSI, ASTM, International Labor Office, European Economic Community, and the Canadian government.

The National Information Services Corporation's (NISC Natural Resources Database is now known as the Natural Resources Metabase. This database provides information on natural resources, oil spills, wetlands, and fisheries. A second CD-ROM available from NISC is called Fish and Fisheries Worldwide.

CCINFO has two new environmental CD-ROMs available. OSH Publications, updated semiannually, contains New Jersey fact sheets, case studies and solutions for environmental problems, International Chemical Safety Cards, and Environmental Health Criteria documents from the International Programme on Chemical Safety. CCINFO also has available a CD-ROM called Chemical Advisor. A comprehensive source of regulatory and advisory information on chemicals in the workplace, Chemical Advisor contains the Toxic Substances Control Act of 1976 (TSCA) inventory and the ChemAdvisor Database. Principal health and environmental concerns of substances are highlighted.

The Bureau of National Affairs (BNA) recently premiered a new CD-ROM product called Environmental Library. It offers a very useful scroll-back option and features regulations, statutes, legislative histories, executive orders, court opinions, and administrative opinions. BNA plans to add state regulations as well.

Another CD-ROM featuring environmental regulations is being offered by ERM Computer Services, Inc. 855 Springdale Drive, Exton, PA 19341; 800/544-3118. ENFLEX INFO includes federal statutes, EPA, OSHA, and DOT regulations. Information on the Clean Air Act Amendments is also available, including Congressional reports, bills and final acts, proposed and final regulations, and notices. Approximately 50% of state environmental regulations are available on ENFLEX INFO. A weekly newsletter of the *Federal Register* and state register citations, effective dates, subject areas, and brief descriptions is also mailed to users. Price on this varies according to the number of users in the chosen jurisdiction.

In 1991, the National Pesticide Information Retrieval System (NPIRS) became known as the Center for Environmental and Regulatory Information Systems (CERIS). The NPIRS name will be retained to identify pesticide databases. CERIS-net is available on the Internet. MSDSs from CROPPRO have been added. Plans include the development of a full-text label information database.

A relatively new database managed by EPA's Environmental Finance Program is the Environmental Financing Information Network (EFIN), which provides comprehensive information on environmental financing issues. EFIN contains information on funding alternatives for state and local environmental programs and projects, lists experts in environmental programs and public financing, and identifies sources and methods to raise funds and lower fund-raising costs. Abstracts of publications, case studies, directory of contacts, and calendars are all available through EFIN. Topics featured are wastewater treatment, wetlands, groundwater protection, air quality management, state grants and loans, and local and small community technical assistance. EFIN is currently available through LEGISNET: National Conference of State Legislatures 303/830-2200; Public Technology Inc's Local Exchange 202/626-2400; and the Government Finance Network. State and federal agencies may be able to obtain free access to the systems. Local governments should contact EPA at 202/260-0420 to obtain information on networks that might provide low-cost or free access to them. Discussions are underway to include this selection on the OLS.

MISCELLANEOUS ENVIRONMENTAL INFORMATION

Nonelectronic sources of environmental information are available from the federal government and other organizations. The National Center for Health Statistics of the Centers for Disease Control and Prevention, ATSDR, and EPA have co-produced *Inventory of Exposure-Related Data Systems in the Federal Government*. The book features approximately 100 exposure data systems. Each entry provides the following information: acronym, contact person, environmental data found in the system, and data availability. Subject areas include acid rain, aquatic topics (*e.g.*, fish, drinking water, lakes), air pollution, pesticides, and health effects. *Inventory of Exposure-Related Data* includes databases that are totally or partially federally funded.

Material available at the state level includes "Florida's Hidden Environmental Databases and Bulletin Boards." For more information or to request the publication, contact Stephanie Haas, Information Specialist, Marston Science Library, University of Florida, Gainesville, FL 32611-2020.

Peachpit Press' Ecolinking (ISBN 0-938151-35-5) is written by Don Rittner. The book contains information on global networks, environmental news sources, Internet mailing lists, and gateway services. Another publication, the quarterly newsletter from the Environment and Resources Management Division, Special Libraries Association, has expanded its coverage of electronic resources.

CONCLUSION

The proliferation of available resources in the past year has been tremendous. With increased data sharing across national boundaries, access to international environmental databases will be increasing. The use of the Internet and similar services will become vital to the exchange of this information to aid in finding environmental solutions. The clientele for environmental information is expanding the citizen involvement in finding the solutions. Information professionals can and must be a part of that solution by continuing to seek out and learn about new resources.

E-LAW: THE INTERNET, THE ENVIRONMENT, AND THE LAW

Operating under the premise that information is like water in a desert, a group of environmental lawyers are using the Internet to provide access to scientific and legal information to environmental action groups in the developing world.

Environmental Law Alliance Worldwide (E-LAW) was formed by public interest lawyers in Peru, Ecuador, Australia, Malaysia, Indonesia, the Philippines, Sri Lanka, and the U.S and now includes attorneys in several dozen countries. E-LAW uses email and conferencing, and is distributed throughout the world on the Internet, BITNET, and UUCP. Their success in networking to remote sites and undeveloped regions has been inspiring to other international groups.

E-LAW's position is that speedy access to information, whether scientific studies or other legal actions, helps level the playing field between the people trying to protect fragile resources in remote areas of the world and multinational companies who have worldwide access to information and the resources to press their points of view.

Does it work? According to John Bonine, a professor of Law at the University of Oregon, Ecuadorian public interest lawyers have been fighting to prevent oil drilling in a National Park in the Amazon considered to be the most biologically diverse on the planet. They uncovered information on improper influences in the Ecuadorian judicial system by certain foreign oil companies, drew up a complaint to the U.S. government, and publicized the complaint worldwide on the computer networks." This effort, combined with others, may have persuaded a major oil company to drop the project.

When public interest environmental lawyers in Malaysia were fighting a Japanese company's radioactive waste dump in Malaysia they were having trouble obtaining information about the company. "The answer was to find documents in Japan that undercut the credibility of the very experts who were testifying," Bonine said. "The research revealed that one of them had written a book saying the process they were defending was too dangerous to use in Japan, so they were going to move it to a Third World country."

HUMAN AND ENVIRONMENTAL PROTECTION LINKED

Often advocates of environmental protection are the ones most threatened with violations of human rights. Bonine says, "They are being arrested, beaten, put in jail, and sometimes, in the case of Sri Lanka for example, public interest environmental lawyers there are being murdered. " Bonine feels it is important that E-LAW associates defend the rights of citizens, groups and environmental lawyers to advocate, to speak freely and to press their causes."

The secret of E-LAW is grassroots people, both environmental groups and lawyers, working together to support one another across national boundaries. E-LAW will not itself take cases, but each member of E-LAW can and will argue cases in court.

From an article by John E. Bonine in Internet Society News vol. 1, no. 1 (Winter 1992), p. 26. Published by the Internet Society in Reston, Va.

E-LAW's addresses:

Environmental Law Alliance Worldwide, U.S.
1877 Garden Avenue
Eugene Oregon 97403

Email: elaweugene@igc.org
        beaugene@igc.org (for Bonine)
Fax: 1-503-687-0535
Phone: 1-503-687-8454

B. Periodical Loose-leaf Services

A Partial Compilation of Periodical Loose-Leaf Services Currently Available in the Environmental Law Field

ENVIRONMENTAL LAW – INTERNATIONAL

International Environment Reporter (BNA)
International Protection of the Environment: Treaties and Related Documents 2d Series (Oceana)
International Environmental Law and Regulation: A Practical Guide (Butterworth)
International Environmental Litigation (Clark Boardman Callaghan)
International Water Report (Geraghty and Miller)
World Food Regulation Review (BNA)
World Pharmaceuticals Report (BNA)

ENVIRONMENTAL LAW – GENERAL, MOSTLY U.S. FEDERAL

Air Pollution Control (BNA)
Air Pollution: Federal Law and Analysis (Clark Boardman Callaghan)
CFC Compliance Guide to Regulation of Ozone (Thompson)
Clean Air Act 1990 Amendments: Law and Practice (Wiley Law)
Clean Air Permits: Manager's Guide to the 1990 Clean Air Act (Thompson)
Corporate Counsel's Guide to Environmental Law (Bus. Laws)
Environment Reporter (BNA)
Environmental and Natural Resources Permits (Butterworth)
Environmental Citizen Suits (Butterworth)
Environmental Compliance and Audits (Bus. Laws)
Environmental Crimes (Shepard's)
Environmental Due Diligence Guide (BNA)
Environmental Insurance Coverage: State Law & Regulation (Butterworth)
Environmental Insurance Litigation: Law and Practice (Shepard's)
Environmental Insurance Litigation: Practice Forms (Shepard's)
Environmental Law & Practice (Clark Boardman Callaghan)
Environmental Law: ALR Annotations (Lawyers Coop)
Environmental Law Reporter (ELI)
Environmental Liability - Law and Strategy for Businesses and Corporations (Butterworth)
Environmental Liability Laws (American Insurance Assn.)
Environmental Packaging - U.S. Guide to Green Labeling Packaging and Recycling (Thompson)
Environmental Regulation of Land Use (Clark Boardman Callaghan)
Environmental Regulation of Real Property (Law Journal)
Federal Environmental Regulation (Butterworth)
Funding Wastewater Treatment Facilities: The Complete Resource Guide to the New State Revolving Fund Program (BNA)
Insurance Coverage for Environmental Claims (Bender)
Law of Environmental Protection (Clark Boardman Callaghan)
Law of Solid Waste Management (Clark Boardman Callaghan)
Law of Water Rights and Resources (Clark Boardman Callaghan)
Law of Wetlands Regulation (Clark Boardman Callaghan)

Managing Environmental Risk: Real Estate and Business Transactions (Clark Boardman Callaghan)
Marine Pollution and the Law of the Sea (Hein)
NEPA Law and Litigation (Clark Boardman Callaghan)
Oil Spill Law Information Service (Thompson)
The Oil Spill Planning Manual (Thompson)
RCRA Corrective Action Manual (Thompson)
Reporting Requirements for Environmental Releases (Prentice Hall Law & Business)
Spill Reporting Procedures Guide (BNA Books)
State Environmental Law (Clark Boardman Callaghan)
Stormwater Permit Manual (Thompson)
Superfund: A Legislative History (ELI)
Toxic Substances Control Act-Compliance Guide and Service (Environment Books)
Water Pollution Control (BNA)
Wildlife Law (Lupus Publications)

ENVIRONMENTAL LAW – STATES, GENERALLY AND BY STATE

State Environmental Law (Clark Boardman Callaghan)
Environmental Compliance Management in [State] (IBL)
Environmental Regulations for [State] (IBL)
Environmental Compliance in [various states] (BLR)
Environmental Law of Arkansas (Arkansas Legislative Digest)
BNA California - Environment Report Reference File (BNA)
California Environmental Laws & Land Use Practice (Bender)
Practicing Under the California Environmental Quality Act (Calif. CEB)
Florida Environmental and Land Use Law (Florida Bar)
Environmental Law for Transactional Attorneys (Illinois ICLE)
Issues on Environmental Law (Maryland ICPEL)
Massachusetts Environmental Law (Mass CLE)
Michigan Environmental Law Deskbook (ICLE - Michigan)
Missouri Environmental Law (MoBar)
New Hampshire Environmental Practice: Regulation and Compliance (Butterworth)
ECRA Compliance (New Jersey ICLE)
New Jersey Land Use and Environmental Law (Bender)
Bohannon's New Mexico Environmental Law Handbook (Butterworth)
Environmental Impact Review in New York (Bender)
Texas Air Control Board Rules (RPC)
The Washington State Environmental Policy Act: A Legal and Policy Analysis (Butterworth)

ENVIRONMENTAL LAW – FORMS

Environmental Law Forms Guide (Shepard's)

CHEMICALS

Chemical Process Safety Report (Thompson)
Chemical Regulation Reporter (BNA)
Chemical Substances Control (BNA)
Federal Regulation of the Chemical Industry (Shepard's)
Index to Chemical Regulation (BNA)
Suspect Chemicals Sourcebook (RoyTech)

Toxic Substances Control Act – Compliance Guide and Service (Environment Books)

HAZARDOUS SUBSTANCES

Aboveground Storage Tank Guide (Thompson)
Chemical Crisis Management Guide (Keller)
Chemical Regulation Reporter (BNA)
Chemical Substances Control (BNA)
Community Right-to-Know Manual: Guide to SARA Title III (Thompson)
Guide to Toxic Torts (Bender)
Hazard Communication Compliance Manual: The Complete Guide for Worker Right-to Know (BNA)
Hazard Communication Guide (Keller)
Hazardous Materials Transportation (BNA)
Hazardous Waste (Bender)
Hazardous Waste Compliance Manual for Generators, Transporters, TSDs (Keller)
Hazardous Waste Law and Practice (Wiley)
Hazardous Waste Management Guide: Identification Monitoring, Treatment and Disposal (Keller)
Hazardous Waste Operations & Emergency Response Compliance Manual (Keller)
Hazardous Waste Regulatory Guide (Keller)
Infectious Waste: The Complete Resource Guide (BNA)
The Law of Chemical Regulation and Hazardous Waste (Clark Boardman Callaghan)
Law of Toxic Torts (Clark Boardman Callaghan)
Legal Guide for Handling Toxic Substances in the Workplace (Bus. Laws)
Materials on the Hazard Communication Rule (Bus. Laws)
PCB Compliance Guide for Electrical Equipment (BNA Books)
RCRA and Superfund: A Practice Guide with Forms (Shepard's)
Reporting Requirements for Environmental Releases (Prentice Hall Law & Business)
Right to Know Compliance Manual (Keller)
Right to Know Planning Guide (BNA)
Spill Reporting Procedures Guide (BNA Books)
State & Local Government Solid Waste Management (Clark Boardman Callaghan)
State Hazardous Waste Regulation (Butterworth)
Superfund: A Legislative History (ELI)
Toxic Substances Control Act-Compliance Guide and Service (Environment Books)
Underground Storage Tank Guide (Thompson)
Underground Storage Tank Law (New Jersey ICLE)

HEALTH AND OCCUPATIONAL SAFETY

Biolaw (UPA)
Employment Safety and Health Guide (CCH)
Generic and Innovator Drugs: A Guide to FDA Requirements (Prentice Hall Law & Business)
Handling Occupational Disease Cases (Clark Boardman Callaghan)
Job Safety and Health (BNA)
Occupational Safety & Health Reporter (BNA)
Occupational Safety and Health Act (Bender)

OSHA 1910 Guide (Keller)
OSHA Compliance Encyclopedia (BLR)
OSHA Reference Manual (Merritt)
A Practical Guide to The Occupational Safety & Health Act (Law Journal)

Appendix 3, Federal Environmental Justice Materials
• Executive Order 12898
• Title VI of the 1964 Civil Rights Act
• EPA Title VI Rules

Executive Order 12898

Federal Actions To Address Environmental Justice in Minority Populations and Low-Income Populations

February 11, 1994

By the authority vested in me as President by the Constitution and the laws of the United States of America, it is hereby ordered as follows:

Section 1-1. Implementation.

1-101. Agency Responsibilities. To the greatest extent practicable and permitted by law, and consistent with the principles set forth in the report on the National Performance Review, each Federal agency shall make achieving environmental justice part of its mission by identifying and addressing, as appropriate, disproportionately high and adverse human health or environmental effects of its programs, policies, and activities on minority populations and low-income populations in the United States and its territories and possessions, the District of Columbia, the Commonwealth of Puerto Rico, and the Commonwealth of the Mariana Islands.

1-102. Creation of an Interagency Working Group on Environmental Justice. (a) Within 3 months of the date of this order, the Administrator of the Environmental Protection Agency ("Administrator") or the Administrator's designee shall convene an interagency Federal Working Group on Environmental Justice ("Working Group"). The Working Group shall comprise the heads of the following executive agencies and offices, or their designees: (a) Department of Defense; (b) Department of Health and Human Services; (c) Department of Housing and Urban Development; (d) Department of Labor; (e) Department of Agriculture; (f) Department of Transportation; (g) Department of Justice; (h) Department of the Interior; (i) Department of Commerce; (j) Department of Energy; (k) Environmental Protection Agency; (l) Office of Management and Budget; (m) Office of Science and Technology Policy; (n) Office of the Deputy Assistant to the President for Environmental Policy; (o) Office of the Assistant to the President for Domestic Policy; (p) National Economic Council; (q) Council of Economic Advisers; and (r) such other Government officials as the

President may designate. The Working Group shall report to the President through the Deputy Assistant to the President for Environmental Policy and the Assistant to the President for Domestic Policy.

(b) The Working Group shall: (1) provide guidance to Federal agencies on criteria for identifying disproportionately high and adverse human health or environmental effects on minority populations and low-income populations;

(2) coordinate with, provide guidance to, and serve as a clearinghouse for, each Federal agency as it develops an environmental justice strategy as required by section 1-103 of this order, in order to ensure that the administration, interpretation and enforcement of programs, activities and policies are undertaken in a consistent manner;

(3) assist in coordinating research by, and stimulating cooperation among, the Environmental Protection Agency, the Department of Health and Human Services, the Department of Housing and Urban Development, and other agencies conducting research or other activities in accordance with section 3-3 of this order;

(4) assist in coordinating data collection, required by this order;

(5) examine existing data and studies on environmental justice;

(6) hold public meetings as required in section 5-502(d) of this order; and

(7) develop interagency model projects on environmental justice that evidence cooperation among Federal agencies.

1-103. Development of Agency Strategies. (a) Except as provided in section 6- 605 of this order, each Federal agency shall develop an agency-wide environmental justice strategy, as set forth in subsections (b)-(e) of this section that identifies and addresses disproportionately high and adverse human health or environmental effects of its programs, policies, and activities on minority populations and low-income populations. The environmental justice strategy shall list programs, policies, planning and public participation processes, enforcement, and/or rulemakings related to human health or the environment that should be revised to, at a minimum: (1) promote enforcement of all health and environmental statutes in areas with minority populations and low-income populations; (2) ensure greater public participation; (3) improve research and data collection relating to the health of and environment of minority populations and low-income populations; and (4) identify differential patterns of consumption of natural resources among minority populations and low-income populations. In addition, the environmental justice strategy shall include, where appropriate, a timetable for undertaking identified revisions and consideration of economic and social implications of the revisions.

(b) Within 4 months of the date of this order, each Federal agency shall identify an internal administrative process for developing its environmental justice strategy, and shall inform the Working Group of the process.

(c) Within 6 months of the date of this order, each Federal agency shall provide the Working Group with an outline of its proposed environmental justice strategy.

(d) Within 10 months of the date of this order, each Federal agency shall provide the Working Group with its proposed environmental justice strategy.

(e) Within 12 months of the date of this order, each Federal agency shall finalize its environmental justice strategy and provide a copy and written description of its strategy to the Working Group. During the 12 month period from the date of this order, each Federal agency, as part of its environmental justice strategy, shall identify several specific projects that can be promptly undertaken to address particular concerns identified during the development of the proposed environmental justice strategy, and a schedule for implementing those projects.

(f) Within 24 months of the date of this order, each Federal agency shall report to the Working Group on its progress in implementing its agency-wide environmental justice strategy.

(g) Federal agencies shall provide additional periodic reports to the Working Group as requested by the Working Group.

1-104. Reports to the President. Within 14 months of the date of this order, the Working Group shall submit to the President, through the Office of the Deputy Assistant to the President for Environmental Policy and the Office of the Assistant to the President for Domestic Policy, a report that describes the implementation of this order, and includes the final environmental justice strategies described in section 1-103(e) of this order.

Sec. 2-2. Federal Agency Responsibilities for Federal Programs. Each Federal agency shall conduct its programs, policies, and activities that substantially affect human health or the environment, in a manner that ensures that such programs, policies, and activities do not have the effect of excluding persons (including populations) from participation in, denying persons (including populations) the benefits of, or subjecting persons (including populations) to discrimination under, such programs, policies, and activities, because of their race, color, or national origin.

Sec. 3-3. Research, Data Collection, and Analysis.

3-301. Human Health and Environmental Research and Analysis. (a) Environmental human health research, whenever practicable and appropriate, shall include diverse segments of the population in epidemiological and clinical studies, including segments at high risk from environmental hazards, such as minority populations, low-income populations and workers who may be exposed to substantial environmental hazards.

(b) Environmental human health analyses, whenever practicable and appropriate, shall identify multiple and cumulative exposures.

(c) Federal agencies shall provide minority populations and low-income populations the opportunity to comment on the development and design of research strategies undertaken pursuant to this order.

3-302. Human Health and Environmental Data Collection and Analysis. To the extent permitted by existing law, including the Privacy Act, as amended (5 U.S.C. section 552a): (a) each Federal agency, whenever practicable and appropriate, shall collect, maintain, and analyze information assessing and comparing environmental and human health risks borne by populations identified by race, national origin, or income. To the extent practical and appropriate, Federal agencies shall use this information to determine whether their programs, policies, and activities have disproportionately high and adverse human health or environmental effects on minority populations and low-income populations;

(b) In connection with the development and implementation of agency strategies in section 1-103 of this order, each Federal agency, whenever practicable and appropriate, shall collect, maintain and analyze information on the race, national origin, income level, and other readily accessible and appropriate information for areas surrounding facilities or sites expected to have a substantial environmental, human health, or economic effect on the surrounding populations, when such facilities or sites become the subject of a substantial Federal environmental administrative or judicial action. Such information shall be made available to the public, unless prohibited by law; and

(c) Each Federal agency, whenever practicable and appropriate, shall collect, maintain, and analyze information on the race, national origin, income level, and other readily accessible and appropriate information for areas surrounding Federal facilities that are: (1) subject to the reporting requirements under the Emergency Planning and Community Right-to-Know Act, 42 U.S.C. section 11001-11050 as mandated in Executive Order No. 12856; and (2) expected to have a substantial environmental, human health, or economic effect on surrounding populations. Such information shall be made available to the public, unless prohibited by law.

(d) In carrying out the responsibilities in this section, each Federal agency, whenever practicable and appropriate, shall share information and eliminate unnecessary duplication of efforts through the use of existing data systems and cooperative agreements among Federal agencies and with State, local, and tribal governments.

Sec. 4-4. Subsistence Consumption of Fish and Wildlife.

4-401. Consumption Patterns. In order to assist in identifying the need for ensuring protection of populations with differential patterns of subsistence consumption of fish and wildlife, Federal agencies, whenever practicable and appropriate, shall collect, maintain, and analyze information on the consumption patterns of populations who principally rely on fish and/or wildlife for subsistence. Federal agencies shall communicate to the public the risks of those consumption patterns.

4-402. Guidance. Federal agencies, whenever practicable and appropriate, shall work in a coordinated manner to publish guidance reflecting the latest scientific information available concerning methods for evaluating the human health risks associated with the consumption of pollutant-bearing fish or wildlife. Agencies shall consider such guidance in developing their policies and rules.

Sec. 5-5. Public Participation and Access to Information. (a) The public may submit recommendations to Federal agencies relating to the incorporation of environmental justice principles into Federal agency programs or policies. Each Federal agency shall convey such recommendations to the Working Group.

(b) Each Federal agency may, whenever practicable and appropriate, translate crucial public documents, notices, and hearings relating to human health or the environment for limited English speaking populations.

(c) Each Federal agency shall work to ensure that public documents, notices, and hearings relating to human health or the environment are concise, understandable, and readily accessible to the public.

(d) The Working Group shall hold public meetings, as appropriate, for the purpose of fact-finding, receiving public comments, and conducting inquiries concerning environmental justice. The Working Group shall prepare for public review a summary of the comments and recommendations discussed at the public meetings.

Sec. 6-6. General Provisions.

6-601. Responsibility for Agency Implementation. The head of each Federal agency shall be responsible for ensuring compliance with this order. Each Federal agency shall conduct internal reviews and take such other steps as may be necessary to monitor compliance with this order.

6-602. Executive Order No. 12250. This Executive order is intended to supplement but not supersede Executive Order No. 12250, which requires consistent and effective implementation of various laws prohibiting discriminatory practices in programs receiving Federal financial assistance. Nothing herein shall limit the effect or mandate of Executive Order No. 12250.

6-603. Executive Order No. 12875. This Executive order is not intended to limit the effect or mandate of Executive Order No. 12875.

6-604. Scope. For purposes of this order, Federal agency means any agency on the Working Group, and such other agencies as may be designated by the President, that conducts any Federal program or activity that substantially affects human health or the environment. Independent agencies are requested to comply with the provisions of this order.

6-605. Petitions for Exemptions. The head of a Federal agency may petition the President for an exemption from the requirements of this order on the grounds that all or some of the petitioning agency's programs or activities should not be subject to the requirements of this order.

6-606. Native American Programs. Each Federal agency responsibility set forth under this order shall apply equally to Native American programs. In addition, the Department of the Interior, in coordination with the Working Group, and, after consultation with tribal leaders, shall coordinate steps to be taken pursuant to this order that address Federally-recognized Indian Tribes.

6-607. Costs. Unless otherwise provided by law, Federal agencies shall assume the financial costs of complying with this order.

6-608. General. Federal agencies shall implement this order consistent with, and to the extent permitted by, existing law.

6-609. Judicial Review. This order is intended only to improve the internal management of the executive branch and is not intended to, nor does it create any right, benefit, or trust responsibility, substantive or procedural, enforceable at law or equity by a party against the United States, its agencies, its officers, or any person. This order shall not be construed to create any right to judicial review involving the compliance or noncompliance of the United States, its agencies, its officers, or any other person with this order.

WILLIAM CLINTON

THE WHITE HOUSE,

February 11, 1994.

Exec. Order No. 12898, 59 FR 7629, 1994 WL 43891 (Pres.)

Title VI of the 1964 Civil Rights Act

Title VI of the 1964 federal Civil Rights Act, 42 U.S.C.A. §2000d
Pub.L. 88-352, Title VI, §601, July 2, 1964, 78 Stat. 252, as amended

§2000d. Prohibition against exclusion from participation in, denial of benefits of, and discrimination under Federally assisted programs on ground of race, color, or national origin

No person in the United States shall, on the ground of race, color, or national origin, be excluded from participation in, be denied the benefits of, or be subjected to discrimination under any program or activity receiving Federal financial assistance.

EPA Title VI Rules

40 C.F.R. §7.35

CODE OF FEDERAL REGULATIONS

TITLE 40 — PROTECTION OF ENVIRONMENT

CHAPTER I — ENVIRONMENTAL PROTECTION AGENCY

SUBCHAPTER A — GENERAL

PART 7 — NONDISCRIMINATION IN PROGRAMS RECEIVING FEDERAL ASSISTANCE FROM THE ENVIRONMENTAL PROTECTION AGENCY

SUBPART B — DISCRIMINATION PROHIBITED ON THE BASIS OF RACE, COLOR, NATIONAL ORIGIN OR SEX

§7.35 Specific prohibitions.

(a) As to any program or activity receiving EPA assistance, a recipient shall not directly or through contractual, licensing, or other arrangements on the basis of race, color, national origin or, if applicable, sex:

(1) Deny a person any service, aid or other benefit of the program;

(2) Provide a person any service, aid or other benefit that is different, or is provided differently from that provided to others under the program;

(3) Restrict a person in any way in the enjoyment of any advantage or privilege enjoyed by others receiving any service, aid, or benefit provided by the program;

(4) Subject a person to segregation in any manner or separate treatment in any way related to receiving services or benefits under the program;

(5) Deny a person or any group of persons the opportunity to participate as members of any planning or advisory body which is an integral part of the program, such as a local sanitation board or sewer authority;

(6) Discriminate in employment on the basis of sex in any program subject to Section 13, or on the basis of race, color, or national origin in any program whose purpose is to create employment; or, by means of employment discrimination, deny intended beneficiaries the benefits of the EPA assistance program, or subject the beneficiaries to prohibited discrimination.

(7) In administering a program or activity receiving Federal financial assistance in which the recipient has previously discriminated on the basis of race, color, sex, or national origin, the recipient shall take affirmative action to provide remedies to those who have been injured by the discrimination.

(b) A recipient shall not use criteria or methods of administering its program which have the effect of subjecting individuals to discrimination because of their race, color, national origin, or sex, or have the effect of defeating or substantially impairing accomplishment of the objectives of the program with respect to individuals of a particular race, color, national origin, or sex.

(c) A recipient shall not choose a site or location of a facility that has the purpose or effect of excluding individuals from, denying them the benefits of, or subjecting them to discrimination under any program to which this Part applies on the grounds of race, color, or national origin or sex; or with the purpose or effect of defeating or substantially impairing the accomplishment of the objectives of this subpart....

Appendix 4,   An Environmental Justice Bibliograpy

Because the environmental justice field is so recently developed as a field of active academic and litigative effort, the following bibliography may be particularly helpful in providing a starting point for students interested in exploring the field.

Articles and Books

Anderson, Nancy E., "Notes from the Front Line," 21 Fordham Urban L.J.
        (forthcoming
        1994).

Anderson, Nancy E., "The Visible Spectrum," 21 Fordham Urban L.J.
        (forthcoming
        1994).

Atkinson, Amanda, "Environmental Inequity: An Emerging Concern for
        Government," 5
        Maryland Journal of Contemporary Legal Issues 81 (1994).

Austin, Regina, and Michael Schill, "Black, Brown, Poor and Poisoned:
        Minority
        Grassroots Environmentalism and the Quest for Eco-Justice," 1
        Kansas J. L. &
        Public Policy 69 (1991).

Been, Vicki, "Compensated Siting: Is There a Fox in the Henhouse?" 21
        Fordham Urban
        L.J. (forthcoming 1994).

Been, Vicki, "Conceptions of Fairness in Proposals for Facility Siting," 5
        Maryland
        Journal of Contemporary Legal Issues 13 (1994).

Been, Vicki, "Locally Undesirable Land Uses in Minority Neighborhoods:
        Disproportionate Siting or Market Dynamics?" 103 Yale L. J. 1383
        (1994).

Been, Vicki, "Siting of Locally Undesirable Land Uses: Directions for
        Further Research,"
        5 Maryland Journal of Contemporary Legal Issues 105 (1994).

Been, Vicki, "What's Fairness Got to Do With It? Environmental Justice
        and the Siting of
        Locally Undesirable Land Uses," 78 Cornell L. Rev. 1001 (1993).

Bernstein, "The Siting of Commercial Hazardous Waste Facilities: An
        Evolution of Community Land Use Decisions," 1 Kansas J. L. &
        Public Policy 83 (1991).

Boyle, Edward Patrick, ""It's Not Easy Bein' Green: The Psychology of
        Racism, Environmental Discrimination, and the Argument for
        Modernizing Equal Protection Analysis," 46 Vanderbilt L. Rev. 937
        (1993).

Brion, "An Essay on LULU, NIMBY, and the Problem of Distributive Justice," 15 B.C. Journal of Environmental Affairs 437 (1988).

Bryant, Bunyan, and Paul Mohai, eds., RACE AND THE INCIDENCE OF ENVIRONMENTAL HAZARDS: A TIME FOR DISCOURSE (1992).

Bullard, Robert D. "The Threat of Environmental Racism," 7 Natural Resources & the Environment 23 (1993).

Bullard, Robert D. "Waste and Racism: A Stacked Deck?" Forum for Applied Research and Public Policy 29 (1993).

Bullard, Robert D. and Beverly H. Wright, "Environmentalism and the Politics of Equity: Emergent Trends in the Black Community," Mid-American Review of Sociology 21 (Winter 1987).

Bullard, Robert D., "Race and Environmental Justice in the United States," 18 Yale J. Intl. L. 319 (1993).

Bullard, Robert D., "Solid Waste Sites and the Black Houston Community," 53 Soc. Inquiry 273 (1983).

Bullard, Robert D., DUMPING IN DIXIE: RACE, CLASS & ENVIRONMENTAL QUALITY (1990).

Bullard, Robert D., PEOPLE OF COLOR ENVIRONMENTAL GROUPS, DIRECTORY 1992 (1992).

Change, William son B.C., "The Wasteland' in the Western Exploitation of 'Race' and the Environment," 63 Colorado Law Review 839 (1992).

Chase, Anthony R., 'Assessing and Addressing Problems Posed by Environmental Racism," 45 Rutgers L. Rev. 335 (1993).

Clinton, William J., Executive Order 12898, 59 FR 7629, 1994 WL 43891 (Pres.)
(**See Appendix 3**).

Cole, Luke W. and M. Casey Jarman, "A New Approach to Expanding Resources for Environmental Justice: The Professor-in-Residence," *West Virginia L. Rev.* (forthcoming 1994).

Cole, Luke W. and Susan Senger Bowyer, "Pesticides and the Poor in California," 2 *Race, Poverty & the Environment* 1 (Spring 1991).

Cole, Luke W., "Empowerment as the Means to Environmental Protection: The Need for Environmental Poverty Law," 19 *Ecology Law Quarterly* 619 (1992).

Cole, Luke W., "Environmental Justice in the Classroom: Real Life Lessons for Law Students," *West Virginia Law Review* (forthcoming 1994).

Cole, Luke W., "Environmental Justice Litigation: Another Stone in David's Sling," 21 *Fordham Urban Law* Journal (forthcoming 1994).

Cole, Luke W., "The Anti-Immigration Environmental Alliance: Divide and Conquer at the Border of Racism," 3 *Race, Poverty & The Environment* 13 (Spring 1992).

Cole, Luke W., "The Struggle of Kettleman City for Environmental Justice: Lessons For the Movement," 5 *Maryland Journal of Contemporary Legal Issues* 67 (1994).

Cole, Luke W., Correspondence, "Remedies for Environmental Racism: A View from the Field," 90 *Michigan Law Review* 1991 (1992).

Collin, Robert, "Environmental Equity: A Law and Planning Approach to Environmental Racism, 11 Virginia Environmental Law J. 495 (1992).

Colopy, James, "The Road Less Travelled: Pursuing Environmental Justice Through Title VI of the Civil Rights Act of 1964," 13 Stanford Env. L.J. 125 (1994).

Colquette, Kelly & Michelle Robertson, "Environmental Racism: The Causes, Consequences, and Commendations," 5 Tulane Environmental L. J. 153 (1991).

Denno, Deborah, "Considering Lead Poisoning as a Criminal Defense," 20 Fordham Urban Law J. 377 (1993).

Dubin, Jon C., "From Junkyards to Gentrification: Explicating a Right to Protective Zoning in Low-Income Communities of Color," 77 Minn. L. Rev. 739 (1993).

Duff, Lydia B., "Beyond Environmental LULUs: Thoughts of an Urban Environmental Lawyer, 5 Maryland J. Contemp. Leg. Issues 49 (1994).

Environmental Equity Workgroup, U.S. Environmental Protection Agency (EPA230-R92-008), ENVIRONMENTAL EQUITY: REDUCING RISK FOR ALL COMMUNITIES (1992).

EPA Journal, Volume 18, Number 1, 175N-92-001 (Issue on Environmental Justice) March/April 1992.

Ferris, Deeohn, "A Broad Environmental Justice Agenda: Mandating Change Begins at the Federal Level," 5 Maryland Journal of Contemporary Legal Issues 115 (1994).

Ferris, Deeohn, "Communities of Color and Hazardous Waste Cleanup: Expanding Public Participation in the Federal Superfund Program," 21 Fordham Urban L.J. (forthcoming 1994).

Foster, Sheila, "Race(ial) Matters: The Quest for Environmental Justice," 20 Ecology Law Quarterly 721 (1993).

Freeman, James S. and Godsil, Rachel D. "The Question of Risk: Incorporating Community Perceptions into Environmental Risk Assessments," 21 Fordham Urban Law Journal (forthcoming 1994).

Freudenberg, Nicholas, & Kohn, "The Washington Heights health Action Project: A New Role for Social Service Workers in Community Organizing," 13 Catalyst 7 (1982).

Friedman-Jimenez, George, "Occupational Health and Environmental Justice," 21 Fordham Urban L.J. (forthcoming 1994).

Gelobter, Michel, "The Meaning of Urban Environmental Justice," 21 Fordham Urban L.J. (forthcoming 1994).

Gerrard, Michael, "Fear and Loathing in the Siting of Hazardous and Radioactive Waste Facilities: A Comprehensive Approach to a Misperceived Crisis," 68 Tulane L. Rev. (forthcoming 1994).

Gerrard, Michael, "Who are the Victims of NIMBY?" 21 Fordham Urban L.J. (forthcoming 1994).

Godsil, Rachel, "Remedying Environmental Racism," 90 Michigan L. Rev. 394 (1991).

Godsil, Rachel, and Freeman, James, "Jobs, Trees, and Autonomy: The Convergence of the Environmental Justice Movement and Community Economic Development," 5 Maryland Journal of Contemporary Legal Issues 25 (1994).

Gover, Kevin, and Jana L. Walker, "Escaping Environmental Paternalism: One Tribe's Approach to Developing a Commercial Waste Disposal Project in Indian Country," 63 Colorado Law Review 933 (1992).

Huffman, James L., "An Exploratory Essay on Native Americans and Environmentalism," 63 Colorado Law Review 839 (1992).

Kazis, Richard and Richard L. Grossman, FEAR AT WORK: JOB BLACKMAIL, LABOR, AND THE ENVIRONMENT (1982).

Keeva, Steven, "A Breath of Justice," 80 ABA J. 88 (February 1994).

Lavelle, Marianne, and Marcia Coyle, "Unequal Protection: The Racial Divide in Environmental Law," National Law Journal, September 21, 1992, at S2.

Lawyer," 5 Maryland Journal of Contemporary Legal Issues 49 (1994).

Lazarus, Richard, "Pursuing 'Environmental Justice': The Distributional Effects of Environmental Protection," 87 Northwestern U. L. Rev. 787 (1993).

Lazarus, Richard, "The Meaning and Promotion of Environmental Justice," 5 Maryland Journal of Contemporary Legal Issues 1 (1994).

Lyskowski, Kevin. "Environmental Justice: A Research Guide," (forthcoming 1994).

Mank, Bradford, "What Comes after Technology: Using an 'Exceptions Process' to Improve Residual Risk Regulation of Hazardous Air Pollutants," 13 Stanford Envtl Law J. 263 (1994)(opening up air quality regulation to considerations of highly impacted communities).

McDermot, Charles, "Balancing the Scales of Environmental Justice," 21 Fordham Urban L.J. (forthcoming 1994).

Miller, Vernice, "Planning, Power, and Politics: A Case Study of the Land Use and Siting History of the North River Water Pollution Control Plant," 21 Fordham Urban L.J. (forthcoming 1994).

Mohai, Paul, and Bunyan Bryant, "Environmental Injustice: Weighing Race and Class as Factors in the Distribution of Environmental Hazards," 63 University of Colorado L. Rev. 921 (1992).

Moore, Richard and Arnoldo Garcia, "Environmental Inequities," Crossroads, June 1990, at 16.

Perkins, Jane, "Recognizing and Attacking Environmental Racism," 26 Clearinghouse Review 389 (Aug. 1992).

Portney, Kent, "Environmental Justice and Sustainability: Is there a Critical Nexus?" 21 Fordham Urban L.J. (forthcoming 1994).

Rabin, Yale, "Expulsive Zoning: The Inequitable Legacy of *Euclid*," in ZONING AND THE AMERICAN DREAM (Charles Haar and Jerold Kayden, eds., 1989).

Reath, Viki, [an ongoing series of articles on environmental justice in ENVIRONMENT WEEK].

Reich, Peter L., "Greening the Ghetto: A Theory of Environmental Race Discrimination," 41 Kansas L. Rev. 271 (1992).

Sandman, "Getting to Maybe: Some Communications Aspects of Siting Hazardous Waste Facilities," 9 Seton Hall Legislative Journal 437 (1985).

Seigler, Jane, "Environmental Justice: An Industry Perspective," 5 Maryland Journal of Contemporary Legal Issues 59 (1994).

Shabecoff, Philip, "Environmental Groups Told They Are Racists in Hiring," New York Times, 31 January 1990, A20.

Shepard, Peggy, "Issues of Community Empowerment," 21 Fordham Urban L.J. (forthcoming 1994).

Swanston, Samara, "Race, Gender, & Disproportionate Impact: What Can We Do About the Failure to Protect the Most Vulnerable?" 21 Fordham Urban L.J. (forthcoming 1994).

Tarlock, A. Dan, "City and Countryside: Environmental Equity in Context," 21 Fordham Urban L.J. (forthcoming 1994).

Tarlock, A. Dan, "Environmental Protection: The Potential Misfit Between Equity and Efficiency," 63 Colorado Law Review 839 (1992).

Torres, Gerald, "Environmental Burdens and Democratic Justice," 21 Fordham Urban L.J. (forthcoming 1994).

Torres, Gerald, "Introduction: Understanding Environmental Racism," 63 Colorado Law Review 839 (1992).

Truax, "Beyond White Environmentalism," Environmental Action; Jan./Feb. 1990, p. 21.

Tsao, Naikang, "Ameliorating Environmental Racism," 67 NYU L. Rev. 366 (1992).

United Church of Christ, TOXIC WASTES AND RACE IN THE UNITED STATES (1987).

Vasquez, Xavier Carlos, "The North American Free Trade Agreement and Environmental Racism," 34 Harvard International L.J. 357 (1993).

Willard, Walter. "Environmental Racism: The Merging of Civil Rights and Environmental Activism," 19 Southern University L. Rev. 77 (1992).